THE
Kansas Historical Quarterly

KIRKE MECHEM, Editor
JAMES C. MALIN, Associate Editor

Volume V
1936

(Kansas Historical Collections)
VOL. XXII

Published by
The Kansas State Historical Society
Topeka, Kansas
16-5211

Contents of Volume V

Number 1—February, 1936

	PAGE
THE CHISHOLM TRAIL ....*John Rossel*,	3
KICKAPOO-POTTAWATOMIE GRAND INDIAN JUBILEE..........*Frank A. Root*,	15
FERRIES IN KANSAS: Part IX—Arkansas River..........*George A. Root*,	22
LABOR PROBLEMS DURING THE FIRST YEAR OF GOVERNOR MARTIN'S ADMINISTRATION ....*Edith Walker*,	33

THE ANNUAL MEETING: Containing the Reports of the Secretary, Treasurer, and Executive Committee; the Annual Address of the President, Thomas F. Doran; "The Pony Express," by W. R. Honnell; "The Governors of Kansas," by Thomas A. McNeal; Election of Officers; List of Directors of the Society,
Kirke Mechem, Secretary, 54

RECENT ADDITIONS TO THE LIBRARY,
Compiled by *Helen M. McFarland*, Librarian, 82

KANSAS HISTORY AS PUBLISHED IN THE PRESS........................... 105

KANSAS HISTORICAL NOTES.. 112

Number 2—May, 1936

	PAGE
FRANK HEYWOOD HODDER, 1860-1935.....................*James C. Malin*,	115
ISAAC MCCOY AND THE TREATY OF 1821......................*Lela Barnes*,	122
LETTERS OF A KANSAS PIONEER, 1855-1860................*Thomas C. Wells*,	143
FERRIES IN KANSAS: Part IX—Arkansas River—Concluded, *George A. Root*,	180
LABOR PROBLEMS IN THE SECOND YEAR OF GOVERNOR MARTIN'S ADMINISTRATION ....*Dorothy Leibengood*,	191
THE GRAVE OF SARAH KEYES ON THE OREGON TRAIL......*William E. Smith*,	208
KANSAS HISTORY AS PUBLISHED IN THE PRESS............................	213
KANSAS HISTORICAL NOTES	224

Number 3—August, 1936

JOURNAL OF ISAAC MCCOY FOR THE EXPLORING EXPEDITION OF 1828,
Lela Barnes, 227

THE FIRST KANSAS BAND..........................*Edward Bumgardner*, 278

LETTERS OF A KANSAS PIONEER, 1855-1860—Continued....*Thomas C. Wells*, 282

FERRIES IN KANSAS: Part X—Grasshopper River........*George A. Root*, 319

KANSAS HISTORY AS PUBLISHED IN THE PRESS............................ 325

KANSAS HISTORICAL NOTES 335

Number 4—November, 1936

JOURNAL OF ISAAC MCCOY FOR THE EXPLORING EXPEDITION OF 1830,
Lela Barnes, 339

FERRIES IN KANSAS: Part XI—Great Nemaha River.....*George A. Root*, 378

LETTERS OF A KANSAS PIONEER, 1855-1860—Concluded....*Thomas C. Wells*, 381

KANSAS HISTORY AS PUBLISHED IN THE PRESS............................ 419

KANSAS HISTORICAL NOTES 431

INDEX TO VOLUME V... 435

THE
Kansas Historical Quarterly

Volume V   Number 1

February, 1936

PRINTED BY KANSAS STATE PRINTING PLANT
W. C. AUSTIN, STATE PRINTER
TOPEKA 1936
16-1937

Contributors

JOHN ROSSEL, native of Kansas, is history instructor at Franklin High School, Baltimore, Md.

FRANK ALBERT ROOT was a pioneer newspaperman of Kansas and author of *The Overland Stage to California*. (For a biographical sketch *see* p. 15.)

GEORGE A. ROOT is curator of archives of the Kansas State Historical Society.

EDITH WALKER is an instructor of history in the high school at Eureka.

NOTE.—Articles in the *Quarterly* appear in chronological order without regard to their importance.

The Chisholm Trail

John Rossel

THE Chisholm trail is one of the most important but least known trails in American history. Its story has never been completely told, which accounts, to a large degree, for the many misconceptions which are held concerning it.

At the annual meeting of the Old-Time Trail Drivers' Association in San Antonio there ensues a perennial dispute both as to the origin of the Chisholm trail and its location. At present they seem to be no nearer the solution than at the beginning. In their monumental work entitled, *The Trail Drivers of Texas* (1925 edition), written by the trail drivers themselves, we find on page 289 one explanation, while on page 950 we find an emphatic denial of this, with quite another explanation set forth in no uncertain terms.

Modern scholarship has as yet neglected to deal with the subject in a thorough manner. Thus most that is known concerning the Chisholm trail is from the stories of the trail drivers, whose memories are no doubt dimmed by time, and from various accounts dealing with the cattle industry which treat it only in an indirect manner.

The object of this monograph is to make a critical analysis of available source material concerning the origin and location of the Chisholm trail. It will emphasize material brought out by maps of the period located in the Library of Congress, and bring to light the hitherto unpublished accounts of James R. Mead, an associate of Jesse Chisholm in the early-day trading business. Brief comment concerning the volume of trade that passed over the trail and its end will be in the conclusion.

When the Civil War drew to a close the plains of Texas were swarming with cattle for which there was no ready market. Herds of cattle were offered for sale upon the range at one to two dollars per head without finding a buyer. So critical did the situation become that Joseph G. McCoy, prominent cattleman of the time, was led to remark, "—there dawned a time in Texas that a man's poverty was estimated by the number of cattle he possessed."[1]

But the situation in the North was quite different. A good animal which would bring only a few dollars in Texas would sell for as

---

1. Joseph G. McCoy, *Sketches of the Early Cattle Trade* (Kansas City, 1874), p. 261.

much as ten times that amount in the North.[2] Prior to the Civil War there had been attempts to drive Texas cattle to market, but never on a very large scale.

After the Civil War, towns in southwestern Missouri and southeastern Kansas were the destinations of these early drives. It was not, however, until the railroads began to move westward that the movement was to reach its height. The North was demanding the meat which already existed in Texas. The big problem was to find a connecting link, and in this fact we see the beginnings of the Chisholm trail.

Joseph G. McCoy, a cattle buyer of Illinois, heard of the conditions in Texas and determined to see what he could do to remedy them. He came to Abilene in 1867, which was, as he describes it, ". . . a small dead place, consisting of about a dozen log huts, low, small rude affairs, four fifths of which were covered with dirt for roofing," and determined to establish a cattle terminal there.

The Kansas Pacific Railway had already extended its lines to this place, and McCoy decided that if the proper shipping facilities were set up it would be a comparatively easy matter for the Texas ranchers to drive their cattle overland to market.[3]

He bought 480 acres of land at five dollars an acre, and soon began the construction of shipping-yards, corrals capable of holding 3,000 wild Texas steers, along with chutes, scales, barns, and other equipment.[4] In the short space of two months, from July 1, 1867, to September 1 of the same year, he and his helpers had everything in readiness.[5] But as yet there was no connecting link between Texas and Kansas.

We shall leave the cattle business for the moment and consider the details of the origin and location of the Chisholm trail.

In considering such a problem it is necessary to make use of the many maps which made their appearance before the Civil War. Jefferson Davis, who was appointed Secretary of War in March, 1853, became interested in the extension of railroads to the West, and he had numerous surveys made of the territory in the Mississippi valley and westward. The results of these surveys are carefully preserved by maps in the possession of the Library of Congress.

One of the earliest surveys of this territory was made by a Capt.

---

2. Monthly reports of the *Department of Agriculture*, 1867, pp. 168, 169.
3. McCoy, *Sketches of the Early Cattle Trade*, p. 44.
4. Joseph G. McCoy, "Historic and Biographic Sketch," *Kansas Magazine*, December, 1909.
5. McCoy, *Sketches of the Early Cattle Trade*, p. 50.

R. B. Marcy, between the years 1849-1852.[6] The results were published soon after. He shows in detail the many trails in the West, but the ones we are particularly interested in are those located in the Indian territory, later Oklahoma. He clearly indicates trails originating south of the Wichita mountains, and extending north on both sides. After passing the mountains, they join, swing out into the central part of the Indian territory and extend about half-way. If the trail had extended in the same general direction, it would have entered the Kansas territory at about where Caldwell is now located.

Two very significant facts are noted in this map. First, that the trail indicated by Captain Marcy followed very closely the natural topography of the land, indicating that Indians had early learned the easiest way to traverse the territory, and second, that the trail followed substantially the same path as the later Chisholm trail. Captain Marcy is very careful to note the natural topography. Mountains, rivers and crossings are traced in great detail. The trail, he indicates, simply followed the easiest course through the territory.

From this map we conclude that there were probably many trails traversing the Southwest, originated by the Indians at an early date. Being familiar with the land, they would naturally pick the easiest way through. Later when the white man appeared, he simply made use of the existing trails.

Joseph Stroud, who made many trips over the Chisholm trail, suggests further that many of these trails followed the old routes of the buffalo migrations, from the spring grazing grounds in the North to the winter grounds in the South.[7]

In 1858 another map was made at the instigation of Jefferson Davis.[8] This shows several military trails which assume great importance in the solution of our problem. One is especially significant. Prior to 1858 a Major Merril had left Fort Belknap, Tex., and moved northward, east of the Wichita mountains. At the mountains he swerved eastward into the central part of the Indian territory and headed towards central Kansas. A comparison of this map with the previous one mentioned clearly indicates that this military trail followed closely the course of the earlier Indian trail noted by Captain Marcy.

6. Capt. R. B. Marcy, "Map of Western Trails," Division of Maps, Library of Congress.
7. Joseph Stroud, *Memories of Western Trails*, p. 9, Library of Congress.
8. War Department "Survey Map, 1858," Division of Maps, Library of Congress.

In 1861 federal troops located in the Indian territory were ordered to Fort Leavenworth for mobilization. The federal garrison at Fort Smith, Ark., left its post, and joining with the troops of Fort Washita, the combined garrisons under the command of Col. William H. Emory marched up the valley of the Washita river. Continuing farther, the troops from Fort Arbuckle and later Fort Cobb joined with them, and they all set out for Fort Leavenworth.[9] In doing so they traversed much of the same territory of the Indian trails as indicated by Captain Marcy, and the military trail of Captain Merril. The principal difference is that they went farther north, through the territory near present Wichita, and thence to Fort Leavenworth.

From these facts we arrive at the following conclusions: First, that at an early date Indians had marked out the easiest paths over the territory, following the natural topography of the land; second, that military leaders under their guidance had followed substantially the same paths; and third, that these were later used by Jesse Chisholm in laying out his trail.

In the spring of 1864 the affiliated bands comprising the Wichita Indians, about 1,500 in number, began their trek northward. Their ultimate destination was the mouth of the Little Arkansas river, the site of present Wichita, where they made their village. With them was Jesse Chisholm, a half-breed Cherokee Indian, who established a trading post there in the same year.[10] He was quite familiar with this territory as he had guided a party from Arkansas in search of buried treasure to the mouth of the Little Arkansas in 1836, and had made many subsequent trips.[11]

After Jesse Chisholm had established his trading post at the mouth of the Little Arkansas he immediately began to make plans to trade with the Indian territory. In the spring of 1865, when it

---

9. James R. Mead, "The Chisholm Trail," Wichita *Eagle*, March 1, 1890; letter to author from George Rainey, pioneer of Oklahoma, now a resident of Enid; Joseph G. Thoburn, "The Chisholm Trail," *Rock Island Magazine*, v. XIX (December, 1924), p. 4.

10. Jesse Chisholm was born in Tennessee, 1806. His father was of Scottish extraction, and his mother was a woman of the Cherokee Indian tribe. He settled among the Western Cherokees in Arkansas territory about 1825. Jesse Chisholm accompanied the Leavenworth-Dodge expedition to the country of the Comanche, Kiowa, and Wichita tribes, near Red river, and was one of the interpreters in the great peace council at the Wichita village.

He became a trader among the many Indian tribes of the plains. At the outbreak of the war he was prevailed upon to aid the Confederate authorities in the negotiation of treaties of alliance with various tribes in the Indian territory, but in the latter part of 1861, he was numbered among the loyalist refugees who followed Opothleyahola northward to an asylum.

Soon tiring of life in the refugee camps, he drifted westward to the mouth of the Little Arkansas river, where the Wichita and affiliated tribes, also refugees from the Indian territory, were located, and settled temporarily. There he started in his trading activities again. In order to contact the territory to the south, he laid out the trail which bore his name. However, it did not assume any great importance until the cattle industry started using it.

He was reported to have a speaking knowledge of fourteen Indian languages. He died at his trading camp in what is now Blaine county, Okla., March 4, 1868.

11. Mead, "The Little Arkansas," *Kansas Historical Collections*, v. X (1907-1908), p. 9.

was apparent that the war was drawing to a close, Chisholm invited James R. Mead to join him in a trading venture. Mead accepted the invitation. Together they loaded their wagons, crossed the Arkansas, and slowly drove to the crossing of the North Canadian. There a short side trip was made to Chisholm's trading post at Council Grove, just west of the site of present Oklahoma City, which had been abandoned at the outbreak of the Civil War.[12]

In the summer of 1865 Chisholm collected a herd of 3,000 head of cattle which grazed over the site of present West Wichita, and in the fall drove them to the Sac and Fox agency, and thence to fill government contracts in New Mexico. In December, 1865, Chisholm, purchasing goods from James R. Mead, loaded a number of teams, and in January, 1866, started across the Indian territory to his former trading post on the North Fork of the Canadian river and points south. In April, 1866, he returned over the same route, bringing with him teams loaded with furs and robes and 250 head of cattle.[13]

This trail over which Chisholm traveled included present Wichita, Clearwater, Caldwell, Pond Creek, Jefferson, Skeleton ranch (near Enid), Bison (formerly Buffalo Springs), Kingfisher, mouth of Turkey creek, Cheyenne agency (Darlington), Wichita agency (Anadarko), and Fort Sill.[14]

The historical student today, taking a map and drawing a line along these towns, will note that the trail laid out by Chisholm followed very closely the Indian trails as noted by Captain Marcy, 1853, and the military trails of Captain Merril and Captain Emory as they made their way through the Indian territory. We conclude that Jesse Chisholm simply followed the best paths over the territory, paths that had been used many years earlier by the Indians and by military authorities. This does not in any way detract from the honor due Chisholm. He knew the land well, and guided the traders over the best possible routes to the North.

The trail immediately became known as "Chisholm's trail" (1865) but not "The Chisholm Trail." It did not receive the latter appellation until after it was extensively used by the cattlemen.[15] The reader should note that Chisholm did not lay out a trail for the cattle trade. He laid out a trail for his own private business which

---
12. Stroud, *op. cit.*, p. 5.
13. James R. Mead, "The Chisholm Trail," Wichita *Eagle*, March 1, 1890.
14. Andreas, *History of Kansas*, p. 1385.
15. Stroud, *op. cit.*, p. 9.

was later used by the cattlemen. However, it was the cattle trade which made it famous.

In 1867 William Mathewson, the original "Buffalo Bill," went down over this trail taking two boys he had rescued from the Comanches to the commandant at Fort Arbuckle. There he met Colonel Dougherty of Texas on his way north over the new trail, and guided him as far as the North Canadian. This is the first herd of Texas cattle known to have passed over the Chisholm trail.[16]

On December 5, 1867, William Griffinstein crossed the Arkansas river with a wagon train and went on down the trail. He was followed a little later by Mead, with teams loaded with goods for Jesse Chisholm, who was trading with the Indians at his post on the North Fork of the Canadian river.[17] According to James R. Mead, "Mr. Chisholm's teams and my own were the first which ever passed over that route and marked out what afterward became known as the Chisholm trail."[18]

Before returning to the cattle business at the close of the Civil War, it is interesting to note the present route of the Chicago, Rock Island & Pacific Railway. It passes through Wichita, Caldwell, Pond Creek, Enid, Kingfisher, El Reno, Chickasha, Waurika, and Fort Worth. The Chisholm trail went through Wichita, Caldwell, Pond Creek, Enid, Kingfisher, El Reno, and then branched off to Anadarko and Fort Sill. The railroad engineers recognized that the Chisholm trail was the best possible route through the territory because it followed the natural topography of the land. Thus the similarity of the routes.

As noted before, Joseph G. McCoy had completed his yards at Abilene September 1, 1867. Before he finished his structures he started a man toward southern Kansas and the Indian territory to round up every drover possible and bring him to Abilene. This agent started at Junction City, then went in a southwesterly direction toward the mouth of the Little Arkansas, now Wichita, and then into the Indian territory.[19]

The first herd of cattle to arrive in Abilene was driven from Texas by a Mr. Thompson. He sold them to some dealers in the Indian territory, by the names of Smith, McCord, and Candler, who in turn drove them to Abilene. Another herd owned by

---

16. Mead, "The Chisholm Trail," Wichita *Eagle*, March 1, 1890.
17. *Ibid.*
18. James R. Mead, "Reminiscences of Frontier Life" (1898), p. 75, manuscript in possession of the Kansas State Historical Society, Topeka.
19. McCoy, *Sketches of the Early Cattle Trade*, p. 50.

Wheeler, Wilson, and Hicks, all from California, and en route to the Pacific coast, was located about thirty miles from Abilene. The owners of the cattle were finally persuaded to dispose of them at Abilene, and this little town was on the road to big business.[20]

A total of 35,000 head of Texas cattle were rounded up and disposed of at Abilene in 1867. The first shipment was made September 5, and consisted of a twenty-car train, en route to Chicago.[21]

The cattle shipped from Abilene this first year were rounded up from various places. But it is significant to note that some of the drovers began to use the newly laid-out Chisholm trading trail.

McCoy was just getting started. During the winter of 1867 and 1868 circulars were sent to every Texas cow man whose address could be secured. These circulars told of the advantages of Abilene as a shipping terminal, and invited all the Texas drovers to bring their cattle to this city. Then, in the further interests of his trade, McCoy sent two men to Texas to advertise Abilene and to make personal contact with as many ranchers as possible. At the same time he was running full-page advertisements in many of the Northern newspapers, urging buyers to come to Abilene to buy their stock. Over five thousand dollars was spent in advertising in these newspapers.[22]

But the climax to McCoy's advertising schemes came when he hired some Spanish cowboys to rope wild buffalo, load them in a reinforced boxcar, and ship them to Chicago. On the sides of the cars were huge circulars advertising Abilene and urging cattlemen to come there to buy their cattle.[23]

Since the Chisholm trading trail reached only to Wichita, McCoy hired a civil engineer by the name of T. F. Hersey, with a group of flagmen and workers, to extend the trail to Abilene. They took along spades and threw up mounds of dirt, thus completing the trail to its northern terminal. This task accomplished, McCoy placed a workman, W. W. Suggs, at the mouth of the Little Arkansas to direct the herds over the new trail, so that they would be sure to come to Abilene and not to some other point.[24]

Thus we see the Chisholm trading trail being extended in length, and being used more continuously by the cattlemen.

Evidence of McCoy's success is shown by the fact that in 1868

---

20. *Ibid.*, p. 51.
21. *Ibid.*
22. *Ibid.*, pp. 114, 115.
23. *Ibid.*, pp. 180-182.
24. *Ibid.*, p. 116.

75,000 cattle arrived in Abilene for shipment,[25] and that in 1869 150,000 were driven there.[26] These figures correspond quite closely with those given in the *Second Annual Report of the Bureau of Animal Husbandry* for the total number driven to market during these years, and they establish the importance of Abilene as a cattle terminal.[27] According to McCoy there was no place in the west five times as large as Abilene that was doing one half the business. Her cattle business amounted to more than three million dollars annually, aside from an immense trade in camp supplies.[28]

It should be clearly understood that McCoy had very little to do with the origin of the Chisholm trail. His great contribution was to establish a terminal at Abilene, and then by successful advertising to cause the Texas rancher and Northern buyer to meet there. The connecting link was the trail laid out by Chisholm earlier for his own trading ventures.

Now let us consider the completion of the trail to the south. At this time, 1867, there were a multitude of cattle trails in Texas. A map issued by the Kansas Pacific Railway in 1874, and now in possession of the Kansas State Historical Society, Topeka, shows a large network of trails, embracing the entire state of Texas, resembling somewhat a huge fan. However, nearly all crossed the Red river at a place known as Red River station, near the present town of Terral. From there the trail followed a course almost due north, crossing the Washita river near the present town of Alex, the South Canadian near Tuttle, and the North Canadian just west of Yukon. From the North Canadian it inclined slightly westward and joined the Chisholm trading trail at the crossing of the Cimarron between Kingfisher and Dover. Inasmuch as the cattle trail from Texas and the Chisholm trail were thus joined together in the Indian territory, the name Chisholm trail soon came to be applied popularly, if not accurately, to the trail throughout its entire length from its beginning in Texas to Abilene.[29]

Now let us consider the disputes concerning both the origin of the trail and its location. Reviewing briefly the material which we have already covered there can be little doubt that the Chisholm trail received its name from Jesse Chisholm, the half-breed Indian trader, who laid out a trail between his trading post at the mouth

25. *Ibid.*, p. 131.
26. *Ibid.*, p. 186.
27. *Second Annual Report of the Bureau of Animal Husbandry* (1885), p. 300.
28. McCoy, *Sketches of the Early Cattle Trade*, p. 204.
29. Stroud, *op. cit.*, p. 6.

of the Little Arkansas, now Wichita, to the Indian territory. We have already seen how the cattlemen later made use of this trail and extended it northward to Abilene, and southward to Texas.

But some of the pioneer cattlemen insist that the Chisholm trail received its name from John Chisum (sometimes incorrectly spelled Chisholm), a large cattle owner of New Mexico.[30] This Chisum was a frontier stockman who was said to have been one of the first to drive cattle over the trail. He formerly lived at Paris, Tex., and had many thousand head of cattle on the ranges in the southern part of the state.[31] He was the owner of the famous Jingle Bob outfit, and in 1867 he drove his herds into New Mexico from Texas, up the Pecos river, and located ranches near the present town of Roswell, N. Mex. It is said he did not know himself how many cattle he possessed, but a conservative estimate puts the total at over 75,000. Chisum trailed many cattle to Arizona and to various points in New Mexico to fill army and Indian agency beef contracts.

Charles Goodnight, who was the partner of John Chisum for several years says, "In conversation with me, he (John Chisum) said that one Chisholm, in no way related to him, did pilot 600 steers from the Texas frontier to old Fort Cobb, and he presumed that this was the origin of the name of the Chisholm trail."[32] And Goodnight adds, "I positively know that no trail north was laid out by John Chisum."[33]

This should clarify the issue as to whether the Chisholm trail received its name from Jesse Chisholm or John Chisum.[34]

Turning our attention to the location of the Chisholm trail, we have what on the surface appears to be a complicated situation, but actually it is relatively simple.

---

30. John Simpson Chisum was born in Hardeman county, Tennessee. His father's name had been Chisholm and the altered spelling is said to date from the time of the battle of New Orleans. Claiborne Chisum, with his family, moved to Texas in 1837.
In 1854 John Chisum started in the cattle business in Lamar county, but three years later moved to Denton county, where he remained until 1863. In that year he drove a herd, estimated at 10,000 head, into Concho county, where he engaged in business with a number of other men on shares. In the late fall of 1866 he drove a herd up the Pecos to Bosque Grande, about thirty miles north of Roswell, N. Mex., and in the following spring disposed of it to the government contractors for the Navajo and Mescalero Apache reservations.
He then formed a connection with Charles Goodnight by which for three years he continued to drive cattle from Texas to Bosque Grande. His herds multiplied and estimates of the number of cattle owned by him vary from 60,000 to 100,000. It seems certain that he was the largest owner in the United States, and may well have held the same title for the world.
He died at Eureka Springs, Ark., leaving an estate valued at $500,000. For many years he had been known as "the cattle king of America."—*Dictionary of American Biography*, v. IV, p. 77.

31. Charles Moreau Harger, "Cattle Trails of the Prairies," *Scribner's Magazine*, v. XI (June, 1892), p. 734.

32. Charles Goodnight, "More About the Chisholm Trail," in *Trail Drivers of Texas*, pp. 950-952.

33. *Ibid.*

34. The reader should call to mind that the Chisholm trail received its name approximately two years before cattle were driven north to Abilene.

The existence of any point as a cow town must of necessity have been brief. As the settlers came in, they found their interests in direct conflict with those of the cattlemen. And it was the cattlemen who had to give way. Thus we see the cattle trails of the prairies shifting westward before the vanguard of civilization. The northern end of the Chisholm trail was located first at Abilene. Then it shifted to Newton, Wichita, and Caldwell in rapid succession. But finally population became so dense in the central part of Kansas that a branch trail was laid out, leaving the Chisholm trail near Elm Spring, Indian territory, going northwest into western Kansas and ending in Dodge City.[35]

This explains the conflict as to the location of the Chisholm trail. As W. P. Anderson, railroad agent at Abilene during its heyday as a cow town, comments, "Nominally every man that came up the trail felt as though he had traversed the old Chisholm trail. Each westward movement of the cattle industry necessitated a new trail, yet so strong was the force of habit, each in succession continued to be known as the Chisholm trail." [36]

Separating myth and fantasy from historical fact, the issue is clear. In 1865, Jesse Chisholm, the half-breed Indian trader, established a trail from Wichita to Indian territory. At the close of the Civil War it became necessary to find a market for the Texas cattle. The Kansas Pacific Railway had extended its lines westward to Abilene. Joseph G. McCoy, recognizing the possibility of driving cattle to market, established shipping facilities there, and by a series of advertising activities, succeeded in persuading the cattlemen to drive their cattle there. His contribution to the Chisholm trail was its extension north from Wichita to Abilene. Texas cattlemen extended the trail from Indian territory to Texas.

As population increased it became necessary to find a new shipping terminal. This caused the laying out of a branch trail, leaving the Chisholm trail at Elm Spring, Indian territory, and ending at Dodge City. But this was not the Chisholm trail. Desire for historical importance, or any other reason, cannot alter the fact that the Chisholm trail extended from Indian territory to Wichita, and thence north to Abilene. Although the trail drivers may have believed and are now willing to argue that they were traveling over the Chisholm trail, when traversing the western route, this cannot change historical fact.

35. Harger, *op. cit.*, p. 735.
36. Letter from W. P. Anderson to Luther A. Lawhon, secretary of the Trail Drivers Association, quoted in *Trail Drivers of Texas*, p. 14.

Dodge City became the last and probably the most famous of all the pioneer cattle towns. Abilene had held the center of the trade from 1867 to 1870; Newton, 1871; Wichita, 1872; Ellsworth and Caldwell, 1873; and then Dodge City to the close of the long drive.

Robert M. Wright, pioneer cattle dealer of Dodge City, insists that ". . . there were more cattle driven to Dodge any and every year that Dodge held it, than to any other town, and for about ten years, Dodge City was the greatest cattle market in the world."[37]

But even Dodge City was beginning to be affected by the advance of civilization. Harry Norman of the New York *World*, passing through Dodge City in 1925, says, "Gone are the buffalo, the longhorn steers, the badmen, from this once rip-roaring town, the center of a vast region of which it was once said, that 'all they raised was cattle and hell.' "[38]

With the passing of the range cattle industry necessarily came the passing of the Chisholm trail. This trail was followed continuously for more than twenty years, and since it has been estimated that between five and six million head of cattle were driven north from Texas, we can see the volume of business that passed over it.[39]

Probably no greater or more vivid description has ever been given of the Chisholm trail than that of Charles Moreau Harger, writing in 1892:

> From two hundred to four hundred yards wide, beaten into the bare earth, it reached over hill and through valley for over six hundred miles, a chocolate band amid the green prairies, uniting the North and the South. As the marching hoofs wore it down and the wind blew and the waters washed the earth away it became lower than the surrounding territory, and was flanked by little banks of sand, drifted there by the wind. Bleaching skulls and skeletons of weary brutes who had perished on the journey gleamed along its borders, and here and there was a low mound showing where some cowboy had literally "died with his boots on." Occasionally a dilapidated wagon frame told of a break down, and spotting the emerald reaches on either side were the barren circle-like "bedding-grounds," each a record that a great herd had there spent a night.
>
> The wealth of an empire passed over the trail, leaving its mark for decades to come. The traveler of today sees the wide trough-like course, with ridges being washed down by the rains, and with fences and farms of the settlers and

---

37. Robert M. Wright, *Dodge City, the Cowboy Capital* (Wichita, 1913), p. 260.
38. Harry Norman in the New York *World*, quoted in *The Literary Digest*, August 22, 1925, p. 46.
39. *Second Annual Report of Bureau of Animal Husbandry* (1885), p. 300.

the more civilized redmen intercepting its track and forgets the wild and arduous life of which it was the exponent.[40]

In the New York *Times* for December 7, 1930, we find the future of this historic old highway:

The famous cattle trail from Texas to Kansas, celebrated in the galloping measures of the songs crooned by all cowboys a generation ago and now broadcast to the far corners of the land—has recently acquired belated but official recognition from the Lone Star state. For the state highway commission has authorized the Chisholm Trail Association to name two highways and mark them at historical spots with long-horned steer heads. By this action the most important of the south to north trails, linking parts of the Far West before the coming of the railroads, takes its place with the Santa Fé and Oregon in the nation's history.[41]

Progress has been made in marking out the trail, and Oklahoma and Kansas have joined in. Thus we see the gradual wearing away of the Chisholm trail, ". . . that legendary highway acclaimed in song and story as most celebrated of the Old West's premier cowland."

[40]. Harger, *op. cit.*, p. 734. The accurate historical scholar would probably question Mr. Harger's statement that the trail was a "beaten path." This would be true only where the topography of the country necessitated a limited trail. In order to feed the vast herds, the drovers naturally had to spread out over the prairie wherever possible. However, this does not detract from the merit of Mr. Harger's description.

[41]. Carl L. Cannon, "The Chisholm Trail Lives Again," in the New York *Times*, December 7, 1930.

Kickapoo-Pottawatomie Grand Indian Jubilee

FRANK A. ROOT [1]

DURING the last year of overland staging out of Atchison, it was my privilege on a hot day in the month of July, 1867, to be present at and witness the festivities connected with a grand Indian tournament and pow-wow. The festival took place on the Kickapoo reserve in northeastern Kansas, in the southwestern corner of Brown county, something over thirty miles a little north of west from Atchison. The chosen spot was only a short distance from the great overland wagon road built across the plains and over which the Concord stage to California passed. The pow-wow was gotten up on quite an elaborate scale. Of the Indians who were ~sent and took part, there were less than one hundred Pottawato-
es and fully twice that number of Kickapoos, while the white
ests in attendance were little more than half a dozen.

The event to be celebrated had for a long time been in practice by these two tribes. It was the regular annual visit of the Pottawatomies [2] to their old-time friends, the Kickapoos. For a long time it had been the custom of these two tribes, from their intimate relations, to alternately visit each other once a year, on which occasion there would be a sort of jubilee and a general rejoicing, and this would be followed by an exchange of presents between the members of each tribe.

I was present at this aboriginal entertainment through an invitation extended by Judge F. G. Adams, agent of the Kickapoos in the latter '60's, as his guest. This was an opportunity I had long sought. I had frequently heard about their pow-wows, and, while I had seen

---

1. Frank Albert Root was born in Binghamton, N. Y., July 3, 1837. He attended school in New York and Pennsylvania, and entered the printing business at Wellsboro, Pa., where he completed his apprenticeship. In April, 1857, he came to Kansas, and worked in newspaper offices in Lawrence, Quindaro, Highland and Atchison. He served as assistant postmaster at Atchison, and also was city clerk. Later he was appointed express messenger on the Holladay Overland Stage line, and during 1863-1864 he was in the service of the government as Overland mail agent at Latham station, Weld county, Colorado territory, handling mails brought in from the Pacific slope. He retired from the Overland service in 1865. That year he became part owner of the Atchison *Daily Free Press*. Later he became a partner of John A. Martin in the publication of the Atchison *Daily* and *Weekly Champion and Press*. He was one of the first route agents on the Central Branch line of the Union Pacific from Atchison to Waterville. He started newspapers in Waterville, Seneca, Holton, Topeka, North Topeka, and Gunnison, Colo., and is author of *The Overland Stage to California*. He died in Topeka on June 20, 1926. The paper published here was written in the early 1890's.

2. Since about 1819 or 1820, a number of Pottawatomies had been living with the Kickapoos, and had intermarried with them. By a treaty or national compact, in 1851, they had been adopted into the Kickapoo tribe. This accounted for the friendly relations existing between the two tribes.

(15)

several thousands of the "noble red men" in a stretch of more than five hundred miles on the plains, I never had spent a day among them in the country. Being on the ground in person and witnessing the weird festivities that followed this annual gathering, was indeed a rare pleasure.

The exercises were held at the wigwams of Ke-o-Quack,[3] near the west bank of Walnut creek, a handsome stream that courses down through the Kickapoo reservation. The spot selected—near the southwest corner of the reserve—was a very beautiful one, no doubt one of the finest to be found in that lovely portion of Kansas. It was an elevated section of prairie, surrounded on the east, north and south sides with belts of elm, oak and walnut timber, while on the west an unbroken view was had for a considerable distance over the green landscape. The prairies were decked with a profusion of choice wild flowers and this added much to the appearance of the surroundings.

The Indians had assembled on the premises a short time bef[ore] I reached there, having come from almost every direction. In a fe[w] minutes, dividing up into four parties, they were each arranged in a different position on the ground they had selected for the exercises. Beginning their program, a party of between thirty and forty Pottawatomies on foot were stationed on the west side. They began by hopping and jumping several feet above the ground, at the same time hooting and yelling at the tops of their voices at every jump. At the same time they chanted a number of their peculiar tribal songs, to the strains of the most outlandish sounding music, their orchestra comprising a sort of drum that had been gotten up for the occasion by stretching the skin of some animal over the top of an old paint keg. I listened, of course, to the music, but the discordant sounds that came from this improvised instrument were little less than torturing to all the pale-face guests. The drum was placed on the ground and surrounding it were seated as many squaws and bucks as could comfortably get around it, each one being provided with a set of sticks. These musicians thumped away industriously on their instrument, at the same time chanting some of their hideous-sounding airs. It was a rum-dum, rum-dum, rum-dum, for several hours, and nothing I had ever before heard was so monotonous.

While this musical part of the program was being gone over, a dozen or more of the bucks were out in front dancing, while another

---

3. Ke-o-Quack, Kickapoo, married a daughter of Wathena, a Kickapoo chief.

band was singing and dancing near by. During this part of the exercises a number of the braves were flourishing above their heads scalping knives, tomahawks, and several other promiscuous war trophies they were in possession of. On the south side of the inclosure was another delegation of Pottawatomies—mostly squaws, boys and papooses. The squaws and boys were left in charge of the ponies belonging to that tribe. On the north side was still another delegation on foot, but to which tribe they belonged I did not learn, for nearly all the Indians looked alike though dressed differently. Stationed at the east end and nearest the wigwams were the Kickapoos, the whole number, as arranged on the grounds, representing three sides of a rectangle, or perhaps more properly, a sort of oblong square. The most of the Kickapoos engaged in these exercises were mounted upon their fleetest ponies.

The costumes worn by the Indians were varied and numerous. They consisted of a great variety of outlandish and ludicrous styles, while their dusky faces, and in many cases a goodly portion of their bodies, were daubed and striped with several different colors of paint. What seemed to me the strangest thing about the whole business was that no two of the Indians assembled were dressed exactly alike. Many of them had their heads ornamented in styles simply ridiculous, while some of them were indescribable. A few were fixed up with gaily colored ribbons and cords with tassels of gaudy colors streaming from their slouch hats; a few had bead ornaments, with wild turkey, hawk and buzzard feathers in the tops of their hats and caps; some had plug hats with different kinds and styles of overcoats; one had on a pair of fine doeskin pants and a yellow calico blouse; some were attired in leggins, with blankets of various colors wrapped around them. One tall fellow waltzed around with one foot bare, clad in a heavy buffalo overcoat, while the mercury was soaring in the 90's. One brave was carelessly wrapped in a heavy red blanket doubled and tied around his body, on his feet were stogy [4] shoes, while his head was covered with a chip hat, striped off in several colors of paint with a few feathers sticking out of the top. Another fellow was attired in a calico shirt, a pair of leggins, and on one foot was a buckskin moccasin, while a heavy cowhide shoe was on the other; another was dressed in corduroy pants and stogy boots with heavy spurs attached to them; another cut a big swell, clad in a long, turkey-red shirt and moccasins, his

---

4. "Stogies" was the common name of the coarse, heavy cowhide boots and shoes made for rough manual labor and farm work. This designation was a common one up to about the last decade of the nineteenth century.

head covered with a dilapidated old plug hat; another wore a red shirt, white hat and blue pants. Another was in a gaudy calico shirt with buckskin leggins, while on his head was one of the ugliest looking caps imaginable; it was made from the fur of a beaver, and was minus the crown; in its front was a buffalo horn sticking out about eight inches, while the tail of a buffalo dangled down his back. Another was cutting up all sorts of queer antics, attired solely in a breech-clout; another was dressed in a peculiarly odd-looking suit with a string of fancy beads around his neck and three crescents made of tin or German silver, which dangled behind. Still another— and his was the most beautiful dress in the entire outfit—wore a fur cape made of otter and silk, tapering down to a point, which dragged at least a foot on the ground. This was fixed up with a variety of silver ornaments of various shapes and sizes and tapered all the way down from the neck to the bottom of the lovely rich garment. A pair of buffalo horns protruded from the head of one of the Pottawatomie braves, while around his neck was a rather singular looking ornament—a necklace manufactured from the claws of wolves. This made him look fierce enough, still he may have been as gentle and innocent as a lamb.

It is hardly necessary to describe more than a few of the varied costumes worn by the Indians at this pow-wow. Some of them were extremely ridiculous and decidedly funny; two or three were perfectly hideous; a number of them were ludicrous in the extreme. Such a contrast in styles and garments in an equal number of visitors from two tribes of "noble reds" may never have been seen in Kansas before or will ever be seen again. In a great measure the exercises became somewhat tiresome, still I rather enjoyed the dusky reunion as one of the rarest treats of the kind my eyes had ever feasted upon.

The plan for distributing the presents was an interesting feature and this part of the exercises I also enjoyed. A short time after the arrival of our pale-face party on the premises, one of the Kickapoos, mounted upon a fine horse and dressed in an elaborate costume, galloped around the band of Pottawatomies stationed on the west side of the "square," at the same time going through all manner of gestures known to but few besides the members of the two tribes, finally returning to the spot from whence he started. A young man—John C. Anderson [5]—a fine-looking half-breed who had been educated and spoke English fluently, was employed as the Kickapoo interpreter. He informed the writer that the exercises I had just

---

5. John C. Anderson was government interpreter for the Kickapoo Indians, with headquarters at the Kickapoo and Pottawatomie and Great Nemaha agency, during the 1860's.

witnessed was the first "sign." It signified that a pony was to be donated by the fellow mounted on the fine horse to one of the Pottawatomie visitors. In the various exercises that followed at intervals of a few minutes, some thirty Kickapoos rode around the band stationed at the west end, each giving away a pony at the conclusion of the ride. A number rode up to within a few feet of the Pottawatomie line and returned without going outside and around to the rear of the dusky visitors. This was a "sign" that the gifts they were about to bestow upon their guests were of another nature, intrinsically worth considerably less than the price of a pony.

In going through the various exercises out on the open prairie where the delegations formed the hollow square the time consumed was less than an hour. Following these the leader of the band of Kickapoos—Ke-o-Quack—rode forward on his fine horse and, in his native tongue, made a brief speech to his men. At the conclusion of his remarks all of the Indians then repaired to the wigwams which had been neatly arranged in the Walnut creek bottom, where they seated themselves, some on the fence, some on benches, stools, boxes, barrels, logs, etc., while a number were squatted around promiscuously on the grass. It seemed that there was not a breath of air stirring at one time and the heat from the broiling sun became oppressive. Repairing to one of the wigwams close by was a relief to me, for there I was out of the intense heat and was able for several hours to watch the exercises that followed with a far greater degree of comfort than at any time before.

Ali-co-the—one of the prominent Kickapoos—made a neat little speech in his native tongue. In his talk he took occasion to remind his brethren not to forget to be liberal in the donations to their visitors; at the same time he also reminded them that the time would swiftly pass when they would next become the guests of the Pottawatomie visitors. At the conclusion of his remarks another and not less interesting part of the program followed, that of "smoking" for the presents. This feature of the exercises was done in the following manner: A Kickapoo with a pipe—the stem of which is at least three feet long—desires to present a favorite small Pottawatomie boy with a substantial gift. Walking over to the little fellow he places the pipe to the lad's lips for a few seconds; then taking it away, he repairs a short distance to one side. In a minute or two he returns, leading a handsome pony which the young aborigine accepts, without even a smile—no expression on his face indicating the least sign of gratification by the gift. The next "smoking" was done by an Indian clad in his favorite (though not very becoming) suit—a breechclout—his entire covering being little more than enough to wad an old flint-lock musket. In his practically-naked condition the Indian was presented with a gunny sack filled with clothing—under the circumstances quite an appropriate gift. A young squaw put the pipe to the lips of one of her female visitors and presented her with a piece of calico. She next unhooked and took off her skirt and gave *that* to her also. One old gray-headed, gray-bearded man—Mo-she-no [6]—whose make-up appeared to be about three-quarters French and one-quarter Pottawatomie, was a rather conspicuous and somewhat prominent character on the scene. He was present bare-headed, with nothing but a calico shirt on his back and a pair of moccasins on his feet. After smoking a whiff or two he was presented with a skunk's skin stuffed with tobacco, something doubtlessly relished by the thinly-clad recipient. In addition to the various ponies presented there were a goodly number of other gifts bestowed, still the greater portion of them were of slight value.

At the conclusion of the presentation of gifts by the "smoking" plan, the next exercises consisted of dancing. An Indian carpet made of rushes and flag (or iris) leaves was spread out on the ground near the host's home and in front of the large wigwam the drum was placed. A half dozen or more Indians at once seated themselves around this instrument of torture and soon there was "music" in earnest. A few taps on the "drum" was the signal, and those seated around it at once began to render another selection of vocal and instrumental music in true aboriginal style. Almost instantly a dozen or more Prairie Pottawatomies jumped up and began dancing around the musicians. This was a scene interspersed with a number of antics that would do credit to an ordinary circus acrobat. Only a faint idea can be given of these dances; no two of the dancers resembled each other in dress. The exercises embraced at least half a dozen different dances, but the motions and gestures made by the participants as the various figures were being gone through, were decidedly ludicrous. One of the Indian braves had an old-style rifle and a horse pistol; another a flint-lock musket; another had a pistol of the Colt patent; several had bows with quivers filled with arrows; two or three had lances; some had tomahawks and several flourished hunting or scalping knives; a few had war clubs, while the balance were provided with a variety of other weapons. Some fearful shouts

---

6. Mo-she-no (Ma-she-nah) or the Elk Horns, was with Tecumseh, in his confederation against the whites. He took part in the battle of Tippecanoe, and later moved to Kansas with the tribe and lived at Kickapoo for twenty-two years.—Remsburg, Geo. J., "Scrap Books," v. B, p. 5, in library of the Kansas State Historical Society.

arose when dancing begun. It seemed as if one was in the midst of a weird pandemonium. At first they would leap several feet into the air, coming down and alighting first on one foot and alternately on the other, at the same time flourishing their guns, knives, pistols, tomahawks, etc., in savage warlike fashion, and all the while yelling at the top of their voices. At the conclusion of each dance a volley of doleful yells and the most hideous whoops and shouts would be sent up which sounded almost deafening.

As the exercises connected with the festival were held on the premises of Ke-o-Quack, courtesy naturally gave this popular Kickapoo the position of "captain," "marshal," "great mogul," or "high-cock-a-lorum" of the day. He was an exceedingly bright Indian— one of the most useful, intelligent, deserving and prosperous members of the tribe. He was past the half century mark in age when this "blowout" took place. His squaw was a prominent lady in the tribe, being the daughter of "Wa-the-na," after whom one of the prominent towns and the first county seat of Doniphan county was named in the latter '50's. Previous to the treaty of 1854—the year the Kansas-Nebraska bill passed Congress—she resided where that handsome town named for her father now stands, six miles west of the Missouri river from St. Joseph.

From the "spirited" condition of some of the Indians appearing at this gathering, it would seem that the festival might more properly have been called a regular old-fashioned jamboree. It is a fact that quite a number of the members of both tribes had provided themselves with an ample supply of the vilest liquor. During the exercises they had been slipping away to secretly imbibe of this hidden store, and from the quantity they had gotten away with at this time, it was evident that they were not behind the pale faces in learning how to get their booze.

In late years a religious form of worship, embracing a portion of the doctrines of a number of the Christian churches has appeared and is now practiced by some of the members of both the Kickapoo and Pottawatomie tribes. Only a few of these, however, are said to be earnest, consistent members of this church; yet they are an honor to their tribes. The most of them still believe in and practice the aboriginal doctrines taught by their "illustrious predecessors." The annual feasts connected with their jubilees and dances, which usually continue for several days, are illustrations of the manner in which the Indians express their loyalty and devotion to the one who, in their belief, they will join when they drop off and finally enter their new home in the "happy hunting ground."

Ferries in Kansas

Part IX—Arkansas River

George A. Root

NO EARLIER mention of the Arkansas river has been found than that in narratives of the Coronado expedition of 1540-1541. The river was first sighted by the Spaniards accompanying the expedition on June 29, 1541. This being the day of St. Peter and St. Paul, the name was given the river. One of the expedition's members called the stream the "River of Quivera."[1] Marquette, the French explorer, called the stream the "Akansa." Mexicans called it the "Rio Napete." William Delisle, on his map of 1700, called it the "Acansa." Emanuel Bowen's map of 1752 lists it as the "Rio des Acansas." LePage du Pratz's map of 1757 designates the stream as the "Arkansas," this probably being one of the earliest spellings of the name as we have it today.[2]

The Arkansas has been termed the "Nile of America," traversing the miles of sandy country to the east of the Rocky Mountains. This appellation may have been applied to the river by Marshall M. Murdock, founder of the Wichita *Eagle*, who many years ago wrote a classic under that title which has been widely read and copied. Mr. Murdock also frequently referred in a jocular way to the stream in the columns of the *Eagle* as the "Rackensack."

The Arkansas river rises in central Colorado, in a pocket of peaks in Lake county, near present Leadville, at an altitude of 10,000 feet. After leaving that county it takes a southerly course for about seventy miles, makes a turn to the east, through the celebrated Royal Gorge, then flows on and across the Great Plains region. Up to the early 1880's there was always an abundance of water in the river, and the channel, even down to the ever-flowing Little Arkansas, near Wichita, was usually filled. Occasionally, however, the river was a bed of dry sand above the mouth of the Little Arkansas for a couple of months in the fall.[3]

After leaving Lake county, Colorado, the river flows through Fremont, Pueblo, Otero, Bent and Prowers counties before it leaves that state, and enters Kansas near Coolidge, in Hamilton county.

---

1. *Kansas Historical Collections*, v. 12, p. 223.
2. Spellings and names taken from old maps and volumes in library of the Kansas State Historical Society.
3. James R. Mead, "A Dying River," in *Transactions of Kansas Academy of Science*, v. 14, p. 113.

From here it crosses that county and the counties of Kearny, Finney, Gray, Ford, Edwards, Pawnee, Barton, Rice, Reno, Sedgwick, Sumner and Cowley, leaving Kansas at a point about eight miles southeast of Arkansas City. From here the stream cuts across northeastern Oklahoma, bisects Arkansas and joins the Mississippi at present Napoleon.

In that portion of Colorado east of the Rocky Mountains and in Kansas, the course of the Arkansas is through gently rolling sandy soil, the bed of the river making up in width what it lacks in depth—in some places being about a mile wide.

Ordinarily the river receives but little water from its tributaries, except in times of flood. These usually occur in the spring, when the snows of the mountains begin to melt and spring rains set in. The most disastrous flood of this sort occurred in the upper river in Colorado, reaching Pueblo early in June, 1921, causing the death of over 500 persons and the destruction of property worth $10,000,000 or more.

Lowest stages of water in the river occur from August to December. During prolonged dry spells water in the channel has been known to disappear suddenly, only to make its reappearance as unexpectedly within the next day or two. This phenomenon was recorded by one of the early Sedgwick county newspapers, which, having mentioned that the river was dry, discovered water in the channel the next day. A short time later the water again disappeared, and reappearing just before the paper went to press caused the scribe to record an item to the effect that "The Arkansas wet its bed again last night." Low water was not unheard of even in the lower reaches of the river, for the Junction City *Union,* of November 9, 1867, citing the Fort Smith (Ark.) *Herald* as authority, said that "the Arkansas river was so low above that place last week that a drove of cows stopping to drink in it, drank the river in two." Another instance of the scarcity of water in the channel occurred during the past two decades, when the city of Hutchinson made an appropriation to cover the expense of sprinkling the bed of the river for the purpose of keeping down the dust.

The drainage area of the Arkansas is variously given as 177,510 square miles by the U. S. Weather Bureau, and from 185,000 to 188,000 square miles by standard encyclopedias,[4] this being greater than the area drained by the upper Mississippi. The stream is the greatest western affluent of the Missouri-Mississippi system, and

---

4. *Encyclopedia Britannica,* v. 2, p. 371. *New International Encyclopedia,* v. 2, p. 129.

its length is variously given as 1,477 miles by the Weather Bureau, and approximately 2,000 miles by the encyclopedias.

It has been common knowledge for years that there is an underflow of the Arkansas river. Probably this underflow was first noticed in June, 1860, the year of the great trans-Mississippi drought. That year M. M. Murdock dug down in the valley and found water. He dug a series of holes on different nights, and one night he sprinkled bran on the surface of the water and next morning when he got up the bran was on the south or southwest side of the hole. He called the attention of a government man to it, who said he had noticed the same thing. This government agent reported that the underflow was moving at the rate of eight or nine feet in every twenty-four hours.[5] Further investigations of this flow were made in the year 1904, by representatives of the U. S. Geological Survey, and some interesting facts were brought out. This underflow moves at an average rate of eight feet every twenty-four hours, in the general direction of the valley. The water plane slopes to the east at the rate of 7.5 feet per mile and towards the river at the rate of two to three feet per mile. The moving ground water extends several miles north from the river valley. No north or south limit was found. The underflow has its origin in the rainfall on the sand hills to the south of the river and on the bottom lands and plains north of the river. The influence of the floods in the river upon the ground-water level does not extend one half mile north or south of the channel. A heavy rain contributes more water to the underflow than a flood.[6]

With the settlement of that portion of Kansas lying along the river between Dodge City and the west line of the state, the pioneers in irrigation began construction of canals and ditches, and the waters of the Arkansas were diverted for irrigation purposes. Miles and miles of canals and ditches were constructed between the 100th meridian and the Colorado line. With the influx of settlers in the valley from the base of the mountains eastward to the Kansas line, so much of the flow of the river was diverted for agricultural purposes that by the time the river reached Kansas the stream was dry.[7] This action by farm owners in Colorado was the cause of ruining many farmers living along the river in western Kansas, and finally resulted in a suit brought by the state of Kansas against Colorado

---

5. Testimony of M. M. Murdock in the supreme court of the United States, in the Kansas-Colorado water suit.—Abstract of evidence, pp. 11, 12, in Archives division, Kansas State Historical Society.
6. *Water Supply and Irrigation Papers*, No. 153, p. 5.
7. *Transactions of Kansas Academy of Science*, v. 14, p. 113.

for a more equal distribution of the Arkansas' waters. This case was fought through the United States courts, but was decided against Kansas.

While the lower portion of the river is navigable as far as Fort Smith, early writers had stated that the head of navigation on the stream was twenty-four miles below old Fort Mann, this being about south of present Kinsley, in Edwards county. However, navigation to that point could only have been accomplished during a period of flood, and only then by boats of light draft. Some attempts at navigation had been made during the 1870's, and a small steamboat—the *Aunt Sally*—reached Arkansas City and was moored there on Sunday morning, June 30, 1878. During the early 1880's several small craft had managed to navigate from the lower river up as far as Wichita, but these attempts to prove the navigability of the river were disappointing to those most vitally interested. Dreams of being able to market surplus farm crops down the river by use of ferryboats, flat boats and steamers did not always materialize, for many cargoes shipped by water were stranded on sand bars en route. After a few trials these attempts were discontinued, owing to the shifting channel, sand bars and lack of water.

Ferries on the river north of the Oklahoma-Kansas line, with possibly one or two exceptions, do not antedate the establishment of towns in Cowley county about the year 1870. The first ferry encountered after crossing the boundary line was probably near Delphi, now Arkansas City.

On January 8, 1870, the Arkansas River Ferry Co. received a charter from the state of Kansas for a ferry near the town of Delphi, and in the vicinity of the mouth of the Walnut river—about two miles above it and south of the town. The incorporators of this company were H. B. Morton, G. H. Norton, W. R. Brown, E. C. Manning, P. B. Plumb, C. V. Eskridge and L. B. Kellogg.[8] The principal office of the company was to be located at or in the vicinity of Delphi. Capital stock was placed at $2,000, with shares $100 each. This charter was filed with the secretary of state January 10,

---

8. Of the projectors of this ferry, three were prominent in the newspaper business and one was a noted educator. Manning arrived in Kansas in 1859 and published papers in Marysville, Manhattan and Winfield. He served in both branches of the legislature, and was a president of the Kansas State Historical Society. Plumb arrived in Kansas in 1856, and in December that year became foreman of the *Herald of Freedom*, Lawrence. In June, 1857, he founded the *Kanzas News*, at Emporia. He helped organize the Eleventh Kansas cavalry, and became its lieutenant colonel. He held many positions of trust in the state and county and was one of Kansas' United States senators from 1877 up to the time of his death on December 20, 1891. Eskridge was editor and publisher of the Emporia *Republican*, served as lieutenant governor and also as a member of the board of regents of the Emporia State Normal School. Kellogg was attorney general, 1889-1891, and prominent in the State Teachers' Association.

1870.[9] More than likely this company never functioned, as no further history has been located.

According to county commissioners' records, the first ferry license for the Arkansas river within Cowley county was issued April 11, 1871, to W. H. Speers and others. This ferry was located at the point where the South Sixth street bridge of later date crossed the river, and was one of the busiest ferries in the county. The crossing was where the old Shoo Fly trail [10] from the west entered Arkansas City, and also where a few years later the Ponca trail [11] from the south reached the town.[12]

Various authorities agree that there was very little water in the Arkansas river in 1871, and the probabilities are that the ferryboat did not operate very much that year, if at all. There also appears to be a difference of opinion as to who operated the first ferry. According to Mrs. E. A. Eaton, who has been a resident of Arkansas City since 1871, the ferry was located at South Sixth street and Lincoln avenue, which is west of the main part of the city and to the south. A. A. Davis, known as "Peg Leg" Davis, was the operator, being assisted by his son Adley, a lad in his teens.[13] According to Mrs. Eaton, Davis operated the ferry up to the time the first bridge was built, probably in 1873 or 1874, at the site of the ferry location.[14] His boat was large enough to carry four horses and two boomer wagons, by unhitching the horses. It was operated

---

9. Corporations, v. 2, p. 206.

10. This trail went west between townships 34 and 35 to the Sumner county line, and was named for a Sumner county creek which received its name from some travelers who were camped there one night on their return from the settlements where they had first heard a new song entitled "Shoo Fly." This trail led to the southwest and was used as a freight route and stage line to Hunnewell and Caldwell, and like all other trails branched south and west.—Statement of Bert Moore, Winfield, in letters to author, dated January 10, 26, 1936.

11. The Ponca trail, Mr. Moore says, went south on the one half mile section line through sections 1, 12 and 13 to the Indian territory. It "was not named until placing of the Ponca Indians on their reservation in the years 1877 or 1878; was the trail from Arkansas City to Ponca agency on the Salt Fork river, being about forty miles long. Many trails branched from it leading to Indian agencies, cow camps and soldiers' camps. This trail also became a stage line until the building of the Santa Fé in 1886. This trail crossed at right angles the old Black Dog Osage trail near the village of Kildare, Okla. It was over this Ponca trail the homeseekers traveled in April, 1889, to reach the first land opened for settlement in Oklahoma. For several days after they were permitted to cross the Kansas-Indian territory line this trail was one broken line of covered wagons, all going south."—Letter of Bert Moore, January 26, 1936, to author.

12. Cowley county, "Commissioners' Journal," 1871.

13. "Census of 1875," Cowley county, Creswell township, Arkansas City post office, p. 11, gives the following: "A. A. Davis, 42; farmer; native of Ohio; from Wisconsin to Kansas. Wife, Sophia Davis, 38; native of Ohio. Adley, 18; born Wisconsin."

14. Fred C. DeMott, president of the Union State Bank, of Arkansas City, and a resident of that city for sixty-five years, in a letter to the author states that there was no way to cross the river until the bridge was built by subscription and opened as a toll bridge. "Amsley Davis, an old veteran who had taken a claim right by the approach of the bridge was given the job as toll-keeper. He was known as 'Peg Leg Davis' because he had a peg leg. When the bridge was carried away about 1877-'78, a man by the name of Boone Hartsock, who had some former experience in ferries, operated a cable ferry. After awhile there was a sand bar in the middle of the river and the ferry could not be operated clear across this part of the river, so they moved it up to the west part of town, a little north of Madison avenue, in S. 36, T. 34, R. 3 E., and operated it there until the bridge was repaired and built over.

by means of pulleys on a cable which was attached to trees on either side of the river, the boat having a large spoke wheel, like the old-fashioned steamboats. There were many Indians in the vicinity during those early days, but very few made use of the ferry, and then not very frequently, as Mr. Davis would not trust them.

After the building of the first bridge, the ferry south of town was moved up the river to a location immediately west of town. This first bridge was carried away or partially destroyed on several occasions. Lacking opportunity to consult commissioners' journals or early Cowley county newspapers, we are unable to give all dates when floods caused damage. However, the river was at flood stage, being bank full early in April, 1876. On July 12,[15] following, the river was reported to be twenty-six feet high at Little Rock, Ark., and full to the top of the bank at Arkansas City.

Unprecedently high waters in the river during late May, 1877, carried away or disabled all the bridges on the lower Arkansas, every one in Cowley county being put out of commission. A portion of the Sixth street bridge—two spans on the south—was all that survived the flood. A temporary ferry service was soon established at this point, the local paper making the following announcement: "A wagon will carry parties to and from the river free of charge. They will also convey them across the river in a boat. The rope has been sent for and the boat is building, so that before many days the ferry will be running." [16]

About this time William H. Speers, mill operator, inaugurated a temporary free service, announcing that he "has a new boat and is carrying all parties with grists for his mill free of charge across the Arkansas." [17] Mr. Speers is listed in the "Census of 1875," Cowley county, Creswell township, p. 18, as being 37 years of age; a miller, and a native of Ohio. He came to Kansas from Illinois.

Lack of bridges was a serious handicap to the town and county, as settlers were coming into the region every day. The following, from a local paper, describes conditions:

> The clerk of this township engaged a boat last week and went down the Arkansas as far as Deer creek, in search of the missing bridge. On the island at the mouth of the Walnut he found one bottom cord and part of the flooring lodged in the trees. The next lot, one whole span, was found on an island near Mr. Myers' in good condition. Someone had been taking it to pieces, and some of the iron was carried away. About two miles this side of Deer creek

---

15. Arkansas City *Traveler,* April 5, July 12, 1876.
16. *Ibid.,* May 30, 1877.
17. *Ibid.,* July 6, 1877.

another lot was found, badly broken. Fully one half of the missing part was found, and information gained that one span and a half had lodged near the Kaw agency. They also learned that a considerable portion of a red painted bridge was lying at the mouth of Deer creek.[18]

Preparations for the ferry south of town went steadily on. Lumber for the boat and a cable to stretch across the river had been ordered. The lumber arrived on June 20, and as all necessary arrangements had been completed, the ferry was expected to be in running order very shortly. By this time, however, the free rides from town to the Arkansas had come to a stop, the local paper, in mentioning the matter, stating that "the sturdy yeoman is compelled to take a little exercise between the river and town."[19] This ferry apparently was sponsored by the city and was to be a free ferry, and in getting it in shape to operate, volunteer help was solicited, as the following would indicate: "Our neighbor merchant came into the office yesterday and demanded that we supply some of our loose men to help fix the ferry. The boys were all loose and not in condition to work."[20]

The ferry was completed early in July, and at a meeting of the city council, July 6, it was decided to employ C. R. Bridges to run the boat for one month at $1 per day. The ferry was to be free to anyone during that time.[21] Another notice regarding the ferry, evidently for the benefit of patrons living on the opposite side of the river, read: "Free ferry on the Arkansas at this place. Come and go as often as you please without costing you a cent, as long as it is daylight. After sundown toll will be charged."[22]

Occasionally something happened on a ferryboat to break the monotony. The following could almost be classed among the "believe it or not" items so frequently found in papers of today:

A stranger drove on the ferryboat last week with a wagon and a woman sitting in the bottom of it. He had heard that the boat only went half way across the river bed, and when the boat stopped in the middle of the stream a minute he drove off. The horses went down almost out of sight, and the wagon sank until the woman's head was all that was out of the water. She sat calmly in the bottom, however, until she reached the shore. It is hardly worth while to add she got wet.[23]

Following the high water another ferry had been started west of town. This was a toll ferry, and as such, was not popular. At a

18. *Ibid.*, June 6, 1877.
19. *Ibid.*, June 30, 1877.
20. *Ibid.*
21. *Ibid.*, July 11, 1877.
22. *Ibid.*
23. *Ibid.*, August 8, 1877

meeting of the city council on July 2, 1877, an order was issued to pay $250 for the ferryboat west of town and to convert it into a free ferry.[24]

Another ferryboat had been built for the Arkansas following the flood, which had not been put to use at the time. This boat was about thirty-five feet long by twelve feet eight inches wide. It had a cabin at each end. On the Fourth of July this year the boat was tied up at the west ferry landing with five tons of chattels. Doctor Trichen, of Wichita, was in command of the boat and was moving his entire stock of drugs from the railroad terminus in Sedgwick county to Fort Smith, Ark. Thirteen persons besides the skipper were en route with him.[25]

About this time Jacob Parr started a ferry across the Arkansas. Just where this ferry was located has not been learned, other than it was at Denton's ford. The announcement as published in the local paper was as follows:

Jacob Parr will cross parties over the Arkansas at Denton's ford in a small boat for five cents each. He has a team that can be hired for $2 per day, and will run it two days a week, hauling passengers to town, and charging only enough to make the required two dollars.[26]

The next two items apply to one of the Arkansas City ferries, but which location we are unable to determine:

On and after August 1st toll will be charged on the ferry for crossing the Arkansas river near Arkansas City as follows, from sunrise to sunset: One single or double team, round trip 10 cents; one passenger on foot or horseback, round trip, 5 cents; each additional span of horses or yoke of cattle, round trip, 10 cents. After sunset 25 cents per trip will be charged.[27]

Ferry tickets are sold at I. H. Bonsall's office. Single crossing on horseback, two and one half cents. Single crossing with wagon, five cents. With four-horse team, 10 cents. After sunset 25 cents.[28]

During August the ferry boat west of town was moved to a location south of town where the bridge formerly stood. This move evidently met with some popular approval and the local paper commented that it was much easier to get at, and added further:

Since the ferry has been moved from the west to the south of town, many persons, especially those of East Bolton, express themselves well pleased. We crossed on it last Sunday and found that less than half the distance over sand has to be traveled. If an inclined platform was built to the remaining part of the bridge now, it would help it a great deal more.[29]

24. *Ibid.*, July 4, 1877.
25. *Ibid.*, July 4, 1877.
26. *Ibid.*, July 25, 1877.
27. *Ibid.*, August 1, 1877.
28. *Ibid.*, August 15, 1877.
29. *Ibid.*, August 22, 1877.

That the removal did not satisfy everyone may be inferred by the following item published the succeeding week: "The ferry is moved," says a Creswell man. "D- -n the ferryboat," says a Bolton man.

The ferries at this time were well patronized. There was much freighting from Arkansas City, Winfield, Wichita and other points along the north side of the river. It was not an uncommon occurrence to arrive at a ferry and find a large number of teams and outfits awaiting their turn to be crossed. Each was anxious to get across and delays of any sort were not popular.

Early in November, 1877, a project was on foot to place another ferry over the Arkansas west of town. The local paper in mentioning the matter commented that the enterprise would be a paying investment to the owners as well as a benefit to the town.[30] Two weeks later the same authority stated that "arrangements have been about completed to place another ferry west of town."[31] No further mention of this is found this year than a laconic item in the issue of December 26, which stated that "the new ferry west of town floats like a swan." Two weeks later, the *Traveler* recorded that "the ferry west of town is running all right again," but failed to mention why it had not been running. This ferry was located between Secs. 26 and 35, T. 34, R. 3 E., and was in operation after the Sixth Street bridge was built, as it saved a drive around the bend of the river.[32] It was projected by Speers and Walton. Early in April, 1878, they announced that their boat was to be operated by steam, the local paper stating that "the engine used on Christy's steam thresher is to be placed on the ferryboat west of town by Speers and Walton, to try the experiment of ferrying by steam."[33] The same authority, in issue of April 23, following, said: "Speer and Walton will have their steam ferryboat ready to run this week, and before long will make a trial trip to Oxford, El Paso and Wichita."[34]

The owners named their boat the *Arkansas Traveler,* and by early in May it was engaged in ferrying as far upstream as Wichita, its cargoes being somewhat diversified—ranging from excursionists to sawlogs and cordwood. On Sunday, May 5, 1878, the boat took a load of excursionists up to Salt City, making the trip without

30. *Ibid.,* November 14, 1877.
31. *Ibid.,* November 28, 1877.
32. Statement of F. M. Arnott to Bert Moore, January 10, 1936.—Letter of Mr. Moore to author.
33. Arkansas City *Traveler,* April 3, 1878.
34. Kansas State Board of Agriculture, *First Biennial Report, 1877-1878,* p. 159.

trouble of any kind. Being overconfident they tried going on after dark, when their boat stuck on a sandbar. There they remained until morning, compelling many of the anxious excursionists to find their way back home on foot. On the return trip the next morning the boat made the distance from Salt City to Arkansas City, seven miles, in three quarters of an hour.[35]

During June, 1878, high waters in the Arkansas again caused inconvenience to the residents of the county. Even ferry service was temporarily disrupted. The *Traveler* of June 19 said the river had risen some four feet over the bridge pilings at that place, but also conveyed the good news that "the ferry across the Arkansas is in good running order again, and ready for business."

Down the river there was always a good market for surplus grain, flour, produce, etc. During the late 1870's it was not always an easy matter to sell surplus crops; the railroad was too far away, and the river afforded the most convenient route to a market, so ferryboats were utilized for conveying such crops. A boat, under the command of Capt. H. B. Pruden, built early in 1879 at Arkansas City for the Pawnee agency, left on April 2 with a cargo of 12,000 pounds of potatoes.[36]

High water late in 1879 or early in 1880 must have put the bridge at this location out of commission and necessitated the use of the ferry for a time. This was no doubt followed by a shortage of water in the channel, for the local paper said: "The ferry west of town at the present stage of water has assumed more the shape of a bridge than a boat, since it spans the channel from shore to shore."[37] Midsummer brought good rains to the west and the Arkansas went "on a bender," rendering fords useless and ferries somewhat bothersome.[38]

Following the disastrous flood of May 27, 1877, which swept away all the bridges in the county, the only action taken was to call an election to be held on August 18, following, for the purpose of voting bonds for building and repairing the bridges on the Arkansas. This measure carried, but up to late in November nothing definite had been decided on. Early in March, 1878, Bolton township voted $2,000 in bonds to be used towards rehabilitating the old bridge, and a contract was let. Within the next six weeks a force was at work and it was thought that within sixty days teams would be crossing.[39]

35. Arkansas City *Traveler*, May 8, 1878.
36. *Ibid.*, April 2, 1879.
37. *Ibid.*, April 4, 1880.
38. *Ibid.*, August 11, 1880.
39. *Ibid.*, November 14, 1877; February 12, March 27, April 24, 1878.

By early May about half the piles had been driven and work on the spans had commenced. A week later the local paper reported progress as follows:

> The piling on the Arkansas river bridge is about completed, and the floor will be laid in a few more days. Everybody will be glad of it, as it is not a pleasant matter to "stick on a sandbar" about the time the other party is getting away with your hotel grub. Then if Boone Hartsock was not a religious man the language of the boatman might be obnoxious.[40]

Two months later the bridge was not yet ready for use, and the ferry was still the only means for crossing. It was thought, however, that within two more weeks the ferry could be dispensed with. There was also a growing feeling that the portion of the bridge on the Bolton side was not safe. The new section had been built some four or five feet higher than the old part, and township authorities were called upon to remedy this situation before the bridge was opened to traffic.[41] Before this, however, the local paper once more called attention to its unsafe condition and advocated that it should be nailed up and repaired before use. It was finally opened about the middle of September, 1878, about fifteen months after being wrecked by the flood. In August, 1879, the township trustee published a warning that the bridge was unsafe for heavily loaded wagons, and that any wagons carrying two tons must cross at their own risk.[42] The *Traveler* continued its fight until a new bridge was built.

Roads were one of the requisites of the newly established Arkansas City, and during the session of the 1871 legislature three state roads were established to connect with the town. One, 89¼ miles in length, ran from Florence, in Marion county, via El Dorado, Augusta, Douglass, Rock City, Polk's, Walnut City and Winfield. Another, 76 miles in length, ran from Humboldt, via Fredonia, Longton, Elk Falls, Greenfield and Tisdale. The third road, 57 miles long, ran from Wichita to Arkansas City.[43] In 1877 another road was established, running from Arkansas City to Independence, via Cedar Vale and Sedan, this being a little over 82 miles in length.[44]

---

40. *Ibid.*, May 15, 1878.
41. *Ibid.*, August 7, 14, 1878.
42. *Ibid.*, September 4, 25, October 16, 1878; August 13, 1879.
43. *Laws*, 1871, p. 432. Plats, field notes, etc., of the first two roads, and commissioners' report of the last, are on file in the Archives division of the Kansas State Historical Society.
44. *Laws*, 1877, p. 221. Field notes, plat and commissioners' report in Archives division.

(*Part IX—Arkansas River Ferries—to be concluded in the May Quarterly.*)

Labor Problems During the First Year of Governor Martin's Administration

Edith Walker

Labor Legislation in 1885

ALTHOUGH the force of economic change was not felt with the same degree of intensity in Kansas as in the older sections of the country, still rapid changes in economic conditions were taking place during the eighties. The development in the fields of mining, transportation, and manufacturing increased the number of workers in the state having special need for protective legislation.[1] In 1884 the General Assembly of the Knights of Labor formulated a platform and declaration of principles in which the state legislatures were urged to establish bureaus of labor.[2] The following year such a department was established in Kansas.[3]

The sponsor of the bill creating a bureau of labor was Sen. W. J. Buchan, of Wyandotte, who had gone to work as a boy in Ohio when he was twelve years old. He served as a clerk in a drug store for several years and enlisted in the Union forces at the age of eighteen. After coming to Kansas in 1867 he worked for a time as a brakeman on the Kansas Pacific Railway before his admission to the bar in 1871.[4]

He introduced the measure into the senate January 19, 1885, where it was debated vigorously. Sen. R. M. Crane, of Marion, proposed, for the sake of economy, that it be amended and the duties contemplated by the bill be added to the work of the bureau of agriculture. In this endeavor he was supported by Sen. C. H. Kimball, of Parsons, who explained that the duties of the secretary of the board of agriculture were concerned with labor. He cautioned the senators to think carefully before they passed legislation which would increase the expenses of the state. Sen. W. M. Congdon, a farmer from Sedgwick county, who opposed the establishment of a labor bureau, explained that Ohio, which suffered from serious industrial conflicts, had such a bureau which was probably the cause of labor riots there.[5] Moreover, he was satisfied that the measure was useless and simply a move to provide someone with a job.

---

1. Kansas Bureau of Labor and Industrial Statistics, *First Annual Report* (1885), p. 4.
2. Ibid., *Fourth Annual Report* (1888), p. 36.
3. *Laws*, Kansas, 1885, ch. 188.
4. Kansas state senate, *Directory* (1889), p. 9.
5. *The Daily Commonwealth*, Topeka, February 18, 1885.

Senator Buchan, in defense of his measure, maintained that forty percent of the citizens of Kansas merited more than a mere recognition of their existence by placing the work proposed by the bill in the department of agriculture. The very nature of the work, he insisted, demanded a person especially fitted for the task.[6] Sen. Frank S. Jennings of Winfield claimed that the welfare of the Kansas laborer was entirely neglected. He was convinced that it was to the interest of all Kansas citizens to create an independent department to better the condition of the workingman and that the time had come to establish it.[7] Efforts to amend the bill were unsuccessful, and it passed the senate providing for the creation of a labor bureau coördinate with the bureau of agriculture.[8] After an uneventful course in the house, where it encountered little opposition, it became a law March 5, 1885.[9]

It provided for the establishment of a bureau of labor and industrial statistics under the direction of a commissioner who was to be appointed by the governor for a term of two years. The duties of the bureau were to collect, assort, and present to the governor, in annual reports, statistics relating to all departments of labor and industry in the state, especially in their relation to the commercial, industrial, social, educational, and sanitary condition of the laboring classes. The commissioner was given the power to take and preserve testimony, examine witnesses under oath, and while discharging his duty to enter any factory, workshop or mine, and compel persons to answer questions. The state, city, county, and township officers were required to furnish him information upon request.[10]

F. H. Betton, who was indorsed for the position by the Knights of Labor, was appointed in April as the first commissioner of the labor bureau.[11] He had engaged in the lumber and milling business for years, took up the duties of the new office with that knowledge of the labor problem which comes from actual experience.[12]

A disastrous fire in a mine at Carbondale in 1883 had aroused the Kansas miners to action. The enactment of a law designed to protect their health and safety and to provide for the inspection of the mines was the result.[13] The code was revised March 13, 1885,

6. Topeka *Daily Capital,* February 18, 1885.
7. *The Daily Commonwealth,* Topeka, February 18, 1885.
8. Topeka *Daily Capital,* February 18, 1885.
9. *House Journal,* 1885, pp. 728, 748, 843.
10. *Laws,* Kansas, 1885, ch. 188.
11. Topeka *Daily Capital,* April 18, 1885.
12. Editorial in the Atchison *Daily Champion,* April 19, 1885.
13. Kansas State Inspector of Mines, *First Annual Report* (1884), pp. 3-5.

and minor changes made. The annual number of visits the mine inspector was required to make to each mine in the state was reduced from four to two. The revised law required all coal operators to make quarterly reports to the inspector of the amount of coal mined and the number of persons employed. An annual report to the governor supplanted monthly reports originally made by the inspector to the secretary of the board of agriculture. To further protect the miners a clause was added limiting the amount of explosives which each miner was allowed to take into the mine at one time, and stating that this material was to be kept in a tight box.[14]

In June, 1885, John R. Braidwood of Pittsburg[15] was appointed inspector of mines.[16] As a practical miner and civil engineer he was well fitted for the position[17] and was recommended by the Knights of Labor as well as by others interested in Kansas mines and miners.[18] Both Mr. Braidwood and Gov. John A. Martin, who appointed him, were eager to see that the law was obeyed and the health and lives of the miners protected. Moreover, they hoped that the mine inspector, in the course of his duties, might be able to maintain harmonious relations between mine owners and employees, thus eliminating a resort to strikes.[19]

On January 16, 1885, Sen. John N. Ritter, of Columbus, introduced a bill to secure to the industrial workers of Kansas the payment of their wages every month in lawful money of the United States.[20] It was referred to the committee on mines and mining of which Sen. T. L. Marshall, of Osage City, was chairman.[21] Senator Marshall worked diligently in the senate in favor of the measure, where it was passed by unanimous vote.[22]

The house, however, was reluctant to enact a law which might discourage the development of Kansas industries. J. R. Burton, of Dickinson county, felt that the lawmakers should do everything in their power to help build the state and not discourage its industrial development.[23] Toward the close of the session the house amended

---

14. *Laws,* Kansas, 1885, ch. 143.
15. Editorial in *Labor's Tribune,* Weir City, June 18, 1885.
16. Letter from Gov. John A. Martin to J. R. Braidwood, June 13, 1885, in "Correspondence of Kansas Governors, Martin" (Letterpress books), v. II, p. 151, Archives division, Kansas State Historical Society. Hereafter, the various forms of this correspondence will be cited "C. K. G."
17. Editorial in Parsons *Daily Sun,* June 27, 1885.
18. Editorial in *The Daily Citizen,* Topeka, June 13, 1885.
19. Letter of J. R. Braidwood, Pittsburg, June 15, 1885, in "C. K. G., Martin" (Personal), v. III. Also letter of Governor Martin to J. R. Braidwood, June 16, 1885, in *ibid.* (Official), v. LVIII, pp. 436, 437.
20. *Senate Journal,* 1885, p. 164.
21. *Ibid.,* p. 257.
22. *Ibid.,* p. 507.
23. Topeka *Daily Capital,* February 22, 1885.

the bill to the point of destroying its intent.[24] Two conference committees were appointed to work out the differences existing between the two houses, but they proved unsuccessful and the bill failed to become a law.[25]

THE MISSOURI PACIFIC RAILWAY STRIKE

Early in March, 1885, a strike occurred on the Missouri Pacific Railway which arrested the operation of the trains upon that company's lines in Kansas, Missouri and Texas, except the passenger trains carrying the United States mails. Thus all freight traffic was entirely suspended and the railway system practically paralyzed for a period of nine days.[26]

On October 10, 1884, a notice had been posted informing the mechanics and other employees in the shops of a ten percent reduction in their wages. This cut was to take effect from the first of the month. This, together with earlier reductions, brought their wages below the level paid by other railway companies in Kansas, Missouri and Texas. In addition, the hours had also been reduced, with less pay in proportion.[27] In February, 1885, with increase in business and consequent greater demand for rolling stock, full time had been restored.[28] The low wages remained, however, and the indignant workers demanded a restoration of the wage scale of September, 1884. Their action was not impulsive, but taken only after consideration. They maintained that they could not live on less than the former wage, and that sickness or any emergency made it impossible to live on that.[29] In March, 1885, fully aware of their opportunity to impair disastrously the services of the company, they walked out.[30]

Those included in this action were the shopmen employed at Atchison and Parsons in Kansas, at Sedalia and Kansas City in Missouri, and at Fort Worth and Denison in Texas—points that practically commanded the entire railroad system of this company. They refused to work any longer until the matter of which they complained was arranged to their satisfaction.[31] On the afternoon of March 7, at the signal of a whistle, 300 men at Parsons dropped

---

24. Editorial in *The Daily Commonwealth,* Topeka, March 8, 1885.
25. *Senate Journal,* 1885, p. 855.
26. Kansas Board of Railroad Commissioners, *Third Annual Report* (1885), p. 22.
27. Kansas Bureau of Labor and Industrial Statistics, *Second Annual Report* (1886), p. 21.
28. Parsons *Daily Sun,* February 12, 1885.
29. Atchison *Daily Champion,* March 10, 1885.
30. Kansas City (Mo.) *Daily Journal,* March 9, 1885.
31. Kansas Board of Railroad Commissioners, *Third Annual Report* (1885), p. 22.

their work and walked out of the shops. That evening, acting upon orders from Sedalia, Mo., between 200 and 300 shopmen struck at Atchison.[32] Two days later the mechanical employees of the Missouri Pacific Railway at West Kansas City joined the ranks of the strikers.[33]

Members of the Knights of Labor had charge of the strike at Atchison, where they had a strong organization.[34] A meeting was called Saturday evening, March 7, where committees and leaders were chosen, and the details necessary to conduct a successful strike were carefully worked out.

On March 9 the company tendered the workmen their pay up to the time they quit work and notified them of their discharge. They refused to receive the one or to recognize the other. They would not work nor would they vacate their places.[35]

From the beginning of the controversy every movement was directed by the executive committee representing the strikers, and a perfect police system was maintained, under which the property of the railroad company and private individuals was fully protected. The yards were closely guarded and two engines kept in readiness for any emergency. The strikers were determined to hold the freight engines. They were equally determined, however, that no violence should occur, and as a pledge of their intention not to destroy any property, offered to detail twenty-five or fifty of their men to be sworn in as special deputy constables.[36]

Soon after the trouble developed the railway authorities at Atchison filed notices of the controversy with the local officers and called upon them for protection of the company's property from the rioters.[37] There was no violence on the part of the employees, no attempt to destroy property, nor was there any record of any complaint having been filed charging the rioters with the violation of any law or resistance to arrest. The local officers, however, promptly stated that they were powerless to act.[38] Both the mayor of Atchison and the sheriff of Atchison county immediately informed the governor that an organized mob was in possession of the trains and engines of the Missouri Pacific Railway, and the latter called upon the governor to furnish sufficient militia to put down the

32. Atchison *Daily Champion*, March 8, 1885.
33. *Ibid.*, March 10, 1885.
34. Kansas City (Mo.) *Daily Journal*, March 9, 1885.
35. Atchison *Daily Champion*, March 10, 1885.
36. *Ibid.*, March 11, 1885.
37. *Ibid.*, March 10, 1885.
38. *Ibid.*, March 11, 1885.

riot and disperse the mob.[39] Superintendent Fagan notified Governor Martin that the passenger and freight trains were in the hands of a mob and the passengers driven from the trains. He explained that the city and county officials could do nothing, and he appealed to the governor to take immediate action to furnish military protection for the railroad property.[40] H. M. Hoxie of St. Louis, third vice-president of the Missouri Pacific Railway, not only requested but demanded that Governor Martin take steps necessary to protect the company's property in the state of Kansas and thus make it possible for the railroad to continue to serve the public.[41] The following day, March 10, he again wrote to the governor explaining that the local authorities had expressed themselves to be powerless. Consequently, he requested immediate aid in order to avoid loss to the railway and to the shippers. Unless the state authorities stepped in, he insisted the people would soon suffer from lack of coal and other provisions. Gov. J. S. Marmaduke, of Missouri, he pointed out, had ordered out the state militia. In closing, he informed the governor that he had directed the attorneys representing the company at Atchison and Parsons to communicate to him the seriousness of the situation.[42]

Rumors were rife that the company intended soon to abandon attempts at conciliation and appeal to the federal government for protection. If the state admitted itself powerless then the federal soldiers would be called upon.[43] Although the strikers laughed at the talk of ordering out the state militia, they realized that the use of federal troops was a far more serious matter. The men were determined to win, but it was believed that they would disperse rather than come into conflict with the regular soldiers.[44]

The situation facing the governor was a grave one. Local authorities and railroad officials alike had insisted that only the use of force could suppress the riot. Governor Martin realized fully that a serious outbreak resulting in the loss of life and destruction of property might occur. Still, the use of force might provoke a conflict with equally disastrous results.

Determined to ascertain fully his duties and powers before taking

---

39. Telegram of Mayor C. C. Burns to Governor Martin, March 9, 1885, in "C. K. G., Martin" (Official), 1884-1885. Also telegram of Sheriff L. B. Hargrove to Governor Martin, March 9, 1885, *ibid.*
40. Telegram of W. W. Fagan, division superintendent of the Missouri Pacific Railway Co., Atchison, to Governor Martin, March 9, 1885, *ibid.*
41. Telegram and letter of H. M. Hoxie to Governor Martin, March 9, 1885, *ibid.*
42. Telegram of H. M. Hoxie to Governor Martin, March 10, 1885, *ibid.*
43. Atchison *Daily Champion,* March 10, 1885.
44. Kansas City (Mo.) *Daily Journal,* March 10, 1885.

any hasty action in the controversy,[45] Governor Martin submitted to the attorney general eight definite propositions covering the perplexing problems which confronted him. Thus he learned first, that, according to Kansas laws, in case of invasion, insurrection, or breach of the peace, the executive authority of a state was authorized and required to call out the militia. The constable and sheriff had the power to call to their aid all able-bodied citizens of their township and county in enforcing the law. Until they had done so, and thus exhausted every effort, they were not entitled to the aid of the militia. Second, no statute provided that any civil officer had the right to call on the executive for the militia. In the third place, in the case of a call from local officers for military aid, it was the duty of the governor to investigate first, and if he felt the militia unnecessary he might refuse to comply with the call. Fourth, a constable's and sheriff's authority was almost unlimited and only as a last resort might military aid be used. Fifth, military aid was justified when a mob prevented the legal serving of writs and rendered useless lawful court orders. Sixth, the governor must be satisfied on more substantial grounds, however, than rumor or newspaper reports, that the local officers were unable to do their duty. Seventh, like individuals, railway companies must use care in protecting their property. If molested they must first rely upon civil or criminal remedies. If the use of the railway property was interfered with by strikers it was the duty of the railroad authorities to file complaints and swear out warrants for the apprehension of the offenders. If the civil officers were powerless to do their duty, then they might call upon the commanding military officer, and he, in turn, upon the executive. Finally, no officer of a railroad had the legal right to demand of the executive the use of the militia.[46]

To the alarmed sheriff of Atchison county the governor pointed out his duty to preserve peace, and informed him that he was empowered to call to his aid as many deputies as he felt necessary. He also cited the laws, the provisions of which set forth the sheriff's powers. If these laws were faithfully carried out, and an effort made to coöperate with the city officials, who were given like powers, need for executive action would be rendered unnecessary.[47] The sheriff promptly answered, and still insisted that he was powerless.[48]

45. Atchison *Daily Champion*, March 10, 1885.
46. Attorney General of the State of Kansas, *Fifth Biennial Report* (1886), pp. 101-104.
47. Letter of Governor Martin to Sheriff L. B. Hargrove, Atchison, March 9, 1885, "C. K. G., Martin" (Letterpress books, Official), v. LVI, p. 432.
48. Telegram of Sheriff L. B. Hargrove to Governor Martin, March 9, 1885, *ibid.* (Official), 1884-1885.

To these insistent demands for help the governor did not respond with troops, but he did investigate the facts. He dispatched Adjutant General Alexander B. Campbell to Parsons,[49] and requested the board of railroad commissioners to proceed to Atchison. In writing to the commissioners he described the situation, and explained that although he was fully aware of the fact that legally they had no power to act in such an emergency, he believed their presence in Atchison would have a salutary effect. Therefore, he urged them to investigate the trouble there and see whether their services as mediators would be accepted by both parties. In this emergency, only one other course was left open, and that was to call out the militia—a move he was very anxious to avoid.[50] He then informed the attorney representing the company at Atchison of his move in the direction of mediation through the agency of the railroad commissioners, and asked him if his company would accept their services as arbiters.[51] In reply, the attorney ignored the governor's proposal and merely stated that the Missouri Pacific Railway Co. refused to yield to the demands of the strikers.[52]

After seeking information concerning wages paid by other railroads operated in Missouri, Kansas, and Texas,[53] Governor Martin endeavored to get in direct touch with the committee representing the strikers at Atchison. When informed that that committee was reluctant to leave the men without control,[54] he hastened to Atchison. Here he held a long conference with the executive committee, and though according the strikers his sympathy, he informed them that he was unable, as governor, to sympathize with the methods they employed to gain their point. Later, at a conference including representatives of all the parties in the controversy, the governor proposed that the railroad commissioners serve as arbitrators and said that he believed that the matter would be fairly adjusted if submitted to them. After careful consideration the striking employees expressed their willingness to accept the services of the commissioners, but subject to conditions which amounted to dictating

49. Letter of Governor Martin to Adj. Gen. A. B. Campbell, Fort Scott, March 10, 1885, *ibid.* (Letterpress books, Official), v. LVI, p. 468.
50. Letter of Governor Martin to the board of railway commissioners, March 10, 1885, *ibid.*, pp. 459-462.
51. Letter of Governor Martin to B. P. Waggener, Atchison, March 10, 1885, *ibid.*, p. 465.
52. Letter of Everest and Waggener, Atchison, to Governor Martin, March 10, 1885, *ibid.* (Official), 1884-1885.
53. Kansas Board of Railroad Commissioners, *Third Annual Report* (1885), p. 23.
54. Telegram of N. L. Prentis, Atchison, to Governor Martin, March 10, 1885, "C. K. G., Martin" (Official), 1884-1885.

the terms of settlement. On the other hand, the Missouri Pacific Company made no reply whatever to the governor's proposal.

The plan to arbitrate was abandoned, and the prospects of an immediate settlement seemed, indeed, discouraging. However, the governor made another attempt to adjust the difficulty and bring about an amicable settlement. At his suggestion committees representing the strikers at the various railroad centers were appointed and prepared to go to St. Louis to confer with the railway officials there. While at no time during the deadlock was there any danger to either the property of the public or the company, nevertheless, every hour the strike was prolonged increased the difficulty for both the strikers and the company.[55]

While the governor was in Atchison awaiting developments he sent a long telegram to Mr. Hoxie describing the situation in Kansas in which he said:

. . . Nothing whatever has been done by the strikers, either here or elsewhere in the state to justify a call for troops, or their use either by the state or the United States. This opinion is confirmed by the railroad commissioners, two of whom, you know, are lawyers.

Second, I fear you do not comprehend the extent and character of the strike; ostensibly, it is confined to the shopmen. In fact, as I am convinced, it extends to the employees of every branch of your service.

Third, the strike is, in all its features, phenomenal in the history of strikes. The strikers are sober, intelligent, orderly men, who have always, heretofore, been loyal to their employers. They are such employees as any private citizen would be glad to have. Their character and intelligence deserves respect.

Fourth, There is not the slightest danger that the men engaged in the strike will destroy any property. The only danger is, that the lawless elements, who always gather where trouble prevails, may do so.

Fifth, The men believe they have been wronged, and I am impelled to say that I believe the universal sentiment of the state sympathizes with them in this opinion.

For all of these reasons, I appeal to you to abandon any purpose of provoking a collision, if you entertain it, and to endeavor to arrange terms for amicable settlement with your employees. I believe the men would promptly and gladly accept overtures looking to such a settlement.

Mr. Hoxie replied that he appreciated fully the situation at Atchison. He wrote, ". . . if the men who have been in our employ . . . will permit us to resume business . . . we will discuss and arrange wages with them . . . for their future employment. . . ." The company demanded absolute submission to its terms. Feeling that it was fruitless to remain any longer

55. Editorial in Atchison *Daily Champion*, March 12, 1885.

in Atchison, in view of this position, Governor Martin informed Mr. Hoxie of his intentions to return to Topeka.

The situation at Atchison was characteristic of the condition of things existing at other places where the strike prevailed. Adjutant General Campbell informed the governor that the situation at Parsons, though peculiar, was entirely safe so far as public peace was concerned.[56] At Kansas City the engines stood idle and the force in the freight department, though kept on duty, had very little work to do. Meetings were held regularly at Armourdale, and committees appointed to carry on the strike.[57]

The representative appointed by the strikers left Atchison Friday, March 13, for Sedalia, to join similar representatives from Sedalia and Parsons. They planned to go on to St. Louis, providing the railroad officials there would give them an audience. With both parties to the contest demanding surrender to their terms, considerable attention was focused upon the committee on its way to St. Louis. The prospects of an amicable settlement, however, seemed discouraging, and especially so when the representative of the Atchison strikers returned the same night from Sedalia, having accomplished nothing.[58] Mr. Hoxie expressed no willingness to meet the committee and so the men abandoned the plan of going on to St. Louis.[59]

The situation presented a real difficulty. If compliance with the demands of the strikers had been the only problem it would have been an easy matter to end the strike. But other questions of much greater importance had arisen in the progress of the conflict. The striking employees illegally held the property of the company, and refused to permit the owners to gain possession of it.[60] The company had tendered them full pay in discharge of its obligations to them.[61] Hence, for the Missouri Pacific company to treat directly with them now would amount to an abdication, on its part, of the management and direction of its own affairs. The company's chief executive officers believed the majority of their employees to be loyal to the company's interests; still it was felt that the strikers had placed themselves under the direction of ambitious and unscrupulous leaders whose growing arrogance in the future would

56. Letter of A. B. Campbell, Fort Scott, to Governor Martin, March 11, 1885, "C. K. G.," 1884-1885.
57. Kansas City (Mo.) *Daily Journal,* March 12, 1885.
58. Atchison *Daily Champion,* March 14, 1885.
59. *Ibid.,* March 15, 1885.
60. Kansas City (Mo.) *Daily Journal,* March 12, 1885.
61. Atchison *Daily Champion,* March 10, 1885.

render impossible the efficient management of the property, and place the master in the position of servant.[62]

On Friday, the day that Governor Martin returned to Topeka, Mr. Fagan, division superintendent at Atchison, wrote him that Mr. Hoxie wished to meet him and the board of railroad commissioners at St. Louis. In reply the Kansas executive explained that he and the commissioners would cheerfully go to St. Louis to meet with Mr. Hoxie if terms for a friendly settlement of the strike were open for discussion. But if the terms announced by Mr. Hoxie in his last dispatch were final, Governor Martin failed to see how he and the commissioners could be of any service. Mr. Fagan replied that the general manager of the Missouri Pacific company had stated that he would be glad to confer with the Kansas authorities in order to bring about an adjustment of the strike.

The Kansas governor and railroad commissioners were joined in this conference at St. Louis, Sunday morning, March 15, by the following Missouri officials: Gov. J. S. Marmaduke, Attorney General J. C. Jamison, and Oscar Kochtitzky, commissioner of labor statistics. R. S. Hayes, first vice-president of the Missouri Pacific company, served as spokesman for the Gould system. After a long discussion of the situation, during which the facts were presented, the representatives of the two states formulated a proposition which they believed a just settlement. They recommended its acceptance by the company and the striking employees. They proposed that the company restore the wage scale of September, 1884, including one and one half price for extra time worked, and reëmploy the men without prejudice on account of the strike. The railway officials immediately accepted this proposition and stated that the wage scale would go into effect March 16 and would not be changed except after thirty days' notice. Thus they yielded every point demanded by the strikers.[63]

The news that the intercession of the representatives of Kansas and Missouri had resulted in their favor reached the employees Sunday evening, March 15. The next morning the shopmen returned to their regular posts, but before work was resumed, the leaders insisted that it was necessary to hear from headquarters at Sedalia. The command from the leaders at that point to return to work was received in the afternoon. The central committee had spoken; the strike was over.[64]

62. Kansas City (Mo.) *Daily Journal*, March 17, 1885.
63. Kansas Board of Railroad Commissioners, *Third Annual Report* (1885), p. 24.
64. Kansas City (Mo.) *Daily Journal*, March 16, 1885. Also Atchison *Daily Champion*, March 17, 1885.

The strike involved more than the employees and employers, for it reached the people through their business interests. Nevertheless, public sentiment arrayed itself very generally with the strikers, for it was believed that they had a just grievance, and their good conduct throughout the controversy created sympathy for them. Moreover, the actions of Governor Martin won for him the good will of the laboring man[65] as well as the approval of other Kansas citizens.[66]

Although no other strike occurred during the year affecting any railroad operated in Kansas, it was evident that the relations existing between employers and employees continued to be of so strained a character as to excite great uneasiness. Measures of retrenchment and economy adopted by the larger railroad companies produced dissatisfaction among the army of railroad workers.[67] Following the strike conflicting reports reflecting the apprehension felt by the railroad workers appeared from time to time in the Parsons newspapers.[68] At one time it was feared that another strike was imminent.[69] In May, Governor Martin instituted careful inquiries concerning a complaint sent him by a committee representing the railroad men at Parsons that certain employees had been discharged for participation in the strike.[70] He urged the board of railroad commissioners to go to that point, giving them definite instructions to make a full and impartial investigation of the alleged violation of the company's agreement.[71] At the same time, he informed Vice-president Hayes of the matter, urging him to give it his careful attention, for he was convinced that a violation of the terms of the agreement made by the company with the Kansas authorities would seriously undermine the confidence of the public in the railway corporation. Moreover, he concluded, such a violation would be an act of bad faith, not only to the employees, but also to the state officers who undertook to negotiate the terms of the settlement at the express request of the company.[72] Mr. Hayes, in his reply, ex-

65. Letter of R. H. Semple, secretary of Franklin Assembly 2557, Knights of Labor, to Governor Martin, April 14, 1885, "C. K. G., Martin," v. II. Also letter from Cigarmaker's Union, No. 36, of Cigarmaker's International Union, to Governor Martin, April 21, 1885, *ibid.*
66. Editorial in Topeka *Daily Capital*, March 13, 1885.
67. Kansas Board of Railroad Commissioners, *Third Annual Report* (1885), p. 25.
68. Parsons *Daily Sun*, March 26, April 29, May 2, 1885. Also Parsons *Daily Eclipse*, March 30, 31, May 4, 1885.
69. Parsons *Daily Sun*, April 15, 1885.
70. Letter of Governor Martin to W. Quarles, J. McFeely, and others, committee, Parsons, May 13, 1885, "C. K. G., Martin" (Letterpress books, Official), v. LVIII, pp. 181-184.
71. Letter of Governor Martin to board of railroad commissioners, May 13, 1885, *ibid.*, pp. 173-176.
72. Letter of Governor Martin to Capt. R. S. Hayes, first vice-president of Missouri Pacific Railroad Co., May 14, 1885, *ibid.*, pp. 177-180.

pressed his doubt concerning the truth of the report, but promised to investigate, and assured Governor Martin that the agreement of March would be complied with by the company. Investigation disclosed the fact that the trouble which the Kansas authorities had been led to believe existed at Parsons, and which caused them no little concern, was actually located in Texas.[73] The railroad commissioners assured the governor that they believed a conference called at St. Louis would adjust the difficulty satisfactorily.[74]

Rumors in August of a strike on the Wabash line alarmed the public.[75] The road, which was in the hands of a receiver, reduced the force of men in the shops at Moberly, Mo., to a point which meant a lockout of the members of the Knights of Labor. As a result, the executive board of the Knights of Labor issued an order forbidding the members of the organization to repair any stock of that road.[76] At Parsons, where the Missouri Pacific employees watched the movement with interest, a notice was posted forbidding the Knights to handle Wabash cars,[77] while those employed on the Union Pacific Railway were awaiting orders from their labor headquarters at Denver before refusing to do the work. Mr. Betton, commissioner of labor, after a meeting at Wyandotte with a committee representing the Knights of Labor employed on the Union Pacific Railway, expressed his uneasiness concerning the gravity of the situation in a letter to Governor Martin.[78] The order of the executive board if fully carried out would affect over 20,000 miles of railroad, and a strike equal in dimensions to the one of 1877 would be the result.

Jay Gould was unwilling to risk a general strike. Consequently, he arranged a conference between the executive board of the Knights of Labor and the managers of the Missouri Pacific and Wabash railroads. Here he assured the Knights that he believed in labor organizations. At length, he brought pressure to bear upon the managers of the Wabash and a settlement was effected. An order was issued directing the superintendents in filling vacancies to give the men who had formerly been employed preference over the strangers and to ask no questions concerning membership in the Knights of Labor or any other organization.

73. Letter of Wm. Quarles, S. Gladwin, and others, executive committee, Parsons, to Governor Martin, May 14, 1885, "C. K. G., Martin."
74. Letter of J. Humphrey, A. Gillett, Parsons, to Governor Martin, May 17, 1885, *ibid*.
75. Parsons *Daily Eclipse*, August 18, 1885.
76. Commons, *History of Labour in the United States*.
77. Parsons *Daily Sun*, August 23, 1885.
78. Letter of F. H. Betton, Wyandotte, to Governor Martin, August 27, 1885, "C. K. G., Martin" (Personal), v. IV.

The Knights of Labor had dealt on an equal footing with Jay Gould, a man who in the minds of some people was more powerful than the United States government. The order stood out as a championship of the masses. As a result, with an exaggerated notion of its power, many hastened to join this mighty organization.[79]

Boycotts in Kansas

The boycott movement of the years 1884 and 1885 was truly nation wide, and during the latter year reached the epidemic stage.[80] Such a method of coercion had the advantage over the strike of entailing little cost or effort to the laborer who supported it. Moreover, it was frequently used to render strikes more effective.

In Kansas, during 1885, two boycotts of importance were inaugurated at the instigation of the typographical union and sanctioned and aggressively carried on by the Knights of Labor. One, directed against the Kansas City *Daily Journal*, originated in Missouri but was actively supported by Kansas Knights. The other, ordered by the Knights of Topeka, was carried on against *The Daily Commonwealth* of that city.

Although the Kansas City *Daily Journal* was published in Missouri it had a large circulation in Kansas, and maintained agents in the principal Kansas cities. The boycott on both its advertising business and its circulation was actively supported by Kansas Knights. The original trouble dated back to 1883, when the union printers employed on the Kansas City *Daily Journal*, claiming that they were treated unfairly, walked out. The boycott in Kansas, however, was not instituted until the spring of 1885, when the Kansas Knights of Wyandotte county indorsed it. From that point it spread to those cities where the *Journal* was patronized, until it reached practically every part of the state where assemblies of the Knights were located. Much ill feeling was created by the zeal of the Knights, who forbade the business men to subscribe or advertise in the offending journal under penalty of a withdrawal of patronage. The boycott was rigidly enforced until the spring of 1886, and undoubtedly affected the interests of the paper to a considerable extent. Although it continued into the year 1886 the bitterness diminished.

The cause of the controversy in which the Topeka paper was involved centered about the employment of a foreman who had

---

79. Commons, *History of Labour in the United States*, pp. 369, 370.
80. *Ibid.*, p. 365.

been expelled from the typographical union. The union printers protested against his employment and walked out when they failed to induce the owner of the *Commonwealth* company to discharge him. This occurred on April 7. Early the next morning the company put a new force of men to work.

The striking printers, seeing their action fail, appealed to the Knights for assistance. In response, Local Assembly 1800 appointed a committee on April 13 to investigate the grievances of the printers and act as a board of arbitration between the typographical union and the proprietor of *The Daily Commonwealth*.[81] A few days later, at a special meeting, this assembly accepted the committee's recommendation that the printers be upheld in their action by every trade union, and more particularly by the Knights of Labor.[82] As a result, a boycott was declared against *The Daily Commonwealth* by the local assemblies of the Topeka Knights and championed by the senior Assembly 1800.

Organized labor in Topeka earnestly set about to wage a successful campaign against the offending firm. Merchants and others who advertised in the offending paper were visited and requested to withdraw their patronage from it under penalty of loss of the trade of the Knights of Labor.[83] Early in the controversy the striking printers established an evening paper entitled *The Citizen*,[84] and the first issue appeared on April 11. It set forth in its columns the methods of boycotting and urged those who subscribed for *The Daily Commonwealth* or bought goods from dealers advertising in that paper, to stop doing so at once until the company employed union men.[85] It achieved a wide circulation in Topeka, and by the middle of July claimed the largest circulation of any paper in the city.[86] *The Citizen* urged the business men to stop dealing with *The Daily Commonwealth* until the difficulty was settled, and those who refused were warned that they would be remembered in the future.[87] Although *The Citizen* declared that it did not propose to dictate to the business men of the city it did intend to stand by its friends.[88] The executive committee of the Knights of Labor issued

81. Kansas Bureau of Labor and Industrial Statistics, *Second Annual Report* (1886), pp. 76-94.
82. *The Citizen*, Topeka, April 20, 1885.
83. *Ibid.*, April 11, 1885.
84. Kansas Bureau of Labor and Industrial Statistics, *Second Annual Report* (1886), pp. 81, 89.
85. *The Citizen*, Topeka, April 11, 1885.
86. *Ibid.*, editorial, July 14, 1885.
87. *Ibid.*, editorial, April 11, 1885.
88. *Ibid.*, editorial, December 31, 1885.

a special paper called the *Boycotter* which was devoted to the task of carrying on the boycott against the *Commonwealth*.

A state-wide boycott was entered upon. Circulars were sent out by Topeka Knights to sister assemblies in other parts of the state urging them to take action against the *Commonwealth*.[89] The *Trades-Union*, a labor paper published in Atchison, carried notices urging its readers to boycott the Topeka journal.

As a result of this persistent industrial warfare[90] organized labor claimed that it succeeded in seriously crippling the firm. In June *The Citizen* stated that the advertising patronage of the *Commonwealth* was daily growing less, and that merchants who advertised in it were beginning to notice a decrease in their trade. On the other hand, the owners of the paper asserted that it made no noticeable difference in their business.

The controversy continued throughout 1885. On Sunday, February 7, 1886, C. U. Spencer of Emporia organized the printers of *The Daily Commonwealth* into a printers' assembly of the Knights of Labor. This action called forth a protest from Local Assembly 1800 which was sent February 10 to the general executive board of the Knights of Labor at Philadelphia. A week later, February 17, representatives from all the labor organizations in Topeka, including the new assembly of printers, met in conference at the office of the commissioner of labor. Here it was agreed to refer the difficulty to the local assemblies, and arbitration as a solution of the problem was recommended. On February 24 the *Commonwealth* printers answered the protest of Local Assembly 1800 against the organization of Printers' Assembly 5314 in a statement termed "Our Vindication." They, too, appealed to the general executive board at Philadelphia and asked for approval of their organization. The two protesting groups were attached to District Assembly 69. Consequently, the general executive board referred the matter to the officials of this district assembly, who met in Topeka March 2 to March 6 to settle the controversy. Here, March 5, they agreed unanimously that the boycott on *The Daily Commonwealth* should be lifted. Typographical Union No. 121 of Topeka objected strenuously to this action. The members issued a statement in which they set forth the opinion of T. V. Powderly expressed at Cleveland in May, 1886, concerning the relations of the trade unions to the Order. This statement read that "the only serious trouble between the

---

89. Kansas Bureau of Labor and Industrial Statistics, *Second Annual Report* (1886), pp. 81, 89.
90. *The Trades-Union*, Atchison, December 5, 12, 19, 1885.

Knights of Labor and the trades unions, outside of the trouble with the cigarmakers' union, was the supposed granting of a charter to a number of 'rats' at Topeka, Kansas." Consequently, the typographical union felt justified in refusing to accept, as final, the decision of District Assembly 69.

In his second annual report the commissioner of labor said:

> In a general way . . . the boycott on the *Commonwealth* by the Knights of Labor extended over a period of time commencing in the latter part of April, 1885, and terminating March 5, 1886, by order of the Executive Board of District Assembly No. 69. . . . In explanation it may be proper to add that while the boycott . . . has ended as far as the Knights of Labor are concerned, the original trouble remains unsettled and Typographical Union No. 121 still continues to consider it a "rat" office, although negotiations are now pending that may result in an amicable settlement. . . . An amnesty has been agreed upon, and far more friendly feelings prevail.[91]

LEGISLATION PROVIDING FOR TRIBUNALS OF VOLUNTARY ARBITRATION

The public was thoroughly aroused during the course of the railroad strike and convinced of the need of setting up effective machinery for the prevention of industrial conflicts. It was argued that if the public demanded the services of the railway employees then it was the duty of the state to see that those employed received a reasonable compensation for their work.[92] Moreover, it was declared that a corporation undertaking to serve the public should submit to such regulations as would secure the safe performance of its work.[93] Some even contended that the public interest in strikes was great and important enough to justify the adoption of any measures to prevent their recurrence.[94]

Many were confident that the creation of a state tribunal would avert industrial controversies.[95] The establishment of a board to arbitrate these differences would practically abolish strikes throughout the state, it was believed. The part played by the board of railroad commissioners in the actual settlement of the Missouri Pacific strike suggested a solution which seemed practicable to many. It was proposed that the law which provided for the establishment of the board of railroad commissioners be amended so as to empower the commissioners to act as referees in cases of serious difficulty between employer and employees.[96]

---

91. Kansas Bureau of Labor and Industrial Statistics, *Second Annual Report* (1886), pp. 83-90.
92. Editorial in Topeka *Daily Capital,* March 13, 1885.
93. Editorial in Topeka *Daily Journal,* March 15, 1885.
94. Editorial in Topeka *Daily Capital,* March 14, 1885.
95. *The Trades-Union,* Atchison, December 19, 1885.
96. Editorial in Atchison *Daily Champion,* March 18, 1885.

Governor Martin believed that the public interest in uninterrupted commerce was as great, if not greater, than that of the employees and the railway corporation. He felt that the welfare of the people, who were in no way responsible for the strike, should be considered. Consequently, with their welfare as well as that of the employees and employers in mind, he urged some action which would bring about industrial peace,[97] and agreed that the law which provided for the adjustment of differences between shippers and the railway corporations might be extended to arbitrate differences between railway companies and their employees.[98] During the course of the strike Governor Martin advanced the proposition to the railroad commissioners that in certain emergencies, due to the relation of the railroads to the public, it might become necessary for the state to take charge of the railroads and operate them. Such a step was not necessary, but it was his opinion that some legal measures should be provided enabling the state to intervene and settle controversies.[99] In a letter to an assembly of Knights of Labor written soon after the strike Governor Martin said that if afforded an opportunity to address another legislature, he would certainly stress the need for legislation providing some method of arbitrating industrial disputes.[100]

When the legislature convened in special session in January, 1886, the governor, in his message, reviewed the history of the strike and pointed out the difficulty of bridging the gap between the wage earner and the corporation. He said that the strikers were industrious and law-respecting citizens who felt that the only way to gain relief from undesirable conditions was a resort to force, which they deplored, for they realized fully the losses a strike involved. Therefore he earnestly recommended the passage of a law providing regulations to govern the arbitration of disputes between employers and employees.[101]

A group of Kansas Knights, eager to coöperate with the lawmakers and likewise express their views, met January 25 and 26, 1886, at the office of the commissioner of labor in Topeka. This group recommended the creation of a board of arbitration composed of the commissioner of labor, who should serve as chairman, and two

---

97. Letter of Governor Martin to W. S. Smith, Marysville, March 18, 1885, "C. K. G., Martin" (Letterpress books, Official), v. I, pp. 187-189.
98. Letter of Governor Martin to Gen. T. M. Carroll, Paola, March 19, 1885, *ibid.*, p. 203.
99. Letter of Governor Martin to W. S. Smith, Marysville, March 18, 1885, *ibid.*, pp. 187-189.
100. Letter of Governor Martin to R. H. Semple, secretary of the Franklin Assembly 2557, Knights of Labor, Ottawa, April 21, 1885, *ibid.*, pp. 337, 338.
101. *Special Message of John A. Martin, Governor, to the Legislature of Kansas* (1886).

others, appointed by the governor, representing labor and capital. It was also agreed to present to the legislature a resolution requesting the appointment of a standing committee on labor.

On the second day of the meeting a bill providing for arbitration was discussed. After careful deliberation it was agreed that not only was the group too small to assume responsibility for such important legislation, but also the time allowed the delegates was too limited to frame an effective law. Moreover, since the time of the legislators was limited by the special session the delegates opposed immediate action on such important legislation. They feared that a crude bill might result from too hasty action, which would do more harm than good. Consequently, this meeting of the Knights of Labor adopted a resolution which provided, first, that all local assemblies in the state should take steps toward drafting bills of arbitration, and second that a convention representing each local assembly in Kansas should assemble in Topeka September 7, 1886. It seemed to organized labor that the better plan, at that time, would be for the legislature to appoint a committee of labor with the authority to meet and study the problem, and report in 1887. As a result the subject would be better understood and a valuable law enacted.[102]

However, the legislators, recognizing the need of bringing labor and capital together, and desiring to erase the ill feeling between the two factions, immediately set about to solve the problem. On January 27, 1886, a bill providing for the arbitration of industrial controversies, the first on this subject ever placed before a Kansas legislature,[103] was introduced into the house by Rodolph Hatfield, a young attorney of Wichita.[104] On the following day, in compliance with the resolution passed by Kansas Knights in Topeka January 25,[105] the house adopted the resolution offered by J. J. Cox of Douglas county recommending the appointment of a committee of five to consider the rights and duties of Kansas labor. Mr. Hatfield's bill was referred to this committee and on February 10 the house adopted its recommendation that the measure be passed and that its consideration be made the special order of business for the following afternoon.[106] Mr. Hatfield eloquently upheld his measure, emphasizing the importance of the subject to the people of Kansas.

102. *The Trades-Union*, Atchison, January 30, 1886.
103. *The Daily Commonwealth*, Topeka, February 12, 1886.
104. *House Journal*, 1886, p. 303.
105. *The Trades-Union*, Atchison, January 30, 1886.
106. *House Journal*, 1886, pp. 287, 565.

He pointed out the fact that the problem of the relation of labor and capital was assuming great proportions, and demanded the attention of legislative bodies. He explained that in spite of the fact that the two factors were vitally related to and dependent upon each other, each was suspicious of and bitter toward the other. He said that he knew what it was to work ten, twelve, and fourteen hours a day. As a disinterested advocate of a measure of paramount importance to Kansas, he hoped the special session would enact a law which would stand as a monument in the march of civilization.

Mr. David Overmyer of Shawnee county said in defense of that feature of the law which provided for voluntary arbitration that the Kansas constitution prohibited the establishment of a tribunal which would compel Kansas citizens to arbitrate their industrial difficulties. However, he explained that the bill provided that when both parties voluntarily placed their disputes before the tribunal its decision was final. His motion to suspend the rules and read the bill a third time while its provisions were well in mind was adopted.[107] The measure passed without a dissenting vote, February 11,[108] and was sent to the senate.

By request, Sen. A. J. Harwi of Atchison introduced a bill on the same subject on the day Mr. Hatfield introduced his measure in the house. The senate bill, however, was not reported from committee, and on February 11 the measure framed by the house was read in the senate for the first time. A week later, February 18, on the motion of L. U. Humphrey of Independence, the rules of the senate were suspended in order to advance the bill to its third reading. As in the lower house, the measure was passed, not a single vote being cast against it.[109]

The governor signed the bill February 19, 1886, and thus machinery was set up which it was hoped would insure industrial peace in Kansas.[110] It embodied the principle of voluntary arbitration and applied to disputes between laborers and employers in manufacturing, mechanical, mining, and other industries. It provided that the district court of each county, when petitioned by parties to a labor dispute, should establish a tribunal of voluntary arbitration and appoint an umpire for that tribunal. It required the signature of at least five employees or two employers to the petition

---

107. *The Daily Commonwealth,* Topeka, February 12, 1886.
108. *House Journal,* 1886, p. 602.
109. *Senate Journal,* 1886, pp. 253, 522, 527, 703.
110. *House Journal,* 1886, p. 969.

praying for a tribunal, the establishment of which might be denied if the court found that the required number of petitioners were not as represented in the petition. It provided that the decision of the tribunal, which was to be composed of two employers and two employees, all residents of the county, should be final. In case the members of the tribunal failed to agree, they might submit the questions in dispute to the umpire, whose award was final only on those matters properly submitted to him by the court of arbitration or the parties to the dispute. It gave the tribunal and the umpire the power to question witnesses under oath, and to examine any documents or material pertaining to the matter before them and belonging to the parties in the dispute. The court of arbitration, when established, remained in existence for one year.[111]

111. *Laws,* Kansas, 1886, ch. 28.

The Annual Meeting

THE sixtieth annual meeting of the Kansas State Historical Society and board of directors was held in the rooms of the Society on October 15, 1935.

The meeting was called to order at 10 a. m. by the president, Thomas F. Doran.

The first business was the reading of the annual report of the secretary:

REPORT OF THE SECRETARY, YEAR ENDING OCTOBER 15, 1935

The experience of this Society confirms reports from other historical agencies that the past few years have shown a material growth in popular interest in local and state history. The increased use of our facilities and the greater demand for information, which were noted in last year's report, have continued throughout the year. The study of local history was featured by many schools in small towns and rural communities, who wrote for detailed historical data about their towns and counties. The staff has been kept busy with routine work and much that should have been done in cataloguing and organizing books and other collections was postponed. The supervision of KERC workers took much time from regular tasks. This increase in the work of the Society is also reflected in the fact that the volume of our correspondence is nearly twenty-five percent greater than it was five years ago. This is a healthy and gratifying condition, but it emphasizes the statement, made last year, that the present staff is inadequate and that additional employees are needed.

EXECUTIVE COMMITTEE

The executive committee, consisting of W. W. Denison, E. A. Austin, John S. Dawson, Thomas Amory Lee and T. M. Lillard, met regularly except during the summer months. Advice of the members was sought in all matters of consequence, and in accordance with the constitution and by-laws they approved all expenditures. The committee and the Society suffered a great loss on July 5 in the death of W. W. Denison. For many years he served on the executive committee and at the time of his death was its chairman. A memorial in the form of a resolution, written by Thomas F. Doran, was adopted by the committee at its September meeting, and a copy was sent to Mrs. Denison.

APPROPRIATIONS AND THE LEGISLATURE

Appropriations requested for the biennium beginning July 1, 1935, were filed with the budget director in September. Our requests included $1,800 for additional newspaper racks and an increase of $500 a year in the contingent fund, which had been reduced from $2,500 to $1,500 by the legislature of 1933. Restoration of salary cuts was not asked for and no additional clerks were requested, although much needed. In his recommendation to the legislature the budget director disallowed both requests. Fortunately, however, we were able to secure from the legislature $900 for new newspaper racks and an increase of $250 a year in the contingent fund.

The reduction of $1,000 a year in the contingent fund, which became effective July 1, 1933, worked a hardship on the Society and made it necessary to apply the limited income from memberships on operating expenses. Due to increased demands on the Society and additional costs incident to supervising KERC workers these expenses have been greater than ever before. The income from memberships has naturally decreased during the depression years. While the restoration of $250 a year in the contingent fund will help, the full amount should be restored, and it is hoped also that it will be possible to increase the revenue from memberships.

It will be noted in the treasurer's report that on April 11, 1935, bonds in the amount of $2,500 were sold and the proceeds placed in the membership fund. These bonds were called by the government and had to be sold or exchanged for others bearing a much lower rate of interest. This action was authorized by the executive committee after careful consideration. The Society possesses invaluable collections of manuscripts, pictures and other documents which must be catalogued, calendared and otherwise organized to be made useful. Part of the proceeds from the sale of the bonds will be applied on this work and part will be available for the purchase of books and other historical material. It must not be supposed that this fund will enable us to complete the organization of our collections; on the contrary this will require thousands of dollars and years of work. But much can be done now, and should be done, to make our collections serve the purpose for which they were intended.

KERC PROJECT

Application for a new project to continue the work begun under the Civil Works Administration project, which operated from January 15 to March 22, 1934, was submitted to the Kansas Emergency Relief Committee September 20, 1934. The committee approved the application, calling for an expenditure of $10,769 by the federal government in salaries for the equivalent of twenty-seven full-time workers for twenty-two weeks.

Considerable freedom had been granted us under the CWA in selecting persons from other counties when the local county relief rolls could not supply the class of workers needed. Under the KERC regulations, however, it was specified that all project workers must be selected from the list of available relief clients on local county relief rolls. It was apparent from the start that this ruling was to interfere seriously with a successful operation of the project. No trained librarians were on the Shawnee county relief rolls; therefore the positions could not be filled. A further handicap was the fact that only a few days' time a month was allowed each worker, conditioned by the budget allowance set for the client by his case worker.

At no time was the Society able to approach maximum employment. With the workers averaging from three to ten days' work a month, it would have been necessary to employ at least eighty persons to fill our quota. The county relief administration did its best to furnish suitable workers, but the total never exceeded twenty-two in any one month. Approximately $150 was expended by the Society for working materials and rental of typewriters.

With the establishment of the Works Progress Administration in Kansas, relief work provided under the KERC was discontinued last month. Workers were called off the Society's project the evening of September 3. Of the original government grant of $10,769, $4,652.50 was actually spent. Since the

KERC seems to be definitely out of the picture as a project supervisor, the $6,116.50 balance probably has been wiped off the books.

Tasks were assigned KERC workers in accordance with their abilities. The project typists were employed copying fragile documents and manuscripts needed for immediate use by the general public. They also copied indexes of the first fourteen volumes of the *Kansas Historical Collections,* a preliminary step necessary to the preparation of a general index of the seventeen volumes. Mention of other work started or accomplished by workers on this project appears in this report under the department headings. Due to the inability of relief headquarters to furnish persons with library experience the Society was compelled to abandon temporarily a catalogue of the picture collection and special cataloguing in the library annex begun last year.

Through the courtesy of Dr. Philip C. King, president of Washburn College, the Society was permitted to use three Washburn students part time from September, 1934, through May, 1935. The students, working under a college-student employment project, were paid from KERC funds. Two students have been supplied the Society during the present college year through a similar project sponsored by Washburn under the National Youth Administration.

PROPOSED WPA PROJECT

Upon the advice of the Shawnee County Relief Administration the Society made application for a project to operate under the Works Progress Administration. It calls for the expenditure of $8,900 by the government in salaries for the employment of fourteen full-time persons for ten months. The application was submitted to the WPA first district office August 24. We have been informed that it has been approved by both the first district office and the state office and that it is now in Washington. To date we have had no information on Washington's disposition of the plans. Application was made in this project for two librarians to continue the work started under the CWA. If approved, work will be continued along the same lines as previously scheduled under the other setups.

LIBRARY

The library received over three thousand requests for information, the greatest number being for Kansas subjects, and next for family history. Information was supplied to schools throughout the state on the history of their communities, which was a phase of their study in history. This often required the compilation and copying of material, and took much time.

The KERC workers assigned to the library were not trained librarians and it was impossible to continue the work of cataloguing and classifying taken up the year before. However, much was accomplished in the physical care of the library: 8,648 books were relabeled; 4,829 leather-bound volumes were oiled to preserve the leather; 280 pamphlets were inclosed in binders; 436 maps and broadsides were mounted; 150 books and pamphlets were repaired; 200 pamphlet boxes and 37 adjustable binders were made; 331 pages of clippings were pasted, and 6,000 cards cataloguing the biographies in Andreas' *History of Kansas* were typed.

Under the college-student employment project two Washburn students were received. Their work consisted of arranging and filing Kansas supreme court briefs, and filing cards in the Library of Congress depository catalogue.

SUBJECTS OF RESEARCH

The limits of this report prevent a detailed statement of the variety and number of requests for information received by the Society. The public considers it the depository of facts and relics pertaining to every conceivable subject. We are offered accessions ranging from live, two-headed snakes, as was the case only last week, to collections of current newspapers from every foreign country, as was the case only last month. To refuse material often incurs hostility, but it is obvious that the policy of confining the scope of the Society principally within the limits of Kansas and the Mid-west and their related subjects is a necessary one. In its field the holdings of the Society are not excelled by those of any other state association, and it is a constant source of gratification, and often of surprise, to be able to meet the thousands of demands for out-of-the-way information.

The Society is used principally by students and writers of history, newspaper men, lawyers, students of genealogy and writers on general subjects. During the past year researchers for the Kansas State Planning Board and representatives of investment companies made much use of the collections for special studies. A list of the subjects on which extended research was made include the following: Early literature in Kansas; Jotham Meeker; county histories; blue-sky legislation; Holladay stage-coach lines; forts of Ford county; early missions; Union Pacific Railroad; Jedediah Smith; United States Indian Superintendency, St. Louis; John Brown; Pony Express; William Allen White; Cyrus K. Holliday; Atchison, Topeka & Santa Fé Railroad; Populist uprising; primary elections; Kansas Industrial court; John A. Anderson; Cherokee strip; early history of telephones in Kansas; early mail routes; Robert J. Walker; state agricultural department; population studies; history and development of schools in Doniphan county; histories of academies in Kansas; Kansas poetry; Methodist Indian missions in Kansas; James H. Lane; Baptist church; *Beadle's Dime Library;* Kansas landmarks; Osawatomie; events in Topeka history for cartoons; historic pictures; Indian art.

PRIVATE MANUSCRIPTS

In this department 665 manuscripts and 53 manuscript volumes were accessioned, in addition to two large collections—those given by Miss Bessie Boughton and the Rev. J. E. Bartholomew—which have not yet been completely inventoried. Of particular interest are:

The papers of Thomas C. Stevens, obtained from Mrs. Frank McIntire. Stevens was at one time a partner of Thomas Carney in the merchandising business in Leavenworth. The papers contain some references to this partnership and cover later business activities of Stevens. Also there are letters and telegrams to and from Carney on military matters in Kansas during the period 1863-1864. An interesting group of papers in the collection is that composed of statements of the steamboat *Mollie Dozier* which plied the Missouri river in 1865.

The Elam Batholomew collection containing letters from leading scientists in all parts of the country on the subject of fungi. Doctor Bartholomew was an authority in this field. For many years he conducted experiments on his large farm in Phillips county. In 1929 he became curator of the mycological museum at the Fort Hays State College. His death occurred in November 1934.

The collection given by the Wilder S. Metcalf estate containing twenty-eight diaries of General Metcalf, three of them covering the period of his service in the Spanish-American War.

The sixteen scrapbooks of John Pierce St. John, governor of Kansas, 1879-1883. These contain clippings and letters relating largely to his activities in public life.

The papers of John C. McCoy and Woodson McCoy, a gift of Spencer McCoy. In the collection are 158 documents—deeds, mortgages, contracts, etc.—relating to land matters in Jackson county, Mo., and Johnson county, Kan., 1836-1905; and account book of the firm of McCoy & Martin, Kansas City, Mo., 1847-1848.

Work done in the manuscripts division by FERA help includes 11,900 manuscripts chronologized and 1,750 manuscripts cleaned and pressed.

Donors of manuscripts during the year were: The Rev. J. E. Batholomew, George F. Beezley, Bessie Boughton, Mrs. Thomas R. Bowman, James B. Brinsmaid, Dr. Edward Bumgardner, Harvey Myers Cary, F. F. Clinger, S. N. Dudley, Edward T. Fay, Lulu R. Fuhr, W. W. Gear, I. D. Graham, Mrs. Almira Belden Hall, Eusebia Mudge Irish, Mrs. Samuel J. Kelly, Davis Harold McCleave, Spencer McCoy, Mrs. Frank McIntire, the Wilder S. Metcalf estate, Martie Millikan, Mrs. Emma Wattles Morse, Effie Parker, Paul Parrish, F. C. Penfield, H. C. Raynesford, W. P. Reese, J. C. Ruppenthal, Floyd B. Streeter, Harriet Thurman, William Allen White, Wichita City Library, Neale Wright, Walker D. Wyman, Lillian Way.

STATE ARCHIVES

There were no accessions in this department during the fiscal year. This month, however, we received the statistical rolls of the counties for the years 1924 to 1928 consisting of approximately 8,500 manuscript return books. These were prepared under the supervision of the State Board of Agriculture and include the decennial state census returns for Kansas, 1925. This is the last state census which will be taken, the 1935 legislature having repealed the law that provided for it. These returns were received from the Kansas State College at Manhattan, where they were used by the federal government in estimating farm allotments. According to a recent agreement between the Board of Agriculture, the Kansas State College and the Historical Society, all statistical rolls in the future will be deposited with the Society after they have been used five years by the State College. Heretofore there had been no definite agreement as to the permanent disposition of these valuable records.

NEWSPAPER SECTION

The usual recommendation was made in our 1934 budget estimate for adequate shelving for the out-of-Kansas newspaper collection which has been stored on boxes and benches in our basement for nearly two decades. The state budget director did not include the request in the revised budget he submitted to the legislature. Three members of the house ways and means committee visited the building, however, saw the need for the shelving, and wrote an item for $900 into the appropriation bill to permit the Society to make a start toward a proper storage of these newspaper volumes. The appropriation was allowed and the fixtures were installed in July of this year. Room was provided in these shelves for nearly half of the volumes previously stacked on boxes and benches. KERC workers assisted in the reassembling of this collection in the new shelving.

The 1935 annual *List of Kansas Newspapers and Periodicals* received by the Kansas State Historical Society was published in September. The edition listed 741 newspapers and periodicals which were being received regularly for filing. Of these, 60 are dailies, 11 semiweeklies, 512 weeklies, 21 fortnightlies, 15 semimonthlies, two once every three weeks, 73 monthlies, nine bimonthlies, 23 quarterlies, 12 occasionals, two semiannuals and one annual, coming from all the 105 Kansas counties. Of the 741 publications, 181 are listed republican, 42 democratic, 294 independent of politics, 76 school or college, and 148 miscellaneous. In this list were included 452 weekly community newspapers. On January 1 the collection of Kansas newspapers totaled 42,783 bound volumes.

Ninety issues of the *Squatter Sovereign,* Atchison's first newspaper, were acquired by the Society in February, one of the most important newspaper accessions in recent years. These issues, obtained from Howard F. Kelley, of Seattle, Wash., a son of one of the editors of the paper, date from the founding of the newspaper on February 3, 1855, to March 3, 1857, and represent most of the period during which the *Sovereign* was proslavery in politics. A volume of *The Democratic Platform,* of Liberty, Mo., dating from March 23 to October 5, 1854, and a volume of the *Herald of Freedom,* of Lawrence, from January 13, 1855, to February 2, 1856, were also received from Mr. Kelley.

Included among other newspaper accessions for the year were: *The Madisonian,* Washington, D. C., October 12, 1837, to September 21, 1841, from Mrs. E. L. Holmes, of Lawrence; Columbus (Miss.) *Press,* November 1, 1873, to April 15, 1876, from Mrs. Hiram Lewis, of Wichita; *The National Tribune,* Washington, D. C., August 20, 1881, to October 4, 1888, from Mr. and Mrs. W. R. Carrie, of Topeka; a large assortment of miscellaneous southeast Kansas newspapers dated in the latter 1870's to 1909, from H. M. Sender, of Kansas City, Mo.; copies of the Hampden *Expositor,* July 9, 1864, and *The Neosho Valley Register,* Burlington, January 3, 1860, October 17 and 24, 1861, from Mrs. Marian Kent Race, of Chicago, Ill.; miscellaneous national agricultural and livestock journals, 1928 to 1933, from the Kansas State Board of Agriculture; miscellaneous newspapers (mostly Kansas) from Mildred Berry, of Topeka, Anna Meluish, of Ottawa, and Mrs. E. L. Holmes, of Lawrence. Camp newspapers of several Civilian Conservation Corps companies located in the state have been furnished the Society by the corps area educational adviser of Omaha.

MUSEUM

The attendance in the museum for the year ending July 1, 1935, was 30,392.

Among the interesting accessions of the year were a physician's saddle bag belonging to Dr. Charles W. Hardy, of Ottawa, who came to Kansas in 1886 and used the bag until 1892, when he began using a horse and buggy in his country practice. Lloyd Hill, Topeka, gave a censor's stamp which was used by officers in censoring soldiers' mail in the 137th (all-Kansas) infantry in France. A silver watch which had belonged to the Rev. Isaac McCoy, Baptist Indian missionary who came to Kansas in 1829, was donated by his great-grandson, Spencer McCoy.

With the help of two FERA workers much cleaning and renovating was done. Five hundred labels and signs were made with pen and brush, seventy-nine display cases and more than 30,000 relics were cleaned, a number of pieces of furniture were repaired, many pictures and frames were restored, and the contents of three storerooms were cleaned and checked with the records. Through the courtesy of Dr. Chas. D. Bunker, of the University of Kansas, the birds in one of the largest cases belonging to the Goss collection were repaired and cleaned.

ACCESSIONS

Total accessions to the Society's collections for the year ending June 30, 1935, were as follows:

Library:
- Books (volumes) 1,180
- Pamphlets 5,350
- Magazines (bound volumes) 539
- Archives .... none
- Printed maps, atlases and charts 160
- Newspapers (bound volumes) 935
- Pictures 185
- Museum objects 20

Private manuscripts:
- Separate manuscripts 665
- Volumes 53

These accessions bring the totals in the possession of the Society to the following figures:

- Books, pamphlets, bound newspapers and magazines 361,066
- Separate manuscripts (archives) 924,795
- Manuscript volumes 27,223
- Manuscript maps 501
- Printed maps, atlases and charts 10,525
- Pictures 15,328
- Museum objects 32,800

THE QUARTERLY

The *Quarterly*, now completing its fourth year, has established itself among the leading state historical magazines of the country. The fact that more articles are being submitted than can be printed gives the editors a wider selection of material and enables them to maintain an increasingly higher standard of scholarship. One of the most popular features of the magazine is the department headed, "Kansas History as Published in the Press," edited by Nyle H. Miller, the Society's newspaper clerk. These items consist of a quarterly review of articles on Kansas history appearing in the state's newspapers. Heretofore no record of this valuable material had ever been made.

OLD SHAWNEE METHODIST MISSION

This property, consisting of twelve acres of ground and three large brick buildings now nearly one hundred years old, was purchased by the state in 1927 at an expense of about $50,000. The caretaker receives a salary of $1,000 a year and $750 a year is allowed for maintenance. This sum is inadequate, but it has been impossible to secure an increase from the legislature. Our request for 1936-1937 called for $4,000 a year for maintenance, but it was disallowed.

The secretary and the state architect prepared a project request for the restoration of the north building, calling for an expenditure out of federal funds of $30,000. No action was taken on this request by the authorities and presumably it was not allowed. Until money can be secured to restore this building all that can be done is to prevent further deterioration.

There are five organizations coöperating with the Society at the mission: the Daughters of the American Revolution, the Colonial Dames, the Daughters of American Colonists, the Daughters of 1812 and the Shawnee Mission Indian Historical Society. These organizations have done much to improve the east building. At their own expense they have repaired and redecorated the rooms which were assigned to them. Only a personal inspection can give an adequate idea of the debt this Society owes them for this assistance.

Last summer the unsightly frame garage was torn down and a brick garage and workshop was erected in its place. The state architect prepared plans which harmonized with the existing buildings and helped to supervise the work of construction. Brick from an old building in Olathe were used in an effort to match the other buildings. Despite the drought the grounds present a better appearance than they have since the state acquired the site.

FIRST CAPITOL OF KANSAS

More persons visited the first capitol building than at any time since it was restored by the Union Pacific Railroad Co. and placed under the supervision of the Historical Society. During the year ending September 30, 1935, there were 15,142 visitors, as compared with 6,647 last year and 11,546 the preceding year. Approximately forty percent were from other states.

The 1935 legislature appropriated only $75 a year for the maintenance of this building. Last summer it was necessary to repaint the exterior woodwork and the box car which the caretaker uses when the weather is cold. This exhausted the fund for the year and it will now be necessary to pay maintenance costs for the balance of the year out of the Society's membership fund. The salary of the caretaker, who is required to be in attendance every day, including Sundays, was reduced by the legislature of 1933 to $37.50 a month. A request for increases in these wholly inadequate appropriations was turned down by the 1935 legislature.

PIKE PAWNEE PARK

The monument commemorating the visit of Zebulon M. Pike to the Pawnee Indian camp at this site in Republic county was blown down during a storm in 1934. A bill appropriating $1,600 for its replacement was allowed by the 1935 legislature. Bids under plans drawn by the state architect were received by the Society this month and it is hoped the repairs will be completed within the next sixty days.

LOCAL AND COUNTY HISTORICAL SOCIETIES

County historical societies have done good work during the year in gathering and preserving historical documents and relics. An exceptional record was made by the newly organized Chase County Historical Society. In December of 1934 their first meeting was held with 154 charter members. Last July they sponsored the first annual picnic of Chase county pioneers and invited the secretary to make an address on the work of the state society. More than one thousand were in attendance.

MARKING HISTORIC SITES

The Society this year began the work of locating all the historic sites in Kansas. More than 300 have been tentatively listed, and as soon as possible they will be indicated by colored pins on a large mounted map of the state. The sites in each county will be numbered, and pins bearing these numbers will appear on the map. A loose-leaf book attached to the map will explain the significance of each site. Red pins will indicate that the site is unmarked, and yellow pins will show that there is a marker of some kind already in place. In this way the map will serve as a progress report of the marking of these sites throughout the state.

The task of erecting markers on the sites must be the duty of the counties and communities in which they are located. The Kansas Chamber of Commerce, the Woman's Kansas Day Club and the Kansas department of the D. A. R. are coöperating with the Society in encouraging local communities and individuals to place suitable tablets or monuments on their sites. When a sufficient number have been marked it is hoped that the state highway commission will install highway signs directing motorists to the sites. When this is done the Kansas Chamber of Commerce expects to publish a map that will be a valuable guide to all the places of historic interest in the state.

This report must not be concluded without an expression of appreciation for the services of the members of the staff of this Society. They are uniformly courteous, loyal and conscientious. The secretary acknowledges his indebtedness to them for what has been accomplished in the past year.

Respectfully submitted,

KIRKE MECHEM, *Secretary.*

Upon the conclusion of the reading of the report of the secretary it was moved by E. A. Austin that it be approved and accepted. Seconded by John S. Dean. Carried.

The president then called for the report of the treasurer, Mrs. Mary Embree, which follows:

REPORT OF THE TREASURER

STATEMENT OF MEMBERSHIP FEE FUND

From October 12, 1934, to October 15, 1935

Balance, October 12, 1934	$486.83
Treasury bonds bearing 3¼ percent	3,500.00
Proceeds from sale of 4¼ percent Liberty bonds placed in membership fee fund	2,500.00
Life membership fees	180.00
Annual membership dues	161.00
Interest on bonds	277.56
Refund of money advanced for postage	170.00
Refund of overpayment of bills	3.23
Postage sent in for *Quarterly*	.25
Books purchased from the Society	5.00
Refund to Society of money advanced to pay for clerk hire	21.00
Total receipts	$7,304.87

Expenditures:

Traveling expenses	$207.10
Extra clerk hire	321.00
Purchase of old books, newspapers, etc.	185.00
Subscriptions	75.75
Filing reports with secretary of state	2.00
Flowers	25.90

Miscellaneous expenses	$46.25
Elliott Addressing Machine Co.	118.30
Transferred to State Savings Bank funds which had by mistake been deposited in the National Bank of Topeka	20.39
Balance on contract for painting at First Capitol	14.50
Gifts to janitors	13.50
Rent of safe-deposit box	3.30
Expenses of annual meeting	19.80
Premium on bonds of secretary and treasurer	10.00
Money advanced for postage	247.00
Premium on treasury notes	24.78
Total expenditures	$1,334.57
Balance, October 15, 1935	5,970.30
	$7,304.87

Balance consists of

Treasury bonds	$3,500.00
Cash	2,470.30
	$5,970.30

JONATHAN PECKER BEQUEST FUND

Principal, Liberty bonds, $950, exchange for 2⅞ percent treasury bonds	$950.00
Balance, interest, October 12, 1934	$41.34
Interest from October 12, 1934, to October 15, 1935	36.90
Total amount received	$78.24

Expenditures:

New Hampshire Historical Society, for vols. 33 and 34 of *Provincial and State Papers*	9.00
Balance on hand October 15, 1935	$69.24

JOHN BOOTH BEQUEST FUND

Principal, Liberty bonds, $500, exchanged for 2⅞ percent treasury bonds	$500.00
Balance, interest, October 12, 1934	$0.53
Interest from October 12, 1934, to October 15, 1935	18.94
Total amount received	$19.47

No expenditures for the year.

THOMAS H. BOWLUS FUND

Principal, Liberty bond for $1,000, converted into treasury bonds bearing 2⅞ percent. Interest included in membership fund.

Respectfully submitted,

MARY EMBREE, *Treasurer.*

On motion of F. H. Hodder, seconded by John S. Dean, the treasurer's report was approved.

The president called for the report of the executive committee. In the absence of E. A. Austin, who had been appointed to act for the committee, the secretary was asked to read the report:

REPORT OF THE EXECUTIVE COMMITTEE

OCTOBER 15, 1935.

To the Board of Directors, Kansas State Historical Society:

Having been appointed to examine the accounts of the treasurer, I find that her accounts agree with the state accountant's report and same is hereby approved. EDWIN A. AUSTIN, *Member of Executive Committee.*

On motion of J. M. Challiss, seconded by F. H. Hodder, the report of the executive committee was approved and accepted.

In the absence of Mrs. Henry F. Mason, chairman of the nominating committee, the report of the committee was read by the secretary as follows:

REPORT OF THE NOMINATING COMMITTEE

OCTOBER 15, 1935.

To the Board of Directors, Kansas State Historical Society:

Your committee on nominations beg leave to submit the following report for officers of the Kansas State Historical Society:

For president, F. H. Hodder, Lawrence; first vice-president, E. E. Kelley, Garden City; second vice-president, E. A. Austin, Topeka.

Respectfully submitted,
MRS. HENRY F. MASON,
JAMES C. MALIN,
ISABELLE C. HARVEY,
ERNEST A. RYAN, *Committee.*

On motion of Thomas A. Lee, seconded by Mrs. Flora I. Godsey, the report of the nominating committee was accepted.

There being no further business for the board of directors, the meeting adjourned.

ANNUAL MEETING OF THE SOCIETY

The annual meeting of the Kansas State Historical Society convened at 2 o'clock p. m. The meeting was called to order by the president.

The secretary read telegrams and letters from members who were unable to be present.

Thomas F. Doran gave the annual address of the president, which follows:

ADDRESS OF THE PRESIDENT

I wish to thank the Kansas State Historical Society for permitting me to act as its president during the year now closing. I would indeed be lacking in gratitude should I fail to express my appreciation of the distinct honor thus conferred upon me.

The territory now comprising our state was carved from the plains sloping eastward from the Rocky Mountains, formerly known as the Great American desert. I fear that it is still so considered by many untutored people living east of the Allegheny mountains who read only the headlines of the daily papers, magnifying blizzards, grasshoppers, drought and dust storms, forgetting that their daily bread comes largely from the wheat fields of Kansas and that a substantial portion of their best beef and pork comes from the feed lots and pastures of this state.

Until the first half of the nineteenth century, this land had been inhabited by Indians and by countless millions of buffalo, deer, antelope and other wild life, furnishing a happy hunting ground for these nomadic tribes who pitched their tents in its wooded valleys and roamed its boundless prairies at will. However, about the middle of the last century trappers, adventurers and pioneer settlers seeking homes, drifted into this plethoric but untried land. They began the struggle, encountered by all pioneers, against the loneliness and deprivations of the wilderness and the desert; against the brassy skies, burning droughts and hot winds of summer; against the blizzards and bleak and dreary death of winter; and, both winter and summer, living in terror of attacks from savage Indians.

The trials of such a life can be comprehended only by those who have endured its bitterness and enjoyed its luxuries. The freedom and charm of such a life lured the pioneer and gave him a feeling of independence and happiness found nowhere else on earth. Its memory is his heritage.

Kansas came into existence as one of the United States in 1861. Its birth was almost coincident with the beginning of the greatest and most sanguinary civil war of all history.

The admission of Kansas into the Union and the Civil War followed a bitter and bloody border war between the forces and factions of slavery from the South and the forces and factions of antislavery from the North. They met along the border line between Missouri and Kansas in their struggle to determine by squatter sovereignty whether this state should be free or slave.

The geographical location of Kansas and the character and conflicting ideas of its pioneer settlers made it the pivotal point of conflict between the North and South over the extension of slavery. The record of the struggles and tragedies of the period of the Kansas-Missouri border war presents one of the most absorbing and thrilling chapters of our nation's history.

The names of John Brown, James Montgomery, James H. Lane, George W. Brown, Gaius Jenkins, Charles Robinson, William A. Phillips, Amos A. Lawrence, Eli Thayer, and countless other Abolitionists from the North, with David R. Atchison, Benjamin F. Stringfellow, the Andersons, George W. Clarke, and C. A. Hamelton, leader in the cold-blooded massacre of eleven Free-State settlers on the Marais des Cygnes; the massacre of five Proslavery settlers at Dutch Henry's crossing of the Pottawatomie by John Brown; the marauding bands known as the "Jayhawkers," the "Red Legs" and "Bushwhackers"; the Battles of Blackjack, Hickory Point, Osawatomie, and a score of others, and in 1863 the burning of Lawrence by Quantrill and his men—all these incidents of the Border War bring up a flood of historic memories so thrilling and tragic as to constitute a story of real life unequalled in fiction. This often written and rewritten story is preserved in many forms in the records of this Society and should be read by all who are not familiar with it.

Following the Civil War came the building of our state, physically and politically. We started with the ox wagon. We now have stream-line railroad trains, automobiles and airplanes. In the beginning, our folks had to travel six miles on foot to summon a doctor. There were no telephones. We now have telephones and radios in almost every home. In those early days, the mention of a radio would have been a just cause for the execution of the mentioner as a witch.

In the development of this state, there have been seasons of drought and seasons of flood; years of famine and years of abundance. We have tried Republicans and Democrats; Pops and pretenders; rags and riches; Jerry Simpson and Mary Ellen Lease; poverty and Peffer. We tried whisky in the original package and then fell for absolute prohibition. Violations of this law were rigidly prosecuted for a generation, aided by Carrie Nation and her hatchet, but, despite our efforts to redeem the world from sin, a few fallen Kansans still indulge in an occasional glass of 3.2 beer.

Through the cycle of the seasons, Kansas always has produced, and always will produce, an abundance. Indeed, the present federal administration says we produce too much, and is now paying us fabulous sums of money for what we could, but are forbidden to, produce. We are told that scarcity of products will give us abundance, and that poverty will make us rich; that prosperity and happiness are found, not in economy and thrift, but in extravagance and debt. Senator Ingalls once said: "Kansas can come nearer going to Hell than any country on earth, and then redeem itself." It may even recover from this.

We are anxious to learn, however, what Alf Landon will do if and when he becomes President of the United States. His slogan now is: "Balance the budget and don't spend what you haven't got."

What is the answer? We are just sticking around to find out. The Historical Society is keeping the minutes and will correctly record the result.

Following the reading of his address, the president called upon the secretary to introduce W. R. Honnell, of Kansas City, who spoke on the "Pony Express."

In his introduction Mr. Mechem said:

Mr. Honnell used to live in a neighborhood on the route of the Pony Express. For the past several years he has been collecting data for the preparation of this map which we have on display here. You will note that it traces the entire route covered by the Pony Express, gives the names of riders, locates all the stations and gives other pertinent information. This map has been in such demand since Mr. Honnell prepared it that he has already been repaid for the many hours he spent in research. He has made a most valuable contribution to the recorded history of one of the most romantic phases of the story of Kansas. It gives me pleasure to introduce Mr. Honnell.

THE PONY EXPRESS

I am not indifferent for the invitation and this opportunity of speaking to this group of men and women representing the intellectuals of Kansas. I am especially pleased with my place on the program just before Tom McNeal, for I know you will all stay to hear his address on "The Governors of Kansas," and you might all leave when he had finished.

In northeastern Kansas twenty-five miles west of the Missouri river is the location of one of the lost towns of Kansas; a town that in the territorial days was known from the Missouri river to the Rocky Mountains. It derived its name from an Indian who was known as Kennekuk, for many years chief of the Kickapoo tribe of Indians. At this town three overland trails came together—a stagecoach and Pony Express trail from St. Joseph, Mo.; an overland freighting and stagecoach road from Atchison; and a military road from Fort Leavenworth over which Gen. Sidney Johnston moved an army of 5,000 soldiers in 1857 to quell the Mormon uprising in Utah. There were located here at this time a United States Indian agency for the Kickapoo tribe of Indians; an Indian mission, at which my parents were married in 1855; two rather commodious hotels, a large livery barn, a blacksmith shop, a wagon shop, two stores, and a post office. It is said that Abraham Lincoln stayed all night at the Baldwin House when he visited Kansas in December, 1859, so you see that Kennekuk was a place of some historical importance besides the fact that I was born there.

On New Year's day I received an invitation from an old Kennekuk Anti-Horse Thief Association to speak at a celebration of the seventy-fifth anniversary of the Pony Express. This association has degenerated from its former noble purpose of holding necktie parties into an old settlers' reunion. At this meeting were a number of people from Kansas City, Mo., among whom was Ben Majors, a son of Alexander Majors, who, with his associates, built and operated the Pony Express. He is ninety years of age, and he brought with him some of the original records kept by the Pony Express officials. I was interested in reading from a printed page the rules and regulations governing the conduct of their employees which said that they must not drink, swear, quarrel, or fight with other employees of the company.

Mr. Majors now lives on the state line in a rather palatial old home built by his father in 1855. It has seven fireplaces and seven gables. Mr. Majors frequently crossed the plains with the overland freight trains of his father, and was present when the golden spike was driven into the mahogany tie that linked the eastern and western divisions of the Union Pacific.

There are three things that make a nation great—fertile soil, busy workshops, and easy means of transportation for men and goods. The years preceding and those immediately following the Civil War were the years of the greatest activity in transportation, and no means of transportation was more romantic or more spectacular than the Pony Express which carried the mail on horseback from St. Joseph, Mo., to Sacramento City, Cal., a distance of 2,000 miles on a schedule of ten days. This reduced the time of the Butterfield stagecoaches through the south, and the Overland stagecoaches through the north by more than one half. At this time there were more than half a million people west of the Rocky Mountains isolated from all communication under thirty days, which brought about the demand and necessity for the Pony Express. It was a privately owned concern, built and operated by Russell, Majors & Waddell, one of the most outstanding firms of their day, at an expense of $750,000. No firm had a higher or more deserved reputation for integrity in the fulfillment of their contracts. It operated eighteen months, and the total receipts did not exceed $500,000.

On this trail there were 190 stations on an average of ten or twelve miles apart. It took approximately 450 horses, and 400 station keepers and helpers, of which 80 were riders, 40 always going east, and 40 always going west. All the equipment, supplies, grain and food had to be transported from the Missouri river to the various stations by ox teams. Hay cost from fifty to eighty dollars per ton, and grain cost from ten to twenty-five cents a pound. The charge for carrying mail was five dollars per one half ounce, so there weren't many love letters written at that time. The riders were chosen with the greatest care from among young lads reared on the frontier, and known to be expert horsemen, capable of thinking and acting quickly in moments of great personal danger. Their mounts were selected with no less care than the riders. Most of them were cayuses and bronchos, the same breed of horses only under a different name—a distinction without a difference. They were descendants from the horses brought to this country by Cortez and Coronado, and their ancestors grazed on the steppes of Arabia. They were clean of limb, deep of chest, and outlaws in disposition, and had to be broken each time they were ridden.

These horses were the fleetest mounts the company could buy, and were well groomed and cared for, thus giving the rider an advantage over the Redskins, with their horses that subsisted entirely upon the grass. The horses of the Redskins could not maintain a long pursuit, and would soon be outdistanced by the company's horses. The riders were instructed to outrun the Indians wherever possible, and only give battle where there was no other alternative. Each rider was armed, usually carrying two revolvers, a knife and extra cartridges. The whole equipment, including saddle and bridle, did not exceed thirteen pounds. They carried the mail in what was known as a "mochila," which was a leather blanket about four feet square, to which were sewed four small mail sacks about nine by twelve inches. Two of these were in front of the rider's legs and two behind, so he was always sitting upon his mail sack.

When arriving at a station the rider found his change of mount ready and waiting. He quickly changed his mail sack to the fresh horse, and was on his way. These riders received salaries ranging from $80 to $125 per month, and the station keepers and helpers received from $50 to $100 per month, including their board.

Alex Carlisle was the first rider out of St. Joseph, Mo. He was a consumptive and the pace was too much for him, so he soon resigned. The next rider was Johnnie Frye, who was a little Irish boy raised in Buchanan county, Missouri. He was an expert horseman before he entered this greatest school of horsemanship. The third station west of St. Joseph was Cold Springs ranch, kept by a homesteader who had three daughters, young, good-looking and vivacious. They would bake cookies, pie, and good things to eat and hand them to Johnnie Frye when he went by. They say Johnnie, on his three days' lay-over, used to go out to Cold Springs ranch to fish (I suppose that's what he went for). These girls were engaged in making a log-cabin quilt, and they desired to have Johnnie's red necktie to use as a pattern in their quilt. But Johnnie declined to accommodate them. Then the oldest girl, who was a good horsewoman, decided she would waylay Johnnie, and with her fresh horse ride along the trail beside him and grab his red necktie. After a few efforts, she was unsuccessful, and Johnnie's horse began to show greater speed than hers, so she made a last lunge at the necktie, and tore off a part of Johnnie's shirt. If you would visit today the descendants of this romantic girl, they would take great pleasure and delight in showing you the old log-cabin quilt, and indicating that a certain pattern was a part of Johnnie Frye's shirt tail.

Among the more famous riders of this trail was Jack Keetley, who rode from Rock Creek, the first station in Nebraska, to St. Joseph, Mo., and then doubled back to Rock Creek and returned to Seneca, without taking time out. He covered more than three hundred miles of continuous riding. Another rider by the name of Jim Moore rode from Midway station in Nebraska to Old Julesburg in the northeast corner of Colorado, and returned to Midway, covering a distance of 280 miles.

One of the longest authenticated rides was made by "Buffalo Bill," whose regular run was from Red Butte to Three Crossings, in Wyoming. When he arrived at Three Crossings the rider who should have taken the mail west had been killed, and the division superintendent sent him on to Rock Ridge, 85 miles farther. This rider who should have returned with the mail had gone out hunting during his lay-over and the Indians had raised his hair, so "Buffalo Bill" had to double back to Red Butte, a distance of 322 miles without rest, through a very rough, lonely and dangerous region.

Another of the old pioneers in this western country, who was in the employ of the Pony Express, was "Wild Bill" Hickok, who had charge of the station at Rock Creek, Neb. During the time he worked there he and his helper engaged in a fight with one of the local bad men and his associates, and are alleged to have killed four of them. They were tried for murder, but were later acquitted. Hickok was a remarkable marksman, and is alleged to have already killed forty-three men when he was appointed marshal of Abilene, these killings, however, being in the line of duty.

Another interesting story concerning "Buffalo Bill" was this: On one of his rides he had to carry a large amount of money, and being fully aware that numerous outlaws and thieves lurked in the region through which he had to pass, this courageous rider used two "mochilas," placing the one containing the valuables under his saddle, and the other, containing nothing but worthless paper, over the saddle. After he had gone but a few miles, two men jumped out from ambush and demanded the sack, covering him with their guns. "Buffalo Bill" gave them the worthless sack, and as they relaxed their watch on him, he shot and killed one of the men and the other ran away. He got back the other "mochila," although its contents were valueless.

There are many others who performed feats of great courage and endurance in getting the mail through on time, which had become to these young riders a religious duty.

Some of the beneficial results of this romantic and thrilling enterprise are as follows. It saved California to the Union, and proved that a line of communication could be maintained during all seasons of the year from the Missouri river to the Pacific coast. It encouraged the building of a telegraph line and hastened the completion of the Union Pacific Railroad.

The Pony Express started on the evening of the third of April, 1860, from St. Joseph, Mo., going west, and from Sacramento, Cal., going east. It continued until the completion of a telegraph line eighteen months later, which put the Pony Express out of business, for as swift as they were, they were not able to compete with lightning. This romantic and spectacular event in the early transportation and development of the great new West has increased in interest through the passing years. Having been born and reared on this trail, I have always had a sympathetic interest in its events, which led me to endeavor to reproduce this trail on a map, 24" x 48". This map gives the names of all the riders, alphabetically arranged, practically all of the 190 stations, as well as the Oregon trail from South Pass to the Northwest. It shows numerous illustrated incidents of the trail and a correct location of the Santa Fé trail as taken from the original survey by the government in 1825. Their field notes say that they crossed into Kansas nine miles south of where the Kaw river empties into the Missouri river. The map shows the location of Council Grove, Fort Zarah, Fort Dodge, Cimarron crossing, Bent's fort, and old Pawnee Rock, the cornerstone of many of the tragedies of the plains. Many of the public schools, libraries, universities and historical societies have availed themselves of this map for the information it contains.

These ponies and their riders were the air mail of 1860 and 1861. They traveled 650,000 miles, or twenty-six times around the world. They rendered faithful service to the people on the far Pacific coast, bringing them tidings from their friends and loved ones far away; tidings of the nation's struggle for freedom, and of battles won and battles lost.

Like a weaver's shuttle, they glided to and fro until the task was done. Through winter and summer, sunshine and storm, day and night, they pressed on across swollen streams, wind-swept plains, and desert waste, through warring bands of blood-thirsty savages, renegade outlaws, stampeding herds of buffaloes, and droves of hungry coyotes, the ghouls of the prairie, always seeking whom they might devour. On they went, through the dark and stormy nights, without even a friendly star to guide them on their lonely way, singing their love songs to the rhythm of their galloping ponies, with the ever-present danger of their ponies stepping into badger holes or prairie dog dens, throwing both horse and rider, often crippling the ponies. Then it became the painful duty of the rider to dispatch his pony as a friendly act, rather than to leave him to be devoured alive by the hungry coyotes. Quickly removing his "mochila" containing its precious burden, he trudged on afoot to the next station where a fresh mount sent the mail on towards its destination.

When the full-blooded Indian historian writes the story of the swift decline of his people and of the civilization that he loved and was centuries in building, he will date it from the advent of the Pony Express and the completion of the telegraph line and the Union Pacific Railroad.

The principal address was made by Thomas A. McNeal, of Topeka. He was introduced by President Doran, who said:

Now, members and friends, I wouldn't be unkind enough to our preceding speaker to say that the best always comes last, but we have with us the greatest reporter and finest story-teller in Kansas, and probably the most beloved citizen of our great commonwealth. I know that is a very broad statement, but had you been with us last night, with the other gentlemen who attended the eighty-second birthday meeting held in honor of the next speaker, you would realize the truth of what I have just said.

I am now living on borrowed time. The Scriptural span of life, which would have ended my career three years ago, has passed, and in all that time I have never seen such whole-hearted, honest and moving tribute paid to any man as was paid to the next speaker at that meeting. I want to say to him that, like Cleopatra, "age cannot wither him, nor custom stale, his infinite variety."

It is with the greatest pleasure that I introduce to you our most wonderful story-teller, greatest writer, and most beloved and honored citizen, Tom A. McNeal.

THE GOVERNORS OF KANSAS

According to the old theological concept you can divide humanity into two groups—the sheep and the goats, yet I have known quite a lot of goats who got mixed in with the sheep, and a few sheep who were mingled with the goats. No man I have ever known was absolutely honest, and, on the other hand, while I have known a number of damned scoundrels, I knew none who was wholly dishonest. I have never known any man who was wholly truthful, nor any man who was entirely a liar. There is no such thing as living up to an oath to tell the truth, the whole truth, and nothing but the truth. Nobody ever did that on all occasions and under all circumstances and if he did he would be a damned fool, and would very likely get himself into a lot of trouble.

I was put down on your program to talk on "Governors of Kansas."

Now, I don't know that there is so very much inspiration or interest in that particular subject, but it so happens that I have met, shaken hands with and talked a little with every governor of the state of Kansas. It happened in this way. In 1886, Kansas held a twenty-fifth anniversary celebration of the admission of Kansas into the Union. Gov. John A. Martin was then the chief executive. All the governors who had served up to that time were still alive. They met here in Topeka, and I happened to be in Topeka as a member of the legislature, so I met all of these governors, and I have known all of the governors serving since that time.

The first governor of Kansas was Charles Robinson. He was born in the state of Massachusetts in 1818, was educated to be a doctor, but his eyes failed him and he was terribly discouraged—thought his life was going to be a failure. In 1849 there was tremendous excitement throughout the country, because a miller by the name of Sutter discovered gold in his mill race near Sacramento, Cal. Immediately men of all classes and conditions began a race toward that land of promise, hoping to get a share of the precious yellow metal. They went by horseback, by boat, by wagon, and by stage; some crossed the Rocky Mountains and some sailed around Cape Horn. Many of them died, but a good many of them got to California, and so Doctor Robinson decided he would go to California.

He took what was the easiest but the longest way 'round, going by boat around Cape Horn to San Francisco. When he arrived at San Francisco a marvelous physical change had taken place in Doctor Robinson. He had gained much weight, and being a large man, standing about 6 feet, 2 inches in height, he was really a magnificent looking fellow.

In fact, he had changed almost as much on that sea voyage as did an old man I heard of who came out to Kansas, and let our wonderful climate work on him. I am going to relate that particular instance because it shows what Kansas can do.

There was an old gentleman in my native state who was ninety years of age; he had lost his sight, couldn't hear any too well, had lost all of his teeth, and didn't have enough hair left to make a collarette for a katydid. He had the rheumatism terribly bad, in fact he was stove up in every way, shape and form. He had a son who had settled out in western Kansas, and the old man took a notion that he would like to see his son before he died, and, as the old man had considerable property, the son was rather anxious to see him before he died. Well, the old man went out to see his son, and his people began to hear from him. In six months he had entirely recovered from his rheumatism, and in a year he had recovered his hearing and eyesight, and raised a new set of teeth, had a new crop of hair, and had joined the Boy Scouts, and a year and a half later had become the most proficient buck and wing dancer in the whole country roundabout. Then his folks didn't hear from him any more, and the son had apparently moved away from there, so they wrote to the postmaster, and asked him to tell them what had become of old man Badger. The postmaster answered that he regretted to tell them that the old man was dead. He had gone out with the Boy Scouts and taken an active part in most of their youthful sports, had contracted infantile paralysis and died as a result.

Going back to Doctor Robinson; when he arrived there it was to find that there was almost a war going on in California. The lands there were held almost altogether under Spanish grants. And all this influx of gold seekers took gold digging without having leases from those holding the land, and went to digging gold, or panning rather than digging. The authorities of California tried to arrest these squatters; to eject them from their diggings. Doctor Robinson joined the squatters, led them against those who sought to eject them, and there was a battle. So, while the landholders had a semblance of authority, they could not enforce it, but they indicted our first governor for treason. He stayed there for two or three years, and then went back home, where he became interested in any question arising which appealed to his sense of adventure. About that time there was a tremendous struggle going on between the forces of freedom and slavery. Massachusetts had an emigrant aid society, and he entered heart and soul into the struggle which was eventually to lead to the Civil War.

He came to Kansas, with his young wife, in 1854, and became a leader in that movement. He was a natural born leader, but the forces of slavery were too strong for him, and so again Doctor Robinson was arrested, charged with treason, put in jail at Lecompton, and kept there for, I think, four months. He regained his freedom when there came a change in the administration, the Free State forces having the upper hand.

Then came the Wyandotte constitutional convention, with its constitution, still our constitution, which was ratified by a considerable majority of the citizens of Kansas. This seemed to be admitted at Washington to be a fair election, but Kansas was not yet admitted to the Union. The Southern senators had not withdrawn from the senate, and they did not propose to ratify the admission of a free state into the Union, so Kansas was left hanging in the air. An election had been called under this new constitution, and Governor Robinson was the first governor elected. He was elected for a two-year term, but it was almost a year before the Southern senators got out of the senate. Buchanan was still sitting in the presidential chair, apparently not knowing what to do. I never believed that James Buchanan was a traitor to his country, but he might just as well have been, so far as results were concerned.

On the 29th day of January, 1861, Kansas was made a state. Robinson had been elected more than a year before that time, but when the word came from Washington that Kansas was finally admitted to the Union, he, as governor, called the legislature into session on the 26th day of March, 1861. Already the skies were overcast with the dark clouds of war. On account of this delay in taking the oath of office by Governor Robinson, there resulted one of the first and greatest cases in our supreme court. It was claimed that his term had expired at the close of the two-year term for which he was elected, although he had not actually been inducted into office until more than a year after his election. The case was decided in favor of Robinson, and he served out his full two years. He had trouble all the time. There was the Robinson faction and the Lane faction. The state was poor, and bonds were issued with a provision that they were not to be sold for less than eighty cents on the dollar. It was claimed that the governor, secretary of state, also named Robinson, through a man named Stevens, and the state auditor sold these bonds for about fifty cents on the dollar defrauding the state out of thousands of dollars. It finally resulted in the impeachment of the governor, the secretary of state, and the auditor.

One of the members of the committee on impeachment became the second governor of Kansas. They were all tried before the senate. Robinson was acquitted on all counts. The secretary of state and auditor were convicted, but these proceedings ruined Robinson's career, so in 1863 a groceryman named Thomas Carney, more often called Tom Carney, became governor. He was born in my own state of Ohio in 1827. There was nothing striking about him. I guess he was a pretty good business man. His administration was troublous, of course, but along with his many enemies he had many friends. He tried to be renominated but failed, and in 1865 Samuel J. Crawford became the third governor of Kansas.

He was born on the 15th day of April, 1835, and came to Kansas in 1858 settling at Garnett. When the war broke out he became a captain in the Second Kansas infantry, and fought with Lyon at Wilson's creek. He was a great soldier, and his book, *Kansas in the Sixties,* would indicate that he had a fine sense of military strategy. He was afterwards commissioned colonel of the U. S. Eighty-third Colored infantry. At that time it was a very unpopular thing for a white man to officer a colored regiment. The South had raised the black flag against them, and issued an order that no quarter was to be given to officers or men of colored regiments. When Colonel Crawford learned of that order it so happened that he had captured quite a number of officers belonging to the Southern army. He sent word to General Hindman, of the Southern army, saying, "I wish to respectfully tell you that I have (I have forgotten how many) men and officers of your command here as my prisoners, and unless that order that no quarter be given officers or men of colored regiments is rescinded, I intend to stand these men up and shoot them."

These officers and men didn't want to be shot; the Southern army didn't want these prisoners shot, and after a great deal of blustering, the order of no quarter was canceled. It was said that Governor Crawford had the best trained regiment in the western army. How true that was I do not know.

Came 1864, and the country was still in a state of war. In the fall of that year, September, the time was approaching for the election of another governor. The war was pretty nearly over, and without his solicitation, possibly without his knowledge, Colonel Crawford was nominated by the Republicans for governor, and was elected in the fall of 1864, as the third governor of Kansas. He was the youngest governor that ever served in this state, being only twenty-nine years of age.

He was a magnificent looking soldier; a man of great courage and intelligence. The state was in a chaotic state financially, the people were poor; few crops had been raised, hardly more than enough to keep the people alive. Armies had marched across the state cleaning up everything as they went; in addition to that, heretofore peaceful tribes of Indians went on the warpath, with the result that more than 100 peaceful citizens in western Kansas were slaughtered in a most barbarous manner. The war was not yet over, and as I have said, the state was poor and ravaged, and yet out of it all Governor Crawford must be given credit for laying the foundation of all the great institutions of the state which have become so efficient and powerful in Kansas. He founded the university, the penitentiary, and the beginnings of our great agricultural college. In addition to that he did a great work in bringing peace to the border. He was continually after the government to help him to bring about peace. Sherman and Sheridan helped him, and he gave himself heart and soul to bringing about peace between the Indians and settlers.

In 1868, near the close of his second term, he resigned to take the position of colonel of the Nineteenth Kansas and led it to the border in one of the most thrilling campaigns ever made. Governor Crawford always felt that he was not given the credit he should have had for bringing an end to the Indian troubles, and in the calling of the great peace council, near where my old town of Medicine Lodge was afterward located, where 15,000 Indians gathered, all full of hostility and treachery. The story goes, and I suppose it is true, that Governor Crawford noticed that the Indians far outnumbered the government troops and he didn't like the way the Indians were behaving. He suggested that the whole command form a hollow square as the best means of repelling any attack, and that when the Indians saw that they decided they wouldn't try to attack.

Along with Crawford there was elected a Methodist, or he may have been a Presbyterian, preacher named Nehemiah Green, as lieutenant governor. You know people do not pay much attention to a lieutenant governor—hardly anybody knows who he is. I once asked one of our former lieutenant governors whether he had heard about that mysterious case near Buffalo, N. Y., and he said he hadn't, so I said, "Well, they found a man dead up there, and they couldn't find a thing upon him to identify him, so they said that probably he was a lieutenant governor of some state." I think he didn't like that story a bit.

That was the only case in Kansas where a lieutenant governor became a governor during the term of the man who was elected governor, and he was the only preacher who became a governor.

After him came James M. Harvey. He was elected in that year, 1868. He served four years, and then he was elected to the United States senate. He was the first governor to go from the governor's chair to the United States senate. He stayed there three years and then he was knocked out by Senator Plumb, who served about seventeen years.

Governor Harvey was born, I think, in the state of Virginia. He was a farmer and lived, I believe, in Riley county. He was succeeded by Thomas A. Osborn, who was born in Pennsylvania in the year 1836. He moved to Doniphan county and was elected to the state senate from there. I don't know how he got into Leavenworth, but he was there in 1872. He served for four years as governor, and was succeeded by George T. Anthony. Anthony had everything that it takes to make a great governor except diplomacy and tact. He was a man of great ability. I loved him. He was one of the greatest men I ever knew, but he would offend a politician by too plain speech. The result was that he served only one term. He was born in New York in 1824. He served two years and then his enemies, led by his own cousin, Col. Dan Anthony, defeated him for renomination. There was a bitter feud between these two powerful cousins. They hated each other as long as they lived, and how much longer I don't know, but anyway they hated each other. Col. Dan Anthony, as editor of the Leavenworth *Times,* marshalled his forces for John A. Martin, but he didn't have quite enough force to succeed in getting the nomination, so George T. Anthony, after battling for several days, threw his influence behind John P. St. John and nominated him.

Then started a new page in the history of the state. John P. St. John was called by his enemies "the man with the painted mustache." He had what was called a walrus mustache and they claimed he dyed it. Maybe he did. It was his mustache and I suppose it was his right and privilege to dye it if he wanted to. He was a stalwart, rugged man, six feet or more in height, and a man of great courage and uprightness. He had a son who had been ruined by liquor and he was bitterly opposed to its sale.

He intended when he took the governor's chair to seek the strengthening of the liquor law, but did not ask for constitutional prohibition. His enemies thought they could checkmate him by proposing a prohibitory amendment to the constitution, passed the resolution in the senate but expected to defeat it in the house. They didn't think that the people would vote for a prohibition amendment if submitted, nor did they believe that the lower house of the legislature would vote to submit such an amendment to a vote of the people. They were fooled on both counts. After an intense campaign, John P. St. John was reëlected as governor, and the liquor amendment carried by about 8,000 majority, so St. John became the head of the prohibition movement, not only in Kansas, but in the United States. The bolt that had been launched to kill his political career was like a boomerang in its reaction on his enemies. However, he had raised up a mighty flock of enemies and they were not idle. When St. John was foolish enough to aspire to a third term they raised the cry of usurpation—claimed that he was disrupting the state, with the consequence that George W. Glick became the first Democratic governor of Kansas.

Glick served two years and then the state swung back to the Republican party, and John A. Martin achieved the ambition of his life by being elected governor. He was secretary of the Wyandotte convention when only twenty years of age. When the war broke out he became the colonel of the Eighth Kansas infantry, and made a magnificent record in the war. He was only twenty-two years old when he and his regiment made a record at Chickamauga, and in many other battles he proved his valor and courage as a soldier and leader of men. When he became governor he rather leaned to the anti-prohibition side, but before he got through with his four years of service he was one of the most intense prohibitionists I ever saw. He always felt, however, a little disappointed; he felt that he was through—that life was over for him. He had tasted the intoxicating wine of power and life seemed very flat and tasteless afterwards. I think he died long before his time, as he was a comparatively young man.

He was succeeded by a lawyer from Independence, Lyman U. Humphrey, elected by a large majority, about 80,000. Before he got through his first term it was nip and tuck whether he would ever get a second term, and his enemies claimed that tuck had it. Humphrey was reëlected by a small plurality. The first governor of Kansas, Charles Robinson, had left his party and became the leader of the independent party which called themselves the "Free Silver and Anti-Prohibition Party." He was nominated for governor by a coalition of antiprohibition Republicans and Democrats who wouldn't go with the Populists. He received about 90,000 votes, most of which would have gone to Willets, so Humphrey was reëlected.

To show you how complete was the political revolution of 1890, in 1889 there were not enough Democrats to hold a caucus in the lower house of the legislature and two years afterwards there were hardly enough Republicans left in the lower house to hold a caucus. The house was overwhelmingly Populist. In 1892 L. D. Lewelling, a school teacher from Iowa, was elected governor by a small majority. Then came the legislative war when the question was raised as to whether we had a Populist legislature under the rule of J. M. Dunsmore or a Republican legislature under the rule of George L. Douglass of Wichita. Well, that is all history and you know that eventually the "Bald Hornet" Dunsmore and his crowd were ousted.

In 1894 the Republicans nominated Edmund N. Morrill, of Hiawatha. He was born in Maine in 1834, and was a fine man, but he lacked the chief qualification for a governor, he couldn't say no. A man would come to him and ask for a job, and he would put his arm around his shoulder and tell him that he was a mighty good fellow and he didn't know any one he would rather give a job to than him. And the man would go away, sure that he had it, and the next day he would learn that some one else had the job. Well, of course, Morrill got to be known as something of a hypocrite, and although most of us are hypocrites to some extent, we don't like the other fellow to be one. So the result was that the governorship in 1896 was in the name of John W. Leedy, of Coffey county. He was nominated for governor at the Abilene convention and one of our most eloquent speakers of that day, Ed. C. Little, made a stirring speech pledging his support after the manner of Ruth to her mother-in-law, "Whither Thou goest I will go; where Thou liest I will lie; Thy people shall be my people and where Thou diest there will I be buried." However, Ed didn't lie with the Populists very long and I know he didn't die with them. John W. Leedy served two years and was defeated by W. E. Stanley, of Wichita. He was a fine chap, able to trim his sails and make himself popular with the church people and with the politicians, better than any other man I have known. He could talk to the Sunday schools and they believed he was a prohibitionist, and when he spoke officially he kept on both sides of the question.

Following him came Willis J. Bailey. After serving two years Bailey was defeated for renomination by a newspaperman, E. W. Hoch, who was a native of Kentucky, born in 1849. I happened to be for a while his secretary and I know he had plenty of troubles.

After him came the misnamed redheaded governor. He was not a redhead, he was flaxen polled, but he acted like a redhead most of the time, Walter Roscoe Stubbs. Just about that time along came the Bull Moose movement, led by the immortal Teddy Roosevelt, and this division in the Republican party resulted in the defeat of Stubbs for the U. S. senate.

George H. Hodges, the second Democrat to be elected governor, served two years, and was defeated by Arthur Capper, who served four years, and then went to the United States senate and is now serving his third term there.

After Capper came Henry J. Allen, who managed to stir up among labor unions a very intense hatred. He served four years, and then came a farmer from Bourbon, Jonathan M. Davis, a Democrat, who defeated our Republican candidate, W. Y. Morgan, by about 20,000 votes. Davis served two years and was succeeded by Ben S. Paulen, who served four years. He was not born in Kansas, but he told me that if he had it to do over again he would have waited and been born in Kansas. He went out just as popular as when he became governor.

And then came Clyde M. Reed, an able man, but one who could make more men mad without half trying than any one I have ever known. Reed served two years and then was defeated by Harry H. Woodring, a Democrat who is now our present assistant secretary of war.

And last, but far from least, we have our present governor, Alf M. Landon, who actually has a chance to be elected president of the United States.

Of those twenty-six men I have mentioned, all are dead except Hodges, Capper, Allen, Davis, Paulen, Reed, Woodring and the present acting governor. Eighteen of them have passed away. Of those that are left Sen. Arthur Capper leads in point of age, being seventy years old last July; Hodges will be seventy next February; Allen sixty-eight next September, Paulen sixty-seven next July, and the others are just kids.

I don't know, ladies and gentlemen, whether this has bored you or not. It may have seemed to you more like a somewhat remarkable feat of memory than anything else. The governors I have known have been nearly all good men who did, I think, the best they knew, and guided the state through troublous times to the best of their ability. And through those troublous times and good times our state has grown, but it has grown through many hardships and vicissitudes. I have lived here for fifty-six years and have seen it in all its phases. I have seen it dry, so dry that you had to prime the mourners at a funeral so they could shed tears for the departed. I have seen the wind blow so hard that any intelligent dog when he wanted to bark turned away from the wind because if he turned the other way it would have turned him inside out. In fact, I knew of this kind of an accident. In the midst of a terrific wind storm a dog which loved to bark, forgot his caution and turned and barked right into the wind, and the wind went down his throat and promptly turned him inside out, and one of his enemies got at him and chewed up his insides. That dog didn't get over it for months, even when he was turned back the right way, and he never seemed quite the same dog afterwards.

This is Kansas, the poorest state when it is poor, and the richest when it is rich; whose people are, as a rule, brave and loyal citizens. There is no state in the Union that comes nearer being inhabited by simon pure Americans than this our own state of Kansas. This fact gives me new faith in humanity—new faith in our country, faith that this republic of ours is not going down but will go on and on and our children's children will still live under its starry banner, enjoying the blessings of its freedom and its opportunities.

At the conclusion of Mr. McNeal's address Mr. Doran said:

After listening to Mr. McNeal's address I know you feel that it justified every word I said about Tom, and inspires me to make another speech.

It is from such men as Tom McNeal, and our early pioneers, from the worthy men who have governed this state, who have been a part of its history and have added luster to its already bright name, that we learn to appreciate, to know the truth of the motto on our great seal of the state, "Through difficulties to the stars."

I would like to go on and on forever, telling you about the progress of Kansas; about its wonderful people; about its wonderful climate, about the joy of living in this unique state, and I want to say here and now that one of the greatest joys of my life is to have known and loved Tom McNeal, and I am glad to have this opportunity of saying it to him, before the hand of death has been laid upon our lives. Praise of the dead is most fitting, but falls on deaf ears; praise of the living finds willing and open ears, and brings a glow to the heart of the giver.

President Doran then called for the report of the committee on nominations for directors. In the absence of the chairman, Mrs. Henry F. Mason, the secretary, read the report as follows:

The Annual Meeting

October 15, 1935.

To the Kansas State Historical Society:

Your committee on nominations beg leave to submit the following report and recommendations for directors of the Society for the term of three years ending October, 1938:

Aitchison, R. T., Wichita.
Capper, Arthur, Topeka.
Carson, F. L., Wichita.
Challiss, J. M., Atchison.
Dawson, John S., Hill City.
Doerr, Mrs. Laura P. V., Larned.
Doran, Thos. F., Topeka.
Ellenbecker, John G., Marysville.
Hobble, Frank A., Dodge City.
Hodder, F. H., Lawrence.
Hogin, John C., Belleville.
Huggins, Wm. L., Emporia.
Johnston, Mrs. W. A., Topeka.
Knapp, Dallas W., Coffeyville.
Lilleston, W. F., Wichita.
McLean, Milton R., Topeka.
McNeal, Thos. A., Topeka.
Malin, James C., Lawrence.
Mason, Mrs. Henry F., Topeka.
Moore, Russell, Wichita.
Morehouse, Geo. P., Topeka.
Price, Ralph R., Manhattan.
Raynesford, H. C., Ellis.
Russell, W. J., Topeka.
Smith, Wm. E., Wamego.
Solander, Mrs. T. T., Osawatomie.
Spratt, O. M., Baxter Springs.
Stevens, Caroline F., Lawrence.
Thompson, W. F., Topeka.
Van Tuyl, Mrs. Effie H., Leavenworth.
Walker, Mrs. Ida M., Norton.
White, William Allen, Emporia.
Wilson, John H., Salina.

Respectfully submitted,
Mrs. Henry F. Mason,
James C. Malin,
Isabelle C. Harvey,
Ernest A. Ryan,
E. E. Kelley, *Committee.*

On motion of J. W. Berryman, seconded by E. A. Austin, these directors were unanimously elected for the term ending October, 1938.

President Doran then called for the report of the Shawnee Mission Indian Historical Society. The report was read by the secretary. On motion of J. W. Berryman, seconded by E. A. Austin, it was voted to accept and file the report.

Mr. Doran called for the report of the Chase County Historical Society, which was given verbally by its president, C. W. Hawkins. President Doran said, "This splendid report will be accepted and approved and filed in the records of the state Society, and it is so ordered."

President Doran called for the report of the Riley County Historical Society. Mrs. Caroline A. Smith of Manhattan responded and read the report which had been written by Mrs. George Failyer. At the conclusion of the reading of the report President Doran said, "We are very glad to have this excellent report. It is accepted and will be filed in the records of the state Society."

President Doran called for the report of the Pawnee County Historical Society. This report was given verbally by Mrs. Laura P. V. Doerr of Larned. At the conclusion of Mrs. Doerr's report President Doran said, "We thank you, and your report, when written, will be filed in the records of the state Society."

There being no further business, the annual meeting of the Society adjourned.

MEETING OF THE BOARD OF DIRECTORS

The afternoon meeting of the board of directors was called to order by the president. He asked for a re-reading of the report of the nominating committee for the officers of the Society. The following were then unanimously elected:

For a one-year term: F. H. Hodder, president; E. E. Kelley, first vice-president; E. A. Austin, second vice-president.

There being no further business, the meeting adjourned.

KIRKE MECHEM, *Secretary*.

DIRECTORS OF THE KANSAS STATE HISTORICAL SOCIETY AS OF OCTOBER, 1935

DIRECTORS FOR YEAR ENDING OCTOBER, 1936

Beeks, Charles E., Baldwin.
Beezley, George F., Girard.
Bonebrake, Fred B., Topeka.
Bowlus, Thomas H., Iola.
Browne, Charles H., Horton.
Dean, John S., Topeka.
Embree, Mrs. Mary, Topeka.
Gray, John M., Kirwin.
Harger, Charles M., Abilene.
Harvey, Mrs. Isabelle C., Topeka.
Haucke, Frank, Council Grove.
Kagey, Charles L., Wichita.
Kinkel, John M., Topeka.
Lee, Thomas Amory, Topeka.
McFarland, Helen M., Topeka.
McFarland, Horace E., Junction City.
Malone, James, Topeka.
Mechem, Kirke, Topeka.
Morrison, T. F., Chanute.
Norris, Mrs. George, Arkansas City.
O'Neil, Ralph T., Topeka.
Philip, Mrs. W. D., Hays.
Rankin, Robert C., Lawrence.
Ruppenthal, J. C., Russell.
Ryan, Ernest A., Topeka.
Sawtell, James H., Topeka.
Simons, W. C., Lawrence.
Soller, August, Washington.
Stanley, W. E., Wichita.
Stone, Robert, Topeka.
Trembly, W. B., Kansas City.
Walker, B. P., Topeka.
Woodward, Chester, Topeka.

THE ANNUAL MEETING

DIRECTORS FOR YEAR ENDING OCTOBER, 1937

Austin, E. A., Topeka.
Berryman, J. W., Ashland.
Brigham, Mrs. Lalla M., Council Grove.
Brokaw, C. L., Kansas City, Kan.
Bumgardner, Edward, Lawrence.
Correll, Charles M., Manhattan.
Davis, John W., Dodge City.
Denious, Jess C., Dodge City.
Fay, Mrs. Mamie Axline, Pratt.
Frizell, E. E., Larned.
Godsey, Mrs. Flora R., Emporia.
Hall, Mrs. Carrie A., Leavenworth.
Hamilton, Clad, Topeka.
Haskin, S. B., Olathe.
Hegler, Ben F., Wichita.
Jones, Horace, Lyons.
Kelley, E. E., Garden City.
Lillard, T. M., Topeka.
Lindsley, H. K., Wichita.
McCarter, Mrs. Margaret Hill, Topeka.
Mercer, J. H., Topeka.
Oliver, Hannah P., Lawrence.
Patrick, Mrs. Mae C., Satanta.
Reed, Clyde M., Parsons.
Rupp, Mrs. W. E., Hillsboro.
Scott, Charles F., Iola.
Schultz, Floyd B., Clay Center.
Shirer, H. L., Topeka.
Van de Mark, M. V. B., Concordia.
Wark, George H., Caney.
Wheeler, Mrs. B. R., Topeka.
Woolard, Sam F., Wichita.
Wooster, Lorraine E., Salina.

DIRECTORS FOR YEAR ENDING OCTOBER, 1938

Aitchison, R. T., Wichita.
Capper, Arthur, Topeka.
Carson, F. L., Wichita.
Challiss, J. M., Atchison.
Dawson, John S., Hill City.
Doerr, Mrs. Laura P. V., Larned.
Doran, Thos. F., Topeka.
Ellenbecker, John G., Marysville.
Hobble, Frank A., Dodge City.
Hodder, F. H., Lawrence.
Hogin, John C., Belleville.
Huggins, Wm. L., Emporia.
Johnston, Mrs. W. A., Topeka.
Knapp, Dallas W., Coffeyville.
Lilleston, W. F., Wichita.
McLean, Milton R., Topeka.
McNeal, Thos. A., Topeka.
Malin, James C., Lawrence.
Mason, Mrs. Henry F., Topeka.
Moore, Russell, Wichita.
Morehouse, Geo. P., Topeka.
Price, Ralph R., Manhattan.
Raynesford, H. C., Ellis.
Russell, W. J., Topeka.
Smith, Wm. E., Wamego.
Solander, Mrs. T. T., Osawatomie.
Spratt, O. M., Baxter Springs.
Stevens, Caroline F., Lawrence.
Thompson, W. F., Topeka.
Van Tuyl, Mrs. Effie H., Leavenworth.
Walker, Mrs. Ida M., Norton.
White, William Allen, Emporia.
Wilson, John H., Salina.

Recent Additions to the Library

Compiled by HELEN M. McFARLAND, Librarian

IN ORDER that members of the Kansas State Historical Society and others interested in historical study may know the class of books we are receiving, a list is printed annually of the books accessioned in our specialized fields.

These books come to us from three sources, purchase, gift and exchange, and fall into the following classes: books by Kansans and about Kansas; books on the West, including explorations, overland journeys and personal narratives; genealogy and local history; and books on the Indians of North America, United States history and biography.

We receive regularly the publications of many historical societies by exchange, and subscribe to other historical and genealogical publications which are needed in reference work.

The following is a partial list of books which were added to the library from October 1, 1934, to October 1, 1935. Government and state official publications and some books of a general nature are not included. The total number of books accessioned appears in the report of the secretary in this issue of the *Quarterly*.

KANSAS

ALEXANDER, MRS. LILLIAN M., *Candy*. New York, Dodd, Meade & Company, 1934.

ALLEN, E. L., *The Spiritual Conflict. A Memorial Discourse Delivered at Lane, Franklin County, Kansas, May 26, 1887*. Kansas City, Mo., J. H. Smart & Company, 1887.

ALLISON, GEORGE WILLIAM, and others, *With Christ in Kansas; a History of the First Presbyterian Church of Topeka, Kansas, 1859 to 1934*. Topeka, Committee on the Seventy-fifth Anniversary, 1934.

AMERICAN LEGION, Kansas department, Thomas Hopkins Post No. 4, Wichita, *The American Legion Membership Directory, 1934, 1935*. No impr.

ANDERSON, MRS. BERNICE (GOUDY), *Topsy Turvy and the Tin Clown*. New York, Rand McNally [c1932].

—— *Topsy Turvy's Pigtails*. New York, Rand McNally [c1930].

ATWOOD, FREDERICK, *Kansas Rhymes and Other Lyrics*. Topeka, Crane & Company, 1902.

BASKA, SISTER MARY REGINA, *The Benedictine Congregation of Saint Scholastica; Its Foundation and Development (1852-1930)*. Washington, D. C., Catholic University of America, 1935. (*Studies in American Church History*, vol. 20.)

BECK, STEPHEN C., *A True Sketch of His Army Life.* No impr.
BECKER, EDNA, *Pickpocket Songs.* Caldwell, Idaho, The Caxton Printers, 1935.
BOYLE, L. C., *"Kansas," Toast, Kansas City Commercial Club Banquet, Coates House, December 19, 1898.* No impr.
BRYAN, S. A., *Memorial Reminiscences; Sketches of Civil War Veterans of the Waterville Community.* N. p., 1935.
BURKE, JOHN M., comp., *"Buffalo Bill" From Prairie to Palace; an Authentic History of the Wild West.* Chicago, Rand McNally, 1893.
BURRES, MARJORIE (BAKER), and PAUL WILLIAM BURRES, *Thrills and Heartthrobs of Europe.* Philadelphia, Dorrance & Company [c1934].
CADMAN, W. K., *Kansas Natural Gas; a Report to the Kansas State Planning Board.* Wichita, 1934. Mimeographed.
CARPENTER, FRANK M., *The Lower Permian Insects of Kansas.* Parts 1-6. Publisher varies. 1930-1933.
CHITTENDEN DIRECTORY CO., comps. and pubs., *Chanute and Neosho County, Kansas, Directory, 1903-1904.* St. Louis, Chittenden Directory Company, 1903.
COULTER, O. H., *Roster of Illinois Soldiers Residing in Kansas.* Topeka, *Western Veteran* [1889].
CRARY, ALBERT M., *The A. M. Crary Memoirs and Memoranda, Written by Himself.* Herington, Herington *Times* [c1915].
DAIL, C. C., *Adam Answered.* No impr.
DAVIS, ISABEL, *Kansas Poems.* N. p. [Turner] 1914.
DILL, WILLIAM ADELBERT, *The Newspaper's Family Tree.* Rev. ed. Lawrence, University of Kansas, Department of Journalism, 1934.
DUNSMORE, J. M., *Dedicatory Address, Delivered September 12, 1889, at the Unveiling of the Monument Erected to Mark the Position Held by the 116th Regiment, Pennsylvania Volunteers, in the Battle of Gettysburg, Pennsylvania, July 2, 1863.* No impr.
EDMONDS, MRS. MARY (MYERS), *Historical Survey of Social Service in Wichita, Kansas, From 1870 to 1934.* A dissertation submitted to the graduate faculty of the University of Wichita in candidacy for the degree of Master of Arts, department of sociology. Typed, 1934.
EMMERT, DAVID B., comp., *Wichita City Directory and Immigrants Guide, 1878.* Kansas City, Mo., Tiernan & Wainwright, 1878.
ESTEY, STEPHEN SEWALL, *Laugh, and Love, and Lift.* New York, Fleming H. Revell Company [c1934].
FARNHAM, MRS. MATEEL (HOWE), *Great Riches.* New York, Dodd, Mead & Company, 1934.
FIFTH KANSAS CAVALRY ASSOCIATION, *Regimental Roster, 1911.* No impr.
FULLING, KATHARINE PAINTER, *Trail Blazers; a Kansas Day Play for Children, in One Act.* Typed, 1935.
GANDY, LEWIS CASS, *The Tabors; a Footnote of Western History.* New York, Press of the Pioneers, Inc., 1934.

GEARY COUNTY PLANNING COMMITTEE, "The Next Twenty Years." A Report to the Kansas State Planning Board. Junction City, 1935. Mimeographed.

GRANT, BLANCHE CHLOE, When Old Trails Were New; the Story of Taos. New York, Press of the Pioneers, 1934.

HALL, MRS. CARRIE A., and ROSE G. KRETSINGER, The Romance of the Patchwork Quilt in America . . . Caldwell, Idaho, Caxton Printers, Ltd., 1935.

HARRINGTON, GRANT W., Historic Spots or Mile-stones in the Progress of Wyandotte County, Kansas. [Merriam, Kan., The Mission Press] 1935.

HARRIS, CECIL H., Cecil's Poems. [Wichita, Composed and Printed by Cecil H. Harris] n. d.

HEDGES, J. EDWARD, The Advertising of Fabricated Parts in Consumer Media. Lawrence, University of Kansas, 1934. (Kansas Studies in Business, No. 16.)

HINSHAW, DAVID, Will Republican Government Disappear? N. p. [1935.]

HOINVILLE, JULIA SIMONS, The Purple Velvet Gown; a Christmas Story Reaching from Hodgeman County and Larned, Kansas, to Chicago and Back Again. N. p. [1930.]

HOLTON, ORDINANCES, Revised Ordinances and Rules of the Council, 1898. Holton, Signal Job Printing House, 1898.

HOY, ELLA COMPTON, The Church Moths. Baltimore, Md., Saulsbury Publishing Company [c1919].

ISELY, MRS. ELISE (DUBACH), Sunbonnet Days, by Elise Dubach Isely as Told to Her Son Bliss Isely. Caldwell, Idaho, The Caxton Printers, 1935.

JEFFREY, ORLANDO, Folks and Fairies in Poesy. [Marion, Kan., Printed by the Marion Record, c1931.]

John Brown, and "The Union Right or Wrong" Songster: Containing All the Celebrated "John Brown" & "Union Songs" . . . San Francisco, D. E. Appleton & Company, 1862.

JOHNSON, W. A., Address to the Citizens of Fredonia, Wilson County, Kansas. Delivered July 4, 1896. No impr.

JOHNSTON, WILLIAM, Petition for Review Before the Secretary of the Interior; Settlers on the Osage Purchase in Kansas vs. Railroad Companies. Supplemental Argument for Petitioners. Washington, D. C., Judd & Detweiler, 1870.

KANSAS ACADEMY OF SCIENCE, Transactions of the 66th Annual Meeting, April 13-15, 1934, vol. 37. Topeka, Kansas State Printing Plant, 1934.

KANSAS CATHOLIC HISTORICAL SOCIETY, Annals, May 1931, No. 1. No impr.

KANSAS CITY, KANSAS, COUNCIL OF RELIGIOUS EDUCATION, Decennial; Weekday Church Schools of Kansas City, Kansas, 1923-1933. [Kansas City, Kansas, 1934.]

KANSAS COÖPERATIVE LEAGUE, Kansas, Our State. [Topeka, Kansas Coöperative League, 1934.]

KANSAS CRIME PREVENTION COMMITTEE, Safety for Kansas. Topeka, Kansas Crime Prevention Committee [1935].

KANSAS EDUCATORS CLUB, The Kansas Educator, Yearbook, February 1, 1935. Mimeographed.

KANSAS EMERGENCY RELIEF COMMITTEE, *Public Welfare Service in Kansas; a Ten-year Report, 1924-1933.* Topeka, Committee, 1934. (*KERC Bulletin,* No. 127.)

Kansas Farmer and Mail and Breeze, pub., *Directory of Franklin and Douglas Counties, Kansas.* Topeka, Kansas Farmer and Mail and Breeze [c1920].

Kansas Magazine, 1935: Essay, Short Story, Verse, Kansas Art. [Manhattan, Kansas State College Press, 1935.]

KANSAS SOCIETY OF CERTIFIED PUBLIC ACCOUNTANTS, *Membership Roster, Constitution and By-laws of the Society, C. P. A. Law, C. P. A. Certificates Issued Under Provisions of State Law.* No impr.

KANSAS STATE PLANNING BOARD, *Before Building Reservoirs or Levees; Some Important Considerations.* Topeka, 1935. Mimeographed.

—— *The Coördination of Transport; a Study of Interstate Motor Traffic Into and Through Kansas, 1934. A Report of the Kansas State Planning Board.* Topeka, 1935. Mimeographed.

—— *Inventory of Public Works; a Study of Possibilities in Kansas. A Report of the Kansas State Planning Board.* Topeka, 1935. Mimeographed.

—— *Progress Report, September, 1934.* Mimeographed.

—— *Progress Report, March, 1935.* Mimeographed.

—— *Rural Schools in Kansas; a Study of Their Physical Condition and Recreational Equipment. A Report of the Kansas State Planning Board.* Topeka, 1935. Mimeographed.

KARSNER, DAVID, *John Brown, Terrible "Saint"* . . . New York, Dodd, Mead & Company, 1934.

KEPLINGER, L. W., *Address at Oak Grove Cemetery, Kansas City, Kansas, May 30, 1922.* No impr.

KIMBALL, MRS. MARIA PORTER (BRACE), *My Eighty Years.* Privately Printed, 1934.

KINNEY, A. M., *Kansas Prairies and Other Poems.* [Kansas City, Mo., Stockyards Printing Company, c1935.]

KISTLER, JOHN J., *The Installation and Operation of a Cost-Finding System for Printers.* Lawrence, University of Kansas, Department of Journalism, 1934.

KOEPSEL, LOUIS HERMAN, *The Life Supreme; Being the Real and True Biography of Jesus Christ.* Parsons, Foley Railway Printing Company, 1904.

KOESTER, EDWARD A., *Development of the Oil and Gas Resources of Kansas in 1931 and 1932.* Topeka, Kansas State Printing Plant, 1934. (State Geological Survey of Kansas, *Mineral Resources,* Circular 3.)

LANGSDORF, EDGAR, *The Teachings of Jesus and the Treaty of Versailles.* [Lawrence] University of Kansas, 1934. (*Hattie Elizabeth Lewis Memorial,* No. 15.)

LEAVENWORTH, ORDINANCES, *Charter and Ordinances of the City of Leavenworth,* compiled and revised by William Stanley. Leavenworth, Kansas Territory, Frank F. Barclay's English, French and German Printing Establishment, 1859.

LEWIS, SINCLAIR, and LLOYD LEWIS, *Jayhawker; A Play in Three Acts.* Garden City, N. Y., Doubleday, Doran & Company, 1935.

[LOOMIS, N. H.], *Directory of Saline County, Kansas, 1882.* Lawrence, J. S. Boughton [1882].

MCCLEAVE, DAVID HAROLD, *History of the Indian Missions of the Presbyterian Church in Kansas*, being a Thesis Presented to the Graduate Faculty [of the Fort Hays Kansas State College] in Partial Fulfillment for the Degree of Master of Science. Typed.

MCDANIEL, CHARLES W., *Telephone Reminiscences.* Mimeographed.

MCKEEVER, WILLIAM ARCH, *Getting Ahead Financially.* [Topeka, School of Creative Psychology] c1925. (*His Creative Psychology* [Series], Book One.)

——— *Leaves of Healing.* Topeka, School of Psychology Press, 1927. (*His Creative Psychology Series*, Book Two.)

MADDEN, JOHN B., *Just Who Is Stabbing Prohibition in Kansas! "The Story Behind the Story" Now Told for the First Time . . . to Henry L. Carey.* N. p. [c1934.]

MARKLEY, WALT, *Builders of Topeka.* Topeka, Capper Printing Company, 1934.

MATHENA, MRS. J. B., *History of the Methodist Episcopal Church of Willis, Kansas, 1872-1933.* No impr.

MAYBERRY, JAMES W., *Physiology, Hygiene and Sanitation.* Dallas, Tex., Southern Publishing Company, 1913.

MAYBERRY, JAMES W., and LAWRENCE W. MAYBERRY, *Primary Physiology, Hygiene and Sanitation.* Topeka, Kansas State Printing Plant, 1927.

MILLER, A. Q., *Logical Flood Control Program for Kansas.* 1935. Broadside.

MORRISON, [THOMAS] F., *The Forgotten Hero.* Typed.

MORSE, ADELAIDE JANE, *History of First Baptist Church of Emporia, Kansas.* No impr.

NATIONAL HIGHWAY USERS CONFERENCE, *The Kansas Port of Entry Law; a Study of the Practical Effect of Its Actual Operation.* Washington, D. C., National Highway Users Conference, 1934. (*Highway Users Series*, No. R1.)

NORTH, F. A., compiler and publisher, *Fifth Annual Directory of the City of Wichita for 1889.* Wichita, *Eagle* Job Office and Bindery, 1889.

——— *Sixth Annual Directory of the City of Wichita for 1890.* Wichita, *Eagle* Job Office and Bindery, 1890.

OSWALD, A. LEWIS, *Troop One Marches On!* Hutchinson, Kan., Rotherwood Press [c1934].

OTTAWA, BOARD OF EDUCATION, *Annual Report for the Year Ending July 31, 1884.* Ottawa, Kessler & M'Allister, 1884.

——— *A Manual for the Government and Regulation of the Public Schools of Ottawa, Kansas . . .* Ottawa, N. Waring, 1882.

PEACOCK, ARTHUR SHELDON, *Trego County, Kansas; a Brief History.* [WaKeeney, 1914.]

Polk's Coffeyville (Kansas) City Directory, 1930. Kansas City, Mo., R. L. Polk & Company, c1930.

Polk's Emporia (Kansas) City Directory, 1932. Kansas City, Mo., R. L. Polk & Company, c1932.

Polk's Kansas City (Kansas) Directory, 1932. Kansas City, Mo., R. L. Polk & Company, c1932.

Polk's Leavenworth (Kansas) City Directory, 1930, Including Leavenworth County. Kansas City, Mo., R. L. Polk & Company, c1930.

Polk's Pittsburg (Kansas) City Directory, 1930. Kansas City, Mo., R. L. Polk & Company, c1930.

Polk's Topeka City Directory, 1935. Kansas City, Mo., R. L. Polk & Company, 1935.

Polk's Wichita (Kansas) City Directory, 1933, 1934. Kansas City, Mo., R. L. Polk & Company, c1933, 1934.

RAYNESFORD, H. C., *Kansas; an Address Given by H. C. Raynesford at the Kansas Day Banquet, Ellis, Kansas, January 29, 1930.* Typed.

—— *Smoky Hill Trail.* Typed.

REASONER, J. W., *What Is Man?* N. p., c1930.

RICE, MARTIN, *Rural Rhymes, and Folks and Tales of Older Times* . . . Kansas City, Mo., Ramsey, Millett & Hudson, 1882.

RITTER, C. S., *The Origin of Thought and the Law of Memory.* Iola, 1928.

ROSEBERRY & FROGUE, *About Neosho County, Kansas, and Erie, the County Seat.* N. p., 1912.

SATTERLEE, ELBERT E., *If Jesus Came.* No impr.

SCOTT, CHARLES F., *Why We Are Fighting and What We Are Fighting For; an Address Delivered at the Old Soldiers' Reunion at Cherryvale, Kansas, August 20, 1917.* Iola, Press of the Iola *Daily Register*, n. d.

Semi-Centennial Celebration; Judge Nelson Case, Oswego, Kansas, May 15, 1919. Commemorating the Fiftieth Anniversary of His Continuous Practice as a Lawyer at Oswego, Labette County, Kan. No impr.

SHANNON, FRED ALBERT, *Economic History of the People of the United States.* New York, Macmillan, 1934.

SHELDON, CHARLES MONROE, *In His Steps Today.* Elgin, Ill., David C. Cook, n. d.

SHERBON, DR. FLORENCE (BROWN), *The Child; His Origin, Development and Care.* New York, McGraw-Hill Book Company, 1934.

SHINN, J. F., *The Laws Governing the Orbital Distribution of the Solar System.* Fredonia, Wm. D. Christman, 1897.

SHOUSE, JOUETT, *The Constitution Still Stands. Speech Delivered Under the Auspices of the Young Men's Hebrew Association at St. Louis, Missouri, February 12, 1935.* Washington, D. C., 1935.

—— *Democracy or Bureaucracy. Speech Before the Philadelphia County League of Women Voters, February 4, 1935.* Washington, D. C. [1935].

—— *Progress vs. Change. Speech Before the Bond Club of New York, November 20, 1934.* Washington, D. C. [1934].

—— *Recovery, Relief and the Constitution. Speech Before the Beacon Society of Boston, December 8, 1934.* Washington, D. C. [1934].

—— *Why? The American Liberty League.* Washington, D. C., The American Liberty League [1934].

——— *You Are the Government.* Boston, Little, Brown & Company, 1935.
SIEGELE, HERMAN H., *Twigs of Thought.* Emporia, 1934.
SLEMMER, E. G., *Behold the Man!* N. p., Author, n. d.
——— *The Buying Machine as the "Heart" of Business.* Winfield, Townsend Club, n. d.
Social Register, Wichita, 1921. [Wichita, Wichita *Eagle* Press] n. d.
STEUNENBERG, GEORGE E., *Songs of a Soldier.* Kansas City, Mo., Franklin Hudson Press, 1914.
STILWELL, ARTHUR E., and J. E. ROBERTS, editors and publishers, *The Demonetization of the Mule.* Kansas City, Mo., n. d. (*Stilwell's Political Fables.*)
——— *The Mystic 16 to 1.* N. p., c1896. (*Stilwell's Political Fables.*)
STRATFORD, JESSIE PERRY, *Butler County's Eighty Years, 1855-1935.* N. p. [c1934.]
TOPEKA ENGINEERS CLUB and TOPEKA CHAMBER OF COMMERCE, "*A Twenty-five Year Plan" for Shawnee County and the City of Topeka. A Report to the Kansas State Planning Board.* Topeka, 1935. Mimeographed.
TOPEKA PROVIDENT ASSOCIATION, *Annual Report for the Year Ending December 31, 1934.* No impr.
——— [*The Story of the Topeka Provident Association.*] [Topeka, 1934.]
TUCKER, HENRY HARRISON, JR., *Standard Against Uncle Sam.* Kansas City, Kan. [c1907].
UNITED SPANISH WAR VETERANS, *Souvenir Book and U. S. W. V. History; Twenty-eighth Annual Encampment, May 12-13-14, 1935, Hutchinson, Kansas.* [Hutchinson, Southworth Printing Company, 1935.]
VESTAL, STANLEY, *New Sources of Indian History, 1850-1891; the Ghost Dance—the Prairie Sioux; a Miscellany.* Norman, Okla., University of Oklahoma Press, 1934.
WALKER, D. W., *Stevens County, Kansas.* Typed.
WALKER, WILLIS H., *Franco-American Commercial Relations, 1820-1850.* Hays, Author, n. d.
WARE, EUGENE FITCH, *Ancient Lawyers.* From the Proceedings of the Twenty-fourth Annual Meeting of the Missouri Bar Association, held at St. Joseph, Mo., September 28, 1906. Columbia, Mo., E. W. Stephens Publishing Company, 1907.
——— tr., *Roman Water Law.* Translated from the Pandects of Justinian. St. Paul, West Publishing Company, 1905.
WELLMAN, MANLY WADE, *Builders of Wichita.* Typed.
WELLMAN, PAUL I., *Death in the Desert; the Fifty Years' War for the Great Southwest.* New York, Macmillan Company, 1935.
WELLS, WILLIAM M., *The Desert's Hidden Wealth.* 3d and 4th eds. N. p., 1934.
WESTGATE, MRS. INEZ WHEELER, *Memorial Volume of Selected Poems.* No impr.

WHITTEMORE, MARGARET, and EDNA BECKER, *Trees;* Woodcuts and Linoleum Blocks by Margaret Whittemore, Verse by Edna Becker. Boston, Bruce Humphries, Inc. [c1935].

WICHITA INDEPENDENT BUSINESS MEN'S ASSOCIATION, *"Builders of Wichita";* a Historical Pageant in Commemoration of the 64th Anniversary of Wichita. N. p., 1935.

WILSON, LUCIA S., and EDWARD B. WILSON, *The Good Old Rule.* Boston, Meador Publishing Company, 1935.

THE WEST

ADAMS, WINONA, ed., *An Indian Girl's Story of a Trading Expedition to the Southwest About 1841.* Missoula, Mont., University of Montana, n. d. (State University of Montana, *Sources of Northwest History,* No. 11.)

ARESE, FRANCESCO, Conte, *A Trip to the Prairies in the Interior of North America (1837-1838).* Travel Notes . . . Now First Translated from the Original French by Andrew Evans. New York, Harbor Press, 1934.

BARROWS, JOHN R., *A Wisconsin Youth in Montana, 1880-1882.* Missoula, Mont., University of Montana, 1932. (State University of Montana, *Sources of Northwest History,* No. 1.)

BEALL, JOHN BRAMBETT, *In Barrack and Field; Poems and Sketches of Army Life.* Nashville, Tenn., Publishing House of M. E. Church, South, 1906.

BECKWOURTH, JAMES P., *The Life and Adventures of James P. Beckwourth,* edited by T. D. Bonner. New York, Alfred A. Knopf, 1931.

BIDDLE, MRS. ELLEN MCGOWAN, *Reminiscences of a Soldier's Wife.* Philadelphia, J. B. Lippincott Company, 1907.

BOOTH, MARGARET, ed., *Overland From Indiana to Oregon; the Dinwiddie Journal.* Missoula, Mont., University of Montana, n. d. (State University of Montana, *Sources of Northwest History,* No. 2.)

BROOKS, ELISHA, *A Pioneer Mother of California.* San Francisco, Harr Wagner Publishing Company, 1922.

CADY, JOHN HENRY, *Arizona's Yesterdays, Being the Narrative of John H. Cady, Pioneer.* N. p. [c1916.]

CARDINELL, CHARLES, *Adventures on the Plains.* San Francisco, California Historical Society, 1922.

CELIZ, FRAY FRANCISCO, *Diary of the Alarcon Expedition Into Texas, 1718-1719.* Los Angeles, Quivira Society, 1935. (Quivira Society *Publications,* vol. 5.)

CHITTENDEN, HIRAM MARTIN, *The American Fur Trade of the Far West.* New York, The Press of the Pioneers, Inc., 1935. 2 vols.

CLOUGH, WILSON O., ed., *Fort Russell and Fort Laramie Peace Commission in 1867.* Missoula, Mont., University of Montana, n. d. (State University of Montana, *Sources of Northwest History,* No. 14.)

DRIGGS, HOWARD R., *The Pony Express Goes Through; an American Saga Told by Its Heroes.* New York, Frederick A. Stokes Company, 1935.

DUNN, JACOB PIATT, *Massacres of the Mountains; a History of the Indian Wars of the Far West.* New York, Harper & Brothers, 1886.

FLINT, TIMOTHY, *Recollections of the Last Ten Years, Passed in Occasional Residences and Journeyings in the Valley of the Mississippi, From Pittsburg and the Missouri to the Gulf of Mexico, and From Florida to the Spanish Frontier; in a Series of Letters.* Boston, Cummings, Hilliard & Company, 1826.

FULLER, HENRY C., *Adventures of Bill Longley* . . . Nacogdoches, Tex., n. d.

GALE, GEORGE, *Upper Mississippi; or, Historical Sketches of the Mound Builders, the Indian Tribes, and the Progress of Civilization in the Northwest.* Chicago, Clarke and Company, 1867.

GARCÉS, FRANCISCO, *On the Trail of a Spanish Pioneer; the Diary and Itinerary of Francisco Garcés in His Travels Through Sonora, Arizona and California, 1775-1776.* New York, Harper, 1900. 2 vols.

GIBSON, GEORGE RUTLEDGE, *Journal of a Soldier Under Kearny and Doniphan, 1846-1847.* Glendale, Cal., Arthur H. Clark Company, 1935. (*Southwest Historical Series*, vol. 3.)

GOLDER, FRANK ALFRED, *The March of the Mormon Battalion From Council Bluffs to California; Taken From the Journal of Henry Standage;* by Frank Alfred Golder, in collaboration with Thomas A. Bailey and J. Lyman Smith. New York, Century Company [c1928].

HICKMAN, RICHARD OWEN, *An Overland Journey to California in 1852.* Missoula, University of Montana, n. d. (State University of Montana, *Sources of Northwest History*, No. 6.)

HOLDEN, WILLIAM CURRY, *Alkali Trails; or, Social and Economic Movements of the Texas Frontier, 1846-1900* . . . Dallas, Southwest Press [c1930].

———— *Rollie Burns; or, An Account of the Ranching Industry on the South Plains* . . . Dallas, Tex., Southwest Press [c1932].

———— *The Spur Ranch; a Study of the Inclosed Ranch Phase of the Cattle Industry in Texas* . . . Boston, Christopher Publishing House [c1934].

HOUSMAN, ROBERT L., *The Beginnings of Journalism in Frontier Montana.* Missoula, Mont., University of Montana, n. d. (State University of Montana, *Sources of Northwest History*, No. 22.)

HULBERT, ARCHER BUTLER, ed., *The Call of the Columbia; Iron Men and Saints Take the Oregon Trail* . . . [Colorado Springs] The Stewart Commission of Colorado College; [Denver] Denver Public Library [1934]. (*Overland to the Pacific,* vol. 4.)

———— *1830-1930, the Oregon Trail Centennial: The Documentary Background of the Days of the First Wagon Train on the Road to Oregon.* Missoula, University of Montana, n. d. (State University of Montana, *Sources of Northwest History*, No. 9.)

————, and Dorothy Printup Hulbert, eds., *The Oregon Crusade; Across Land and Sea to Oregon.* [Colorado Springs] The Stewart Commission of Colorado College; [Denver] Denver Public Library [1933]. (*Overland to the Pacific,* vol. 5.)

KIRKPATRICK, JAMES, *A Reminiscence of John Bozeman.* Missoula, Mont., University of Montana, n. d. (State University of Montana, *Sources of Northwest History*, No. 8.)

Koch, Peter, *Journal of, 1869-1870.* Missoula, University of Montana, n. d. (State University of Montana, *Sources of Northwest History,* No. 5.)

Larocque, Francois Antoine, *Journal of . . . From the Assiniboine River to the Yellowstone, 1805.* Missoula, University of Montana, n. d. (State University of Montana, *Sources of Northwest History,* No. 20.)

Lee, Daniel, and J. H. Frost, *Ten Years in Oregon . . .* New York, Authors, 1844.

Maerdian, Otto, *Pioneer Ranching in Central Montana From the Letters of Otto Maerdian, Written in 1882-1883.* Missoula, Mont., University of Montana, n. d. (State University of Montana, *Sources of Northwest History,* No. 10.)

Milner, Joe E., and Earl R. Forrest, *California Joe, Noted Scout and Indian Fighter, With an Authentic Account of Custer's Last Fight.* Caldwell, Idaho, Caxton Printers, 1935.

Mokler, Alfred James, *History of Natrona County, Wyoming, 1888-1922.* Chicago, R. R. Donnelley & Sons Company, 1923.

Mullan, John, *Journal From Fort Dalles O. T. to Fort Wallah Wallah W. T., July, 1858.* Missoula, Mont., University of Montana, n. d. (State University of Montana, *Sources of Northwest History,* No. 18.)

Murray, Mrs. Genevieve, *Marias Pass, Its Part in the History and Development of the Northwest.* Missoula, Mont., University of Montana, n. d. (State University of Montana, *Sources of Northwest History,* No. 12.)

Otero, Miguel Antonio, *My Life on the Frontier, 1864-1882; Incidents and Characters of the Period When Kansas, Colorado, and New Mexico Were Passing Through the Last of Their Wild and Romantic Years.* New York, The Press of the Pioneers, Inc., 1935.

Pacific Coast Annual Mining Review and Stock Ledger . . . and A Series of Finance Articles by Colonel Henry S. Fitch. San Francisco, Francis & Valentine, 1878.

Phillips, Paul C., ed., *"The Battle of the Big Hole," an Episode in the Nez Perce War.* Missoula, University of Montana, n. d. (State University of Montana, *Sources of Northwest History,* No. 8.)

———, and W. S. Lewis, eds., *The Oregon Missions as Shown in the Walker Letters, 1839-1851.* Missoula, Mont., University of Montana, n. d. (State University of Montana, *Sources of Northwest History,* No. 13.)

Remington, Frederic, *Remington's Frontier Sketches.* Chicago, Werner Company [c1898].

Sabin, Edwin Legrand, *Kit Carson Days, 1809-1868 . . .* Revised Edition with New Matter. New York, The Press of the Pioneers, Inc., 1935. 2 vols.

Shaw, David Augustus, *Eldorado, or California as Seen by a Pioneer, 1850-1900.* Los Angeles, B. R. Baumgardt, 1900.

Shea, John Gilmary, *Early Voyages Up and Down the Mississippi by Cavelier, St. Cosme, Le Sueur, Gravier, and Guignas.* Albany, Joel Munsell, 1861.

Smith, Jedediah Strong, *The Travels of Jedediah Smith; a Documentary Outline Including the Journal of the Great American Pathfinder,* by Maurice S. Sullivan. Santa Ana, Cal., Fine Arts Press, 1934.

STEPHENS, L. DOW, *Life Sketches of a Jayhawker of '49.* N. p., 1916.

TAYLOR, LANDON, *The Battle Field Reviewed* . . . Chicago, Published for the Author, 1881.

THOMAS, ALFRED BARNABY, tr. and ed., *After Coronado; Spanish Exploration Northeast of New Mexico, 1696-1727.* Documents From the Archives of Spain, Mexico and New Mexico. Norman, University of Oklahoma Press, 1935.

UPHAM, HIRAM D., *Upham Letters From the Upper Missouri, 1865.* Missoula, Mont., University of Montana, n. d. (State University of Montana, *Sources of Northwest History,* No. 19.)

WALKER, MARY RICHARDSON, *The Diary of Mary Richardson Walker, June 10 - December 21, 1838.* Missoula, Mont., University of Montana, n. d. (State University of Montana, *Sources of Northwest History,* No. 15.)

Western Tourist and Emigrant's Guide Through the States of Ohio, Michigan, Indiana, Illinois, Missouri, Iowa, and Wisconsin, and the Territories of Minnesota, Missouri, and Nebraska . . . New York, J. H. Colton and Company, 1855.

WHITAKER, ARTHUR PRESTON, *The Mississippi Question, 1795-1803; a Study in Trade, Politics, and Diplomacy* . . . New York, Appleton-Century Company [c1934].

——— *The Spanish-American Frontier, 1783-1795; the Westward Movement and the Spanish Retreat in the Mississippi Valley* . . . Boston, Houghton Mifflin Company, 1927.

WILLIAMS, CHAUNCEY PRATT, *Lone Elk, The Life Story of Bill Williams, Trapper and Guide of the Far West.* Denver, John Van Male, 1935. (*The Old West Series,* No. 6.)

WILLIAMS, HENRY T., ed., *The Pacific Tourist. Williams' Illustrated Trans-Continental Guide of Travel, From the Atlantic to the Pacific Ocean* . . . New York, Author, 1878.

WILLISON, GEORGE FINDLAY, *Here They Dug the Gold.* New York, Brentano's [c1931].

GENEALOGY AND LOCAL HISTORY

ACKERMAN, ARTHUR WILMOT, *Reverend John White of Dorchester, England, and His Participation in Founding the Massachusetts Bay Colony.* Boston, 1929. (*Publications of the Governor and Company of Massachusetts Bay in New England,* No. 1.)

AMERICAN ANTIQUARIAN SOCIETY, *Proceedings at the Semiannual Meeting Held in Boston, April 18, 1934.* Worcester, Mass., Society, 1935.

ANDREWS, CHARLES MCLEAN, *The Beginnings of Connecticut, 1632-1662.* [New Haven] Published for the Tercentenary Commission of the State of Connecticut by the Yale University Press, 1934.

ATKINSON, JOSEPH, *History of Newark, New Jersey; Being a Narrative of its Rise and Progress, From the Settlement in May, 1666, by Emigrants From Connecticut, to the Present Time* . . . Newark, William B. Guild, 1878.

Augusta, Me., *Vital Records of Augusta, Maine, to the Year 1892* . . . Published Under Authority of the Maine Historical Society. [Auburn, Me., Press of Merrill & Webber Company] 1933-1934. 2 vols.

Bagley Family. Asbury Park, N. J., Martin & Allardyce, 1916.

BARBER, LUCIUS ISRAEL, *Record and Documentary History of Simsbury [Connecticut].* Simsbury, Abigail Phelps Chapter, Daughters of the American Revolution, 1931.

BARRETT, WILLIAM, *Genealogy of Some of the Descendants of Thomas Barrett, Sen., of Braintree, Mass., 1635.* Saint Paul, D. Ramaley & Son, 1888.

BELL, EDMUND HAYES, and MARY HALL COLWELL, comps. and eds., *James Patterson of Conestoga Manor and His Descendants.* Lancaster, Pa., Wickersham Printing Company, 1925.

BURNS, LEE, *Early Architects and Builders of Indiana.* Indianapolis, Indiana Historical Society, 1935.

Caldwell Chronicle. Vol. 1, Nos. 1-5; October 19, 1899 - March, 1900. Providence, R. I., A. Caldwell, 1899-1900.

CHAFFIN, WILLIAM LADD, *History of Robert Chaffin and His Descendants and of the Other Chaffins in America.* New York, F. H. Hitchcock [1913].

Colonial and Revolutionary Families of Pennsylvania . . . Vols. I-III. New York, Lewis, 1911.

COLUMBIA HISTORICAL SOCIETY, *Records.* Vols. 35-36. Washington, D. C., Published by the Society, 1935.

CONNECTICUT HISTORICAL SOCIETY, *Annual Report; Reports and Papers Presented at the Annual Meeting, May 21, 1935. Also a List of Officers and Members and of Donations for the Year.* Hartford, Published by the Society, 1935.

COOPER, W. ROSS, *Notes on the Jackson Family From Various Sources.* Typed [1934].

CORNELL, JOHN, *Genealogy of the Cornell Family; Being an Account of the Descendants of Thomas Cornell of Portsmouth, R. I.* New York, T. A. Wright, 1902.

CRAFTS, JAMES MONROE, and WILLIAM FRANCIS CRAFTS, *The Crafts Family; a Genealogical and Biographical History of the Descendants of Griffin and Alice Craft, of Roxbury, Mass., 1630-1890.* Northampton, Mass., Gazette Printing Company, 1893.

CURTISS, FREDERICK HAINES, *A Genealogy of the Curtiss Family; Being a Record of the Descendants of Widow Elizabeth Curtiss Who Settled in Stratford, Conn., 1639-'40.* Boston, Rockwell and Churchill Press, 1903.

DAUGHTERS OF THE AMERICAN REVOLUTION, *Lineage Books,* vols. 139-144. Washington, D. C. [Press of Judd and Detweiler, Inc.] 1934-1935.

DODD, BETHUEL LEWIS, and JOHN R. BURNET, *Genealogies of the Male Descendants of Daniel Dod, of Branford, Conn., a Native of England, 1646-1863.* Newark, N. J., *Daily Advertiser* Office, 1864.

DUDLEY, DEAN, *The History of the Dudley Family, Containing the Genealogy of Each Branch in Various Countries* . . . Montrose, Mass., Author, 1894. 3 vols.

DUNHAM, SAMUEL, *An Historical Discourse Delivered at West Brookfield, Mass., on Occasion of the One Hundred and Fiftieth Anniversary of the First Church in Brookfield, October 16, 1867.* Springfield, Mass., Samuel Bowles & Company, 1867.

Duxbury, Mass., *Copy of the Old Records of the Town of Duxbury, Mass., From 1642 to 1770.* Plymouth, Avery & Doten, 1893.

ELY, EZRA E., *A Biographical History of Waterloo Township and Other Townships of the County* . . . Berlin, Canada, 1895. 2 vols.

Encyclopedia of Pennsylvania Biography, vol. 21. New York, Lewis Historical Publishing Company, 1934.

EVANS, NELSON WILEY, *History of Scioto County, Ohio, Together With a Pioneer Record of Southern Ohio* . . . Portsmouth, O., N. W. Evans, 1903.

FERNALD, CHARLES AUGUSTUS, *Genealogy of the Ancient Fernald Family.* 1899. Chart.

HARPER, MRS. LILLIE DU PUY (VAN CULIN), *Colonial Men and Times, Containing the Journal of Col. Daniel Trabue* . . . *the Huguenots, Genealogy, With Brief Sketches of the Allied Families.* Philadelphia, Innes & Sons, 1916.

HAYES, LYMAN SIMPSON, *History of the Town of Rockingham, Vermont, Including the Villages of Bellows Falls, Saxtons River, Rockingham, Cambridgeport and Bartonsville* . . . *With Family Genealogies.* Bellows Falls, Published by the Town, 1907.

HERRICK, WILLIAM DODGE, *History of the Town of Gardner, Worcester County, Mass.* . . Gardner, Published by the Committee, 1878.

History of Cumberland and Adams Counties, Pennsylvania . . . Chicago, Warner, Beers & Company, 1886.

History of Litchfield County, Connecticut, With Illustrations and Biographical Sketches of its Prominent Men and Pioneers. Philadelphia, J. W. Lewis & Company, 1881.

History of Warren County, Ohio . . . Chicago, W. H. Beers & Company, 1882.

HONEYMAN, ABRAHAM VAN DOREN, *Joannes Nevius* . . . *and His Descendants, A. D. 1627-1900.* Plainfield, N. J., Honeyman & Company, 1900.

HOPKINS, TIMOTHY, *The Kelloggs in the Old World and the New.* San Francisco, Sunset Press and Photo Engraving Company, 1903. 3 vols.

HOTTEN, JOHN CAMDEN, ed., *The Original Lists of Persons of Quality* . . . *and Others Who Went From Great Britain to the American Plantations, 1600-1700* . . . London, John Camden Hotten, 1874. Reprinted: Empire State Book Company, New York, n. d.

HUGUENOT SOCIETY OF SOUTH CAROLINA, *Transactions,* No. 39. Charleston, Published by Order of the Society, 1934.

IDAHO STATE HISTORICAL SOCIETY, *Fourteenth Biennial Report of the Board of Trustees.* Boise, 1934.

ILLINOIS STATE HISTORICAL LIBRARY, *The French Foundations, 1680-1693. French Series,* vol. 1. (*Collections* of the Illinois State Historical Library, vol. 23.)

ILLINOIS STATE HISTORICAL SOCIETY, *Transactions for the Year 1934: Proceedings of the Annual Meeting and Papers Presented at That Time.* Printed by Authority of the State of Illinois. (Illinois State Historical Library Publication, No. 41.)

INDIANA (TERRITORY) LAWS, STATUTES, ETC., *The Laws of Indiana Territory, 1809-1816.* Indianapolis, Indiana Historical Bureau, 1934.

KAY COUNTY GAS COMPANY, KAY COUNTY, OKLAHOMA. Ponca City, Kay County Gas Company [c1919].

KELLOGG, LUCY CUTLER, *History of the Town of Bernardston, Franklin County, Massachusetts, 1736-1900, With Genealogies.* Greenfield, Mass., E. A. Hall & Company, 1902.

KILBOURNE, PAYNE KENYON, *The History and Antiquities of the Name and Family of Kilbourn.* New Haven, Durrie & Peck, 1856.

KIRKLAND, THOMAS J., and ROBERT M. KENNEDY, *Historic Camden [S. C.] Part Two, Nineteenth Century.* Columbia, S. C., State Company, 1926.

LAMAR, MRS. CLARINDA (PENDLETON), *A History of the National Society of the Colonial Dames of America From 1891 to 1933.* [Atlanta, Walter W. Brown Publishing Company, 1934.]

LAWRENCE, MRS. GLADYS (WILKINSON), *Rees History.* N. p. [c1932].

―――― *Wilkinson and Irvine.* No impr.

LEA, ALBERT MILLER, *Notes on the Wisconsin Territory, With a Map.* Philadelphia, H. S. Tanner, 1836. [Reprint by State Historical Society of Iowa, 1935.]

LITTLE, MRS. CYNTHIA MARIA (JONES) ATWOOD, *History of the Clan MacFarlane (Macfarlane) MacFarlan, MacFarland, MacFarlin.* Tottenville, N. Y., Author, 1893.

MCMURTRIE, DOUGLAS CRAWFORD, *Early Printing in Dayton, Ohio.* Dayton, Printing House Craftsmen's Club of Dayton and Vicinity, 1935.

MARYLAND, COURT OF CHANCERY, *Proceedings of 1669-1679.* Baltimore, Maryland Historical Society, 1934.

MASSACHUSETTS, ADJUTANT GENERAL, *Massachusetts Soldiers, Sailors, and Marines in the Civil War,* vol. 7. Norwood, Mass., Norwood Press, 1933.

MATHEWS, ALFRED, and AUSTIN N. HUNGERFORD, *History of the Counties of Lehigh and Carbon in the Commonwealth of Pennsylvania.* Philadelphia, Everts & Richards, 1884.

MATSON, NEHEMIAH, *Reminiscences of Bureau County [Illinois].* Princeton, Ill., *Republican* Book and Job Office, 1872.

MELLON, MRS. RACHEL HUGHEY (LARIMER), *The Larimer, McMasters and Allied Families.* Philadelphia, Printed for Private Circulation by J. B. Lippincott Company, 1903.

MORRELL, FRANCIS VANDERVOORT, *Ancestry of Daniel Morrell of Hartford With His Descendants and Some Contemporary Families.* [Hartford, Conn.] J. W. Morrell, 1916.

MORRISON, LEONARD ALLISON, *History of the Alison or Allison Family in Europe and America, A. D. 1135 to 1893; Giving an Account of the Family in Scot-*

land, England, Ireland, Australia, Canada and the United States. Boston, Damrell & Upham, 1893.

The National Society Magna Charta Dames, Instituted March 1, 1909. June 1, 1935. No impr.

NATIONAL SOCIETY DAUGHTERS OF FOUNDERS AND PATRIOTS OF AMERICA, *Lineage Book*, vols. 22-24. [West Somerville, Mass., Somerville Printing Company, c1934-1935.]

—— Ohio Chapter, *Ohio Chapter of the National Society Daughters of Founders and Patriots of America.* N. p., 1935.

NEILL, EDWARD DUFFIELD, *The Fairfaxes of England and America in the Seventeenth and Eighteenth Centuries* . . . Albany, N. Y., J. Munsell, 1868.

NEW ENGLAND SOCIETY IN THE CITY OF NEW YORK, *One Hundred and Twenty-Ninth Annual Report for the Year 1934.* No impr.

NEW HAMPSHIRE (PROVINCE), *Probate Records of the Province of New Hampshire*, vol. 3, *1741-1749;* vol. 4, *1750-1753. (State Papers Series*, vols. 33-34.)

NEW JERSEY, SECRETARY OF STATE, *Index of Wills, Inventories, etc., in the Office of the Secretary of State Prior to 1901.* N. p. 1912-1913. 3 vols.

NEW MEXICO HISTORICAL SOCIETY, *Old Santa Fé and Vicinity; Points of Interest and Convenient Trips.* [Santa Fé] El Palacio Press, 1930.

NEWFANE, VT., *Centennial Proceedings and Other Historical Facts and Incidents Relating to Newfane, the County Seat of Windham County, Vermont.* Brattleboro, D. Leonard, 1877.

NEWTON, CLAIR ALONZO HEMENWAY, *Ralph Hemmenway of Roxbury, Mass., 1634, and His Descendants.* Naperville, Ill., 1932.

NORTH CAROLINA HISTORICAL COMMISSION, *Fifteenth Biennial Report, July 1, 1932, to June 30, 1934.* Raleigh, North Carolina Historical Commission, 1934.

NUTE, GRACE LEE, and GERTRUDE W. ACKERMAN, *Guide to the Personal Papers in the Manuscript Collections of the Minnesota Historical Society.* Saint Paul, Minnesota Historical Society, 1935.

ORCUTT, SAMUEL, *The History of the Old Town of Derby, Connecticut, 1642-1880, With Biographies and Genealogies* . . . Springfield, Mass., Springfield Printing Company, 1880.

Organization and the Execution of the Selective Service Act in the State of West Virginia. Charleston, W. Va., *Tribune* Printing Company, n. d.

Panhandle-Plains Historical Review, vols. 7-8. Canyon, Tex., Panhandle-Plains Historical Society, 1934-1935.

PECK, EPAPHRODITUS, *The Loyalists of Connecticut.* [New Haven] Published for the Tercentenary Commission of the State of Connecticut by the Yale University Press, 1934.

PIERCE, FREDERICK CLIFTON, *Fiske and Fisk Family; Being the Record of the Descendants of Symond Fiske* . . . *Suffolk County, England* . . . Chicago, Author, 1896.

Polk's Council Bluffs (Pottawatamie County, Ia.) City Directory, 1933. Detroit, R. L. Polk & Company, c1933.

Recent Additions to the Library

Polk's Des Moines (Iowa) City Directory, 1933. Des Moines, R. L. Polk & Company, c1932.

Polk's Jefferson City (Missouri) Directory, 1931. St. Louis, R. L. Polk & Company, c1931.

Polk's Kansas City (Missouri) Directory, 1933. Kansas City, Mo., Gate City Directory Company, c1933.

Polk's Lincoln (Nebraska) City Directory, 1932. Kansas City, Mo., R. L. Polk & Company, c1932.

Polk's Omaha (Douglas County, Neb.) City Directory, 1933. Detroit, R. L. Polk & Company, c1933.

Polk's Sioux City (Iowa) Directory, 1933. Detroit, R. L. Polk & Company, c1932.

Polk's Springfield (Greene County, Mo.) City Directory, 1933. Kansas City, Mo., R. L. Polk & Company, c1933.

PORTER, W. ARTHUR, comp., *A History of Union Presbyterian Church, Walnut Township, Montgomery County, Indiana, 1834-1934.* No impr.

Portrait and Biographical Album of Knox County, Illinois . . . Chicago, Biographical Publishing Company, 1886.

Portrait and Biographical Album of Mahaska County, Iowa . . . Chicago, Chapman Brothers, 1887.

PRICE, BENJAMIN LUTHER, *John Price the Emigrant, Jamestown Colony, 1620, With Some of His Descendants.* N. p. [preface, 1910].

PUCKETT, JAMES LOUIS, and ELLEN PUCKETT, *History of Oklahoma and Indian Territory and Homeseekers' Guide.* Vinita, Okla., *Chieftain* Publishing Company, 1906.

ROE, JOSEPH WICKHAM, *Connecticut Inventors.* [New Haven] Published for the Tercentenary Commission of the State of Connecticut by the Yale University Press, 1934.

SEYMOUR, ORIGEN STORRS, *The Beginnings of the Episcopal Church in Connecticut.* [New Haven] Published for the Tercentenary Commission of the State of Connecticut by the Yale University Press, 1934.

SHOWERMAN, GRANT, *The Indian Stream Republic and Luther Parker.* Concord, N. H., New Hampshire Historical Society, 1915. (*Collections* of the New Hampshire Historical Society, vol. 11.)

SMITHTOWN, N. Y., *Records of the Town of Smithtown, Long Island, N. Y., With Other Ancient Documents of Historic Value.* Published by Authority of the Town, 1898.

SOCIETY OF THE CINCINNATI, *Rules of the State Societies for Admission to Membership.* Washington, D. C., Society, 1934.

SOCIETY OF THE WAR OF 1812 in the District of Columbia [*Year Book, 1934*]. Washington, D. C., 1934.

Some Account of the Park Family, and Especially of the Rev. Joseph Park, M. A., 1705-1777, and Benjamin Parke, LL. D., 1801-1882. Westerly, R. I., Westerly Historical Society, 1917.

Some Tennessee Heroes of the Revolution, Compiled From Pension Statements. Pamphlet No. 2. Chattanooga, *Lookout* Publishing Company, n. d.

SONS OF THE REVOLUTION in the State of New York. *Reports and Proceedings, July 1, 1933, to June 30, 1934.* No impr.

SPOONER, THOMAS, *Records of William Spooner, of Plymouth, Mass., and His Descendants.* Vol. 1. Cincinnati, 1883.

SPRINGER, MOSES C., *A Genealogical Table and History of the Springer Family in Europe and North America.* Vol. 1. Amesbury, Mass., Guild & Cameron [1917].

SWISHER, JACOB ARMSTRONG, *The Legislation of the Forty-fifth General Assembly of Iowa, Extra Session.* Iowa City, State Historical Society of Iowa, 1934. (*Iowa Monograph Series,* No. 7.)

SWISSHELM, JANE GREY, *Crusader and Feminist; Letters of Jane Grey Swisshelm, 1858-1865.* St. Paul, Minnesota Historical Society, 1934.

TAYLOR, OLIVER, *Historic Sullivan; A History of Sullivan County, Tennessee, With Brief Biographies of the Makers of History.* Bristol, Tenn., King Printing Company, 1909.

UNITED DAUGHTERS OF THE CONFEDERACY, Georgia division, Willie Hunt Smith Chapter, Barnesville, *History of Lamar County* [Georgia]. Barnesville, Barnesville *News-Gazette,* 1932.

UPHAM, CHARLES WENTWORTH, *Salem Witchcraft; With an Account of Salem Village, and a History of Opinions on Witchcraft and Kindred Subjects.* Boston, Wiggin and Lunt, 1867. 2 vols.

VAN RENSSELAER, MARIA, *Correspondence of* . . . *1669-1689.* Albany, University of the State of New York, 1935.

VERMONT, ADJUTANT GENERAL, *Roster of Soldiers in the War of 1812-'14.* [St. Albans, Vt., The *Messenger* Press, 1933.]

—— *Roster of Vermont Men and Women in the Military and Naval Service of the United States and Allies in the World War, 1917-1919.* Montpelier, 1927.

VINELAND HISTORICAL AND ANTIQUARIAN SOCIETY, *Annual Report for the Year Ending October 2, 1934.* Vineland, N. J. [The Society] 1934.

VINTON, JOHN ADAMS, *The Symmes Memorial. A Biographical Sketch of Rev. Zechariah Symmes, Minister of Charlestown, 1634-1671, With a Genealogy and Brief Memoirs of Some of His Descendants* . . . Boston, Printed for the Author by David Clapp & Son, 1873.

WEBSTER, NOAH, *Webster Genealogy* . . . *New Haven, 1836. With Notes and Corrections by His Great-Grandson, Paul Leicester Ford.* Brooklyn, N. Y., Privately Printed, 1876.

WHITE, HENRY, *The Early History of New England, Illustrated by Numerous Interesting Incidents.* Concord, N. H., I. S. Boyd, 1842.

WHITEBREAD, S. A., comp. and pub., *Genealogy of the Whitebread Family in America.* Ottawa, Kan., Newman Waring, The Printer, 1902.

WHITSITT, WILLIAM HETH, *Genealogy of Jefferson Davis and of Samuel Davies.* New York, Neale Publishing Company, 1910.

WILEY, SAMUEL T., and W. SCOTT GARNER, eds., *Biographical and Portrait Cyclopedia of Blair County, Pennsylvania.* Philadelphia, Gresham Publishing Company, 1892.

WOMEN'S CANADIAN HISTORICAL SOCIETY OF OTTAWA. *Annual Report, 1933-1934.* Mimeographed.

[WOODIN, WALLACE I.], *Descendants of Amos Woodin.* Mimeographed [1934].

WOOLSEY, C. M., *History of the Town of Marlborough, Ulster County, New York, From Its Earliest Discovery.* Albany, J. B. Lyon Company, 1908.

WORCESTER HISTORICAL SOCIETY, *Publications, New Series,* vol. 1, No. 8. Worcester, Mass., Worcester Historical Society, 1935.

WRIGHT, FREDERICK H., [*Brownlee Family*] *Brownlees in Scotland and Brownlees in America.* Typed.

WYOMING COMMEMORATIVE ASSOCIATION, *Proceedings, 1934.* No impr.

GENERAL

ADAMS, JAMES TRUSLOW, *America's Tragedy.* New York, Charles Scribner's Sons, 1934.

ALLSOPP, FREDERICK WILLIAM, *Albert Pike; a Biography.* Little Rock, Ark., Parke-Harper Company, 1928.

BAILEY, WILLIAM FRANCIS, *The Story of the First Trans-Continental Railroad.* [Pittsburgh, Pa., 1906.]

BARAGA, FRIEDRICH, bp., *Katolik anamie-Masinaigan. A Catholic Prayerbook and Catechism in the Otchipwe-Indian Language . . . With an Appendix of the Mass and Vespers in Latin; and Prayers in the Ottawa-Indian Language, by Rev. John B. Weikamp* . . . New York, Benziger Brothers, n. d.

BATTERSON, JAMES GOODWIN, *Gold and Silver as Currency in the Light of Experience, Historical, Economical, and Practical: a Series of Papers Written for the Travelers Record* . . . Hartford, Conn., Press of Case, Lockwood & Brainard, 1896.

BEAGLEHOLE, ERNEST, and PEARL BEAGLEHOLE, *Hopi of the Second Mesa.* Menasha, Wis., American Anthropological Association, 1935. (*Memoirs,* No. 44.)

BEARD, CHARLES AUSTIN, and MRS. MARY (RITTER) BEARD, *American Citizenship.* New York, Macmillan Company, 1915.

BEARD, CHARLES AUSTIN, and GEORGE HOWARD EDWARD SMITH, *The Open Door at Home, a Trial Philosophy of National Interest.* New York, The Macmillan Company, 1935.

BEECHER, HENRY WARD, *Lectures to Young Men, on Various Important Subjects.* New ed. With Additional Lectures. New York, Derby & Jackson, 1860.

BERRY, CHESTER D., *Loss of the Sultana and Reminiscences of Survivors.* Lansing, Mich., Darius D. Thorp, 1892.

CARNEGIE ENDOWMENT FOR INTERNATIONAL PEACE, *Yearbook,* 1934-1935. Washington, Endowment, 1934-1935. 2 vols.

—— Division of Intercourse and Education, *International Conciliation, Documents for the Year 1934.* Worcester, Mass., Carnegie Endowment for International Peace, n. d.

CARTER, CLARENCE EDWIN, ed., *The Territorial Papers of the United States.* Vols. 1-3. Washington, D. C., Government Printing Office, 1934.

CAUGHEY, JOHN WALTON, *Bernardo De Galvez in Louisiana, 1776-1783.* Berkeley, University of California Press, 1934. (*Publications of the University of California at Los Angeles in Social Sciences,* vol. 4.)

CHAMPION, RICHARD, *The American Correspondence of a Bristol Merchant, 1766-1776.* Berkeley, University of California Press, 1934. (*University of California Publications in History,* vol. 22, No. 1.)

COBERN, CAMDEN MCCORMACK, *The New Archaeological Discoveries and Their Bearing Upon the New Testament and Upon the Life and Times of the Primitive Church.* New York, Funk & Wagnalls, 1917.

CONFERENCE OF TEACHERS OF INTERNATIONAL LAW AND RELATED SUBJECTS, *Proceedings of the Fifth Conference Held at Washington, D. C., April 26-27, 1933.* Washington, D. C., Carnegie Endowment for International Peace, 1933.

DEBO, ANGIE, *The Rise and Fall of the Choctaw Republic.* Norman, Okla., University of Oklahoma Press, 1934.

Dictionary of American Biography, vols. 15-16. New York, Charles Scribner's Sons, 1935.

DODGE, GRENVILLE MELLEN, *Address to Army Associations and Miscellaneous Papers Relating to Civil and Spanish Wars.* New York, Unz & Company, 1904.

DYER, BRAINERD, *The Public Career of William M. Evarts.* Berkeley, University of California Press, 1933. (*Publications of the University of California at Los Angeles in Social Sciences,* vol. 2.)

Encyclopedia of American Biography, New Series, vols. 2-3. New York, American Historical Society, Inc., 1934-1935.

FERGUSON, HENRY LEE, *Archaeological Exploration of Fishers Island, New York.* New York, Museum of the American Indian, Heye Foundation, 1935. (*Indian Notes and Monographs,* vol. 11, No. 1.)

FIELD MUSEUM OF NATURAL HISTORY, *Annual Report of the Director to the Board of Trustees for the Year 1934.* Chicago, 1935.

FISKE, JOHN, *The Critical Period of American History, 1783-1789.* Boston, Houghton Mifflin and Company, 1898.

——— *The Dutch and Quaker Colonies in America.* Boston, Houghton Mifflin and Company, 1903. 2 vols.

FOREMAN, GRANT, *The Five Civilized Tribes.* Norman, University of Oklahoma Press, 1934.

FREEMAN, DOUGLAS SOUTHALL, *R. E. Lee; a Biography.* New York, Charles Scribner's Sons, 1934. 4 vols.

GESSNER, ROBERT, *Massacre; a Survey of Today's American Indian.* New York, Jonathan Cape and Harrison Smith [c1931].

GRAHAM, MALBONE WATSON, *The League of Nations; the Recognition of States.* Berkeley, University of California Press, 1933. (*Publications of the University of California at Los Angeles in Social Sciences,* vol. 3, pp. 1-76.)

GRAY, CARL RAYMOND, *The Significance of the Pacific Railroads.* Princeton University, The Cyrus Fogg Brockett Lectureship, April 9, 1935.

HAINES, CHARLES GROVE, *The American Doctrine of Judicial Supremacy.* Berkeley, University of California Press, 1932. (*Publications of the University of California at Los Angeles,* vol. 1.)

HALE, WILLIAM JAY, *The Farm Chemurgic; Farmward the Star of Destiny Lights Our Way* . . . Boston, Stratford Company [c1934].

HARLOW, ALVIN FAY, *Old Waybills; the Romance of the Express Companies.* New York, Appleton-Century Company, 1934.

HENDERSON, HAROLD GOULD, *The Bamboo Broom; an Introduction to Japanese Haiku.* Boston, Houghton Mifflin Company, 1934.

HOOVER, HERBERT, *Challenge to Liberty.* New York, Charles Scribner's Sons, 1934.

HOWARD, JOHN TASKER, *Stephen Foster, America's Troubadour.* . . . New York, Thomas Y. Crowell [c1934].

HUSSEY, ROLAND DENNIS, *The Caracas Company, 1728-1784; a Study in the History of Spanish Monopolistic Trade.* Cambridge, Harvard University Press, 1934.

HYDE, GEORGE E., *The Pawnee Indians, Part Two. 1680-1770.* Denver, John Van Male, 1934. (*The Old West Series,* No. 5.)

INDIAN RIGHTS ASSOCIATION, *Fifty-first and Fifty-second Annual Reports of the Board of Directors for the Two Years Ending December 15, 1934.* Philadelphia, 1935.

JOHNSON, GERALD WHITE, *The Secession of the Southern States.* New York, G. P. Putnam's Sons, 1933.

A Joint Catalogue of the Periodicals and Serials in the Libraries of the City of Toronto. [4th ed.] Toronto, Printed and Published by the King's Printer, 1934.

JONES, ALONZO TREVIER, *Civil Government and Religion, or, Christianity and the American Constitution.* Chicago, American Sentinel, 1889.

JONES, DANIEL WEBSTER, *Forty Years Among the Indians.* . . . Salt Lake City, Juvenile Instructor Office, 1890.

JONES, ELECTA FIDELIA, *Stockbridge, Past and Present; or, Records of an Old Mission Station.* Springfield, Samuel Bowles & Company, 1854.

KELSEY, D. M., *Deeds of Daring by Both Blue and Gray* . . . *During the Great Civil War.* Philadelphia, Scammell & Company, 1884.

KENNELLY, ARTHUR EDWIN, *Vestiges of Pre-Metric Weights and Measures Persisting in Metric-System Europe, 1926-1927.* New York, The Macmillan Company, 1928.

KNIFFEN, FRED, and others, *Walapai Ethnography.* Menasha, Wis., American Anthropological Association, 1935. (*Memoirs,* No. 42.)

LADAS, STEPHEN PERICLES, *The Exchange of Minorities; Bulgaria, Greece and Turkey.* New York, The Macmillan Company, 1932.

LEA, firm, publishers, Philadelphia, *One Hundred and Fifty Years of Publishing, 1785-1935.* Philadelphia, Lea & Febiger, 1935.

LEE, DWIGHT ERWIN, *Great Britain and the Cyprus Convention Policy of 1878.* Cambridge, Harvard University Press, 1934.

LOMAX, JOHN A., and ALAN LOMAX, comps., *American Ballads and Folk Songs*. New York, Macmillan, 1934.

MANLEY, INZA JANE, *Effects of the Germanic Invasions on Gaul, 234-284 A. D.* Berkeley, University of California Press, 1934. (*University of California Publications in History*, vol. 17, No. 2.)

MANNING, WILLIAM RAY, *Diplomatic Correspondence of the United States, Inter-American Affairs, 1831-1860*. Vols. 3-6. Washington, Carnegie Endowment for International Peace, 1934-1935.

MASTERSON, WILLIAM EDWARD, *Jurisdiction in Marginal Seas With Special Reference to Smuggling*. New York, The Macmillan Company, 1929.

MEACHAM, ALFRED BENJAMEN, *We-Ne-Ma (the Woman-Chief)*. Hartford, American Publishing Company, 1876.

MILTON, GEORGE FORT, *The Eve of Conflict; Stephen A. Douglas and the Needless War* . . . Boston, Houghton Mifflin Company, 1934.

MORRIS, T. A., *Miscellany: Consisting of Essays, Biographical Sketches and Notes of Travel*. Cincinnati, L. Swormstedt & A. Poe, 1853.

MOUNT VERNON LADIES' ASSOCIATION OF THE UNION, *Annual Report, 1934*. No impr.

MUSEUM OF THE CITY OF NEW YORK, *Annual Report of the Trustees, 1934*. New York, 1935.

National Cyclopaedia of American Biography, Current Volume D. New York, James T. White & Company, 1934.

National Cyclopaedia of American Biography Indexes. New York, James T. White & Company, 1935.

New York Times Index . . . *Annual Cumulative Volume, Year 1934*. New York, New York *Times* Company, 1935.

NORBY, CHARLES H., and W. D. WYMAN, *A Topical Guide to the Mississippi Valley Historical Review, Vols. 1-19, 1914-1932, and the Mississippi Valley Historical Association Proceedings, Vols. 1-11, 1907-1924*. N. p. The Mississippi Valley Historical Association, 1934.

ORDER OF INDIAN WARS OF THE UNITED STATES, *Proceedings of the Annual Meeting and Dinner* . . . *January 26, 1929*. No impr.

O'RELL, MAX, *John Bull and His Island*. New York, Norman L. Munro [c1884].

Pacific Coast Annual Mining Review . . . October, 1878. San Francisco, 1878.

PANELLE, MICHAEL ANTHONY, ed., *Contemporary American Lyricists*. San Francisco, Author, n. d.

Patterson's American Educational Directory, vol. 32. Chicago, American Educational Company, 1935.

PEARSON, HENRY CLEMENS, *Pneumatic Tires; Automobile, Truck, Airplane, Motorcycle, Bicycle; an Encyclopedia of Tire Manufacture* . . . New York, India Rubber Publishing Company [c1922].

PENNYPACKER MEMORIAL COMMISSION OF PENNSYLVANIA, *The Memorial to Brevet Major General Galusha Pennypacker* . . . N. p. [The Commission] 1934.

POLITIS, NICOLAS, *La Neutralite et la Paix.* Paris, Librairie Hachette, 1935.

Polk's Dental Register and Directory of the United States and Canada . . . 7th ed. Detroit, 1906-'07.

POOLE, DEWITT CLINTON, *Among the Sioux of Dakota; Eighteen Months' Experience as an Indian Agent.* New York, D. Van Nostrand, 1881.

PORTER, DAVID DIXON, *The Naval History of the Civil War.* New York, Sherman Publishing Company, 1886.

PRESBYTERIAN CHURCH, General Assembly, *Minutes, Third Series—Volume 14— 1935* . . . Philadelphia, Office of the General Assembly, 1935.

SCHUH, H. J., *David Zeisberger, the Moravian Missionary to the American Indians.* Columbus, The Book Concern, n. d.

SCOTT, JAMES BROWN, *The Spanish Conception of International Law and of Sanctions.* Washington, Carnegie Endowment for International Peace, 1934.

SELLERS, JAMES LEE, *James R. Doolittle.* [Evansville, Antes Press, n. d.] (Reprinted from the *Wisconsin Magazine of History.* Vol. 17, Nos. 2, 3, 4, and vol. 18, Nos. 1, 2. December, 1933-December, 1934.)

SHEPHERD, WILLIAM ROBERT, *Historical Atlas* . . . 7th edition, Revised and Enlarged. New York, Henry Holt & Company, 1929.

SIMPSON, MATTHEW, ed., *Cyclopaedia of Methodism, Embracing Sketches of Its Rise, Progress, and Present Condition, With Biographical Notices* . . . Philadelphia, Everts & Stewart, 1878.

SPOONER, LYSANDER, *The Constitution of No Authority.* Boston, Author, 1870. (*No Treason,* No. 6.)

STEPHENSON, WENDELL HOLMES, *Alexander Porter, Whig Planter of Old Louisiana.* Baton Rouge, Louisiana State University Press, 1934. (*University Studies,* No. 16.)

[STEVENSON, WILLIAM G.], *Thirteen Months in the Rebel Army; Being a Narrative of Personal Adventures in the Infantry, Ordnance, Cavalry, Courier, and Hospital Services* . . . *by an Impressed New Yorker.* New York, A. S. Barnes & Burr, 1862.

[STYLEPARK HATS, INCORPORATED], *Hats of the World.* [Philadelphia, Bingham Company, c1935.]

THOMANN, GALLUS, *Real and Imaginary Effects of Intemperance.* New York, The United States Brewers' Association, 1864.

TRUEBLOOD, BENJAMIN FRANKLIN, *The Development of the Peace Idea and Other Essays* . . . Boston, 1932.

VAN DE WATER, FREDERIC F., *Glory-Hunter; a Life of General Custer* . . . Indianapolis, N. Y., Bobbs-Merrill Company [c1934].

WALKER, ROBERT SPARKS, *Torchlights to the Cherokees: the Brainerd Mission.* New York, Macmillan Company, 1931.

WALLACE, W. STEWART, ed., *Documents Relating to the North West Company.* Toronto, Champlain Society, 1934. (*Publications* of the Champlain Society, vol. 22.)

WELLCOME FOUNDATION, LTD., London, *The Wellcome Research Institution and the Affiliated Research Laboratories and Museums Founded by Sir Henry Wellcome* . . . London, Eng., Wellcome Foundation, Ltd., 1934.

WHITE, LESLIE A., *The Pueblo of Santo Domingo, New Mexico.* Menasha, Wis., American Anthropological Association, 1935. (*Memoirs,* No. 43.)

Who's Who Among North American Authors . . . Vol. 6, 1933-'34-'35. Los Angeles, Golden Syndicate Publishing Company [c1935].

Who's Who in America, a Biographical Dictionary of Notable Living Men and Women of the United States. Vol. 18, 1934-1935. Chicago, A. N. Marquis Company, 1934.

WILLCOX, JOHN, *The Approaching Conflict: a Brief Sketch of the Object and Aims of Human Government* . . . Chicago, Hazlitt & Reed, 1873.

The World Almanac and Book of Facts for 1935. New York, New York World-Telegram, **1935.**

YOUNG, JAMES CAPERS, *Liberia Rediscovered.* Garden City, N. Y., Doubleday, Doran & Company, 1934.

Kansas History as Published in the Press

Phillips county history is being discussed at length in W. M. Parham's column, for some time a regular feature of the Logan *Republican*.

Allamead community of Lincoln county in 1882, and Boston Corbett as a preacher, were recalled by A. Boyer in the *Seneca County Press*, of Seneca Falls, N. Y., January 23, 1935. The article was republished in the Lincoln *Sentinel-Republican* and *The Lincoln County News* February 21. More information about Boston Corbett's activities were contributed by Gomer T. Davies in a letter in the *News* February 28.

Cawker City's library history, by Mrs. Adele Jennings, librarian, appeared in the Cawker City *News* in its issues from February 21 to May 2, 1935, inclusive.

The rivalry of Glen Elder and Beloit for the county seat of Mitchell county was recounted briefly in the Glen Elder *Sentinel* February 28, 1935.

Pioneer life in north-central Kansas was described by Mrs. Mary E. Darrow in the Simpson *News* March 7, 1935.

"Early County Genealogy" is the title of a regular column in the *McPherson County Advertiser*, of McPherson. It began in the issue of March 22, 1935.

The early history of the Simpson Baptist Church was reviewed in the Simpson *News* April 4, 1935. The church observed its fiftieth anniversary March 31.

Early school days at Rocky Hill district, Lincoln county, were recalled in *The Lincoln County News*, of Lincoln, April 4, 1935. The school dates from the early 1870's.

A stockade erected near present Alexander on the old Fort Hays-Fort Dodge trail was described briefly by Nels Olson in the La Crosse *Republican* May 2, 1935.

The story of the migration from Mexico in 1900 of eighty German-Russians to join their kinsmen in Russell was related in *The Russell County News*, of Russell, May 16, 1935.

A résumé of an article describing the first acid treatment of oil wells in Kansas, published in the *Oil and Gas Journal* of Tulsa, Okla., was printed in the Russell *Record* May 16, 1935. The first well treated in Russell county was on January 22, 1933. Another article on this subject was contributed by John G. Staudt to the *Record* August 8.

St. John Lutheran Church of Kensington observed the fiftieth anniversary of its founding last spring. A history of the organization was sketched in the Kensington *Mirror* May 16, 1935.

Brief histories of the municipal bands of Russell, Lucas, Luray, Osborne, Beloit, Sylvan Grove and Cawker City appeared in the "Band Convention Issue" of the Lucas *Independent* June 6, 1935.

The diary of T. P. Alexander, pioneer hardware merchant of Florence, is being printed serially in the Florence *Bulletin*, starting with the issue of June 13, 1935. The diary runs from August 11, 1883, to a short time before Mr. Alexander's death in 1912.

Several stories about men and women who helped to build the Southwest were contributed by Mrs. India H. Simmons to the Dodge City *Daily Globe* during the summer months of 1935. Commencing with the issue of November 23, the *Globe* began a new series by Mrs. Simmons called "Southwest History Corner." These articles, published weekly, feature the narratives of pioneer men and women of the Southwest.

The early history of the Presbyterian church at Minneapolis and the organization of the Presbyterian church at Bennington were recounted in *The Lincoln County News*, of Lincoln, July 4, 1935. The article, by Rev. Wm. B. Cary, was reprinted from the New York *Observer* of July 22, 1874.

Early-day Cawker City was briefly described by Katherine Green in the Cawker City *Ledger* July 18, 1935.

Reminiscences of Harry H. Wolcott as a printer on T. E. Leftwich's Larned *Optic* were recorded in a three-column article in the Larned *Chronoscope* July 25, 1935.

The first annual convention of Kansas county clerks was held in Topeka January 19, 1887. *The Kansas Official*, of Topeka, made a brief report of this meeting in its August, 1935, issue.

Kansas' early forts were named and described briefly in the Dodge City *Journal* August 1, 1935.

"Tragedies," a story recalling several fatal accidents in the Luray community during the past thirty years, was printed in the Luray *Herald* August 1, 1935.

An account of the relief furnished Harvey county during the winter of 1874-1875 as recorded in the diary of C. W. Ives, pioneer resident, was published in the Marion *Review* September 11, 1935.

The fiftieth anniversary of the founding of Oakley was celebrated September 12, 1935. Historical articles and early-day pictures, in addition to a regular series contributed by Clarence Mershon, were printed for several months preceding the event, in the Oakley *Graphic*. Mr. Mershon's "History of Oakley" still continues as a weekly feature.

Horton history was outlined in the Horton *Headlight* and *The Tri-County News* in their issues of September 16, 1935. Horton was incorporated September 20, 1887.

A history of School District No. 9, Grant township, Marion county, by Mrs. Edith Phillips Collett, appeared in the Marion *Record* September 19, 1935.

The fiftieth anniversary of the founding of the Syracuse Presbyterian Church was observed September 22, 1935. The Syracuse *Journal* gave a brief review of the church's history on September 20.

"Some Lost Towns of Western Kansas," by Rebecca Wells Taylor, and "Rabbit Drives in Kansas," by L. D. Wooster, were historical features of *The Aerend*, quarterly publication of the Fort Hays Kansas State College, in its fall, 1935, issue.

A series of articles entitled "Early Day History of Hamilton County" was contributed by George F. Rinehart, of Glendora, Calif., to the Syracuse *Journal* for several weeks beginning September 27, 1935. Mr. Rinehart was a resident of Syracuse in the middle 1880's.

Bethel School, District No. 8, east of Lincolnville, celebrated the fiftieth anniversary of the erection of its present building with a special program September 27, 1935. The history of the school was sketched in the Marion *Review* and *Record* October 3.

Notes on old Plymouth and Lane's fort in Brown county by George A. Root and George J. Remsburg appeared in an article by Mr. Remsburg in the Horton *Headlight* October 3, 1935.

Garden City during the "boom" of the 1880's was described briefly in the Garden City *Daily Telegram* October 3, 1935.

Several dead post offices of Russell county were listed in *The Russell County News*, of Russell, October 3, 1935.

Arrington history was reviewed in *The Tri-County News*, of Horton, October 3, 1935. The leading article, "Community History of Arrington," was by J. M. Miller.

Early-day history of New Malden community, Atchison county, was recounted by G. W. Carpenter, of Horton, in the Horton *Headlight* October 7, 1935.

The organization and early history of Haskell county's Sunday schools were discussed in the Sublette *Monitor* October 10, 1935.

Bunkerhill in 1875 was described briefly in the Bunkerhill *Advertiser* October 10, 1935.

The Meade *Globe-News* issued a special historical edition October 24, 1935, celebrating the fiftieth anniversary of the incorporation of Meade Center as a third-class city. Leading articles were: "Carrie S. Anshutz Tells of the Early Settlement of Meade County," "Frank Fuhr Gives Partial List of Business Men on Square," and "Meade Center Incorporated as Third-class City October 21, 1885."

Early-day Kirwin is being described by F. E. Young, of Stockton, in the Phillipsburg *News*. His articles began October 31, 1935.

Meade county's early boundaries were discussed in the Meade *Globe-News* October 31, 1935. The county was organized November 4, 1885, with its present boundaries.

John R. Walden's column, "Early History of Clark County," has been revived and is appearing regularly in *The Clark County Clipper*, of Ashland, starting October 31, 1935. The previous series began September 13, 1934.

Early observances of Thanksgiving in Kansas were mentioned by Kirke Mechem in *Progress in Kansas*, of Topeka, in its issue of November, 1935, and by Cecil Howes in the Kansas City (Mo.) *Times* November 28, 1935.

Hays high-school history was sketched by Kathryn McLain in the Hays *Daily News* November 11, 1935. High-school subjects were first available to Hays students in 1885.

"Dramatic Kansas," a paper read by Olin Templin of Kansas University in Iola November 18, 1935, was reviewed in the Iola *Daily Register* November 19. It sketched the territorial history of Kansas.

Wichita banking history from 1877 to 1916 as compiled by Frank O. Carr was discussed in Victor Murdock's front-page feature article in the Wichita (Evening) *Eagle* November 19, 1935.

A history of the Ellsworth *Reporter* was briefly sketched in its issue of November 21, 1935. The *Reporter* has been published sixty-four years.

The Hornet, mimeographed organ of the Sun City schools, issued an attractive sixteen-page edition November 21, 1935, featuring the history of Sun City and vicinity.

Kansans in Congress during the first thirty years of statehood were discussed by David D. Leahy in the Wichita *Sunday Eagle* in its issues from November 24 to December 15, 1935, inclusive.

"Can't Agree on Ware Poem" was the title of a short article by Cecil Howes in the Kansas City (Mo.) *Star* November 26, 1935, reviewing several accounts of how and where Eugene Ware wrote his poem commemorating Admiral Dewey's victory in Manila Bay.

Excerpts from Saline county's official minute books of 1860 and 1861 were printed in the Salina *Journal* November 26, 1935.

"Thanksgiving Often Came in Midst of Hard Times, But Old-Timers Celebrated Anyway," was the title of Harry Johnson's article in the Garnett *Review* November 28, 1935. Mr. Johnson is a frequent contributor of historical articles to the *Review*.

Arthur Selleck's reminiscences of his experiences in Cloud and Mitchell counties in the 1870's as written for a meeting of the Mitchell county old settlers were printed in the Simpson *News*, November 28, 1935.

The history of the Garden Plain Methodist Church was briefly reviewed in the Cheney *Sentinel* November 28, 1935. The church was organized in 1885 by the Rev. E. C. Beach.

"Buffalo, Once Here in Millions, Now Almost Vanished From Earth," was the title of an article by John G. Ellenbecker in the *Marshall County News*, of Marysville, November 28, 1935.

An Indian scare in Kirwin and vicinity in the fall of 1878 was mentioned in the Kirwin *Kansan* November 28, 1935.

Some of the first automobiles in Dodge City and their owners were recalled in the Dodge City *Daily Globe* November 28, 1935.

A two-column history of the Cultus Club, a woman's organization of Phillipsburg, was printed in *The Phillips County Review* November 28, 1935.

Springs in the Flint Hills and the part they played in the early history of Kansas were discussed by Milton Tabor in the Topeka *Daily Capital* December 1, 1935.

Two Allen county churches—the First Methodist Church of Iola and the Humboldt Methodist Church—celebrated the seventy-fifth anniversaries of their founding during the week starting December 2, 1935. Brief histories of the organizations were published in the Iola *Daily Register* December 2. A sketch of the Humboldt church was also printed in the Humboldt *Union* December 12.

Names of Russell county court reporters of the twenty-third judicial district were listed in *The Russell County News*, of Russell, December 5, 1935.

"The Lot of the Territorial Governor in Kansas Was Not an Enviable One" was the title of an article briefly reviewing the administrations of Kansas' ten territorial governors, published in the Kansas City (Mo.) *Star* December 11, 1935.

A history of education in Edwards county as written by L. R. Clark was featured in the Kinsley *Graphic's* twenty-six page "Christmas Special," December 12, 1935.

Biographies of several Lewis pioneers appeared in the Christmas edition of the Lewis *Press*, December 12, 1935.

Salina's history and the story of its city government were outlined by J. R. Epp at a meeting of the Salina Chamber of Commerce, December 12, 1935. The Salina *Journal* reviewed the speech on December 12.

"Col. Jack Potter Recalls Fight Near Dodge City," "An Early Day Doctor," Dr. G. W. Hollembeak's story as told to Ida Ellen Cox; "The Heart of the Pioneer," by W. C. Pearce, of Garden City, and "Famous Cowboy Band Mixed Fun and Music," were the titles of historical articles featured in the Dodge City *Daily Globe* December 24, 1935.

Christmas in Salina in the early days was recalled by Mrs. N. H. Loomis, of Omaha, Neb., in a letter to the Salina *Journal*, printed December 25, 1935.

A brief history of Cheney by John I. Saunders appeared in the Cheney *Sentinel* December 26, 1935.

Russell in 1874-1876 was described by Thomas H. McGill in *The Russell County News*, of Russell, December 26, 1935.

A history of Naomi Rebekah Lodge No. 61, of Minneapolis, as written and presented by John Hartley at the anniversary meeting, was published in the Minneapolis *Better Way* December 26, 1935. The lodge was founded in 1872.

The history of the Kansas Frontier Historical Park, located on part of the old Fort Hays military reservation, was reviewed in the Topeka *Daily Capital* December 29, 1935.

Articles describing the blizzard of 1886 were featured in several Kansas newspapers in January, 1936, on the fiftieth anniversary of the event.

"Some Notes on the Wyandotte Constitutional Convention," by Kirke Mechem, appeared in *Progress in Kansas*, of Topeka, in its January, 1936, issue.

"Passing of Old Salem Church Revives Memories of Early Days," was an article in the Emporia *Gazette* January 1, 1936. The church, located south of Emporia, was erected in 1870 and was destroyed by fire in December, 1935.

The story of Fredonia's courthouse, now fifty years old, was reviewed in the Fredonia *Daily Herald* January 11, 1936.

Three articles by Cecil Howes in the Kansas City (Mo.) *Times* were: "County Seat Wars Provide a Lurid Addition to the History of Kansas," January 11, 1936; "Appearance of Topeka Scrip Issued in 1856 Recalls Kansas Conflict," January 17, and "Group of Kansans Traveling Together Gave the Populists Their Title," February 4. An article describing the career of "Fighting Fred" Funston, written by Herbert E. Smith for *Foreign Service*, of Kansas City, Mo., was reprinted in the *Times* January 14.

Excerpts from the narrative of Prince Paul of Wurttemberg, who visited at the mouth of the Kansas river in 1823, were published in the Kansas City (Mo.) *Star* January 19, 1936. The account of his explorations was originally printed in German; the *Star's* English translation was by Robert M. Snyder, Jr.

A history of the Wichita Business College was sketched in the Wichita (Evening) *Eagle* January 24, 1936. It was founded in 1883.

Kansas Historical Notes

Eight of the nine directors of the Lindsborg Historical Society were reëlected to their offices October 28, 1935, at the annual meeting of the society. The new member is E. O. Deere, who succeeded Henry Olson. Members reëlected for another year were: J. A. Holmberg, Birger Sandzen, C. A. Nelson, G. E. Eberhardt, John Altenborg, A. W. Carlson, H. J. Thorstenberg, and C. R. Rooth.

All officers of the Ness County Historical Society were reëlected at the annual meeting in Ness City November 5, 1935. The officers were: Lea Maranville, president; Grace Beardslee, secretary, and Martha Borthwick, treasurer.

Sen. Arthur Capper addressed the annual meeting of the Shawnee County Old Settlers' Association in Topeka December 5, 1935. Newly elected officers of the organization are: Miss M. L. Addis, president; Mrs. Luther Smith, vice-president, and Mrs. Frank Kambach, secretary-treasurer.

Olin Templin was the featured speaker at the annual meeting of the Douglas County Historical Society in Lawrence December 11, 1935. Officers elected to serve during 1936 include: Mrs. E. M. Owen, president; Mrs. Ida Lyons, first vice-president; F. N. Raymond, second vice-president; Mrs. Caroline B. Spangler, secretary, and Walter Varnum, treasurer.

Kirke Mechem, secretary of the Kansas State Historical Society, addressed the Memorial Craftsmen of Kansas in Salina January 10, 1935.

THE
Kansas Historical Quarterly

Volume V   Number 2

May, 1936

PRINTED BY KANSAS STATE PRINTING PLANT
W. C. AUSTIN, STATE PRINTER
TOPEKA 1936
16-3057

Contributors

JAMES C. MALIN, associate editor of *The Kansas Historical Quarterly*, is associate professor of history at the University of Kansas, at Lawrence.

LELA BARNES is curator of manuscripts of the Kansas State Historical Society.

THOMAS CLARKE WELLS, who died in 1907, was an early settler in the Manhattan vicinity. A biographical sketch appears on page 143.

GEORGE A. ROOT is curator of archives of the Kansas State Historical Society.

DOROTHY LEIBENGOOD is social science instructor in the Oak Street Junior High School at Burlington, Iowa.

WILLIAM E. SMITH is an attorney at Wamego and a director of the Kansas State Historical Society.

Frank Heywood Hodder, 1860-1935

THE death of the president of the Kansas State Historical Society, Prof. Frank Heywood Hodder, on December 27, 1935, brought to a close the career of one who has meant more to the cause of history in Kansas than any other man. Born at Aurora, Ill., November 6, 1860, his early life was identified with that town. He was graduated from the University of Michigan in 1883; spent part of the next two years at Washington in civil service; served as instructor in history and economics at Cornell University, 1885-1889, under his former teacher, Charles Kendall Adams, who had moved from Michigan; became assistant professor of economics, 1889-1890; studied in Germany at the universities of Goettingen and Freiburg, 1890-1891; came to the University of Kansas as associate professor of American history, 1891. After two years he was promoted to the position of professor of American history and political science and became head of the department of history in 1908.

At the time when Hodder was beginning his historical studies several of the great teachers were urging young students to begin with the investigation of the history and development of local institutions in their own communities. Hodder's first recorded research work was of this type, "The City Government of Chicago," which was scheduled to be published in the Johns Hopkins University *Studies in History and Political Science;*[1] but for some reason not now determinable was not included in the volume of that series devoted to municipal government. This monograph was the first evidence of his interest in the historical development of Chicago, and for that reason is of importance, because that city was to be the focus of the studies in which he made his greatest contribution to historical knowledge during his later career.

On locating in Kansas he undertook the study of the history and government of his adopted state, and in 1895 published his *Government of the People of Kansas*.[2] This little book combined Kansas history, as a background and introduction, with the study of state government. It illustrated his unusual ability to digest the conflicting materials of this most controversial of states and to present the

---

1. H. B. Adams, *The Study of History in American Colleges,* p. 111. United States Bureau of Education *Circulars of Information,* 1887, number 2.
2. Frank Heywood Hodder, *The Government of the People of Kansas* (Philadelphia, Eldredge & Brother, 1895).

results with simplicity and balanced perspective. In spite of the careful work that went into the book it did not please certain factions then prominent in Kansas political life. An attack of intense bitterness was made upon the book and its author, led by John Speer. The formal statement of the charges is to be found in the presidential address delivered by Speer at the annual meeting of the Kansas State Historical Society January 18, 1898, entitled "Accuracy in History."[3] There is no point to discussing here the merits of the historical question in controversy. The matter that was at stake for a young professor of history was his position in the university. Some friends advised him to fight it out with Speer, while others pointed to the extremes of the controversies in which Speer and his contemporaries had so often engaged, the power which Speer and his friends wielded in political circles and among newspaper men, and warned Hodder that it would be better to drop the subject. After full consideration he decided on the latter course, abandoning Kansas history as a major field of historical work for himself and his students—and thereby the state of Kansas has been the loser.[4] Hodder had intended to review the whole question in his presidential address in October, 1936. The present reference to the subject is in no sense intended as a substitute, neither is it intended to revive the old controversy in any form, but is introduced only because it became a turning point in Hodder's career and in justice to him and to the history of research in and the writing of Kansas history it is necessary to give this much of explanation in order to complete the record.

For many years the only instructor in American history at the University of Kansas, Hodder devoted his energies to the development of courses which covered the whole subject, rather than to concentration on a single phase or period as was possible in the history departments of some of the larger and wealthier institutions. The guides to these courses were published in two small volumes, and as he was constantly engaged in original investigation, they

---

3. *Collections* of the Kansas State Historical Society, v. VI, pp. 60-69.

4. The few Kansas items he published include "Some Aspects of the English Bill," in the *Report* of the American Historical Association, 1906, pp. 201-210, and reprinted in the *Collections* of the Kansas State Historical Society, v. X, pp. 224-232; "Kansas, 1910-1920," in the supplement to *The Encyclopedia Britannica*, 1922; "The John Brown Pikes," in *The Kansas Historical Quarterly*, v. II, pp. 386-390, and a review of W. E. Connelley's *History of Kansas, State and People* in *The American Historical Review*, v. XXXIV, pp. 663-664.

The publication of theses on Kansas and related subjects, written by students under his supervision include: Rosa M. Perdue, "The Sources of the Constitution of Kansas" in the *Collections* of the Kansas State Historical Society, v. VII, pp. 130-151; Anna H. Abel, "Indian Reservations in Kansas and the Extinguishment of Their Title," *ibid.*, v. VIII, pp. 72-109; Helen G. Gill, "The Establishment of Counties in Kansas," *ibid.*, v. VIII, pp. 449-472; James C. Malin, "Indian Policy and Westward Expansion," University of Kansas *Humanistic Studies*, v. II, pp. 261-358.

were frequently revised.[5] His interest was primarily in the analysis of special problems—historical criticism—rather than factual narrative or philosophical synthesis. Although he labeled his courses as primarily political, they were not narrowly so. He was opposed to the separation of history into compartments, political, diplomatic, economic, social and cultural; all phases should be studied together as they were lived—as a whole. If he had any prejudices which anyone might point to as coloring his presentation of history, it was an abiding abomination of those inseparable twins—war and intolerance.

He added to his courses, or changed them in many details, each year, and for some periods more than others. There was scarcely a topic to which he did not contribute something from his own investigation. He did not rush into print with every new thing, but he taught these new things to a long succession of students. He was reluctant to publish, even when to others it seemed that the problem had been completed, and much or most of his work was never printed. On some problems where he did not publish, his mastery of the subject is attested beyond question by brilliant book reviews.

Every student who worked with Hodder remembers problems, such as those dealing with Columbus, Cabot, the cause of the American Revolution, the Missouri compromises, the Oregon question, the compromise of 1850, Douglas, the Pacific railroad and the Kansas-Nebraska act, the Dred Scott decision, John Brown, and the Grant-Johnson controversy. His success in dealing with these problems of historical criticism was derived from certain special talents of the man—his faculty for analysis, by which he was able to fix upon the crucial point at issue; his unusual power of discrimination in dealing with masses of conflicting materials; and a mastery of the bibliography of his subject. These are essentials of every good historian, but he possessed them more fully than most men. When he had arrived at his conclusions, they were stated briefly. What many historians would require a book to present, he would condense into a magazine article. For these same reasons he was without a superior in the historical profession as a book reviewer.[6] His talents included also a rare ability to interpret maps, portraits and cartoons for historical purposes.

Among his earliest works was the *Outline Historical Atlas of the*

---

5. F. H. Hodder, *Outlines of American Colonial History* (c. 1910, 1914, 1917). Seven printings. *Outlines of American Political History* (c. 1911, 1915). Five printings.

6. Beginning in 1898, he wrote book reviews for *The Dial* (Chicago) until 1904, his first review article being "An American Chancellor of Law," a review of William Kent, *Memoirs and Letters of James Kent, LL. D., Dial*, v. XXIV, pp. 376-377.

United States, illustrating territorial growth and organization.[7] This was revised and perfected from time to time, going through five editions. As a recognized authority on the subject he reviewed several publications of similar nature for *The American Historical Review.*[8] He contributed also to two sections of the monumental *Atlas of the Historical Geography of the United States* published jointly in 1932 by the Carnegie Institution at Washington and the American Geographical Society of New York.

In the utilization of portraiture as a source material for history Hodder published little,[9] but he acquired an extensive knowledge of portraits, especially those of Lincoln. He prepared lantern slides of the most significant Lincoln material for presentation in illustrated lectures.[10] Similar series of lantern slides and lectures were prepared to illustrate the development of the use of cartoons for political purposes. A short sketch of this subject was published,[11] but the book he had in preparation was not completed.

Among his published articles, one that aroused as much comment as any was the paper entitled "Propaganda as a Source of American History."[12] Starting with the Columbian tradition, he indicated how it was established by propaganda, and except in a limited number of works, is perpetuated in the standard histories of today. Other episodes were selected in successive periods down to and including Woodrow Wilson, to illustrate how similar influences determined in one way or another many of the established versions of history.

The Columbus problem attracted Hodder's attention early in his career, and he was still working on it at the time of his death. The only publications which indicate the extent of his mastery of that complicated question are book reviews of 1904.[13] The Cabot problem is not so complicated, but is one of unusual interest to the student of exploration, cartography and commerce. In a review of Beazley's *John and Sebastian Cabot,* he pointed out that Sebastian Cabot's Muscovy company voyage of 1553 was the first application of the trading corporation to the purposes of discovery.[14]

On the period of the American Revolution there are four book

7. Boston, Ginn and Company, 1899, 1901, 1913, 1921, 1929.
8. *American Historical Review,* v. VII, pp. 569-572; v. VIII, pp. 561-562; v. X, pp. 215-216.
9. F. H. Hodder, "Lincoln Portraits," New York *Times,* February 26, 1922; "Healey's Portrait of Lincoln," *ibid.,* March 13, 1927.
10. Mrs. Hodder presented this Lincoln material to the Kansas State Historical Society.
11. F. H. Hodder, "Some Early Political Cartoons," *The Historical Outlook,* v. XIX, pp. 261-264.
12. *Mississippi Valley Historical Review,* v. IX, pp. 3-18.
13. *Dial,* v. XXXVII, pp. 12-13, 85-87, 363-366.
14. *Ibid.,* v. XXV, pp. 342-343.

reviews of his, two of which are of particular importance, the reviews of the books of Van Tyne and McIlwain.[15] These are most excellent examples of his best work, as well as outstanding illustrations of what a book review ought to be. The review of the Van Tyne book, for example, traced the history of how the history of the American Revolution had been written, the multiplication of monographic studies, the place of the book as a new synthesis, and, lastly, the criticism of the work in detail.

There is a considerable list of book reviews and there are a few articles on expansion and foreign policy. Particularly, however, he was interested in the internal development of western territory. He was primarily a historian of the Trans-Mississippi West. As an editor of original narratives he prepared the introduction and notes for an edition of Pittman's *The Present State of the European Settlements on the Mississippi* (ca. 1763-1770), and of Audubon's *Western Journal, 1849-1850*, both published in 1906. He reviewed in detail Chittenden's *The American Fur Trade* (1902) and Nevin's *Fremont, the World's Greatest Adventurer* (1928).[16] Incidentally the Fremont review must be ranked along with the Van Tyne and McIlwain reviews. The Oregon question was another which engaged his interest over a long period, although he did not publish his results, except as they came out in connection with book reviews.[17]

For the middle period of the nineteenth century the westward movement in its relations to railroads and slavery was the theme of Hodder's most important work. His earliest article on the anti-slavery movement was "Some Early Anti-Slavery Publications" in which he traced chronologically the publications of antislavery books prior to the book of Lydia Childs in 1833.[18] This kind of a bibliographical discussion is familiar to all students who heard his lectures. It was one of the distinctive features of his teaching.

The Missouri compromises were the subject of three research papers [19] and two book reviews. The first published record of Hod-

15. Review of Claude H. Van Tyne, *The Causes of the War of Independence, Mississippi Valley Historical Review*, v. X, pp. 472-475; review of Charles H. McIlwain, *The American Revolution*, ibid., v. XI, pp. 271-274; review of S. E. Morrison, *Documents Relative to the American Revolution*, ibid., v. XI, pp. 441-442; review of Paul C. Phillips, *The West in the Diplomacy of the American Revolution*, ibid., v. I, pp. 302-304.

16. *Dial*, v. XXXII, pp. 412-414, and *Mississippi Valley Historical Review*, v. XV, pp. 266-269.

17. Review of E. G. Bourne, *Essays in Historical Criticism, Dial*, v. XXXII, pp. 40-43; review of W. I. Marshall, *History vs. The Whitman Saved Oregon Story, American Historical Review*, v. X, pp. 451-452; Joseph Schafer, *A History of the Pacific Northwest*, ibid., v. XI, pp. 949-950; J. C. Bell, *The Opening of the Highway to the Pacific, Mississippi Valley Historical Review*, v. IX, pp. 243-244.

18. *Dial*, v. XXXI, pp. 310-311.

19. F. H. Hodder, "An Omitted Chapter in the History of the Second Missouri Compromise," abstract published in *The American Historical Review*, v. VI, p. 421; "Side-Lights on the Second Missouri Compromise," *Report* of the American Historical Association, 1909,

der's interest in Stephen A. Douglas is found in a book review of W. G. Brown, *Stephen Arnold Douglas* (1903).[20] About this time he planned a biography of Douglas. For various reasons the book was not written, but two phases of his research on the problem have been published. A part of his work on the compromise of 1850 was condensed into an article read at the Lincoln, Neb., meeting of the Mississippi Valley Historical Association in 1932, but was not published until after his death.[21] In this he pointed out conclusively, what he had taught for so many years, that the two points contributed by Henry Clay to the compromise were both rejected, that Clay was absent when the principal decisions were reached, and that Douglas was the chief author of the measures passed and the determining influence in securing the acceptance of the compromise.

The first published clue to Hodder's interest in the Kansas-Nebraska act is found in his review of Mrs. Archibald Dixon's book, *The True History of the Missouri Compromise and Its Repeal* (1899).[22] An appreciation of the ramifications of this problem and Hodder's approach may be made more complete by reference to preliminary influences. His interest in exploration, the contributions of exploration to geographical knowledge, the incorporation of such information into maps, all tended to focus on the importance to history of natural highways and of the instruments of transportation. His appreciation of the work of Hulbert on historic highways of America is evident in his review article on the work of that author.[23] Hodder's own interest in highways was focused on railways and a railway interpretation of American history, especially as associated with the Kansas-Nebraska problem and the Pacific railroad project. The key to the situation was Douglas' interest in the Pacific railroad, of which Chicago was to be the beneficiary. The South wanted such a railroad also, and as a result of the Mexican War and the Gadsden Purchase appeared to be about to realize its objective. After ten years of advocacy Douglas secured the enactment of his bill to organize the territories of Kansas and Nebraska and to open them to settlement preparatory to the final contest for the authorization of the building of his Pacific railroad, as he hoped,

pp. 151-161; the same also in *The Missouri Historical Review*, v. III, pp. 138-149; "Dough-Faces; the Occasion Upon Which John Randolph Coined the Phrase and a Discussion of Its Source and Meaning," *Nation*, v. C, p. 245; review of F. C. Shoemaker, *Missouri's Struggle for Statehood*, *American Historical Review*, v. XXII, p. 404; review of E. S. Brown, *The Missouri Compromise*, *Mississippi Valley Historical Review*, v. XIII, pp. 284-286.

20. Review in *American Historical Review*, v. VIII, p. 390.
21. F. H. Hodder, "The Authorship of the Compromise of 1850," *Mississippi Valley Historical Review*, v. XXII, pp. 525-536.
22. *Dial*, v. XXVII, pp. 124-126.
23. *Ibid.*, v. XXXV, pp. 214-215.

by the northern or the central route connecting with Chicago, rather than by the southern route.[24]

Nowhere is Hodder's scholarship more brilliantly expressed than in his study of the Dred Scott case. For many years constitutional law was one of his major courses as a teacher, and he possessed a type of mind admirably suited to interpretation of the law. Most students of constitutional law know little history, and most historians know little law. Hodder knew both. He demonstrated beyond question that practically every point in the traditional anti-slavery accounts of the case was wrong; the motives for originating the case, its course through the courts, the responsibility for the political character of the opinions, the charges of delay in the decision, and the soundness of the legal argument in the opinions of the judges. From the standpoint of legal analysis, precision of statement and literary form it exhibits a standard of quality which is rarely equaled.

In spite of the regular burden of teaching and administrative duties, with a limited time for research and writing, Hodder participated in most of the activities of a historical character in the state. Especially he attended regularly and participated in the meetings of teachers of history in the public school system.

On account of the limited facilities of the University of Kansas, most of his graduate students were urged to go to Eastern universities. For this reason many history students who completed their work in the East and are credited to such institutions, received their major training in Kansas. In his profession he was never a member of a clique or faction; his interest was primarily in scholarly work. Especially he was interested in the work of the younger men, whether or not they were his own students. He gave unselfishly to them of his time, energy and knowledge. Much of the time he had on hand one or more historical manuscripts submitted to him from all parts of the country for his friendly and constructive criticism. It is not in one activity alone or in one locality that his influence has been felt; his was a well-rounded career in which substantial and permanent contributions were made which place him in the rank of the nation's foremost scholars and teachers.

JAMES C. MALIN.

---

24. Two other historians, W. E. Dodd and Allen Johnson, about the same time, recognized the relation of Douglas to railroads, but Hodder was the first to work out the problem in detail. His published articles are: "The Genesis of the Kansas-Nebraska Act," *Proceedings of the State Historical Society of Wisconsin for 1912*, pp. 69-86; "When the Railroads Came to Chicago," abstract in the *Report of the American Historical Review*, v. XX, p. 517; "The Railroad Background of the Kansas-Nebraska Act," *Mississippi Valley Historical Review*, v. XII, pp. 3-22. Review of Allen Johnson, *Stephen A. Douglas, American Historical Review*, v. XIV, p. 369.

Isaac McCoy and the Treaty of 1821

LELA BARNES

ISAAC McCOY, Baptist missionary to the Indians, was an outstanding figure in the development of the Indian removal policy of the United States. He began his missionary work on the western frontier of Indiana in 1817 and spent the twelve years following with the tribes of Indiana and Michigan. By 1823 he was convinced that the ultimate decline and ruin of the Indians could be avoided only by removing them from the encroaching whites and by colonization in lands west of Missouri. The following year he submitted his conclusions to the Baptist Mission Board and was authorized to present the matter at Washington. Secretary of War John C. Calhoun, whose department was at that time in charge of Indian affairs, approved McCoy's plans and became a supporter of the measure. McCoy worked unceasingly for the program and published in 1827 his *Remarks on the Practicability of Indian Reform,* in which he urged concentration of the perishing tribes in some suitable portion of the country under proper guardianship of the government.[1]

By 1828 many of the tribes had migrated to the West and in that year an exploring expedition was ordered by the government to permit certain other tribes to examine the country west of the Mississippi and select locations. McCoy was appointed one of the commissioners. Two tours were made and delegations of Pottawatomies, Ottawas, Creeks, Chickasaws and Choctaws were taken into the territory. In 1830 McCoy was appointed surveyor and agent to assist in the migration westward, and devoted more than ten years to the work. During this period he spent much time in what is now Kansas selecting and surveying locations for the tribes and establishing missions and schools. Much of the early recorded history of the state relates to the settling of the Indians within its borders and subsequent efforts of mission groups to introduce the ways of civilization.

This paper is a brief sketch of McCoy's life up to 1823, when he began his work at Carey mission, near St. Joseph's river, Michigan.

---

1. Isaac McCoy was born near Uniontown, Pa., June 13, 1784. He died at Louisville, Ky., June 21, 1846. His published works include: *Remarks on the Practicability of Indian Reform Embracing Their Colonization,* 1827; *The Annual Register of Indian Affairs Within the Indian (or Western) Territory,* 1835-1838; *A History of the Baptist Indian Missions,* 1840.

Although the establishment of this mission was the result of many years of directed effort, it hinged at the last upon the terms of the Treaty of 1821, whereby the government sought to purchase lands from the Ottawa, Chippewa and Pottawatomie nations. McCoy's hopes depended on the adoption of a provision for the establishment of a school for the Pottawatomies in Michigan territory and his own subsequent appointment as teacher. He planned, of course, to combine teaching and religious instruction. The treaty, as concluded, provided for the school, and upon its ratification McCoy received his appointment. But he had struggled with many deterring forces by the time this end was reached.

McCoy's determination to "labor" in the Indian country runs like a vein of iron through the account of his life. Before his twentieth year the idea of going to Vincennes, Indiana territory, had taken definite form in his mind, strengthened by a mystical experience in which he was directed by a luminous spot in a cloud-darkened sky to that place.[2] Soon after this occurrence he married Christiana Polke, and in the year 1804 set out from Shelby county, Kentucky, with his sixteen-year old bride, for the territory of the Wabash. Here he settled on public land about seven miles above Vincennes, later removing to the settlement where he prepared to follow the art of making spinning wheels, which he had learned from his father. But the climate of the region was not favorable and in 1805 the little family (there was by now a small daughter) removed to Clark county, Indiana territory, and settled on Silver creek.

Throughout his journal for this period are references to mental perturbation on the subject of preaching. By 1808 he had been regularly licensed. In 1809 he was again visited by "agitations of the mind" respecting preaching at Vincennes, and with the consent of his wife—who expected never to be settled until he had accomplished his purpose of laboring at that place—the family returned to the country of the Wabash where, in the year following, McCoy became pastor of Maria church. Here life was filled with peril and hardship. The family suffered much illness; only a bare existence was possible on the small earnings from wheel-making; and the Indians were a constant menace, forcing them at times to live at the forts. But in spite of all this McCoy planned to enlarge the field of his work and by 1815 had conceived the idea of forming a

---

2. Statement of the events of his life, addressed to his brother-in-law, William Polke. Isaac McCoy's journals, correspondence and manuscripts referred to in this article are part of the McCoy collection of manuscripts belonging to the Kansas State Historical Society. The journal covers, with some gaps, the years 1817-1841; the correspondence begins with the year 1808 and continues until McCoy's death.

society for domestic missions. He later found that the idea had been developed elsewhere, yet "such was the obscurity of my situation," he recorded, "that I had never heard of it. . . . I concluded it would not be foreign from the general Missionary Cause, for these western regions to turn their attention in part to the destitute [who] were immediately under their notice. I had no sooner conceived the plan than I felt pretty much transported with the idea." [3] As a result of perseverance he was given an opportunity in 1816 by the Longrun (Kentucky) Association to a make a three months' tour in the territories of Illinois and Missouri. This tour took him to what he describes as the heart of the devil's empire—a place less menacing in aspect after 120 years, known as St. Louis.

The enthusiasm of the Longrun Association for domestic missions had declined, however, by the time the tour was over. There were but few members then favoring the project and these, wrote McCoy, could not obtain for the expiring scheme a decent funeral. The cause of foreign missions was then in the ascendency. A period of despair followed, out of which came the idea that he must so improve his financial condition as to be able to give all his time to preaching—seemingly an impossible goal, since time already spent in the ministry had brought him to a state of poverty. Restlessness filled his heart and his constant prayer was for a larger sphere in which to work. "I have thought," he wrote, "that if a suitable opportunity should offer I would offer my services to the Baptist Board of Foreign Missions—to travel under their auspices in these western regions." [4]

Hearing that the Massachusetts Baptist Missionary Society was contemplating a mission in the West, McCoy made known his desire for an appointment. Also he informed the Baptist Board of Foreign Missions for the United States of his desire to become a missionary, suggesting St. Louis as a field. But the board did not favor his request and selected two others for the St. Louis post. News of this action came when his fortunes were at low ebb, when he was afraid "to go in company" lest he should see a creditor, and when the needs of eight children pressed down upon him. Fever, which failed to respond to "physick and barks" burned his strength and energies, and he believed that he was dying. Then, when matters had reached the lowest point during this time of trial, he received notice from the Baptist board of his selection as missionary to the Wabash country

3. *Ibid.*
4. Journal of Isaac McCoy, January 12, 1817. Hereinafter cited as Journal.

for the period of a year. This was in August, 1817. His field was defined as the counties of Edwards and Crawford, Illinois territory; Knox, Sullivan and Daviess counties, Indiana territory.[5]

McCoy received the appointment in October, following, and assumed his duties at once. His journal record of distances traveled indicates his determination to carry the message to remote corners of the assigned territory. But his program of work did not permit him to spend much time with the Indians and, since he had by now decided to dedicate the remainder of his life to their earthly and eternal welfare, he set about to devise means. Late in 1817 he visited Thomas Posey, Indian agent at Vincennes, and informed him of his plans. Posey was friendly and offered assistance, suggesting that McCoy defer any trips to the Indian villages until after his desire to work among them had been presented in council. Early the following year McCoy visited Territorial Judge Benjamin Parke. He recorded the interview as follows:

> I rode to Vincennes and conversed with Judge Parke on the introduction of civilized habits among the Indians, he having been in the service of government in Indian affairs, is well acquainted with their character, altho. he thinks their civilization practicable, he supposes it will require say 15 or 20 years to effect any thing of consequence, but I hope that this dis-heartening opinion of his is owing to his want of faith.[6]

Judge Parke's lack of enthusiasm did not act as a deterrent. In a short time McCoy wrote, "My feelings are all alive with the Subject of introducing the Gospel among the Indians";[7] and he set out on a tour with a view of preparing for the meeting of the Indians. But at this point, the death of Agent Thomas Posey halted his plans. In considering the situation it occurred to McCoy that it would be desirable to have a missionary appointed to the position of agent. This plan, he reasoned—

> would bring the whole business with the Indians under the Control of the Board, in a way that our Benevolent measures would not be liable to be thwarted by an ill-natured Agent, and every movement in the Agency might be rendered subservient to their Civilization. The Indians might be persuaded to accept of such articles as part of their annuities, as incline them to Civilization such as Cattle, hogs, etc. . . . and knowing that he could obtain stock, and implements of husbandry, he [the Indian] would hardly fail to become a farmer, a Citizen of the U. S. *A Christian*.[8]

McCoy found no means of putting the plan into operation, how-

---

5. Letter, William Staughton, corresponding secretary Baptist Board of Foreign Missions, to Isaac McCoy, September 16, 1817.
6. Journal, January 24, 1818.
7. *Ibid.*, March 7, 1818.
8. *Ibid.*, March 30, 1818.

ever, and was obliged to wait for the development of favorable circumstances. Judge Benjamin Parke, acting as temporary agent following the death of Posey, was clearly out of sympathy. With the appointment of William Prince as agent, McCoy's outlook became brighter. Prince favored the project of an Indian school and arranged a meeting with the Weas for June, 1818, at which time McCoy set forth his plans. The Indians appeared to favor the proposal.

Although his appointment as missionary had been for a period of one year only, and had implied no desire on the part of the Baptist board to locate him permanently, McCoy determined to establish himself in the Indian country. He wrote of his decision: "We resolved to show to those to whom it might concern, that when we spoke of laboring for the benefit of the Indians, we meant precisely what we said; and having actually made a beginning among them, we hoped that if the Baptist board of missions should not continue its patronage, help would be obtained from some other source." [9] He fixed upon a site for the mission on Raccoon creek, Parke county, Indiana, and erected two log cabins. By this time—October, 1818—his commission had expired, and he went into the wilderness with Christiana and their seven children (the eldest had died of typhus) with no more tangible support in the venture than the hope that Heaven would dispose the hearts of some to lend them aid. This naive faith was rewarded by a pledge of assistance from the board, given in a letter from the corresponding secretary to McCoy dated at Philadelphia, December 2, 1818. He wrote:

> The drafts you have sent on have been duly honoured and will continue to be so. . . . The Board is anxious to see the cause of the Redeemer spread through the nations and in a peculiar degree to hear of its influence on the Indian bosom. It also wishes its missionaries to be comfortable to the utmost extent of its ability. . . . It might be a matter of question whether one broad Indian station might not be preferable as to the prospect of ultimate success than several more limited ones. The latter however seems demanded by reason that the funds come in a greater or less degree from all parts of the Union. . . . It [the board] nevertheless confides much in the wisdom, piety and prudence of its Missionaries, and I may add has a high sense of the zeal, disinterestedness and discretion of their beloved Brother McCoy. The expenses attendant on the preparing a mission house you will state and had better draw on us, so as not to feel the least embarrassment. The idea of the Board was to supply you with $500 annually, leaving you to devote as much of your time to the mission as you could command from family demands. . . . I can only in general observe that the board will ever be happy that you state to them what your comfort will require at their hand,

---

9. McCoy, Isaac, *History of Baptist Indian Missions*, p. 46.

and I am convinced you will ever find the principles on which they act are liberal, sympathizing and evangelic. . . . An assistant will be sent as soon as the Lord shall provide a suitable character.

McCoy notes the receipt of this letter in his journal entry for January 19, 1819:

> On the 9th inst. I received a letter from the Board, which, although its contents did not fully come up to our desires, gladdened our hearts by an assurance of the patronage of the Board. While I fear that our mission will be restricted in its operations on account of the fearfulness of the Board that they will incur too great an expense, I feel much pleasure in finding them disposed to adhere to a cautious frugality in the expenditure of the moneys entrusted to them and in the very affectionate & friendly manner in which they write to me. The sincerity of these assurances of friendship is confirmed by their desire & labor to afford me a colleague.

A very practical idea now entered into McCoy's planning. He had been unable to attract more than a few Indian pupils to the school on Raccoon creek and as a consequence had made but a poor showing. The board, he reasoned, would soon suggest a discontinuance of his labors unless he widened his activities. Therefore he directed his efforts towards securing a location where he could increase the number of pupils, and reach, as well, a larger number of adults. It was this determination that led, later, to his intense interest in the 1821 treaty, and his eventual location on St. Joseph's river. But before this removal to St. Joseph's there was a season of work at Fort Wayne.

Immediately after his arrival at Raccoon creek, McCoy had journeyed to the frontiers of Ohio with the view of extending his acquaintance with the Indians and finding, if possible, a field for his labors. A few months later he made a second tour, having in the meantime received permission from the Secretary of War to settle in the Indian country. After consideration of two possible locations, one at the Miami Mississinewa villages, the other at Fort Wayne, he decided upon the latter place as more favorable. He was offered here the gratuitous use of public buildings and assured of the coöperation of William Turner, agent to the Miamis.

In May, 1820, therefore, the family removed to Fort Wayne. They were accompanied by two Indians, one white man—Johnston Lykins, teacher—fifteen head of cattle and forty-three swine. Their household goods were conveyed by a batteau, poled up the Wabash river by four men. School was opened on May 29 with ten English pupils, six French, eight Indian and one Negro (who, it was hoped, would in time find his way to Liberia).

Life here was marked by opposition from the Indians, difficulties attendant upon remoteness from supply stations, and steadily increasing financial problems. There was also criticism of his plans. To one critic, Samuel Dedman of Pike county, Indiana, McCoy announced his stand. It may be taken as an answer to all objectors.

I have patiently heard the advice you gave us to relinquish our missionary pursuits, & have weighed the arguments by which you have enforced it, and must say that what you have said is among the many things which are calculated to make us doubt the correctness of our present and intended movements. . . . When I look among the Indians, I find them barbarous & wild, ignorant, cruel & deceitful. If I live among them I must bear with their uncouth manners & insults, I must be exposed to hunger, wet, & cold. I must, with small exceptions be denied the luxuries of life, the comforts of society, the aid of physicians, & the consoling voice of friends. I shall never hereafter lay up, by personal service, a shilling for the widow & orphans which I shall probably in a few years, leave in the wilds of wabash, or arkansas, & lastly I must probably die without seeing much fruit of my labours, only that I have prepared the way for others to follow. This colouring, my brother is not too high. . . . I assure you, my brother, that every opposing difficulty, the opposition of the assn. not excepted, has only tended to increase my missionary ardour. May my merciful God forgive me if I be wrong, and set me right. I would rather be a missionary to the Indians, than fill the President's chair, or sit on the throne of Alexander, emperour of Russia. I would rather preach Jesus to the poor Indians in a bark camp, than address the thousands who assemble in Sansom Street meeting hous, philadel. Something has turned my attention towards the Indians, & every feeling of my soul is enlisted in their cause, yet still I may be wrong. But I feel not the least inclination to turn back, but would drive on with the vehemence of Peter, the meekness of Moses, & the wisdom of Solomon.[10]

McCoy's financial troubles at this time were due in part to the fact that the board placed no money in his hands for the purchase of supplies. Accounts were submitted for payment if approved. The distraught missionary lived in constant dread of the refusal of that body to settle for goods delivered to him by more optimistic merchants. He had learned indirectly of the surprise occasioned by some of his expenditures. The consumption of pork in the wilderness, for example, had seemed beyond reason to those sitting at Philadelphia. Throughout his journal for these dark months are expressions of despair. Debts piled up; he borrowed money with which to pay them; he then came to that financial extremity—borrowing money to pay back borrowed money that had gone to settle debts. In spite of discouragement and uncertainty, however, his mind leaped constantly to possibilities for fruitful work, and even in the shadow of the necessity to terminate his labor he made

10. Draft of letter, January 12, 1820.

plans for continuing. He wrote to John Kinzie[11] and Alexander Wolcott[12] at Chicago inquiring about the possibility of attracting Indian children of that region to the school at Fort Wayne. Their replies are suggestive of obstacles to Indian reform.

Sir,　　　　　　　　　　　　　　　Chicago Illinois January 3d, 1821

I have great pleasure in acknowledging the receipt of your favor of the twenty fourth ultimo, by our express which arrived yesterday. I rejoice that your school has been opened and continued under such favorable auspices. The task you have undertaken is really a formidable one. To soothe, to correct, or subdue the perversness and capriciousness of the Indian disposition, increased as those qualities are by the unlimited indulgence with which children are treated by their parents from earliest infancy, requires a command of temper, a degree of patience and perseverance, which few men possess. The meliorating of the condition of the Indians must be always an object of great interest to the philanthropist; and, at this time, when we have such extended and growing relations with them, must be peculiarly important to the American people. Institutions of pure benevolence, such as that over which you preside, reflect honor on all concerned in them, and I truly hope that you, and those under whose directions you act, will find your efforts rewarded with distinguished success. Whenever it shall be in my power to do anything to promote the interests of your school you may depend upon my zealous cooperation. But I cannot promise you any considerable additions to your number from this quarter. There are it is true, several half breeds here of a proper age and who are much in want both of the training and instruction which they would receive if placed under your care, and the parents of some, perhaps of all of them, might be easily prevailed on to send them to fort Wayne; but then their parents are for the most part Indian traders, and doubtless intend to bring their sons up to the same employment, so that whatever instruction their sons may receive, though it may be of great benefit to them individually, will be wholly lost as regards the improvement of the Indians, which I take to be the grand object of your institution. The savages of this neighborhood are remarkably indolent, holding all labors, except those of the chase, in utter contempt. They have moreover a strong affection for their children, and can seldom be brought to part with them even to those whites whom they know and in whom they have confidence. They say that obliging them to labor is reducing them to a state of slavery, which they consider the greatest of evils. There is another objection which will perhaps operate with equal force upon the Indians of this vicinity. They would be very unwilling to send their children into the country of the Miamis, with whom they have been often engaged in hostilities, and towards whom their feelings are never very cordial. Should the association of which you are a member ever so far extend its views as to think of establishing a school in this place, it is very possible that, when the Indians see it before them, and are made to understand its advantages, their repugnance to parting with their children may be more easily overcome. As it is, I think it very improbable

11. Pioneer who settled at Fort Dearborn in 1804.
12. United States Indian agent at Chicago, 1820-1830.

that any of them can be prevailed on to send their children to Fort Wayne. I will however make the experiment, and use my influence to effect that object when the Indians shall return in the spring from their hunting-grounds. At present there is not one in this neighborhood.

With the best wishes for your success

I have the honor to be
Very Respectfully
Your Obedient Servant

Revd. Isaac McCoy
Fort Wayne.

Alex. Wolcott Jr.

Mr. John Mackoy   Chicago January 27 1821
Sir—

I have not had an opportunity to see any of the Principle men of the different tribes of Indians resident in this Agency since I had the pleasure of your favor and without a discourse with them on the subject you wrote on I would not pretend to give my Opinion Positive. I expect that Doctor Wolcott will Introduce the subject to them as soon as opportunity will offer and that cannot well be untill sometime in May as they will not be into their respective Villages untill then. I consider it a part of my duty to inculcate into the breast of the savage the great benefits they will derive from education, and I think that there are a few that might be led to believe its benefits. You must know that your residence at Fort Wayne is immediately in the neighborhood of the Miamis, and as they are different tribe the Indians of this place might not wish to send their Children so far out of their country, this I know will be one objection, not but they are confident they would be treated with all the kindness in your Power but the Ignorance of the savage is such, that they would constantly be in dread of some revenge from some former acts of Violence that have been committed by this Nation on the Miamis and all I could say to the contrary would not have the good effect required, but I am still of opinion was there a school opened here that a small portion of children might be prevailed on to be educated. However you must not expect to effect this good and benevolent purpose in a day or two pray the society to hold on some time and probably their expectations and wishes may be reallized this is my sincere wish and I shall not fail to get the Opinion of the Principals as soon as I shall have the seeing of them.

With respect believe me D Sir
Your Most Obt. Servt
John Kinzie

Acting upon a suggestion that assistance might be obtained from the government, McCoy went to Detroit in February, 1821, and placed the details of his situation before Gov. Lewis Cass. He received aid in the form of food and clothing, and the promise of gratuitous work at the Fort Wayne smithery. At this meeting he told Governor Cass of his desire to settle farther in the Indian country. Cass thought permission of the Indians to do so might be obtained at the contemplated treaty. A single statement in Mc-

Coy's writings introduces the subject of this treaty, but it now became the point of concentration in his planning.

While deeply thankful for assistance given by the government, McCoy realized that it would serve to alleviate only temporarily his great distress. He wrote on February 28, on the journey back to Fort Wayne: "I am returning home with an aching heart. The mission never appeared to me to be in a more precarious situation. Unless we obtain pecuniary assistance in a short time from the Board or from some other source a few months will put a period to the Mission unless God almost miraculously preserve it." [13]

Immediately after his return from Detroit he formulated plans for having incorporated into the proposed treaty provisions for educational work among the nations. "In all this I was careful," he wrote, "to ascertain that I acted in accordance with the views of those who would be the principal agents of the U. S. in the negotiations." [14] He believed that a tour among the Pottawatomies would promote his ends. The specific objects of the tour were set forth in his journal entry for June 6, 1821. He wrote:

> The objects of my journey are to convince the Indians that I am what I profess to be— To look out a suitable site for our Mission establishment when we shall wish to leave this, and to persuade the Indians to invite me on to it— To endeavour to persuade them to do something for the benefit of their children at the contemplated treaty— to encourage them to send their children to our school, and to adopt civilized habits, and especially to talk to them about the way of life & salvation thro. our Lord Jesus Christ.

Hope had been fired by the intelligence that several of the Pottawatomie chiefs had determined to invite him to settle at St. Joseph of the Lake.

This tour took McCoy to the village of the Pottawatomie chief, Topenebee, where he had a talk with leaders of the tribe. He presented his plans with considerable caution, emphasizing the advantages of education and his desire to establish a school, but leaving other phases of his program unannounced. From this village he went to the shore of Lake Michigan where a stop was made at the residence of the Burnetts, relatives of the Indian, Abraham, who accompanied him. On the return journey he selected a site on the Elkhart river as suitable for the location of the mission.

The tour ended on June 19. Christiana McCoy, expecting shortly the birth of another child, set out a few days later with her three young daughters for a journey down the Wabash to the settled

13. Journal.
14. *History of Baptist Indian Missions*, p. 100.

country. The trip was made in an open canoe, a distance of between three and four hundred miles. McCoy was thus left with the entire responsibility of the mission establishment. Farm, house and forty-seven pupils required his constant supervision and these manifold duties prevented him from attending the treaty. He formulated his plans carefully, however, and recorded them under date of July 18, 1821, as follows:

I do not wish to thwart the plans of government, and I am confident that my plans must accord with the righteous course which it is hoped government will pursue with the Indians.

If the Putawatomies should sell their lands at the contemplated treaty, I hope they will reserve at least 30 miles square on Elksheart, including the large prarie on the road to Chicago, 40 miles square would be still preferable. On to this reservation I wish the Putawatomies to invite me to establish our School. Even ten miles square would be desirable, But a large Reservation would prevent white population from crowding their clashing interests in the way of our operations.

Whether the Putawatomies sell their land or not, I am very desirous that they should give me permission to establish our School in the above mentioned prarie. The 1st of next October I shall report the progress of the Missions to the President of the U. S. I wish, if possible to get the consent of the Indians before that time, so that I may be able to say to the Prest. that I am going on to build on said prarie immediately. In which case the Prest., agreeably to letters I have lately received, would defray two thirds of the expense of erecting the necessary buildings.

I have never yet told the Indians that I wished to live at that place, I wish my good friends to endeavour to prevail on the Chiefs to grant me permission. Were I to ask permission to settle there, they might be led to suspect the purity of my motives. I therefore wish my good friends to convince the Chiefs that it would be greatly to their advantage for us to have our school more immediately in their country, and that the above mentioned prarie would be the most suitable site for the establishment. I shall not ask a title to the land, I only want permission to live on their land so long as they remain satisfied with the school, and with the objects of the mission.

I wish them, if they sell, to say at the treaty that two, or three or four Townships of land, of good quality, which they may sell to government, shall be sold, and the proceeds of the sale, laid out in educating their children, and for other purposes of civilization. This would be no material loss to government, because they would get the land, which is the main object.—It would be a great benefit to the Indians, because it would enable us to hold out to them such inducements to civilized and religious habits, that their most inflexible jealousies, and prejudices could not resist.

Unfortunately for the Indians, most of the Agents consider their reformation impracticable, and are therefore somewhat indifferent to it. For these reasons, if the Indians were to provide for the education of their children in the manner suggested above, the money would be liable to be placed in the hands of men who would not promptly dispose of it to their advantage, and the whole might be squandered to no purpose. I would therefore propose that they say that the said money shall be laid out for their benefit at the time and place, and in the manner, that I, or a succeeding missionary in my place, should deem expedient for their welfare. I would of course be under the necessity of obtaining the approbation of the Prest. for every appropriation which I would wish to make. Government would keep the money in their own hands, and issue to me in such sums as they might think proper in order to avoid abuse, or extravagance on my part.

If the Indians consent to my living among them for these purposes, government cannot object to their taking the above measures in order to increase my usefulness. The presumption is that such a course would be perfectly congenial to the humane wishes of the Prest. Nevertheless the Commissioners as Agents of government might feel it their duty to make as good a bargain as possible for their employers. They would not therefore make these proposals themselves to the Indians, but would cheerfully consent to them if the Indians made the request. Isaac McCoy[15]
July 18, 1821.

With detailed instructions regarding the best methods of obtaining desired ends, Robert Montgomery, teacher at the mission, was sent to represent McCoy at Chicago. Montgomery left Fort Wayne on August 2, but had proceded only a short distance when that enemy of the traveler in the wilderness, ague, struck him down and imperiled the entire cause. But he so far recovered as to reach the treaty grounds. Two letters addressed to McCoy from Chicago give details of his work there.

Chicago. Illinois State
Augt. 12th 1821

Revd. Isaac McCoy
My Dear Sir
Your letter of the 4th Inst. has just come to hand, also one from John Johnston, Rice McCoy, &c. I return you my sincere thanks for the Interest you manifest in your Letter for my welfare, and comfort. *God* in his providence has permitted me to reach this place, and I desire to act as pope directs, "Why charge to heaven in those, in these acquit? In both to reason right, is to submit." Mr John Burnett had the goodness to present me with his "Essay on Man," which I peruse with much Interest.

As I have plenty of time, I will proceed to give you a minute description of my proceedings since I left Mr Bertrands. That day my ague paroxism was worse than it had been before, was quite deranged, for some time, Abram was much alarmed. The next day we left Mr Bertrands where we were kindly treated, and arrived in the evening at John Burnetts. he was laying with the Fever the next day I took Emetic which did not vomit me any though purged me well. this day I felt nothing like the ague, nor have I since. I however concluded to continue here three days and was kindly treated by the family during which time I took profusely of the Bark. The Second day the principal chief Topash, arrived. he stayed one day. I had a talk with him on the sub-

15. MS. statement.

ject of our business, his only reply was that they would council on the subject when they arrived at this place. I stop my narrative Topash, and chebas come into my room. After the usual salutations, I quit writing, and holding your letter in my hand, told Mr. Bobia,[16] my Landlord, to inform them, it was from you, that you thought often of them &c, was desirous to come nearer them, and hoped they would permit you to do so, that I would come out to their camps and see them, to which they replied that they would do every thing they could, that I would hear them talk to Govr. Cass &c. I gave them some tobacco and they went away. To continue. On thursday Mr Burnett and myself being better we set out for this place, though I was quite weak and still am. We arrived here on Saturday, which was yesterday, without any material difficulty, but the Journey fatigued me very much, in my weak State, and our horses are much Jaded indeed. I call'd at Mr Kinzie's, but his house being entirely occupied by the public he could not accommodate me, was very friendly, and permitted me to put my horses in his pasture, which is not very good, and dispatched his son over to my present Lodging to request him to afford me every comfort in his power, as I was his particular friend. My accommodations are reasonably good, and quite high. Abraham went out to his brothers yesterday and has not since returned. my health is improving and hope, (unless a relapse) that it will soon be restored again.

Govr. Cass[17] has not yet arrived, but is hourly expected. It is expected the Treaty will be tardy, perhaps may be the 1st of Sept. before I will get to leave this place Unfortunately I cannot do any business of a decisive nature, untill the result of the Treaty is known, because if I were to enter into a contract with them to locate at a certain Spot, they might afterwards dispose of the Same, thus you will at once discover my difficulty in the case. this will necessarily detain me untill all is over.

I have concluded if they should sell their country generally, and make but small reserves, and if they should be unwilling to give us liberty to settle thereon, to endeavour to get them to make a reserve of 2, 4 or 6 miles square (as near their principal reserve as possible) for the exclusive use and benefit of the Society, and Mission, adjoining if practicable, and we could locate thereon.

If all other attempts should prove abortive, and I should succeed in this dernier alternative, I hope it may meet your approbation. Should like your council, which is altogether out of the question.

If the Indians refuse, it will not be because they are opposed to the Mission. it will be from a fear of Monopoly, but rest assured my *dear Sir* I will use every exertion to effect the objects of my agency, to what I shall consider to be the most advantageous to the Mission——

Mr. John Burnet is quite friendly and says he will afford me all the aid which is in his power. he is with them in their private councils, and will use his influence. I depend much on his interposition in our behalf. told him in our first interview that I would be govd. by his advice on which he promised me. Appearances are not unfavourable at present, but not sufficient to justify an opinion on as to the result. I hope for success. If I should have to return

---

16. Probably phonetic spelling of Beaubien.
17. Lewis Cass, governor of Michigan territory and ex officio superintendent of Indian affairs for that region, and Solomon Sibley, pioneer and jurist, acted as United States commissioners at the treaty.

to Fort Wayne without success, after spending so much time, money, jading my Horses &c. I shall be much chagrin'd indeed.

This morning several of my friends called in to see me amongst whom was Maj. Phillips paymr. of the Army, and Doct. Woolcot, Indian Agent here, two of my particular friends. There are about 1900 Hundred Indians now here, Putaws. Chippys. & Ottaways. The object is, as far as I can learn, to purchase all the Land laying in the Michigan Territory but I am rather of the opinion th[ey] will not dispose of all within those bound[aries].

I am happy to discover that your confidence is strong in myself. Your confidence in my ability to perform may be misplaced, but your confidence in my disposition to use every exertion, cannot be. Any assistince you might have sent, would not have added much to my comfort, nor could they have been much benefit towards effecting the object, only have incurred an expense which you will think enough by the time I return, though am under obligations to you, for your disposition to render me comfortable. Make yourself easy about me. I trust I shall again see you, though much doubted it when I wrote you last. Give my Love to Miss Delilah, and Miss Rachel, and the family generally, and in addition tender Miss R. my unfeigned respects, tell her that I am gratified to think, that the news of my distress, should excite in her susceptible heart, emotions of sympathy, and sorrow—I feel grateful to her. I should be glad to hear from you by return express though I may have left it by that time if not I will write you.   I remain
                 Truly Yrs
                 R. Montgomery

Revd. & Dear Sir,   Chicago 22d Augt. 1821

Capt Hackly goes in the morning I have delay'd writing until the last hour, in order to give you the latest information, relative to the objects of my Agency, which to my regret and deep sorrow, is not flattering. I need not give you a detail of my proceedings, inasmuch as I shall (if spared) be home so soon.

I recd yours of different dates. have had many interviews with Col. Trimble,[18] he is a fine man & is much advantage to me here. The Indians were not collected previous to his arrivel Gen. T. & I did not wish to make any comm. indeed I could not untill Govr. Cass had made his propositions to them. Mr Trimble & myself visited their camps together. concluded as his object or business & mine were simular that we would comm together. He made his first, which was a handsome prelude & paved the way for mine, he requested to know if the Indians wished any change in relation to the Factory system, if they wished Blacksmith, schools &c among them. and closed with saying that he knew Mr. McCoy & myself that we were good men and that they might depend on any thing I would say to them. I then made my comm touching lightly on reserves to which they replyed that they would give us answers at a few days. We have heard from them frequently since, which is rather unfavourable, and as an evidence that our propositions did not relish well, they have not given either of us an answer, and Col. Trimble has since that time frequently reqt. it, stating that he was going away

---

18. William A. Trimble, U. S. senator from Ohio. Trimble visited McCoy at Fort Wayne on his way to the treaty and promised support of McCoy's program.

soon. he starts on tomorrow, without any answer to Green Bay in a Birch Canoe, in company with Major Biddle. I much regret his leaving me.

The objection is what I stated, "fear of Monopoly." I anticipated this and guarded against it in my speech to them. but they state that though we want no Land at the present time, after some time we will creep in to get some. Col. Trimble says he has no hopes of my succeeding, but we must pursad them by degrees, gradually overcoming their strong prejudices, and allaying their suspicion, by a course of conduct corresponding with our professions, towards them, in doing them good. That this circumstance though somewhat thwarting our plans at the present, ought not to discourage, or cause an abandonment of so laudable, and rightious an undertaking. That God in his wisdom & goodness, will provide ways and means to carry on so good a work, which are at present unforseen by us. The above observations were no doubt made as a consolation to my mind which he discovd. was much agitated, by the appearance of an unfavourable result. It is indeed much distressed. This morning Col. Trimble, Gov. Cass and myself had a conversation on the subject, and the conclusion was as a last effort that Govr. Cass would at his last council with them, make the request, to get permission to settle in their country that I yet have hope, but not much ground therefor. Mr. Burnet has not as much influence as I expected, and he has much business of his own. I have altogether given up any reserves. Col. Trimble says it is not material. The Govt. will afford means sufficient. I have had frequent talks with the chiefs since my first one. Govr. Cass & Mr. Sibley are quite favourable. There has been much councelling about the Treaty. I apprehend a cession will be made though some think otherwise. A few days will determine. I hope to be able to leave here in a few days, say monday next. My Horses are [rec]uperaiting some. I have procured some corn for them. my health is nearly restored for which I feel grateful. I hope you all enjoy good health. refer you to Capt. Hackly for particulars. I am happy to hear of the arrival of assistince in the *arduous,* I say *arduous* work of Indian r[e]form, prejudices & suspicions (which are not natural to such a degree, but excited,) to bear with. The latter are augmented if not produced by the former, bearing with them and endeavouring to remove them, requires the exercise of adequate qualifications, which unfortunately few of us possess. Give my respects to Miss Delala & Rachel, and all friends—hoping that I may be blest with health sufficient to return, may find you all in health and spirits. I subscribe myself,
Yr. affectionate friend
Robt. Montgomery

The treaty had formally opened on August 17. For several days the Indians had been gathering upon the plain. Schoolcraft, returning from his tour of the Mississippi valley, arrived August 14 and recorded the total number encamped at the opening of negotiations as about three thousand.[19] The vast scene was one of moving color, rimmed by the blue splendor of Lake Michigan. Records of the talks indicate that the Indians were reluctant to deal, partly be-

---

19. Schoolcraft, Henry R., *Travels in the Central Portions of the Mississippi Valley* (New York, 1825), p. 336.

cause of dissatisfaction over the outcome of the St. Mary's Treaty of 1819, and partly because of general aversion to disposing of the lands. Terms were finally arranged for the ceding of certain tracts, and the treaty was concluded on August 29.

Article 4 of the treaty specified that one mile square should be selected under the direction of the President, on the north side of the Grand river, and one mile square on the south side of the St. Joseph, within the Indian lands not ceded, upon which blacksmiths and teachers for the Ottawas and Pottawatomies, respectively, should reside. Immediately upon the return of Montgomery from Chicago with news of this provision, McCoy leaped into action. He addressed a letter to Governor Cass:

Dear Sir   Fort Wayne, Sep. 2d 1821

As the Putawatomies have asked for a teacher and blacksmith to be stationed on a section of land appropriated for that purpose, it is desirable that this mission should realize the advantages arising from this arrangement. A smith, it is expected, will shortly be united with us.

The Board of Missions have authorized me to enlarge the sphere of our labours. It would, therefore, be truly gratifying for some of our missionaries who will shortly be connected with this mission, to be appointed, teacher, farmer, & blacksmith, for the Ottaways. The two establishments, so far as they would be under the control of the board of Missions, would be placed under one superintendent, and would mutually assist each other.

I shall report the state of the mission to the Department of War, the 1st of Oct. and shall solicit a proper share of the $10,000 annual appropriation for Indn. reform. Now, sir, permit me, in behalf of the society which I serve, to solicit most earnestly your good offices in obtaining the above mentioned objects.

A few lines from you, before you leave Detroit for Washington, would be a singular favour.   Most respectfully
His Excellency L. Cass   Your Humble Servt.
                                                    Isaac McCoy[20]

Details of his plans were placed before the Board of Baptist Missions in this communication to the secretary, William Staughton:

Rev. bro.   Fort Wayne, Sep. 6, 1821

To obtain a permanent and eligible site for the mission establishment, and to induce the Indians to aid somewhat in the support of schools among them, I have been labouring a long time. Thro. the good providence of God I have at length succeeded in a good degree.

At a treaty last month at Chicago, when the Indians were ceding to the U. S. about 4,000,000 of acres of land in Michigan Territory, the Putawatomies obligated government to furnish them with a teacher, and a blacksmith and to

20. Draft of letter.

expend in supporting them $1,000 annually for 15 years. For the residence of those men, or in other words, for a Mission plantation, they gave one mile square of land to be selected by the Prest. of the U. S. any where in their country.

This arrangement is the result of plans which I had formed long since, and for the accomplishment of which I had felt much solicitude, and had put up many prayers. Should the government choose to appoint me teacher for the Putawatomies, and allow me to nominate the blacksmith, I beg leave to accept those offers, and permission to remove the establishment to the appropriated spot, so soon as the state of our funds and other circumstances shall justify.

Nothing can be certainly known respecting those appointments, and nothing can be done relative to removing from this place, until the treaty shall have been retified by Congress. My present wishes are, to commence at the new site next March, make a crop of corn &c. build cabins, and in the fall remove thither the family and school, having grain & vegetables at the place for the subsistince of the family, which will save a deal of cost. Government I trust will defray most of the expense of building.

Permit me to say that the Commissioners of Government expect the Board to avail themselves of the facilities offered to missionaries by their treaty with those natives, & the Indians themselves consider that we are under obligations to do so.

The site which I would prefer, & which I hope will be selected is about 50 miles N. W. of this, and that much further from white settlements.

When we shall settle at our more permanent residence, It is my wish to vary a little from the ordinary course of Missionaries among the Indians. I wish to lay off a town, not very compact, Let the houses be, say 20 poles apart, so that each family could have room for feeding cattle, horses, hogs, sheep & poultry. The missionaries would form one family. In this town I would invite all well disposed Indians to settle, preventing, as much as possible the Introduction of ardent spirits. Our fields would be a little back. at the mission house would be the place for public worship & for the school.

Anticipating the arrangements made at the late treaty, I have for almost one year, been pursuing measures to prepare the minds of a number of Indian families to settle with us, and I am encouraged to expect emigrants from 4 different sources so soon as I shall say I am ready to receive them. The head of one family, who speaks english, has agreed to be our interpreter being a citizen Himself and his children attending school, his services will occasion no expense to the Mission, except on particular occasions.

The Ottaways at the same time contracted with the U. S. for a teacher, a farmer, and a blacksmith, for the support of whom government is to allow $1,500 annually for 10 years, and also to furnish the nation with a number of cattle.

The demands of these two tribes astonished the Commissioners in as much as the like had never before occurred with any of the Indians N. W. of Ohio, or west of Mississippi.

As the arrangement of the Ottaways offer such facilities to Missionary I hope the Board will endeavour to avail themselves of them, all those persons whom the Indians have asked for to assist them, will be appointed by government, and I have already petitioned the proper persons, to appoint some of our missionaries, I presume that men of the proper characters may be obtained in the course of one year from this time. The establishment among the Ottaways could be located at a place not more than 100 North [*sic*] of that among the Putawatomies, and, if the Board pleased, the former might be an apendage to the latter.

These two tribes speak the same language with very trifling variations. The establishments being near to each other, and connected in their labours, would always act in unison, and would mutually assist each other. If the Board should not choose to expend any thing on the branch among the Ottaways, It would be no objection to my plan, for it would be better for us to have three missionaries living there on the annual salary of $500 each, than to risk an establishment which might not favour our views. Farming utensils, blacksmith tools, and even stock to work upon, would, I conclude be furnished by government. However, if the board will please to say that they approve the measure, provided the teacher, farmer & blacksmith can be supported at the station by the salary they shall receive from government, or, rather if they could afford to say that after bearing the expense of conveying the missionaries to the ground, they could afterwards allow that department the annual sum of $1000 towards defraying the current expenses, I would then if they please, make the best possible arrangement with government, after which we would be enabled to decide on the eligibility of the plan.

I fear that my worthy patrons will think that I am likely to run on precipitately & extravagantly in business, but I assure them that my present requests are the results of sober reflection and, as I said before, of much labour.

It is however uncertain whether with all our labour & pains we shall be able to get a footing among the Ottaways. At the moment when the Putawatomies requested the teacher &c. a Roman catholic, who was interpreting for the commissioners had the audacity to say in publick council, that the Indians desired government to furnish them with a Roman catholic teacher. The indians being informed of what the interpreter had said, immediately contradicted him, and declared that *I was the man whom they wanted.* From this circumstances you will perceive, dear sir, what vigilence, and care are necessary to secure the best interests of the mission.

It is also very desirable that a teacher farmer & blacksmith be located among the Miamies, say 40 miles southeast of the plantation among the Putawatomies. The Miamies are already entitled to a smith. I trust they will yet be prevailed upon to request of government the other two persons. The prospects around us, are brightening. Shall I ask pardon for wishing to improve every opportunity which presents itself for putting the mission into extensive operation? But we are liable to disappointment.

In order to render our plans effective and to secure a liberal share of patronage from government, I have thought it would be well for me to visit Washington at the next session of Congress, provided the business of the establishment would admit of my leaving home. I could then more fully explain to the proper persons my wishes, and more hopefully press upon them my requests. I would not, however, like to take such a journey, without the permission of the Board. I have written to a particular friend, who is a member of the Senate, to know at what time I had better attend. Should the Board permit me to go to Washington, perhaps they may instruct me to meet them before I return, that our plans may be more fully developed, and the best measures adopted. . . .

I have received the last Annual Report, and your late affectionate letters. I feel sensibly affected with the sympathy and liberality of the Board, I subscribe myself   Your Obedient Humble Sevt.
                       Isaac McCoy
Rev. Wm. Staughton Corr. Sec. &c.
Ps. The necessity of an answer as soon as possible to the foregoing will readily occur to you.   I. M.[21]

The attitude of the board, as expressed by its secretary, was one of qualified encouragement. Mr. Staughton wrote on September 29: "The plan you propose seems a good one, but, I do not think the Board is favorable to frequent changes. Circumstances may sometimes require them, but in general the best rule, to use the words of Dr. Young is 'in fixing, fix.' Or as Franklin expresses himself 'a rolling stone gathers no moss.'" Another letter dated October 18 transmitted information that the board had declined to take action on McCoy's proposed move until he could appear before that body; nor was it deemed advisable that he solicit aid from the government before visiting the board. Frequent removals it was felt, were undesirable, having usually an ill effect upon the public mind. Mr. Staughton again recommended the axiom of Dr. Young.

Following instructions from the board to appear before the group, McCoy set out upon a journey by horseback to Philadelphia on December 4. On January 7 he made a statement of his work and plans. His entire program was approved, including three proposed missionary stations, one among the Pottawatomies, one among the Ottawas and one among the Miamis. He was given full authority to select workers and to remove from Fort Wayne when he deemed it expedient to do so. In view of the indifference of the board before his personal visit, it must be concluded that McCoy spoke with convincing fervor. Before his return to Fort Wayne, he visited the Secretary of War in Washington and obtained assurances of aid insofar as it could be given when the treaty should be ratified.

It must not be assumed that McCoy was seeking the slightest pecuniary advantage for himself in asking the appointment as teacher to the Pottawatomies, which position he expected to fill while acting also as representative of the Baptist board. Although he should be drawing money from two sources under that arrangement, all was to be applied to the work of the mission. Two rules

21. Draft of letter.

from "General Rules for the Fort Wayne Mission Family" indicate the sincerity of these laborers in the wilderness:

2d. We agree that our whole time, talents, and labours, shall be dedicated to the obtaining of this object [to meliorate the condition of the Indians], and shall all be bestowed gratis, so that the mission cannot become indebted to any missionary for his or her services.

3d. We agree that all remittances from the board of missions, and all money and property accruing to any of us, by salaries from Government, by smith shops, by schools, by donations, or from whatever quarter it may arise, shall be thrown into the common missionary fund, and be sacredly applied to the cause of *this* mission; and that no part of the property held by us at our stations is ours, or belongs to any of us, but it belongs to the General Convention which we serve, and is held in trust by us, so long as said society shall continue us in their employment: Provided that nothing herein contained shall affect the right of any to private inheritance, &c.[22]

The treaty was ratified March 25, 1822. In July, following, McCoy visited Governor Cass at Detroit and subsequently received his appointment and full instructions. A small portion of an appropriation by Congress of $10,000 for the purposes of Indian reform was allotted to the new station.

The location finally determined upon was not exactly that desired by McCoy, but he yielded to the wishes of the Indians in the matter. The site was about one mile west of the present city of Niles, Berrien county, Mich., one hundred and eighty miles from a settlement and an even greater distance from a mill. The mission was called Carey, honoring a celebrated Baptist missionary.

Preparations were immediately started for removal. In August McCoy took workers to the new location where hay was prepared for the stock. In October a company left Fort Wayne and began the erection of buildings at Carey. And on December 9 the mission family departed from the old station. The train consisted of three wagons drawn by oxen and one by horses. There were thirty-two persons—seven members of the McCoy family, one assistant, six work hands and eighteen Indians. Fifty hogs and five cows were driven with difficulty over the icy ground. The journey was completed in eleven days.

The concerns of life were altogether too serious and pressing to admit of any period of relaxation upon their arrival at the goal. The cabins were unfinished and the school not yet begun; it was necessary to butcher the hogs because there was no grain with which to feed them; the Indians immediately demanded work at the

22. *History of Baptist Indian Missions*, p. 170.

smithery; and food stuffs had to be hauled from the settlement—a trip of four hundred miles for the wagons.

It was deemed expedient, however, to pause from labor at the beginning of the new year and extend a welcome to the neighbors of the region. McCoy wrote in his journal on January 1, 1823:

> Chebass & Topenebee, chiefs, and others, men, women & children, about 40 in all, called in to congratulate us on the opening of the New Year. Shaking of hands and kissing are among the ceremonies which prevail among them on this day. In conforming to the former we felt no embarrassment. But we dispensed with the latter, as it was a perfor[mance] which we could not very well relish. Their observance of holidays is not an original custom among them, but is derived from the French traders among them. Smoked the pipe of peace and friendship together, after which we sat down together and partook of a dinner we had prepared for them. All appeared remarkably cheerful and well pleased. Some of the principal men expressed to our interpreter the greatest satisfaction in the manner we had received them. Said they could not think there were any more such good men among the whites, and that our kindness should be rewarded by presents of sugar, or something else by and by.

Life and work had begun at Carey mission. The story of the years that followed differs little from that of the years that went before. There were hardships, always, obstacles and discouragement. But there was also a new and stronger purpose—the removal of the tribes to the region beyond the Mississippi. And it was in his application to this purpose that McCoy became in time a leader in the movement to better the condition of the Indian.

Letters of a Kansas Pioneer
1855-1860
Thomas C. Wells [1]

My Dear Father,   Waites Hotel Prov. Mar. 12, 1855.

I HARDLY know what to write you or what to do. I met James at the depot in Providence and he had found the tickets at the Express Office. I must say I had really hoped that he would not get them and that would furnish a reason for returning home,—not that I shrink from any hardships, real or imaginary which I might be called to endure in Kansas, but I do find it hard to leave *you* and *Mother & sister,* Herbert, &c at home.

I say again I do not know what to do, I have prayed that I might be guided in the right way, and I trust that I shall be thus guided. James seems to be as eager to go as ever. I shall probably go on to Boston tomorrow, at least, and shall have a plain talk with him, and tell him just what I think about it. I may yet see it best to return and not go at all, but if I do go I may not stay—or but a short time at any rate. I certainly will not stay—(and would not go did I know that you felt so) if you feel the need of me greatly at home, and if you think that I ought to come back or that you cannot get along *comfortably* without *me* (I did not think that I was so important) I *do* hope that you will write me so and I will *gladly* return and be contented and not only contented but esteem it a priviledge to remain with you and mother and try to be a comfort to you as long as you or I shall live.

---

1. Thomas Clarke Wells, the son of Thomas Potter Wells and Sarah Elizabeth Clarke, was the eighth and last Thomas Wells born in direct line, descendants of Nathaniel Wells who emigrated to this country in 1629 from Essex county, England. His mother died in 1834 and his father made two subsequent marriages, the first to Clarissa Sherman in 1836, who died in 1846, and the second to Julia Esther Johnson in 1848. Two children were born of each marriage. They were: (1st) Thomas Clarke, 1832, and Frances Elizabeth, 1834; (2nd) George Henry, 1837, and Theodore Backus, 1840; (3rd) Herbert Johnson, 1850, and Helen May, 1861.

Mr. Wells was born April 26, 1832, in Hopkinton, R. I., spent his early life in Kingston and Wakefield and at the academy of East Greenwich, and as a young man planned to enter his father's bank. Ill health, however, forced him to leave the Atlantic coast and in 1855 he came West, taking a claim near Juniata, and subsequently one near Manhattan. On October 30, 1856, he was married to Miss Eleanor Bemis of Holliston, Mass., who lived on a near-by claim. As the accompanying letters written to his father, stepmother and half brothers show, Mr. Wells was a Free-State man, on one occasion joining a party which started to the defense of Lawrence, and was active in the affairs of the community, particularly in the work of the Congregational church in Manhattan where he was a charter member. He died in Manhattan, January 9, 1907.

The originals of the letters published here are preserved in the Manuscript division of the Kansas State Historical Society. They were presented by Elizabeth J. and Emily P. Wells, of Kingston, R. I., nieces of Thomas C. Wells, daughters of the Herbert J. Wells who is mentioned in the letters. Included in the series are several letters written by Eleanor Bemis Wells to her new relatives. Spelling and punctuation as contained in the original letters have been followed throughout.

But if you find it easier to get along without me than you thought at first then it may be best for me to stay a year or two in Kanzas if I should ever reach that country.

James says that he has learned of two printers who he thinks might suit you and they will probably write you soon.

But I must bid you goodnight Do not be troubled on my account— I doubt but that all will in the end be for the best though what the end may be I am sure I cannot now tell

Yours affectionately in haste
T. C. Wells

Dear Father

I have just been to wash my face &c and when I came back I found James just directing a letter to you, and I will add two or three words and more soon.

We have been on the railroad all night stuck fast for three or four hours in a snow bank on Mount Holly in Vermont A strange way to get to Albany through Fitchburg Mass., Keen, N. H., Bellows Falls, and Rutland Ver., but we shall have a chance to see the country, for the last hour we have been going [through] the Mountain hills— this is the most broken roughest country I have ever seen. I should think there were as many as three hundred on their way to Kanzas with us, some thirty or forty Women some whole families. We expect to arrive at Albany at about six (6) this evening or rather we arrive three or four hours before that and start from there at six. If you wish to write before I get in Kanzas you may direct to the care of Samuel C. Pomeroy,[2] Esq., Kanzas City, Mo. and I shall get them as soon as they can be forwarded, If it should be necessary you can communicate with me by telegraph directing to the care of same person in Kanzas City as there is a telegraph there. Yours affectionately,
Will write more soon as can. T. C. Wells.

Detroit Michigan

Dear Father, Mar. 16-55

Here we are in Detroit Start for Chicago at ¼ to nine this eve'g. We arrived at Albany at about seven Thursday evening, and a mean dirty place it is—around the depot at least—if I am any judge.

We left Albany at ½ past eleven at night for Suspension Bridge, Niagara Falls where we arrived at about ½ past four yesterday

---

2. Samuel C. Pomeroy was United States senator from Kansas from 1861 to 1873. For biographical sketch see *Kansas Historical Collections*, v. VIII, p. 278.

afternoon; we took a walk up to the falls on the Canada side. I will not attempt to describe them, the pictures which I have seen of them give as good an idea as you could expect to get on paper. The river below the falls is quite narrow but deep and rushes along furiously under the suspension bridge, two or three hundred feet below the carriage path. Two or three of us went down a long flight of steps and clambered down the bank of the river, clear to the water's edge and drank of the river directly under the bridge. Those standing on the edge of the bank, which was almost perpendicular, looked like mere monkeys in size. The Susp. Bridge is most as great an artificial wonder and curiosity as the Falls is a natural.

We left Niagara at 11½ o'clock last night and arrived in Detroit at about 2 o'clock this afternoon. It seems to be a fixed fact that we travel nights and "lay by" if we lay by at all, in the day time.

My health is as good as it has been at any time for a year past, but I shall be glad when we get to Kanzas or somewhere where one can "stretch his weary limbs" once more, for though I am not very tired, yet sleeping for three or four successive nights in the cars is not the most comfortable way of resting, especially when cramped up with two on a seat all night. I cannot write many particulars now as I have hardly time and am crowded up in "Johnson's Hotel," about 75 or 100 men talking all around me.

We have great times with our baggage, hunting for it every time we change cars, and generally, as it has happened, in the dark. I keep a little minature sort of a journal as we go along, and will write more fully of our journey when I get a chance.

Have you found a printer yet? I hope I shall find a letter from home at Kanzas City when I get there. I might go and back again while we are going, we might as [well] sail around Cape Horn as to go this way. I send a copy of today's Tribune.

Yours in haste,
T. C. Wells.

Steamer Lonora Missouri River
My dear father, Saturday March 24, 1855

It is several days since I sent a letter to you and I suppose you would like to hear from us once more. At about noon last Tuesday we left St. Louis on the "Steamer Lonora" with about 300 passengers on board, and when you know that the *steamers* this way are *flat bottom* and those of the larger size among which our boat may be ranked, are only about one hundred feet long, you will not *imagine* but know that we are rather short for room and accommodations. This steamboating up the Missouri, when the water is as low as it is now, in a crowded boat is just the meanest way of getting along that ever I tried. By far the greater portion of us have to sleep on mattresses on the floor, and I believe that we should be more comfortable and less liable to catch cold if we slept out of doors. As it is I do not believe there are a dozen on board who have not taken a severe cold and I have not escaped. For two or three days it made me most or quite sick and that is the reason why I have not written before since I have been on the river. I am much better now, however, and feel about well today.

If we have good luck and don't get stuck in a sand bar we shall get to Kansas City a little after noon today. The Missouri is a strange river, at least it seems so to us Eastern people. Every few minutes we run against a snag which one would think would knock a hole through the bottom of the boat, and every day, and sometimes several times a day we are delayed from half an hour to three or four hours on a sand bar. Yesterday we remained stationary for full half a day on this account and after all had been done that the captain thought best he sent about 250 of us ashore, most of us without our dinner, and we had to [walk] five or six miles around to a point while the steamer worked her way across the bar. We got our dinner and supper together. Our Yankees say that they expected to meet with some hardships in Kanzas and have prepared for it, but such hard times in the cars and on the boat is something that they had no reason to expect. They did not bargain or pay for it, and I assure you they do not like it. We have formed an association among ourselves and shall probably, quite a large number of us, settle together. We expect to hear from Mr. Goodnow[3] in Kansas City and can then tell perhaps about where we shall go. The Missourians, some of them, are making a tremendous row about the *"pauper Yankees,"* as they call them, coming out to make Kanzas a free state; but some of them talk very reasonable on the subject. I think there is more danger of being frightened than hurt by them. How do you all do? I want to hear from you *very much*, and hope I shall when I get to K. C.

It is most time for dinner and the servants, *not slaves*, will want the tables and chairs, and I must stop writing. We have just been

---

3. For biographical sketch of Isaac T. Goodnow, one of the founders of Bluemont College, see *Kansas Historical Collections*, v. VII, p. 170.

walking over a bad bar on "stilts," I call them, two long, strong, pieces of timber by means of which they walk over sand bars, sticking one end in the sand, and with rope and tackle raising the boat up while the paddle wheels drive the boat along. I will try to write to mother soon and give a sort of history of my journey. Love to all. Yours affectionately in haste,

T. C. Wells

Dear Mother, Kansas City, Mo. Sunday
March 25, 1855.

We did not arrive at this place until after dusk last evening, owing to snags, etc. in the river. indeed we have been behind time and had to wait for trains and boat at almost every station so that instead of coming here in eight days as we ought to and as many do when the trains connect we have been twelve days tossed about with night and day without decent accommodations, and without stoping a single night to rest ones weary bones, even on the boat we had to sleep on the floor, and I doubt not but that I should have felt better and stronger had I remained in a chair by the stove, as, indeed, I did one night. Last night for the first time, more fortunate than some of the company, I obtained a good bed on a bedstead with only three other persons in the room, and I assure you I enjoyed it. It is a luxury which those only know how to value who have been for some days deprived of it. My cold has not entirely left me, I cough a little, but hope soon to be well. But enough of the *blue* in the past, now for a word on the prospects of the future. We have not heard definitely from Mr. Goodnow, but know that he has gone up the river toward Fort Riley, and the company have good reason to expect to see him in Lawrence, about fifty miles from here, for which place most of them expect to start tomorrow, though I am sorry to say that quite a large number started today. We have a goodly number of very fine men, and women too, but we have also a large number of such as I have no desire to associate with, many of whom I expect and hope will separate from the company and some go back home. I am not yet decided whether to go with the company toward Fort Riley or independent of them start for Council City. Am strongly inclined to the latter place. It is highly spoken of by all who have been there, both as to the character of the people and its situation. It is on an elevated prairie country at a distance from the river, and the low bottom lands having wells of the best water in the territory, and on either side is a stream of clear running water, and there is a good opportunity for selecting a good *claim* and a city lot by paying five dollars for a share of the company's stock. I did [not] hear anything from home here. Perhaps you have not received a letter from me, though I have sent three before these and a paper.

I feel rather tired and sleepy and fear that I shall not be able to secure a bed unless I occupy it soon "Squatter Law," or rather *grab* law is supreme in this part of the country and has been with us ever since we started from Boston.

I hope that the next time that I write I shall be able to inform you where to direct letters to your humble servant and affectionate son, T. C. Wells

Remember me kindly to friends, and tell *some* of them that I shall try to write to them when I can find an opportunity to do so.

T. C. W.

According to *directions* I send a feather from the banks of the Missouri and a piece of the inside bark of a tree near the far famed Kansas river.

Hope all are well.

Please Write direct Topeka Kanzas Ter. (and I will find your letters)

My Dear Mother, Topeka, K. T., April 1, 55.

Here I am in the far famed Kanzas Territory, we left Kanzas city on Monday last at about noon, and passing through Westport, a large Missourian town, we soon came upon the *Indian reserve* (belonging to the Shawnee's) which extends for thirty miles up the Kanzas or Kaw river. We went as far as Mill Creek the first day, called about twenty miles from Kanzas, and there we hired for the night an old log cabin of the Indians, made a good fire in the old fireplace, made some coffee, which we drank with our crackers and gingerbread, and then we all, seven in number, spread down our blankets etc., pulled off our boots and overcoats, and, tried to go to sleep. 'Twas a pretty cold night, the wind whistled through the holes in the old cabin, which was thoroughly ventilated, as we could put both hands between most any of the logs, but we fastened our tent up on the windy side, and slept quite comfortably. The next morning we started for Lawrence City about thirty miles further up the river. We found the ground frozen in the morning, but it grew warmer as soon as the sun was well up, and we had quite a good day for traveling. We found no settlements on the road, except once in a while an Indian cabin, but we saw a plenty of rich rolling prairie, with here and there a ravine skirted with timber, and generally a spring or brook at the bottom. We traveled nearly all day among a large party of *Missourians,* number about 200, who were going to Lawrence to *vote* and a pretty rough looking set they were, some on horseback, some in covered wagons, and others on foot, all hardy, sunburnt, frontier men, and all well armed with guns, revolvers and bowie knives. We were often asked what *county* (in Missouri) we came from, and when they learned that we were from the East we had the *pleasure* of being called *"damned Yankees,"* etc., but they did not succeed in frightening us or in driving us back, though they assured us that they could fire some twenty shots each, and that they had a six pounder with them. The thing which I was most afraid of was a barrel of whisky which we discovered in one of their wagons. They all stoped at the Wakarusha, where we pased their camp toward Lawrence about five mile distant but I can tell you those five miles were long ones, for although we hired a team to carry our luggage we had to walk ourselves, and thirty miles is something of a walk for a beginer especially when we had come twenty miles the afternoon before. However we arrived at L. at near sunset, a little after and put up at Page's Hotel, the best in the City but poor enough at that. For breakfast, dinner, and supper we had fried pork, and very *poor bread, biscuit* and *cornbread,* a little miserable butter, and molasses. We were not able to procure a team to carry us further on our journey, and were therefore obliged to remain several days in L.

I will describe L. to you in my next if nothing prevents. We came here (Topeka) yesterday, and start for Big Blue, where Mr. Goodnow is, tomorrow. We are both well. James has gone to sleep.

Yours affectionately in haste,
T. C. Wells

Dear Father   Cedar Creek, May 28, 1855.

In my letter to mother a few days ago I expressed a wish for you to send me some money and suggested that you send it in your letters to me in fifty dollar notes on Wa[kefield] Bank. But as letters come so irregularly here I do not think it will be safe to send money thus, and I do not know as you can send to me at all unless you can procure a check, payable to my order, on some banking house in St. Louis. I suppose I can get along without the money, but I am and shall be pretty short of funds until I either raise something on my claim to sell, or else sell the "claim" itself.

As to the last I have thought that I should not try very much to do it until toward fall, as it is hardly safe to go down the river now on account of cholera, and I think it will be much easier to find a purchaser in three or four months from now than at present.

I like the country here very much, it is beautiful now that every thing is green; but I do *not* like the *idea* much more the reality of having no letters or communication from home, neither do I like to think that you may be sick and have no one to assist you.

For these reasons I feel often that I ought to come home though if it were not for these I could get along very well here for two or three years, but I should want very much to see you all before the end of that time.

I have no doubt but that letters have been mailed to me from home often but I have received but one as yet—that dated March 22.

I have also written home about once a week ever since I came here, I do not know whether you receive them regularly or not.

Three deer ran by the cabin a few days ago, I have seen quite a number since I have been here, but not near enough to get a shot at them.

I shot a turtle in the creek last Saturday which weighed twenty one lbs. I should like to get another of the "Narragansett Times," I heard while down to Mr. Dyer's[4] to meeting yesterday that there was a paper there for me, but it could not be found then, perhaps I may get it today. We have preaching somewhere within a dozen miles twice each Sabbath and a Sunday School has just been started at Mr. Dyer's. But we have no prayer meetings here and I miss them very much more than almost any thing else. We are so much scattered here that it is hardly possible to get together more than once in a week and that of course is on the Sabbath.

Does the interest continue in the meetings at Wakefield? And

---

4. Samuel D. Dyer, a native of Tennessee, came to Kansas in 1843, settling at Fort Scott, where he worked for the government as a mechanic. In 1853 he was transferred to Juniata to operate a ferry across the Blue river on the military road between Fort Leavenworth and Fort Riley, and he later collected toll on the bridge that replaced the ferry. He had served as a major in the Black Hawk war and was already an old man when he came to what is now Pottawatomie county.

Mr. Dyer homesteaded land at the mouth of Cedar creek where old Juniata was located. His house served for several years as a voting precinct and also as a preaching place for ministers of all denominations. The first county jail was the cellar under a little store kept by him. He was noted for his generosity and his place was designated as a free hotel. Politically he was a Free-State Democrat. He was elected justice of the peace in 1858 and held this office for a number of years. Mr. and Mrs. Dyer were the parents of eleven children. He lived on his farm until his death February 1, 1875. For another biographical sketch of Mr. Dyer, see *The Kansas Historical Quarterly*, v. III, pp. 120-123.

how is the state of religious feeling in Kingston? I wish that they might have a real genuine revival there.

James has not left me yet and he may not for some time but if he should I do not know but I should be obliged to give up *keeping house* as it would be *rather* lonely for often we do not see another person for several days, sometimes for more than a week, unless we happen off three or four miles to look for them.

Love to all friends, and hoping that *you* and *yours* are well

I am yours affectionately,

T. C. Wells

My dear Mother,   Cedar Creek, June 11 55

I found at Mr. Dyer's yesterday, when I went down to meeting, a letter from you, and three papers all "Narragansett Times" I assure you I was not at all sorry to get them all but especially glad was I to get the letter.

James was down to Dyer's this morning and brought me a letter from Lizzie which had lodged for sometime in the P. O. at the Catholic Mission[5] and would have remained in those comfortable, quarters, *no-one* knows how long, if an acquaintence of mine had not passed through there and spying it out brought it up to me. The Mission is about thirty miles from here and why in the name of reason the [letter] should stop there I cannot tell, for it was plainly directed to the care of S. D. Dyer, &c. I was glad to get a letter from Lizzie too and will try to answer it soon. Yesterday was the second time that I have received either letter or paper since I left home and "good news from a far country" is worth having I can tell you. James, too, has been favoured with letters, he received *three* from Prov. yesterday which were very acceptable though he would have prefered *one* from home.

A man from Topeka says that there are two or three letters there for me which the P. M. would not let him have as he did not remember my whole name. I am going to start after them tomorrow if nothing happens to prevent. What would you think in the East of going over *fifty miles* after one or two letters and that on horse back? but we do not think so much of riding fifty miles here as you *eastern* people would of going two, provided we both have the same mode of conveyance. James has heard that there is a letter for him at the Mission and I can stop and get it for him.

. . . You tell me in your letter of a number of things that you

---

5. Doubtless St. Mary's mission, established in 1848.

"want to know" and I will try to inform you though perhaps, I have already given some of the desired information in previous letters that you have not yet received. But to the point. I *do* cook myself, sometimes James cooks but I generally do that part of the business. We make wheat bread, biscuit griddle cakes, (flapjacks west) puddings, etc., soups out of turtles and squirrels, boil duck, snipe and other birds and sometimes ham and also eggs.—and we fry ham and fish. Of course I have a good cook stove. We have made nothing but what we could eat and tasted good; have not had sour bread once, neither have we burnt it up, had nothing to throw away because 'twas not good. Can you beat that? We do most of our own washing also though we carry some of our shirts, pants, etc., which need starching and ironing about a mile over the bluffs where we get them "done up" for us at $1 a doz. as for coats and vests they remain in our trunks the most of the time walk out perhaps once a week or so, that's all. I have a very good garden, but more than that I did not get ploughed as the man whom I engaged to "break up" for me disappointed me; he could not make it go. We do have meeting once a day on the Sabbath at Mr. Dyer's also an interesting S. School both conducted by Methodists. There are meetings held in other places in the neighborhood but too far off for us to attend as we should have to go nine or ten miles each way and that takes too long Sunday afternoon. I am glad you and father had an opportunity to *take the air* while Henry was at home. Every one says that I look much better than when I came here. Indeed, I *know* that I am better, am not sick at all now. The country agrees with me well, and all the people here to whom I have spoken of leaving say that they don't want me to go, and that I ought not to leave the country but I think I shall come home before Spring.

Yours aff———

T. C. Wells

Mrs. Thos. P. Wells,   Cedar Creek July 21/55
    My Dear Mother,   Juniata Kansas Ter.

I received two letters last Tuesday morning, one from you and one from Henry both of the same date June 18. May 11th was the date of the last letter which I had received, it was from Lizzie. It seemed a long time since I had heard from home—more than nine weeks. I am glad you all had so nice a visit in East Lynne and hope grandfather will soon get well.

So I have two new cousins, have I? that is good but I am sorry to hear that aunts E. and L. are so sick, hope to hear that they are better in the next letter.

Thus it is joy and sorrow are mingled here below, but even while sad we may yet be really happy and looking beyond above these present sorrows expect a life of eternal joy. May we not only expect but receive that life.

I have received every number of the "Times" as far as June 23rd. No. 8 and they are very welcome visitors, especially when one lives alone. A family moved in above me yesterday, consisting of a father, mother, and four daughters; they are three fourths of a mile from my cabin and out of sight behind the bluffs.

My horse was found a few days after he was lost, about thirty miles down the river. He was not just such a horse as I wanted and I traded him off together with my wagon for a pair of steers and another horse. In less than an hour afterwards I sold the steers for more than the horse was worth, and I can sell the horse that I have now for all that I could have got for the wagon; he is worth more to me than the one that I had before.

I do not like to have father so closely confined and feel badly every time I think about him; but it does not seem to me best to return home quite yet. Even if it was perfectly safe going down the Missouri, I fear that my ill health might return if I should go east now and then I should be of little use to any one, but I am so well here that I hope if I remain until cold weather I shall have so entirely recovered that my health will not be affected by the Atlantic fogs. The Missourians are circulating all kinds of evil reports about Kanzas, to discourage northern imigration, but they are not founded in fact. We feel in no danger whatever from hostile indians or cholera. It is very healthy here, and, in this section at least, the crops look finely and promise a plentiful harvest. I hope the South Kingston people will succeed in establishing a good public Library and erect a suitable building.

I am obliged to Joanna for her kind wishes. Tell her that I get along nicely cooking for myself and dog which is my only companion now. I did cook the turtle I shot and it was very good. Tell father that, Providence permitting, I will come home as soon as I well can and take [care] of the printing office, paper, or bank, and, if possible, all together for a while and let him rest a little. Tell Lizzie if *it* does not happen before Thanksgiving I will try to be there.

I am glad father did not send any money. I wrote for him not to send it in another letter immediately afterward. Did he not get it.

We have had a real rainy day just such as we have in the east, here the rain usually comes in thunder showers and rains very hard. Love to all, not forgetting Fanny Burdick. She sent love to me in one of your former letters and I neglected to *acknowledge the receipt* of it, so I send a *double portion* now to *make up*.

Yours affectionately   T. C. Wells

Mrs. Thos. P. Wells,   Juniata, Kanzas T., Aug. 9, 1855.

Dear Mother,

I am happy to say that I get your letters quite regularly now; the last reached me in less than a month after it was written.

It would have given me much pleasure to have made one of your pic-nic party on the *fourth* no doubt you all had a very fine time. I am sorry, on father's account that I shall not be able to settle up my affairs so as to go home before the middle or last of November.

I still sleep in my log cabin, but take my meals in Mr. Hanna's family, three quarters of a mile up the creek.

I began to get quite lonely and after my cow was gone I decided not to keep house for myself any longer for the present.

I received a very good offer for my horse and cow, and thought best to sell as I might not again get so good an opportunity.

I "reckon" $45. dollars is a good price to get for a cow and calf in Kanzas when you can buy as many as you please for from $15, to $25. in Missouri but mine was a little extra.

The cholera has been raging terribly at Fort Reiley, chiefly among the soldiers who were in the habit of drinking large quantities of whiskey. Some forty five or fifty persons died there last week. I believe there have been no cases since Sunday.

There is but little sickness in this part of the territory—no cholera.

We have not had a "wet" season but have been favored with sufficient rain to make the corn fields look finely.

I picked a ripe tomato in my garden today, the first I have seen this season, I shall have plenty of them soon. I have no lack of garden vegetables, except beans which don't do very well here this season, and I turn them in, in part pay for my board.

You ask—How long it takes me to go fifty miles. It is about fifty five miles from Topeka here, and I rode home on a very hard riding horse, in a day and half, with an easy riding horse it would not take as long.

I had an invitation to go on a grape hunt last Monday, with about a dozen young people of both sexes and had a nice time. I may tell you more about it some other time. They were the smallest grapes I ever saw, not much larger than our whortleberries, but when ripe are quite good.

Wild plums grow about here, I have found some plum bushes up the creek that hang very full indeed but they are not yet ripe.

Our *Missouri* Legislature has adjourned without accomplishing anything. The governor would not recognize them as a legal body while at the Shawnee Mission, and the people will not trouble themselves to obey any laws passed by such a sham Legislature.

The truth is many of the members were Missourians, elected by fraud and mob force, and some of [them] now live in Missouri.

Yours affectionately
T. C. Wells

Mrs. Thomas P. Wells,   Juniata, Kanzas T., Aug. 29/55
    My Dear Mother,

I have neglected writing to you for some time past, waiting to receive a letter from you first, but it does not come and I will put off writing no longer. It is eight weeks tomorrow since your last letter was written and the mail will not be here again under ten days or a fortnight.

I soon became tired of sleeping alone in my cabin and taking my meals, so far away, and so I determined to move up to Mr. Hanna's altogether and for the last three weeks have been "camping out" with them.

I am now in the little tent that I brought from home, it has been quite useful both to me and others. If I should tell you how we live here you would think we had rather a hard time—you could not bear it,—'twould kill you, etc., but I like it very well especially in pleasant weather 'tis not quite so pleasant when it storms. The cooking is all done over the fire out of doors, something as yould cook at a picnic in the east. We set our table under a large oak tree and under its shade we sit and talk or read when we have nothing else to do. We had a wedding here last week out of doors! one of Mr. Hanna's daughters was married to a Mr. Dyer who lives at Juniata about four miles from here, he is a son of the old man Dyer who is spoken of in Boynton's "Journey through Kanzas," which you saw while I was at home. The *knot* was tied at four o'clock last Thursday evening.

Everything was prepared before hand as well as could be done under the circumstances. A long table was set under the trees, loaded with cake of various kinds, tarts made from native grapes, which by the way are much smaller than the wild grapes of the east, custards, preserves etc., while at a side table was roast pork, mutton and chicken in abundance. At about three o'clock the bridegroom and his friends with the "preacher" came a part in two large two horse wagons and others on horse-back. The bridegroom was dressed in black coat and pants with white vest and the bride in pure white with a head dress also of white. At the appointed hour the relations and friends formed a semicircle; the bride and bridegroom stood up alone in front and the minister before them. After they had promised to love, respect, obey, etc., as long as they both should live they were pronounced man and wife. The minister then made a prayer commending them and their friends to the care of God and asking *his* blessing upon them. Then all the party were invited to partake of the refreshments prepared for them. Two young men were selected to carve the meat etc., for the first table. When they were through others who could not find room at first together with the carvers took their places and were waited on in turn. After dinner all were invited to the "infare" or second wedding at the house of Mr. Dyer on the morrow.

After a little while most of the friends went home, but the bride and bridegroom with one of his sisters and two or three others remained all night.

On the next morning I had the pleasure of riding down with them to the *infare* where we remained until nearly night. This time the table was set in a large log house, a story and a half high, containing four rooms with a kitchen built on one side, this is a first class house in Kansas.

We were supplied with a greater variety of nice things than we had the day before. More than fifty persons were there to take dinner with them.

After dinner some of the company took a walk to the water melon patch, eat as many as they wished and went back loaded with melons for those that they had left behind. We had no dancing, no instrumental music but considerable time was spent in singing *sacred* songs. So you have a brief description of a wedding in Kanzas.

They say that there will be a number of weddings more in a short time, as all of the young men have become tired of keeping batchelor's hall.

A number of [us] went a plumming yesterday, I have been once before. We had a pleasant time and came home loaded with as many plums as we could bring.

They grow on bushes not much larger than our current bushes, they would grow larger, but the prairie fires keep them down. The plums were very thick and so ripe that we could scarcely touch the bushes without shaking them to the ground. These plums are of a yellowish red when ripe, are nearly as large as our tame plums and are very sweet and good. I have saved some of the seed to carry east.

I have had about six acres of prairie broken and shall probably have ten or twelve in all, which will make quite a good start for *some one* next spring. It may possibly be me for if my health should not continue good in the east this winter I do not know what I can do better than return here and go to farming in earnest.

I have spoken with two or three physicians and they together with all the old people who have lived in different parts of the country, say that I am very foolish to think of returning east to live and that the first cold I catch there will bring on my former sickness as bad or worse than ever. I intend however to go home this fall, and try it next winter, though I do not expect to be as well in the east. I have made up my mind not to sell my claim this fall unless I am offered a very good price but leave it in the care of some friend until spring and then if I remain in the east I can get them to sell it for me or if I decide to come back it will be ready for me. If I should return here again I wish you and father, etc, would come too. It would be much better for father's health and I think you could all be happy. It will not cost much to live out here after the first year, and it may be good for your health too. There have been one hundred and thirty or forty deaths of cholera at Fort Reilly but in this part of the country it has continued quite healthy. The cholera has not appeared at all here I believe.

I hope to hear from you soon.

My health continues good and I expect to be on my way home in a little more than two months. I have written to Amos [?] but have not yet heard from him. Love to all,

Yours affectionately

T. C. Wells

Thos. P. Wells Esq.,   Juniata, Kansas Territory
    My dear Father,   Oct. 12th, 1855.

    I was very glad to receive a letter from you about ten days ago, the first you have written me since I have been in Kansas.

    I received five or six other letters at the same time and as many papers. I have not been well for a part of the time since having had two pretty severe attacks of *fever* and *ague,* I have also had to spend considerable time in my garden, gathering beans, fixing fence etc., and have not had an opportunity to answer your letter before now.

    I have got over the ague entirely I hope for there is nothing pleasant about it.

    A lot of unruly oxen broke into my garden and destroyed some thirty dollars worth of things—most too bad!

    Your paper takes so much of your time that I am almost sorry that you ever commenced publishing it for even if it paid well your health is worth much more to you than money.

    Had I known two months before how you felt about my remaining here I would have made arrangements to stay here a year or two at least for although I have been much better here than I was in the east yet I do not feel that I have entirely recovered, and to tell the truth I am almost afraid to return home. I intend to start next month however and spend the winter with you if I am able but I think I will have to return here in the spring. We will talk about this when we see each other if we are permitted to meet again.

    You ask about Mr. Goodnow;—he and his wife live about ten miles from me, but I see them occasionally, they both have been sick for sometime past. Mr. G. has got pretty well but his wife is very poorly yet. Three claims have been taken on our creek since I first settled here—two above me and one on a small branch half a mile southeast of my claim.

    The emigration comes in rather slowly this fall as yet, owing to our political troubles, the doings of our *sham legislature* and the border ruffians under Atchison and Stringfellow, but people need not fear to come to Kanzas the *Missouri* laws are a *dead letter* to Kanzas freemen, their hirelings *dare* not enforce them There are eight free state men to two who are in favor of slavery in the territory and the ratio is constantly increasing in favor of freedom *Kanzas must* and *will* be *free.* Nearly every one who comes here wants a claim and so houses are seldom built nearer than half a mile of each other, but at Manhattan, ten miles from me, there are fifteen or eighteen houses and there is a good prospect of soon having quite a town there.

There are but two or three families very near Mr. Dyer's but he has a fine situation for trading and probably others will build near him. He lives 2½ or 3 miles from me. Nearly all our meal and flour is ground in the States 110 to 130 miles from here, but there are mills at Lawrance, 80 miles, and at Topeka 55 miles, and we shall have mills here this fall. There are persons who make a business of going to the States after provisions, of course we purchase here.

Cattle will sometimes get there [sic] living here without feeding, but it is best to allow them about a ton of hay to the head, which is quite sufficient for them to winter on. We can cut plenty of hay here on the prairies. Do not direct any more letters to me at this place, as I shall not be here when they arrive. I hope to write mother soon. I have also unanswered letters from Henry, Amos, and Theodore which I will try to remember soon.

Yours Affectionately
Thomas C. Wells

Mrs. Thos. P. Wells,   Juniata, Kanzas Ter. Oct. 26/54. [1855]
My Dear Mother

If you had ever spent a month or two "camping out" in tents you would excuse me for not being more regular in writing home of late.

But beside living in tents I have had two or three touches of fever and ague within a few weeks and have not felt much like writing or doing much of anything else for a good part of the time.

I have now three unanswered letters of yours before me, but have received none since I wrote father a few days ago. The last letter I have had was from Henry, dated Sept 11.

We have just moved into a *house*, that is a pile of logs with a roof on the top of them. The spaces between the logs are not filled up yet, but we have a tent cloth, wagon cover, quilts, comforters, etc hung up around the sides to keep off the wind for the present, and have, also, a tent set up inside of the house; we have no chimney but build our fires on the ground in one corner of the house. Of course we have no cellar or second story, and old mother earth serves us for a floor. But this is a great improvement on "camping out" as we have done Now we are quite comfortable although we have some cold, frosty, weather. I suppose however, that if you could look in upon us and see just how we live, you would think that you could not endure it for a week, " 'twould kill you."

. . . My letter will not be very well connected this time for I read your letters and then write down whatever thought they suggest in the same order that they come into my head. . . .

You say I have written nothing about the flowers in this country. We have some that are very pretty, and I have saved seeds of as many as I could so that if nothing happens to prevent you may yet see some of the Kanzas flowers in the east. I intend, also, to bring with me some garden seeds. . . .

You and Henry and Theodore keep wishing me to "write for the "Times", but really that is out of my line of business. I know not what I could write that would be interesting to the people, the newspapers are all so full about Kanzas that I could hardly write anything new on that subject, and I conclude that the "Times" has correspondents enough without me. . . .

The two Kansas elections have just come off, the pro-slavery election, called by the sham Legislature occurred one week before the free state election which was called by the people assembled in convention.

We did not have pro-slavery men enough in our precinct to hold an election, but there were seventy nine free State votes cast.

In the whole territory the pro-slavery people report 1,800 votes cast for Gen. Whitefield [John W. Whitfield] and probably half of them were foreign votes.

Gov. Reeder the free state candidate received more than 4,000 votes! I think congress will hardly refuse to receive him as delegate from Kanzas, if they do there will be a *fuss*.

You may not get any more letters from me, as I shall probably start for the east in a few days, and shall be able to travel as fast as a letter. I may be delayed on the way, however, and you need not expect to see me much befor the first of Dec. I shall not bring home but a few of my things as I shall expect to come back in the Spring even if I remain here only through another summer.

Yours affectionately
Thomas C. Wells.

Mrs Thomas P. Wells

Johnston's Hotel, Detroit
Mich, 2½ o'clock Mar 27/56

My Dear Mother,

We arrived here at about half past one this P. M. four hours behind our time owing to the immense length of our train. I think we had on fourteen cars.

We crossed Susp bridge at about midnight and last night, we did not have time to go to the falls but caught a glimpse of them as we crossed the bridge a little before dark. I made a mistake in saying above that we crossed at midnight that was the time that we started for Detroit.

We were behind on the Hudson River R. R. and have been behind ever since, so that we have to lay by and wait for trains in the day time and travel nights in order to reach St Louis before Sunday which we wish to do if possible.

Theodore gets so excited at what he sees sometimes that he can hardly control himself; coming through western Canada this morning he almost jumped up and down at the sight of the prairie we were passing through, I don't know what he will do with himself when he sees the immense prairies of Illinois, the Missisipi and Missouri rivers etc. etc.

Detroit is a beautiful city in my opinion, it is regularly laid out in straight, wide streets, well paved and good side walks, and contains several very fine churches, and hotels. I hope I shall get a letter from you as soon as I reach Juniata and would like very much to receive letters from father, Henry, and others in Wakefield whom I might mention Write me what father is going to do about the Times as soon as he decides.

Do you feel any better than when we left?—you were most sick then I hope all are well.

We are not sick, but are rather tired of traveling night and day in the cars; we shall finish that business, however, for the present, in two or three days.

Theodore is so full of *seeing* that he thought he could not write now. There is a great deal of snow in western N. Y. and in Canada, and I am afraid that we are too early to drive stock up into the territory if so we shall go right along and attend to something else first and come down to the States again in a few weeks to get our cows oxen etc

Yours truly, in haste

I enclose a few spring flowers

Thomas C. Wells

Apr 3, 1856,
Steamer Jas H Lucas
Missouri River.

My dear Mother

I believe my last letter home was written from Detroit Mich. but Theodore has written you since. We left the beautiful city of Detroit one week ago to-day, at six o'clock P. M. and arrived in Chicago, the "Garden City of the West," at about eight o'clock the next morning.

As we had two or three hours to ourselves before the train started for St. Louis, we went to the American Hotel and took breakfast. Theodore and myself then started up State St to find our old friend Benj Watson while, our companion Mr Wilson went in another part of the city to hunt up an old acquaintance of his.

We found Ben at the store door and as may be imagined somewhat surprised to see us, for though he had heard that we were coming and had expected us two or three weeks before he had, I think, quite given us up, thinking that we [had] gone some other rout or passed through the city without seeing him. After talking a few minutes he started with us for the Depot which is about a mile from his store, and there he introduced us to one of his partners, the yonger Mr. Otis, who happened to be on the spot.

I received a much more favorable impression of Chicago this time than at either of my previous visits—the mud was all frozen up and I had a better opportunity to run around.

At half past nine we started on the Chicago, Alton, and St Louis R. R. for St Louis and were accompanied for thirty or forty miles by Mr Otis who had business in a little village at that distance from Chicago. We found him very sociable and agreable.

We arrived among the one hundred and forty thousand inhabitants of St Louis at a little before three o'clock A. M. and immediately proceeded to the Missouri Hotel, went to bed and slept soundly until late breakfast time. This was the first time we had enjoyed a bed since we left the Commodore's births in L Island sound.

On Saturday we spent the time in hunting up a Missouri River boat, and doing some of our shopping. Sunday was quite unpleasant, cloudy damp, and in the afternoon it snowed hard for two or three hours, accompanied by considerable *thunder* and *lightening,* a new thing in my experience—thunder and lightening in a snow storm. I did not feel at all well, having taken a very bad cold, on my journey, and did not go to meeting in the day time, but was persuaded [to go to] Dr. Rice's church in the evening by a yong man who had heard the Dr. preach in the morning and was very much pleased with him. I was disappointed in not hearing him as a stranger preached in the evening.

We went on board the Steamer J. H. Lucas on Monday Morning and engaged passage for Kansas City. The Lucas is a very fine boat, the *fastest* on the river, has a very gentlemanly Master and clerk and good accomodations. We were so fortunate as to obtain good State rooms, many of the passengers have to sleep on mattrasses on the floor. As the[y] did not advertise to start until Tuesday at 4 o'clk, we had plenty of time to walk about St Louis, *spend* as much *money* as we chose at the stores and hear more swaring and profane talking than we could in the same time in any other city with which I am acquainted.

An immense quantity of business is done in St L. I can liken the appearance of the levee to nothing than B. Way in N. Y. in a very busy time, only instead being enclosed by two rows of buildings, it is bounded of one side by a long line of splendid Steamers on the Missisippi river.

St L. is a good market, anything can be purchased there for money, though sometimes a good deal of that useful article is required.

We live finely on board the boat. The table is set nearly the whole length of the cabin, and at dinner time is loaded with almost every thing in the eatable sort. Beef, pork, ham, veal, turky, chicken duck fish etc cooked in every style, pies of apple, peach, plums, prunes, blackberries, cranberries, etc various kinds of puddings tarts, fruit, nuts, etc. Today we had fresh greens, yesterday lettuce, you would enjoy it I know especially as you would not be seasick on the river.

Quite a number of people are on board from South Carolina and Georgia going to Kansas. What think you of that? I will tell you what I think. Nine tenths of them will return home, or at least leave Kansas before they have been there three months. They have left their old homes in beautiful Springtime, all nature looking green and luxuriant—their warm and suny homes in the South, for the windy plains of Kansas, as yet brown with the frosts of winter. They have taken the wrong time to emigrate and the new country will not suit them.

And of those who do remain, nine out of ten will ere long turn free state men. They will find it for their interest to do so, and when their interest decides against slavery they will both see and acknowledge that the whole system is entirely wrong. We anticipate no trouble from them. And indeed we expect that the worst trouble is over and that we shall be left comparatively to ourselves, at least we hope so.

The free state people must eventually conquor—the South cannot compete with the North in sending emigrants, and—very few of the small number who come from the South dare to bring Slaves with them Theodore is not very well but is better than he has been.

Remember me to inquiring friends, I shall try to write some of them when I get to the end of my journey, and should in the mean time be very happy to have about a dozen of them write me. The jarring of the boat makes it quite difficult to write distinctly and I have written considerably in haste in order to finish before supper time Yours affect'ly

Juniata Kansas Ter.

Apr 13th. I expected to have sent this letter long ago, and you will doubtless wonder before you get it why I do not write.

The mail leaves here tomorrow and I will just write a little more, and send this and write again some other day and give more particulars. We landed at Leavenworth City, instead of Lexington or Kansas. Leavenworth is 50 miles further up the river than Kansas City, and is 15 or 20 miles nearer the Blue than K. The road is also much better, it being the Government road from Fort L. to Fort Reiley. I was quite sick at Leavenworth had a little touch of the chills and a pretty high fever, together with a very bad cold and cough which I caught in the cars. I felt so miserably that I did not undertake to write or even send this letter which I had already partly written on the boat. Theodore was not much better off. I wrote you that he was not very well, and he was [missing] care of himself while at Leavenworth but he is getting better now quite fast. I did not buy any cows or oxen in Missouri as the grass was not high enough to keep them.

I bought a waggon in St Louis and also a plow, harrow, cultivator etc and at Weston Missouri I purchased two very good horses which brought us and a part of our things up from Leavenworth. I have got to go down to L again in a few days and get the rest of our things. There has been more trouble in Kansas this winter than I had supposed; the wrongs of the free state people have not been exagerated in the papers. The Lawrance people especially have suffered immensely. For a long time no one could go to or from Kansas City without having his baggage searched, and even now the Missourians frequently break open heavy trunks or boxes to search for Sharps rifles of which they stand in great fear. I think they must feel rather cheap at times, however, when the[y] find what the contents of the boxes really are. One which they opened in Kansas contained a *piano,* and a chest which they had opened at Leavenworth while we were there was full of books, surveyor's instruments and a few articles of clothing, and this was done at the request of the *mayor* and marshall of the city—shame on such proceedings.

When we arrived at Juniata we found the Government bridge across the Blue had been carried away by the ice. We have to cross on a ferry boat now which is rather expensive and not very pleasant business. Mr. Dyer has turned strong pro slavery and they have got a pro slavery minister there of the Methodist Church South, who says "he would as leave sell a nigger as an ox." They have organized a church under pro slavery influence and intend to do all they can to bring slaves into Kansas and drive out the yankees "for," they say, "they do not want eastern men to rule the territory."

They may do their best however, and they will not succeed, they have a class of people to deal with that are not frightened at trifles, and not withstanding their threats and their struggles Kansas will be a *free state* and and [*sic*] the territory will be ruled by eastern men.

I do not consider my claim half as valuable as I did last fall and I think I shall sell out and take one on the other side of the blue.

The claim is really an excellent one but the society is not such as I would choose it being mostly composed of western and Southern people, some of them very good neighbors in their way, and others pretty strongly tinctured with pro slavery notions, while the greater part of the settlers on the west side of the Blue are eastern men.

I have an excellent opportunity to get a claim within half a mile or so of Manhattan, only a little way from Mr. Goodnow's with eleven acres plowed land and a good spring on it. There is no wood on it, but in a few years if it is not already, it will be more valuable than my old claim.

I shall be much nearer churches—schools, stores, Post Office etc than if I remained on my old claim. I have written much more than I intended to when I commenced, but I have hard work to write any thing straight. I must either be thick-headed today or my mind if full of something else, in either case I had better stop. I hope I shall get another letter from you soon.

Yours truly
T. C. Wells

Juniata, K. T. Monday, May 5th 1856.

Mrs Thos. P. Wells

My dear Mother,

I commenced to write a letter home last Friday noon but had to leave to go to plowing and have had no opportunity to finish it until now, so I concluded to begin again and write a new letter. It rained nearly all night so that the ground is too wet to work today and I am going to improve the time in writing two or three letters.

I believe I wrote that I was going to sell my old claim and take another on the prairie. My new claim is situated about three miles west of, or rather south-west of, the ferry across the Big Blue at Juniata and about one or one and one half miles N.N.W. of Manhattan which in all probability will be much the largest town any where in this vicinity. There are at present not more than twenty five homes in Manhattan, including two stores, and one very good saw-mill with grist-mill attached which work very well. Quite a large number of houses are going up very soon, some of them will be built of stone, and another saw mill is going up within two miles of the "*city*." We expect that a Cong. Church will be built in Manhattan during the summer.

I did not remain here but two or three days after I first arrived, before I again returned to the "States" to get the rest of my things which I left at Leavenworth City.

The distance from Juniata each way is about 110 miles and I assure you it is no small undertaking to make such a journey in a two horse wagon, putting up nights at any little cabin you may chance to find on the road, making your supper and breakfast of corn-bread and bacon, with strong coffee to wash them down and eating crackers and cheese, by the roadside, for your dinner. We generally have good appetites, however, and can make a hearty meal out of the plainest fare and are tired enough at [night] to sleep well on the hardest beds even though we should be obliged to roll ourselves up in a blanket or buffalo skin and lay on the floor. Mr. Wilson went down to L with me and bought four yoke of oxen, which we took turns in driving up, and I assure you we were both pretty well tired out by the time we got back to the Blue, one week ago last Friday evening. I had a hard chill next day, and a worse one Sunday. Monday I got some quinine etc had only a very light chill and have had none since.

I hope I shall not be troubled with the chills any more, I enjoy better health now than I have done before for two months at least.

I was very glad to find some letters waiting for me when I returned from L one each, from you (enclosing one from Mr Goodnow—Did you attempt to read his hieroglyphics?—and a sort of one from Henry for which I enclose a one cent stamp—please deliver it,) Lissie, and N. A. Reed, Jun. I am sorry you have been so unwell and hope that now you have got better you will continue to improve You seem to have poor luck in getting help. Have you found no one to suit you yet?

We have received two copies of the "Times," the last first, and also two copies of the "Puritan Recorder"

We were surprised to see a notice of Mr Reynolds' death in one of the "Times." You ask about Mr Wilsons family, they did *not* come out with him and he will return east again in the fall.

I shall not get much if any more for my old claim than I shall have to give for my new one. There are no improvements on my new claim except eleven acres of broken land which I intend to plant mostly in corn this season. I want to get twenty-five or thirty acres more broken this summer and sow a part of it in wheat in the fall. I want to put a good fence around the whole which will cost me from two hundred and fifty to three hundred dollars; and I must put me up a little house which will cost me as much more. The house will be small (good size for this country) only 16x24 and a story and a half high, but it costs a sight to build here where poor lumber is worth $40. a thousand and carpenter's wages are $2.50 per day. I must also build a small stable in the fall, large enough to shelter two horses and one or two cows.

I believe I wrote that I bought a wagon and harnesses at St Louis and two horses in Weston Mo. My whole team costing me nearly $400. so you see that it costs *something* to *start* even in this country. I find that I shall come short of cash and I wish father would sell ten shares of my stock in Landholders Bank as soon as he can and send the proceeds out by Amos if he concludes to come this way, in bills of Wakefield Bank if he chooses and I will give it as good a circulation as I can. If he can not send it by Amos he may send it by letter in hundred dollar checks on Hanover Bank N. Y. and I can get them cashed here.

We are boarding for the present, and until my house is finished, which will be ten or twelve weeks perhaps, with a young couple by the name of Browning from Fitchburg Mass. We like them very much they are both members of the Cong Church organized here a few weeks ago and have family prayers morning and evening. They live in a stone house on the claim just east of mine, belonging to Mr. Wilson Mr. B. will not be able to get a house up on his own claim, which is a little further north, before fall.

We have to pay three dollars, each, per week for board and get pretty plain fair at that, but Mr. B. expects to get a cow in a few days and then we shall live somewhat better. We could board ourselves for half the expense if we had a place to live in.

The season is much more forward than it was last year; the trees have put out their leaves and the prairies are covered with the green grass and flowers. Changing claims and going a second time to the states has made me late with my garden. I have planted nothing as yet except a few seeds in a box, but as we are boarding we shall have no need for a very early garden. I intend to commence planting tomorrow. Mr & Mrs Browning and Theodore have all gone six or seven miles up the Wild Cat Creek today to get some seed corn and potatoes. The corn costs $1.50 and the potatoes *only* $4.00 per bushel.

I will stop now and write to some one else, but as this letter cannot go until next Monday I shall probably add a few lines before I send it.

Sunday, May 11th, I have been so busy plowing and planting my garden, and drawing lumber for my house, that I have not been able to add anything to this letter until now, and as it is Sunday and we have about two miles to go to meeting this morning I shall write but little today. Our mail goes out Monday mornings and comes Friday afternoon.

I recd another letter from Henry yesterday morning and quite a good one too which I will answer as soon as I can get time. I'll send no stamp now.

Theodore seems to really like the country and he is very well. I think I am getting stronger and in better health every day.

I do not remember whether I wrote you that I had had a private surveyor run the lines on my claim. I do not suppose that they will correspond exactly with the government lines, but they will not probably vary more than a few rods, so that I may be pretty sure to get all the improvements which I make before the regular survey on my own claim. There is a prayer meeting at Mr Blood's this afternoon and a church meeting of the Congregational Church. A Mrs Flagg is coming before the church as a candidate for admission. She has experienced religion within a few weeks. I expect to unite with the church (by letter) at the same time.

Yours truly, in haste
Thomas C Wells

Dear Brother,   Juniata, K. T. June 21/56

I received a letter from you a long time ago, and it should have been answered long ere this, but my time has been very much occupied and besides your letter has been mislaid and I cannot find it.

Perhaps you laugh because I make want of time an excuse for not writing and say that there are odd times enough when I might write if I chose to—might write a little at a time even if I could not finish a letter at once.

All that will do very well to talk and, indeed, I frequently have to improve such odd times or write Sundays, which I do not like to do, if I write at all, but I find very few leisure hours when I have nothing else to do but write letters.

But enough of such talk no doubt you would like to hear how we get along and the Kansas news.

Just now we are getting along finely Both of us enjoy excellent health, you would hardly know either of us. We are strong and hearty, in good flesh and burnt as black as Indians. Our corn field and garden looks well except that the grasshoppers have eaten up some things that we planted in the beds. Although every thing was planted very late, we already begin to get things from the garden—shall have peas fit to pick in a week or ten ds.

Shall commence to build my house next week—will not finish it off very nicely at present—will move into it as soon as 'tis done which will probably be in a month at most after it is commenced.

We *have had* pretty hard times in our territory since we have been here. The "border ruffians" accompanied by a large number of Southerners have been over here with the intention of either driving the Yankees home or making them submit to the laws of the *bogus legislature neither* of which they have been able to do. Gov. Shannon has enrolled the names of these mob-ocrats as part of the Kansas militia—some 500 of them, though they do not claim to be citizens of this territory.

1000 of them according to there own reports, but probably not quite so many, have been for a long time encamped in the vicinity, commiting all sorts of depredations, stealing cattle, robbing private houses, and searching, and taking whatever they wished from, every wagon or individual that attempted to pass by them, and they killed several men and took others prisoners. About the middle of May they threatened to destroy the city of Lawrance and drive the inhabitants from the territory, and we received a call from the Lawrance people for help. Although it was a very busy time for farmers and it seemed almost impossible for any one to leave, about forty of us from this vicinity took what arms we could muster and started for Lawrance. When we reached Topeka 55 miles from here and within 25 of L we heard that the Missourians had done nothing more than *threaten* the destruction of the town etc and probably would not as Col Sumner at the head of a large number of U. S. troops had threatened to fire upon the party that made the first attack.

This prevented an open fight and as we could not afford to remain a long time at Topeka for nothing we returned home, but the Missourians were permitted to remain where they were committing every kind of outrage upon the free state people.

But not content with robbing the emigrant and baggage wagons that passed along the road, and the private homes near them, and taking prisoners whom they chose of the passers by, they got five *men* (?) Shannon, Atchison, the U. S. Marshall, Gen Stringfellow, and the bogus Sheriff Jones to lead them on, marched upon Lawrance, and demanded the public and *private* arms of the people and the privilege of making what arrests they desired. The U. S. Marshall was premitted to make arrests and the public arms were given up, but the people refused to give up their private arms.

So these five men (?) with these foreign highway men to back them destroyed the free state hotel, worth with its furniture which was also destroyed $28,000., the two printing offices and the House of Dr. Robinson with all its contents, and ransacked and robbed private dwellings.

There has been some small skirmishing, but nothing of much consequence has occurred within two or three weeks that I have heard of We hear various reports—that Shannon has been removed, that Col. Sumner is at the head of affairs, and that the Territory is now under Marshall law, but do not know what to believe.

As yet all is peaceable where we are, but we know not how long it will remain so, yet it seems that the present state of things cannot last long or if it does there will be civil war between the whole North and South and then we shall be as well off here as elsewhere.

We can but hope however that these troubles will soon cease, and we trust that Christians in the east will unite their prayers with ours to the great Ruler of the Universe for a return of peace and prosperity to this part of our country and for the removal from our midst of that great evil which has caused so much disturbance— American Slavery.

The prairies look beautifully now, and you do not know how I wish father could come out here and spend two or three weeks, at least, with us. It would do him good, and I really believe he would want to move out here immediately.

I wonder if he has sent the money that I sent for on the first of May? The letter may have been miscarried. I wanted him to sell half my stock in Landholders bank and send me the proceeds either in Wakefield bills, or drafts payable to my order on Hanover bank, N. Y., I am expecting the money every week and need it very much. It costs considerable to start the first year, but if father should come out here it need not cost him half what it has me for obvious reasons.

Our last letter from home was mailed May 28th. We were very sorry to hear that Mr Burdick was so dangerously ill—is he no better?

Our letters and papers are sometimes unaccountably delayed but we have no reason to believe that the mail has ever been robbed.

Give my love to inquiring friends and tell them that when I get over my hurry (poor prospect at present) I intent to write lots of letters

Please write again soon   Your truly
To G. H. Wells   T. C. Wells.
  Wakefield, R. I.

                             Sunday morning, Juniata
My dear Mother,   K. T. July 27th 1856

I used to think it wrong to write letters of any kind on the Sabbath day, but I have somewhat changed my opinion of late, and although I would not spend Sunday in writing business letters, I do not think it wrong to spend an hour or two in writing letters to your friends any more than it would be to spend the same time in talking with them.

We recd a letter from you a week ago last Friday written just after your return from a visit to Lynne; also a note from Henry enclosed. We are glad you had a good visit. I should love to look in upon you and have a little talk with you all. I could tell you more in half an hour than I could write in all day.

Sorry the Kanzas flower seed did not come up—will try to send more this fall. I am glad you think that ambrotype so good. I wish that you and father and Herbert would have yours taken all together and send to me in the mail; it would cost but little and I should be very glad of it indeed. Theodore likes the country as well as ever, talks a little about going home once in a while, but generally sets the time as far off as a year from next fall.

We recd a letter from bro Samuel and Lissie last Friday, also one from father, both which we were very glad to get and I will try to answer them soon. Father's letter contained a draft on N. Y. for $132 9/100 which I very much needed just then. I wish father would write oftener.

The cabins or houses here are so small generally that we frequently have our meeting on the Sabbath under a tree in the woods when pleasant weather and find it much more agreeable than to be shut up in a small room. Last Sabbath the Methodists held their quarterly meeting in a grove two or three miles from here, and as there was no other preaching a great many were there. They had a "love feast," preaching by their presiding elder, (very good) administered the Sacrament of the Lord's Supper and invited all members in good standing of every evangelical church to partake, and then another sermon by the Rev. Mr. Lovejoy who has just returned from a tour to the east to raise money to build churches for his denomination in Kansas The day was pleasant and the services very interesting.

We are enjoying a time of comparative peace and quiet, though the Missourians, Georgians, etc seem to hold a grudge against Manhattan and threaten to destroy the town and arrest those who went down to Topeka, but we do not feel much in fear of them. Our field and garden look nicely and we get along with our house very well but slowly.

What do you think of what I wrote father in my last letter home? I do not think I shall keep *batch* a great while in my new house I think it will be much pleasanter having a *home,* and so does——— *somebody* else. The more I know her the better I like her. I believe she is truly a good Christian and think that you and father would both love her if you knew her.

I hope you will write often, we expect a letter from home every week.

Love to Herbert and tell him he must write once in a while to his brothers in Kansas.

Mrs. Thomas P. Wells
Wakefield, R. I.

Yours truly
Thomas C. Wells

My dear father,   Juniata, Kanzas T. Aug 2d 1856

I was very glad to get a letter from you last week, glad both for what was written and for the dft enclosed.

You speak of your garden and say that you do not see that we have vegetables any earlier than you do. Our garden was planted very late, some of our neighbors had vegetables three or four weeks earlier than we. I plant in all this season about eleven acres; nine of it in western field corn, and an acre and a half is a garden planted with potatoes, sweet corn, beans, vines, etc, etc and Browning has about half an acre in one corner for a garden I keep no other *stock* at present than two horses, 1 cow and calf some hens and a *dog*, which last is almost indispensable here to keep off the prairie wolves from the chickens etc.

We board not more than quarter of a mile from the eastern line of my claim.

I hope Henry will be successful in finding business, and when he gets a good situation I hope he will stick to it long enough to do him some good Please remember me to Morton Sweet Much obliged for the papers that you sent.

I find that it costs a great deal more to get started here than I supposed, and I shall have to raise yet more money than I have heretofore sent for. You may think that I could get along with less, but I will mention some of the principal items of expense which I have had and shall have to meet and then you may judge for yourself whether I can well get along with less.

First our fare out here cost me full	$100
1 two horse wagon and harnesses in St Louis	100
2 horses in Weston Mo	300
Plow, harrow, cultivator, rifle, & necessary sundries stove, corn planter, crockery, corn for horses etc	200
Second trip to Leavenworth for bal of things	40
board since we have been here $6.00 per week	75
It will cost me to finish my house at least	500

for my claim, due next Month............................... 150
must have a well dug and stoned up........................ 60
must build a barn this fall..................................... 250
must pay for rails, stapes, etc to fence field.................... 100
must buy provisions *some* furniture etc, etc.................... 1,875

etc. etc. etc. to commence keeping house the amt of which I cannot estimate exactly but we shall be very prudent and get along with as little as possible until we have more means to do with. I have mentioned only some of the chief things for which I have to pay money and have not estimated largely in any case; everything costs more, here than in the east, except what we can raise ourselves, and be as prudent and careful as you will it must cost a good deal to make a fair *start* and *live*. In the east the yong man just begining life for himself finds very many things already done for him by those who have gone before him; but here the land alone is given to us we have every thing to do to make a home. I started from home with about $1050. and recd a dft from you for $132.97, I shall have to take pay for my old claim mostly in breaking prairie which I shall want done for another year. I suppose I shall receive from you when that stock is sold dfts to the amt of about $550. I suppose, also, that my stock in Prov has been sold and the proceeds applied to my note at Landholders Bank, if so, I would like to have you sell the remainder of my stock in L Bank and send me the proceeds, after paying the balance of my not[e] there. With that I can, I think, get along very comfortably, I hope to raise enough corn this season to pay for my land when it comes into market and together with what we can earn by our work support us comfortably until we can gather another crop.

I would love dearly to see you out here and talk over my plans with you and would love to have you make us a visit—I might say mother and Herbert too—but suppose it would be useless to think of their coming.

A very fine man living in our vicinity formerly from Wonsocket, R. I. is going east in a week or two after his wife and sister and will return as soon as possible. I think he would be perfectly willing to take charge of any dfts that you may want to send me and I would like to have you go up there and see him if you can, as he could give you more information about Kansas affairs and how I am geting along etc in an hour or two than I could by writing a week. I will write you when he is expecting to reach R. I. or give him a letter to you to drop in the P. O. when he gets there so that you may know when to go. His name is Ambrose Todd.

I have written in much haste, you will please excuse the unsightly appearance of the letter.

Love to Mother, Herbert, and friends.

Thos. P. Wells, esq. Yours truly
Wakefield, R. I. Thomas C. Wells

My dear Mother Juniata, Aug last, 1856

We were so glad to receive a letter from you last Friday, dated Aug 10th. We received one from Henry a week or two ago and have not answered it yet—we do not know where to direct.

I feel almost ashamed to date most all of my letters to you on Sunday, but I get very little time to write during the week, and am obliged to remain at home half the day each Sabbath because, for fear of the cattle we dare not leave the corn, therefore I frequently take that time to write.

So you think it "surprising news," do you, that I am "really engaged" to be married? Did you think that I was going to remain a bachelor all my days, and live and improve my claim alone among these western wilds? If you did you are much mistaken, why I *never thought of such a thing.*

To be sure I tried that way of living last summer, but 'twas only an experiment and an experiment tried of necessity and the result proved, to my mind at least, that "it is not good for man to be alone."

Were I in different circumstances I might, perhaps, have chosen a wife among my acquaintance in the east, but one who would have made a very *pleasant* companion for a man in an eastern village, in the midst of schools and churches and the comforts and conveniences of civilization, might be poorly suited to endure the hardships and privations incident to a border life and illcontented withal.

And now I suppose you would like to have me write you a "full description" of my lady—I will try and do the best I can, and first I will endeavor to answer your questions.

She is the youngest of quite a large family of children, all of whom with the exception of herself continue to life, either married or single, near their native place not far from the centre of old Massachusetts.

Her father is still living but she lost her mother when only eleven years of age I think her father and her brothers and sisters are in comfortable circumstances though not wealthy—I have not asked and do not know the business of any of them. She is nearly as tall as myself and well proportioned, neither very light nor very dark complexion, and according to my notion very good looking. Her name is Eleanor S. Bemis. Your questions are answered.

At an early age she lost her mother as I have informed you, her health was very poor until sixteen and for four years from that time she was employed in keeping house for her father consequently her advantages for obtaining an education have been very limited in comparison with those of most young ladies in New England, though I believe they have been well improved. She is a woman of good sense and good temper and I doubt not a Christian. She is a member of the Methodist E. Church

She has no relations in Kansas but many friends. I can write no more about her at present as 'tis about time for me to go to church, and send this letter to the P. O.

We both are in good health. Theo. says he does not care much whether he goes home this fall or not but I think he would be much disapointed if he should be obliged to remain here though it may be best that he should.

My love to all the friends and please write where Henry is, and write often as you can. Yours truly in haste

T. C. Wells

Dear parents Juniata, K. T. Sept 14/56

We were very glad to get a letter from you last Friday, and to hear that you were well etc.

We are and ought to be thankful that the mail continues to come quite regularly in these troublous times. I have no reason to think that we have not recd every letter that has been sent to us from home as yet—I have recd but *one*, however, from N. A. Reed, Jr. and no papers, and but one from Amos, both of which I have answered but it is probable that Amos left the west before his letter arrived at Hastings Min. the place to which it was directed.

I will endeavor to write Nathan again soon and would write to Amos too did I know where to direct. Where is Henry now? We had a letter from him a week ago Friday written while he was in Beloit, Wis.

You must not think too much of the newspaper accts of what the pro-slavery people are going to do in Kansas, or of what either party have done or are doing here very many of them have little foundation in fact; for instance, in the last N. Y. Tribune we saw it stated that a large party of Southerners had been up in this part of Kansas, had a battle with the people of Reilley County near, Manhattan, were defeated, driven back, etc etc all of which is false, except that a party of armed Southerners did march up the Blue a few weeks ago and have returned without doing any damage that I have heard of.

There have been several battles down below between the free State and pro slavery parties in which I believe the free State parties usually if not always came off conquorors, but our news from below is rather indefinite at present and we do not know exactly what is the state of things. It is said that our new Governor has come and is intending to enforce the bogus laws, which [he] or any other man *cannot do, the people will not* acknowledge them as binding on them and they *will* remain a *dead letter* do what they may. *We* that is *Ella* and myself are not prepared to leave Kansas yet. we still live in hope and believe that we shall soon see the end of these troubles—as soon as we get another President at least if not before; but should this state of [uncertainty?] continue still longer we would endeavor to seek some more *peacable* though we would not expect to find a more healthy or fertile, country. Really I did not think of being uncle to any body quite so soon, but I suppose it is so. I am afraid it will be quite a long time before little *Susan* will see her *uncle Thomas,* but she may see uncle *Theodore* this fall. Theodore is very impatient to hear your decision with respect to his coming home this fall.

He ought to be somewhere—where he will be *under authority!* we get along pretty well together, generally, but once in a while he will get some foolish notion into his head which I can neither coax or reason out of him, for he is of just that age when young lads *think* that they know a *little* more about every thing than any one can tell them; but *after all* T. is a pretty good boy.

You complain that I have written very little about my lady *Ella,* but really I was not aware that I had been so very silent, yet I should doubtless have written more if I had not had so much else to attend to and consequently but little time to write, and I would want considerable time to give a full description of *her.* But really I do not know what to write, I answered a lot of your questions about her a while ago and wrote much more besides. What shall I say now?

Do not think that I have lost all my *common sense* (I trust I had a little though none to bost of.) since I have been in Kansas; and that in my *haste* to get a wife I have engaged myself to one *unworthy* of me or of whom after *longer acquaintance* I am *ashamed* Truly such is not the fact. The more I know of Ella—the better I become acquainted with her—the better I like her, yes the more I *love* her and am satisfied that she is just the woman to make me happy—to be, *indeed,* a *help* to me both in a temporal and spiritual sense. I surely have no reason to regret my choice and trust that I shall never have. I only wish that you could see her and get acquainted with her. I believe you both would love her and the more the better you knew her. I do not suppose that *every one* would like her, and I doubt not many would think me a foolish young man to choose a young lady for a wife *without property* or even a *finished education,* but I beg leave to be my own judge in such matters, and shall be satisfied if every body is not suited, so long as I believe that we are suited to each other. If Ella has not *wealth,* she has what is better an *affectionate heart* and good *sound sense;* and if her *school* education has been somewhat deficient, she has an *independent* and *energetic mind* that knows how to *think* for *itself* and turn to good advantage the knowledge it does possess, and she has a *home* education that few of our eastern girls possess.

Did father go to Woonsocket and see Mr. Todd? I really hope he did for he is well acquainted with Ella and has seen her folks in Mass. which I have not, and could give him more information in a conversation of a few minutes than I could in a dozen letters. He could tell also just how I am situated. I would rather give ten dollars than that father should not see him. It is strange that aunt Marian did not get her letter before I wrote her about *affairs* in particular at about the same time that I wrote you.

In seeking some business by which he can pay his own way Henry has done just as I would have done myself, only I think I should never have attempted any other way at first. I really hope he will be successfull.

It is very dry here now, we have had but very little rain for a long time I have just had a well dug and stoned up near my house—an excellent time now it has been so long dry—and have *seven* feet of *very good* water in it. I think it will not dry up very soon. This the worst month for sickness here, in the whole year very many have bilious fevers and fever and ague in verious forms. Theodore continues well, and I am well too. I had a little chill about ten days ago, but my health has been very good throughout the whole summer.

Excuse the blots on the first page I do not know how they came there.

Mr. Thomas P. Wells,   Yours truly
   Wakefield, R. I.   Thomas C Wells

I send you two flowers that *Ella* pressed; the larger one is called the "devil's shoe string" on acc't of its long tough roots which are troublesome in plowing

(To be continued in the August Quarterly)

Ferries in Kansas

PART IX—ARKANSAS RIVER—CONCLUDED

GEORGE A. ROOT

THE next ferry location upstream was near Salt City, Cowley county, between seven and eight miles from Arkansas City. On June 12, 1871, the Salt Springs Ferry Co. was chartered, its incorporators including C. R. Sipes, William Wright, W. J. Walpole, M. J. Martin and E. A. Fish. This company was capitalized at $200, with shares at $10 each. The principal office of the company was at Arkansas City, and the company proposed to operate a ferry on the river at the N. W. ¼ S. 8, T. 34, R. 3 W. This corporation was to exist for ten years, the charter being filed with the secretary of state June 17, 1871.[45]

Mr. Walpole received a license from Cowley county to operate a ferry at Salt Springs (now Geuda Springs) four miles north and five miles west of Arkansas City on August 22, 1871. Evidently Walpole did not operate for any length of time, as John Murray was given a license to operate at Salt Springs on August 22, 1872. Ferry charges were usually the same as established for the Thomas Night ferry which were: Two-horse team and wagon, 75 cents. One-horse team, 50 cents. Horse and buggy, 25 cents. One horse, 15 cents. Footman, 10 cents. Loose horses and cattle, 15 cents. Sheep and hogs, 5 cents each.[46]

In the Geuda Springs *News* of June 15, 1933, George M. Briggs related some of his experiences, and mentioned a ferry operated by a John Conley over the Arkansas at a point nearly a mile east of Geuda Springs about the year 1874, when a bridge was completed at this place.

During the flood in the river on May 20, 1877, bridges at Arkansas City, El Paso and Wichita were carried away. A similar condition must have occurred at Salt City the same year, for the Oxford *Independent* of September 6, stated that "a flat boat is being constructed upon the west side of the river and will be sent to Salt City, where it will be used in the absence of a bridge."

Just how early this ferry went into operation has not been learned. However, the *Traveler* early in October, 1877, stated that it "is well

---

45. Corporations, v. 3, p. 368.
46. Letter of Bert Moore, office of county clerk, Winfield, to author, January 9, 1936.

patronized and meets the favor of every one." In the issue of October 21, the following complimentary notice was printed:

> In another column will be seen the advertisement of the Salt City ferry offering to cross parties at any time of night or day for the small sum of twenty-five cents. The route by the way of Salt City is a good one, and generally favored by freighters going to the Indian agencies in the territory.

The advertisement follows:

> SALT CITY FERRY.—This ferry is located on one of the best crossing points on the Arkansas river, within one mile from Salt City, and on the most direct route to Caldwell and the Indian agencies. Teams or horsemen taken across at any hour of the day or night. Good shelter for stock and ample accommodations for travelers at the city.

This ferry must have operated for a number of years at this location, and is shown in Edwards' *Atlas of Cowley County, 1882*. The following are the last mentions of this enterprise we have located: "A ferryboat is to be placed on the Arkansas east of Salt City. Wm. Berkey has the contract for constructing it."—Arkansas City *Traveler*, August 29, 1877. "The boat formerly used as a ferry at Salt City will be loaded with wheat and floated down the river to Little Rock."—*Sumner County Press*, Wellington, July 25, 1878.

The next point above Salt City where a ferry operated was at the town of Oxford, about five miles distant. This town was settled in the fall of 1870, and was first known as Napawalla or Neptawa, for an Osage chief.[47]

Locally, Oxford was known as "Big Cottonwood Crossing," no doubt from the large trees bordering the river at this point. The name was changed in 1871 to Oxford. One of the first conveyances for crossing the river there was a rude dug-out or skiff, about fourteen feet long, fashioned from white ash, made about 1871 by John and Lafe Binkley and A. Morrill. The Binkley brothers operated the first store opened in the town, and the boat was probably a convenience for patrons who lived on the opposite side of the river before the ferry was put in operation.[48]

On July 1, 1871, the Oxford Ferry Co. was organized, T. J. Barton, E. S. Tonance, W. M. Boyer, J. H. Nyton and J. M. Patterson being incorporators. The capital stock of this enterprise was listed at $3,000, with shares $50 each. The principal place of business evidently had not been decided on at the time of incorporation, as the charter stated it would be at any point in the state of Kansas as best suited the convenience of the directors. T. J. Barton, Wil-

---

47. Oxford *Weekly*, 1880 or 1881. Andreas, *History of Kansas*, p. 1507.
48. Andreas, *op. cit.*, pp. 1495, 1507.

liam Barton and I. T. Confan, of Belle Plaine, and J. Romine and R. Walker, of Oxford, were named as directors for the first year. This charter was filed with the secretary of state July 5, 1871.[49] It will be seen that the company did not give any specific location for the ferry, and may not have operated one.

Just sixteen days later the Oxford Ferry and Bridge Co. was organized, the incorporators being O. E. Kimball, John G. David, Charles Tilton, John Dunlap and Thomas M. Moss. This company had a capital stock of $50,000, with shares at $100 each. The principal place of business of the new company was at Oxford, and its ferry was to be located at or near the crossing of the state road leading from Labette City, Labette county, to Meridian, Sumner county, at or near the south line of S. 12, T. 32, R. 2 E. of the Sixth P. M., the west landing adjoining the townsite. This charter was filed with the secretary of state July 21, 1871.[50]

This company obtained a license from Cowley county on July 16, 1871, and operated the ferry about a year.[51]

The following pertains to the ferry at this point and gives a good idea of the volume of travel that came to the ferry in the early days: "Mr. A. J. Keeley, the ferryman, informed the editor that on Monday (July 15) he had ferried over the river twenty-two two-horse teams, eighteen horsemen, fourteen footmen, four buggies, two four-horse teams and nineteen head of loose stock." [52]

During 1872 a toll bridge built at this point supplanted the ferry. Toll rates were 35 cents for two-horse team, Winfield charging 50 cents for a similar service. This bridge, as well as every other one in the county was destroyed by the big flood of 1877.

Several years later another ferry was started at this point. A neighboring paper mentioning the new enterprise said that "the ferry boat at Oxford tipped up and put one man in the river." A subsequent item from the same source reported the ferryboat as doing a fine business crossing freight and passengers.[53]

This ferry was supplanted by a pontoon bridge, which was in running order late in 1877 or early in 1878. An item in the Oxford *Independent*, copied in the Arkansas City *Traveler*, of January 23, 1878, said:

> The new pontoon bridge is now in place and proves to be a great success.

---

49. Corporations, v. 3, p. 412.
50. *Ibid.*, p. 435.
51. "Commissioners' Journal," Cowley county, 1871.
52. Oxford *Weekly Press*, July 17, 1872; republished in *Monitor-Press*, Wellington, July 17, 1912.
53. Arkansas City *Traveler*, June 6, 27, 1877.

The crossing of the Arkansas at this place was never better or safer in our most prosperous days.

The pontoons, five in number, are safely anchored, and stayed by strong guy ropes, and the intervening spaces covered by portable but broad, safe bridges, with bannisters running the entire length.

Why can't we do the same thing at this place?

This bridge had scarcely been gotten into usable shape when a sudden rise in the river tore it loose and broke it up, crossing being suspended for about a year.[54] Apparently nothing was done to remedy the situation until early in 1879. On January 30 the Arkansas River Bridge and Ferry Co. was incorporated, its promoters being John Murphy, Angus Carroll, Clark Scott, John F. Coldwell and William Sherburne. This organization was capitalized for $5,000, with shares of $100 each. The principal place of business was at Oxford and the charter was for twenty years. The company proposed the construction and maintenance of a toll bridge and ferry across the Arkansas river at Oxford, at a point on the river within a distance of 200 feet south of the site of the bridge erected by the Oxford Bridge and Ferry Co. in the year 1872. This charter was filed with the secretary of state January 31, 1879.[55]

The last mention we have located concerning a ferry at Oxford is in 1881, the Oxford *Weekly* of March 11 stating: "Mr. Richardson sailed through town last Saturday on the ferryboat on wheels, with the stars and stripes flying, and safely launched the same at its old moorings. Mr. R. generally accomplishes what he undertakes."

A new concrete bridge 575 feet long, with seven spans of 77 feet each, was completed just east of Oxford and dedicated on June 20, 1930, with Gov. Clyde M. Reed, as the principal speaker. The bridge cost $55,000. It was erected on the site of the old ferry landing of 1871, and appropriately marks U. S. Highway No. 130. At the christening it was planned to use a bottle of wine for this time-honored ceremony, but as the sheriff declined to furnish anything more potent, a bottle of water was used instead.

The next ferry up-river was in the vicinity of the town of Ninnescah. On February 21, 1871, the Arkansas and Ninnescah Ferry was chartered, the incorporators being Silas Rain, Marion McCoy, E. H. Prentice, John A. Henry, and Mahlon Barr. This company was capitalized at $2,000, with shares $50 each. It was proposed to operate a ferry across the Arkansas river at any point desired between the mouths of the Ninnescah river and Cowskin creek,

54. *Ibid.,* February 20, 1878.
55. Corporations, v. 9, pp. 326-328.

their principal office to be at any point within the limits of the state of Kansas as best suited the convenience of the board of directors. Directors chosen for the first year were T. J. Barton, William Barton, James Hamilton, George Hamilton and Walter Smith, all of Augusta.[56] There is some doubt whether this ferry ever operated, the charter probably having been secured for speculative purposes.

Just one week later, March 1, 1871, the Ninnescah Ferry Co. was chartered by L. B. Wansley (Wamsley?), Ernest Palmer, R. C. Gordon, Burr Mosier and C. M. Kellogg. The principal office of the company was at a point opposite the town of Ninnescah, and its purpose was to operate a ferry across the Arkansas river above the mouth of the Ninnescah river, and extending four miles in Sumner county. Capital stock of the enterprise was $500, divided into five shares. This charter was filed with the secretary of state March 5, 1871.[57] No further history of this enterprise has been located.

The first ferry across the Arkansas river in present Sumner county was started January 25, 1871, by David Richards. It was located at a point opposite present Belle Plaine, on S. 35, T. 30, R. 1 E.[58] Just how long this enterprise functioned we have not discovered.

El Paso, now Derby, about five miles north of the Sumner-Sedgwick county line was the next point to have a ferry. This town was started in the fall of 1870 by John Haufbauer and J. Hont Minnich, and during the spring of 1871 they operated a ferry, having been granted a license for that purpose on March 4. They were required to file a $1,000 bond for the ferry privilege and pay a $10 license fee to the county.[59] At a meeting of the board of commissioners on April 7, 1871, the following ferriage rates were established:

For one span of horses and loaded wagon, 75 cents; each additional span 15 cents; one span of horses and empty wagon or other vehicle, 50 cents; horse and rider, 25 cents; each foot passenger, 20 cents; two yoke of oxen and loaded wagon, $1.00; each additional yoke, 20 cents.[60]

There appears to have been very little water in the Arkansas' channel during 1871, but this ferry operated up to 1873, when a toll bridge was built by the El Paso Bridge Co. The structure was ready for traffic by July 7, the county commissioners approving the following schedule of toll rates:

For wagon and two horses, or one yoke of oxen, 25 cents, for each additional horse or ox 10 cents. For horsemen 10 cents. For footmen, 5 cents. For

---

56. *Ibid.*, v. 3, p. 171.
57. *Ibid.*, v. 3, p. 198.
58. Andreas, *History of Kansas*, p. 1495.
59. *Ibid.*, p. 1402. "Commissioners' Journal," Sedgwick county, Book A, p. 12.
60. *Ibid.*, p. 14.

loose cattle or horses, per head, 5 cents. For loose cattle, hogs and sheep, 2½ cents per head.[61]

During the flood of 1877, this bridge was washed away. A new bridge was completed during the winter of 1879-1880.[62]

Wichita was the next point up the river to have a ferry. During the special session of the legislature of 1860 a bill was introduced in the council to establish a ferry across the Arkansas at a point near the mouth of the Little Arkansas. Samuel F. Wright, John Sharkey, John McShane, H. Harrison Updegraff, John Frame and their associates were to have exclusive right and privilege of maintaining and keeping a ferry at that point for a term of twenty years, no other company being permitted to operate within four miles of the point selected. This ferry franchise was no doubt obtained for speculative purposes, for "section 2" of the act specified that the company should have five years from the date of the passage of the act, or sooner if the interests of the traveling public required it, to keep and maintain a good boat or boats, sufficient to cross the traveling public in a reasonable time; failure to do so would forfeit the charter. It was provided that in case of accident they should have time to replace or repair their boats. Neither Sedgwick county nor Wichita had yet been organized and the act provided that the county board nearest the ferry should fix toll rates, etc. The bill was introduced in the council by Senator Updegraff and passed that body on February 6. It was messaged to the house of representatives that afternoon and was referred to committee. In time it was referred back to the house without amendment, for passage, but for some unexplained reason the measure received no further consideration from that body.[63]

A recent history of early Wichita states that records of the government survey of June 28, 1867, mention a ferry and ford across the river between present First and Second streets. This survey locates the east bank of the river where the present Missouri Pacific depot is now located. The Arkansas river that year was said to be bank full all season. Indians who had occasion to cross ferried their families over in "tubs" fashioned of a single buffalo hide, and swam their horses. Those "tubs" were probably the "bull" boats, much in vogue in early days on western streams where buffalo were plentiful.[64]

61. *Ibid.*, p. 136.
62. Andreas, *History of Kansas*, p. 1402. Bentley, *History of Sedgwick County*, p. 626.
63. *Council Journal*, 1860, special session. *House Journal*, 1860, special session, pp. 224, 228, 297.
64. *Illustrated History of Early Wichita* (Eunice Sterling chapter, D. A. R., publisher), p. 16.

On March 6, 1868, a company composed of E. P. Bancroft, B. O. Carr, M. Greenway and James R. Mead, organized the Arkansas River Bridge and Ferry Co., with a capital stock of $20,000, divided into shares of $100 each. The company proposed to operate bridges and ferries across the Arkansas river at any and all points within the boundaries of Sedgwick county. Their charter was filed with the secretary of state March 16, 1868.[65]

This probably was the first ferry that operated at Wichita, and Greenway was the individual who ran the boat for the company. L. C. Fouquet, of Chandler, Okla., an early resident of Wichita, has the following to say of Greenway in an article published in the Humboldt *Union* of July 5, 1934:

Greenway was a friesky, funny entertaining fellow. I could tell you of how at one time while entertaining a crowd at F. Shattner's saloon, butcher knife in one hand, singing a combination of war and scalping songs and dancing, he, with a ferocious face at its finishing part, scared them pretty bad. (Me too.) I was watching from behind the spectators and as he was somewhat under the influence of liquor and was getting apparently more ferocious in the way of handling that butcher or scalping knife most of them realized that he was now crazy and was likely to at once put the knife into use. He started on one, but one of the cowboys quickly got on the floor behind him and pulled one of his feet which caused him to fall down. He got up in a ferocious rage, and somehow managed to get out of doors. I did too and run clear out of danger, booh . . . I never tried to find out how they managed to quiet him. However, he always was a nice friendly fellow to me and others when sober. But he always had a bottle with him. Perhaps you might say, how did you know. Well, he was the owner of the ferry boat and I run it for him. . . . On a beautiful Sunday he came up the river in his little canoe, perhaps to see how I was getting along. But everything was at a standstill. So he invited me to take a ride with him in his little thing which he rowed from one side with a peculiar oar.

Me, particularly adventurous, was tickled to accept the chance of getting an Indian ride. As I got in he had a most friendly and pleased smile. He pulled a bottle out of his coat pocket and offered me a drink. I drank a little and he took a big one. Oh, he was happy. He started to row and sing at the same time. It was a wonder to me how he could run that little boat so straight from only one side. We had got at what I guessed to be one mile when he stopped and turned it around so as to go back to the ferry. Then he dropped the oar, got his bottle and most politely handed it to me, after taking the cork out. Oh, but I didn't want any more. But as in France it is very unmannerly to refuse, I took it and let on that I was taking several swallows. He received the bottle and ho how he did drink. He was having a happy time, becoming real gay, and singing in English and sometime in Indian. Then he once more dropped the oar and he again took a drink. I was surprised and glad that he forgot to pass it to me. We finally got close to the ferry but he stopped in mid water, took another drink and then again took hold of the

65. Corporations, v. 1, p. 492.

oar, and as I remembered of his doings in the saloon I was glad to think that we'd go to the landing, but instead of using it he dropped it and again started singing in English, then in Indian. He didn't sing any scalping songs as at the saloon. I enjoyed his gay face and Indian song until he had a finish to it with a sound like Aihai Gah Aihahhah. He had placed one hand on each side of the canoe when he said Aihai Gah. He would push on the left side and hallowed Aihai Gah, he would push on the right side, which made it swing up and down, up and down and getting worse. Oh, gee, I realized that it would soon turn over. And that, though I had crossed the Atlantic ocean several times without fear, I never knew how to swim, I sure got scared. And I knew from what he had done in the saloon that to scare a white man was his hobby. But I didn't let on that I was. Although my following words gave him a beginning touch of enjoyment. I shouted, oh, say, you are going to turn it over. With a most pleased face and words he answered, oh, what of it? Then I shouted hay, hay, hay. But you have your Sunday clothes on. He at once stopped with a sigh, and said, oh, I forgot. Then he pulled the bottle out of his pocket, handed it to me saying. Oh, you dear boy, take a drink. And I took a little bit, and oh goody we finally landed.

Victor Murdock, in the Wichita *Evening Eagle*, of November 17, 1932, gave the recollections of S. L. Dunkin, and had the following to say of the old Wichita ferry:

The river at Wichita was once very wide, carried a lot of water and was measurably free from "islands." The eastern end of the ferry was somewhere east of the Broadview hotel of this day. Incidentally the first plat of this addition shows the present corner of Waco and Douglas as nonexistent. It was river bank then. The western end of the ferry was north of the present Midland station. On each bank was a wooden tower and from tower to tower stretched rope. The raft was attached to this trolley rope by two ropes, these ropes equipped with wheels. The raft had no power. It crossed and recrossed the stream by a manipulation of the current of water. Going from east to west the rope on the west side of the craft was slackened, and going from west to east this rope was tightened and the rope on the east end of the raft slackened. The force of the current did the rest in either trip.

The ferry went into operation May, 1871, to pick up trade incident to the spring rise. The fare was 10 cents for foot passengers, 50 cents for one team and an unloaded wagon; one dollar for one team and loaded wagon.

Now a year later the ferry was no more. For in the fall of 1871 work had begun on the bridge at this point and the bridge was in use in the spring of 1872.

The bridge was a long one, had nine spans. The approach on the east bank was 125 feet; the one on the west was 75 feet. The material for the bridge came from St. Joe., Mo., and by December, 1871, the work was taking shape.

The bridge charged a toll for crossing. It ended the ferry business as soon as it went into operation.

If the ferry business was as good in 1870 as the prices for ferriage, operators must have been able to "clean up" handsomely. Commissioners' records recite:

At a special meeting of the board of county commissioners held at Wichita, June 13th, A. D. 1870, the rates of toll for the Arkansas ferry were fixed for crossing—footmen each 20c. For man and horse, 40c. For two-horse team, 75c. For four-horse team, $1.50. For freighting teams, $5. . . . Ordered that the license fee for the Arkansas Ferry be fixed at $10 per year and clerk issue license therefor. Board adjourned. J. M. Steele, clerk. C. S. Roe, Dpty. Co. Clerk.[66]

The next mention of the Wichita Ferry in commissioners' proceedings was on July 1, 1872, when W. A. Sayles was granted a license on payment of $10 for a year's privilege.[67]

The first move for bridges within Sedgwick county was taken by the board of county commissioners at a meeting held on November 11, 1870, when—

It was ordered that a special election be held on the first Tuesday in April, 1871, at which the following questions shall be submitted to the people. Shall the county commissioners be authorized to issue county bonds for the purpose of building bridges. $1500 to build a bridge across the Little Arkansas river on the township line between Ranges 24 and 25, Range 1 West. $500 to build a bridge across Chisholm creek on the section line east through Section 22, Township 27. $500 to build a bridge across Spring creek on the quarter section line running East through Sec. 13, Towns. 29, Range 1 East. . . . J. M. Steele, Co. Clerk per Fred Schattner, clerk. N. A. English, Chairman Board Co. Comm.[68]

On March 4, 1871, Fred A. Sowers, county clerk, recorded that the commissioners "Ordered the publication of a notice calling a vote for the issuing of bonds to build bridges in the sum of $3,000. $1,500 for bridge over Little Arkansas; $500 for bridge over Chisholm creek and $500 for bridge over Spring creek." [69]

Within the limits of Wichita, the first bridge to span the Arkansas was a toll bridge on the line of Douglas avenue, erected by private enterprise, William Griffenstein, N. A. English, James R. Mead, Nelson McClees and Charles Gilbert being its projectors. This was a combination of wood and iron, and had eight spans of 100 feet each, with a 16-foot roadway and a toll house at each end. The bridge had stone piers and abutments resting on foundations of piling driven deep into the river bed. The contract price of the structure was $29,000. It had been said the company was short of cash when the bridge was opened for traffic, June 12, 1872, and that they traded in some town lots in part payment. Just five days before the bridge was opened the board of county commissioners adopted the following rates of toll:

66. "Commissioners' Journal," Sedgwick county, Book A, p. 2.
67. *Ibid.*, p. 12.
68. *Ibid.*, p. 8.
69. *Ibid.*, p. 12.

Two-horse or mule team and wagon, 50 cents. Each additional team, 10 cents. Four-horse or mule team and wagon, 75 cents. Six-horse or mule team and wagon, $1. One horse or mule with buggy, 25 cents. One yoke of oxen and wagon, 50 cents. Each additional yoke, 10 cents. "Two" or "Three" yoke of oxen and wagon, 75 cents. "Five" or "Six" yoke of oxen and wagon, $1.25. Empty wagon, (extra) 25 cents. Loaded wagon, (extra) 50 cents. Lead horse or mule, 10 cents. Horse-man, 15 cents. Footman, 5 cents. Cattle per head, 5 cents. Sheep and hogs, per head, 2 cents. No charge shall be made for team recrossing same day.[70]

By the latter part of 1874 there was a growing sentiment in favor of making this a free bridge. At a meeting of the county commissioners, on December 12, that year, it was ordered that a donation of one thousand dollars be granted to the Wichita Bridge Co., upon condition that the bridge be made free within a period of three months. At this same time an election was ordered by the commissioners to be held February 6, 1877, in order to purchase the bridge.[71] This met with popular approval and the bridge was taken over, the county paying $6,400.[72]

Wichita did not have many early-day roads. Several trails entered the county before its organization in 1870. One of these branched off from the Osage or Black Dog trail in Chautauqua county, turned northwest, crossing the southwest corner of Butler county and the northeast corner of Sedgwick county a few miles east of old Camp Beecher, site of present Wichita. Another road or trail ran from Fort Harker, southeast through Wichita, and down the east side of the Arkansas river, to Fort Gibson, in the Indian territory. The Chisholm cattle trail ran north from the Indian territory and ended at Wichita. This trail was later extended from Wichita to Abilene by Joseph G. McCoy, where McCoy had persuaded a number of large Texas cattlemen to drive their cattle for shipment east over the Kansas Pacific railroad. In 1869 a state road running from Humboldt to Wichita was established by the legislature. This road was 112 miles in length, and ran through Allen, Woodson, Greenwood, Butler and Sedgwick counties.[73] In 1871 another state road was provided for by the legislature, to run from Solomon City to Wichita. This road, seventy-five miles long, ran through Dickinson, Saline, McPherson, Marion, and Sedgwick counties.[74] That same year a petition was presented to the board of county commissioners for a road running from the south line of

70. *Ibid.*, p. 95.
71. *Ibid.*
72. Wichita *Beacon*, July 14, 1909.
73. *Laws*, 1869, p. 222.
74. *Ibid.*, 1871, p. 303.

the county to a point on the Arkansas river opposite the Wichita ferry. Messrs. S. K. Davis, S. Mann and A. S. Dodge were appointed as viewers, and their report was accepted and the road ordered.[75]

The next mention of a ferry above Wichita was in the vicinity of the Cimarron crossing of the Arkansas, in present Gray county. An early writer mentions that the river at this point in times of freshets was crossed by means of a rope ferry, the boat or scow being a wagon bed rendered watertight by being covered with skins.[76]

The westernmost ferry on the Arkansas within limits of present Kansas was at Pierceville, on the line of the old Santa Fé trail. This point was a post office as early as 1873, being located then in old Sequoyah county—later Finney county. This point is in the eastern edge of the county, on S. 13, T. 25, R. 31 W. A road crossed the river here, ran parallel with the river westward a few miles, thence across the sand hills to the southwest.[77] This ferry was started in 1879 and was operated till about the fall of 1886. The following is from Leola Howard Blanchard's *Conquest of the Southwest*, pp. 198-199:

> The Barton Brothers operated a ferry during those years [1879-1886], which made it possible for people south of the river to trade at Pierceville. They could haul a load of four tons and made trips whenever teams and wagons appeared on the opposite bank and hailed the ferry. They used a saddle horse to pull away from the bank, by tying a rope to the saddle horn. Once out in the current, a sail was hoisted and it didn't take much paddling to get the boat across. The fall of '86 they started across with five tons of coal, there was a strong wind blowing, and in spite of its big load the boat was carried along at a rapid rate. The sail was dropped as usual when within thirty feet of the bank, but the boat refused to stop, and shot clear over the bank, wrecking it beyond repair.

During the session of the Territorial Legislature of 1860 several bills were introduced for the establishment of ferries on the river close to the mountains, in territory then Kansas but now Colorado. One of these provided for a ferry at the mouth of the Fountain Qui Bouille, and the other at the town of Huerfano. The projectors of this last-named enterprise were to have the power to charge such rates of toll as might be prescribed by the tribunal transacting business for Arapahoe county, Kansas.[78] No further history of this enterprise has been located.

---

75. "Commissioners' Journal," Sedgwick county, Book A, p. 14.
76. Max Greene, *The Kanzas Region*, p. 131.
77. Everts, *Atlas of Kansas*, p. 316.
78. *House Journal*, Kansas, 1860, special session, pp. 69, 98. *Council Journal*, 1860, special session, p. 42.

Labor Problems in the Second Year of Governor Martin's Administration

DOROTHY LEIBENGOOD

THE year 1886 was a period of great labor unrest in Kansas as well as the United States as a whole. It saw the inauguration of many unsuccessful strikes, boycotts, and agitations by the Knights of Labor, which marked the beginning of the decline of that order. In presenting the labor problems of Kansas for this year the purely local strikes will be reviewed, then the Gould Southwestern strike which affected not only Kansas but Missouri, Arkansas, Texas, and Illinois, and finally the effect of this strike in Kansas, particularly in the gubernatorial campaign of that year and upon the legislation of 1887.

Purely local strikes were few and unimportant. The most serious probably was the strike at the Kansas City Smelting and Refining Co. at Argentine. This establishment engaged in the business of refining lead and silver ores, receiving supplies principally from Colorado, and employed in the neighborhood of two hundred men.[1]

On May 15, 1886, the employees struck, demanding a reduction of hours from twelve to eight with no decrease in pay.[2] As the nature of the employment required day and night work this meant the substitution of three shifts for two, or an increase in the working force of thirty-three and one third percent. Among other grievances was the imposition of a hospital tax of one dollar a month.

Sheriff James Ferguson of Wyandotte county went to Argentine early the morning of the fifteenth and placed a strong guard of deputy sheriffs so that every portion of the property was protected.[3] On the night of May 17 twenty men were sent from Kansas City, at the expense of the smelting works, to stand guard over the premises.[4] The next day F. H. Betton, commissioner of labor statistics, went to Argentine in response to a telegram, and held conferences with both parties.[5]

The men claimed that the labor was severe, unhealthy and exhausting, and that twelve hours was longer than men ought or should

---

1. Kansas Bureau of Labor and Industrial Statistics, *Second Annual Report* (1886).
2. Kansas City (Mo.) *Daily Journal*, May 16, 1886. (Notes from Argentine.)
3. *Ibid.*
4. *Ibid.*, May 18, 1886.
5. F. H. Betton to John A. Martin, May 20, 1886, in "Correspondence of Kansas Governors, Martin (Official)," Archives division, Kansas State Historical Society. Hereafter this reference will be cited as C. K. G., Martin.

be required to work, and longer than they were able to work for any considerable length of time and retain their health. Concerning the hospital tax the men said that the company had no hospital and that in case of sickness it was difficult to secure the company physician, as he resided in Kansas City. In many instances they were forced to employ a physician at their own expense. When a man was "leaded," as they termed a disease often incidental to smelting work, he had no time to send to Kansas City for a doctor, but needed relief at once. On general principles they preferred to select their own doctor, and to pay him themselves. They also claimed that in some instances a double tax, or two dollars, was expected as the hospital fee for one month.[6]

H. A. Meyer, president of the smelting company was in Mexico at the time of the strike.[7] A. F. Snyder, the superintendent, stated that the business was run on a very close margin and would not justify the large increase in wages. He said he would have been willing, had the men continued at work, to substitute three shifts for two, if the men had agreed to scale their wages to eight hours. Since they had abandoned the works and subjected the company to great loss and inconvenience he would refuse to grant any concessions whatever, for he had given the men ample time to return and they had failed to do so. He would not reëmploy them at all, but if any of them wanted to go to work they would have to apply individually to the foreman as any other new man would have to do. If the foreman needed more men and saw fit to employ them he might do so. The superintendent admitted that the work was hard and the hours long, and that in some cases it was also unhealthy, but he thought that the men who abstained from liquor were in no great danger from lead poison. Concerning the hospital tax, he said that when the company first established their works at Argentine the nearest physicians were at Kansas City. He did not think the fee was excessive since it was virtually a guarantee to pay a man's medical attendance, or to insure such attendance if needed, for twelve dollars a year. Since there were now plenty of physicians living in Argentine he did not know but that he would favor the abolishment of the hospital tax, but he could promise only to submit the matter to the president of the company.[8]

After a lengthy conference between Mr. Betton and the strikers, the strike was declared off. The strikers returned to work on the

---
6. Kansas Bureau of Labor and Industrial Statistics, *Second Annual Report* (1886).
7. Kansas City (Mo.) *Daily Journal*, May 18, 1886.
8. Kansas Bureau of Labor and Industrial Statistics, *Second Annual Report* (1886).

old basis, excepting the ringleaders, whom the company refused to take back.[9] Armed guards, hired by the company to protect its property, continued on duty several days. The wages paid at the time of the strike were generally one dollar and thirty-five cents to one dollar and fifty cents per day, very little skilled labor being required. Labor Commissioner Betton seemed to think that if the workers had understood the arbitration law passed by the legislature in 1886 the strike might have been avoided.[10]

A so-called strike or suspension of work, lasting about three weeks, took place in the coal mines at Osage City, Scranton, Peterton, and Burlingame, in Osage county, starting September 14, 1886, because of the refusal of the operators to pay the usual advance, on September 1, of one cent a bushel.[11] The Osage miners' delegate convention had met at Burlingame, September 10, and while in session decided that the miners of Osage county should ask for the advance, to commence September 15. If the operators refused the miners were to suspend work.[12] The mine operators failed to accede to the demands of the miners, and they left their work September 14.

The operators felt they were unable to give the increase because of the competition of coal companies outside of Osage county. Competition had been great on coal hauled long distances, from Wyoming territory, eastern Iowa, Illinois, and Colorado, on which a very low freight rate was charged by the railroads. Southern Kansas coal, too, was competing with Osage county coal in Topeka and Emporia. Southern Kansas railroads seem to have given their coal men better rates than the mine operators of Osage county could obtain from the Santa Fé. The operators found that the market, which had been taken by foreign coals, would not react in favor of Osage county coal quickly enough to enable them to raise the price sufficiently to comply with the demands of the miners.[13]

The people of Osage county thought the strike was inopportune, since hundreds of miners had not earned enough during the summer to support their families, and also because at that time there was not much demand for coal, and the companies could afford to let the mines lay idle for a time.[14] The Osage City *Free Press* blamed the railroad companies for the trouble. It thought that a settlement

9. *The Kansas Democrat*, Topeka, May 20, 1886.
10. F. H. Betton to John A. Martin, May 19, 1886, in C. K. G., Martin (Official).
11. Kansas Bureau of Labor and Industrial Statistics, *Second Annual Report* (1886).
12. Burlingame *Independent*, September 16, 1886.
13. Kansas Bureau of Labor and Industrial Statistics, *Second Annual Report* (1886).
14. *Osage County Democrat*, Burlingame, September 18, 1886.

could be reached between the operators and miners if the railroads were compelled to confine themselves exclusively to the business of hauling freight and passengers.[15]

The several companies posted notices that they would give one half cent more per bushel on October first, and one half cent more per bushel on November first, so that the price of mining would be six and one half and seven cents per bushel respectively.[16] Many of the miners seemed not to care whether they worked, for they felt that at the prices they were not able to make a living. However, they finally accepted the terms of the company and went to work at the wages stated above.[17]

The Gould Southwestern Strike

The Southwestern strike of 1886 was begun at Marshall, Texas, March 1, by the men in the Texas and Pacific shops.[18] The reason given was the discharge of C. A. Hall, foreman of the woodworkers of the Texas and Pacific car shops at Marshall.[19] It is alleged that he had secured a leave of absence from his immediate superior to attend a four-day convention of District Assembly 101 of the Knights of Labor, which met at Marshall February 15. At noon of the last day he returned to work but was discharged that evening for being absent without leave. The local committee demanded his reinstatement and the company refused. The executive board again asked for reinstatement and threatened in case of refusal to call out all the men on the Gould system.[20] Ex-Governor J. C. Brown, one of the receivers of the Texas and Pacific, said that Hall was incompetent, that he had obtained leave from the master mechanic to be absent only three hours, and that he was absent three or four days without further permission.[21] On March 6 the employees of the Missouri Pacific were called out.[22]

Prior to this, as early as January, the executive committee of District Assembly 101, Knights of Labor, had been authorized to order a strike. At that time Martin Irons, district master workman, issued a circular to the locals of that assembly asking if they would sustain the executive board in demanding $1.50 a day minimum for unskilled labor and the recognition of the employees as Knights of

---

15. Osage City *Free Press*, October 7, 1886.
16. *Ibid.*
17. *Osage County Democrat*, Burlingame, October 2, 1886.
18. Kansas Bureau of Labor and Industrial Statistics, *Second Annual Report* (1886).
19. Topeka *Daily Capital*, March 7, 1886.
20. Editorial in Parsons *Daily Sun*, April 4, 1886.
21. *The Daily Commonwealth*, Topeka, March 10, 1886.
22. *Daily Eclipse*, Parsons. March 6, 1886.

Labor.[23] Ex-Governor Brown said that this refusal of the receivers to sign an agreement recognizing the employees as Knights of Labor was the sole cause of the subsequent strike, and that any other allegation of cause was an afterthought.[24]

On March 16 Vice-President H. M. Hoxie of the Missouri Pacific Railway received a letter from Martin Irons asking him to meet a committee of Knights of Labor to confer in regard to difficulties that existed between the employees and the railroad companies composing the Gould Southwestern system.[25] Hoxie replied that he could not see that a meeting with a committee could adjust the trouble since the cause for the strike was the discharge of C. A. Hall by the Texas and Pacific Railway Co., a road which was not under his control but in the hands of a receiver. He added that the action taken by their late employees had so reduced the traffic that they soon would not require as many men in the shops as before.[26] On March 18 Grand Master Workman T. V. Powderly, of the Knights of Labor, arrived in Kansas City for a conference with delegates from five districts.[27] He telegraphed Mr. Hoxie for a conference but was refused.[28]

Frank H. Betton, commissioner of Labor for Kansas, telegraphed to Martin Irons on March 15 asking if the services of the governors of Missouri and Kansas could not be invoked as mediators to settle the differences between the company and its employees.[29] Irons replied that he would be pleased to have the two governors act as mediators.[30] On March 19 the two governors met at Kansas City and after a conference with strike leaders suggested that the Missouri Pacific continue the agreement made with the management of the road on March 15, 1885. This was to restore to the striking employees in Missouri and Kansas the same wages paid them in September, 1884, including one and one half price for extra time worked, and to restore to all employees their respective employments without prejudice because of the strike. The governors assured Mr. Hoxie that the strike could not have been, and was not based on a violation of the terms of the agreement of March 15, 1885, by the management of the Missouri Pacific Railway Co. in its dealings

23. Kansas Bureau of Labor and Industrial Statistics, *Second Annual Report* (1886).
24. *The Daily Commonwealth,* Topeka, March 10, 1886.
25. Topeka *Daily Capital,* March 17, 1886.
26. Ibid.
27. *Ibid.,* March 19, 1886.
28. *The Standard,* Leavenworth, March 20, 1886.
29. Kansas Bureau of Labor and Industrial Statistics, *Second Annual Report* (1886).
30. Martin Irons to Frank H. Betton, March 15, 1886, in C. K. G., Martin (Personal), v. 6, p. 436.

with its employees of Missouri and Kansas.[31] Mr. Hoxie accepted the proposition but said that while the company would take back all strikers necessary to do the work it would not discharge men who had been employed meanwhile.[32] The agreement was then presented to the executive committee of District 101 of the Knights of Labor. But though Governors Martin and J. S. Marmaduke called in person on Martin Irons urging him to accept the plan, he refused the terms.[33]

On March 28 Mr. Powderly had an interview with Jay Gould which resulted in the executive board ordering the men back to work with the understanding that arbitration would follow. Mr. Hoxie, however, refused to meet any committee for arbitration except one made up of actual employees. As the general executive board believed this to be a direct violation of the agreement between Gould and Powderly to arbitrate the differences between the Gould Southwestern system and the Knights of Labor, they recalled the order given the men to return to work.[34]

On April 12 Ex-Governor A. G. Curtin of Pennsylvania introduced a resolution in Congress, which was passed, authorizing the appointment of a committee to investigate the labor troubles in Missouri, Arkansas, Kansas, Texas, and Illinois.[35] The Curtin committee was formed and examined many witnesses.[36] On the evening of May 1 correspondence was begun between the executive board of the Knights of Labor and members of the committee, resulting in declaring off the strike on May 4.[37]

The Strike in Kansas

The general course of the strike throughout the Southwest and the role of Governor Martin in attempting a settlement has been mentioned. In Kansas the main points of the strike were at Atchison, Kansas City, and Parsons. The strike did not reach Atchison until March 8, but due to the walk-out at Kansas City below and at Hiawatha above only local freight was received at Atchison.[38] Governor Martin was in Atchison March 10 and urged settlement by the arbitration law of the state, but the committee refused to

---

31. H. M. Hoxie's "An Address to the Employees of the Missouri Pacific Railway Co.," March 8, 1886, *ibid.*, p. 17a.
32. *The Standard*, Leavenworth, March 31, 1886.
33. Topeka *Daily Capital*, March 23, 1886.
34. *Ibid.*, April 6, 1886.
35. "Investigation of Labor Troubles in Missouri, Arkansas, Kansas, Texas, and Illinois," in *Reports of Committees of the House of Representatives*, No. 4174, v. III, 49 Cong. 2 sess.
36. *Ibid.*
37. *Ibid.*
38. Kansas City (Mo.) *Daily Journal*, March 7, 1886.

accept the proposition without orders from the district assembly at Sedalia.[39] On March 12 an attempt was made by the company to send a freight train west but they had to abandon the attempt because of the determined resistance of a force of strikers at the round house.[40] Many people were applying for work but they were deterred by fear of violence.[41] On the night of March 21 masked men drove the engineer and watchmen out of the Central Branch round house and armed men stood guard over them while the gang damaged as many as twenty-three engines.[42] The strikers denied any knowledge of the affair.[43] On March 26 F. E. Shaw, sheriff of Atchison county, wrote Governor Martin that he would extend to the Missouri Pacific property in that county all the needed protection if the company would furnish the men to do their work.[44] By March 30 the situation apparently began to improve at Atchison. Two trains were taken out that day without objection. A force of men was employed at the shops all the night before and repaired thirteen engines. But on the night of March 31 a mob of at least one hundred masked men visited the Central Branch machine shops and proceeded to make a total wreck of all the costly machinery in that building.[45] The Knights of Labor of Atchison hastened to pass a resolution condemning these acts of violence.[46] By April 3 the strike was over at Atchison, the Missouri Pacific Co. having reëmployed forty or fifty of its former workmen.[47]

The strike on the Missouri Pacific system at Kansas City was inaugurated the morning of March 5. The strikers took possession of the yards at the state line and of Cypress round house, and killed all engines save those needed for passenger service, which were not molested.[48] Attempts were made to get the local assemblies to appeal to the arbitration law of Kansas, but without success.[49] Many deeds of violence were committed during the strike. On the morning of April 26 some unknown parties fired several shots into a

39. *The Daily Commonwealth*, Topeka, March 11, 1886.
40. *Daily Eclipse*, Parsons, March 13, 1886.
41. Prentis to John A. Martin, March 12, 1886, C. K. G., Martin (Personal), v. 5, p. 343.
42. Telegram, Prentis to John A. Martin, March 23, 1886, *ibid.*, v. 6, p. 31.
43. J. T. Cougher to John A. Martin, March 26, 1886, C. K. G., Martin (Official).
44. F. E. Shaw to John A. Martin, March 26, 1886, C. K. G., Martin (Personal), v. 6, p. 456.
45. A. H. Martin to John A. Martin, March 31, 1886, *ibid.*, p. 466.
46. *Kansas Daily State Journal*, Topeka, April 3, 1886.
47. John A. Martin to Col. A. B. Campbell, April 3, 1886, C. K. G., Martin (Personal), v. 6, p. 495.
48. Kansas City (Mo.) *Daily Journal*, May 4, 1886.
49. F. H. Betton to John A. Martin, March 25, 1886, C. K. G., Martin (Personal), v. 6, p. 45.

freight train as it was passing near Cypress yards. Later in the morning, between Cypress yards and Wyandotte, a freight train was thrown from the track and the train generally piled up. The fireman and brakeman were killed.[50] The accident was the result of malicious tampering with the rails,[51] and Governor Martin issued a proclamation offering a reward for the arrest and conviction of the guilty parties.[52] The train wreckers were arrested in July. At the preliminary hearing, which started July 29, evidence showed that the scheme was concocted in the lodge of the Knights of Labor.[53]

The strike at Parsons began at ten o'clock the morning of March 6. The strike was inaugurated in conformity with demands made by the officers of the Knights of Labor at Sedalia, and in unison with employees of all the Gould system.[54] On March 7 operators, clerks and men in the freight departments who were not on strike were indefinitely suspended from duty by the company.[55] On March 12 the city of Parsons was notified by officials of the Missouri Pacific Co. that a body of men without authority were in possession of the company's property, and that the officials would hold the city of Parsons strictly accountable at law for all damages.[56] The same day Supt. T. V. Golden, of the Missouri Pacific, asked A. O. Brown, mayor of Parsons, to appoint eighteen special policemen to guard the property of the company. Mayor Brown replied that while by ordinance he and the council had authority to appoint special policemen to guard the property of railway companies, they were authorized to make only such appointments as were recommended by the superintendent of the railway company. Mayor Brown said he would be willing to appoint any fit persons upon Mr. Golden's recommendation.[57] On March 13 C. B. Woodford, sheriff of Labette county, telegraphed Governor Martin asking for military assistance to aid him at Parsons in preserving peace and enforcing the laws.[58] The same day David Kelso, attorney for the Missouri Pacific, telegraphed Governor Martin that the civil authorities were wholly unable to cope with the situation. That day a mob had forcibly taken a freight engine which the sheriff was endeavoring to protect, and

50. Jas. Ferguson to John A. Martin, April 26, 1886, C. K. G., Martin (Official).
51. Topeka *Daily Capital*, April 27, 1886.
52. *The Trades-Union*, Atchison, April 30, 1886.
53. *Daily Eclipse*, Parsons, July 30, 1886.
54. *Ibid.*, March 6, 1886.
55. *Ibid.*, March 7, 1886.
56. *Ibid.*, March 12, 1886.
57. Parsons *Daily Sun*, March 13, 1886.
58. C. B. Woodford to John A. Martin, March 13, 1886, C. K. G., Martin (Personal), v. 6, p. 433.

had disabled the engine in the sheriff's presence. Mr. Kelso asked the governor's interference to see that the laws were executed.[59] Governor Martin wired Kelso that the sheriff should exhaust all the civil powers of his office, then, if he were unlawfully resisted in the performance of his duty, he should notify the governor.[60] On March 14 Governor Martin telegraphed Col. A. B. Campbell, adjutant general of Kansas, to go to Parsons to determine whether the civil authorities had exhausted their remedies and if such disturbances justified the use of military power. Mr. Campbell was to order Brig. Gen. J. N. Roberts to accompany him and to effect a peaceable settlement if possible. The governor emphasized the fact that the military forces of the state would not be used unless the processes of law were resisted and the authority of the civil officers was defied.[61] Colonel Campbell went to Parsons March 15, accompanied by Brigadier-General Roberts. They remained in Parsons during the fifteenth and found no necessity for the presence of troops at that time and no prospect of immediate settlement of the labor troubles. They returned home the next day.[62] That night a citizens' meeting was held in Parsons wherein resolutions were passed condemning the strike on the Gould system as being detrimental to the best interests of the city and charging that false statements had been prepared by paid agents of the company to induce Governor Martin to invoke military protection in time of profound peace, regardless of the wishes of business men and citizens generally. The meeting resolved that civil authorities were able to protect the lives and property without the aid of the militia.[63] On March 17 the sheriff served injunctions on the strikers, enjoining them from interfering with the property or business of the Missouri Pacific. The application was filed in the district court of Labette county by Judge Kelso, the attorney for the Missouri Pacific Railway Co.[64]

On March 29 David Kelso again telegraphed the governor that no train would move out of Parsons for some time unless aided by the military forces, because of the action of the strikers.[65] The same day C. E. Faulkner sent a dispatch to Governor Martin saying that he thought the presence of the military power was the only solution to

59. David Kelso to John A. Martin, March 13, 1886, *ibid.*, p. 432.
60. John A. Martin to David Kelso, March 13, 1886, *ibid.*, p. 434.
61. John A. Martin to A. B. Campbell, March 14, 1886, *ibid.*, p. 435.
62. Adjutant General of the State of Kansas, *Fifth Biennial Report* (1885-1886).
63. Parsons *Daily Sun,* March 17, 1886.
64. *Daily Eclipse,* Parsons, March 18, 1886.
65. David Kelso to John A. Martin, March 29, 1886, C. K. G., Martin (Personal), v. 6, p. 459.

the question of moving the trains.[66] Also the mayor of Parsons and the sheriff of Labette county communicated with the governor the same day. They stated that all attempts to move trains had been successfully resisted. They asked him to order five hundred militiamen to Parsons at once.[67]

Governor Martin replied that the strike had ended elsewhere, having been ordered off by Mr. Powderly, and presumed there would be no further trouble.[68] In a telegram to Governor Martin on March 30, however, Mayor Brown renewed his request for troops. He said that the strikers had orders from their committee not to yield. The night before a passenger train approaching Parsons had been ditched.[69] Governor Martin again replied that he expected the trouble would be peaceably and finally settled that day. He thought it better to wait twenty-four hours than to provoke a conflict just as the strike seemed to be approaching an end.[70] David Kelso and C. H. Kimball sent dispatches to the governor telling of the lawlessness of the strikers.[71] The governor again ordered the adjutant general to Parsons to examine the situation and to report to him. This time he found the situation much worse. The proclamation of the governor, the writs of the courts, and the officers of the law had been defied. Many engines had been killed and disabled.[72]

On March 31 the adjutant general had a long conference with the local committee in charge of the strike, in which he urged them to make no further resistance to the movement of trains. The company then attempted to resume operations. The first train was permitted to go, but the second engine was killed. Colonel Campbell then addressed the strikers directly asking them to make no further resistance. They asked for a conference with Mr. Golden, division superintendent, and the adjutant general, that evening, at their committee room. The meeting was held but nothing was accomplished toward settlement of the trouble.[73] On April 1 another unsuccessful attempt was made to move trains, whereupon Colonel Campbell wired the governor, as also did the mayor, sheriff, deputy county

---

66. C. E. Faulkner to John A. Martin, March 29, 1886, C. K. G., Martin (Official).
67. C. B. Woodford and A. O. Brown to John A. Martin, March 29, 1886, C. K. G. Martin (Personal), v. 6, p. 460.
68. John A. Martin to Mayor of Parsons, March 29, 1886, *ibid.*, p. 462.
69. A. O. Brown to John A. Martin, March 30, 1886, *ibid.*, p. 465.
70. John A. Martin to A. O. Brown, March 30, 1886, *ibid.*, p. 468.
71. C. H. Kimball and David Kelso to John A. Martin, March 30, 1886, *ibid.*, p. 472.
72. Adjutant General of the State of Kansas, *Fifth Biennial Report* (1885-1886).
73. *Ibid.*

attorney and others. They asked him to send from six hundred to one thousand soldiers to Parsons.[74]

Governor Martin wired Colonel Campbell authority to move Colonel Patrick to Parsons with all the force necessary to sustain the civil officers in the performance of their duties.[75] Colonel Campbell ordered Colonel Patrick to place the entire First regiment under marching orders, and then went to Kansas City to arrange transportation.[76] By nine o'clock on the evening of April 2 the First regiment was in Parsons.[77]

The presence of this militia had the desired effect, for by April 6 traffic on the Missouri Pacific had assumed almost its usual proportions.[78] A Law and Order League, made up of citizens of Parsons, was organized April 5, with arms secured by the adjutant general. This body was to place its entire force at the disposal of the mayor and sheriff to enforce law, preserve order, keep the peace and protect property. Individually the members agreed to use their names to resist boycotting.[79]

On April 7 one half the First regiment was sent home. It was thought best not to have a sudden withdrawal of all the troops, as the strikers might attempt to stop trains as soon as they left.[80] On April 14 the remaining troops broke camp.[81] Thereafter there was little trouble in Parsons.

THE LABOR ELEMENT IN THE GUBERNATORIAL CAMPAIGN OF 1886 AND LABOR LEGISLATION OF 1887

While the Missouri Pacific strike was in progress the press was commenting on the effect the labor question would have on Governor Martin's chances for reëlection. Some papers claimed that his lack of action in the strike was a bid for the Knights of Labor vote. Others felt that because he was so closely associated with the Typographical union he dared not say a word against the strikers.[82] Many papers expressed the belief that the Knights of Labor were against him because he ordered the militia to Parsons while the

74. Sheriff Woodford, Mayor Brown and others to John A. Martin, April 1, 1886, C. K. G., Martin (Official).
75. John A. Martin to Col. A. H. Campbell, April 1, 1886, C. K. G., Martin (Personal), v. 6, p. 482.
76. Adjutant General of the State of Kansas, *Fifth Biennial Report* (1885-1886).
77. Ibid.
78. *Daily Eclipse*, Parsons, April 6, 1886.
79. Ibid.
80. A. B. Campbell to John A. Martin, April 9, 1886, C. K. G., Martin (Personal), v. 6, p. 503.
81. *Ibid.*, April 13, 1886, p. 504.
82. Leavenworth *Times*, April 24, 1886.

friends of the Missouri Pacific were opposed to him because he did not order the militia out at Atchison. They thought because of the labor question the Democrats might select the next governor of Kansas.[83]

Governor Martin was afraid of the opposition of the Knights of Labor in the campaign. He wrote to Senators Plumb and Ingalls that many of the leading men of the Knights of Labor were the old leaders of the Greenback and Anti-Monopoly parties, and they would endeavor to shape their forces against the Republican party, perhaps in an alliance with the Democrats. He asked the senators to help him in the campaign by taking an active part in the canvass, if he were nominated.[84] He also wrote to James G. Blaine, asking him to devote one week to the canvass in Kansas, that fall, making speeches at several of the more important centers. He explained to Blaine that the labor question complicated matters; that the leaders of the labor movement, being old Greenbackers, who would use all their influence to alienate the labor vote from the Republican party.[85] Later he wrote Senator Plumb and asked him to get some speakers from out of the state, men like Blaine, Sherman, Logan, Hawley, and others, who, by their presence, could stir up enthusiasm. He felt that the elements of discontent and discord were numerous and that the Republicans would have a hard fight to win the campaign.[86]

Gen. Hugh Cameron, organizer and member of the corporation board of the Knights of Labor, up to the time Governor Martin called out the troops in the Missouri Pacific strike, had felt very kindly toward him, and would have generously supported him; but it was felt that this action had been entirely unnecessary and constituted a menace and insult to the order. But for this fact labor would have been well disposed toward Governor Martin.[87]

Martin was nominated by acclamation at the Republican state convention in July.[88] The platform adopted had several provisions concerning labor. In the resolutions the party pointed to the past record of the Republicans on labor. They asserted that the Republicans had abolished slavery and had ever contended for the protection of American labor and had been against the importation of

---

83. *The Standard,* Leavenworth, May 7, 1886.
84. John A. Martin to P. B. Plumb and John J. Ingalls, June 17, 1886, C. K. G., Martin (Personal), v. 7, pp. 172-180.
85. John A. Martin to Jas. G. Blaine, June 18, 1886, *ibid.,* pp. 187-190.
86. John A. Martin to P. B. Plumb, June 29, 1886, *ibid.,* pp. 239-245.
87. *Daily Eclipse,* Parsons, June 24, 1886.
88. *The Kansas Democrat,* Topeka, July 8, 1886.

foreign pauper competition. In the following resolutions they gave the record of the Republican party of Kansas on the labor question:

The Republican party of Kansas has embodied in the constitution of the state and in various legislative enactments:
First, Protection to the homesteads and wages of the laborer.
Second, A liberal exemption to the small manufacturer and dealer.
Third, A mechanics lien law, broad enough in its provisions to amply secure the payment of any just demand for work and material.
Fourth, The establishment of a bureau of labor statistics, so that a correct knowledge of the educational, moral, and financial condition of the laboring masses can be obtained.
Fifth, A general incorporation law under which all associations organized by the workingmen to improve their condition and protect their rights can be perpetuated.

In addition the Republican party stated that it was in favor of all other legislation tending to secure to the laborers their just proportion of the proceeds of their work, to protect them against the encroachments of organized capital, and to provide easy and speedy redress for all wrongs suffered by them, or threatened to them. And while it endorsed and espoused all just demands of the laboring masses, it was unalterably opposed to the doctrines of the communists and the red flag of the anarchists. It acknowledged allegiance to no flag but the red, white and blue of the United States, under whose beneficent folds every American must and should enjoy the blessing of a stable government, with every right enforced and every wrong redressed in peace and good order, each moulding his own life, controlling his own property, enjoying his own liberty, subject only to such legal restrictions as the general welfare demands.[89]

The Democratic state convention was held in August at Leavenworth and Thomas Moonlight of Leavenworth was nominated for governor. The platform adopted by the party had the following resolutions on labor:

Resolved, That we recognize labor as the source of all wealth, and demand for the working classes such remuneration for their services as will enable them, with economy and sobriety, to increase their social and financial condition; further, we condemn the policy of the Republican party in building up monopolies and classes by special legislation hostile to the best interests of the masses.

Resolved, That difference between labor and capital be settled by a board of arbitration in each state, and general supervising board, appointed by the United States as a final board of appeal, so that the persecutions of corporate powers and the retaliation of labor strikers may cease and justice prevail.

89. *Ibid.*

Resolved, That the present railroad law should be so amended, as to prevent the railroad companies from charging the people excessive rates of freight to pay the interest on watered stock; should provide for reasonable compensation for services rendered and no more; and the commissioners, if there be, should have the power to enforce their decisions in the name of the state.

Resolved, That we are opposed to convict labor or pauper labor and demand the most stringent legislation on the subject.[90]

An Anti-Monopolist convention met at Topeka on August 25. The convention made no nominations for executive offices but delegates were instructed to work for the election of such candidates as would pledge themselves to secure the adoption of all the measures for the relief of labor and the great producing class that were in harmony with the Anti-Monopolist, Greenback, and Knights of Labor declaration of principles.[91]

On September 15 Governor Martin delivered his opening speech of the campaign at Crawford's opera house in Topeka. He said that the Democratic party was the enemy of honest labor, as was shown by the fact that the Homestead Law was repeatedly defeated by Democratic congressmen and was never enacted until the Republicans came into power. He stated that every attempt of the Democratic party to legislate on the subject of the tariff was in the interest of foreign capital and low-priced labor, and against home enterprise and American workingmen. He asserted that the Republican party had always been the friend of working men; it had freed the slaves, established a protective tariff and passed the Homestead Law. In this speech he also reviewed the laws of Kansas that had been passed in the interest of the workingmen.[92]

Col. D. R. Anthony, editor of the Leavenworth *Times,* repeatedly assailed the Knights of Labor, and assured them that their votes were not wanted by the Republican party.[93] The action of Governor Martin in calling out the militia was commented upon and used to prejudice all members of the Knights of Labor.[94] Some of the Democrats had the Knights of Labor issue a circular bearing the semblance of authority, urging members of the order to support Moonlight for governor. It went out as an official document, but was not made up in such an official manner as to get any of the perpetrators into trouble.[95]

90. *The Standard,* Leavenworth, August 5, 1886.
91. *The Trades-Union,* Atchison, September 2, 1886.
92. *The Daily Commonwealth,* Topeka, September 16, 1886. Governor Martin's speech in full on the editorial page.
93. Leavenworth *Times,* October 3, 1886.
94. Atchison *Daily Champion,* September 25, 1886.
95. W. P. Hackney to John A. Martin, October 18, 1886, C. K. G., Martin (Personal).

The Knights of Labor of Atchison in commenting upon Martin and Moonlight as candidates for governor said that in the strike Governor Martin had refused to place the lives of citizen workingmen in Kansas in danger and had refrained from inciting a spirit of destructiveness by a show of unnecessary power. He had stepped to the front on behalf of the citizens of Kansas and had investigated the Missouri Pacific strike by personal inquiry and had submitted a plan of settlement. They said that Governor Martin's course could be summed up in three sentences.

> The employees had exhausted their individual and organized efforts to obtain a settlement of the cause of the strike. Governor Martin's services were called to see if the contract of 1885 had been violated, and he made a personal investigation. He effected an agreed settlement which was honorable to the men.

They called attention to the fact that during Governor Martin's administration five and one half of the eleven demands made in the Knights of Labor platform had become laws in the state of Kansas. They felt that Governor Martin's opponents in the campaign had nothing to offer but promises.[96]

A reporter interviewed W. S. Anderson, state master workman of the Knights of Labor in Kansas. He said that Mr. Martin had made a good, just, perhaps conservative, yet fearless governor, and was entitled to a second term.[97] He believed there was no truth in the statements that the Knights of Labor would vote for Colonel Moonlight.

In many of his speeches Colonel Moonlight, the Democratic candidate, stated that he was in full sympathy with the aims and aspirations of the workingman. He said he believed in elevating the condition of the laboring man so as to benefit him morally, socially, and financially. To prevent strikes between capital and labor he would appoint a board of arbitration composed of one member from each great political party, one from the commercial interests, and one from the laboring interests.[98] The Republicans pointed out that they had an arbitration law quite as good as the one Colonel Moonlight suggested.[99]

There were reports that the Typographical union was going back on Governor Martin because he was supported by the Kansas City *Journal* and the Leavenworth *Times*, two newspapers that employed

96. Atchison *Daily Champion*, October 23, 1886.
97. Topeka *Daily Capital*, October 24, 1886.
98. *Osage County Democrat*, Burlingame, October 23, 1886.
99. Topeka *Daily Capital*, October 22, 1886.

nonunion men.[100] However, these organizations supported him, contrary to the expectations and claims of some of the Democratic newspapers.

Governor Martin was elected by a large majority. The legislature met in regular session on January 11, 1887,[101] and in his message Martin recommended the repeal of sections 28, 29, 30 of the militia law of 1885. This was a result of the Missouri Pacific strike of 1886. The governor felt that the law conferred dangerous powers upon officers of the national guard, sheriffs and mayors of cities by authorizing them to use military force at their own discretion. He contended that this was in violation of the state constitution which confers upon the governor the sole power to call out the militia to execute the laws, to supress insurrection, and repel invasion. He mentioned the fact that the statute books of Kansas had an unusually large number of acts designed to secure laboring men against the encroachment of capital, and to provide remedies for injustice done them. This, he said, should continue until the removal of abuses was complete.[102]

There were many bills concerning labor and laboring men introduced in this session. Among those that became laws were: A mechanic's liens act, an act encouraging the formation of coöperative societies, an act securing payment to miners and laborers in lawful money, and an act exempting pension money from garnishment. The first of these, an act to protect mechanics, laborers and persons furnishing material for the construction of public buildings and public improvements, provided that when any public officer contracts for such work in any sum exceeding one hundred dollars he must secure a bond from the contractor guaranteeing the payment of all indebtedness for labor or material furnished.[103] The act encouraging the creation of coöperative societies provided that twenty or more persons might organize for the purpose of more successfully promoting and conducting any industrial pursuit, and that every society when so organized should enjoy all the rights, privileges, and powers conferred by law on other chartered or incorporated companies in the state.[104] The act relating to the payment of wages to laborers provided that laborers in and about coal mines and factories should be paid their wages at regular intervals, and in law-

---

100. *The Kansas Democrat,* Topeka, October 30, 1886.
101. Topeka *Daily Capital,* January 11, 1887.
102. *Biennial Message of John A. Martin, Governor, to the Legislature of Kansas* (1887).
103. *Laws of Kansas,* 1887, Ch. CLXXIX.
104. Topeka *Daily Capital,* March 19, 1887.

ful money. Wages paid in scrip, checks, etc., might be recovered in money from the person or firm issuing; coercion of employees to purchase goods from particular firms was to be punished by fine or imprisonment or both.[105] The law relating to garnishment and attachments provided that United States pension money received by a debtor within three months before the garnishment process, could not be applied on his debts when it was shown to be necessary for the maintenance of a family, supported wholly or in part by the pension money.[106]

Some of the bills introduced in the legislature of 1887 that failed to pass were: An act establishing eight hours as a legal day's work, an act providing for the safety and health of persons mining coal, and an act to prevent unjust discrimination against employees of corporations, compounds, or individuals. A great many other bills were introduced concerning the welfare of the working classes, not directly connected with the labor problem.

105. *Laws of Kansas,* 1887, Ch. CLXXI.
106. *Ibid.,* Ch. CLXI.

The Grave of Sarah Keyes on the Oregon Trail

WILLIAM E. SMITH

IN APRIL, 1830, more than 100 years ago, the first wagons passed over the Oregon trail.[1] Sixteen years later the ill-starred Donner party toiled along the trail across Kansas, to meet disaster in the winter snows of the Sierra Nevada mountains. Here forty-two of the ninety died from starvation and cold, and a portion of the remainder barely kept alive by subsisting on human flesh.[2]

The parties composing this caravan left Independence, Mo., about May 1, 1846. A short distance out of Independence it consisted of the following: Sixty-three wagons; one hundred nineteen men; fifty-nine women; one hundred ten children; bread stuffs, 58,484 lbs.; bacon, 38,080 lbs.; powder, 1,065 lbs.; lead, 2,557 lbs.; guns, 144; pistols, 94; 700 head of cattle and 150 head of horses. This was an unusually large caravan and later divided itself into two or three trains.[3]

After crossing the Kansas river the company was increased by two. A Mrs. Hall, the wife of one of the immigrants, gave birth to twins. On the morning of May 19, a new census of the party was taken and it was found to consist of ninety-eight fighting men, fifty women, forty-six wagons, and 350 head of cattle. Two divisions were made for convenience of marching. On this day nine wagons from Illinois belonging to Messrs. Reed and Donner and their families joined.

The caravan moved slowly, seldom more than fifteen miles per day, and on May 26, 1846, the band of immigrants reached the Big Blue in what is now Marshall county, at what is called Independence crossing. The river was very much swollen and they were forced to remain at this camp from May 26 until nine o'clock p. m. on the 31st, when the wagons, oxen and horses were safely landed on the west bank. Because of the continued high water a crude ferry boat, named *Blue River Rover* was constructed by making dugouts of large cottonwood trees. Two of these dugouts were framed together so that the wheels of the wagons rested in the

---

1. Joseph G. Masters, *Oregon Trail Memorial Association Centenary Celebration* (Pamphlet).
2. C. F. McGlashan, *History of the Donner Party*, p. 236.
3. Edwin Bryant, *Rocky Mountain Adventures*, p. 2.

canoes. Lines were attached to both ends and the raft was pulled back and forth by hand.

While the emigrants were waiting to cross the river they were saddened by the death of Sarah Keyes, whose grave as it is today is described in this paper. Their activities of these few days are well depicted by Edwin Bryant in his *Rocky Mountain Adventures,* on which this article is principally based.

On the 26th the women washed clothes and some of the men fished, one catch being a catfish three feet long. There had been some contention among the leaders of the caravan, and the evening of that day was given over to a public meeting in an effort to prepare a system of law for the purpose of preserving order. The day had been delightful, nothing disagreeable had happened, perfect harmony prevailed. After sunset a new moon appeared above the tree tops to the west of the camp, but later, however, a terrific thunder storm and heavy rain came up. Of this, Mr. Bryant says:

> A terrific thunder storm roared and raged, and poured out its floods of water throughout a great portion of the night. But for the protection against the violence of the wind, afforded by the bluffs on one side and the timber on the other, our tents would have been swept away by the storm. The whole arch of the heavens for a time was wrapped in a sheet of flame, and the almost deafening crashes of thunder, following each other with scarcely an intermission between, seemed as if they would rend the solid earth, or topple it from its axis. A more sublime and awful meteoric display, I never witnessed or could conceive.

The morning of the 27th was clear, cloudless and peaceful, just as we have seen it many times in Kansas after a thunderstorm. The rain caused the river to rise several feet. Mr. Grayson, who was a member of the party, and others went out to search for bee trees and they returned with several baskets of honey.

It was on the morning of May 29, 1846, when Mrs. Keyes died. Mr. Bryant says:

> Last night Mrs. Sarah Keyes, a lady aged seventy, a member of the family of Mr. J. H. Reed, of Illinois, and his mother-in-law, died. Mr. Reed, with his family, is emigrating to California. The deceased Mrs. Keyes, however, did not intend to accompany him farther than Fort Hall, where she expected to meet her son who emigrated to Oregon two or three years since. Her health, from disease and the debility of age, was so feeble, that when she left her home she entertained but faint hopes of being able to endure the hardships of the journey. Her physicians had announced to her that she could live but a short time, and this time she determined to devote to an effort to see her only son once more on earth. Such is a mother's affection! The effort, however, was vain. She expired without seeing her child.
>
> The event . . . cast a shade of gloom over our whole encampment.

. . . All recreations were suspended, out of respect for the dead, and to make preparations for the funeral. A cottonwood tree was felled, and the trunk of it split into planks, which being first hewn with an axe and then planed, were constructed into a coffin, in which the remains of the deceased were deposited. A grave was excavated a short distance from the camp, under an oak tree on the right hand side of the trail. A stone was procured, the surface of which being smoothed, it was fashioned into the shape of a tombstone, and the name and age, and the date of the death of the deceased were graved upon it.

At 2 o'clock P. M., a funeral procession was formed, in which nearly every man, woman and child of the company united, and the corpse of the deceased lady was conveyed to its last resting place in this desolate but beautiful wilderness. Her coffin was lowered into the grave. A prayer was offered to the Throne of Grace by the Rev. Mr. Cornwall. An appropriate hymn was sung by the congregation with much pathos and expression. A funeral discourse was then pronounced by the officiating clergyman, and the services were concluded by another hymn and a benediction. The grave was then closed and carefully sodded with the green turf of the prairie, from whence annually will spring and bloom its brilliant and many-colored flowers. The inscription on the tombstone, and on the tree beneath which is the grave, is as follows: "Mrs. Sarah Keyes, Died May 29, 1846; Aged 70."

The night is perfectly calm. The crescent moon sheds her pale rays over the dim landscape; the whippoorwill is chanting its lamentations in the neighboring grove; the low and mournful hooting of the owl is heard at a far off distance, and altogether the scene, with its adjuncts around us, is one of peace, beauty and enjoyment.

Mr. Bryant described the Blue at Independence crossing as being a stream about one hundred yards wide, with turbid water and strong and rapid current. When he saw it it was in flood time. He mentions a small spring branch which empties into the Blue just above the ford. He followed up this small branch, he says, about three quarters of a mile from the camp, where he found a large spring of water, ice-cold and pure. From the shelving rock projecting over a basin a beautiful cascade of water fell some ten or twelve feet. This spring was named by them, "Alcove Spring," and many names were graven on the rocks, and on the trunks of trees surrounding it.

On March 16, 1930, the writer visited Independence crossing. The river was normal and the crossing was about fifty yards wide, with a gravelly bottom on the east side. Numerous floods had left a high bank on the west side. I am informed that this crossing was used a great deal up to the flood of 1903. The small stream emptying into the river just above the ford is still there, although at the time I visited it, it was dry. I followed the little creek up to Alcove Springs, which is about one half mile from the crossing, practically due east. No doubt the spring has changed considerably since Mr. Bryant saw it in 1846. No water was running over the ledge. The stones upon which the names were graven had broken from the ledge and had been washed down the stream a short distance. There were two very fine springs coming out of the ground on the east side. The following names and dates were engraved upon the rocks:

Alcove Spring

Engraved by Edwin Bryant

May 28, 1846

J. F. Reed

May 26, 1846

The small stream is called Alcove Springs creek. The grave of Sarah Keyes is between Alcove Springs and the crossing, as nearly as I can judge, about half way or a quarter of a mile from the springs and a quarter of a mile from the crossing. It is located on a sloping hill on the north side of Alcove Springs creek, about fifty yards from the wagon road. It is on the side of the bluffs and this ground is still virgin prairie, used for pasture. The grave is beside an oak tree, which now consists of three trees growing from the same stump. They are not very large, being about one foot in diameter in the largest place, although the stump from which they sprang is about two and one half to three feet thick. Apparently the parent tree was blown or cut down and these sprouts came up from the stump and grew together at the base and formed three trees. The stone which was fashioned into a headstone is still standing, the upper portion rounding. Apparently all markings are obliterated; neither did I find any markings on the tree as described by Bryant. This, however, is not strange, as eighty-four years had passed and the markings would have long since been grown over.

Independence crossing, the grave, and Alcove Springs are all in the southeast quarter of section thirty-one, Elm Creek township, in Marshall county. They may be easily reached by automobile, by driving to Blue Rapids, taking the Marysville road from there, and after crossing the Big Blue, taking the first road to the left and driving up the river to within two miles of Shroyer. This wagon road passes very close to the crossing and one can drive into the pasture, by the grave, and up to Alcove Springs.

One can only hazard a guess why this was called Independence crossing. Presumably it was named for Independence, Mo., where those traveling on the Oregon trail in the early days outfitted themselves for the journey across the plains. The Donner party named Alcove Springs. The early writers on the Donner party often referred to this grave as being near Manhattan, and in the Kansas City (Mo.) *Star* of Wednesday, June 11, 1930, in an article, "Death Takes the Last Survivor of the Donner Party," the following appears: "On May 29, Grandmother Keyes died and she was buried under a big oak tree where was later the city cemetery of Manhattan."

This of course is not true, as this grave is located about eight miles south of Marysville and about fifty-two miles north of Manhattan.

It may be of interest to know that Sarah Keyes was a great-aunt of James Madison Harvey, governor of Kansas in the early 1870's. Two sons and three daughters of ex-Governor Harvey still reside on the one hundred sixty acres preëmpted by him in Riley county in 1859.

Kansas History as Published in the Press

"The Story of the Queen's Daughters in the City of Wichita," by Mrs. Sophia Kramer Joy, was printed serially in *The Catholic Advance,* of Wichita, from January 12 to June 1, 1935. Persons interested in Kansas Catholic church history will find considerable material in the *Advance* which frequently publishes historical sketches of the various churches in the state.

A two-column history of School District No. 76, near Summerfield, appeared in the Summerfield *Sun* February 14, 1935.

Electors of the first election held in Corinth township, Osborne county, on November 4, 1873, were named in the Downs *News* February 21, 1935.

A history of Lone Tree school, Pottawatomie county, by Orman L. Miller, was printed in the Onaga *Herald* February 21 and 28, 1935. A list of teachers from 1875 to date was included.

Early Natoma history was discussed in articles published under the heading "Pioneer Gleanings" in the Natoma *Independent* February 28 and March 21, 1935.

Brief historical sketches of St. John's Evangelical Lutheran Church of Lincolnville, by the Rev. K. J. Karstensen, were printed in the Marion *Review* May 8, 1935, and the Marion *Record* May 9. The congregation was organized in 1877.

The Marion Methodist Episcopal Church observed the sixty-sixth anniversary of its founding with a week of special programs beginning May 19, 1935. A brief historical sketch of the church appeared in the Marion *Review* May 15. A more detailed history compiled by Mrs. William Rupp was published in the Marion *Record* May 16 and 23.

Reminiscences of Robert Banks, who settled in Kansas in 1854, as told to Mrs. R. C. Moseley, were contributed by her to the Wamego *Reporter* June 6, 1935.

Jefferson's Methodist Church history was briefly outlined in the Independence *South Kansas Tribune* June 12, 1935. The church building was dedicated June 7, 1885.

Clearwater's First Presbyterian Church history was briefly sketched by Mrs. Bessie Colver in the Clearwater *News* June 27, 1935. The church was organized in February, 1874.

An "old-fashioned" Fourth of July held in Altamont in 1905 was described in the Altamont *Journal* July 4, 1935.

The story of Camp Gardner, Johnson county transient camp, was contributed by Jack Chesbro to the Gardner *Gazette* July 31, 1935. The camp was established May 16, 1934.

Histories of the municipal bands of Belleville, Beloit, Bennington, Cuba, Ellsworth, Minneapolis and Salina were briefly sketched in the Ellsworth *Messenger* August 1, 1935.

Life in early Kiowa county as experienced by Mrs. Mary Evans and Charles Isham was described in an article appearing in the Greensburg *News* August 1, 1935. In the August 15 issue, James Briggs, another pioneer, recounted his experiences.

Several articles of historical interest were contributed by A. H. Stewart to Goodland newspapers in recent months. Titles of some of these stories and the dates of their publication were: "The Murder of Corley and Lynching of the McKinleys, Father and Son . . . Wallace County's Peak of Tragedy," *News-Republic*, August 7, 1935; "The Battle With the Train Robbers; a Stirring Event of 35 Years Ago," August 8, "Goodland Man Tells Interesting Facts About Early Day Droughts," September 5, and "Battle of Arickaree Was Section's Great Incident in Struggle for Prairies," September 12, in *The Sherman County Herald*.

"Methodism in Conway Springs" was the title of a three-column article written by F. H. Poore and L. E. McNeil for the Conway Springs *Star* August 8, 1935.

Arrival of the grasshoppers in Harvey county in 1874 was described by John S. Biggs, of Washington, D. C., in a two-column article appearing in the Sedgwick *Pantagraph* August 15, 1935.

The fifty-fifth anniversary of the founding of the Oneida Christian Church was celebrated August 18, 1935. A brief history of the church, which was organized by Elder R. C. Barrows on August 22, 1880, was published in the Seneca *Times* and *The Courier-Tribune* in their issues of August 15 and 22.

Subjects discussed by "Old-Timer" in recent issues of the Protection *Post* and the dates of their publication were: Red Bluff and

Protection townsites, August 15, 1935; preparations for Indian raid, September 5; a trip through the blizzard in the middle 1880's, December 12; early days in Protection, February 6, 1936, and the city's first newspaper, February 20.

Brief histories of the Kingman county farm bureau and 4-H clubs were printed in *The Leader-Courier,* of Kingman, August 16, 1935.

Frank D. Tomson's impressions and reminiscences of Burlingame were recorded in *The Enterprise-Chronicle,* Burlingame, August 29, 1935.

Norcatur's Methodist Episcopal Church celebrated the fiftieth anniversary of its founding September 1, 1935. Its history was briefly sketched in the Norcatur *Dispatch* August 29.

A twenty-page souvenir historical edition of the Potwin *Ledger* was issued September 5, 1935, commemorating the founding of the Potwin Methodist Episcopal Church fifty years ago.

The history of St. Augustine's church at Fidelity was reviewed in the Fairview *Enterprise* September 5, 1935. The first church edifice was built in the middle 1860's.

Gove county teachers for the 1935-1936 school term were named in the *Gove County Republican-Gazette,* of Gove City, September 12, 1935.

"Antecedents of Osage Mission," an article written in 1897 by the Rev. Paul M. Ponziglione, S. J., was printed in the St. Paul *Journal* September 12, 1935.

Excerpts from the diary of Stephen J. Wilson describing three guerilla "visits" to Gardner during the Civil War were published in the Gardner *Gazette* September 18, 25, and October 2, 1935. The raids, as reported by Mr. Wilson, occurred on October 22, 1861; in May, 1862; and on August 23, 1863.

A twenty-page souvenir edition of the Sedgwick *Pantagraph* was issued September 19, 1935, in commemoration of the incorporation of the Sedgwick Methodist Church on October 22, 1875.

The history of the Holy Trinity Catholic Church of Paola was briefly sketched in *The Western Spirit,* Paola, September 20, 1935. The church held special services October 10 in observance of the seventy-fifth anniversary of its founding.

A five-column illustrated history of the Coldwater Methodist Episcopal Church was published in *The Western Star*, of Coldwater, September 20, 1935. The church was organized in April, 1885.

Barton county's rural teachers for the 1935-1936 term were named in the Hoisington *Dispatch* September 26, 1935.

Early Altamont history as recorded in the city's first minute book was briefly recounted in the Altamont *Journal* October 3, 1935. The city was incorporated in September, 1884.

A series of articles on pioneer days in Kingman county as written by P. J. Conklin, early Kingman newspaperman in the fall of 1915 for *The Leader-Courier*, Kingman, was republished in issues dated from October 11 to November 15, 1935, inclusive.

Trego county teachers for the 1935-1936 school term were named in the *Western Kansas World*, Wakeeney, October 17, 1935.

The fiftieth anniversary of the dedication of the present Solomon Methodist Episcopal church building was celebrated October 25, 1935. A brief history of the organization, including names of pastors serving the church from 1870 to date, was published in the Solomon *Tribune* October 24. A more detailed history of the church by Ethel Vanderwilt followed in the *Tribune* in its issues of November 7 and 14.

Salem Lutheran Church of Lenexa celebrated its golden jubilee October 27, 1935. A history of the church as read at the anniversary meeting by the Rev. George W. Busch, pastor, was published in the Olathe *Mirror* and *The Johnson County Democrat* in their issues of October 31.

Life in early-day Rooks county as recalled by Mr. and Mrs. J. A. Hebrew, who came to Kansas in 1872, was published in W. F. Hughes' column "Facts and Comments" in the *Rooks County Record*, of Stockton, October 31 and November 7, 1935. The county's first election in 1872 was discussed in another article printed in the latter issue.

The killing of Stafford county's last wild buffalo in 1879 was described in the Topeka *Daily Capital* November 24, 1935.

Twenty-five years of reporting for the Bonner Springs *Chieftain* were recalled by Mrs. Frances Zumwalt Vaughn, its editor, in the issue of November 28, 1935.

"Memories of Four Mile in the Early Eighties," was the title of a one-column article by Ed A. Smies, of Manhattan, appearing in *The Times*, of Clay Center, December 26, 1935.

The history of the Quinter Church of the Brethren was sketched in *The Gove County Advocate*, of Quinter, December 26, 1935. The church was organized August 14, 1886.

"A Trip to Kansas and Return," the day-by-day account of Benjamin F. Pearson's journey from Iowa, May 20 to June 27, 1872, was published in the *Annals of Iowa*, Des Moines, in the January, 1936, issue. Mr. Pearson entered Kansas through Doniphan county and traveled west to Jewell county before returning.

A train robbery in Atchison in 1882 was described by Fred E. Sutton in an article printed in the Atchison *Daily Globe* January 1, 1936.

The Broken Treaty, a story of the Osage country, by W. W. Graves, publisher of the St. Paul *Journal*, is appearing serially in the *Journal* starting with the issue of January 2, 1936. The story was issued in book form in December, 1935.

Osborne county's log stockade, constructed in the early 1870's by pioneers for protection against the Indians, was described by Mrs. R. R. Hays in the Topeka *Daily Capital* January 5, 1936. Frank Rothenberger, of Osborne, is the only old-timer yet alive, Mrs. Hays related.

A history of *The Empire-Journal*, of Osborne, was briefly sketched in its issue of January 16, 1936. *The Empire-Journal* is a consolidation of the Alton *Empire* and the Osborne *Journal*.

Historic spots in Osborne county were mentioned in the *Osborne County Farmer*, of Osborne, January 16, 1936.

Recollections of Atchison in the latter part of the nineteenth century were recorded by Joseph Kathrens, of West Milton, Ohio, in letters printed in the Atchison *Daily Globe* January 20 and February 17, 1936.

St. Paul's Episcopal Church of Clay Center, established fifty-five years ago, observed its anniversary with special services January 23, 1936. The history of the church was reviewed in the Clay Center *Dispatch*, January 21, *The Economist*, January 22, and *The Times* January 23.

"L. H. Thorp Owned First Bicycle Ever Brought to Larned," the Larned *Chronoscope* reported in its issue of January 23, 1936. The first wheel was made in Pawnee county in 1881 and the first mail-order purchase arrived in the county late in December, 1882.

A history of the Masonic lodge of Larned was briefly sketched in *The Tiller and Toiler*, Larned, January 23, 1936. The lodge was organized in January 1876.

Several newspapers recently published brief histories of the telephone in their communities. Among these were: The Larned *Chronoscope* and *The Tiller and Toiler*, January 23, 1936; Council Grove *Republican*, January 27; Clifton *News*, January 30, and the Chanute *Tribune*, February 3.

An advertising circular of the Atchison Board of Trade, citing the early advantages of Atchison, was reprinted in the Atchison *Daily Globe* January 24, 1936. The circular was dated November 1, 1864.

"Buffalo Bill" Cody's life in Kansas—particularly in Leavenworth county—was recounted in the Leavenworth *Times* January 26, 1936. It has been proposed in Leavenworth to erect a bronze statue honoring Cody on Highway 73, northwest of the city, near the spot where he spent his boyhood days.

The story of the invention of basketball was told in a two-column article printed in the Topeka *Daily Capital* January 26, 1936. Dr. James A. Naismith, now of Kansas University, devised the game while a staff member of the Y. M. C. A. college at Springfield, Mass. "Kansas Women's Republican Club's Six Years of Service," by Margaret Hill McCarter, was another historical feature of this issue of the *Capital*.

A horseback ride from Wakefield to Manhattan and back in the winter of 1872 was described by Dr. Charles Hewitt, of Manhattan, in *The Economist*, of Clay Center, January 29, 1936.

Leavenworth's reception of the news that Kansas had been admitted to the Union was recounted in the Kansas City (Mo.) *Star* January 29, 1936, under the title "Dan Anthony Scooped His Own Paper When Kansas Entered the Union."

Kansas history was reviewed in Kansas Day editions of Topeka's dailies issued January 29, 1936. Articles by Milton Tabor entitled "Highlights of Kansas History From Coronado to Now" and "Modern Day Topekans Owe Much to Pioneers," were featured in the *Daily Capital*. In the *State Journal* special articles on the early history of the Kansas Day Club by Frank S. Crane, Leonard S. Ferry, Charles F. Scott, George A. Clark, Charles M. Harger, Charles S. Elliott and Ewing Herbert were prominently displayed. Titles of other articles included "First Press, 1833," by Eileen Reinhardt; "Topeka in 1861," and "When Kansas Heard 'Flash' of Statehood," by George A. Root, and "Farm Growth Since 1861 Is Story of Toil."

The history of Kanwaka community, Douglas county, was outlined in the Lawrence *Daily Journal-World* January 30, 1936. The sketch was a review of a paper presented by Mrs. Nellie Colman Brigsby at a meeting of the Douglas County Historical Society on January 29.

Histories of Summerfield and its newspaper, the *Sun*, were briefly reviewed in the Summerfield *Sun* January 30, 1936.

Spearville's history was reviewed by Carol Jean Nelson in the Spearville *News* January 30, 1936.

Pleasant Hour Club of Paola observed the sixtieth anniversary of its founding at a meeting held January 30, 1936. The history of the organization was sketched in *The Miami Republican*, of Paola, January 31.

The Leon *News'* "Fifth Annual M. E. Booster Edition," featuring histories of the church and city, was issued January 31, 1936.

Le Roy Methodist Church history was reviewed in the Le Roy *Reporter* January 31, 1936. The congregation was regularly established as the Le Roy mission in 1858.

"Chronology of the *Farmer's* Ten Years of Existence in Rolla," by A. B. Edson, and "Morton County Pioneers Recall the Early History of Morton County," as compiled by Bertha Carpenter, were feature articles of *The Morton County Farmer*, of Rolla, January 31, 1936.

Celebrating Kansas' seventy-fifth birthday, the *Graduate Magazine* of the University of Kansas at Lawrence issued a "Kansas Day Number" in February, 1936. "Kansas Before the Indians," by Kenneth K. Landes, and "Some Notes on the University's Progress," by Fred Ellsworth, were features.

A sawmill boiler explosion in Leavenworth county in 1861 which fatally injured eight men was recalled in the Leavenworth *Times* February 2, 1936.

The Kansas City *Kansan* issued its special "1936 Yearly Progress Edition" February 2, 1936, observing the fifteenth anniversary of the taking over of the *Kansan* by the present management, the fiftieth anniversary of the city of Kansas City, and the seventy-fifth anniversary of the state.

Instances of American Indian tribes sanctioning public ownership of utilities, free public school systems, woman's suffrage, fraternal organizations and prohibition were related by Grant W. Harrington in a letter published in *The Masonic News*, of Kansas City, February 7, 1936.

Two articles contributed by George J. Remsburg to the Leavenworth *Times* and published in recent issues were: "A Century Ago in and Around Leavenworth," appearing February 9, 1936, and "Kapioma, a Kickapoo Chief, Killed by Texans in the '60's," printed February 14.

A history of the Holyrood *Gazette* was reviewed by John Russmann, editor, in the issue of February 12, 1936. An article on the origin of the city's name was another feature of this edition.

Stockton's old log hotel built in 1871 by Joseph McNulty was mentioned by W. F. Hughes in the *Rooks County Record*, of Stockton, February 13, 1936.

Pioneer memories of James Barton, of Cuba, who settled in Republic county in 1871 were published in the Belleville *Telescope* February 13, 20, and 27, 1936.

"Tracing the March of Coronado Through Kansas to Find His Tomb in Mexico," as told by Paul Jones, of Lyons, to A. B. MacDonald, was the title of an article printed in the Kansas City (Mo.) *Star* February 16, 1936.

Highlights in the history of the Frankfort *Daily Index*, founded on February 26, 1906, were recounted by Jim Reed in the Topeka *State Journal* February 20, 1936. H. H. and A. P. Hartman, sons of F. M. Hartman, one of the cofounders, are the publishers.

The history of School District No. 66 near Summerfield was outlined in the Summerfield *Sun* February 20, 1936. District 66 was formed from a division of Districts 47 and 22 in 1885.

"Great frauds in connection with the adoption of the Lecompton constitution came to light through the revelations of Charlie Torry," the Kansas City (Mo.) *Times* reported in a two-column illustrated article appearing in its issue of February 21, 1936. Torry, who was a clerk in the office of the surveyor general at Lecompton, witnessed the hiding of fraudulent election returns and revealed their whereabouts in time for the subsequent publicity to prevent the adoption of the constitution by Congress.

Several letters describing Clay Center's street cars which were operated in the late 1880's were published in the Clay Center *Dispatch* starting February 24, 1936.

The Pratt *Daily Tribune* printed a forty-four page "Yearly Progress Edition" February 26, 1936, featuring stories and photographs of Pratt's leading institutions and business houses and pictures of several prominent citizens.

A "Cornerstone Edition" of the Caldwell *Daily Messenger* was issued February 26, 1936, announcing the program for the cornerstone laying of Caldwell's new city building on February 27. "City Founded 65 Years Ago by Wichita Group" and "Oil Found Here After 40 Years" were the titles of two historical articles in the edition.

Some of the more important historical documents and collections preserved by the Kansas State Historical Society were discussed by Cecil Howes in a two-column article in the Kansas City (Mo.) *Times* March 6, 1936. Included among other recent articles by Mr. Howes were: "Eighty Years Ago 'Beecher's Bibles' Made Their Appearance in Kansas," published in the *Times*, February 26, and "Marker Sought for Site of Lone Tree Indian Massacre in Southwest Kansas," in the *Star* of March 28.

Linn history was sketched by Mrs. Vern Sizemore in a paper delivered at a recent meeting of the Linn Study Club and published in the Linn-Palmer *Record* February 28, 1936. Linn, which was established in 1877, was originally called Summit.

Henry W. Kandt's reminiscences of early-day Kansas and Dickinson county in particular were related in the Abilene *Daily Reflector* February 29, 1936. Mr. Kandt arrived in the territory in 1859.

"Rise and Fall of Most Famous 'Ghost Town' in Kansas," was the title of Harold C. Place's brief sketch of Minneola in the March, 1936, issue of *Progress in Kansas*, published at Topeka.

Included among the historical articles printed in recent issues of the *Pony Express Courier*, of Placerville, Calif., were: "Curing Buffalo Meat," by John G. Ellenbecker, "Guittard Station and Its Founder," and "Abe Lincoln [while in Atchison in 1859] Made Jack Slade Laugh," in the March, 1936, number; "The Pony Express Service and Harry Roff," by Frances Fairchild, and "Daniel Montgomery Drumheller," a Pony Express rider, by John G. Ellenbecker, in the April issue.

"The Father of Governor Landon Points With Paternal Pride" was the title of a five-column interview A. B. MacDonald had with John M. Landon published in the Kansas City (Mo.) *Star* March 1, 1936.

Notes on the history of the Republican party in Kansas, and biographical sketches of several prominent members of the party, past and present, were included in a special thirty-two page Republican supplement issued by the Wichita *Beacon* March 4, 1936. On April 28 the *Beacon* issued its Democratic party supplement, featuring biographies of national and state Democratic leaders.

A history of the Wilson State Bank was sketched in the Wilson *World* March 4, 1936. The bank was chartered July 16, 1886.

Twenty-two Republic county ghost towns were named in the Belleville *Telescope* March 5, 1936.

Marquette Mission Covenant Church observed the thirty-fifth anniversary of its founding March 6 to 8, 1936. A two-column history of the organization by Edwin T. Clemens was published in the Marquette *Tribune* March 5, 1936.

A brief history of Charity Masonic Lodge No. 263 was printed in the Hazelton *Herald* March 6, 1936. The lodge was organized on June 30, 1885.

"Plow Not to Blame for Dust Storms Say Old-Time Western Kansans," the Kansas City (Mo.) *Star* reported in its issue of March 9, 1936. The article included quotations from the journals of early explorers who had encountered dust storms in this region.

The route of the Chisholm trail was discussed by T. E. Beck writing in a recent issue of the *Grant County Journal*, of Medford, Okla.

His observations were reprinted in the Wichita (Evening) *Eagle* March 11, 1936.

Several Kansans who are prominent in theater or radio professions were named by Phil Zimmerman, of Lindsborg, in a short article published in the Topeka *State Journal's* radio column March 12, 1936.

Early-day recollections of Anderson county as told by B. F. Reiber to the editor of the Kincaid *Dispatch* were printed in the *Dispatch* March 12, 1936. Mr. Reiber settled in eastern Kansas in 1870.

The history of the Beloit *Gazette* was briefly reviewed in its issue of March 12, 1936. The *Gazette* is now entering its sixty-fifth year.

"How Nova School in Carmi Township Received Its Name," by M. H. Long, was the title of a one-column article in the Preston *News* March 13, 1936.

The twenty-fifth anniversary of the Independence Methodist Episcopal Church, six miles southeast of Goddard, was observed March 15, 1936. Pictures and a brief history of the church were printed in the Wichita *Beacon* March 15.

"Orders for Founding Fort on West Bank of Missouri River Issued in March, 109 Years Ago," was the title of an article recounting the early history of Fort Leavenworth in the Leavenworth *Times* March 15, 1936.

The early history of old Paxico, near present Paxico, Wabaunsee county, was reviewed by E. B. Chapman in the Topeka *State Journal* March 19, 1936.

Augusta's newspaper history was sketched in the Augusta *Journal* March 20, 1936. The *Journal* was founded on March 17, 1887.

Seven families of Amish farmers have moved from their frontier homesteads at Yoder (now an oil producing center) to Iowa. In an interview with members of the settlement Pliny Castanien, Wichita *Eagle* newsman, relates in the *Sunday Eagle* of March 22, 1936, that "Tractors, Not Oil, Cause Kansas Amish to Migrate."

The history of the Henry Rohr chapter, Order of the Eastern Star, was reviewed by Mrs. Isabel Mace Gillmore for the St. John *News* March 26, 1936.

Kansas Historical Notes

The federal government is sponsoring several projects in the historical field of interest to Kansans. In addition to local projects under the Works Progress Administration and the National Youth Administration operating under the sponsorship of the Kansas State Historical Society at the Society's rooms in Topeka are three of state-wide and national scope. The American Guide Manual, a writers' project of the WPA, is employing persons in all sections of the state to prepare material for the Kansas section of a manual to be published in five regional volumes. The topics to be included in the manual are: Topography, fauna, flora, history, Indian tribes and reservations, folks, monuments, literature, music, art, education, religion, libraries, museums, health and social work, recreation, transportation, hotels, industries, products, markets, organizations, waterways and conservation. A Historical Records Survey, to include city, county and state archives, was recently instituted by the Kansas WPA. Work is also progressing in several cities of the state on a Federal Archives survey. It is planned under the latter organizations to compile a catalogue showing the nature and location of documents and historical material throughout the state. Other projects of a local historical nature are being sponsored in several Kansas communities. A local project to index the contents of all Russell county newspaper files was recently started under the supervision of Judge J. C. Ruppenthal, of Russell. The Fort Hays Kansas State College library is also working on an index of several western Kansas newspapers, files of which are preserved at Hays.

THE
Kansas Historical Quarterly

Volume V   Number 3

August, 1936

PRINTED BY KANSAS STATE PRINTING PLANT
W. C. AUSTIN, STATE PRINTER
TOPEKA 1936
16-3875

Contributors

LELA BARNES is curator of manuscripts of the Kansas State Historical Society.

DR. EDWARD BUMGARDNER, dentist by profession and a long-time member of the Kansas State Historical Society, is a resident of Lawrence.

THOMAS CLARKE WELLS, who died in 1907, was an early settler near Manhattan. For a biographical sketch see page 143 of the May number.

GEORGE A. ROOT is curator of archives of the Kansas State Historical Society.

NOTE.—Articles in the *Quarterly* appear in chronological order without regard to their importance.

Journal of Isaac McCoy for the Exploring Expedition of 1828

Lela Barnes

I. Introduction

WITH the purchase of Louisiana by the United States in 1803, removal of eastern Indians to unoccupied territory became a feasible plan, but it was not until the election of Andrew Jackson that settlement of the tribes on lands west of the Mississippi river became established as a national policy. By this time several tribes had removed to the West under treaty arrangements; removal of those remaining was legalized by the act of Congress of 1830.

A step in the development of this program was an exploring expedition ordered in 1828 to permit certain tribes to examine the country west of the Mississippi and select locations. Isaac McCoy, Baptist missionary at Carey, Michigan, was appointed commissioner to accompany representatives of the tribes.[1] His appointment and instructions were contained in a letter from Thomas L. McKenney, superintendent of Indian trade:

Department of War,
Off: Ind: Affairs,
10th June, 1828.

To The Revd.
Isaac McCoy,
Supt. Indian School,
Carey, via Fort Wayne, Indiana.—
Sir,

The Congress having appropriated fifteen thousand Dollars to defray the expense of an exploring party of Indians, and you having made known the desire of certain Potawatomies to visit the Country west of the Mississippi, the Secretary of War directs me to inform you that you are appointed to accompany the party, and that you are at liberty to take with you three Potawatomies, and if necessary an Interpreter. To you is confided the trust of expending the means provided for the expense of the undertaking. You will be particular therefore in the exercise of a rigid economy, and in keeping regular and properly vouched accounts of the expenditures. Of the fifteen thousand Dollars, I am directed to authorize you to draw for Ten thousand on the Secretary of War, at sight, accompanying the bill with a letter of advice.

You will repair to St. Louis as early as possible, and report to Genl. Wm. Clark, Supt. Ind: Affairs, who has instructions upon the subject, and who will name a leader of the party, and in general give the necessary detailed instructions for the government of your route and movements.

---

1. For a sketch of McCoy's work with the Indians of Indiana and Michigan, from which developed his interest in Indian reform, see "Isaac McCoy and the Treaty of 1821," *The Kansas Historical Quarterly*, May, 1936.

Should it be found indispensable to use more than ten thousand Dollars, in paying the necessary expenses of the undertaking, Genl. Clark will arrange with you at St. Louis for the remainder of the appropriation by placing it within your reach, which, however it is expected will be so managed as to cover the cost of the agents, including your own pay, and which will be made equivalent, as far as that may be possible, to the nature and value of the services which you may render.

The Chickasaws and Choctaws are notified to be off as soon as possible. You had better drop Genl. Clark, at St. Louis, a line saying when you will be there. *Move quick.* I am

Very Respectfully
Yr Obt. Servt.
Tho: L. McKenney[2]

McCoy's acceptance was as follows:

Carey, 100 Miles N. West of
Fort Wayne, Ind. July 1, 1828

Sir

Yesterday I had the honor to receive your favour of the 10th ult. authorizing and instructing me to accompany an exploring party of Indians to West of Mississippi.

In obedience to your instruction, I shall set out tomorrow for St. Louis accompanied by several Indians.

Most Respectfully
Sir Your Obt. Sevt.
Isaac McCoy[3]

Thomas L. McKenney Esq.
  Department of War,
  Off. Ind. Affairs,
  Washington.

With representatives of the Pottawatomie and Ottawa tribes McCoy set out for St. Louis on July 2, 1828. Upon arrival there it was found that delegations from the southern tribes would not reach the city for some time. Fearing that the entire project would have to be abandoned if it became necessary to postpone the starting date until late in the season, McCoy persuaded General Clark to authorize two tours, one for the Pottawatomie and Ottawa representatives who were already on the ground, and a later tour for the Creeks, Choctaws and Chickasaws should representatives of the two last named tribes arrive in time.

McCoy's journal here reproduced covers the journey from Michigan to St. Louis and the first tour with the northern Indians.[4] A second tour was made, but the journal record is missing.

Following the journal entries are various statements of account,

---

2. Isaac McCoy collection of manuscripts, Kansas State Historical Society.
3. *Ibid.* Autograph draft signed.
4. *Ibid.*

provision lists and receipts, suggestive of the needs and costs of the expedition. Unless marked as original these documents are duplicates retained by McCoy for his own records and preserved with his correspondence.

II. ENTRIES FROM THE JOURNAL: JULY 2 TO OCTOBER 12, 1828

At Camp, Wednesday, July 2d. 1828 Shawaunukwuk, one of the Putawatomies who are to accompany me, went day before yesterday to see some of his friends, and commenced drinking. Yesterday I sent twice after him, but could not get him home. This morning I sent for him early He came but had sold his shirt which we had given him a few days since, for whiskey, and had abused an outer garment which I had lent him.

At ten o'clock I made a short address to our company and set out on our journey to west of Mississippi. Our company consisted of, Naoquah Kozhuk, Gosa, & Wesauogana, Ottawas, and Magaukwok, & Shawaunukwuk, Puts. & Shadenoy, who is half Putawatomie for an interpreter. Several of the neighbors were present at our starting. My wife and child, and Mr. Bay accompanied us this day, and will spend the night with us, and return tomorrow. By the Secretary of War we are directed to proceed to St. Louis, & report to Genl. Clark, of whom we shall receive further instructions.

Wednesday July 3 I was quite sick during the night, became worse at daylight—took medicine and at 9 o'clock took my leave of my wife and babe, our brother Bay. They started back and we proceeded. I was scarcely able to set on my horse. At 12 better, at which time I write this. After taking some food, and rest, felt better and proceeded. Encamped beside a small Creek.

Friday July 4 Swam our horses across Calemink, mired one at [an]other place, and with some difficulty got him a[nd] the others across that and similar rivers, and encamped at the mouth of the Calemink.

Saturday July 5 Having some writing to do we [c]ould not leave our camp before 9 o'clock. It was fortunate for us that we were near an encampment of Indians. Of them we obtained a Canoe, in which we crossed the Calemink ourselves and baggage, & swam the horses. We reached Chicago about 12, wh[ere] we found a few articles which we needed, & transacted some other business. I have written the governor requesting, for reasons assigned, that the treaty on St. Joseph be deferred till October in the hope that by that time

I may be back. The Putawatomies with me having seen the new country may be of service at this treaty. Mr. Reed, subagent at Carey has promised to write Gov. Cass to the same effect. I had hoped also that the agt. and subagt. A[lexande]r Wolcott and Mr. Doyle of this place, would also commend the same to the Governor but this they declined for reasons which they did not assign. I am of opinion that these gentlemen, tho. very friendly to me personally are unfriendly to the project of the removal of the Indians. Mr. Siliman the Governor's nephew, now on a commission to the Winabago & others, will do what he can for us in relation to the treaty.

Spent some time swimming our horses across Chicago river, and crossed our baggage in a very small Canoe, and encamped on the river Auplain, 12 miles from Chicago Fort, or Fort Dearbourn. Every day we pass Indians traveling or encamped. We are now near an encampment.

River Auplain[5]
12 miles from Chicago
Sunday July 6
1828

Here we are resting. At half past 8 o'clock commenced Service in Ottawa, which consisted of a hymn & prayer a discourse, & concluded with another Hymn. In the evening we had a Hymn & prayer. Having little to do, am afforded time for reflection on the awful responsibility which at this time devolves upon me. This is increased [by] a view of the peculiar and very merciful dealings of Providence [in] relation to our affairs.

The measure of alocating the Indians in a country of *their own* under suitable provisions of our government, is the only one in which we can discover grounds to hope for their preservation. This measure is warmly opposed by many in authority. Zealous efforts on the part of a few worthy advocates, obtained for it a majority in the House of Representatives in Congress merely of *ten votes*. We have laboured more than five years on the subject, and do now rejoice to see that it has gained an ascendency over opposition, and, the more to be dreaded apathy of too many, even in the small degree which authorizes this expedition. Should some disaster, or some mismanagement occur—Should the Indians be dissatisfied with the country they shall see, the business might receive such a check that it could not be resusitated until too late for many almost expiring tribes! We are going to look [for] a home for a homeless people—a people who were once lords of all the Continent of America, and whose just claims have never been acknowledged by others, nor conveyed away by themselves. Half the United States say the

---

5. Des Plaines river.

southern Indians shall not come north of the degree of 36-30 N. latitude. Or in other words we are limited to the regions west of Arkansas territory, and Missouri State. Should the inhospitableness of that country deny them a place there, they will be left destitute unless mercy provides by means unseen to short sighted mortals.

I feel myself inadequate to these responsibilities. The particulars of this inadequacy need not be entered in my journal. But under a sense of dependence on God I have asked of *Him* the appointment which I now have received—and to *Him* I look for ability to perform its duties. To *Him alone* must be ascribed the Kingdom and the power and the *Glory* for ever Amen!

River Auplain Left camp at six oclock At noon halted for dinner
Monday, July 7 near the river. Passed this morning a curious rock singly in the prarie, porous, with holes large enough to admit Dozens of apartments for snakes, and convenient passages from one to the other. The rock is about 9 feet long 7 wide, & 4 feet higher than the surface of the ground. Three or four striped snakes were basking in the sunshine on the top, which retired on our approach, others or the same were seen passing at pleasure through their habitation.

In the afternoon passed a singular hill rising about 40 feet in the level prarie, mentioned by Schoolcraft.[6] Encamped at the River Page.

Tuesday Arrived at 12—encamped at the mouth of Fox river
July 8 about this place reside a few distressed looking white people

Wednesday 9 Crossed Illinois river in a canoe, and swam our horses. Passed several huts of poor looking white people, near one of which we halted for dinner—tired of bacon, we have been able to take a few pigions, & the like, but cannot get either beef, venison, or chicken, of the few inhabitants. Travelled ten miles without the appearance of a road, steering our way thro. the praries. Encamped earlier than usual for the sake of water—four of our men Hunted till dark, but killed nothing.

Thursday As usual halted an hour and a half at noon. Encamped
July 10 about 10 miles South of Fort Clark. Bot. some bacon, and a fowl today, at one of the two houses we have passed. Travelled several miles without a road.

6. Schoolcraft, Henry R., *Travels in the Central Portion of the Mississippi Valley* (New York, 1825), pp. 330, 331. See, also, "Mount Joliet: Its Place in Illinois History and Its Location," by Robert Knight and Lucius Zeuch, in *Journal of the Illinois Historical Society*, April, 1930.

Friday July 11 We commonly set out at 6 oclock in the morning. Since we passed Chicago we have travelled about 14 miles of every 15 in Prarie. Since we left Illinois river Praries have been more extensive. To our left there is only now and then a small grove or streak of timber along water courses. We usually encamp in the open Prarie contiguous to wood for fuel. Dews fall heavy on us. Where there is no fear of rain I merely pitch my musquito bar, this morning it was so wet that water could be wrung out of it.

We dined in a Prarie where no fuel could be obtained within a long distance except pieces of a Broken bridge of which we availed ourselves of as much as cooked our dinner encamped on a branch of Sangamo[n].

Saturday July 12 Dined near a whiteman's house, where we obtained a kettle to aid in preparing our dinner. passed Springfield near Sangamo[n] river. The inhabitants and people around the place may be denominated unmannerly or without manners at all. Bot. a little sugar & flour. Encamped on a branch of Sangamo[n]. We are yet 93 miles from St. Louis.

Sunday July 13 I halted here last evening with a severe pain in the head which continued the greater part of this day. I have had a sick day. About 10 in the morning took a potion of Rheubarb & Magnesia. So sick that we could have no other service morning and evening than a hymn and prayer. Confined to my tent most of the day.

The difficulties attendant on such tours as this seem small while in tolerable health compared with the magnitude to which they swell in sickness. The parting with my dear wife and babe after they had accompanied us one day & night, was rendered doubly hard by the circumstance of my being so sick as to be scarcely able to sit on my horse at the time of our adieus. My poor wife had mounted her horse—and waited to see me seated on mine then rode off without once looking back.

Monday July 14 Set off at 6 a. m. quite unwell, yet rode 22 miles before we halted for dinner. Ate very little, proceeded 18 miles further and encamped near one of the 3 houses we have passed to-day. I am so tired of our travelling food that my appetite will not take it. Tried here to get something more palatable, but could obtain nothing but 3 eggs, of two of these I prepared a pudding which I tied up in a cloth & boiled, and ate with sweetened water. I have just finished my repast. I am saving my third egg for my breakfast. My health more comfortable. Two men out looking for deer.

Tuesday July 15   A young man left camp early to look for Deer, joined a mile or two from camp but had taken nothing. Dined in a prarie where scarcely a few small bushes could be found along a rivulet, sufficient to prepare our dinner, two small willows were found and placed in the ground so as with the assistance of my umbrella, to shelter me from the sun. The flies bad—the road remarkably dusty, water found at eight and nine miles distance, houses not so frequent, until evening we reached Edwardsville. The settlement now compact. Encamped two miles South of Edwardsville.

Wednesday July 16   By a disagreeable ride thro. the praries, sunbeams, and *dust,* of 18 miles we reached Mississippi opposite St. Louis about 12 o'clock, after waiting an hour for the boat we crossed, and pitched our tents a mile above the town. I returned and made my call on Genl. Clark. He presently introduced me to a Captain Kennerly[7] who has been appointed leader of the party.

The Southern deputations of Indians have not yet arrived. Some preparations are making for the tour, and it is thought we may leave this by the 27th and return in the course of 50 or 60 days.

Cap. Kennerly appears to be a pleasant man. He has lately resigned an Indian Agency up the Missouri. He is well acquainted with the Country & people we expect to visit. He was spoken of by the Department of war as suitable for our leader, at the same time an opinion was expressed by the Department that he would likely not accept the appointment, and in that case Genl. Clark to whom the trust of appointing was confided was to appoint another person. But he has accepted, and I trust will do well.

In the evening we brought our horses into town to have them fed, and I took lodgings at the City Hotel. The company sleep in their tents tonight.

Thursday July 17   Wish'd to procure lodgings for our Indians in town but did not succeed. Wrote many letters.

Friday July 18   Made arrangements for lodgings for our Indians. Sent out for them and their baggage, when to my grief I learnt that some of them had become intoxicated. Noonday & Wesauogana came in, expressed great grief that the thing had oc-

---

7. George Hancock Kennerly.

curred. These were sober. Chandonois & the others kept away in order to get sober and through the day, came to their lodgings and lay down. They had not been much drunk, except Chandonois who came in the evening much intoxicated Mr. Forsythe saw him and as he was taking him up stairs to their lodgings, Chandonois fell and wounded his face. About that time I went into the room.. He was becoming noisy as a drunken Indian, when I took hold on him and told him to lay down & become quiet which he did. I was much mortified at this circumstance.

Dined at Genl. Clark's in company of Col. Menard going on to treaties at Green Bay & Carey.

Saturday July 19 This morning early I was attacked with a bowel complaint supposed to be chiefly the effect of the water of this place, which to my taste is unpalateable, and always warm except when cooled with ice. I had a poor day confined to my room until evening when I rode out a short distance.

Sunday July 20 Feel in better health this morning. I have talked with Chandonois and the Indians and they say they think the error will not be repeated. Chandonois says he knows he has done wrong, and that he will not repeat it here. The Indians blame him for leading them into the error. Gosa pleads that he did not expose himself, that he drank a little and lay down until he had recovered and then came into town. Went to hear a Presbyterian preach in company of several of our Indians.

Monday July 20 [21] Among other business gave drafts on Sec. War to the amount of $5000. Wrote home by Maj. Forsythe & Col. Menard who are going to attend the treaties.

Tuesday July 21 [22] Rode into the country ten or 12 miles to seek for accommodations for ourselves and horses, this measure I believed would tend to the improvement of the condition of our horses, the preservation of our health and would be much more economical. Lodged at H. Walton's. On this day at my instance Cap. Kennerly & Genl. Clark sent a man in a steam boat to inquire after the southern Indians. Genl. Clark gave him instructions.

Wednesday July 23 This morning I pursued my inquiries, breakfasted at J. Walton's rode into St. Louis at one oclock p. m. Having engaged horsekeeping and boarding at a Mr. Brown's, by which the 22 horses, and eight persons now here on expenses very high could be accomodated at a saving of $58.50 for every week.

On arriving in town I communicated this inteligence to Cap. Kennerly and Genl. Clark, both of whom approved of the arrangement, though about four of the horses they suppose will be needed in town and will not be sent out.

Thursday July 24   I took our company of Indians and our horses and rode out into the country ten miles, to Mr. Brown's where I had procured quarters. Cap. Kennerly has promised to send out ten of the other horses today, keeping four in town for other uses.

Friday July 25   The other horses from town have not arrived Wrote several letters, and also wrote some Indian.

Saturday July 26   Cap. Kennerly sent out to my care 9 horses. We are comfortably situated here, and our horses have a fine situation. Thankful for a letter from my son Calvin in Ohio, by which I heard from my Dear children scattered in three different places among strangers.

While in St. Louis Wesauogana met with a cousin of his, a girl of about 11 years of age, whose parents were dead, and she had fallen into the hand of some poor Sauks. The child wept and begged him to help her. The people whom she was following also desired to get rid of her. On being informed of this and asked by Wesauogana if I would do any thing for her, I obtained the consent of Mrs. Brown to take her in here. Weasauogana and Gosa went into St. Louis today, reached the camp of the Sauks a little before they left the place. And brot. her hither. The child is very sick of a fever. Wesauogana put her on his horse, and led him, but it would have been with difficulty she could have reached this, had not young Mr. Brown, who was returning in a Dearbourne, kindly taken her into his carriage. I have hired Mr. Brown's to take care of her until we return from our tour to the west, when we design to take her with us to one of our schools.

Sunday 27, July   Rode three miles to a Baptist meeting house, heard sermon and preached myself from Prov. 1. 32, 33.

Monday 28   Rode to St. Louis. Heard no news of the rest of our party, transacted some business.

Tuesday 29 & Wednes. 30   Employed busily in drawing a map of the country west of Arkansas Ter. & State of Missouri, and S. West of Missouri river.

Thursday 31   Went into St. Louis—no news from the rest of our company.

Friday Aug. 1　　Worked faithfully on my map.
Saturday Aug. 2

Sunday, 3　　Preached at the place at which I reside, a funeral sermon on the recent deaths two sisters who died within a few hours of each other and were buried at the same time and place, one of whom was buried with an infant in her arms. A congregation respectable for numbers and attention attended.

Monday Aug. 4　　Received a letter from my Son Rice in Kentucky, containing the very satisfactory inteligence that my daughter Sarah at School in Cincinnati with a younger sister, herself about 13 years of age, had lately been Baptized by Rev. Vardeman of Kentucky. This little girl is the first of my children which has made public profession of religion. I cannot conceive of any other kind of inteligence that I could have received that would have afforded equal satisfaction, or equally conferred on me a sense [of] gratitude to God. The circumstance seems to have inspired new hopes in relation to my other dear children, and increased fervour to prayers in their behalf. The necessity of having our children scattered, not among relatives & particular friends, but as I may say, among strangers, has given their good mother and me much uneasiness. But hitherto the Lord has been very merciful to us in relation to our children.

Tuesday Aug. 5　　Yesterday three of our Indians went into St. Louis. I had requested a gentleman to take care of them. He sent them out of town in time but at some wretched whiskey-shops on the road they obtained liquor and came home drunk. Two of them capable of taking care of themselves, the other was brot. home by Mr. Brown in his little wagon who found them drinking by the road side about four miles from this.

I was in bed before they arrived, and on hearing a noise went into the Indians' apartment to quiet the drunkard. He obeyed me in undressing and laying down, but as soon as he supposed I had left the room he would again begin his noise, and it was with difficulty that a young man could hold him. I at length with the assistance of the young Indian tied his hands and feet, and left him to loosen him when he would become quiet. They lost a few articles they had bot. in St. Louis.

This day I completed my map of the country proposed for Indian territory. It is 2 feet 7 inches by about 3 feet.

Wednesday—　　Wrote—not much to do.

Thursday— Cap. Kennerly sent me a letter he had received from the man sent to the Southern Indians. Information he had received on the way was calculated to cause fears that those Indians would not come at all. The man himself may be back in a few days.

Friday Aug. 8 — I rode to St. Louis. Recd. a letter from Mr. Simerwell[s] in Boston informing that a Mr. Bingham had been appointed a missionary to Saut De St. Marie. We had hoped that Mr. Bingham would have come to Carey[9] for the assistance of that place after the departure of Mr. Lykins[10] and myself. A Mr. Stannard whom we hoped would engage with us, or at St. Marie, is in a state of health too poor to engage. We are in much want of missionary aid for Carey.

Saturday & Sunday 10 — Remained at home. Sunday had a prayer, &c. for such as understand English, and a service in Indian.

Monday— Tuesday— Wednesday 13 — I have had little to do this week, and this day above all others since I left home, I am tired of delay, lonesome, & homesick. I cannot be contented in idleness, and our delay here must make sad havoc of some of our favourite plans of the coming autumn.

Thursday Aug. 14 — I went into St. Louis. Met a note from Cap. Kennerly informing that Mr. Blake and three Creek Indians & an interpreter had arrived. Their horses are sent out to our place. I introduced 3 of our Indians with me to the Creeks—hope they will consent to come into the country.

Thankful for a letter from my Son at Carey, 16 days after I left home, and that all were well.

I called on Col. Benton,[11] a Senator, and Chairman of the Committee on Indian affairs, whose aid was last winter solicited and afforded in support of the exploring bill.

Friday & Saturday — I did little except write Indian

Sunday— Rode out to hear a Presbyterian preach—preached myself from the parable of the talents.

---

8. Robert Simerwell, Baptist missionary. See *The Kansas Historical Quarterly*, February, 1932, p. 91, footnote 6.

9. Carey mission, on St. Joseph's river, Michigan. For an account of the founding of this mission see *ibid.*, May, 1936.

10. Johnston Lykins, Baptist missionary.—*Ibid.*, February, 1932, p. 90, footnote 3.

11. Thomas Hart Benton (1782-1858), American statesman, U. S. senator from Missouri 1820-1850.

This evening I received a letter from Cap. Kennerly saying the man whom we had sent to inquire the cause of delay of the Chickesaws, & Choctaws, returned on Saturday, with a letter from Colbert, Principal Chief of the Chickesaws, saying that they and the Choctaws had decided not to go on the exploring expedition until next March. The reasons assigned by him for this conclusion were, it had become so late in the season that cold weather wo[ul]d overtake them, and there would be no grass for horses, it would be severe on the men, and the ground would be covered with snow so that its quality could not be determined. They said that they had received no orders to march from the war Department, and knew nothing of the time to go, &c. until our express arrived.

Blake who came in the other day with the Creeks, saw the Agent & Subagent of the Chickasaws, on his way. He said they were at variance with each other on the subject.

It is hardly possible that the Sec. War has omitted to give them notice of the time to start—more probable that he wrote orders to the Agent, who is the proper medium and that he, unwilling that the Indians should go, and ultimately remove, and he would lose his salary of $1600 pr. annum, had never informed the Indians.

Monday Aug. 18   I went into St. Louis, and found that Mr. Blake had expressed an opinion that if he could visit those Indians he could yet bring them this fall. He was much inclined to make the trial. Genl. Clark and Cap. Kennerly seemed willing he should.

I could not approve the course because I did not believe Blake would succeed. If he should, it would be six weeks before he could return, during all that time all who were already here must lay by at great expense and much trouble to some of us on account of the disposition of the Indians to drink. Should Blake not bring the Indians, it would then be too late for our Indians to make the tour— Therefore after all the expense of this summer's work *nothing* would be done, and the Indians who had come this far would return to their homes disappointed and displeased.

I thought that those of us who had already arrived had better proceed, then the business so far as related to them would be done, and let the others make the tour next Spring as they proposed. To going next spring all seemed opposed. They said the flies, high waters, and mires would render it almost impracticable. I plead that I travelled in the wilderness at all seasons. And if they set out next Spring, they would have time to extend the rout[e] as far as they pleased, whereas to go late this fall, their time would be limitted by the approach of winter.

However, when I saw their determination to send again for those Indians, I proposed proceeding on a tour of six weeks, the time they supposed it would require to bring those from the south, with our five Indians. If on my return I met the Southern deputations, send home our Putawatomies, and Ottawas, and I would turn about and make a second tour. If this could not be allowed, I thought our Indians had better go home now. It would cost less for us to make this tour now, and then discharge our Indians, than to lay by here six weeks and then make the tour.

This course was approved by Genl. Clark & Cap. Kennerly, but a difficulty arose out of the circumstance of the Sec. of War having directed that none should move until the Chickasaws arrived. On this account neither Genl. Clark nor Cap. Kennerly will assume the responsibility of giving me direct instructions to go. I therefore take upon myself the entire responsibility of this measure.

Dr. Todson[12] also pleads that he cannot go without order to that effect given in direct terms.

I shall hire two young men to assist, and take in an interpreter about 250 miles from this. I sent out to have 12 horses brought in for shoeing, while I remain in town to prepare for the expedition.

Mr. Blake started in a steam boat this afternoon. His three Creeks & interpreter have gone out to spend the six weeks at our place in the country.

St. Louis Tuesday Aug. 19   Our people brought in the horses, and two of the Creeks came with them. The Creeks and Chandonois got into a notion of drinking, and gave me much trouble. I had a hard days work of it, procuring my out-fit, &c. I started some of the Indians home before me. It was almost sundown when I and two of them left St. Louis— We then had 13 miles to ride. The drunken part had went ahead of the rest. I overtook the companies in different places, the last were the drunkards who had stopped at a whiskey house 4 miles from ours. They had slept in the yard. I alighted to search for whiskey but could find none and the wretch who lives by this base traffic after receiving a very severe reprimand from me, which he did with great submission, for selling whiskey to our people, declared they had drank only water there. Some of them were unwilling to leave the house but I insisted, and took them with me. One of the Creeks gave me much trouble. He fell off his horse two or three times.

---

12. Dr. George P. Todsen was employed as physician and surgeon to accompany the exploring party.

Wednesday preparing to start— Genl. Clark sent me the following
Aug. 20   instructions, for which I am very thankful. Cap Kennerly also has given me a number of introductory letters to persons on the frontiers.

Superintendency of Indian Affairs
St. Louis, Aug. 20, 1828

Revd. I. McCoy
Dr. Sir

As the exploring party of Chickasaws is not expected before the 20th of next month, & should they arrive will not be in advance of this state until the 1st of October, and as the Putawatomies & Ottawas who accompanied you to this place are unwilling to delay, I would, in accordance with your suggestions recommend that you proceed with your party, and explore a portion of the country purchased of the Osage & Kansas West of the State of Missouri, & between the Osage & Shawanoe reservations, and north of the Kansas Reservation, taking care not to go so far west as to endanger your party by falling in with war parties of the Panis,[13] and other Tribes who are at War with the Osage & Kansas.

The Indian Agents in your direction are informed of your movements & will afford you every aid & assistance in their power.

You will take Noel Mongrain a half-breed Osage, who is acquainted with the country,—the routes of the Indians, & speaks the Osage & Kansas languages.

I must request the favor of you to write to me from Harmony Mission,[14] & on your return to Camp Leavenworth, or the out settlements, & state your views & wishes, that I may be enabled to afford such aid as may be necessary.

Accept the assurance of my best wishes.   Yours sincerely
Wm. Clark

1828   I set out from my lodgings at Browns, 13 miles from
Thursday 21   St. Louis. Our company consists of Chandonois the
August 21   Interpreter, five Indians and two hired white men in
all 9. We have 12 horses, one of which is to place an interpreter & guide on, whom we expect to take from Harmony mission Station. We are all armed with guns, and besides I have a brace of horse pistols. We proceeded 14 miles & spent the night at Fishwaters'. The men lodged in their tents, but I lodged in the house.

Friday   We nooned in the woods, & lodged in our tents, near a
Aug. 22   house where we obtained some food for ourselves, but
could not obtain a grain of corn for our horses, though we sent two of our men to another house in the neighborhood

---

13. Pawnee.

14. A mission in Bates county, Missouri, established in 1821 by the United Foreign Missionary Society.

Saturday   We stopped in a little village—Union, obtained breakfast
Aug. 23   and a feed for our horses. Nooned in the woods— In
the afternoon met a man in the wilderness going 13 miles to mill, &
prevailed on him to let us have about one bushel of corn for which I
gave him 75 cts. This was all the grain we had for our horses at
camp at night.

Sunday   We proceeded from Camp about 4 miles and pitched our
Aug. 24   tents about ¼ of a mile from a solitary and wretched hut,
at which we obtained a little food for ourselves, but none for our
horses.

After breakfast, and the morning Service I laid down to rest &
fell asleep, In the course of an hour & a half I arose and discovered
that my beast was absent from the company. I immediately sent
a young man on horseback in pursuit of her. He instead of pursue-
ing the road we had come, listened to an idle story of the woman of
the house and went in search of the beast in a direction of all the
others the least promising. I had but just started this man when I
mounted a horse myself and taking Chandonois, went in pursuit.
The man at the house had that moment returned from the rout[e]
the beast went—said two travellers had stopped at the farther side
of a prarie a mile distant, to feed their horses— They had told him
that the beast had passed them, but the man who had come along
the road had not met her. We proceeded in a gallop and passed the
men before they had set off. They told me the beast had not been
gone more than 15 minutes, & that she went directly along the road.
We galloped on, believing she would stop where we had encamped
the night before, and had fed the horses on the ground.

But she had not passed that way, we returned and kept three or
four persons searching for her till dark Beleiving that the two men
who had seen her had caught her and concealed her in the woods.
We thought so because, they stopped at an undesirable place to
graze or feed—no traveller acquainted with the road as they were,
would have stopped there—because they could see a long distance
back if any one was persueing the beast, because it was not likely
that the beast would so soon have left theirs especially as they were
feeding, ours being hungry for grain—because she would not likely
have left the road. We suspected the man near whose house we
had stopped for having a hand in it, and we set three men to watch
his house. They watched until some time in the night thinking he
might go out in the night to convey the beast further off. But they

made no discoveries. Those two men whom we had suspected had but two horses, yet our men discovered three places where horses had been fed, hence we inferred that one place was where they had caught our beast.

I scolded some about the carelessness of the men while I was asleep.

Monday Aug. 25 1828 — Those two suspected men said they were going to a certain house on the road— This evening a man overtook us who had lodged at the same house, and said the men had not been there. I am confirmed in the opinion that they stole the beast and conveyed her away in the night. I regret the loss much. I had bot. her myself, and for my own use on the tour.

We nooned at the usual hour, and sleep I know not where.

Tuesday Aug. 26 — Sent some hunters ahead early, but without success. One killed one Turkey. Rested at noon—reached the house of a white man near which we encamped—& of whom we obtained corn for our horses, & our Suppers. We are on Gasconade river, about 40 miles below the mills

Wednesday Aug. 27 — I bought a horse of Harrison for $45. By Banson of St. Louis who has travelled a day with us, I wrote to a number of persons respecting our lost beast, requesting aid in her recovery, and offering a reward of $10. We found a house at which we obtained something to eat for ourselves & horses. Encamped on a branch of Gasconade.

Thursday Aug. 28 — Our new horse attempted to escape I sent two men after him before day who caught him in the course of a few miles—found another house today at which we obtained food for selves & horses. Encamped on the waters of grand Auglaize, a branch of the Osage river.

Our Indians have daily tried to take some game but the grass and bushes are so high and thick that they had taken nothing larger than one turkey—Until dark this evening, Gosa brought in a young bear, and reported that he had wounded the dam. This circumstance has raised the Spirits of them all

Friday Aug. 29 — Three men went out & brought in the bear shot last night or rather the hams & shoulders—and even these were scarcely eatible—it was so lean.

On leaving our camp Noonday carefully covered the feet & some other pieces of the bears that were left, with brushes at the root of a tree. When I asked the reason for this Chandonois answered it was the Indian fashion—that the bear in the symetry of its person so much resembled a human being that they were deemed a species of man, and on this account it was becoming in us to bury the remains of such as we killed.

Yesterday we met in the wilderness a fair delicate looking youth in Shirt and panteloons, hat and moccasins. I made some inquiries respecting the way, and he did the same of me. At one o'clock today we reached a house on Osage river & learnt that the youth was a female who lived five miles below, who had taken it into her head, without letting the cause be known, to escape from her father's house in this disguise. Her parents were absent. Her friends had searched for her, particularly in the river supposing she had killed herself— They at length noticed that some of her brothers clothes were missing, and thought they had discovered her track. Their first inteligence of her was received from us. She had told me she was going to Gasconade. She had 25 miles to walk to the 1st house and about the same distance to the next.

Soon after leaving St. Louis we fell into a poor hill country exceedingly stony. The stones in the road remarkably severe on our horses feet—They are all square & pointed. They diminish in size from the very large rocks down to those of the size of a pea, and all the smaller resemble stone broken by the hammer for making a turnpike—none assume a globular form. They are generally white flint. Among these sterile hills a few people are scattered, most of whom seem to have taken pains to settle remote from every body else. It is not surprising that such inhabitants should be less moral & refined than in many other countries, and that among them a female could undertake an exploit which would scarcely be ventured upon by her sex elsewhere.

We crossed Osage river at 12 o'clock, nooned on Gravois Creek & ascended and encamped on the same.

Saturday Aug. 30 Just as I was ready to leave camp an old white man one of the few in this wilderness, came to request some medicine for a son sick of a fever, for which he said he had nothing to pay. I sent on the company, except one, unpacked a horse to get at the medicine and gave what I deemed appropriate. We had encamped near a family of free blacks, one of whom I hired to pilot us 11 miles. Here we intersected a waggon road leading from the settlements on Missouri river to Harmony Mission Station. Had we crossed Missouri at St. Charles & ascended on the north side—

and re-crossed at Jefferson City we should have had a settled country all the way except about [blank in MS.] miles of the road we are now on. Today we left the poor hilly country and have entered a beautiful, rolling, healthy looking region, delightfully varied with praries & wood-lands. We nooned at a creek, and encamped a little before night on account of water. Our hunters killed two turkies and a squirril, and wounded two deer neither of the latter was found.

Sunday Aug. 31 We rest in our tents—attend the usual religious services of the day— Had rain till noon. The weather has been very warm since we left St. Louis, and it is now the most sickly and unpleasant season of the whole year in these regions, yet my health, and that of all the company are preserved. I find myself, however, growing home-sick & impatient. The Indians also feel too much so. It is discouraging to us all, to be detained so long from entering the country we came to see. I feel anxiety about my people & place at home— Lord take care of them and me!

Monday Sep. 1 passed without any noticeable occurrence. Encamped on Grand river.

Tuesday Sep. 2 In haste to get on to the Mission Station, did not unsaddle at noon— Near night reached the Harmony mission. Sorry that three of the missionaries were absent. Was treated with kindness by those at the place—pleased to see the place, apparantly & without doubt consecrated to promote the interests of religion, & especially among the poor Indians. If from appearances I was to Judge, I would say the preference in praise of the management should be given to the female department— This has been obvious at other stations as well as this. While females labour in more obscurity than the other sex & under greater trials & discouragements they, I believe, usually perform their part best.

At this place we had expected to furnish ourselves with supplies for 30 days. But such is the state of things that to our grief, we are told that we can obtain of flour no more than 30 pounds. The only alternative appears to be parched corn. I have stated the case to our company, and all declare their willingness to encounter the journey, and be satisfied with the fare. And say the flour shall be saved for me, while they will live on corn.

Wednesday Sep. 3. 1828 I saw Noel Mograin an old man of 65—a half Osage. Speaks French—but English imperfectly. He agreed to go with me as interpreter & guide, but insisted that I should take another old Osage. He said he had not expected to go the rout[e] I was taking—that he was not well acquainted with the country. I at length consented to take the other old man. I inquired where his horse was, when Mograin pointed to the old man's legs and said there was his horse, one he had used many years. Our tent is pitched about half a mile from the mission on account of grass. Attended a prayer with the missionaries having breakfasted & dined with Mr. & Mrs. Austin—& drank tea with Mrs. Jones.

Thursday Sep. 4. At day light a poor wretched Osage woman came to camp sat down by our fire, & set up a hideous crying or howling. This we understand to be her method of begging. We had nothing to give, except a little of our food.

To our joy we obtained 69 pounds of flour instead of 30, & 100 lb. corn meal—this with our corn we hope will be such as we can do with tolerably well. We procured pork, & salt, but no sugar—we have partly a supply of our old stock. From this place I have, in obedience to instruction, written to Genl. Clark— Wrote also to Mr. Bolles & to my wife— I have been exceedingly hurried since I arrived here. Am much fatigued, and some distressed for want of sleep.

About 9 oclock we set off—our company now consisting of 11 persons—with 13 horses & Mograin's dog. Our old Osage had agreed to walk. He had Deerskin Moccasins and leggings, and the usual cloth, but was destitute of shirt, or any covering for head or body above the loins. Even hair on his head was scarce. He carried an old gun which I had had repaired for him, a horn and pouch & an additional pair of moccasins. His blanket, which was a mere rag, was thrown across his shoulder under his gun. A small bag that would contain a pint containing his smoking apparatus, was hitched under the belt of his cloth. Thus this almost naked old man of 60 set out on a six week's tour. We steered a little north of west, and soon were without any road.

The weather which had been very hot since we left St. Louis, became cool on Sunday night. on Monday it was almost disagreeably cold in the praries. Tuesday night and Wednesday night there fell white frosts which has killed the vegetation considerably.

The season has been so exceedingly dry in this country that vegetation has become so dried that we can see the praries burning in two or three directions at the same time.

About noon we passed two Osage women, a girl, 2 boys, & two infants. They had three small horses, on one was seated a naked child of a year and a half old, and led by the mother. On another was seated the girl—and on the third, a mother naked above the loins, & scarcely covered any where, and carrying in her arms a naked infant the hairs of all hung loosely. The above description approaches near enough to that of the others. The boys were naked —one carried an old gun, & the other a bow. These wretched people were going in search of roots. In our Lake country the men & children are commonly naked in summer, but the females wear shirts. Most of the Osage women I have seen have been destitute of shirt.

We did not stop until evening when we encamped on the Miry De-Sein—or Miry Swan river[15]—which is the main branch of Osage river. A sluggish, muddy stream, though we are encamped on a limestone bank, & at a pretty ripple.

We have now left the State of Missouri, & entered the Territories west. It therefore becomes my duty to describe the country through which we pass. So far it is a beautiful rolling prarie country, happily diversified with streaks of woodlands. Limestone appears on the sides of hills, and in the rivulets.

This evening I was attacked with Dysentery. But had been so much fatigued with my two past day's labour, that when I could obtain a moment's rest, I slept soundly. At 3 oclock in the morning took a potion of Rheubarb & Magnesia.

Friday Sep. 5 — Was not able to leave camp befor half past 9, & then scarcely able to sit on my horse. I had noticed yesterday that Mograin manifested some fears that our old Osage would desert us. He often stopped and looked back to see if the old man was on the way. We lent the old fellow a blanket to sleep on last night, & this morning informed him that he should ride part of the time. We had proceeded about a mile & a half, when we noticed that he was not in company. Mograin went back in quest of him, and fearing we should lose Mograin too, I sent Gosa back with him. By his track they discovered he had retraced our steps—but they returned to us without him. I encouraged Mograin that we should get along well enough, & so proceeded. ½ past ten reached a large creek, which was muddy, and detained us an hour & a half in finding a crossing. At 3 oclock crossed another large creek near its Junction with Miry Desein and being very feeble and sick, encamped on the former. Passed thro. a fine Limestone country as yesterday. In a few instances sand stones appear. The timber on

---

15. Marais des Cygnes.

this river appears to be about a mile in width, & that along each large creek half a mile— On smaller branches less—and consisting chiefly of oak & hickory, with sometimes walnut & ash &c. The prarie bottom lands are usually covered with a beautiful grass for hay—but we seldom find a quagmire. We ascended a high natural naked mound from which we saw the country on both sides up the river stocked with timber sufficient for support of a tolerably dense population.

The nature of the soil of the praries may be compared with those on the Illinois river, and generally in the western parts of Illinois State. On the uplands, hills rise up to considerable hight, round— oblong, &c. &c. exhibiting a singular appearance, because each seems to dwell alone, and because in general they are destitute of timber. These hills are peaks of Stone, which appear on the sides—not in large masses, and sometimes on their summits.

Deer are plenty. Yesterday our men had several shoots, as they rose and run before us, but took nothing except a squirril killed for me. Today Chandonois had killed a goose & a turkey before we encamped.

Saturday Sep. 6. Left camp at 7. Hunters last evening & this morning unsuccessful. At 9, passed where some Sauks settled three years ago, but left again in compliance with the requisition of the Osages. We saw at a distance three or four of their old deserted huts. About 11 oclock I thought we were leaving the main river. I therefore turned to the left & descended a steep stony hill to the stream which was our guide. Mograin said it was the main Osage river. I did not think so, but as three of our men were out hunting, & fearing they would find difficulty in overtaking us, we went back into the prarie again and waited till they arrived having twice fired guns for them. When they came up I told Mograin that I believed the river lay more to the southwest, I therefore went ahead—went directly across the stream he had called the main river, & proceeded southwest until we reached the main river. We then turned back into the praries again & proceeded till camping time. I made several attempts to get to the river in which we were prevented by stony bluffs. At a half past 5, we crossed and encamped on the south bank. Four hunters afterwards came up all unsuccessful except the taking of one turkey. My health somewhat improved but I am still afflicted with bowel complaint, and am weak, tho. not in much pain. Wood today has been more abundant than heretofore. High lands coming in nearer the rivers and creeks the timber often stretching out on to the hills. The hills more abrupt on the sides, from their tops spread out a beautiful rolling country. Slopes that wash, steep side hills, and all water courses, disclose a bed of limestone. The stone in appearance may be compared with the condition of limestone in the limestone lands of the middle counties of Kentucky. The soil is almost universally rich—darker than the timbered rich lands of Ky. and possesses the mellowness peculiar to limestone lands. The river, and Creeks here, though still too sluggish, are stony, and more clear than below. Springs we have seen none, along the river & creeks are fertile bottoms of timbered lands, covered with oak, ash, hackberry, walnut, hickory, honey locust &c. &c. But these bottoms in too many instances are subject to inundation.

Sunday Sep. 7 1828   We remain in camp on the south bank of Miry Desein or the Osage river. Attend the usual religious services. But regret that the state of our provisions requires hunting. Three men went out and by 9 oclock brought in two deer, which is an acceptable & ample supply.

    The river here passes about as much water only as would move a common grist mill. In most of the large creeks the water has been merely standing, and all the smaller branches are entirely dry. We have not seen a single spring of water.

Monday Sep. 8.   I took Gosa early & rode into the prarie about three miles in order to view a tract of land three parts surrounded by timber. We are encamped in a bottom of excellent woodland. During our excursion the company had prepared to move. We heartily breakfasted & at ½ past 9 set off recrossed the river, and in a few miles bore to the left to see if we were following the main river, or a tributary. Mograin and Chandonois both inclined to think it was the main river. It was indeed little less, but discharged not more than a 4th so much running water. I steered directly across it & at 5 or 6 miles distance ascended a Naked hill, whence we could observe the course of the river. About one oclock in a woodland crossed a branch that a man could step across, about half a mile from its source in prarie in which was wholesome water with small fish in it, indicating that it had not been dry this exceeding drought. A mile & a half further crossed another similar rivulet with running water. Towards camping time bore towards the river, found it so exceedingly difficult descending a large creek, on account of grass, vines, &c. that we halted at 5. & I took Wesauogana, & went on foot and found the river in less than half a mile. Here the discharge of water is not quite sufficient at this time for a grist mill. It is a large creek in the Spring season. Its waters have assumed a wholesome appearance— Its bed, as also all those of the Creeks & rivulets, is limestone.

Timber today has been rather more plenty than heretofore, and we have passed over the same fertile, rolling, limestone kind of country that we did on Saturday last. My health much improved.

Tuesday Sep. 9. We left camp at a quarter past 8. In the course of about two miles happened on a fine Spring of water running out from limestone rocks. At noon crossed a large creek running along side a steep hill of limestone. Here we stopped half an hour and ate a bite. Timbered bottom half a mile wide, very rich, covered heavily with black walnut, hickory, honey locust—[MS. illegible], oak, some [MS. illegible] tree, mulberry, &c. Afterwards crossed two small creeks each affording water but not running. At 4 reached a large creek, spent an hour in finding a crossing, & at 5 encamped on its west bank. The bottoms of all the creeks wide and rich. The creeks this afternoon more muddy, less stone & less current than yesterday. Timber about the same as yesterday, land the same though with less stone to be seen. The country in which we encamped last night, I supposed to be well watered with Springs.

Wednesday Sep. 10. Left camp a quarter after 8. In the course of four miles crossed two small branches with considerable water, but no perceivable current. At one of them a sandstone rock appeared in the side hill. At one o'clock dined at a rocky creek. Water is now found in most of the rivulets so that it is not necessary to mention each occurrence. Timber was about the same as heretofore until towards noon, when, being near the source of the river, the quantity diminished. Untill at 5 we encamped at the last little grove on the stream we were following up. We had taken this as the main stream which we afterwards found was a mistake. Passed the same kind of high, rolling, limestone, fertile country as heretofore. By my map I had for three parts of the day supposed we were near the road leading from St. Louis to Santa Fee. Unwilling that our trail should be seen on that road, Chandonois and I kept ahead of the company. Seen much sign of Elk, and in the evening Gosa fired on one in a gang of eleven. After camping sent a man back to watch till dusk if any one was following our trail. At 11 we had crossed a large trail made a few days ago, but as it went north it gave us no uneasiness. Did not unstop the bells till morning.

Thursday Sep. 11 — I took Chandonois and early went forth to look for the Santa Fee road, which we found at the distance of about three miles. We left camp at half past 9, In the course of about three miles crossed the stream marked on the map as the river, proceeded north west several miles and crossed the main stream, and proceeded west up the river on the south side and encamped at 5. We have crossed many small streams today, generally with water in them. High country as before, less stone, land rich, but timber scarce. Only a small patch seen here & there, besides that on the river, which is sufficient to admit of a farm to about every three fourths of a mile along the river.

By my map, the measurement of the Santa Fe road, made our encampment last night eighty one miles west of the state of Missouri. We have travelled since we left Harmony mission seven days, we suppose at an average of 24 miles per day making in our turnings 168 miles. Several deer fired on today as they ran, none killed. Magaukwuk found bees in a tree near camp & climbed and cut with a Tomahawk & took considerable honey. The praries are burning a few miles above us, whence we infer that a hunting party is near.

We find it often difficult to get through the briers, brush, & vines along the small streams. Sometimes we use the knife and sometimes the Tomahawk in opening our way through. We keep much in praries where, excepting the water courses, travelling is fine.

I have for myself, a lonesome time. No one is with me who feels interested in the enterprize beyond his own immediate comfort, or with whom I can indulge as an associate. The Indians are exceedingly careless and improvident. Willing to do anything I tell them, but will not put themselves to the trouble of *thinking*. Like children, some of them think the distance great and appear to be somewhat home-sick. I almost daily show them on the map where we are, and whither we are going. Were it not for this, some would be ready to fancy themselves near the edge of the World. Upon the whole, however, they are generally cheerful. The two white men hired as packmen &c. are *poor sticks* & give me trouble. Scarce a day passes that I have not to reprove one of them, and sometimes threaten to discharge them there in the wilderness, I think however, that they are rather improving in their ways. Chandonois performs his part well, and is my main dependence

Friday Sep. 12 — Our venison being exhausted, I informed the men that we must lie here until they could take more. Four hunters went out early & remained till after seven without even seeing any game. This is remarkable since it has been so plenty in the country through which we have travelled, We suppose the cause is the proximity of Hunters, which has made the game scarce. Hunting & rain made it half past ten before we left camp. We proceeded Southwest in order to find a branch of Neosho river. Travelled thro. prarie. It rained on us considerably. At the distance of about 12 miles reached the stream we sought, a large creek with deep water, but at a ripple, at which we cross[ed] there was not enough running water to turn a common grist mill. Timber today seen only in small patches until we came to this stream. Here might be a farm on each side of the river at the distance of half a mile. The country high, and very rich, stone less. We encamped on the southwest bank, at 3 oclock, after our men had shot four raccoons on one oak tree which they had ascended for the sake of the fruit, one of which was lost in the river.

Sent out three hunters who returned at dark without game. Our company, except myself supped bountifully on their raccoons.

We have now left the Osage river. The water in it and its tributaries is too stagnant. Streams for mills are abundant, but mills would be still in the dry season of the year. From our Saturday's encampment upward—a distance of 70 miles on a straight line, there can be no want of spring & well water. below spring water appeared scarce, Timber is in plenty to admit a tolerably dense population for 75 miles west of Missouri State afterwards more scarce. The country promises health, except on the immediate banks of the larger streams, where it will be subject to Agues & fevers. The soil is almost universally fertile, and the whole supplied abundantly with limestone. It is the most sightly country I ever saw. I have seen no coal, but have not had time to search. I examined two banks which at a distance appeared to contain coal, but they were slate.

Saturday Sep. 13. Sent out two hunters who returned unsuccessful. Left camp a[t] half past 8. proceeded southwest in order to reach another large branch of Neosho. In the course of 4 miles we crossed a pretty large creek in which Wesauogana shot a fish, as they said, for my supper. This creek is pretty much wooded, two other streams with timber are in sight, so that the country here will allow a tolerable settlement. We had left the creek about a mile when a large gang of Elk about 20 in number were discovered. A halt was called, and a brief council held, the result of which was that I & the two pack-men returned to the creek with six horses and all the baggage, and the other seven men, thus lightened, went on horseback in quest of the Elk, & while we wait by the baggage I make this note.

At dusk our hunters returned, having taken one elk, and having enjoyed fine sport in chasing and shooting. No set of men could be better pleased than were those. And I was not much less so, for we were in want of meat, and I was very desirous that they should be allowed thus to enjoy themselves. This circumstance will go further in commending the country to them than a million of acres of rich land.

Sunday Sep. 14   We remain in camp. The men happy that they have meat and marrow bones to the full. Religious Services morning and evening as usual on Sundays.

Monday Sep. 15   Rose at daylight & left camp at 7 oclock. The wolves stole some of our elk meat last night, but we still have as much as we can take with us. We had proceeded a few miles when we discovered an Elk, all the men joined in the effort to take him except Mograin & I. Four of them fired at him, but he escaped unhurt, for which I was not sorry as we should have been unable to save the meat. Saw a wolf, & again saw an Antelope, an animal few of us had ever before seen. Shawaunukwuk tried to take him but failed. At half past One reached a large branch of Neosho, which might be compared with St. Marys at Fort Wayne, though something larger. My map appears to be incorrect so that I am not able to decide which branch of Neosho this is. I supposed it to be a middle fork, but Mograin says it is the main Southern branch. We ate a little, and turned to the N. West & encamped on a large creek not many miles from the main river. We travelled W. S. W. until we reached this stream. On Thursday we beleived we travelled 15 miles, on Friday 12 miles, Saturday 4, and this day 27 miles. Gosa shot deer a little before we encamped. We crossed many small creeks today. The country to our left sufficiently timbered to admit a good settlement, but to our right was chiefly prarie. We passed over the same kind of high, limestone, rich country that I have heretofore described, water found in almost all watercourses, even those that are very small. The Bottom lands of this river appear to be full three miles wide. Deer abundant, elk sign plenty.

We had rain today which is disagreeable enough in these praries. About the time we reached the river, we crossed a trail of foot men going south, might suppose them to be 20 or 30 in number. Sign not recent. Supposed by Mograin to be a war party gone against his people, who mostly reside on this river below.

Tuesday Sep. 16   Left camp quarter after 8. proceeded up the creek on which we had s[l]ept, north, about 9 crossed & passed between forks of nearly equal size, Saw three antelopes lying on the side of the hill, stopped the company & three went to take them, but failed. These animals appear remarkably nimble in running. At 11 reached the Santa Fe road, and followed it eastward. Halted at a creek between 12 and one. I wished to ascertain at what point on the road we were and must therefore return until I find distances to correspond with the map. But in following the trail I left the surveyors marks, the latter being that only which would explain the map; we left the trail & bore N. east, separating, in order to find the mounds raised by the surveyors, but we did not succeed, then, bore due east. Near 5 oclock, an elk was discovered a little beyond the creek on which we intended to encamp. The men went in chase, there was a large flock, some of them ran near us. They killed a very large male Elk & one wounded a large Deer. The elk they pronounced too lean & old for use, tho. in fact it was pretty good, but we were not in great want, & brought only the horns to camp. This elk chasing kept us till nearly dark before we encamped. Our Indians are wonderfully delighted with their evening's sport.

Mograin is a good natured, simple old man, of no manner of use to us than to add one to our number, & to be our interpreter should we come in contact with Osages or Kanzas, unless we add his capacity for lightening the loads of the packhorses which carry the provision. He says he never before travelled through this country which we are exploring. I am my own pilot solely. Yesterday we recrossed the Indian trail which we crossed on monday, & which Mograin pronounced the trail of a war party. Today I alighted and examined the trail myself and found it to be made in part by horses—am sure therefore it is not the track of a war party, but of a hunting party, no doubt of Kanzas as it comes from that direction.

The country today not quite so well timbered as heretofore, though sufficiently so to allow considerable population. In respect to soil, limestone, and situation, it resembles what we have heretofore described.

Wednesday Sep. 17   Four men went to search for the Deer wounded yesterday, but did not find him. It was near 10 before we could leave camp. We proceeded east until we again reached the Santa Fe road, which we kept until I supposed I had ascertained the point at which we were, which was 122 miles, due west, from the western boundary of State of Missouri. Here we steered north, from 12 till five o'clock, when we encamped as I beleived on the waters of Ne[os]ho which we had descended about two miles. Poor old Mograin is fairly lost, and supposed we were here on the waters of a large Creek we crossed the third day's travel from Harmony.

This day's journey lying across the land dividing Neosho & Osage rivers from Kanzas, I had expected to find the country almost wholly destitute of wood. In this I have been happily disappointed. Timber is more scarce than formerly but the country will admit a tolerable settlement the whole way. The country rises to the dividing lands. Then descends towards Kanzas. Still high, rich, and abounding in limestone. One of our horses lame, so that one man has to walk. Tuesday we travelled, we suppose 17—today 20.

We have now left Neosho waters, which country needs no other description than to say it resembles that on the Osage, rather less timber, & perhaps better watered. It may justly be pronounced an excellent country so far as I saw it.

Thursday Sep. 18 Left camp before 8. In an hour's ride fell in with a Kanza hunting, by whom learnt we were not far from a village. We found much difficulty in crossing a large Creek & some other branches. On the top of a high natural mount we discovered an artificial mound of stone, apparently constructed from the same principles on which our earthen mounds are to the east.

Coming in sight of two houses about two miles from the principal village, the inhabitants became alarmed, some of the women & children hid in the brush, and one man came running to a wood towards us for the purpose of securing his horses. He did not reach his horse until we were within fifty yards of him. I sent Mograin to speak to him who soon allayed his fears. We halted to take some refreshment half a mile from the houses, & sent the man, with some tobacco to inform the main village that we were coming to smoke with them. A woman presently came from the two houses with a kettle of boiled corn. After an hour we proceeded and after much delay to wait Mograin's tedious, & tiresome talkativeness to every one of the many Indians that met us, we encamped a mile & a half from town & went upon foot to talk, leaving the baggage in charge of the two hired men. At camp and every where else, men, women, children & dogs swarmed about us. We were shown into a large bark hut, which was immediately crowded as thick as it could be, with exception of a little room at each fire, such a scene of crowding, of men women & children, talking, scolding, crying of children, a few good mothers singing to quiet them, dogs fighting & the conquered begging aloud for quarters, I never before witnessed. Boiled corn in two large wooden bowls, supplied with a few Buffaloe horn spoons & ladles, were placed before us.

Sixteen Pawnees had been there, who on hearing of our approach had left except three. I enquired for them, & as they were in a hurry to be gone, I gave them some tobacco, and a little friendly talk, to which they replied in similar friendship, and they departed. The Pawnees & Osages are hostile to each other. The Kanzaus are identified in language & friendship with the Osages. They are indeed a band of the same tribe, they are afraid of the Pawnees, but appear to dread them less than do their brethren. I suppose these Pawnees thought I had some Osages in company, & on this account left as they did, leaving three of their numbers to learn the circumstances of our visit &c.

We smoked with the Kanzaus, & gave them some tobacco, & a little friendly talk. We were obliged to extend our voices in order to be heard amidst the continued noise & confusion.

I then went to view the river. I should judge it to be over a quarter of a mile wide at this place, deep, the water of a milky appearance, & running slowly between sand banks. It much resembles Missouri, tho. so much less, & is less rapid, & muddy. It passes between pretty high hills, & the country, as might be expected, is more broken & hilly near the river. The land fertile, no limestone seen, but plenty of freestone, Timber too scarce but sufficient to allow a very considerable population.

It was dark when I reached camp, the principal Chief & his wife both aged people, and many others came to camp. I had the chief to eat supper with me, gave his wife also, and a little to some others, gave the chief two or three pounds of flour at his request. And on preparing for rest, they all left us. One old fellow on our arrival had offered his service to assist in the work, &c. We accepted his offer merely for his gratification, & rewarded him with food & tobacco.

The Kanzas appear to be more wretched than even the Osages. Men generally naked with exception of the small cloth & sometimes a blanket thrown over their shoulders. The women with a ragged piece of cloth about the middle, and some of them with a narrow piece of cloth passing awry over one shoulder & under the other arm, to conceal the breasts, which is commonly held over them with one hand. But many of the women were wholly uncovered above the waist & below the knee. Boys entirely naked, girls, with a piece of cloth about the middly. They were much pleased with our visit, & very friendly.

I am instructed to pass thro. the country north of this river, but, it is remarkable that, I cannot hear of one single canoe, or other craft for crossing anywhere on the river. These people, if ever they cross, swim or cross on rafts, With my lazy company I do not think we should be able to construct rafts, & get ourselves, &c. across in less than four days. I cannot lose this time. Indeed the time allowed me is so far gone that I must bend my course towards St. Louis. This is the upper Indian town on the river, & consists of about 15 houses. It is 125 miles due west of Missouri State.

Friday Sep. 19 Left camp before 8, took a road down the river, a few miles from it, towards other villages. In the course of 10 miles passed between two small villages, travelling a little north of east. At one oclock, stopped to dine, sent some tobacco to the principal Kanzau village, now in sight, say 7 miles off, by two Indians who have accompanied us from above. While we left the road & bore south east, in order to see the country on some large creek, which lay before us, and, to endeavor to procure some meat. It was dusk when we reached a suitable camping place.

We had travelled five or six miles after we parted with the messenger sent with tobacco to the village, when an Indian came riding to us at full speed, from the village, which now must have been seven or eight miles distant, He was entirely naked from head to heels except the breech cloth. Had no other business he said than to get a little tobacco. This we gave him and went on. An old chief he said had started with him, but finding the chase too long had become discourage[d], & went back.

Timber of the Kanza river is sufficient to allow a dense settlement for four or five miles on each side. It appears well watered. Small creeks, & rivulets are numerous, and wooded, and watered.

Saturday Sep. 20 The rain which commenced in the night continueing the men were not called up early. It was so wet that they seemed disinclined to hunt. Chandonois killed a turkey near camp, & at 10 we proceeded on our way, eastwardly crossed a large creek near camp. On this creek we find both limestone & free stone. The wind blew all day so severely that travelling in the prarie was almost impracticable. About the middle of the afternoon a violent wind and rain overtook us. We were favored in being at that moment in a wood, & being able to secure most of the baggage from wet.

Six of the men were hunting three came to us half an hour after the storm. The other three were a little lost, but reached us afterwards with a fine deer. We are much favored by providence, in being allowed to stop at a place favourable for resting on tomorrow, being well supplied with grass for horses, and we are now well supplied with meat.

The country continues the same in appearance. Except that the lands, though excellent, I think are not quite so rich as on Neosho. Wood scattered in streaks & groves all over the country. We are now about 70 miles due west of State of Missouri, & 15 south of Kanza river Yesterday I suppose we travelled 30 miles, and today, 20.

Since we left Neosho, Mograin has said he supposed, from the circumstance of our seeing antelopes, &c. that we were near to the Buffaloe. He says he was afraid to tell us so at the time lest we should be inclined to go further west, which he was afraid to do, lest we should fall in with enemies. He had all along given it as his opinion that it was a long distance to Buffalos. The night we lay farthest west some ravens were croaking about us till pretty late in the evening. The old man said that from that circumstance he judged that enemies were near.

Sunday Sep. 21   Remained in camp, religious Service morning & evening as usual on Sabbaths.

Monday Sep. 22   Left camp at 8   Steered eastwardly, but at length found the hills so steep & rocky, and the brush & vines so thick, that we bore to the south west in order to head some branches. We were in sight of Kanza river, tho. perhaps ten or 12 miles distant. About 12 oclock we fell into the Santa Fe road unexpectedly for, by the map the road at this place was 35 miles from the river, and we had been turned off from the river by the broken land which bordered there on. The road appears not to correspond with the map. We followed it till after 4, a south east, or rather S. S. east course when we turned to the North east, found an encamping place & halted. While in the road we were on the dividing ridge between Kanza & Osage rivers. The country descended with gentle slopes toward Osage, but broke of[f] in abrupt hills towards Kanza. The hills are generally two or three times as high as the trees in the low grounds, very steep & rocky the vales covered with timber, stretching frequently to the tops of the hills. From the hilltops the land passes off beautifully rolling—level enough for cultivation. Between the hills on which we were & Kanza there appeared a large tract chiefly prarie, 150, or 200 feet lower than the hills. Along the hills facing Kanza is more wood than is common at the sources of the streams. We are encamped in a tract of woodland along side of which I think we have travelled ten miles. This woodland lies across the sources of many small rivulets. Wood today has been much more plenty than we have heretofore seen it. The country high, healthy, & rich with abundance of limestone. This excellent tract of Kanza land lies adjoining the better parts of Osage, which we were on about the 7th 8th & 9th September. Much sign of Elk & Deer, Hunters brought in three turkeys in the evening

Tuesday Sep. 23   Left camp at 8 and by the compass travelled all day North east, stopped at 12 rested ¾ of an hour and encamped at 5. In the forenoon we had freestone, and land somewhat sandy, In the afternoon limestone. Crossed many small creeks, & lesser streams in all which was water. Country high & rich resembling the better part of Osage. Timber about as plenty as seen on the more plentiful days.

Wednesday Sep. 24   Left camp at quarter past eight. Rested ¾ an hour at noon. Followed a trail made in the summer until about 11 oclock when we fell into an old Indian road which we kept until 3 oclock we reached the first Shawanoe village. The men mostly were absent, hunting, &c. We gave them some tobacco & proceeded to another settlement of Shawanoes on the line of Missouri. Sorry that Shane the Interpreter was absent. His wife, who is a member of the Church at Carey, was absent in the neighborhood. We pitched our tents a little way off.

After a few miles in the morning, wood has been plenty though it might be said that we were in the wood of the river, extending 8 or 10 miles therefrom, tho. not in a solid body. The country high & rich with Limestone in abundance

Travelled on monday 27 miles—Tuesday 25—Wednesday 28.

I have now returned to the border of the Indian Territory. It is proper therefore to take a retrospect of our tour therein.

I have been favoured, in general with good health—have been favoured with pleasant weather, have been comfortably supplied with food, and not allowed to meet any material accident or loss. Our horses look nearly as well as when we left St. Louis.

The country we have explored, I am ready [to] pronounce excellent. It is admitted that timber is too scarce, but by a judicious arrangement in settlement, a vast population can be conveniently situated. There is great sameness in appearance of the country. High, rich, healthy in appearance, stone for building, & for lime in abundance. Water without scarcity all over the country, for common use of man & beast. Mill streams in abundance but all fail in the dry season. We might expect water-works to stand still for want of water, in general, 4 or 5 months in the year. There is scarcely a quagmire in all the country. I saw only one pond of water, & that covered about an acre of land. Most travellers seek the higher and more open lands, because it is exceeding troublesome getting thro. the timber, brush, & vines, along the watercourses. The hills rise generally once, twice, & thrice, as high as the trees in the low grounds. The sides of the hill are often abrupt, and on the top becomes sufficiently level for cultivation. On these accounts one may pass at a short distance from a grove of timber at a water course, the streak of wood one fourth, one half—or even a mile in width, and scarcely [MS. illegible] the bough of a tree. The country therefore has been reported to be more scarce of wood and water than is the fact. It is remarkable too that because there is but little timber on the uplands, travellers looking over prarie as far as sight could reach, have fancied the country to be level, when, if the whole country were timbered they would report it to be as high & rolling as the middle counties of Kentucky. The ri[vers?] are broader & the slopes of tillable land more gradual than generally in Kentucky.

Notwithstanding there is so little wet land in the country, yet grass for hay can be obtained in abundance especially on Osage & Neosho.

In settling the country, lands should be so laid out that to each home should be allowed 50 or 80 acres of wood-land, and then as much prarie back as should be necessary. Hogs will thrive in any country while new, but this country will not be particularly favourable to the growth of that kind of stock after the country becomes thickly settled, it is too high & open. It will always be remarkably well adapted to the growth of sheep & cattle. This will be the principal business of farmers. On the settling of Indians there, a small field to each will be sufficient. That is, a little larger than will, in that fertile soil, be enough to furnish his bread and vegetables. The extensive grazing & hay of the praries will supercede the necessity of farm pasturage and meadows.

I extended my tour west of Missouri State 140 miles on a direct line as measured on the map. Say 160 miles the nearest way that could be travelled, and within 60 miles as measured on the map, of the place where the Santa Fe road crosses Arkansas river,[16] and not more than 50 miles from that river at a point lower down. I think I have been enabled to form a pretty just estimate of the country 80 miles in width, and 150 from east to west, making 12,000 square miles or 7,680,000 acres. How much further west the country is inhabitable I am not able from observation to say.

The country of the Shawanoe, near the mouth of Kanzas river is best supplied with timber. On the upper branches of the creek of Kanzas named on the map Wahusa,[17] and opposite, south, & near thereto on Osage river, is the most desirable country for a good settlement, & in that region I am inclined to hope for a mission Station, & perhaps the seat of government of the Indian Territory, say from 30 to 70 miles due west of Missouri.

And now, O thou father of the fatherless & friend of the poor. Grant that in these deserts, where, with a few, I have been allowed the privilege of bowing the knee, and lisping a song, prayers & praises may arise from the thousands of a people *Saved by Thee!* and all the glory—*all the* Glory shall be Thine.

The Shawanoes arrived in this country last Spring late. They consist chiefly of about one half of those who resided at Waupaugkonetta in Ohio, some from Merimack, in this State, some from Lewistown, O. & elsewhere. With some aid from government, chiefly in food & clothing, & farming utensils, they are in three or four settlements or villages putting up with their own hands very neat log cabbins.

Thursday Sep. 25. Took breakfast with our sister Shane, happy to hear her of her own accord readily speak of religion, and lament that there was not much of anything like it in their country. I find too that she maintains an excellent character.

Mograin now chose to return home, & I had no further need of his services. I therefore paid him. But his horse had left the company last night, and having no bell on, could not be found this morning. I was anxious to proceed to the town of Liberty, to which place I had directed all my papers to be sent. At 11, I therefore took one man, and leaving the company to search for the horse, set out, crossed Missouri about six miles below the mouth of Kanza river. The Kanzas do not pronounce this as usually written. Their pro-

---

16. McCoy probably referred to the first point at which the Santa Fé trail touched the Arkansas river, in present Barton county. The first crossing was in present Ford county, about 280 miles west of the western line of Missouri.

17. Wakarusa.

nunciation is truly Kan'-zau, & for Osages Wos-soshe'. We travelled 21 miles & reached Liberty at sun-setting. No news of the southern Indians. Seven letters from various members of my family, and one from Rev. Cone.[18] Thankful to hear of the health & comfort of my family. Cone manifests his usual interest in our affairs, and assures me of his readiness to co-operate in carrying forward our designs.

Friday Sep. 26   I remained at Liberty. In the evening the company arrived having found Mograins horse. The old prophet & other Shawanoes called on our people after I left them and had considerable talk, some of our Indians accepted an invitation of the Shawanoes to attend a dance with them that night. I left tobacco for the Shawanoes, some of which I left in care of Shane.

Saturday Sep. 27   Left Liberty about 8 oclock and travelled about 28 miles to near Richmond (Martin's)

Sunday Sep. 28   Did not travel.

Monday Sep. 29   Set off at 7 crossed Missouri, travelled till 5, and made 32 miles—Lodged at Estis'.

Tuesday Sep. 30   Left at 7 oclock, travelled 32 miles to Shackleford's.

Wednesday October 1   It was a half past 9 before we could be ready to travel, Crossed Missouri Near Chanton and reached Fayette sun an hour high. I sent the company on a few miles, as we had only travelled 21 miles today, and because it is unpleasant stopping them in a town where there is whisky, which Chandonois and the hired hands are as much inclined to drink, as the Indians.

  Hoping that I and Mr. Lykins with our families will be able to come to this country next Spring for the purpose of commencing our missionary operations in the west. It is desirable that we, ere that time, have some place selected at which we may temporarily locate our families while we prepare houses for them in the wilderness, and that we have a friend to whose care we may, if we choose, direct some property. I had hoped to find an eligible situation nearer the frontier, but was discouraged in the attempt by the apparent sickliness of the country above. Pleased with the situation of this town and country I have stopped here tonight to attend to that business. I engaged Mr. Wm. Wright of this place, & he commends a Mr. Samuel of Franklin as consignee.

18. Spencer H. Cone, member of the American Baptist Board of Foreign Missions.

Thursday Oct. 2   I set off very early. In about 4 miles overtook my company, breakfasted with them and proceeded about in all today, 33 miles, to Wilburn's, where I stopped very much fatigued. I feel much worn down with my journeyings, and greatly in want of rest.

Friday Oct. 3   Resumed our journey at a half past six, and travelled 39 miles to McMurtry's.

Saturday Oct. 4   Set off at 7 and made 42 miles, to Taylors. Today I met A. Shane, Interpreter for Shawanoes, on his way home. Sometime ago I heard that Shane was much dissatisfied with me. In my absence to the east in 1823-4 Mr. Polke, then a missionary, employed Shane to accompany him to see the Ottawas on Grand river, and encouraged Shane to expect a situation, in the mission which circumstances afterwards did not admit of. Shane left his place 40 miles east of Fort Wayne, & brought his wife and children to Carey, where I found them on my return, but about that time they concluded to return. Neither Shane, nor any one else, told me the amount of his expectations. I paid him for his services to Mr. Polke to the extent of the agreement. Mr. Polke did this with the best intentions, but fact proved it to be an unfortunate plan and I was sorry to hear that Shane, who has influence with the Shawanoes in this country should be dissatisfied with me. Yesterday I conversed with him on various subjects, & I mentioned what I had heard he had said in Ohio respecting me, and let him know that I was confident that I had always acted as his sincere friend. He appeared abashed, as well he might be. Did not deny, nor pretend to justify what he had said, nor even repeat the reasons for his dissatisfaction. But said, "We'll drop it," reached to me his hand in token of friendship, of which he re-iterated assurances, and declared that he had always spoken well of me in this country.

I am glad to have this matter settled, which was one (& I viewed it as a serious one) of the difficulties which had grown out of the circumstance of employing unsuccessful missionaries.

Shane informs me that the southern Indians are daily expected at St. Louis. There is therefore great probability that instead of being allowed to proceed direct to the embraces of my family, I must turn about and make another tour in the deserts. Disappointments & delays, and the supposed state of affairs at Carey & Thomas,[19] render me distressed. A treaty has been held there since I left, which

---

19. Baptist mission for the Ottawa Indians on Grand river, 40 miles east of Lake Michigan, established by Isaac McCoy in 1826.

circumstance deeply involved the interests of the Mission. I have heard that Mr. Slater, dissatisfied that he could not be allowed to do as he pleased, had gone to New England to see the Board. I had heard of his being on the way back, & that Dr. Bolles[20] was in company intending to examine the state of things at the stations, and to attend the treaty. The burden of affairs have been greatly increased on the brethren at the stations, particularly at Carey, and more especially must the labours of Mrs. McCoy & our daughter, have been increased. Mrs. Simerwell has been absent, with Mr. S—& Mr. Bay has been a journey to Ohio which must have taken several weeks so that much of the time no male missionary was there except Lykins, and for a long time no female missionaries except my wife and Mrs. Lykins.

I had hoped to be able to be at Washington next winter and to have visited the Board, &c. and to have reprinted an enlarged edition of My Remarks on Indian Reform,[21] preparatory to our coming to this country, & to provide for the situation of Mrs. L—and to afford a little rest to my wife, during my almost constant absence, I had hoped to remove them from Carey, to Ohio, or elsewhere for a few weeks, & then allow them time to visit their relations What now will become of our plans, & arrangements, I cannot guess. My mind is filled with anxiety. I am unworthy of favour, yet I am in many respects favoured—to *Him* with tears, I appeal for help, for myself & family—to Him who has been our help in days that are past, and who is our hope for days to come. O what should I do had I not a God to go to, and to whose care to commit my dear—lonely—companion, and our dear babes, the mission & all connected therewith! Here alone I find comfort. But since the friends of the Indians are so few—their miseries so great, & their destruction so menacing—who would not toil & suffer in support of this work of benevolence! O that God would prepare me for all the duties of this service.

Since I left St. Louis I have not employed much religion. I have had a troublesome company to manage. Have had no associate, I have been very lonely. My mind seems to have assimilated too nearly to the wildness of the wilderness. I cannot generally enjoy myself in prayer. Prayer and other religious services are accom-

---

20. Lucius Bolles, corresponding secretary, American Baptist Board of Foreign Missions.
21. The first edition of this pamphlet was printed by Lincoln & Edwards, Boston, December, 1827; a second edition, with appendix, was printed by Gray & Bruce, 224 Cherry street, New York, 1829. The expense of printing the latter was borne by McCoy, the Baptist Board of Foreign Missions having declined to pay costs because of disapproval of certain statements in the appendix. The manuscript of the work is owned by the Kansas State Historical Society.

panied by too little reverence for him whom I profess to serve. Sometimes however I am blest with a comfortable engagedness.

Monday Oct. 6   We set off very early, Crossed Missouri at St. Charles, travelled hard, and till in the night, made 46 miles and reached Mr. Browns, my former lodgings 12 miles from St. Louis. Here my acquaintances received me with much friendship. It has been forty seven days since I set out from this place. The beast that escaped from me on the [24th of] Aug. had been brought in to St. Louis and is safe. The four Creek Indians whom I left here when I started, are still here.

Tuesday Oct. 7   After over-hauling our baggage & making some arrangements preparatory to sending my company of Indians home, I rode in to St. Louis, and made a brief written report to Genl. Clarke. *This is the 50th day since I left this place.*

The southern Indians have not yet arrived but are daily expected. I have therefore no prospect but of being under the necessity of turning about and making another tour.

(Copy of my Report to Genl. Clark)

St. Louis, Mo. Oct. 7, 1828.

"Sir

In obedience to your instructions I wrote you from Harmony mission station. I informed that I had commenced my tour at St. Louis the 19th August. I have this day returned to this place, having been absent 49 days.

On leaving the State of Missouri I proceeded westwardly up the Osage river, generally on the north side. Passing the sources of Osage we bore South west across the upper branches of Neosho until we intersected the main river at a point eighty miles south, and 127 west of the mouth of Kanzas river, and [a]bout 25 miles southeast of the Santa Fe road. We then bore north west until we reached the Santa Fe road sixty miles from Arkansas river, and 140 due west of this State. These estimates are made according to measurement on the map, and not according to distances travelled, survey of the road, &c. We turned eastward along and near to the Santa Fe road, to a point due South of the upper Kanzas village, then travelled north to said village on the Kanzas river, 125 miles west of this State.

I had been instructed to cross Kanzas river and to return on the north side thereof, but the Indians informed me that there was not a canoe or other craft on the river. My time was then so far consumed that I deemed it inadvisable to incur the delay that would be occasioned by crossing on rafts. I therefore proceeded eastwardly near to the southern limits of the Kanzas reservation, and came down to the Shawanoe settlement near the mouth of the Kanzas river, varying in our journey north and south 40 miles. Thence I came on the most direct rout[e] to this place.

There is great similarity in the appearance of all parts of the country we explored. It is generally a high rolling country, exhibiting a healthy appearance. Stone, and almost universally limestone sufficiently abundant for use. The soil exceedingly fertile with scarcely the occurrence of an exception, and possessing the mellowness peculiar to limestone lands. We suffered no inconvenience from want of water, but found it happily distributed in the creeks & smaller streams all over the country, though not much running. Streams for mills and other water-works are abundant, but all these would fail in the more dry season of the year. Wood is too scarce, especially beyond the distance of sixty miles west of this State; and ten miles south of Kanzas river, nevertheless I suppose the whole country is supplied with groves, and streaks of timber sufficient to sustain a considerable population, if judiciously located. I persuade myself that the scarcity of timber in this country is not so great as has been sometimes reported. The wood is chiefly along the watercourses. The hills, which sometimes are abrupt though sufficiently level on top, and other uplands formed by gentle ascent generally rise once, twice, or thrice as high as the timber in the low grounds. Travellers usually avoid crossing the watercourses as much as practicable because of the unevenness of the way, the brush, and the rocks, and hence most of the timber is unseen by one passing hastily through the country uninterested in the matter of wood. It would be fortunate for this country, if, in its settlement surveys should be so made that to each farm should be allotted so much timber *only* as would be necessary, and let the residue be prarie.

The Putawatomies and Ottawas whom I conducted, while they lament the scarcity of wood, and especially the almost total absence of the sugar tree, pronounce it a fine country.

On our tour we came in contact with Osages, Kanzas, Pawnees, and Shawanoes, the kind treatment received from all whom is pleasantly acknowledged by our party.

With the exception of a few warm days at the commencement of our tour, the whole has been pleasant and our Indians, I am happy to say, have returned with fine feelings.

I have the honour to be
With great respect, Sir,
Your Obt. Servt.
Isaac McCoy"

Genl. William Clarke
    Present."

Tuesday Oct. 7. 1828   Since our return to the settlements I asked Noonday if he thought the country on Osage river, &c. was a suitable place to settle the pupils of our schools, and for the location of the southern Indians, &c, and he replied in direct terms, "yes, it is a good country for such purpose." He cannot bear the idea of leaving Michigan. Having discovered the others pleased with the country he had repeatedly mentioned objections, such as the scarcity of wood, of sugar tree—of bark for bags and twine, and of bulrushes for mats, &c. Gosa tells me all that passes among them, and I had occasionally made remarks which were intended as replys to his objections. Gosa goes so far as to say that Chandonois also has endeavoured to discourage them, and has not only found fault with the country but said that should the Indians settle in it, they would soon be driven thence by the influx of white population. Notwithstanding all which Gosa has, of his own accord, frequently told me that he had resolved to come to this country should I come. He further assures me that Wesauogana, Magaukwuk, and Shawaunukwuk, also, all say the same. I am bound to be thankful that I have so much reason to beleive that, notwithstanding all the disadvantages under which the tour from Michigan has been made, appearances so far promise the result desired.

Wednesday October 8 Col. Manard one of the Commissioners who treated with the Putawatomies at Carey since I left has brought me a brief communication from Mr. Lykins. I am sorry it is so short, but it was written at the breaking up of the treaty & when all no doubt were much hurried—which is the apology for its shortness. Some land has been purchased of the Indians, & some favourable provisions made for the mission.[22] The particulars will be inserted when they are better known. I was exceedingly busy till 12, when not waiting to dine, I rode back to my lodgings in the country, 13 miles. Where I was busy till bed time.

Thursday Oct. 9 I took eight horses, and fixed our five Indians & the little girl whom the Ottawas found here in the summer, and who has ever since resided at Mr. Browns where I provided a place for her, and after a busy morning, set off at 11 o'clock for St. Louis, intending to send the Indians home. Chandonois last Sunday, with Magaukwuk went ahead to spend the time with some acquaintances. The former has received a fall from his horse, and is unable to travel. Both, no doubt were drunk, Magaukwuk has lost several articles. Shawaunukwuk got drunk yesterday in my absence. The Creeks here drink very much also. I am glad that our Indians are likely to go without Chandonois. He is a murderous fellow, and in a frollick on the road might kill some of them. His horse has a severe wound on the head made no doubt with a tomahawk in an attempt of Chandonois to kill him.

On reaching St. Louis I entered upon business of fitting out our party &c. & continued busy till bed time.

---

22. Article 5 of the treaty which was concluded September 20, 1828, and ratified January 7, 1829, was as follows: "Circumstances rendering it probable that the missionary establishment now located upon the St. Joseph, may be compelled to remove west of the Mississippi, it is agreed that when they remove, the value of their buildings and other improvements shall be estimated, and the amount paid by the United States. But, as the location is upon the Indian reservation, the commissioners are unwilling to assume the responsibility of making this provision absolute, and therefore its rejection is not to affect any other part of the treaty."—*Treaties Between the United States of America and the Several Indian Tribes from 1778 to 1837*, compiled by the Commissioner of Indian Affairs, Washington, 1837.

Friday Oct. 10   I paid our Indians according to agreement at the rate of $10. pr. month from the time of leaving their homes until they can return, In addition to this they have received Clothing to a considerable amount, each of them a new gun—blankets, & sundry small articles for travelling. To Noonday I gave an old horse saddle, & bridle, &c. and to the others horses at half their value so that to each one was given $15—20, or 25, in the value of their horse, besides, saddle, &c. &c. So that each has received, since he entered by service near $200. in cash, clothing, &c. &c.

I was extremely anxious to get started today, lest the Putawatomies should begin to drink. I had prepared every thing by one oclock, when they said they wished to see Genl. Clarke, I went with them. After they said they were ready to go, they loitered so that it was near night before we crossed Mississippi. I rode about 5 miles and slept at Belsha's at which place we arrived in the night.

As I am much worn with riding on horseback, Cap. Kennerly has lent me a horse & gig.

They had considerable talk with Genl. Clarke after I left them. I suppose they had begged something of him. I returned to hurry them off and the Genl. told me he thought I had better give them an additional blanket and perhaps something else. I told him that they had already been amply rewarded. However at his suggestion I gave each of them a first rate blanket, and one good one to the girl.

Saturday Oct. 11   I made about 25 miles. White inhabitants on the road are now scattering. Here I have completed my supply of provisions for them. Gave them additionally $10. to bear their travelling expenses, and, as they were anxious to be going, and deemed it most advisable for them to be on the road, at 11 o'clock on

Sunday Oct. 12   They proceeded. Here we parted—they and I both expressing & feeling affection. I trust the Lord will return them in safety to their people. I have go[od] reason to beleive that their journey will be a means of promoting in no small degree, the objects of our labours among them. All except Noonday say they are determined to go to the west, and that they will take with them some of their friends. Two of them told me this morning that by me on my visiting Washington, they wished to make a communication on this subject to the President, in which they would be joined by many of their friends.

I have great reason to be thankful to God that notwithstanding all the disappointments and delays, so that none others have yet seen the country we were to explore, yet all the objects of the tour in relation to the Putawatomies & Ottawas have been fully accomplished, and promise a favourable result.

By these I have written home to my dear family & brethren from whom, for a few years past I have been much absent. This is a great privation! I feel much anxiety of mind. O that the Lord would strengthen me for my work, and enable me to endure hardness as a good soldier! No one not in similar circumstances can form an idea of my anxiety. O Lord sustain my lonely companion in life, & preserve our dear babes and older children!

III. Statements of Expenses of the Tour

Carey, July 1. 1828.

The following articles were furnished by the Mission for the use of Indians on the exploring expedition being second hand *and* repaired.

3 Coats, 5 vests and 3 pr. pantaloons
5 pair socks and 2 pair suspenders
2 Shot pouch straps 1 hunting shirt & Coat
1 vest and 2 pair Socks
1 pair pantaloons Belt & shot pouch Strap
6 Saddles 3 saddle Bags, 6 Bridles 6 saddle blankets &
6 circingles—
1 saddle, saddle bags, bridle saddle Blanket circingle
and Buffalo robe
1 Pack saddle circingle & Bridle
5 Bell Collars & 2 Leather hobbles
9 Bags Buffalo Robe Deer & Bear skin
100 lb flour 4 Tin Kettles 1 pan 8 cups 1 canteen
2 spoons & pepper Box
one musquito Bar
2 Rifles & 1 heavy shot gun with pouches & horns
1 lb Tea 2 lb Coffee 1 pr socks & 14 lb sugar
2 blankets

For the above mentioned articles McCoy Received of the U. States $261.81¼ which is accordingly Credited on the mission book for Sep. 1829.

Fayette, Mo. Sep. 8. 1829
Isaac McCoy

   Isaac McCoy
    to David Walker
1828 To Ferriage of 7 men & 8 horses
July 10 mouth Fox river .... .50 cts
              Recd payment
              David Walker

Isaac McCoy Bot of
William Holland
22¾ lb. bacon............ @ 8 cts. $2.81¼
                      Recd. payment
                      Farm Creek, near Fort Clark
                      July 10. 1828
                          Wm. Holland.

Springfield, Ill. July 12. 1828
    Bot. of A. G. Herndon
12 lb. sugar 2.00
20 " flour .... .40
                                                  2.40
                      Recd. payment
                      A. G. Herndon

Isaac McCoy
    To Samuel Wiggins .... Dr.
    For ferriage at St. Louis 8 horses & 7 men............. $3.87½
St. Louis, July 16, 1828.   Recd. payment for Samuel Wiggins
                      Benjamin Ground

Isaac McCoy
    to John Cormack   Dr.
For keeping 8 horses one night, & for provisions
  for company $1.25
                      Recd. payment
[MS. torn] Edwardsville, Ill. July 16, 1828
                      John Cormack

Isaac McCoy Dr.
    to J. Baum
July 22   Repairing Coat for Gosa, Ottawa...................... 2.00
            1 Sett Buttons 1.00
                                                  $3.00
                      Recd. pay St. Louis, July 23, 1828
    [Original]   J. Baum

                St. Louis, City Hotel
The Revd. Isaac McCoy   Dr.
    To G. S. Greene
Expenses necessarily incurred for entertainment of self
and a party of Indians on an exploring expedition to the
west.

1828
July 16   To supper & lodgings for self.......................... .62½
    17   " one bottle Madiera Wine.......................... 2.00
          " washing of peices .... .56¼
          " Do.   24 Do. for Indians.................... 1.50
    22   " Do.   8 Do. for self........................ .50
    23   " Two bottles Madeira Wine 4.00
          " 7 days board and lodgings for self.................. 7.00
          " 6 days entertainment for one interpreter and five Indians at $1. pr. diem for each person as pr. contract 36.00

                                                                         $52.18¾
      "   " one weeks keep of 1 Horse........................ 2.00

                                                                          54.18¾
                                                     Received Payment
                                                          Geo. S. Greene

                                      St. Louis, Aug. 14. 1828.
Magaukwok......Coat $6.50
3 brevetts 1.00
Wesauogana......Hkf. .... .50
Noonday........Hkf. .... .50
Shawaunukwuk...vest 2.00

                                                                10.50
                                                 Recd. Payment
                                                 Saml. Waddell

    The United States
                                    To Henry Crossle......Dr.
For the following No of Horses furnished Capt George H. Kennerly as leader of a party of Indians &c on an exploring party west of the State of Missouri & Territory of Arkansas authorized by the last Session of Congress.
For   1 Roan Mare $38.00
  "   1 Gray Horse 40.00
  "   1 Roan Horse 75.00
  "   1 Bay Horse 35.00

                                                          $188.00
St. Louis August 14th 1828
    Received of the Revd. I. McCoy One Hundred and eighty eight dollars in full of the above a/c
$188.   Henry Crossle

The United States
                          To Robert Payne......Dr.
For the following No. of horses furnished Capt Geo H Kennerly as Leader of a party of Indians &c on an exploring party west of the State of Missouri & Territory of Arkansas. Authorized by the last Session of congress.

For   1 Large Sorrel Horse $80.00
"   1 Dark Bay Horse 60.00
"   1 Light Sorrel Horse 75.00
"   1 Dark Sorrel 65.00
"   Light Bay ditto 95.00
"   1 Dark Gray ditto 83.00
"   1 Black ditto 65.00

$523.00

St. Louis August 14th 1828.

Received of the Revd. I. McCoy Five Hundred & Twenty three dollars in full of the above a/c.

R. Payne
Approved   [Signed duplicate]
Wm Clark S. I. Af.

For the service of an expedition to the West Isaac McCoy Bought of me one Horse for which I have this day received sixty Dollars.

St. Louis County, Missouri,
August 15, 1828
$60.00   (Duplicate)   Lewellyn Brown

Revd. Isaac McCoy
Bot. of Joseph Charless Senr.

¼ lb. Best Lima Bark .... @ 1........ $ .25
2 oz. Blister Plaister .... 18¾........ .37½
3 Nutmegs .... .12½
4 oz. Ess. Peppermint & Phial....................... .31¼
2 oz. Calomel & vial................................ .37
1 oz. Jallap & vial............................ [MS. torn]
½ lb. Epsom Salt .... [MS. torn]
1 Small bottle Cas [MS. torn]   [MS. torn]
2 drs. Opium .... [MS. torn]
$2.23

Recd. Payment
St. Louis, Aug. 19. 1828.
Jos. Charless Senr.

Isaac McCoy
    To Samuel Worthington   Dr.
For accommodations for himself and party of eight, with 12 horses, night & morning $3.62½

Recd. Payment
St. Louis County, Missouri
Aug. 22, 1828
Saml. L. Worthington

The Reverend Isaac McCoy

Dr.

1828
July 24   on an exploring expidition to the west, To John Brown
          To boarding self & 5 indians four weeks
            at 175c per week each   42.00
          To Interpreters Board 3 weeks @ 175c   5.25
          To 7 horses kept 4 weeks @ 1$ per week   28.00
          To 1 horse one week   do   1.00
          To 9 horses kept 3 weeks and 5 days @ 1$ pr   33.75
          To keeping sorrell mare one week @   1.00
          To washing 2 doz & 5 pieces per self @ 50c   1.25
          To whng—6½ dozen per Indians @ 62½   4.06¼
          To washing 10 blankets per do @ 10c   1.00
          To heming 2 handkercheifs per do   .12½
          To paid for shoeing 2 horses   2.62½
          To 25 lb flour @ 3c   .75
          To 30 lb Buiscuits @ 5c   1.50
August 25 To 1 Bacon ham 12 lb @ 8 cents   .96
          To 1 Midling bacon 11 lb @ 6¼c   .68¾
          To 3 horses one night @ 25c   .75
          To 2 men 6 meals @ 12½c   .75
          To ¾ lb Tea@   1.00
          " 5 quts Salt @ 25c—1 Rope @ 25c   .50
                                                                   ―――――
                                                                    126.96

Received payment in full of the above account from the Revd Isaac McCoy

[Original]   John Brown

The United States

              To Thornton Grimsley   Dr.
For the following number of Saddles, Bridles, pack Saddles Halters & Hobbles furnished Capt George H Kennerly as leader of a party of Indians &c on an Exploring party west of the State of Missouri and Territory of Arkansas. Authorized by the last Session of Congress., &c

1828
Augt 26th For 6 Common Saddles   @$6.60 $39.00
           1 ditto ditto   10.00
           6 Bridles   50c   3.00
           12 Pack Saddles   3.00   36.00
           1 Bridle   2.50
           14 Halters   1.00   14.00
           12 Hobbles   .50c   6.00
                                                   ―――――
                                                    $110.50

Received St. Louis Augt 26th 1828 of the Revd. I. McCoy One Hundred & ten dollars and fifty cents in full of the above acct.

          (Signed duplicates)
                                        Thornton Grimsley

Isaac McCoy
    To Thomas Gibson   Dr.
For Dinners, horsefeed and 10 lb. bacon.............. $2.50
                                 Received Payment
                                Gasconade, Aug. 27. 1828
                                      Thom. Gibson

Isaac McCoy
    To James Wilson   Dr.
For Dinners & horsefeed for party &
11 lb. pork $2.50
                                 Received Payment
                                Grand Auglaize, Aug. 28. 1828
                                     James Wilson

Isaac McCoy
    To Edmund J. Carter   Dr.
For provisions for party, and piloting
five miles $1.50
                                Received Payment
                              Gravois, Cooper County M.
                                    Aug. 30. 1828
                              Edmund J. Carter

1828   Rev. Mr. McCoy and party Dr. to Harmony Mission
Sep. 4th   To 1 bushel Corn @ 1.00 pr. bush $1.00
            Blacksmith's bill .... .25
                                               ———
                                              1.25
                    Recd. payment for said Mission
                              D. H. Austin

                                     St. Louis September 10th 1828
The United States
                                         To William King Dr.
For Hunting and finding one sorrel mare on the Merrimack
River lost by the Revd. I. McCoy while on an exploring expedition west of the State of Missouri & Territory of Arkansas and bringing her to St. Louis................... $15.00
St. Louis   1828 Recd. of the Revd. I. McCoy
Fifteen dollars in full of the above acct.
            (Signed Duplicate)
                                                    his
                                     William × King
Witness   mark
    Henry Crossle

Isaac McCoy
    To Wm. Everett   Dr.
For ferriage of himself and man & two horses on Sep. 25
and Do. 7 men & two horses on Sep. 26.............. $2.50
                Received payment, Clay Co. Missouri
                          Sep. 25. 1828
                          Wm. Everett

The United States Indian Dept.
    To Leonard Searcy   Dr.
For   2 Gentlemen ten meals.......... $2.50
"   2 Horses thirty six hours........ 1.50
"   8 Horses for one night.......... 1.00
"   7 Suppers and Breakfasts 3.25   8.25

    Recd. Liberty Sept. 27th 1828 of
    the Revd. Isaac McCoy the sum
    of eight dollars and twenty five
    cents in full of the above act.
                          L Searcy

Isaac McCoy
    To Joseph Erwin   Dr.
For ferriage across Missouri river of himself
& eight men and 12 horses........................... $2.50
                    Received payment
                    Jack's ferry, Ray County, Mo.
                    Sep. 29. 1828
                    Joseph Erwin

1828   Isaac McCoy
Sep. 29   To Wm. B. Martin   Dr.
To accomodations for self and eight men &
12 Horses, 2 nights & one day..................... $10.00
                Received, Richmond, Ray County, Mo.
                Payment in full
                    Wm. B. Martin

Isaac McCoy
    To A. A. Evans   Dr.
For ferriage across Tabbo creek of himself &
eight men and twelve horses.
                    Recd. payment
                    La Fayette County, Mo.
                    Sept. 29. 1828
                          Abner A. Evans

Isaac McCoy
  To Littleberry Estes   Dr.
For suppers & breakfasts, &c. for himself &
eight men, and the keeping one night of
twelve horses $7.50
       Received payment
       September 30, 1828
        Little B. Estes

Isaac McCoy
  To Noel Mograin   Dr.
For services as interpreter to Osage & Kanzas, and
for the use of horse from September 3d. to
Sep. 30th inclusive, being twenty eight days at
$1.50 pr. day $42.00
       Received payment in full
       Shawanoe village
       September 30. 1828
         his
       Noel × Mograin
        mark

Isaac McCoy
  To Thornton & Thrash   Dr.
For ferriage of himself and eight men and
twelve horses $3.00
       Received three Dollars in payment
       Chariton County, Mo.
       Oct. 1. 1828
        Thornton & Thrash

Mr. Isaac McCoy
  To William Wright   Dr.

1828   To supper .... .25
Oct. 2   " Horse .... .37½
     " Lodgings .... .12½
                    .75 cts
       Received Payment
       Fayette, Oct. 2. 1828.
        Wm. Wright

Isaac McCoy
  To Jonah H. Shepherd   Dr.
For 4 bush. of corn .... @ 37½ $1.50
    4 Dozen bundles fodder ...... 25 .... 1.00
    Supper for eight .... " 2.00
    Breakfast for nine .... " 2.25
                      $6.75

Received six Dollars 75 Cents
           Howard Co. Mo.
           Oct. 2. 1828
              Jonah H. Shepherd

Isaac McCoy
  To Levy McMurtry   Dr.
9 suppers .... @ 25 .... $2.25
9 breakfasts 2.25
11 horses all night .... 25 .... 2.75
                      $7.25

Received seven Dollars and twenty five Cents in
payment.   Callaway County, Mo.
          Oct. 4. 1828
             Levy McMurtry

Mr. Isaac McCoy
  To Roger Taylor   Dr.
Oct. 4th. 5th. 1828
    9 suppers .... @ 25 .... 2.25
    9 breakfasts .... " 2.25
    1 lodging .... .12½
    12 horses per night .... 25 each........ 3.00
    6 dinners .... 25 .... 1.50
    10 Horses pr. day .... 12½ each....... 1.25
    10 horses per night .... 25 " 2.50
    7 breakfasts .... 25 each........ 1.75
    1 lodging .... .12½
                      14.75

Recd. [MS. torn] 1828 of Mr. Isaac McCoy fourteen
Dollars & seventy [MS. torn] cents, Montgomery
County, State of Missouri
              Roger Taylor

Isaac McCoy
> To George Belsha

For supper & breakfast for himself & six Indians &
for one lodging and the keeping one night of
nine horses $4.87½
Received four Dollars 87½ cts. in full

> St. Clair County Il.
> Oct. 11. 1828
> G. Belsha

Isaac McCoy
> to Gaius Paddock   Dr.

For two meals for six Indians........ @ 25 .... $3.00
     The keeping one night of eight horses.. @ 25 .... 2.00
     63 lb. pork .... @ 2½ cts.... 1.57½
     3 meals, 2 lodgings & keeping horse two nights.... 1.50
                                                    $8.07½

Received eight Dollars 7½ cts. in payment

> Madison County Il.
> Oct. 13. 1828
> Gaius Paddock

The First Kansas Band

Edward Bumgardner

IN THE early records of the Kansas Academy of Science the name of Joseph Savage occurs frequently. He was the pioneer explorer in the fertile field of Kansas paleontology. As a boy he lived at Hartford, Vt., where he was a member of the village brass band. On Sunday, August 26, 1854, he suddenly decided to emigrate to Kansas. One party of New Englanders had already availed themselves of the reduced rates secured by the Emigrant Aid company, and had reached the site of Lawrence. Another party was to leave Boston on the 29th of that month. Mr. Savage made his way to Boston, arriving there on Tuesday. When he went to the station the next day to join the party bound for Kansas he was surprised to find his brother, Forrest Savage, and two cousins named Hazen, who were also members of the Hartford band. At the last moment, they too, had decided to go to Kansas. They were carrying in their hands their four musical instruments—"one e flat copper key bugle, one brass post horn in b flat, one b flat cornet, and one b flat baratone." [1]

There was considerable excitement at the station. A large crowd was on hand to bid the emigrants farewell. Whittier had written a poem especially for the occasion. This had been printed on cards and distributed among the people in the crowd. Some one discovered that the meter of the poem corresponded to "Auld Lang Syne." The four Vermont boys took up that tune wtih their horns, and as the train pulled out the voices of the Kansas emigrants and of the people remaining at the depot, led by the four instruments, were united in singing:

> We cross the prairies as of old
> The Pilgrims crossed the sea,
> To make the West as they the East
> The homestead of the free.

The route of that second party of New Englanders bound for Lawrence was a little different from what it would be today. They went from Boston to Buffalo by rail, from there to Detroit on a lake steamboat, from Detroit to Chicago by rail, to the Mississippi river over the Chicago and Alton Railroad which had just been completed, down the river to St. Louis on a Mississippi steamer, and up the Missouri by boat to Westport Landing.

---

1. *The Kansas Memorial* (Kansas City, Mo., 1880), pp. 160-162.

At different points along the way through the North, people assembled to see the "abolitionists," and were entertained by the playing and singing of the Kansas hymn. The song had become immensely popular as soon as it was published. No sooner had the party boarded the boat at St. Louis, however, than profane threats against the Yankees warned them that the song of freedom must be taboo on the long journey up the Missouri river; but when the little band relieved the monotony by such selections as "Annie Laurie" and "Oft in the Stilly Night" there was no interruption.

At Kansas City wagons and equipment were bought and the emigrants started on the last lap of their journey to Lawrence. Walking beside their loaded wagons, the four Vermont boys led the procession across the Kansas line playing patriotic airs. As they passed Shawnee mission they took up again the song that was not welcome in Missouri.[2]

After arriving at Lawrence they became the nucleus of the first musical organization in Kansas.[3] Often that fall the settlers would assemble on pleasant evenings to listen to national airs played by the little band and to sing hymns and Sunday school songs to its accompaniment.

Gradually new members were added to the band. O. Wilmarth soon came out from Rhode Island with a clarinet, and Mr. Harlow from Vermont with a melodeon. Thus reënforced, they furnished music for the first Fourth of July celebration in Lawrence in 1855. This celebration was held in a grove a mile northwest of the town. It was the first festive occasion after the settlements in Kansas were started. By primitive modes of travel, including a train of wagons from "Kennedy valley"[4] drawn by eleven yoke of oxen, settlers came from every direction until the greatest crowd of white people thus far seen in the territory had assembled. The Delaware and Shawnee Indians had been invited and many of them were present. They appreciated the antislavery attitude of the New Englanders. After he had heard "Home, Sweet Home," "Yankee Doodle" and "Hail Columbia," Pechowkee, a dignified old Delaware chief made a speech of welcome in which he said, "We are glad that our white brothers do not come to us with the trumpets of war, but with the sweet flutes of peace and civilization. The Indian, too, loves

---

2. Susan D. Alford, "The Old Band," *The Atlantic Monthly*, January, 1929, p. 31.
3. Although the author has found no records of them there may have been military bands at Fort Leavenworth or other posts in Kansas territory, but he believes this is the first band of any kind organized in Kansas.
4. Andreas, *History of Kansas*, p. 318.

Liberty; the tree of liberty has been watered by many an Indian with his blood."

It was but a few months afterward that the owners of the cornet and clarinet were called upon to play the Portuguese hymn or "dead march" for the funerals of Thomas Barber, Captain Shombre and other martyrs of the Free-state cause.

By the spring of 1856 the pioneer band was fairly well organized. Samuel, Edward and Fred Kimball, three brothers from New Hampshire, became interested and proved to be good musicians. Samuel Newhall came out from Boston, John Ross beat the bass drum, Abram Wilder the tenor drum, and they were led by Leonard Worcester. Often during the troubles of 1856 they were called upon by Gen. James Lane to provide martial music to stimulate enlistment in the volunteer militia for the protection of the town.

The band grew in numbers and prospered until 1863. In March of that year the Kansas conference of the Methodist Church was held in Lawrence. In honor of the event the Methodist Sunday School arranged for a concert in which the band took a prominent part.[5]

About this time a movement was started to secure new instruments for the band. Gov. Charles Robinson headed a subscription list to raise the necessary funds, and the band gave a series of open-air concerts to encourage contributions. At last their hopes were realized. A set of fine new silver instruments was received from Hall, of Boston. As soon as they had been tested the members of the band were anxious to appear in a public recital with their new equipment. It was a good band. Patient drill had made the members proficient and they were able to render harmonious music under the direction of their new leader, Mr. McCoy, from Ohio. Proudly they assembled on the evening of August 20, 1863, and gave a concert from a platform that had been erected on the spot where the great Shunganunga boulder now stands.

Several times that evening they were called upon to respond to encores. It was high tide for the old band. Little did the players or the listeners dream of impending disaster. The next day Lawrence was destroyed by Quantrill. Fred Kimball, E. P. Fitch and another member of the band were instantly killed, and their director was so injured that he died soon afterward. For more than a year the survivors had but little time or heart for music, but at

---

5. *Kansas State Journal,* Lawrence, March 19, 1863.

the time of the Price raid in October, 1864, they went to the front as a militia band and served on the border for two weeks.

Another noteworthy service was performed in June, 1867, when the old band had the honor of assisting in the exercises of the first commencement of the University of Kansas.

On September 15, 1879, the remaining members of the band assembled and played for the last time. It was the twenty-fifth anniversary of the arrival at Lawrence of that New England party which left Boston in 1854 singing Whittier's "Kansas Emigrants," and they had been called together to furnish music for the old settlers' meeting at Bismarck Grove. Samuel Kimball still lived in Lawrence. Samuel Newhall came from Ouray, Colo., where he was interested in mining. Leonard Worcester came from Greensburg, Ind., where he was a dealer in musical instruments and leader of a band. Forrest Savage and Joseph Savage came in from their farms near Lawrence. The music furnished by the old band was one of the most appreciated features of that quarter-centennial celebration.

The last survivor of the band was Forrest Savage. He died at his home in Lawrence August 17, 1915, in his eighty-ninth year.[6]

6. Lawrence *Journal-World,* August 18, 1915.

Letters of a Kansas Pioneer
1855-1860
(Continued)

THOMAS C. WELLS

Juniata K. T. Sept 28/56

My dear father,

WE ARE as well and as busy as ever, and though we have but little time for letter writing I will try to send a *few lines* home as often as I can, that you may know how we are situated in these troublous times.

As yet we have had no fighting in our neighborhood, and the *war* below affects us, only, in that it cuts off in a great measure communication with the states, making provisions very high, except what we can raise ourselves, and taking all the troops and horses from Ft. Reiley we have not so good a market for our corn etc. I am mistaken it affects us much more than this, it prevents settle[r]s from coming among us, and filling up the country thereby putting [off] for a year or two at least, the growth of our cities and villages, and it tends greatly to discourage the settlers that are here from building churches or school houses, engaging extensively in any business or, indeed, making any improvements.

We do not wonder that you are alarmed for our safety when you read the newspaper accounts from Kansas, they are frequently exagerated however and *more frequently inaccurate* as to names of places and numbers of people engaged in battles etc but they are more always founded in fact and sometimes do not stat[e] the case nearly as bad as the truth would allow.

Sometimes we think that the future looks dark, but generally we keep up good courage and hope for better times   At all events we (I mean our free state settlers) are determined to "stick to the ship until we know she is lost" and whether we remain in Kansas or not we will do all we can, to prevent slavery from coming hither. If we may credit the latest news from below our new governor has turned decidedly against us, has been taking prisinors free state men and calls out the troops to assist the Missourians and their allies in enforcing the *shameful, bogus* laws, and in driving the free state Settlers from their homes.

But whether it be true or not that our governor Sides with our enemies, they are making all the mischief, committing all the outrages & murdering or driving out all the free State people that they can. I am surprized to learn from you that so many, even some of our "near relatives are such blind slaves to party or such selfish seekers for office as not, to believe the stories of or wrongs, or care whether the advocates of liberty or oppression triumph. They may get their reward, but I pity them, and would not give a three cent piece, for their friendship or their patriotism.

But I must close—will write more soon as practicable and I hope to hear frequently from you.

House is not finished yet—getting most out of patience.

Would be glad to have you sell that stock soon as you can for I shall need the money much.

My letters being directed to a pro-slavery P. O. generally come regularly.
Yours truly in haste
T. C. Wells

Manhattan, K. T. Oct 19th 1856

My dear Mother

We very gladly received a letter from you last Friday, we got no letter from any one week before last and by some mistake we got none last week when we first went to the office, but afterwards two letters, one for Theodore from Lissie Sheldon and one from you, were sent to us.

I have been expecting to receive more drafts from home for two or three weeks, and if they do not come soon I shall hardly know how to get along, for I have calculated upon getting them and I really need the money. Theodore has decided to go home this fall, with Mr Wilson, Nealley etc who are going east to spend the winter with their friends; but if I do not receive the drafts from home I do not know how I can get the money for him. It will be as much or more than I ought to spare even if they come.

Everything is quiet now in the territory,—no fighting, and no trouble—hope it will remain thus quiet but I fear that we may have more trouble again after the presidential election in the States. Thus far our new governor seems to act impartially.

I am sorry father was not able to go and see Mr. Todd. He is one of our nearest neighbors and I think he would have liked him much. Mr. T. has returned with his wife and little boy, and his wife's brother—and they are now keeping house on their claim—the third one north of mine.

Providence permitting we shall be married before Theodore starts for home, probably on the Thursday previous. Theodore is the only relation that either of us have in Kansas. Ella wishes she could have some of *her* folks here at that time if at no other.

I expect to harvest my corn this week, I think I shall have 275 or 300 bushels, and I expect to get 25 or 30 bush. potatoes and two or three bush of beans—we have gathered two or three wagon loads of winter, squashes crooknecks etc and have quite a lot of beets yet in the garden.

I wish you and father and little Herbert were here to share some of the good things with us, prairie hens will be *plenty,* once in a while we may get a wild turkey, or a deer, and we can buy dry buffalo meat of the indians; but in the absence of all these we have beef, and there is no beef like that raised on the Kansas prairies.

Is Henry at Beloit now? we have not heard from him in a long time, and we know not where to write to him.

You will be really lonely when Mr. Reeds family and Fannie Burdick go away—I think you had better move out here and settle near us in Kansas;—It would not cost father so much to get started as it has me for he could use my horses, oxen, wagon, plow, etc. etc., that I was obliged to buy, until it may be convenient for him to get such things for himself, and after the first year or so he would have quite an easy time, and I doubt not that both his health and yours would be better here than there.

Come now make up your minds to come out here and bring the Lyme folks with you, or at least, after Theodore gets home and learns enough about the Bank to get along alone for a few weeks— say by next June, send father out west on an exploring expedition. The journey will do him good, even if he should decide to go back and spend his days in R. I. nothing would be lost, and I assure you we should be very glad to see him.

How does Gillies get along with the Printing Office? We recd a letter from him not long ago and I will try to answer it soon.

Is there any prospect of the Baptist Church geting any one to take Mr. Reed's place? Do you have any preaching in the Episcopal church now?

Emigrants come in every week and soon all the good claims will be taken up, so that none can be had without buying. We expect a very large emigration in the Spring.

Love to friends and I hope you will write often and oblige yours truly,
                                                                T. C. Wells.

Manhattan, K. T. Nov. 2d 1856.

Mrs. T. P. Wells

My dear Mother,

I did not write home last week for I had enough else to occupy my time.

The past week has been an eventful one to me, on Thursday evening last (Oct. 30th) Ella and I were married. Everything passed off very pleasantly; 'twas a beautiful day, not a cloud to be seen, and all the guests that were invited came, except two, and they were quite unwell; sixteen, besides ourselves and the family in whose house we were married, were present, and that is doing pretty well for Kansas, for you must know that they all had to come from one to five miles over the prairies in the dark and several of them got lost and wandered about for half an hour or more before they could find the house.

Ella has made her home at Rev. Mr. Traftons during the past six months; he is a Methodist Minister, ordained only week before last at Lawrance; he married us, the first job of the kind he has had, and he did his part well.

Both he and his wife have been very kind to us, and we regard them as our very best friends in this far off land.

We are boarding with them for a few days as our house is not quite ready for us. We hope to move into it toward the last of this week.

We would not have hurried matters quite so much had not Theodore been intending to start for home on Tuesday, next, and as he was the only relation that either of us had out here, we wanted him to be present when we were married.

I assure you that I have no reason to regret my choice, nor do I ever expect to have, and I hope I am, I know that I ought to be, very grateful to my Heavenly Father for so good a wife.

How little do we know of the future! Little did I think two years ago that I should now be living in this distant land, and married to one of whom I had never heard, a perfect stranger, but so it is.

I feel more than ever that all things are ordered by a *higher* power, and He doeth all things well.

I suppose that Theodore will start, with Mr. Wilson and Mr Nealley, for New England, on Tuesday.

I have had considerable trouble in raising the money for him to go, for times are rather hard here now and money is *very scarce*. I tried to collect some in several places where it was due me but was unsuccessfull. I then tried to sell some of my Manhattan stock, but could find no one ready to buy just then. At last I made a raise by hiring it of Mr. Wilson for a few months at a pretty high rate of interest.

Father wrote me a long time ago that he would sell the remainder of my stock at Landholders Bk. and send me the proceeds, and I have been looking for the drafts for several weeks—had they come as I expected I should have had no such trouble.

I[t] takes a great deal to do a little in a new country and I hope the drafts will come soon for I really need them to pay for what I have been obliged to get trusted. I am getting a very good start here now and if I can once more get "squared up" I think I shall have no difficulty in keeping so and doing something better too another season.

My expenses have been much greater than I expected since I have been here this time. I have been obliged to pay a board bill of six dollars a week for myself & Theodore besides one dollar a dozen for washing, and my house has cost me more than I expected etc. etc. and the man who engaged to furnish me with rails disappointed me so that I did not get my field fenced and the stray cattle have harvested considerable of my corn for me which is not very pleasant, but I hope I shall do better another season, for I shall not have quite every thing to do. We shall feel rather bad at parting with Theodore, but I think it best both for him and us that he should go, for though he does as well perhaps as any young fellow of his age would do, yet he needs a father's care, and we do not really need his help. I hope he will have a safe journey home, and that he will do his best to help father this winter.

After a little while now I do not expect to be so driven with work as I have been, and shall try to write more frequently to my eastern friends

How is Doct. Clarke now? I have written him a long while ago but have received no answer.

I wish that you and father could come and make us a good long visit when we get settled in our new home, it would be *so nice;* but I would like still better to see you settled near us in a home of your own. We did not know that Theodore would *certainly* start on Tuesday until yesterday afternoon, for I was not able to get the *cash* for him until then; so that will account for his clothes being in no better condition, but I am glad that he can go now for I would rather he would go with Mr. Wilson than most any one else.

Theodore will tell you all the news when he gets home, so I need not write more. We send a few cards by him, they are not just what we wanted, but you must remember that we are in *Kansas* and we got the best we could, we sent east for some others, but they have not come yet, and we may not get them at all should they come however. I think they will be better than these and we will send you some of them. Give Herbert a kiss for me and remember me to old friends. Where is N. Read Jr now? I would like to know where to direct a letter to him. Ella sends love.

Yours truly from your affc't son,
T. C. Wells.

We are short of envelopes, so I send three cards in yours—one for Lissie and one for Henry, and I will put in two more for Grandfather and grandmother Johnson and *Mr & Mrs* Denison. We did not get as many cards or envelopes as we wanted. We had to send east for them and had to take up with what we could get We can get none printed here. I think you will give me credit for writing a good long letter this time and if I had time I could write as much more. T. C. W.

Mrs. Thos. P. Wells,   Manhattan, K. T. Nov. 16/56

My dear Mother,

I have before me your letter dated Oct. 4th—the last which we have received from home or any where else; I should have said, the last that I have received, for Theodore has left us, and Ella got two letters from her friends last week.

I have been anxiously expecting a letter from home containing drfts. for several weeks past but have been disappointed thus far and if the dfts do not come pretty soon I do not know what I shall do.

I saw Mr. Randolf, the gentleman that carried Theodore and Mr. Wilson etc down to the states, last Friday, and was glad to learn that finding a boat at Leavenworth, they were able to proceed immediately on their journey, without any delay and that he left them all well and in good spirits.

We both miss Theodore a good deal, and should miss him much more had we not so much to occupy our time and thoughts.

We moved into our new house last *Saturday,* Nov 8th rather a queer time to move, I own, but "circumstances alter cases" 'tis said, and we thought that in this case circumstances would justify our moving, and I believe we were right in thinking thus.

'Twas a cold day, the 8th of Nov., the ground was all covered with snow and it seemed very much like winter. The house was just as the carpenters had left it, only partly finished, doors only to one room, neither lathed or plastered, the floors all covered with dirt and shavings, and everything in "sweet confusion."

In the morning Mr. Browning and myself put up the cook stove in our parlor-kitchen-dining room-and-sitting room, and I moved over some of our things from Mr. B.s with an ox team, and with the same I brought over in the afternoon the remainder of our things from Mr. Trafton's, and Ella. We arrived at our house at about four o'clock, and set up a bedstead made a bed, and arranged our things a little, during the evening so that we got along quite comfortably until Monday, and Ella has been very busy all the past week in cleaning up, and arranging our things so that it begins to seem quite like home.

I would not have you think that, every thing is straightened up and fixed to our liking and that there is now nothing more to be done, by no means, but we have made a begining, and a good begining, and we see some prospect of getting done before a great while.

Ella does not *half* do *anything* and what she has done is done thoroughly, so that it will not have to be done over again.

The township surveyors have been along here and the section surveyors will be along in a few days, so that we shall soon know where our claims are. As near as we can judge from the township lines, our claims will go 40 rods further west and six rods further south than we supposed judging from Thurstons survey, if this should be the case nearly all my plowed ground will come on Mr. Wilson's claim which will not be very pleasant as it costs from four to five dollars an acre to break up the soil here for the first time. I think however that Mr Wilson will do the fair thing and break as many acres for me as he gets of mine.

It seems real good to have a home once more, we have both of us been flying about, here and there, settled no where for so long a time that we know how to prize a home now that we have one, and I assure you we do prize and enjoy it.

We have had no meeting today as the minister Rev. Mr. Denison,[6] whose turn it was to preach was sick The peace still continues below, and a little while ago this morning, we saw a large

---

6. Probably Joseph Denison, one of the founders of Bluemont college. He was president of the college when it became a state institution. For a biographical sketch see *Kansas Historical Collections*, v. VII, p. 169.

company, perhaps one hundred and fifty, dragoons returning from below to Fort Reiley.

Ella received a box from home yesterday containing a lot of things which will be both useful and pleasant for us, it came out with Mr Todd's things. I suppose you know long before this who is elected president, we have not heard yet.

I wish you would send us some flower seeds, a few at a time in your letters, we would be very much obliged, indeed, for them.

I think of nothing more of interest at present, please write often. I hope we shall get a letter from you this week.

Ella sends love, and says Tell Theodore I want to see him very much indeed and he must write as soon as he gets home.

Has father got well of his lameness yet. I do so wish some of you could come out and see us, and make us a good long visit.

Yours very truly
T. C. Wells

I enclose a letter from G. I. Robinson to Theodore.

Manhattan K. T.
Nov. 29th, 1856.

Thos. P. Wells, Esq.,

My dear father,

I received a letter from you yesterday, dated Nov 12th with enclosures as stated, and was very glad to get the same and am much obliged to you for the trouble you have had in doing business for me. I had been obliged to borrow some money here at the usual rate of interest, (ten per cent) and also to purchase some things on credit, and was fearful that I should not get the drafts in time to meet my engagements, and pay my honest debts, but they have come at last and all is right To me it is unpleasant to get into debt at all, but it is *very* unpleasant when one does get into such a fix not to be able to see his way out, nothing will make me feel blue sooner I think I can "pay up" and get "square" with the world now and if possible I intend to keep so.

We were very glad to get your letter, for though it contained no news it furnished evidence that some one was still alive in the east and that we were not quite forgotten

We have not heard from home before since Theodore left more than three weeks ago. We have heard nothing from Theodore or Mr. Wilson since they left Leavenworth City and feel almost afraid that something has happened to them.

Another week has nearly gone. It is Saturday evening and we

are glad that another Sabbath is near at hand   We find a great deal to do and feel that we ought to work while we can, but tired with the labors of the week we are glad when that day approaches wherein we *must not* work.

We get along nicely in our new home; true when we moved here we found nothing done, and every thing to do, but we have got a few of the odd jobs off our hands and hope that *sometime* the time will come when we shall not feel quite so hurried.

Our house is quite comfortable as much or more so than any in this region, and yet you would almost as soon think of moving into a barn, in the east, as of moving into an unfinished house like this. I have not heard from Elisabeth, Henry, or Amos, in a long time. What's the matter with them all? It is getting late, and I am getting sleepy as you may judge from this letter so I must close. Do write us a good *old-fashioned* long letter soon.

Yours truly
T. C. Wells

Manhattan, K. T. Dec 14/56

My dear Mother,

You did indeed write me a good long letter this time—it is now just three weeks since it was written—I would like to get as long a letter from you every week. I entirely agree with you in thinking it a "shame" that the Baptist church in Wakefield should let so good a minister as Mr. Reed go and be willing to take up with such preaching as they may chance to get from Sabbath to Sabbath or go without any preaching at all; one would think that their religion was all in their pockets or they would not be satisfied with such a state of things.

We can, indeed, tell a "better" story of Kansas society than you do of Wakefield. There are three little churches formed in our vicinity Methodist, Congregational, and Baptist, each provided with a minister; But each minister preaches at several different places so that we do not hear the same one only once in three Sabbaths, but we have preaching every pleasant Sunday.

And then as I have told you before we have as good neighbors as we could wish, and I very much doubt, whether, in any New England village you would find a less number of objectionable characters than there are in our vicinity.

We have no factory help, no colored people, and very few foreigners of any kind (not to say that there are not often to be found very fine people in each of the classes above named.) But society is not nearly so good in Manhattan, as among the farmers on the prairie.

You are right in saying that "you will be far happier" for being married. I do not know how I could get along without Ella. I *do wish* that you and father and Herbert could come and spend not only a "few days" but a few weeks with us; I know that you would enjoy your visit and we would so love to have you here. If Henry should come home again could not he take charge of the Bank a while in the spring so that father could leave awhile? I do wish you could all come out here and live; there is a claim just north of me, that is not yet, but soon will be, taken if father could only settle on that or some other claim near us, he would then have a home of his own while he lived, and be near, at least, two of his children. I believe he would be far happier, and you too if you would only believe it, than to remain in Wakefield. To be sure father gets a regular salary, you all have enough to eat, drink, and wear, the body is well cared for—but that is not all you want to make you happy here below. " 'Tis not all of life to live." . . . If Dr. Clarke comes out to visit Amos in the spring, we would be very glad to have him come and stay awhile with us; tell him if you see him soon that he owes me a letter and I should be very happy to get it. I hope he will like my "wife" as well and better than he thinks.

We spent last Friday evening at Mr. Todd's and Mr. Trafton and Mr Browning with their wives were also there—we had a very pleasant time. Theodore will tell you who they were.

Tell Sam. he must come and see my wife and then he will know *something* more about her. We got a letter from him and Lizzie yesterday—all well.

I think with him that Kansas will be a free state, and that we shall have little more trouble with "border ruffians;" all continues quiet. Did you save the seeds of that squash that Theodore brought you?

I hope Theodore will really be of much help to father, and will learn all he can about banking; it will be a good thing for him.

I am sorry he was so foolish as to buy a watch, and on credit, too. He seemed to have a fever for a watch all the time he was here, and wanted to sell something that he had and get one or buy one on credit, but I advised him not to do so.

Theodore left a good many clothes here, but none of them were fit for him to wear and we thought it not worth while for him to take them home with him.

Theodore, like all young lads has a great many notions of his own, and thinks he knows all about many things of which he is quite ignorant and he needs the advice and counsel of wiser and older heads He has naturally an affectionate disposition and can be *led* more easily than *driven,* but yet he must know what it is to *obey.*

I am sorry that Henry has had such poor success in getting business, I do not know what he can do. He must not despise the day of small I fear he is trying to get too good a situation and because he cannot find such an one as suits him in every particular will not accept of any. If he wants to learn any kind of business or rather if he wants to get a living and make money at any kind of business he must begin at the begining and learn it, and be content with a small salary at first. If he attempts to commence at the top of the ladder he will surely fail and have to try again and another way

I hope he will soon be successful and find some employment which will be profitable. I wrote him a week or two ago,—directed to care of A. B. Carpenter & Co. Beloit. Will he be likely to get it?

I am sorry that you are going to lose your library; a sort of literary society with a library connected with it is just starting at Manhattan I hope it will succeed.

I have written quite a long letter, and must stop without giving many particulars of our house-keeping, for I was not very well yesterday and today and though I feel pretty well now I am getting tired and feel that I should be better off in bed. I received a letter from Theodore last week and will try to answer it soon. Do write often. A large grey wolf came up quite near the house this afternoon, and two more came quite up to the hay stack about sunset. They will not attack men unless a number of them are together and then only under cover of the night and in winter when half starved.

Yours truly
T. C. Wells

I have written by candle light and cannot see whether I write on the lines or not. I enclose a few cards which you may make such use of as you think best.

Jany 11th 1856 [1857; misdated.]

Mrs. Thos P. Wells   Manhattan, K. T.

    My dear Mother,

It is four weeks since we heard from home and it seems to us a long time. Why is it? because you do not write?—or because the letters are delayed on the way.

Our mail usually comes Fridays and Mondays; I hope we shall

get some letters tomorrow. It is very unpleasant to be so long without hearing from our eastern friends, we do not get homesick, exactly, but, we can but fear that something bad may have happened, and we long to know how they do.

You must not think that because we have come so far from our old homes—to Kansas, and like the country so well, and are contented to live here—that we do not think often of you in the east, feel interested in your welfare and long to see you.

If I do not get a letter soon I shall have to write father to look up some suitable person, in his vicinity, who, for a fair compensation, will inform me regularly of the health and prosperity of my friends and relations in South Kingstown.

We enjoy good health and get along finely. At present a young friend, formerly of R. I. (Frank B. Smith) is staying with us for a few days. He is going to the States, to Davenport, Iowa some time this week; his brother is in business there, G. W. Smith who used to keep the house furnishing store in Providence.

I have a map of Manhattan which I intend to send to father as soon as I can get time to mark the direction and distance from Manhattan of some of our neighbors, and some of the villages near us.

The bogus legislature meets at Lecompton tomorrow. I think they will not do much business except to pass an act authorising the Governor to call an election of delegates to a convention to form a state constitution.

I recd two papers from home last week, the Prov. Journal and N. Y. Evangelist. Much obliged. We had quite a pleasant time at *our house* on New Year's evening. Eleven of our neighbors came by invitation, took supper with us and spent the evening, three remaining with us all night. It was quite stormy nearly all day the wind blew and it half snowed and half rained and the walking was very slippery, but our Kansas neighbors are not afraid of a little rough weather. Perhaps you would like to know something about our friends:— I will tell you who they were and where they come from. First, Harriet Leyman, the young lady who stood up with us when we were married, lives on a claim about three miles N. E. of us; her father-in-law (Mr Childs) brought her in a mule team— she stayed all night. She came from Ill. Mr. and Mrs. Whelden, from Prov. R. I. live on a claim two miles N. E. of us. they walked, and remained all night. Mr. & Mrs. Todd and little boy, and Mrs T's brother Henry Booth (who also stood up with us) from Woonsocket, R. I. Mrs T. and boy rode on a sled drawn by one horse and returned after ten o'clock in evening, they live just west of Mr Whelden one and half miles from here. Mr. and Mrs. Browning living on claim east of us, from Fitchburg Mass. they walked. Mr & Mrs Trafton, claim west of us—walked—from Mass. all very fine people and as good neighbors as we could desire; Theodore can tell you more about them. I have been thus particular to satisfy your curiosity. How does Theodore get along in the bank? Is he a good boy? Is Henry at home?

Is uncle Hagadorn doing well? How does the school prosper in Kingston? Remember me to Dr. Clarke if you see him and tell him I would be glad to have him write. Do you think there is any prospect of his coming out as far as here in the spring? Are you and father well? Do you ever talk (in earnest) of coming west? You see I am full of questions. It is reported that we are going to have a semiweekly mail—hope it is true.

We have not heard very much from Congress yet. I wonder whether they will do anything for Kansas this Session.

But it is getting late and I must stop until another week. Do write soon and often   Yours truly,
Wakefield, R. I.   T. C. Wells

          Manhattan, K. T. Jany 27/57
My dear Mother,

I was very glad to get a letter from you two weeks ago yesterday I received two other letters on the same day, one from Henry and one from Dr. Clarke. I had had no letters for three or four weeks before and have received none since.

I should have answered before but for two or three weeks past, I have been much troubled with the toothache from a decayed tooth and as there was no regular dentist here I dreaded to have it out, but yesterday I went down to Dr Whitehorn's and had it pulled. The Dr. performed the opperation as well as any one could.

You must not "mourn"—you and father,—because we are settled so far away from you; though I confess that I should feel very badly too did I think that we should always be thus separated. I have hoped that you would move out here, and settle on a home of your own near us, and would love to have you do so now; but if that is impossible or even impracticable we must hit upon some other plan. What that plan may be I cannot at present say. I do not think that it would be prudent for me to settle near the sea co[a]st soon and perhaps never, and it may be best for me to remain here one, two, or three years longer. It would be pleasant if we could find business in eastern Ohio, Southwestern N. Y. or Western Penn. and live near each other and near Sam'l and Lizzie too.

My health is very good now, *very much* better than it was one year ago. My lungs do not trouble me at all, and I have had but one "chill" since I have been married and that a very slight one on the day that Theodore left for Leavenworth City.

I intend to continue to improve my claim and work upon it as though I were going to make it my permanent home, but if I should get a good opportunity to sell I should probably sell out and try to find business nearer my eastern friends. Perhaps you may think from the tenor of the above, so different from anything that I have written before, that I am getting homesick or tired of the country. Not in the least, I have as pleasant a home as an affectionate wife can make it and I think none the less of the country as I become more and more acquainted with it. Were not my own and my wife's friends *so far* away I would not think of changing my place of residence.

Father never could have thought more of my society than I of his, & I would love, dearly love, to be where I could see him and you often—but we must " 'bide our time."

Ella frequently says she wishes some of my folks or hers were out here.

She is very much obliged for that collar, it did not reach here as soon as the letter. Please consider what I have written as confidential, I do not want it to go out of the family.

Has father received the map of Manhattan that I sent to him?

What is Theodore doing now? Why does he not write to us? Ella sends her love to him and says she is most tired waiting for that letter that he promised to write her. The lines are so faint on this paper that it is quite difficult to see them by candle light so please excuse the appearance of the writing. I enclose a little letter to Herbert, and a tulip that Ella painted expressly for him. I feel anxious to hear again from Henry, and know how he gets along. I do hope he has been successful. I intend writing him this week.

We have had some very cold weather; one week ago Sunday Mr. Todd says that the mercury was 16 degrees below zero, Mr Blood says that half an hour after sunrise 'twas 24° below zero.

We have been reading Mrs. Robinson's book on "Kansas" it is

very interesting and can be relied on as true; I wish you would get it and read it; it will give you a better idea of what has been done here than anything else that you can find, and it is well worth reading.

Do you have any regular preaching in Wakefield now? It has been so cold and such bad traveling that we have not been to meeting but little for a month or two past. Do write often. Yours affectionately

Mrs. Thos. P. Wells   T. C. Wells
Wakefield, R. I.

Feby 1st. The mail goes tomorrow, I have been writing a letter to father to go in the same mail. Do not urge him to stay I certainly think it will be for the health and happiness of him and you too to acceed to my proposal. If he continues in his present employment and with no one on whom he can *depend* for assistance he will soon be obliged to give up business entirely but if you were here and he should be sick or anything should happen to him you would have some one to look to for help and one too, that would gladly give it.

The male prairie chickens have little tufts of feathers on each side of their heads just back of their ears; they look like little wings Wife cut them off of one that I shot the other day and I enclose one for you. It has been very warm and pleasant for a few days past, it seems as though spring was coming in earnest. I hope we shall have no more very cold weather.

T. C. Wells

Manhattan, K. T. Feb 1/57

My dear father,

Since writing to Mother I have been thinking more about your circumstances and mine and I sincerely hope that you will agree with me in the conclusions to which I have come. It is the afternoon of the Sabbath day but I do not feel that it is wrong for me to write what I am going to for no time ought to be lost.

I came out here, as you know, with very poor health, little experience in the ways of the world and a comparatively small amount of money; I am now settled on a farm of my own (I may call it so, although I have not yet paid the government the nominal price asked for it.) and in my own house; My health is very much improved, indeed it is quite good, and notwithstanding my inexperiance, I have managed to get a comfortable living and the property that I have here now is worth more than all that I had in the east before I came out here. In a most beautiful country I have a very good location, near a growing town which promises to become shortly a large business place; my neighbors are such as no one need be ashamed of, kind hearted, and true, and most of them proffessors of religion (in this respect I think I could never better my situation.); during the coming year we expect to have good schools established and churches built.

All things induce me to stay here and there is only one drawback of any consequence, and that is my friends, my old friends, especially my father and mother, are far, far away,—if they were here wife and I would be perfectly contented to stay here.

Now a word for you. Perhaps I can imagine better than you think your feelings and you[r] situation. Your business is very trying to both your mind and body; it is continually injuring your health, as much so as though you drank daily small quantities of some poisonous mixture; and if you continue in it you will soon be unable to do much at any kind of business. You need to be free from so much perplexing hard work and you ought to have more out of doors exercise You greatly enjoy the society of "congenial spirits," you do not care for very many intimate friends but some you do want and those few you dearly love, in a great measure you are deprived of these, those for whom you cared the most are far away, and this is a cause of many unhappy moments and anxious thoughts. I know that there is little society in Wakefield for you, and I think there is little prospect of any improvement in that respect.

Now in view of these things (and I say not this without consideration) I would earnestly urge you to *resign the cashiership* whether you have any other business in view or not; it seems to me as though your health, and your happiness, and as your family are dependent on you, they too, demand it, for should you be entirely deprived of health you could do little for yourself or them.

And then I would urge you, while mother and Herbert and perhaps Theodore are on a visit to Lyme, to come out here and see the country for yourself and determine whether you could be happy and get a comfortable living here.

I will guarantee that you will not be disappointed, if you are I will agree to pay your expenses here and back with pleasure, if I cannot do so immediately as soon as I can get the ready money. I have no doubt but that should you and mother move out here

Uncle John Denison and his wife and even grandfather and grandmother would soon follow, but even should they not, it cannot be best for you to remain there on that account. It does them no material good for you to remain there except that they occasionally receive a visit from you or mother this *could* be done though perhaps at longer intervals if you were here and the means of communication will continually improve between here and New England, and in a few years it will take but little if any more than half the time that it does now to make the journey. At all events they will not be left alone for uncle J. D. and wife will not leave without them, and under the circumstances they certainly can not want you to stay where you are.

The troubles in the territory are doubtless ended, the free state majority is constantly increasing and we anticipate a very large emigration in the spring.

As for the fever and ague I think you need not fear that with decent care and prudence, many of our citizens have not been troubled with it at all.

And as for the expense of "starting" out here you need not fear, you have enough to give you a *good* start, twice as much as nine tenths of those who move to this far western country; and it need not cost you half what it did me to make a begining. As for cattle and horses and farm implements generally we can use the same in a great measure, and I have a pretty good supply.

Your age is no objection many come from New England older than you, and do well and you could not get them to return

Now the claim north of me is not taken the claim east or south of me can be purchased for much less than they will be worth one year hence but six, perhaps four months from now they will not probably be for sale.

And now my dear father will you not carefully weigh these considerations in your mind and may God be with you and help you to decide aright. I should be overjoyed to see you; it seems as though you must come. Even if you should not, (and I hope such will not be the case,) conclude to remain here the visit and journey will do you much good, and you certainly could find business again *as good, all things considered,* as that you have at present. Please write me very soon in answer to this, and if you conclude to "come and see" start as early as possible in the spring in order to secure a good claim while it may be had. I almost expect you will come. While down to Manhattan to meeting today I got a letter from

Theodore to wife. She will endeavor to answer it next week. I recd a letter from Mr. Wilson also. He says Theodore was a very good boy in going home in doing as he advised him to.

Thos P. Wells Esq Yours most affc'tly
   Wakefield, R. I.   *Do come*   T. C. Wells

[From Ella S. Wells to Theodore]

Mr. T. B. Wells   Manhattan, K. T. Feb 7th/56 [1857].

  My Dear Brother

It is 8 oclock Saturday night and I have but just taken my pen to answer your letter. I was intending to write you a long letter but as I want to send this to the office in the morning fear that I shall not be able to this time. Yours was received last Sabath I was very glad to hear from you and read your letter with pleasure.

I think you must have been tired and glad to get home after your flying journey you have not wished yourself here more than I have. I do want to see you very much I could not realize when I bade you goodbye that I was not to see you for a *long long time*. yet I trust it is all for the best and that you will be very usefull to father We wish very much that he could be induced to come out here if for nothing more to make us a good long visit. his health is of more consequence than anything else. The journey would do him good and we should be glad to see him. You do not speak very flatteringly of Wakefield people I hope there are ten righteous ones left.

Do you like working in the Bank better than working in a Kansas cornfield? Thomas says you cannot locate a land Warrant until the land comes into market but one can be used to pay for a claim if you are settled on it.

I thought I would write you the particulars of our household arrangements as you knew how the house was planed and then you could visit us in your mind's eye but shall not have time to write half I was intending. I will tell you about the sitting room as we spend most of our time in it this cold weather. By much hard rubbing I got the tent so it looks quite white I lined the sitting room over head and also the open space by the stairs with it & I got some thick brown paper to line the rest of the room. The stove sits on the side by the stairs T put up a long black walnut mantle shelf back of it he also has made quite a nice bookcase that holds all our books that is behind the entry door our looking glass hangs to the right of the window that looks towards Mr. Brownings I put a large shelf under that that looks like a table with a cloth on it. The table he got of Mr. Childs sits on the side next the well room. the little one he got at the Fort at the right of the door to the well room   T's trunk at the right of the window that looks towards Mr. Traftons   with 5 chairs & a cricket leaves but little spare room. I got a large stuffed chair of Mr. Whelden which is quite a luxury. the clock sits on the mantle shelf but chooses not to go   the box that my things came in from home sits at the left of the stove & answers for a wood box   Now dear little brother after such a detailed account of one room I think there will be nothing to hinder you from making us a visit.

I must tell you that poor Rover is dead   he died yesterday from repeated blows of an axe first having had one leg shot off   our hens commenced laying in Dec & Rover took a notion to eat the eggs which we preferd to do ourselves. We have a small pupy that Mr. Boasa gave Thomas   we call him Tiger.

Mrs Browning was in and spent the afternoon   she enquired after you   said she would like to see you and wished me to give her love to you when I wrote. Hatty Leyman was here new years   she enquired after you   Mrs Lipher & many others to numerous to mention often ask if we have heard from you & if you are coming out again. I have had a miniature and an ambrotype from the east & this year wish my dear brother would drop his in the ofice for me. Mrs. Trafton wished me to give her love to you when I wrote   she is as well as usual & has Mrs Becknal boarding with her whose husband died at Mr Goodnows soon after you left. It is almost 10 oclock   T is wating very patiently for me & I must close although I have not written half I wanted to. My love to father & mother & a kiss for Herbert. Now do write often. Dear brother, do not ferget for what you are placed here in this world but prepare for the world to come   you know that you will be a great deal happier. I must close.
          Your aff sister,
                    Ella S. Wells.

                              Manhattan, K. T.
My dear mother,   March 14th, 1857.

I have your letter before me, written Feb'y 1st, as yet unanswered; I received it a fortnight ago today, but have been *very busy* of late and have had little time to write. During a part of the time since I wrote you I have been in the woods chopping saw logs which I intend to get sawn into fencing stuff 1 in. x 4 in. A part of the time I have been having a shed put up for a shelter to my horses etc. and a part of the time I have been helping a man draw some cedar posts to his claim and have not finished yet. I can earn three dollars ($3.) a day with my oxen, and wagon. I am going to take my pay for this job in cedar posts. I do not mean to plant any this year unless I can have it fenced. I expect to lose all the plowed ground that I had last year as the lines will probably run between that and my house. My claim is not yet surveyed though I am pretty well satisfied that the line between Wilson and me will run two or three rods east of my house. We expect the surveyors along very soon, and then we shall know where we are, and what we may call our own.

I got a letter from Dr. Clarke this week. He wrote that he had just written father and says that he will come out and visit us this spring if father will. O I do so wish that they would come. It would do both of them good, and us too I assure you. Perhaps father has already decided to come. I hope he has but if not do try and prevail on him to undertake the journey with Dr. I do not love to have him confine himself so closely, I am afraid that if he does his health will get so poor that he will be obliged to give up all business. Do get him to come. *If* he should not come, or if you receive this before he starts, I wish he would send me a statement of my affairs there, bank stock, notes, etc., and also how they stood on January 1st/57. I would like to know how they stand, and if he can I would like to have him buy a one hundred and sixty acre land warrant, for me; and if he cannot raise the money to pay for it, on anything that I have in the east, I will raise it here and send it on to him when I know how much it is. It would save me $45. or $50. to pay for my claim with a land-warrant instead of the *cash*. A *transfer* the name left blank, *must be legally* written upon it and signed by the person to whom the warrant was made out. Since the first week in February we have had very pleasant weather for winter, until within a few days it has been rather cold, but not so that we could not work pretty comfortably out of doors.

We had quite a snow storm last night and this morning.

We do not have so much mud when the frost is coming out of the ground as you in the east it generally drys up most as fast as it thaws, but it is pretty *sticky*, after a heavy rain.

We *did* receive the letter or paper containing a collar for Ella and she is greatly obliged for it. I think I have written you this before. I should think from what you write and from what I can learn from other sources, that you have had a much more cold and tedious winter than we. We certainly have had no such snow storm as you speak of. I am real sorry that the steeple has blown off the meeting house at K. I always liked that steeple. Will they try to build another? You say that many wells in your vicinity are dry we have had no trouble of that sort here. We have had *seven ft* of water in our well all winter. Please remember me to Mr. Reeds folks if you write them soon. It is strange that Lissie has not heard from me since I have been married. I have certainly written her or Samuel and have been wondering why she did not write us. I will try to write again soon. I am very sorry that Henry has such poor success. If he was out here and would hear to reason a little from a friend I could put him in a way to do a good business with $500. capital or even less, but I do not know that it is best to write him so. I am expecting a letter from him soon. I have not had a letter from Amos in five or six months or more. I do not know why. I do not think that West Point would be a good place for Theodore in every respect. He would learn to obey of course, he ought to do that at home, but I fear he would *not* learn *good morrals* there.

We are always glad to get a letter from home and I hope you will write often. Hope Theodore will write. Love to all, & kiss to Herbert.

Yours truly

To Mrs Thos. P. Wells,   T. C. Wells.
  Wakefield, R. I.

Manhattan, K. T. Apr 5th, 1857.

My dear mother,

I was very glad to get a letter from you last Friday, dated Mar. 8th. We had not heard from home in a long time, and were anxious to hear from you once more. I am glad you do not always [wait] for a letter from me before you write, it takes so long for letters to go and come that it will not do to wait one for another.

I used to think that Wakefield promised to be *the* village of the town but should think from your letter than Peacedale was going ahead of it.

We have not heard from Lizzie in a long, long time. Is she and Samuel and little Susy well? Does Henry think of going into business in Rockford? I wish he would write me. I am happy to hear that uncle Hagadorn succeeds so well with his school, would like to get a letter from him.

Dr. Clarke means to do what he thinks right I believe, but I did think he would vote for Buchanan. I thought that "Spiritualism" was about dead or at least on the wane, we seldom hear anything about it hear, and I was much surprised to hear that so many in your neighborhood had turned "Spiritualists."

I sent a map of Manhattan to father at the same time that I mailed the two letters that you write have been received. Has he never got it? I sent one to Dr. Clarke at the same time and he wrote me that he had received it some time ago.

I am exceedingly sorry, and so is Ella, that father thinks he will not be able to come and see us this spring. I hope something will turn up at the annual meeting that will lead him to alter his mind. It is very possible that he could find some other business than farming and even if he should not I do not think he would find it so bad as he anticipates. We do not have to work so much in the hottest weather here as eastern farmers do. I wish he would come and see us at least, and then he could tell better whether it would be well to move out here or not.

Kansas would be just the place for uncle John Denison and aunt Mariann. They would get along finely on a claim here I know, and I often think of them and wish they were here.

The Methodist Church are going to build a college in Kansas. The Conference meets at Nebraska City next week and will decide on the location. Manhattan association have offered large inducements to have it built here, and it will probably be located on the claim south of me. It has been bought and is reserved for that purpose. Should this be done it would increase the value of my claim very much.

The association have also voted ten shares each toward building the Methodist and Congregational churches, and the Cincinnatti Company agree to give 20 lots each for the same. Shares sell at from $50. to $75. each and lots at from $25. to $50. each. We expect both churches will be built before next fall.

A room for a school has also been hired until a school house can be built and a school will be commenced soon. If you should come out here to live you would not know much about a *new* country. All the claims around me and within several miles of the city are taken and can be got only by purchase; they are increasing in value every day. My claim is not yet surveyed by government, and I cannot therefore tell exactly where the lines will be, and on that account I do not intend to plow up any new ground or make any improvements until the lines are run. I think I shall put a temporary fence around the land that I plowed last year and plant that again without any addition.

Ella sends her love, and wants Theodore to write to her. How does Gillies get along with the printing? remember me to him. I do really think that you and father would be better off and better contented after you had been out here two or three years than you ever will be in Wakefield. Yours truly

To Mrs. Thos. P. Wells,   T. C. Wells
    Wakefield, R. I.

Manhattan, Kansas Territory,
May 12th, 1857

My dear father,

Very glad indeed was I to get a good long letter from you last week. I believe you have not written me so long a letter before since I have been in Kansas. I am very much obliged to you for purchasing me a land warrant and sending me a statement of my affairs in the east; perhaps it would give you pleasure if I would send you an account of my affairs in Kansas, and I will try to do so before I close. I am sorry that you and Dr. Clarke could not have come out and visited us this spring, we almost expected you and are really disappointed. As to the bank and the state of your health, you, of course, know your own business better than I, but I have been afraid that the confinement and the perplexity of your business would ruin your health. I am glad that you think your health so good. It was too bad that you should lose so much money (for the present at least) by Henry. I am sorry for Henry and you too. He wrote me that that was the case, since he got his present situation in Beloit, but did not write what his trouble was. I do hope you will be able to make some arrangement so that you can visit us before another year. You ask if Mr Wilson will make the loss of my plowed ground good to me by plowing again? He says that he will, and I am going to have the use of it this year, (the old ground I mean). It is not *absolutely* certain yet that I shall lose my plowed ground. My claim nor Mr. Wilsons (except his eastern line) is not surveyed yet; but as near as we can tell the line will run about two rods east of my house—, it *may possibly* run west of my house; in that case I should hold the quarter section that Mr. Wilson claims and hold not only my plowed ground but his *house* and *well* which I do not want. I do not think there is much danger of that however.

June 20th 1857. I have been waiting now for more than five weeks for a little leisure time, except Sunday, that I might finish this letter to you, but I have tired of waiting and have concluded to *take* the time this afternoon. Since I commenced this letter the surveyors have been along and now our claims are all surveyed; the line runs about three rods east of my house so that I lose all my old plowed ground as I expected, but Mr. Wilson has paid me the cost of breaking as much more and I have the use of the old land this year.

I have my field all *planted* and *fenced* and the corn has come up finely and looks well. I mean to take good care of it and if we have a good season I expect to get six or seven hundred bushels of corn. It is very dry now, however, and if we do not get rain soon I am afraid we shall not have much corn or grass or any thing else, but I hope for the best—we may have a good shower before night. Some of our neighbors have peas fit to eat, but I shall not have any in a good while yet. I put off plowing and planting even a garden, as long as I could, hoping that the surveyors would come along and show me where my claim was and also waiting for Mr Wilson to come out in order to make some arrangement with him about planting my old land if it should come on his claim. You suggest that one inch by four in is too thin for fencing. It is as thick as any of my neighbors use. We set our posts pretty close together, about seven ft apart on the average. When we have to pay $35. and $40 per m. for the cheapest kind of lumber, we have the disposition to make a little go as far as we can. I have not planted any more than I did last year, as I was afraid to have any more land broken until I knew where my claim was. I did not sell more than $30 or $40 dollars worth of last years produce, we had a very cold winter and my stock consumed a great deal, much more than they would have done if I had had a good barn to keep them in. We have had as changable weather here as you write you have had in the east; the spring was very late, three or four weeks later than usual but during this month it has been *very* warm the thermometer ranging at mid day, in the shade, from 95° to 102°, which would be considered rather hot in the east but as we nearly always have a good breeze, even in the hottest weather we manage to keep quite comfortable. And now I will try to give you an idea of what I have here in Kansas, what I am doing and what [I am] intending to do.

I have a good claim of 160 acres within one and one half miles of Manhattan nine tenths of which is suitable to plow and the rest *can* be plowed but is rather uneven. a snug little house 16 ft x 24 ft with an ell 12 x 14 and a good well of water in the ell—cost about $900. a shed 12 x 17 cost $80. about 500 cedar posts worth $100. nearly 1500 ft of fencing lumber at my house (besides nine or ten logs not yet sawed) worth $50. between 1150 and 1200 rails. and stakes and forkes to go with them, worth $150. I have three lots in Manhattan worth at least $50 each. an order for 500 ft of lumber at the mill which I shall get in a few days worth $20. cash on hand $165. due me for sundries $70. and I do not really owe $5. in the world except what I owe the Wa. & La. banks in R. I. I consider my claims with the buildings and fencing materials on it very low at $2500, and would not be willing to take that for it. I have two horses $250 two pr. oxen $225. two cows & calf $100. two pigs $10. & 70 or 80 chickens worth at least $10. Wagon, harnesses, plow, harrow, cultivator & other farming tools $150. household furniture and provisions $100 total $3750.

I have represented everything at less than I really thought it worth and if I wanted to purchase should expect to pay more than I have valued them at. I started from home the first time with about $700. the second time with $1100. and have recd about $700. in drafts since I have been here in all $2500.

And now father, considering my inexperience at farming the expenses of traveling the cost of living in a new country and that I have *married a wife* do you not think that I am getting along pretty well. I enjoy excellent health, am comfortably and pleasantly situated except that I want you and mother and Lizzie and Henry & Theodore & Herbert nearer to us. I do so much wish that you all could come and live near us. You wish you could get acquainted with wife, I wish so too. I believe that the better you knew her the better you would like her. Cannot you possibly come and see us this next fall, say September? Unless the banks are anxious to have the notes paid immediately I do not wish to have the remaining stock sold. I hope to be able to pay something on them before another year. I see that I have skip[p]ed a page, but you will find no difficulty in finding the place I think.

Sunday evening, June 21. We have had beautiful weather for three or four days, warm and pleasant, with just breeze enough to make it comfortable, and the nights comparatively cool. Though we usually have very warm weather here in the summer, we almost always have a good breeze so that we do not suffer so much from the heat as the people in the east, and we have very few nights so warm as to make it difficult, to sleep. We have been down to Manhattan to church today; we have a pretty good congregation usually on the Sabbath, and our church going people, and our citizens generally will compare *favorably* with those of *any* New England town, I do not care where you find it. We had a Sunday School after meeting and I *acted* as Superintendent The Sunday School was organized sometime ago and Mr. Wheldon, who was expected to move into town immediately, was chosen Superintendent and I assistant, but he did not come as anticipated and met with the school only once, and living so far away as I do, on account of bad weather etc I am frequently unable to attend, so that if there were no other reason, I thought best on that account to resign, and a man by the name of Butterfield, much more capable of holding such an office than myself, I think, is going to take charge of the school next Sunday. I hope we shall be able to keep up a good and interesting school, with the blessing of God.

The School house in Manhattan makes quite a show; it is built of limestone, size 32 ft by 48 ft I believe and two stories high. They are now building two large stone hotels and a Methodist Church also of stone the Congregational church has not yet been commenced but we hope will be soon. I did not write you so much as I was intending to about what I was doing and hoping to do, but will try to do so when I write again. It is now quite late and I must close. Ella sends her love. She often expresses the wish that you would come and see us and thinks she should like you.

Why does not Theodore write? We have not had a letter from home in three or four weeks. Hope you will write soon again.

To Thos. P. Wells Esq
    Wakefield, R. I.
                                    Yours truly
                                                  T. C. Wells.

Love to Mother, Theodore, Herbert, etc.

Morton Sweet is in this vicinity, he called here a few days ago. He said you told him to tell me something but he had forgotten what.

I wish James A Ward would pay you what he owes me. I would like to have it applied to my notes in Wa. & La. banks.

                                    Manhattan, May 30/57.
My dear Mother   Kansas Territory

We received your letter of May 3d more than a week ago, and had I not been very busy should have answered it immediately.

I have written to *Samuel* and Henry quite recently, and I sent three papers to father two or three weeks ago but owing to the carelessness of the P. O. master they were sent back to me a day or two ago after the stamp had been defaced and it had been postmarked Manhattan. I will start them again and send more soon. I receive the Prov. Jour. & N. E. Farmer. from home quite often and am very much obliged for them. I find very many good things in the

N. E. Farmer. The season is very late here this year—three or four weeks later than last year I should think; some of our farmers have been and are planting their corn over again as that which was planted early rotted in the ground. Some are planting now for the first time. I have planted all of mine but about one acre and that I intend to plant tomorrow.

Mr. Booth, Mr. Todd's father in law, has just arrived from R. I. He says that the grass is just starting there, We have had good feed for four weeks. Mr. B. was only one week coming from R. I. here, I do not see why it need take three or four weeks for letters to pass between us. Does the weather still continue cold in the east?

I am glad to hear that uncle Hagadorn succeeds so well with his school. How does the Female Seminary prosper? How does Theodore get along in the store? Have you finished planting in the garden yet? Those Crowder peas do not need sticks or brush. If you plant the seeds of the sensitive plant in the house out of the wind it will do better and be more sensitive, they should not be handled while very young.

I do not think we shall be able to get the Cong Meeting house built this season; money commands a high rate of interest, from ten to *fifty* per. cent., and sufficient funds cannot be raised immediately. The surveyors have come along at last, and my claim has been surveyed The lines come better than I feared, east line about four rods east of house, but I loose my plowed ground. Mr. Wilson has paid me enough to get as much more broken up, and I am going to have the use of the old ground this year.

It is getting quite late and I must close.

Wife sends her love to you all Tell Herbert to write us a letter. The election for delegates to Constitutional convention comes off on the 15th of June. we do not anticipate any trouble. Do write often.

Mrs. T. P. Wells   Yours aff'cty.
    Wakefield, R. I.   T. C. Wells

                         Manhattan, K. T.
                          July, 16th 1857.

Dear father & mother,

We were very glad to get a letter, written in part by both of you, last week. Mother thought it was time I had a letter from home even if it was a *"short one,"* So think I; it was four weeks since we heard from you before, but instead of a "short one" we were very glad to get a good long letter. Sorry to hear that Aunt Mariann's health is so poor. I believe she is owing me a letter, I wish she would write, if she does not soon, perhaps I shall take the liberty to write again.

I had forgotten that I made any promise to write grandmother Clarke, but have been intending to write her when I had a little leisure. I will try and write her soon. It has taken about all my spare time to answer my old correspondent's letters.

I am happy to hear that they have settled a minister in Lyme, and one too that gives satisfaction I hope their like for him will continue to increase on acquaintance and that God may bless his labors there to the good of the church and society.

We have not yet commenced building the Congregational Church but intend doing so soon. We have now about three thousand dollars towards building a church, which would pay for a building sufficiently large to accommodate the present congregation, but in this fast growing country we have to calculate a little for the future A church large enough for us today would be too small a year hence.

Do you feel able to help us a little? and do you know of any one in your vicinity that would give us a little?

Our little church now numbers twenty five; ten united with us last Sunday, nine by letter or recommendation from other churches, and one by profession; and there are several more that think of joining us soon.

So it seems that you hear from us once in a while, besides through our letters. Mr. Goodnow says we "are very pleasantly situated" and so we are. I wish you could come and see us you would say so too. And then Judge Woodworth has been in Wakefield; the last man that I should have thought of being there, a queer man.

We have heard nothing of Dr Clarke since he left the east, he owes me a letter and I should be glad to hear from him. I wonder how he liked the *west*. I am sorry that Theodore is out of business again; he will never be easy without some *active business* or without *company*. He never was made to be much alone, I think; and if he *cannot* have *good* companions he *will* have *bad ones*. By *companions* I mean those of near the same age. Perhaps it would be well for him to go to school awhile longer, he might get over his fever for going to sea and take a liking to something else less objectionable. I would have liked to have him stay out here with me, if he would have done as well for me as any one else would. I always liked Theodore and am willing to do much for him, but did not feel that I could afford to keep him with me unless he would take more interest in my affairs. I did not feel as if I could afford it, and yet perhaps he did as well as any young fellow of his age would do under the circumstances. I think he got a little homesick once in a while and that would make him a little careless as to what he did and how he worked.

I would rather try him again than have him go to sea—he might do better the second time; and I think *Ella's* influence over him would be *very good* as they seem to think a good deal of each other. If he *must go to sea* it seems to me that it would be much better for him to go a long voyage under a *good captain* than to go a coasting. I mean if he must *follow* the sea as a means of livelihood, but I think that one short voyage from Wakefield to N. Y. would sicken him of sea life so that he would be glad to remain on land after that. If he should go on a long voyage he might get to liking it before he reached home again. July 18th The thermometer stands 109° in the *shade* rather too warm to work with comfort out of doors and so I will try and finish my letter to you.

We had a fine rain a week ago today after a drouth of five weeks wanting two days. We needed rain very much, the ground was *very* dry and the grass was all drying up. Nearly all the *sod* corn was killed by the drouth. Although considerable water fell the ground was so *very* dry that it soaked it all up and it is getting quite dry again. My corn grows finely and looks as well as anybody's. I have cultivated it twice in each row, both lengthwise and cross wise of the field, making *four* times that I have gone through it with the cultivator. I have also gone through the most of it and pulled off the *suckers,* the soil being stronger we are troubled much more with suckers than you are in the east. The *tobacco* worm has destroyed most of the *potatoes* in this vicinity and as far as I can learn throughout Kansas. Those that were fortunate enough to have their potatoes planted near the house where the *chickens* could get at them will probably have a good crop. I have killed all the worms on mine several times and may get a fair crop from my early ones, but my late ones are, I fear, entirely destroyed.

The spring being so late and the drouth following, our gardens have fared rather hard; many things in the beds that were planted late did not come up and many things that did come up, as cabbages, have been killed by the dry weather and grasshoppers, we have had radishes, and spinage, and a small mess of peas. We have cucumbers and squashes nearly large enough to eat, and our early corn has tasseled. My well holds out finely during the dry time, *seven* feet of water in it all the time. I don't know what we should do without it. Several of the neighbors have to come here after their water. I have had a hired man with me for nearly two months past, find plenty of work all the time. When there is not much to be done on the farm, a man and team (two yoke of oxen and wagon) can get $4. per day drawing stone, sand, or water down to Manhattan. Houses are springing up there like mushrooms, and it will soon be quite a town.

I am glad, if you intend to remain in Wakefield, that you have bought some land; I wish you could put up a snug little house on it and have a nice home of your own, that is if you think it impossible that you can ever come and live out here with us. If you lived one or two hundred miles further *in land* I should entertain strong hopes of sometime selling out here and going east, to live near you again. You say that the farmers there have had to plant over their corn as *we did here.* Many of our farmers had to plant over on account of poor seed, but *I did not,* except a little where the crows pulled it up.

Your garden would not suffer for *warm* weather if you had a few such days as we are having now; the thermometer has gone up a degree since I have been writing it now stands 110°.

I am glad Uncle Hagadorn succeeds so well with his school.

I have no doubt but that my old ground is worth much more than I got for it from Wilson, but that was the best I could do with him. You must consider that Mr. Wilson was not *legally obliged* to pay me anything.

Mr. Wilson has sold his claim for *twelve hundred dollars* and gone east. He has considerable property here yet in the shape of town shares and town lots etc. has left two notes with me, not yet due, to collect. The thermometer has gone up two degrees more; we shall catch afire soon! But we do not suffer nearly so much from extreme heat here as in the damper atmosphere of the east.

July 19; Sunday. The thermometer rose above 114° during yesterday afternoon, but it has not been so warm today by 9° or 10°. We have not been to meeting today James, the man that helps me, went down to his claim, about six miles S. E. of here, yesterday and did not get back until this afternoon. He had one of my horses and the saddle and it was too warm to walk to meeting, so we staid at home and spent most of the time in reading. Do write often and tell Theodore and Bertie to write.

Love to all. Has Lizzie returned to Rochester yet?

Yours truly in haste
T. C. Wells

July 20th No rain yet: very dry.
If you can get anything toward helping us build a church please send to me and I will hand to the treasurer of the society with name of donor.

[Ella S. Wells to Theodore]

Manhattan, K. T. Aug 23rd 1857

Mr. T. B. Wells.

My Dear Brother Theodore,

I have three letters that I ought to answer, but somehow I feel a strong inclination to write to you. I have been thinking for some time it was very strange that you did not write and let us know how you were getting along. I have thought of you more than usual of late especially last week when we went graping. We found them much nicer & thicker than they were last year. I would much rather have had a good time with you if I had not got quite as many grapes. We did not start until after dinner and three of us got as many as two bushels. How I do wish I could see you.

I often think that you would have enjoyed yourself much better had you been here this year insted of last. Do you not think so? I am sometimes silly enough to think that we are as happy and contented as people ever are in this world.

There has been some changes since you left Mr Browning has a house on his claim & has lived there since early last spring. His family now consists of himself wife, & little *daughter*. The neighbors say it is the handsomest *little* girl they ever saw. Mr Todd has a new shop apart from the house his sister that came out last spring is failing very fast I do not think she will live two months. Mrs. Todd now says that she is willing to live here or any where else that Mr. T. can be well; it would kill her to see him suffer as Mary does. Mr. Whelden lives about as usual; he has been below & traded some this summer but he has had quite a number of fits and if they continue it is not safe for him to do so. he has provided for his family better than last year. Hatty Lyman is just as sweet as ever Henry Booth waits upon her some. I have not time to write about all the folks. It is almost bed time, when I get to writing to a *dear friend* it is hard for me to stop. I shall never see my father again; he has left this world of sin for a better clime I trust. I will send you a letter from sister Nancie giving the particulars. Excuse me for so doing, it was so interesting to me it seemed as if it would be to you. Please save it for me until I come home. Now Theodore will you not write and tell us all about yourself. What are you doing? How you enjoy yourself? Are you a good boy and try to please you[r] Heavenly Father and your earthly parents? I hope you are and that you are happy. Naught else will make you so. Much love to father & mother and a kiss for Herbert. I will leave the next page for T. Do write soon I want to hear from you much.

Your Affectionate sis   Ella.

Dear Brother,

Ella has written and wishes me to write you a little on this page. We have wondered why we have not heard from you this long time. Have you been sick We have not heard from Wakefield in four weeks. Do you think of coming out here again at any time?

I hope we shall be able to make a visit east in two or three years, but hope we shall receive a visit from father first. Are father and mother and little Bertie well? Tell Bertie to write us a letter. My Corn looks finely. For two weeks past we have been drawing stone and digging out and walling up our cellar. It will take two or three days more to finish it.

Excuse the appearance of this letter. I could write better with a stick, if it was not very sharp, than with such a pen as this.

Do write us soon

Yours truly

T. C. Wells

Manhattan, Kansas T.
Oct 4th, 1857.

My Dear Mother,

Your letter should have been answered before; we received one from Theodore at the same time and answered that, and as I was pressed for time, concluded to wait a week or two before I answered yours.

Our hired man has left us, his time being out, and now I have to work alone again.

We have been haying for the past two or three weeks, and I have got up two large stacks of excellent hay. My corn is ready to gather, or rather to cut up, it is hardly dry enough to put away in a crib. I expect to have 400 or 500 bushels notwithstanding the injury it received from drought and grasshoppers. My corn suffered less from drought than most other fields around, because I *plowed deeper,* and the grasshoppers did not injure it so much as they did many other fields.

Corn is worth $1. per. bush. here now and will be worth $2. or more in the spring. We shall have plenty of squashes & pumpkins, but very few beets and no potatoes. There are a cartload or more of nice water-melons in the field; you may have as many as you wish if you will come after them.

Our pigs grow finely, and we shall have plenty of fresh pork by & by. We have about 100. hens & chickens from seven or eight last spring, and might spare you a few very well. My cow "Beauty" met with a misfortune the other day, so that she does not look quite so *beautiful* She had been off with some other cattle and was rather fractious, so we tied her up to a post, but she tried hard to get away, twisted herself around the post and broke off one of her horns. We tied a tarred cloth around the wound immediately and it is doing well. Meeting was held in the hall over the new stone school house today; the Lords Supper was administered, and Mr. Parsons, of Ogden, (formerly of Cape Cod,) preached to us from the text They crucified him. Quite a large congregation were out. I think Uncle Hagadorn must be acquainted with this Mr Parsons. You ask if we ever "think" of coming home. Indeed we do, few days pass but what we speak of making a visit east, and if our lives and health are spared we anticipate much pleasure from such a visit before many years.

You speak of Amos being in New York. Has he been there on business or on a visit, or has he left Minnesota? Is grandmother Wells in Kingston now? How does Theodore get along? I think that he is naturally very affect[ion]ate and will do most anything for you if he *really feels* that you *love* him.

I hope I shall have more time, now that long evenings have come, so that I can answer your letters more punctually. Have not had a letter from father in a long time. Does he talk any of coming to see us now? I do wish he would come and make us a visit. Ella sends her love to you and father, and says that you "are all that she can call father and mother now." She also sends love to Theodore. Tell him we want him to write us.

Tomorrow is election day when the great question will be decided whether the people of Kansas shall rule Kansas or not. May God speed the right. Yours truly
Mrs. Thos P. Wells, T. C. Wells
   Wakefield, R. I.

                                           Manhattan K. T.
My dear Mother,   October 25th 1856 [1857]

It is Sabbath evening and I was intending to go down to Manhattan to a prayer meeting this evening, but wife was taken with so bad a tooth ache that she was obliged to go to bed, and I thought it not best to go and leave her.

You have been doing great things in the picnic line in Wakefield. Why did Uncle Christopher leave Norton? Will the boy's school in the Seminary injure uncle H's school?

The Rev. Mr. Kelloch[7] (the one about whom there has been so

---

7. Kalloch, Rev. I. S.—See *Kansas Historical Collections*, v. VIII, p. 79.

much talk in Boston and the papers) a Baptist minister from Boston, preached in Manhattan today, and the best sermon in my judgment that I have heard in a year. He is a fine looking man, and an intimate friend of Dr. Robinson, from Maine, who resides here, and who seems to think as much of Mr. K. as of an own brother. Mr. K. talks some of coming out here to settle in the spring and bring a number of families with him. He is a great advocate of temperance and a very interesting temperance lecturer, and we need such a man here very much.

The Oct. election has resulted in a perfect triumph to the free state party, notwithstanding the disadvantages under which they laboured. They have elected their delegate to Congress and have a working majority in both branches of the legislature. So now I hope the question is settled that we shall have a free state, and there will be no more trouble.

I have traded off one of my horses for a buggy wagon and do not intend to keep but one horse now. I find that one will answer my purpose very well. Oxen are much better to do heavy work with and there is not near so much risk in keeping them as horses. Times are hard here, but not quite so bad as in the east. Money is very scarce. I had $90. dollars to get for a man last week and I never found so hard work to get a little money before. Could not collect a cent where it was due me and found it *very* difficult to borrow or hire for the reason that every bodie's pocket was empty. By perseverance, however, I made out to get it at last. Does the Wakefield Bank still continue to redeem her bills? Some emigrants have come in this fall. The country is continually filling up and cabins and houses are going up all the time. Manhattan *"city"* has got to be considerable of a place.

The Chinese Sugar cane does well here; several barrels of Sirup have been made in this vicinity and they are still making. Next year—I think we shall raise all the sweetening that we need in this part of the country. I can raise sugar cane enough on an eighth acre of land to supply me with Sweetening for a year and it is no more work to raise it than corn. It is said that the seed are as good to make cakes of as buckwheat. You had better come out and live with us on some good claim near by. Do write often.

Mrs. T. P. Wells   Yours truly in haste
    Wakefield, R. I.   T. C. Wells

Manhattan, K. T. Nov. 22/57.

My dear father,

We have been watching the prairie fires for an hour past. The wind is strong from the west, and the fires are quite near on the S. and within four or five miles on S. W. and W. They look fearfully grand in the night, and we have felt somewhat afraid that they might come upon us in the night and do some damage, but it has commenced raining within a few minutes and deadened the fires very much, yet they continue to burn a little.

We have not had a letter from home in a long time, five or six weeks at least; mothers last letter was written sometime in September and was answered within a week or two. Are some of you sick or what has happened that we hear nothing from any of you?

We have had a very stormy fall, some snow and a good deal of rain and most of our farmers are late about harvesting there corn. Some few have theirs all gathered but many have either a part or the whole of their crop still standing in the field. I hope to get mine all secured in a few days.

I do not think there has been much, if any, more corn raised here this year than there was last year, as the drought killed nearly all the sod corn and the grasshoppers very much injured that on the old ground. There are many more people and cattle here, to create a deman[d] for corn, than were here last year, and I doubt not it will be worth from $2.50 to $3. per. bush. before another autumn.

I do not think that there will be much suffering here this winter, as there doubtless will be in the east. Labor is in good demand; common laborers getting from $1.75 to $2. per day while masons, carpenters &c get $2.50 and $3. a day.

I went up to Ogden, a few days ago, and paid for my claim and received the usual certificate or receipt which answers for a deed until I get my patent from Washington. So now I have a farm of my own, secured by government title; and if you will come and live on it I will give you forty acres of it for a home, and you can raise your own corn and wheat, sugar and molasses, and beef and have as much milk and butter and as many chickens and eggs as you choose, and all sorts of garden vegetables, and enough over to furnish your family with suitable clothing. There will be churches, schools and stores, within two and one half miles, and probably there will soon be a college on the claim directly south.

There is little danger of fever and ague on the high prairie, and Kansas is to be a free state. It would be so nice if we could live near each other.

How does Theodore come on? Is he a pretty good boy now? I wish he would write to us oftener.

It is getting late and I must bid you goodnight. Do write soon. Love to mother, Theodore and Herbert.   Yours truly
To Thos. P. Wells Esq.   Thomas C. Wells
    Wakefield, R. I.

Manhattan, K. T. Dec. 20/57.

My dear mother,

I have neglected answering your letter longer than usual on acct of press of business. I have had two or three men helping me get in my corn; there has been so much wet weather this fall and winter that corn has not been dry enough to crib until quite lately. We finished a week ago yesterday. I had between 450 & 500 bushels, which considering the dry weather and the grasshoppers was a good crop—much better than most of my neighbors succeeded in saving. I attribute my success, principally, under the blessing of God, to deep plowing and the frequent and thorough working of the ground with the cultivator, especially during the dry season. How do you like Rev. Albert Palmer, as a preacher and as a neighbor? As well as Mr. Reed? What do you mean by the sentence "When we are thrown out of Wakefield Bank we may *possibly* build a house there"? &c Is there any chance of fathers leaving the Bank? If he ever does I hope he will not settle in Wakefield but will come out west and live near us. He can then have a farm of his own and be as independent as you please. Ella's friends write that they have been afflicted with very bad colds similar to what you say that you and many others have had around Wakefield.

I have not heard from Dr. Clarke in a long time. I presume that he has been busily engaged with business of his own, for Lizzie says, in a letter that I received last week, that he has married again—a sister of Rev. Mr. Clarke's wife of Whitinsville. We hear enough about "failures" "broken banks" &c but they do not trouble us much, except that they make money scarce, for we find it quite difficult to get the cash for dfts on the east.

Uncle Sam is buying considerable corn, however, and will soon make money more plenty here. Lizzie writes that you think the reason Theodore went home was because I "could not manage him," but that is a mistake. I did get *tried* with him sometimes and I presume he did with me; but he went home principally because he was home-sick. He was young, had never been from home but little, had never been used to working much at home, here he had to work a good deal *alone,* and then we were boarding, and did not have things very comfortable, compared with what he had been used to in the east, or we now have it here; altogether it was not strange that he wanted to go home; and I did not discourage him because I did not feel that I needed his help much in the winter and, he and I both felt that father needed his assistance. Theodore felt more free to do as he was a mind to with me than he would with a stranger, and did not seem to interest himself so much in my behalf sometimes as I would have liked, but perhaps he did as well as I could expect one so young as he to do under the circumstances. If father does not need his assistance I would like to have him help me next year, and would pay him reasonable wages. I shall have to get *some one* to help me in the spring, for I shall have forty acres to fence and at least twenty five to plow and plant, and if T. will *try to do right* would rather have him than another.

We have had a very mild winter thus far. Warmer this month than in Nov. the thermometer ranging generally, on the north side of the house, from 30° to 50°.

It is expected that quite a number will unite with the Congregational Church at the next Communion season.

It is very probably that Kansas will be admitted as a state by the present Congress under some sort of a constitution.

At least nine tenths of the people are in favor of a free state; and if Congress attempts to force a pro slavery Constitution upon us there will be civil war. We do not expect any such thing, however, thus far God has been with us, and brought to nought the counsels of those that would tyranize over us and I trust he will not forsake us now. Love to father Theodore and Herbert, would like to have them all write us. Ella sends love.

To Mrs. Thos. P. Wells,   Yours truly in haste,
  Wakefield, R. I.   Thomas C. Wells

Private. Dear father,

I shall want some one to help me in the spring, and I have sometimes thought that, *if* Theodore *cannot* be contented there and *will not* be useful to you, I would be willing to try him here again. Living with us in our own home he might be better contented than before, and I cannot but think that Ella's influence over him would be good.

I simply make this suggestion and want you to [do] just as you think best about it.   Yours truly
                                                  T. C. W.

(*To be concluded in the November Quarterly*)

Ferries in Kansas
Part X—Grasshopper River
George A. Root

GRASSHOPPER (now called Delaware) river is the largest affluent of the Kaw between the Blue river and the Kansas-Missouri border, and has its source in the eastern part of Rock Creek township, Nemaha county, about one and one half miles west of Sabetha. At its head the stream is designated as Grasshopper creek, attaining the dignity of river after it crosses the Brown county line. Its course is to the southeast from Nemaha county, across the southwest corner of Brown, the northeast corner of Jackson, across the southwest portion of Atchison and then south across Jefferson county from north to south, entering the Kaw river on Kaw Half Breed land, Tract No. 20, about one mile due south of Perry. The stream originally was about 91 miles long, of which approximately six and one half miles are in Nemaha, eighteen in Brown, nineteen in Atchison, six and one half in Jackson and forty-one in Jefferson counties. This river has few tributaries of any importance, the principal ones being the Little Grasshopper, in Atchison county, and Cedar, Slough and Rock creeks in Jefferson county. The Delaware drains a section of the state rarely affected by drought. The banks of the stream in some places are low, and the rich bottom lands along its course are easily flooded. In one locality land was flooded every year from 1902 to 1912 and again in 1914. In the latter year, however, the channel in places was straightened, and approximately ten miles of the river's length eliminated.[1]

It is common belief that the stream took its name from some visitation of grasshoppers many years ago. The first printed reference to the stream the writer has been able to locate is a mention by Prof. Thomas Say, of the Long expedition, who camped on its headwaters the night of August 27, 1819. His comment of the stream was that "About Grasshopper creek the soil is fertile, the grass dense and luxuriant."[2] No doubt the name attached long before his visit.

The stream has been known by a number of names during the past 100 years. John C. McCoy, in a reminiscent article published many years ago, says:

> On the morning of October 11 [1856], we reached a stream thirty-four and one-half miles from the military reservation, which the Indians called Nesh-

---

1. Topeka *Daily Capital*, November 30, 1914.
2. *Kansas Historical Collections*, v. 1-2, p. 297.

cosh-cosh-che-ba[3] or Swallow river, seventy-six links wide about which there was a large timber. Another mode of rendering the sounds of this Indian name of this river is Nach-uch-u-te-be, and this is the orthography given on the map which we made of the Delaware reservation. The stream was also called Sautrelle river and also Martin's river, in 1830. In the field notes of our survey it is given as Nesh-cosh-cosh-che-be.[4]

Delaware Indians, according to William E. Connelley, in a letter to George J. Remsburg, called the river the "Chuck-kan-no," meaning "they stopped here." Remsburg wrote an excellent account of the river, which was printed in the Atchison *Daily Globe,* November 29, 1907. He mentions that William P. Badger, agent for the Kickapoos, stated that the stream was called for a Frenchman named Sautrelle, whose name in English signified Grasshopper. The Delawares called the lower part of the river "Hing-gwi-men-o-ken," signifying "Big Muddy." The names "Martin" and "Swallow" river, according to Remsburg, probably originated from the cliff swallows or martins that frequent the banks of the stream. Kaw Indians may have given the stream its name. Bourgmont, the French explorer, camped on the stream a few miles below the site of present Muscotah on the night of July 27, 1724, while en route from the Kanza nation (present Doniphan) to the Padouca nation, in north central Kansas. From an examination of various old maps, atlases and narratives, it would seem that the name Grasshopper river, antedates that of Sautrelle, but from 1830 to well in the 1850's, one name was used about as frequently as the other.

Falls on the river were unknown to the whites until 1852. That year a military train under command of Maj. E. A. Ogden was conveying workmen, mechanics and supplies to Fort Riley, when a Kickapoo Indian informed the major that there was a much better road than the one by the way of Osawkee they were then using. The major tried the route once, but not a second time. Henry Sen accompanied the expedition as a mechanic, and on this trip made the accidental discovery of the falls. The expedition crossed the river at the location where the old road crossed in 1857 and 1858.[5] In 1859 a town was laid out at this point, and named Grasshopper Falls for the river.[6] Following a number of grasshopper visitations which started as early as 1820 and recurred in 1855, 1860, and 1861,[7] the residents of Jefferson county became "fed up" with the name *grasshopper,* and asked the legislature to change the name of the town-

---
3. McCoy's map, survey of 1830, gives spelling as Neesh-cosh-cosh-che-bah.
4. *Kansas Historical Collections,* v. 4, p. 305.
5. Valley Falls *New Era,* May 18, 1878.
6. *Laws,* Kansas, 1859, p. 141.
7. Wilder's *Annals.*

ship, river and city, substituting Sautrelle in place of the despised name. This was done in 1863.[8] This discarding of an ancient name furnished Sol Miller, editor and publisher of *The Kansas Chief*, at White Cloud, with an excuse to have some fun, and he promptly substituted "Sowtail" for Sautrelle, when speaking of the town, river or township. Ridicule is a hard thing to combat, and the populace did not relish being spoken of as residents of a community with such a ridiculous nickname, so the legislature in 1864[9] restored the old name, which was used for the next eleven years. By the irony of fate the worst visitation of grasshoppers came during the summer of 1874, and mention of hoppers was not a popular subject for discussion with the residents of this county, so with the meeting of the legislature of 1875 a bill was introduced in that body, and passed, changing the name of the town to Valley Falls and the township and river to Delaware.[10]

The first ferry location on ascending the river is a matter of speculation. However, a ferry was contemplated and authorized by the legislature of 1861, to be located at or near the junction with the Kansas river. This act gave John C. Bailey the right to maintain a ferry at that point for ten years and have exclusive privilege for a distance of three miles from the mouth of the river.[11] This must have been close to Perryville of later date.

In 1867 Klews & McHenry were granted a license for a ferry over the Grasshopper at or near where the Union Pacific Railway, Eastern division, crosses that stream. Their license was to date from May 1, 1867, and was to continue in force for one year on payment of $10. Ferriage rates established by the commissioners were:

> Two horses and wagon, over, 25 cents; two horses and wagon, over and back on same day, 40 cents. Four horses and wagon, over, 40 cents; four horses and wagon, over and back on same day 40 [50?] cents. One yoke of oxen, over, 25 cents; one yoke of oxen, over and back on same day, 40 cents. For each additional yoke of cattle, 10 cents. A man and horse, both ways, 15 cents. Footman, .05 cents. Sheep and swine per head, .02 cents. Loose horses per head, .05 cents. Loose cattle, .03 cents.[12]

This location was at or close to present Perry, on the river road running west from Jefferson county.

From Wyandotte and the Missouri river points the bulk of travel and freighting of course went over the military road, but a consider-

8. *Laws*, Kansas, 1863, p. 71.
9. *Ibid*, 1864, p. 169.
10. *Ibid*, 1875, p. 178.
11. *Private Laws*, Kansas, 1861, pp. 34, 35.
12. Jefferson county, "Commissioners' Journal," 1863-1869, pp. 406, 407.

able portion of it took the river road. Just how long this ferry was operated is uncertain, no further mention having been located.

The next ferry licensed for this location was on November 11, 1876, when Wm. M. McKinney was granted a license to keep a ferry across the Grasshopper at Perry; also a license for the Lecompton Bridge Company for a bridge across the Kaw river upon the payment of the clerk's fees.[13] McKinney was an old hand at the business, having been engaged in ferrying at Lecompton from 1868 to 1870.[14]

In 1857 a bill was introduced in the council to authorize the building of a bridge at or near the mouth of the Delaware river, but this failed of passage.[15]

Early in 1872 travel must have been sufficient to warrant the installation of a pontoon bridge at this point, since Thomas G. Smith in March, 1872, applied to the board of county commissioners to grant him a license for a private pontoon bridge on payment of $10.[16] Apparently this was the last license issued at this point.

The next ferry location upstream was at Osawkee. In March, 1856, Jefferson Riddle[17] was granted the first license issued by the board of county commissioners to maintain a ferry at that point, paying $10 for the privilege for one year.[18]

This ferry was located at the crossing of the military road, and probably did not operate for more than a year, as W. F. and G. M. Dyer took steps to establish a bridge at this point, Doctor Tebbs introducing a bill in the legislature asking that privilege for them, which became a law.[19]

Osawkee is the oldest town in Jefferson county, and in its early days was settled by Southerners. During the troublous days in 1856 the town was raided by a Free-state party. It was the first county seat, and for a few years was accounted one of the most important towns in the county. The Delaware land sales were held at this point.

13. *Ibid.*, Book C, p. 193.
14. *Kansas Historical Quarterly*, v. 2, p. 345.
15. *Council Journal*, 1857, pp. 196, 220, 230, 243.
16. Jefferson county, "Commissioners' Journal," Book D, p. 41.
17. Mr. Riddle was a wealthy Southerner who settled at Osawkee and engaged in business—operating a ferry on the side. He attended the land sales at that point when the Delaware lands were sold, and bought several farms. On the breaking out of the Civil War he took his family and left for the South, joining the Confederate army. Returning to his old neighborhood in Kansas after the war was over, he had a feeling that he might be taken into custody on account of his Southern sympathies. All his farms with the exception of one were in the possession of others. A daughter of Mr. Riddle, Mrs. Maude DeLong, now resides at Silver Lake, Shawnee county. She was reared by grandparents on her mother's side, who were strong unionists.
18. State Board of Agriculture, *Report, 1877-1878*, p. 240.
19. *House Journal*, 1857, pp. 75, 196, 212; *Council Journal*, 1857, pp. 75, 169, 174, 184, 201; *Laws*, 1857, p. 145.

During the legislature of 1857-1858 Mr. Owens introduced House bill No. 312,[20] for the establishment of a ferry over the Grasshopper. This bill passed both houses, but was vetoed by the governor, who sent the following message to the House, giving his reasons for so doing:

To the House of Representatives:

Gentlemen—I herewith return "An act to establish a ferry at the mouth of the Grasshopper river," without approval, for the reason that the locality does not come within the jurisdiction of the Territorial Government of Kansas. The mouth of the Grasshopper is within the limits of the Delaware Reserve, though the Half-Breeds of the Kansas tribe, by virtue of a prior treaty, have a life estate in the lands at that point, the reversion being to the Delawares. But the Indian title has never been extinguished to those lands, and the Organic Act declares that "all such territory shall be excepted out of the boundaries, and constitute no part of the Territory of Kansas." With a knowledge of these facts, I do not see how I, as Governor of the Territory, can exercise any legislative control over that locality. With these objections the bill is returned to the House in which it originated.

February 11, 1858.   J. W. DENVER, Acting Governor.[21]

At this same session Council bill No. 5 was introduced to incorporate the Grasshopper Bridge Company. A similar measure, House bill 453, was introduced in the House of Representatives, but neither measure passed.[22]

A toll bridge was constructed at Osawkee some time in the 1860's and must have been a paying proposition. No names of anyone connected with the enterprise have been found, and the only reference we have located is that a petition was presented to the board of county commissioners asking for an appropriation of $500 for the purchase of the toll bridge across the Grasshopper at this point.[23]

Grasshopper Falls was the next ferry location, one being in operation at this point in 1859. No mention of a license was found for this enterprise, but a Leavenworth paper refers to a ferry in connection with the relocation of a road from Fort Leavenworth to Fort Riley via Grasshopper Falls.[24] No further notice of this ferry has been located. Late in the fall of 1862 a bridge had been constructed at this point having a span of 123 feet in the clear. C. G. Waite, formerly of Tecumseh, was the architect and builder.[25]

As early as 1855 Grasshopper Falls took steps towards getting roads, the legislature that year establishing one from Leavenworth

---

20. *House Journal,* 1857-1858, pp. 191, 217; *Council Journal,* 1857-1858.
21. *House Journal,* 1858, p. 388.
22. *Ibid.,* 1858-1859, pp. 221, 261, 327.
23. Jefferson county, "Commissioners' Journal," January 11, 1867.
24. *Kansas Weekly Herald,* Leavenworth, March 26, 1859.
25. *Kansas State Journal,* Lawrence, November 27, 1862.

to Indianola, by way of Money creek and Grasshopper Falls. James Frazer, J. B. Ross and Geo. H. Perrin were appointed commissioners to survey and establish the road.[26] At the same session a road was also established from Osawkee to Grasshopper Falls.[27] In 1872 a road was laid out from Grasshopper Falls to Leavenworth, via Winchester.[28]

Probably the uppermost ferry on the Grasshopper was one thought to have been located on S. 28, T. 5, R. 18, five miles north of Effingham, on the military road.[29]

26. *General Statutes,* Kansas, 1855, p. 977.
27. *Ibid.,* p. 949.
28. Jefferson county, "Commissioners' Journal," Book D, p. 244.
29. This ferry was marked on a map of historic spots in Atchison county, prepared by the late Franklin J. Hole, of Effingham. (Map in Archives division of Kansas State Historical Society.) Mrs. Agnes C. (Franklin J.) Hole was not certain about its existence, however, and under date of June 30, 1936, wrote as follows:

"I have talked with James Snyder here in Effingham, who has resided here 68 years. He said the river five miles north of Effingham is the Little Grasshopper, running into the Grasshopper farther west; a very small stream now, even dry at times, but showing evidence that it was larger formerly. He is sure that there was never a ferry at this point, though remembers something of a ford west of Effingham. The military road from Leavenworth to Fort Kearney is about at that point and he remembers much traffic, both military and immigrants, going farther west. There are deep ruts all along this old road that can yet be seen, especially near old Huron. There seems to be some confusion regarding the military road and the Oregon trail; some say they are the same and others say they are separate, but they were at least both near this county.

"I have talked with the Ed. Phillips family, who own a farm five miles north of Effingham and have lived on it for twenty years. Mr. Phillips was born in Leavenworth and is about 70 years old and remembers very well the soldiers and freighters using the old military road, passing through old Huron and Kennekuk. On his place there is evidence of a trail that crosses the place; also large timbers show near the banks of the former stream that look as though they were parts of a large building and possibly a bridge. They remember an old story of a flat boat and that there was a ford at this place; there is sometimes water in this cut, but think it never could have been large enough for a ferry. There seems to be old Indian mounds on the Phillips place and the one directly north of them.

"Mrs. Neva Jackson, telephone operator, heard us talking and volunteered the information that her uncle Abram Bennett was Indian agent at Kennekuk, and that there was an old stage barn there, and she had heard much of the travel, both military and people going west. She said there was a ford on Clear creek, south of Kennekuk, seven or eight miles north and east of Muscotah, on land now farmed by Mark Hardin. She was also quite sure the ferry, if any, must have been on the Big Grasshopper."

Kansas History as Published in the Press

Events in early Kansas history were reviewed in three articles published in the winter, 1936, number of *The Aerend*, of Hays. Titles and authors of the stories were: "A Hero of the Wakarusa War [Capt. Thomas Bickerton]," by F. B. Streeter; "They Gave the Crowd a Thrill," a story of a shooting in the early days of Ulysses, by Bee Jacquart; "In the Bad Old Days," an account of Dr. William Tichenor's encounter with the Sioux Indians in western Kansas in 1876, by Paul King.

Histories of Kansas local lodges of the A. O. U. W. appear from time to time in the *Kansas Workman*, of Erie, the order's official monthly newspaper.

Reminiscences of Troy in the 1870's, by Eliza Johnston Wiggins, of Otego, were recorded in a letter printed in *The Kansas Chief*, of Troy, January 30, 1936.

"A Story About Alma in the Eighties," by D. R. Brummitt, was published in the Alma *Signal* February 6, 1936.

The history of the Montezuma *Press*, founded as the *Chief* in 1914, was briefly reviewed in its issue of February 20, 1936.

Histories of cattle trails through the Indian territory and more particularly of the Chisholm trail, including statements of pioneers regarding its location and a sectional map of its course from the Red river station to the Kansas border, were published in the *Chronicles of Oklahoma*, of Oklahoma City, in March, 1936. The article was prepared by H. S. Tennant of the Oklahoma State Highway Commission.

A fiftieth anniversary celebration of the organization of Mary S. Wells Chapter, No. 41, Order of the Eastern Star of Osborne, was held March 13, 1936. A history of the society was outlined in the *Osborne County Farmer*, March 19.

"Fort Leavenworth Claims Honor of Being the First Kansas Capital," the Leavenworth *Times* reported in an article appearing March 22, 1936. Congress prescribed in 1854 "that the seat of government shall be temporarily located at Fort Leavenworth," according to the *Times*' article, and "Governor Andrew H. Reeder, first territorial governor, established his official residence at Fort Leavenworth in October, 1854." Remaining there "for a little more than six weeks," the *Times* reported, "Governor Reeder and his staff took themselves off to the Shawnee Methodist Indian Mission."

Coats Methodist Church history was reviewed in detail in a special church fiftieth anniversary edition of the Coats *Courant* issued March 26, 1936. Services in commemoration of the founding were held March 25 to 29, inclusive.

David Donoghue, of Fort Worth, Tex., writing in the April, 1936, number of *Mid-America,* of Chicago, limits the location of Quivira to an area immediately to the north of the Canadian river, and makes the "end of Quivira" coincide with the end of the flat plains at or near the North Canadian in Beaver county, Oklahoma. The "Quivira-in-Kansas idea" was discounted by the author.

Early Runnymede was mentioned in Victor Murdock's column in the Wichita (Evening) *Eagle* April 1, 1936.

Names of pioneers registering at the annual meeting of the Barber County Old Settlers' Association held at Medicine Lodge March 27, 1936, were listed in *The Barber County Index,* of Medicine Lodge, April 2.

On April 2, 1936, Wellington observed the sixty-fifth anniversary of its founding. In celebration of the event both the Wellington *Daily News* and *The Sumner County News* issued 14-page editions carrying more than fifty stories of historical interest. *The Monitor-Press,* of Wellington, also featured a short history of the city.

A résumé of a history of the Junction City Methodist Church, edited by the Rev. Lynn H. Rupert, and published in pamphlet form, was printed in the Junction City *Republic* April 2, 1936.

William F. Cody and his old home in Leavenworth county were discussed by A. B. MacDonald in an article entitled, "The Boyhood Home of 'Buffalo Bill' To Be a Memorial to Frontier Heroism," in the Kansas City (Mo.) *Star,* April 5, 1936.

A biographical sketch of Jesse Chisholm and the story of the founding of the trail which bears his name was published in the Wichita *Sunday Eagle* April 5, 1936, under the title "Would Memorialize Chisholm With Monument."

Old buildings at Fort Leavenworth are still preserved, the Leavenworth *Times* reported in an illustrated article April 5, 1936.

Early-day Huntsville was described by Herbert C. Totten in the Hutchinson *Herald* April 5, 1936.

Wichita's first funeral and first Sunday School were recalled by William G. Taylor, of Cleveland, Ohio, in an interview with Victor Murdock in the Wichita (Evening) *Eagle* April 8, 1936. Mr. Taylor discussed the building of the city's first church in the issue of April 10, and earlier history in the April 11 number.

The history of the Hillsboro *Star*, founded May 2, 1924, was printed in its issue of April 9, 1936.

Reminiscences of the late Otto P. Byers, of Chicago, who had a part in the building of eight railroads in Kansas, were published in the Wichita (Evening) *Eagle* April 9, 1936.

"Colonial Ancesters Give Landon Background for Presidency" was the title of a full-page article by Joe Nickell in the Topeka *Daily Capital* April 12, 1936.

A biographical sketch of the Rev. Charles M. Sheldon, author of *In His Steps*, was contributed by Cecil Howes to the Kansas City (Mo.) *Star* in its issue of April 12, 1936. Other articles by Mr. Howes included: "[Edmund G. Ross] Kansas Senator Who Voted to Acquit Andrew Johnson Was Called Betrayer," *Times*, April 17; "Many Saloons in Kansas Smashed Before Carry Nation's Crusade," *Star*, May 18, and "Kansas Is Far From the Treeless Prairie That Many Believe It to Be," *Times*, June 10.

"Early History of Kanwaka," was the title of an article by Mrs. Guy Bigsby which appeared serially in the Lawrence *Democrat* from April 16 to May 21, 1936, inclusive. The article was read at a meeting of the Douglas County Historical Society on January 29.

Margaret Whittemore, of Topeka, has been preparing sketches of early Kansas landmarks which she plans to issue in book form soon. These drawings are being published in the Sunday issues of the Topeka *Daily Capital* starting with the issue of April 19, 1936. Descriptions and histories of the landmarks which accompany the pencil sketches were also written by Miss Whittemore.

A brief history of the History and Literature Club, Horton's oldest woman's society, was related in the Horton *Headlight* April 20, 1936. The club was organized in 1891.

"Early Day Colonization Attempts Found Jewell County Indian Tribe Inhospitable," was the title of an article printed in the Burr Oak *Herald* April 23, 1936.

Histories of the Rule and Hide Out schools in the Fall River vicinity were briefly sketched in the Fall River *Star* April 24, 1936.

The Clay Center First Baptist Church held a celebration April 30, 1936, in observance of the silver anniversary of the dedication of its present building. The church's history was reviewed in the Clay Center *Dispatch, Times* and *Economist* in issues contemporaneous with the event.

Wichita in April, 1886, in the fourth month of its memorable boom year, was described by Victor Murdock in the Wichita (Evening) *Eagle* April 30, 1936.

On April 30, 1936, the Eudora *Weekly News* celebrated its fiftieth anniversary with the issuance of a special twenty-eight page paper in tabloid form. Histories of the *News* and the city's churches, schools, and clubs, biographical sketches of pioneers, and letters and greetings from friends of the newspaper were published. Included in the feature articles were: "Eudora Seventy-nine Years Old," "First Marriage," and "Main Street Fifty Years Ago."

Four letters recalling the early history of Burr Oak were published in the Burr Oak *Herald* on April 30, May 14, 21, and June 4, 1936.

A history of the Woman's Relief Corps of Coffeyville was briefly sketched in the Coffeyville *Leader* May 1, 1936.

The activities of the Anti-Horse Thief Association in Hutchinson in the latter part of the nineteenth century and names of some of the members were recalled by Charles Epley in an interview in the Hutchinson *Record* May 1, 1936.

Hypnotism as it was first introduced in Wichita was discussed by David D. Leahy in the Wichita *Sunday Eagle* May 3, 1936.

The history of the Osborne County Farmers Union, organized on May 11, 1908, was briefly outlined in the *Osborne County Farmer*, of Osborne, May 7, 1936.

A tale of an overdue bill in the late 1860's and Jesse Chisholm's shrewdness was retold by Victor Murdock in the Wichita (Evening) *Eagle* May 7, 1936. Chisholm first lived on the bank of the Little Arkansas river and in 1866 he moved on what is now Chisholm creek, Mr. Murdock reported.

The Sublette *Monitor* issued an eighty-page magazine-size supplement to its regular issue of May 7, 1936, celebrating its fiftieth anniversary. Features of the edition included: "The Story of the Sublette *Monitor* Since Days of the Homesteaders" "Haskell County's Outline of History," and numerous letters and greetings from friends of the newspaper.

A history of the Leon Christian Church was reviewed in the "Christian Endeavor Edition" of the Leon *News* May 8, 1936.

"Kansans Prominent in Consular Service," was the heading for a series of biographical sketches contributed by Frank K. Tiffany to the Topeka *State Journal* in its Saturday issues, May 9 to June 13, 1936, inclusive.

Histories of Wichita's hospitals were briefly reviewed in the Wichita *Sunday Beacon* May 10, 1936.

Prominent Wichita physicians during the first twenty-five years of the city's history were named in an article entitled "Physicians of Early Day Wichita Were Hardy Lot" published in the Wichita *Sunday Eagle* May 10, 1936. The article was reprinted from the *Medical Bulletin,* publication of the Sedgwick County Medical Society. An article by F. S. Vassar, reviewing the Salvation Army's fifty years in Wichita, was another feature of this issue of the *Eagle*. A memorial plaque was embedded in concrete in the 100 block on East Douglas on May 12, marking the place where the Army first met fifty years ago.

"Reminiscences of an Old Republican of 93 Years," by Thomas F. Wilson, and "Recall Early Days at Diamond School District 14," west of Green, were feature articles of *The Times,* Clay Center, May 14, 1936.

The history of St. John's Lutheran Church of Bird City, organized January 8, 1911, was printed in the Bird City *Times* May 14, 1936.

Osborne observed the opening of a new bridge over the Solomon river, the completion of a dam and lake, and the anniversary of the arrival of the Pennsylvania colony with an all-day celebration on May 21, 1936. Historical articles in the *Osborne County Farmer* contemporaneous with the event included: "Enchanted Valley," and "The Village Deacon Recalls a Few Old Settlers," by B. P. Walker, "Migration of the Pennsylvania Colony," "Osborne County Was Organized in 1871," "The County Census of 1870," "Osborne Fire Department Organized in 1888," "An Indian Baby Born Near Present Site of Library," "Original Minutes of the Pennsylvania

Colony," in the May 14, issue, the last-named article being continued for several weeks following; "Covert Community Pioneers," by Sylvia DeWitt Gorham, May 21; "Old Settlers Register," and "Notes of the Celebration," May 28; "Pioneer Tales," by Myrtle Curran Hose, and B. F. Yost's recollections of consular service in Germany, June 4.

A story of the founding of the Hutchinson Typographical Union was related by Ed M. Moore, charter member, in *The Labor Review,* Hutchinson, May 15, 1936.

"The Memory of the Notorious Marais des Cygnes Massacre Is Revived on Anniversary Day," was the title of an article featured in the Fort Scott *Tribune* May 19, 1936. A monument was erected at Trading Post some time ago in memory of the victims of the 1858 massacre.

Early Thomas county history was briefly outlined in the Colby *Free Press-Tribune* May 20, 1936.

"This Month Marks 75th Anniversary of Chisholm Trail to Abilene, Kas.," was the title of an article by Bliss Isely in the Kansas City (Mo.) *Star* May 20, 1936.

Cimarron's Methodist Episcopal Community Church celebrated the fiftieth anniversary of its founding May 21, 1936. The history of the organization was reviewed in the May 21 issue of *The Jacksonian,* of Cimarron.

Names of former teachers and the salaries paid them were featured in a history of Hard Pan School, District No. 3 of Coffey county, contributed by Ben Preston to *The Daily Republican,* of Burlington, in its issue of May 23, 1936.

"Research Has Separated Truth From Myth In History of Marcus Whitman," missionary to Oregon who made the journey from Independence to Oregon in 1836, the Kansas City (Mo.) *Star* reported in a two-column article printed May 23, 1936.

The story of the Beecher Bible and Rifle colony, which founded Wabaunsee, was reviewed by Mrs. Willard Green in the Topeka *Daily Capital* May 24, 1936. The history of Kickapoo parish, which on June 1 celebrated the centenary of the erection of the first Catholic church in Kansas, was contributed by Sue Carmody Jones as another feature of this issue. The story of the church was also recounted in the Kansas City (Mo.) *Times* May 25.

"White Cloud, Kas. Has Retained the Culture of Its Pioneer Founders," was the title of a three-column article by A. B. MacDonald in the Kansas City (Mo.) *Star* May 24, 1936.

"Some Shawnee County History" was the subtitle to E. E. Kelley's "Kansas Grass Roots" column in the Topeka *Daily Capital* May 25, 1936.

More than twelve pages of the Hays *Daily News* of May 26, 1936, was devoted to the activities of the Hays High School during the past year. Featured in the edition were a page history of the school and a list of graduates from 1889 to date.

A monument was erected and unveiled near Colby on May 31, 1936, at the graves of Alfred and Fred Gould who died in an attempt to reach their semi-invalid father who was alone on the homestead during the blizzard of January, 1886. The story of the tragedy was told in the Colby *Free Press-Tribune* May 27. Original notes made by the early surveyors of Thomas county were published in part in another article in this issue.

The Haven *Journal* celebrated Haven's fiftieth birthday with the issuance of a forty-page tabloid edition on May 27, 1936. Histories of Haven and its churches, and several biographical sketches of early settlers were published. Pioneers reminiscing for the issue included: Etta Williams Astle, C. W. Peckham, the Rev. C. V. Priddle, Chris Stecher, F. O. Mott, W. F. Williams, Mrs. Mattie Fisher, and Mrs. Ellen T. Doles. Feature stories included: "Extracts From the Diary of G. S. Bishop," "Haven's First Newspaper and Post-office Building," "Recollections of Haven by Founder of Haven *Journal*," "Organization of the Haven Grade School," "First Haven Free Library," "The Haven Rural High School," and "Farms Taken by Homestead and Still Owned by First Settlers or Families."

An eye-witness account of "Wichita's Last Touch of Shooting Up Town [1880] and What Took Place," by Fernando Robey, pioneer Wichitan, was the subject of Victor Murdock's front-page column in the (Evening) *Eagle* May 28, 1936.

The Kanopolis Methodist Episcopal Church celebrated the fiftieth anniversary of its founding May 31, 1936. Brief histories of the church were sketched in the Ellsworth *Messenger* and *Reporter* in their May 28 issues.

"Richard Cleve," Pony Express rider, by John G. Ellenbecker, and "Wagon Wheels—Reverberations of Wagon Days Caught Along the Old Overland Trails," by George J. Remsburg, were features of the June, 1936, issue of the *Pony Express Courier*, of Placerville, Cal. Articles of interest to Kansans printed in the July issue included: "William F. Cody," by John G. Ellenbecker, and "Bull Wagon Bosses," by George J. Remsburg. In the August issue Mr. Remsburg continued his "Wagon Wheels" column.

A brief history of the Burns consolidated schools including the names of graduates was recorded in the Burns *Citizen* June 4, 1936.

Celebrating fifty years of service to the Gypsum community the Gypsum *Advocate* issued a twenty-eight page anniversary edition June 4, 1936. A detailed early history of Gypsum, and historical sketches of its churches, newspapers, institutions, and clubs were printed. Other features included: "Mail Service in Gypsum"; "Union Veterans Who Lived Here"; "The Gypsum Public Schools," by A. R. Manning; "Gypsum Fire Department"; "From Kentucky to Kansas," by Charles Burnham Manning; "Fragments of Memory," by Ida Tressin; "The Municipal Water System"; "Public Library in Gypsum," by Ulilla Wheatley; "Saline County Fifty Years Ago," by Edith Wellman-Brown; "Forty-Eight Years in Gypsum," by John Schmitter; "City Auditorium"; "Beginnings in Saline County"; "Gypsum Always a Band Town"; "The *Advocate's* First Editor"; "Early Settlers in the Valley," by Ella Tinkler; "When They Met at Island Park," by E. E. Wheatley; "Floods in Gypsum Valley," by G. H. Goodwin; "Disastrous Fires of Past Years"; "Oldest Resident of Our City," by Dorothy Reynolds.

Eighty-year memorial of the Beecher Bible and Rifle colony was held at Wabaunsee May 30, 1936. The history of the colony was reviewed by F. I. Burt in the Alma *Signal* June 4, 1936, and the Wamego *Reporter* June 4 and 11. Another history was published in the *Wabaunsee County Truth*, of Wabaunsee, in its July issue.

A one-column history of *The Kansas Chief*, of Troy, famous weekly newspaper founded in 1857 at White Cloud by Solomon Miller, appeared in the Topeka *State Journal* June 5, 1936.

"It's No Longer the 'Dust Bowl,'" A. B. MacDonald reported in a seven-column article in the Kansas City (Mo.) *Star* June 7, 1936. Mr. MacDonald interviewed many persons in the southwest corner of Kansas who have lived in a part of the so-called dust bowl region through good crop years and bad, and wrote what he saw and heard.

Trinity Lutheran Church near Ludell celebrated its fiftieth anniversary June 7, 1936. A history of the organization was briefly sketched in *The Citizen-Patriot,* of Atwood, June 11.

A history of the First Methodist Church of Burns, organized in 1885, was recorded in detail in the Burns *News,* June 11 and 18, 1936.

Grace Methodist Episcopal Church of Wichita, established in June, 1886, celebrated its fiftieth anniversary during the week commencing June 14, 1936. A history of the organization was printed in the Wichita *Beacon* June 13.

The part Wadsworth Mound, near Greeley, played in Kansas' territorial history was reviewed in an article entitled "Where John Brown Watched for Raiding Enemies" in the Kansas City (Mo.) *Star* June 14, 1936.

A thirty-eight page "Southwest Kansas Resource Edition" was issued by the Garden City *Daily Telegram* June 16, 1936.

The fiftieth anniversary of the founding of the Colby First Methodist Episcopal Church was observed with special services held on June 28, 1936. A history of the church was sketched in the Colby *Free Press-Tribune* June 17.

Ottawa history was reviewed in the Ottawa *Herald's* illustrated "Ottawa Seventieth Anniversary Edition" June 18, 1936. Full-page reproductions of the entire first issue of the *Western Home Journal,* of December 7, 1865, Ottawa's first newspaper, and histories of the city's churches, lodges and clubs were printed. Other feature articles included: "Early Efforts to Bring Rails Into Ottawa"; "Early Cyclone Helped to Make Weather History"; "Memories of Ottawa," from the files of the *Herald;* "Phone Business Grew With Town"; "Atkinson Saved the Infant O. U.," by Claude Webb; "River Has Made Ottawa History by Its Rampages"; "Thrilling Events in Early Days of Franklin County," by Harry Ireland; "Business Firms of Early Times Still Function"; "Ottawa Noted for Chautauqua"; "Doctors Came in Early Days"; "Ottawa's D. A. R. Organized in 1889"; "A Post Office Here in 1864"; "Some Big Fires in City's History"; "Asa S. Lathrop Was Ottawa's First Mayor"; "School District Formed Here on November 12, 1864," by George H. Marshall; "Isaac Kalloch, Pioneer Editor and Minister, a Sharp Dealer," by John P. Harris; "Old Rohrbaugh Still Lives in Theater Memory"; "[Ellis M.] Clarke Recalled the Early

Days"; "Electric Plant Here Four Years After New York," by W. O. Myers; "Roster of 'Boys in Blue' in Franklin County, 1861-1865"; "G. A. R. in 1880"; "Social Doings in Ye Old Time"; "Cut Acreages Back in 1874," by H. A. Biskie; "Historic Spots in Kansas," by Margaret Whittemore; "Reading Club Library Nucleus"; "Artificial Gas Came in 1886"; "Sons of Ireland Founded Emerald," by J. R. Karnowski.

A three-column biography of John D. M. Hamilton, of Topeka, was published in the Kansas City (Mo.) *Star* June 21, 1936. On June 24 the *Star* recalled that members of the Lewis and Clark expedition held the first court session in the Missouri valley at the mouth of the Kansas river in 1804.

The Marion Hill Lutheran Church celebrated the sixtieth anniversary of its organization with special services on June 21, 1936. A history of the church by the Rev. J. J. Richard was outlined in the White City *Register* June 25.

"What Price White Rock?—A Chronical of Northwestern Jewell County" is appearing serially in the Burr Oak *Herald* commencing with its issue of June 25, 1936. The history was prepared by Harry E. Ross, a former editor of the *Herald*.

"First Fourth of July Celebration in Kansas 132 Years Ago," by Harold C. Place, and "The Story of Kansas Salt," were historical features of the July, 1936, issue of the Kansas Chamber of Commerce's *Progress in Kansas*.

Kansas Historical Notes

The tenth annual meeting of the Kansas History Teachers Association was held at McPherson College April 4, 1936. Approximately seventy members were in attendance. Papers read before the association during the day's sessions included: "Foreign Policy of the New Deal and Recovery," Elmer B. Staats; "Some Recovery Methods Being Used in Canada," H. C. Jordan; "The British Road to Recovery," Ernest Mahan; "High-school Social Studies and Recovery," Jessica Smith; "Recent Historical Literature," John Rydjord; "French Diplomacy in the Americas, 1816-1850," W. H. Walker; "A Mid-Nineteenth Century Crisis," E. L. Harshberger, and "The Homestead Act and the Labor Surplus," F. A. Shannon. Tribute was paid to the late Frank H. Hodder by Samuel A. Johnson during the luncheon session. Officers elected for the new year are: H. A. Shumway, El Dorado Junior College, president; T. L. Parrish, Kansas State College, vice-president, and S. A. Johnson, Kansas State Teachers College of Emporia, secretary-treasurer. Other members elected to the executive committee are: J. D. Bright, McPherson College, the retiring president; Robena Pringle, Topeka High School, and Ernest Mahan, Kansas State Teachers College of Pittsburg.

Kansas has erected a monument at the grave of the late John W. Leedy, former governor of the state, who is buried at Edmonton, Alberta. The bronze plate attached to the monument reads:

John W. Leedy
Thirteenth Governor of Kansas
Born in Richland County, Ohio, 1849
Died in Edmonton, Alberta, 1935
Sincere in Purpose, Simple in Manner
Rugged in Speech, His Public Services
Are Here
Commemorated by the People of Kansas

A two-column biographical sketch of Governor Leedy by Cecil Howes was published in the Kansas City (Mo.) *Times*, May 27, 1936. A picture of the bronze tablet appeared in the June 14 issue of the Topeka *Daily Capital*.

A bronze tablet was recently unveiled on the Pioneer monument at Colfax and Broadway, Denver, Colo., bearing the inscription:

"Here was the end of the famous Smoky Hill Trail, Immigrant and Stage Road extending from the Missouri river to Denver. Entered the city by Fifteenth street. Traversed by Pioneers in 1858. Surveyed by W. G. Russell in 1860. Route of Butterfield's Overland Despatch and Wells-Fargo Express. The trail took its human toll—deaths by thirst and by Indian raids. Placed by The State Historical Society of Colorado from the Mrs. J. N. Hall Foundation and by the city and county of Denver. 1936."

Kirke Mechem addressed a meeting of the Shawnee Mission Indian Historical Society at Overland Park April 27, 1936.

A granite marker has been erected on the bank of White's creek southeast of Jamestown bearing the inscription: "White's Creek and Benj. White Homestead, 1867." The stone was erected last winter by Mrs. E. M. French, of Jamestown, a daughter of Benjamin White. Her father, who was one of the earliest pioneers and homesteaders in the vicinity, was killed by the Indians in 1868. Another daughter, now Mrs. Sarah Brooks, was carried off to the Indian territory and held prisoner by the Cheyennes for several months.

Names of Frank P. MacLennan, editor of the Topeka *State Journal,* and George Watson Marble, editor of the Fort Scott *Tribune-Monitor,* each a Kansas newspaper man for half a century, were recently added to the "Kansas Newspaper Hall of Fame" sponsored by the University of Kansas department of journalism and by Sigma Delta Chi, journalism fraternity at the university. Addition of these names brings to thirteen the list which was started five years ago. For names of other Kansas newspapermen who have been nominated to this honor see *The Kansas Historical Quarterly,* v. III, p. 336, and v. IV, p. 223.

The Second U. S. cavalry, now stationed at Fort Riley, celebrated the centennial of its organization with a two-day program held at the fort May 9 and 10, 1936. The Second cavalry was organized as the Second dragoons in Florida May 8, 1836.

Members of the Douglas County Historical Society visited Lecompton June 16, 1936, being the first of a series of historical tours under the auspices of the Society to places of interest in the county.

THE
Kansas Historical Quarterly

Volume V   Number 4

November, 1936

PRINTED BY KANSAS STATE PRINTING PLANT
W. C. AUSTIN, STATE PRINTER
TOPEKA 1936
16-5211

22—5211

Contributors

LELA BARNES is curator of manuscripts of the Kansas State Historical Society.

GEORGE A. ROOT is curator of archives of the Kansas State Historical Society.

THOMAS CLARKE WELLS, who died in 1907, was an early resident of the Manhattan vicinity. For a biographical sketch see page 143 of the May number.

NOTE.—Articles in the *Quarterly* appear in chronological order without regard to their importance.

Journal of Isaac McCoy for the Exploring Expedition of 1830

Lela Barnes

I. Introduction

FOR several months previous to his tour of 1828 into what is now Kansas, Isaac McCoy had been preparing to leave the Baptist missionary station at Carey, Michigan,[1] which he had founded in 1822, and remove to a western field. McCoy had worked indefatigably for the betterment of conditions for the Indian, and his insistence upon the removal of the tribes from the influences of the whites had been a factor in the development of the Indian removal policy of the government. By 1828 this national policy was taking form and McCoy looked to the West as a field for greater service. He had not, however, been able to interest the Baptist mission board in establishing stations in the western territory, the attention of that body being given chiefly to missions in foreign lands. "We did not believe," wrote McCoy, "that they [the board] would grant us permission at that time, to go west, and we therefore did not ask it; for it would have been more painful to go *contrary* to direct orders, than to go *without* orders."[2] He resolved that no work should be undertaken at the *cost* of the board, but that he would follow the course that lay clear before him—the dedication of his remaining years to the assistance of the tribes in the western territory.

August, 1829, found the McCoy family established at Fayette, Mo. From that point McCoy made a short tour into the country beyond the Missouri in the early autumn for the purpose of securing additional information about the lands. He spent the months from November, 1829, until June, 1830, in Washington, Boston, and other Eastern cities, working for the bill which would legalize the removal of the Indians to the country west of the Mississippi. The bill was approved May 28, 1830.

The apportionment of territory to the tribes was the next step in the removal program and McCoy was commissioned to survey lands which had been assigned by treaty to the Delawares. His appointment and instructions were received in a letter from Thomas L. McKenney, superintendent of Indian affairs:

---

1. For a brief history of the founding of Carey mission, see *The Kansas Historical Quarterly*, May, 1936. McCoy's journal entries covering his tour of 1828 may be found in the *Quarterly* for August, 1936.
2. McCoy, Isaac, *History of Baptist Indian Missions* (Washington, 1840), p. 371.

War Department
Office Indian Affairs, June 3, 1830.

Dear Sir: The conditional ratification of a supplementary treaty with the Delaware Indians, by the United States' Senate, requires that certain surveys shall be made. The conditions are stated in the accompanying copy of a resolution of the Senate, and the lines to be run are defined in the first paragraph of the treaty aforesaid,[3] and illustrated by a sketch which accompanies this— No. 1.

The Secretary of War, by the authority of the President of the United States, refers the execution of this trust to you. No detailed instructions are necessary, since these are ample in the treaty and the resolution of the Senate which accompanies it. You will be governed by these; and in every particular. To aid you with a better view of the country, contiguous to that which is to be surveyed and marked by you, I enclose a copy (No. 2) of Mr. Langham's survey of the Kansas reservation.[4]

I am directed by the Secretary of War to say, that your compensation will be at the rate of five dollars a day, for the time that you may be actually engaged in the execution of this trust; that you will be aided by an assistant surveyor, to be chosen by yourself, whose compensation will be at the rate of three dollars a day, whilst actually engaged; and by a corporal's guard, which will be detailed to report to you from Cantonment Leavenworth. This guard will perform the duties of axemen, &c., and marking of the lines, and in aiding in the transportation of your supplies, &c., from place to place.

You will obtain of the Delawares a designation of their agent, for which the resolution of the Senate provides, whose support will be allowed him, or a daily compensation equivalent to it.

You will be careful, in all things, to conform to the provisions of the resolution of the Senate, in obtaining the certificate of the agent who may be appointed by the Delawares, and in transmitting the map of the surveys, &c., to the President of the United States, for his approval and signature, &c. You will be particular in making up your accounts, and these will embrace your own pay, at the rate mentioned, and your assistant, and the number of days the guard may be with you; as to each man, an extra allowance over the pay in the army will be made, at the rate of fifteen cents a day. The voucher will be your own certificate that the whole is correct as stated.

You will engage in fulfilling this trust with as little delay as possible.

I have, &c., &c.,
Thomas L. McKenney.[5]

---

3. Paragraph 1, supplementary article ratified March, 1831, to the Delaware treaty concluded at St. Mary's, in the State of Ohio, on the 3d of October, 1818: "Whereas the foregoing treaty stipulates that the United States shall provide for the Delaware nation, a country to reside in, west of the Mississippi, as the permanent residence of their nation; and whereas the said Delaware nation, are now willing to remove, on the following conditions, from the country on James's fork of White river in the State of Missouri, to the country selected in the fork of the Kansas and Missouri river, as recommended by the government, for the permanent residence of the whole Delaware nation; it is hereby agreed upon by the parties, that the country in the fork of the Kansas and Missouri rivers, extending up the Kansas river, to the Kansas line, and up the Missouri river to Camp Leavenworth, and thence by a line drawn westwardly, leaving a space ten miles wide, north of the Kansas boundary line, for an outlet; shall be conveyed and forever secured by the United States, to the said Delaware nation, as their permanent residence: And the United States hereby pledges the faith of the government to guarantee to the said Delaware nation forever, the quiet and peaceable possession and undisturbed enjoyment of the same, against the claims and assaults of all and every other people whatever."—*Treaties Between the United States of America and the Several Indian Tribes, 1778-1837* (Washington, 1837), p. 444.

4. See footnote No. 28.

5. "Indian Removal," 23d Cong., 1st sess., *S. Doc.* 512, v. 2, p. 5.

That part of McCoy's journal here published covers his tour to establish the Delaware boundaries. The first survey was that of the western line beginning three and one-half miles west of the center of present Topeka where the eastern boundary line of the reservation of the Kansas Indians crossed the Kansas river; thence north to the northeast corner of the northwest quarter of Section 3, Township 6, Range 15 in present Jackson county. A random line was then run southeast to the Missouri river at Cantonment Leavenworth and the military reservation boundaries established. The party returned to the northwest corner of the Delaware reservation and proceeded to establish the boundaries of the outlet, a strip ten miles wide extending 150 miles westward from the western boundary line.

Isaac McCoy's journal and other manuscripts cited are in the possession of the Kansas State Historical Society.

II. Entries from the Journal

Memorandum—I actually commenced making preparations for surveying expedition July 19— Dr. McCoy[6] started to Fort Leavenworth,[7] and Delaware agency July 26.— He returned August, 7th. On his return I ascertained that the decision of the commanding officer at the Fort was such that I must purchase and equip at least five more horses.

1830, Monday, at ½ past 11, o'clock Aug. 16.

I started on my surveying expedition attended by my son Rice as asst. Surveyor, son Calvin as baggage master— Two white-men as chain-carriers, and black man as cook, &c. and a man to help us with the pack horses as far as Can. Leavenworth. We have 14 horses, We are packed with flour, bacon, and all our out-fit.

My wife and child accompanied me six miles, where I took my leave of them.

We rode 13 miles, was able to get corn for our horses but no

---

6. Rice McCoy, eldest son of Isaac McCoy. In his *History of Baptist Indian Missions* (Washington, 1840), Isaac McCoy wrote, regarding his son's participation in the tour: "From the time of our reaching Fayette, my eldest son had been employed in the practice of medicine, and his prospects were flattering, but he cheerfully consented to gratify my desire to see him labouring in some manner in the Indian country, and took an appointment as assistant surveyor."—p. 404.

7. In March of 1827 Col. Henry Leavenworth was ordered by the War Department to select a site for a cantonment on the left bank of the Missouri river, near the mouth of the Little Platte river. Colonel Leavenworth, however, upon examination of the site suggested, did not find it favorable and chose instead a location on the right bank of the Missouri river. This choice was approved and the post was officially designated Cantonment Leavenworth by Department Order No. 56, of 1827. The primary purpose in stationing troops at this point was for protection of the rapidly increasing trade over the Santa Fé trail. Fort Leavenworth (official designation under Department Order No. 11, 1832) figures prominently in the history of the West and the military history of the United States.

accomodations for ourselves, therefore slept without a house, and cooked our own suppers.

Tuesday Aug. 17   Crossed Missouri river near Chariton Village[8]— rested at Smiths, and put up for the night at Mrs. McCafferty's —where I make these Notes.

Wednesday Aug. 18   Breakfasted & fed at Davis's and stopped for the night at Estes's

Thursday Aug. 19   Nooned at Jennings, & nighted at C. Ewing['s].

Friday—20   Nooned at Rennick's, & nighted at Russel's

Saturday 21   Nooned at Flournoys, Independence. Here I saw M. G. Clark the Sub. agent for the Kanzas, took a letter from him to aid me in assuring the Kanzas that I am not about to disturb them in their lands, nor to intercept any promise which the U. S. had made to them; &c. I purchased a few additional articles of out-fit here, as I had done at Lexington. Received a letter from Genl. Clark,[9] of St. Louis, and a Flag which I had requested him to send me for my use on the expedition.

In the evening reached the Shawanoe & Delaware agency, at the house of Maj. J. Campbell the Sub. Agt. by whom we were kindly received.[10] Our tents were pitched for the company, while I accepted an invitation to take quarters with Maj. Campbell.

Cohern, the Shawanoe express sent to the Delawares to bring on their Commissioner to see their lands marked off, has not yet returned— Is expected soon.[11]

Sunday Aug. 22   Our Sister Wiskehelaehqua, alias Mrs. Shane, I am happy to hear conducts like a christian. She expresses a great desire that a mission should be established here among the Shawanoes, at which she could attend and enjoy religious privileges. She expresses great solicitude for the welfare, especially the Spiritual welfare of her people.

Monday Aug. 23   Major John Campbell, the Sub., but now, acting agent for the Shawanoes & Delawares, &c., has requested me, since my arrival, to endeavour to establish a School among the

---

8. Near present Glasgow in Howard county, Missouri. The following notice appeared in *Niles' Register*, v. 17 (1819-1820), p. 30: "*Chariton*, a new town *somewhere* in Missouri, containing about eighty houses, and several *brick* buildings are now erecting. A year ago there were only 'five or six unchinked cabins' on the town plot."

9. William Clark, U. S. Indian superintendent at St. Louis.

10. The agency was located on the E. ½ of the S. E. ¼ of Section 10, and the W. ½ of the S. W. ¼ of Section 11, Township 12, Range 25, in present Johnson county, Kansas.

11. In his abstract of disbursements for the tour, McCoy gave the name of the express as J. Cohon.—"Indian Removals," 23d Cong., 1st sess., *S. Doc.* 512, v. 5, p. 229.

Shawanoes. Shane the Interpreter, who is a half-Indian, united in the request. The Methodists have been talking of forming an establishment among them, but their project seems not likely to succeed. They have done nothing yet.

Today more than twenty Shawanoes assembled in obedience to a call of Major Campbell, to whom I made a pretty lengthy address on the subject of a mission being established among them. My remarks were seconded by remarks from Maj. Campbell, and some from Shane. The celebrated Shawanoe prophet, who was so often heard of in the last war, and was brother to Tecumseh, replied briefly to me, approbating my doctrine.[12]

An answer in form from the tribe is deferred, until I return from my tour in the wilderness. After the council was dissolved, I had an interview with Fish, alone, He is the Chief of a band of them, He assured me that he and his party were in favour of having a mission established among them. They had been desiring it for some time. They would not have come to this place had they not hoped that this would be done for them. He said he had often expressed his opinion to Shane, He was of the same opinion still. He thought that if a School, &c. was once begun those who are now indifferent to the subject would be induced to follow the example of others who are now ready to adopt those measures, and when they would see others sending their children to school, &c. they would be induced to do the same, &c. &c.

I assured him that at his request a mission should be given them, and that I would enter immediately upon the work of bringing it about. Another man of influence said to me alone that he greatly desired a school that he might send his children, and that his brother might be allowed to send his. Another man, one of Fish's party was pointed out to me, who said that if a school could not be established here he would have to send his daughters into the settlements of the whites, which would occasion an expense which he could not well bear.

Cohern the express sent to the Delawares returned today, and with him the agent of their choice. He is an old man named Johnny Quick is second Chief in the tribe. The interpreter Co[nn]or is bearing the message of the Delaware council— he has not yet arrived.

---

12. Shawnee medicine-man, Tenskwatawa, known as the Prophet, commander of the Indian forces at the battle of Tippecanoe. He removed from Cape Girardeau county, Missouri, to the Shawnee reservation in present Kansas in 1828 and located a town known as Prophet Town in what is now Shawnee township, Wyandotte county. For an account of his death, November, 1837, see *Kansas Historical Collections*, v. 9, p. 164, footnote.

Tuesday Aug. 24 I made a formal application thro. Mr. Campbell, for permission from government to establish a mission here. I also communicated this and the circumstance of the case generally to the Board thro. Mr. Cone.[13] These letters are on file, and may be considered as belonging to the mission Journals.

In the afternoon of this day, J. Connor the Delaware interpreter arrived with the written communications of the Chiefs. The substance of which was that they had been in council on the subject of our surveying. Had chosen and sent as their agt. to see the land marked off—John Quick an aged and respectable Chief— They wished to remove on their lands in the course of two months. While we would be surveying their land, they requested that Maj. Campbell their Agent should be purchasing horses, and wagons, &c. to transport them to their new country before cold weather.

They required that the nature of the whole subject be again explained to their Commissioner, and in event of his being satisfied, he was to proceed.— This was done to his satisfaction, and he cheerfully agreed to proceed. But stated that neither the nation nor he wished for him to go farther than to see the bounds of their tract generally marked that they cared not to see their out-let marked. They would be content without it. It would save the agent, who is old, from much fatigue, and would allow him to return in time to aid in removal to their new country.

Wednesday Aug. 25. It was not until the evening of this day that Maj. Campbell could procure a horse for John Quick to ride.

Thursday Aug. 26 We have been detained here until this time waiting for the Delaware Commissioner to prepare. This done we proceeded. As we passed the Shawanoe village we found 35 Kanzas there, assembled to have a talk with the Shawanoes. They said that the Shawanoes had been living two years in the country, that a general talk between them had been expected, and they had now called for that purpose. The Shawanoes invited me to attend their council, as one, as they said, who took a deep interest in Indian affairs, with which I had made myself acquainted, &c. This was a high compliment, of which I cheerfully accepted. I proceeded to the river five miles, directed the company how to encamp, and returned with my son Rice. By this time it was late in the day & their interpreter having not yet arrived, we returned to camp with the understanding that we should meet them on the following day. It was dusk when we reached camp and I was really fatigued &

13. S. H. Cone, Baptist minister of New York, loyal friend and supporter of Isaac McCoy.

hungry. Maj. Campbell, & Mr. Shane and his son are with us accompanying us to the Garrison.

We expected to have to raise a boat that was sunk in the Kanza river here, to enable us to cross, and to this end the Shawanoes to a considerable number, had been invited to help. On arriving here the Indians pronounced the boat unfit for use.

I had bought of an Indian a small beef for their use when helping us, and for our company. We now gave half of it to the Kanzas.— Soon after I had passed them with our packs today, old Plume,[14] sent two persons in great haste after us. We saw them coming running, and halted to hear what news—when we were informed that Plume had sent to get some of our Bacon. Having no disposition to unpack there, and as little disposition to give away our bacon, we went on.

Friday Aug. 27   I left Rice to take on the company, and took Calvin and Mr. Shane, and returned to the Shawanoe village. It was indispensable for me to see the Kanzas to explain to them the nature of our expedition before we commenced surveying. It is favourable that I can see them here and will save us several days hereafter.

I addressed 35 Kanzas, seated on one side of the Council-house and some Shawanoes on the other. A fire in the centre, near which I placed a few twists of tobacco for them all to smoke. I spread out the map before the Kanzas and explained to them what we were about to do, the wishes of the government in relation to settling the Indians in this country, and enjoined on them to be at peace among themselves.

The Kanzas said they had not yet ceded away that country. Why should the U. S. give it to the Delawares without first consulting them.

I told them that they *had* ceded it five years ago—that I was not at the treaty, but so said the paper, to which they had signed their names.[15] They knowing this to be true said no more, especially as

---

14. White Plume, Kansas Chief. See *Kansas Historical Collections*, v. 9, pp. 194-196.

15. Article 1 of the treaty made and concluded at St. Louis, Mo., June 3, 1825, between William Clark, superintendent of Indian Affairs, commissioner on the part of the United States, and representatives of the Kanzas was as follows: "The Kanzas do hereby cede to the United States all the lands lying within the State of Missouri, to which the said nation have title or claim; and do further cede and relinquish, to the said United States, all other lands which they now occupy, or to which they have title or claim, lying west of the said State of Missouri, and within the following boundaries: Beginning at the entrance of the Kanzas river into the Missouri river; from thence north to the northwest corner of the State of Missouri; from thence westwardly to the Nodewa river, thirty miles from its entrance into the Missouri; from thence to the entrance of the Big Nemahaw river into the Missouri, and with that river to its source; from thence to the source of the Kanzas river, leaving the old village of the Pania Republic to the west; from thence, on the ridge dividing the waters of the Kanzas river from those of the Arkansas, to the western boundary of the State line of Missouri, and with that line, thirty miles, to the place of beginning." Article 2 provided for a reservation 30 miles in width on the Kansas river.—*Treaties Between the United States of America and the Several Indian Tribes, 1778-1837* (Washington, 1837), p. 334.

I had told old Plume that he understood it all, for he had last year showed me where their line crossed the Kanza river.

Having gone thro. with my talk with the Kanzas, I was anxious to follow after our company. But the Kanzas asking me to stay and hear what should pass between them and the Shawanoes, I consented to stay.

The speeches of each are on separate sheets from this and may be considered as a part of this Journal.[16]

The packhorses had with difficulty, and some miring in the river, and some wetting of packs, got over. The river is sandy and miry with quick-sands. It is muddy so that the bottom cannot be perceived. Neither of us knew the ford— Shane got thro by wading very deep. Calvin and I took a little to one side of his place, found it more shallow. Calvin went before to try the bottom, &c. His horse mired about the middle of the river, so that he had to dismount, and carry out his saddle bags. His horse relieved of so much of his burthen arose and was led out.

I seeing this, dismounted in the river, tied up my bridle and let my horse follow, With much difficulty he got across. I having my saddle-bags, which were very heavy, and my gun to carry waded slowly after him. Calvin having got his horse and mine safely ashore returned and met me in the river and relieved me of my load.

We stopped at a solitary wigwam at which lived an Old Delaware alone, without any other human being near him on either side of the river. It was now in the afternoon and we began to get pretty hungry. I had found a few ears of green corn in a deserted Indian field. While we dried our clothes wetted in crossing the river, we roasted the corn. We over-took our company in camp at dark. I was very much fatigued.

Saturday Aug. 28   Quick's horse could not be found. We proceeded a few miles and encamped. Son Rice, Shane & I went to Cantonment Leavenworth, three miles from our camp. We saw the Commanding officer, Maj. Davenport,[17] and Maj. Dougherty Agent for the Pawnees,[18] on our business—the history of this interview will be given a few days hence. We came back to our camp, and my two sons again went to the garrison with our papers for the inspection of those officers.

16. Missing from journal.
17. Maj. William Davenport, Sixth infantry.
18. Maj. John Dougherty received his appointment as Indian agent in January, 1827, and began his work at Cantonment Leavenworth in September of that year.

Sunday
Aug. 29
We remain in camp. Receive communications from home. Also a letter from Rev. S. H. Cone, in which among other things he very kindly states that as it is probable that we are in want of funds for the support of my family, I was at liberty to draw on him for one-two-or three hundred Dollars. He does not say how, or when he would expect to be remunerated. This is an act of kindness [and] generosity worth recording, in our Journal, and on our hearts, and one that will be rewarded by Heaven. I am thankful to the Lord for such a friend—and thankful that I am not under the necessity of accepting the offer. True, we had not funds to fit out Mr. Lykins,[19] and to bear his expenses, nor to leave for the use of my family, but the Lord has given us friends, who have, and will let us have what we need on credit in Fayette, until I realize the earnings of my present labours.

Major Dougherty spent most of the day at our camp.

Monday
Aug. 30
Son Rice & myself again visited the garrison, In order to make arrangements for proceeding. We hope to get off on Wednesday next, which will be as soon as we can arrange our business with the commanding officer at the garrison.

When I undertook this work, the Secretary of War was advised that there would probably be some difficulty with the neighbouring Indians, and ordered a Corporal's guard, (10 men) and at my request he then left the matter to the discretion of the commanding officer at Cantonment Leavenworth. I had sent my son to the garrison to arrange with the commander, who then was Maj. Riley,[20] all appeared fair.

A Maj. Davenport had succeeded to the command a day or two before our arrival, and he perceived difficulties in everything.

He first appeard unwilling to furnish any men to help me, said that my surveying company might be completed by my hiring men. That he could not send an escort, because if one were necessary, it would require more men than he had to spare—at least two companies. I stated to him the nature of the case, that a guard had from the first been deemed indispensable, and therefore the Secretary of War had ordered it. I returned to my camp, & wrote him an official notice that I was now engaged in the work and de-

---

19. Johnston Lykins (1800-1876), son-in-law of Isaac McCoy, had been associated with him in missionary work in Indiana and Michigan and at this time was planning to continue his labors in the West. He founded the Shawnee Baptist mission in present Johnson county, Kansas, in 1831. The trip referred to was from Fayette, Mo., to Carey, Michigan, where he arranged for the appraisal of the Baptist mission property at that place, preparatory to the closing of the mission.

20. Maj. Bennet Riley (1787-1853) for whom Fort Riley, Kansas, was named. For a sketch of his life see *Kansas Historical Collections*, v. 12, p. 1, footnote.

sired him to furnish the men needed to complete my surveying company, and also the necessary escort. When he discovered that I was disposed to proceed in a way that would tell, he appeared more obliging. He said he expected some orders on the subject from Genl. Atkinson,[21] near St. Louis, on Sunday. I also sent him on Saturday evening, my Commission & instructions, and the ratification of the treaty by the Senate &c. for his inspection.

[Marginal note.] This took place on Saturday, Aug. 28.

On Sunday, he forwarded me a letter stating that the number of men that I asked for, to aid me for the first three weeks, which was only six, should be in readiness to start at any time, but that he could not furnish an escort, because, if the disposition of the Indians rendered a guard necessary at all, it would require more men than he could spare.

It seems that he had received an order from Genl. Atkinson stating that as there was no appearance of hostility on the frontiers, no escort was necessary. And if needed at all, not more than 20 men could be spared &c. (this was stated to me by Maj. Dougherty).

All this was mere trifling. Atkinson, and every one else in this country knew that not a year for several years had passed, in which those Pawnees did not kill, and rob, and otherwise abuse, more or fewer of the citizens of the U. States who happened to fall into their hands.

The Secretary of War, aware to some extent of the difficulties to be apprehended from the Indians within the vicinity of our surveying, had issued an order to Genl. Clark, Superintendent of Indian affrs. at St. Louis that he should require the Indian Agents for those tribes with whom I should likely come in contact, to notify the Indians of their several charges that I acted under the authority & protection of the U. States, and to require them to treat me with friendship &c. accordingly.[22] Genl. Clark had not given this notice to the agents. He had written to me that he had notified the Sub-agt. of the Kanzas, but he, the Sub-agent, M. G. Clark, told us the other day at Independence that he had *not* been notified. Neither had Maj. Campbell, S. Agt. for the Shawanoes. Both those men acted promptly upon my statements to them.

---

21. Gen. Henry Atkinson, commanding the western army.

22. "War Department, Office Indian Affairs, June 5, 1830. Sir: The Rev. Isaac McCoy is charged by the executive with the duty of running and marking the lines called for by the treaty with the Delawares. You will instruct the agents who have charge of the Indians, owning the country over which Mr. McCoy will have occasion to travel, to inform them of Mr. McCoy's object; that he is under the protection of the United States, and to require their kind and friendly conduct towards him and his party. I have, &c., &c., THOS. L. MCKENNEY. To General Wm. Clark, Superintendent Indian Affairs, &c."—"Indian Removals," 23d Cong., 1st sess., *S. Doc.* 512, v. 2, p. 8.

I brought on the order to Clark from the Sec. War, and knowing that there were many crooked sticks about St. Louis, I had the precaution to take a copy. This I have used to effect with the agents above named. But Dougherty was absent at the time my son was at the Garrison. He was then in St. Louis, was many days in Clark's company, both at St. Louis, then at Prarie-Du Chien, at a treaty, then again at St. Louis. He asked Clark about it, but Clark gave him no information, and intimated that he did not believe that the treaty had been ratified. After Dougherty's return to the garrison, and his hearing that we were certainly going to work, and knowing that the Pawnees were the only Indians from whom we need fear any hostility, wrote to Clark, from whom he has not yet heard. Clark's neglect of duty, and Atkinson's foolish & wicked orders, and Davenport's childishness are partly unaccountable.

Dougherty could omit doing any thing for us, because he had received no orders, but he kindly consented to act. To justify him in doing so, I made a written request for him to notify and endeavour to conciliate the Pawnees. I also inquired if there were any circumstances which had recently occurred which evinced that they were now under the influence of better feelings than formerly, and what those circumstances were if they did exist. I forwarded him a copy of the Sec. War's order to Clark, and also other documents to show to him the full character of the expedition.

He agreed to send immidiately to the Pawnee towns, and bring in some of them to council on the subject. But he had not horses to send, and I was obliged to let him have two of our horses. These I sent up to him today—and his express will start today or tomorrow

Tuesday Aug. 31   I again went, in company of Rice, and conversed with Major Davenport, respecting an escort when we shall commence running our long line. But he appeared to be no more accommodating than before, and wished, as he had stated in his letter, to let the matter rest until we could hear from the Pawnees.

Maj. Dougherty politely replied to my communication and offers to afford all the aid in his power. In reply to my enquiries, "If any recent circumstances evinced that the Pawnees are now under the influence of better feelings than formerly," &c. He stated that he knew of no such favourable circumstances.

Davenport advised me to write to Genl. Atkinson, and state the number of men that I should probably need, &c. This I declined to do.

The neglect of Davenport I attribute to his naturally, disobliging disposition, as he wished to be understood as treating me with politeness. The unreasonable, and foolish opinion expressed by Atkinson, I attribute to the influence of Clark. The neglect of duty on the part of Clark, I attribute in part to his dislike of Dougherty, but chiefly because he dislikes Vashon,[23] and was not pleased that Vashon had made a treaty with the Delawares, and more especially because that treaty does not stipulate for the payment of certain claims of traders against the Delawares.[24]

This is the last treaty to be made with the Delawares respecting land, and those who had hovered about them like crows about a carcase, knew that this was their last draw. After the treaty with Vashon, the Delawares were prevailed on to ask that certain claims to the amount of some thousands of Dollars, should be paid by the U. States. Vashon told them that the U. States had paid their debts at the treaty of St. Marys in 1818 and that ought to suffice. The Indians gave him to understand that they were quite satisfied to let matters rest so, and that they had made the request at the instance of others.

The nature of those claims are generally as follows. Traders credit the Indians, charging three or four prices for their goods, expecting that all will not be collected, and charging so high as to make themselves safe if but a small amount should be collected. They always enter the trade upon their own risk, and have no more right to insurance from the U. States than any other merchants and traders. When a treaty occurs, they come in with these claims. A trifling present or profession of friendship, &c. will induce an Indian to say the claim is just, and must be paid, if he sells his land. If the amount of claims of the claimer, is not equal to what he hopes the U. States will agree to pay, he creates claims by the same means that he has proven his old ones.

Vashon informed me of Clark's displeasure that the treaty had been made, and of the circumstance of those claims.

Such is the character of the people with whom I have to do this business, and such the state of things in relation to the Indians.

The express—two men, will start this day for the Pawnees. Some Kanzas are at the garrison, by these Dougherty sends for the Kanza chiefs to assemble. He is going with us that far, and will talk to

---

23. George Vashon, Indian agent for Cherokees West.
24. Treaty with the Delawares concluded September 24, 1829, ratified March 24, 1831. This was a supplemental article to the Delaware treaty concluded at St. Mary's, Ohio, October 3, 1818, and provided for the cession by the Delawares of all lands in the state of Missouri. George Vashon represented the United States at the treaty.

them on the subject of our surveying. This he deems necessary, notwithstanding the interview I had with some of them the other day.

A band of Kanzas have lately stolen nine horses from the Pawnees, a little previously, the Osages and Pawnees had a fight in which some ten or twelve Pawnees and two or three Osages were slain. Thes[e] circumstances have induced Dougherty to suggest to me the propriety of taking a guard on our first and present tour. This is to extend only sixty miles west of Missouri State, and will last about three weeks. We shall then be led back to this place by our work, and shall re-fit for our more remote and important expidition.

We leave some of our supplies at Canto. Leavenworth and are preparing to proceed on our Journey, tomorrow, which is as early as we have been able to adjust our business with our trifling major.

Maj. Campbell, Shane, & his son, left us yesterday for their place.

Wednesday September 1   At a half past 9 o'clock we left camp, proceeded to Cantonment Leavenworth, where we took into our company a Corporal & eight men with 21 days' provision. We have deposited the balance of our supplies at the garrison. The garrison furnished food for the men from there but we had to furnish horses and bags, &c for transportation. We there borrowed a spade for mound-making, & a tent for the soldiers.

I and Calvin proceeded with the company, at 12— made, about 15 miles and encamped at the Stranger.[25] Rice, Major Dougherty, & Lieut. Cook overtook us at dark, the latter merely to spend the night.

Thursday Sep. 2   Major Dougherty & I proceeded early and left my sons to bring on the company. We reached Boon's,[26] at the Kanza agency at 1 o'clock, soon after, about 20 or 30 Kanza chiefs & others assembled, to whom Dougherty explained the objects of our coming into their country &c. and conversed with them on the subject of their differences with the Pawnees.

A band of [Kansas] have lately stolen 9 horses from the Pawnees — Since that two other parties have gone, one a party of five, which has been out five days, the other a party of four, which have been gone four days. One party have gone to the Republican

25. Stranger creek rises in the central portion of present Atchison county and flows in a southeasterly direction, emptying into the Kansas river at present Linwood, Leavenworth county. The stream was named O-keet-sha by the Kansas Indians, the word meaning stranger.
26. Daniel Morgan Boone, son of Daniel Boone, pioneer, was appointed farmer for the Kansas Indians in 1827 and located seven miles west of present Lawrence, on the north bank of the Kansas river, at the Kansas agency.

Pawnees, and the other to the Grand Pawnees on the great Platt— both to steal horses. This increases the danger to us, of falling in with hostile Pawnees following in after the Kanza thieves, and to avenge their thefts. We shall be in danger of having our horses stolen at least, even while we are near to the Kanza villages.

The Company overtook us at night, & we encamped near Boon's.

Friday Sep. 3   Had further talks with the Kanzas, Maj. Dougherty warned them not to follow our party to beg for provisions, &c. &c. I have hired our interpreter who speaks Kanza. He has agreed to overtake us tomorrow & to accompany us a few days only. An interpreter is necessary, because, otherwise we could not distinguish a friend from a foe as he would approach us. The Kanzas have not yet decided whether they will deliver up the horses they have lately stolen.

[Marginal note.] Connor returned, had not found the Del. Chiefs horse—but brought another.

About 11 o'clock Maj. Dougherty started home— We sent a man with him a days journey. The company started and I and Calvin soon followed, having obtained some smith work on our guns and a horse. Stopped at Plume's, 3 miles from our camp, and borrowed an U. States' flag. Made about eight miles and encamped on Grasshopper creek.[27] Col. Boon accompanies us.

Saturday Sep. 4.   Several Kanzas passed us both ways yesterday and two encamped with us. We started before 8 oclock, saw a considerable number of Kanzas going each end of the road. We encamped on Soldier creek.[28] More than twenty Kanzas came to our camp, many of them seemed anxious to beg some of our provisions or clothing. But we assured them that we had not come to trade— We had come to perform a piece of work for the benefit of their Delaware neighbors, and had brought no more of food or raiment than we needed for our own use. I gave them some tobacco, at dusk they all left us.

We are now within three miles of the line on which we shall com-

27. Now called the Delaware river. The stream flows in a southeasterly direction across present Jefferson county emptying into the Kansas river near present Perry.

28. "The first surveys in what is now the State of Kansas were made in 1826-7 by Maj. Angus L. Langham of St. Louis but previously from Chillicothe, Ohio. These were 1st the meanders of the Kansas river from its mouth to a point twenty leagues due west of the western boundary of Missouri as provided by the treaty of 1825 with the Kansas tribe as the east boundary of their reservation thence south about 13 miles to the S. E. corner thereof, then west two hundred miles marking the south line thereof. He passed the winter of 1826-7 on Soldier creek about four miles north of present Topeka and about three miles east [of] the Kaw village of the 'Fool Chief.' He had with him a small guard of infantry detailed from Fort Osage. Cantonment Leavenworth was not established as a military post until 1827. The name 'Soldier Creek' was adopted afterwards in honor of the flag that proudly waved over the Major's shanty and the warlike aspect of the camp. . . ."—Letter, John C. McCoy to F. G. Adams, February 9, 1885.

mence our work, and not more than four or five miles from the place of our beginning. Jo Jim, the Kanza interpreter whom we hired overtook, and joined our company at camp.

Sunday Sep. 5. We spend the day in camp, My writing desk is the pad of a packsaddle, one board of the saddle being tied fast to a stake on the out-side, the other board necessarily projects from the stake, and forms a kind of shelf. The two pads are then suffered to fall on to the shelf part, and forms a kind of cushioned table.

My seat is formed upon three stakes driven into the ground, with sticks fastened across the top so that the seat is made firm.

Monday Sep. 6. Left Calvin in charge of the camp, and Rice & I commenced our work. We had to go about 5 miles to find the line of the Kanza lands at the crossing of the Kanzas river. We crossed Soldier creek one mile & three quarters from the river. The creek is three rods & fifteen links between the banks.

About a mile and a half north of us between the creek and river is the village of Chachhaa hogeree, *Prarie-village.* It contains about 50 houses, with say three families to the house. All except three or four persons, started yesterday and today, on their hunting excursions. Sent the Kanza interpreter Jo Jim to try to get some sweet corn of them but he was unsuccessful. From the creek, which we could not cross with our horses, I returned to camp with Quick and his interpreter. The surveyors got in at dusk, I having sent horses to meet them.

Tuesday Sep. 7 Sent four men early to take a Bee tree which they had found yesterday. They got no honey of consequence. We left camp a little after 9. The packhorses encamped so far ahead that it was dark before the surveyors came in. We were encamped on a branch of Soldier creek. I had sent a man to meet them, who returned at sundown without having seen them. I took Connor and rode till dark before we met with them.

Wednesday Sep. 8 It rained on us last night, and I omitted to state that I have made some beginning for a mission on Missouri above Cantonment Leavenworth sixty or eighty miles. In June & July a treaty was held with various tribes—viz Sauks, Foxes, Iowas, Otoes, Omaha, and Sioux assembled at Prarie-Du-Chein, at which treaty it was stipulated that $3000. pr. Ann. for ten years, be paid by government for education purposes among those tribes. Dougherty, the Agt., since I met with him at the garrison suggested that a suitable place for a mission would be on a tract of land above the garrison, between the two Nemaha rivers, on the Missouri, about ten miles wide and twenty miles long, which had been set apart at the late treaty for the use and settlement of half-breeds. The land is to be held by them as other Indians hold their lands, though the Prest. of the U. S. may grant to any one of them a tract, not exceeding 640 acres, in fee simple. Maj. Dougherty thought that some or all of the three thousand dollars mentioned above might be obtained to aid an institution there (though I am of opinion that there has been a contrivance among some whites to apply it to Johnson's School)[29] In conference with him, he has assured me that he would do all in his power to promote such an undertaking.

I have stated to him that we would turn our attention to the matter. On Sunday last I wrote to Mr. Cone on the subject, and have requested that he & the Board resolve to enter upon the work. I state to him that in event of the Board not seizing upon these openings, that others of us intend to improve them. See my letter to Cone, which may be considered as part of this Journal.[30]

We left our camp after 12 oclock, passed the surveyors who had commenced their work pretty soon, and encamped on the Soldier creek, left of our line. The surveyors came in at dark.

Thursday Sep. 9   Our work went on as usual— surveyors made seven miles today. We encamped half a mile to the east of our line, on the upper branches of (perhaps) Sotraell creek.[31] Connor and the Delaware Chief went a hunting about 9 o'clock yesterday morning, and have not yet returned. I had been very particular in telling Connor where we intended to encamp.

A little after dark a white man express arrived with dispatches from Genl. Clark & Maj. Dougherty, sent by the latter. Genl. Clark has sent us plats of the meanderings of Missouri and Kanza rivers, the Kanzas reservation &c. He advises that we should *not* run farther west than the Republican river—becaus we should likely run onto Pawnee lands, and because we should be in danger of injury from the Pawnees.

Dougherty wishes to know what I intend to do, and whether we

---

29. Under the terms of the treaty of 1825 with the Choctaw, the sum of six thousand dollars was to be allowed the tribe annually for twenty years for the use of schools. A school for boys was established at Blue Springs, Scott county, Kentucky, under the management of the Baptist church and the sponsorship of Richard M. Johnson. The first students were received in the autumn of 1825. Boys from other tribes were also accepted and for a number of years the institution flourished, but by 1842 the Indians began to withdraw their boys on account of dissatisfaction with the results of the educational plan. Soon thereafter the school closed.

30. Missing from journal.

31. Grasshopper river, later known as the Delaware river, was also at this time called Sautrelle river.

wish him to delay a tour up Missouri on which his business pressingly calls him, to attend our interview with the Pawnees. I am gratified with Clark's attention in this case, Dougherty appears to be very prompt and obliging.

I replied to Dougherty, and early on

Friday—Sep. 10— I started the express back—

Surveyors commenced early. We passed the northeast corner of the Kanzas reserve, and encamped on the sources of Grasshopper river. We have not been able to kill either Deer or Turkeys, or any thing larger than squirrils. We have found wild honey frequently. Today we have found and taken two trees.

Near night Connor & the Chief got in to camp.

Saturday Sep. 11. I went with some hands and enlarged the mound at the north east corner of the Kansa reservation. We had rain. We found trouble to get a good camping ground, which was on Grasshopper creek. Killed a rattle-snake in the midst of our encampment sometime after we had been tramping over it. Surveyors came in at 4 oclock— Jo Jim killed a deer.

Sunday Sep. 12. We spend the day in Camp. Every night we tie up three horses, so that if the Indians should steal the others we might still have some. Our horses sometimes get affrighted and one taking alarm from another, all are put in motion, and soon would leave us, were they not securely hobbled. By tying up some of them there is less danger of the others leaving camp.

Monday Sep. 13 We surveyed to the northern line of Del. lands, and begun a mound ten feet square at the base, & six feet high. Removed our encampment to another branch of Sotrael. Elk sign has been seen for several days. Today a Buck Elk stalked near the camp, Two of the men got each a shoot at him, but he escaped— Found iron ore on Delaware lands near the corner. The Doctor killed three Turkies.

Tuesday Sep. 14 Set our course as nearly towards Cantonment Leavenworth, (which is one of our points) as possible. Finished our mound, and made six miles. Encamped on a small branch of same creek. Two of our men fired on a large flock of Elk.

Wednesday Sep. 15 Moved our encampment a few miles down the same creek. Three men started early hunting. One of them came in, unsuccessful, after dark. The other two remained absent.

Thursday   Found difficulty in crossing two Creeks. Encamped on a
Sep. 16   branch of same creek, Two lost men still out— Fired the prarie, that by the immense, column of smoke that arises by the burning of old grass mingled with the green, they might see where we were. One of our men killed four turkeys.

Friday   Two lost men not returned. We saw a smoke rise not
Sep. 17   many miles from us, and thought it possible that our lost men had given a signal. We answered by kindling two fires in the grass at different times, but heard nothing from them. Found two bee trees, but obtained little honey. Discovered a large flock of Elk at a distance, about middle of afternoon. Stopped & encamped. Called in the surveyors, and four of us remaining to keep camp, the residue of our company made an unsuccessful effort to take an Elk.

Encamped on a branch of Stranger creek as we supposed.

Saturday   Paid Jo Jim our interpreter with Kanzas & others, and
Sep. 18   sent him home, supposing that we should have no further need for him until we should re-fit for another tour. Took a bee tree. Came in sight of Missouri river, say seven miles ahead. Found that we were too far north for the garrison. Turned at right angles southwardly. Found a grove of wood & brush, and encamped on a water of Missouri.

Sunday   No water for our horses, and food poor, we removed four
Sep. 19   or five miles—(without surveying) and encamped on Stranger creek.

Monday   Yesterday my son narrowly escaped serious injury by
Sep. 20   the kick of a horse on his head and arm. Being in want of meat, Jackson shot a fine buck. We brought up our off-set line, and turned towards the garrison again. Encamped on a small stream running into Missouri.

Before we left camp this morning, Cap. John Quick the Delaware Chief told me that he had seen enough to satisfy him. he would go on to the Garrison and wait until I arrived and then go on home. He could not continue longer with us. They wished to come to this country before cold weather— they had many women & children who would suffer much with cold if it should be late in the season, &c. &c.

He has all along indicated no disposition to stay long with us. After he had started I called to him and made a second effort to pursuade him to stay. The day was cloudy and I feared he could not find the garrison. I promised to send a man in with him on the following day. He stayed with us.

Tuesday Sep. 21 — We have kept up one Sentinel at a time during the night for most of the tour. Last night we dispensed with it, and think of not having guard while near the garrison.

Delaware Chief went for the garrison attended by one of our soldiers. Saw at a great distance in the prarie a company of Indians, amounting, to one hundred going towards the garrison.

Found ourselves getting too near Missouri and had to make another off-set. Had to travel at least two miles along a difficult stream to find water for encampment, which was not far from the river.

Wednesday Sep. 22 — Encamped on a branch of Stranger, fired the prarie for a signal to our men sent to the garrison.

Thursday Sep. 23 — Rode out with son and ascertained the best way to get to the garrison. Sent Calvin and a man to the garrison for supplies. Our man returned from the garrison with a large bundle of papers, letters, &c. Altho. we were no more than 12 or 13 miles from the garrison, such had been his awkwardness that he and the Delaware did not reach it until the second day, & they as awkwardly slept out last night on their return.

The Indians we saw passing in were the Pawnees we had sent for. Dougherty & Davenport requesting me to go in as soon as possible to attend the council, I rode to the garrison but it was too late to call the council.

Connor & Vincent, who got lost on the 15th did not go together. Each had made the best of his way to the garrison and after three or four days reached it. Vincent returned to us today with our express. Connor started alone yesterday to find us, crossed our trail more than once, We had fired the prarie, notwithstanding all which he slept alone in the woods and after spending two days, was making his way back to the garrison last night when, a little after dark as I was returning to camp, I met him and took him with me.

Friday Sep. 24 — We moved our encampment further down Salt creek. Went to the garrison. Had a talk with the 100 Pawnee chiefs & Wariours. Dougherty stated I had been sent to survey lands of the Delawares, and that if any of them should meet with any of our party, they must treat us well, &c.[32] I said a few words

---

[32] "Cant: Leavenworth, 22d. Octr. 1830. To Genl. Wm: Clark, Supt. Ind: Affs. Sir, I have the honor to inform you that in obedience to a message that I sent to the Pawnee Republicans, about one hundred of that tribe consisting of their chiefs and head men assembled at this post, on the 24th ult. My object for calling a council of those Indians at

to them, enjoining on them to be peaceable to the Delawares. John Quick made a short speech to them, expressive of friendship &c. Dougherty gave them a considerable amount of presents which was due them, consisting of powder, lead, blankets, tobacco, &c. &c.

Lately the Kanzas sent to Dougherty to say that the 9 horses lately stolen by them from the Pawnees they could not restore, because their hunting party had taken them with them. This is as it usually happens in those cases. Dougherty now told this to the Pawnees, and said the Kanzas have gone to hunt. If you should meet with them I don't wish you to attack them, but if they attack you, I don't want you to *hold down* your heads.

Agents might prevent wars among these tribes. Had the Kanza agent seized the nine horses, or taken nine others of the Kanzas, and forbid a repetition of such tresspass upon a severer penalty, and returned the horses to Pawnee Agt. Dougherty; if the latter had restored them with damages, and forbidden retaliation by the Pawnees upon a penalty of witholding some of their next year's presents, how much better it would have been than for both agents in this indirect way to encourage hostilities among them!

I sent Connor to bring hither Maj. Campbell, to adjust our business with Quick.

Saturday Sep. 25 — The Pawnees set out for their place. They are a naked wretched looking people, more fierce and brave looking than the Kanzas, but not less miserable in appearance.

Quick & I meeting some of them this morning, a chief entered into communication with Quick by signs. It was amusing to see them enquiring of each other how many nights journey they had to their homes, promising to be friendly &c. The Pawnee at length not well understanding the signs of the Delaware, invited him to the garrison where they could obtain an interpreter. I went on & informed

this post, was to apprise them, that the Government had sent the Rev. Isaac McCoy to run the Delaware lines; and to point him out to them, and advise them how they should treat him, should they meet with him. This I conceived necessary as a precautionary measure, to guard against any difficulty which might possibly ensue, should they meet with his party, without any knowledge of its character. They made professions of friendship in general, and furthermore promised, that if they met with Mr McCoy they would treat him friendly; and also would advise their young men to do the same. They informed me that they met with our Santa Fe traders last summer on the Arkansas, smoked and talked with them friendly. They left here shortly after the Council for their village, apparently much gratified, & well pleased with their visit. I thought it the more necessary that I should assemble and talk with the Pawnees, in regard to Mr. McCoy, as the Kanza Indians have recently committed a breach of the treaty of peace between them and the Pawnees, by stealing several horses, and taking one scalp; and supposing it not improbable that the Pawnees would endeavor to retaliate, in which cases their war parties in passing from the Republican to the Kansas village, might possibly fall in with the surveying party, and finding them not far distant from the Kansas village, might without being apprised of their character seriously interrupt them. After hearing of the conduct of the Kansas, I went to the Kansas Sub Agency; on finding Genl. M. G. Clark Sub Agent absent, I requested of the Kansas a return of the Pawnee horses, which they declined doing. I have not been informed that the Pawnees have made any attempt at retaliation. . . . Very Respectfully Your Obt. Servt Jno. Dougherty, Ind. Agt."—U. S. Indian Superintendency MSS., v. 6, pp., 56, 57.

Maj. Dougherty. The chief difficulty was the Pawnee had understood that the Delaware had invited him home with him. Whereas the Del. had only stated that hereafter they should meet and talk more, and that if either should go to the others place, he should be received with friendship, as also their people severally.

Sunday Sep. 26 — Was informed that Maj. Campbell had gone higher up Kanza river (which turned out to be a mistake) Sent express to intercept him, and inform him where we are. We remained in camp. In the evening Shane and Connor arrived. Campbell is sick and cant come.

Monday Sep. 27 — Took Quick and Shane and showed them where we intended to run the lines of the garrison reserve.[33]

Tuesday Sep. 28 — Took a certificate from Quick that he was satisfied with the land, the lines, &c. and he made a written request that government aid them in their new home, in making fields and houses, and in such other respects as the Govt. should perceive their wants required. He stated also that they had exchanged lands with the expectation that here their posterity would be allowed a residence as long as any of them remained on earth. In order to satisfy them that all was secure, they wished to obtain from the U. States such an instrument of writing as that by which the U. States secured land to their own white citizens. This is perhaps the first instance of an Indian tribe asking a patent for their lands.

We had the documents witnessed by several officers in the garrison, and others—and the two interpreters Connor & Shane.— Furnished Connor & Quick with eight days' rations, and, in the afternoon, started them home.

[Marginal note.] For Shane's communication relative to the wish of the Shawanoes for a school, see, page for Note Oct. 17.

Quick on leaving gave many assurances of his satisfaction and friendship, &c. among which he stated, more than once, that he had

---

33. "The treaty which had fixed the boundary of the Delaware country made no provision for reserving to the use of the United States the site of Fort Leavenworth, and to make the survey according to my instructions would have rendered the site ineligible. I therefore assumed the responsibility of making an arrangement with Quick, who acted in behalf of his people, by which a suitable tract was reserved for the use of the garrison. This measure was afterwards approved by the Secretary of War."—*History of Baptist Indian Missions* (Washington, 1840), by Isaac McCoy, p. 407.

"The McCoy party arrived at Cantonment Leavenworth in the fall of 1830. . . . A feeling of uneasiness . . . soon became manifest, for very soon it was discovered that no provision had been made for reserving the land upon which the Cantonment stood. In fact, if Issac McCoy had followed his instructions literally, he would have included the Post in the Delaware reservation. However, upon his own initiative, he arranged a conference with the Post Commander, Major William Davenport of the 6th Infantry, and the Indian Commissioner, John Quick. Through arrangements with them, a survey of the land immediately surrounding the Cantonment was made and limits were established generally paralleling the present boundaries."—*History of Fort Leavenworth*, by Elvid Hunt (Fort Leavenworth, 1926), pp. 39-41.

travelled much, but had never been treated with so much kindness by any as he had by me, and our company.

Wednesday Sep. 29 — We dined with Dr. Bryant[34] and attended to small matters.

Thursday Sep. 30 — Move our encampment a little lower down Salt creek[35] on account of obtaining food for our horses. Surveyors at work—

Friday Oct. 1 — Surveyors, I with them, worked on the lower line of the Military reserve.

Saturday Oct. 2 — Surveyors at work on the lines of the Military Reserve.

Sunday Oct. 3 — Remain in camp.

Monday Oct. 4 — On a hill not far from the garrison we discovered, as we went out a few weeks since, eight mounds or heaps of stone. This morning we examined them, and excavated one. The stones were not hewn—and were placed circular as though a building had been the design. Within was earth. We found in the one excavated human bones, apparently scorched with fire, coalburnt earth, and stone that had been in the fire. The bones were so much decayed that it could scarcely be seen to what part of the body they belonged except the sculs, some of which appeared to have belonged to adults and some to children, and a few other bones. They were situated as exhibited below. [MS. illegible] It was not a mere burying place, because the bodies had been burned. The burning was not intended to reduce the bones to ashes, because this had not been done. It was, I suppose, or rather, they were "High places" in which worship was performed anciently, agreeably to the account in Scripture of heathenish customs. Human sacrifices had been offered on them, or rather *in* them for they had been a kind of kiln, or furnace, surrounded with a stone wall and the corps and fire within. I should think that the victim had been placed upon a wooden scaffold, or among a pile of wood. The corpse, or corpses, part consumed, had lastly been covered with earth, or with vegtable substance and earth mingled.[36]

34. Dr. T. S. Bryant, surgeon of Cantonment Leavenworth.
35. Salt creek flows in a northeasterly direction across present Kickapoo township, Leavenworth county, emptying into the Missouri river.
36. "At frequent intervals along Salt Creek I have found evidences of aboriginal encampments, showing that it was a favorite haunt of prehistoric man. . . . In the northwest quarter of the northwest quarter, section 10, township 8, range 22, is a natural basin of perhaps one-half acre in extent, which was evidently at one time either a largely marshy spring or a small lake. It is situated on the east bank of Salt Creek, just south of the

We then went to examine a coal mine we had discovered a few days before, and found it an extensive stratum in the bottom of Salt creek, a little within the military reserve, and apparently very good.

Tuesday Oct. 5   Two of our horses cant be found. Packed the others, and about two o'clock left camp— In crossing the creek at our encampment one of our horses fell back from a steep bank they had to ascend, into the water. He could not rise until the pack ropes were cut, and the packs removed— packs in the water.

Five of our soldiers are with the surveyor, two of those left too drunk to be of much service. Our packs very heavy, one especially, Calvin had a difficult time to get started and to get on. Overtook surveyors, and encamped on a branch of Salt creek about six miles from garrison.

[Marginal note.] Our company now consists of 15 soldiers, and six of us who came from Fayette, in all 21 with 14 horses— The two that were taken by express to Pawnees, much reduced.

Calvin remained behind, with one of the soldiers to look for the lost horses.

During the time we have been in the vicinity of the garrison, I have had a troublesome time, again, with Maj. Davenport the Commander. He from our first entering upon this work manifested a most disobliging Spirit.

I gave him notice that we should need six additional men to make up our surveying party for our long route, and asked for such an escort as he deemed expedient. He appeared to get into a fever, insinuated that an escort was not necessary, but if one was necessary it wod. require three of his four companies. He said the commanding General Atkinson had ordered that not more than twenty men in all should accompany us. I held all my intercourse with him in writing, so that these papers might speak for themselves.

I at length informed him that I asked for no escort unless he deemed one necessary, I did not think he would have the hardihood [to] say one was not necessary. This however he ventured to say, as by this means he could take advantage of my remark, and not send any. He then endeavoured to keep me from getting the six

public highway leading to Fort Leavenworth. On the shores of this now dessicated depression have probably been found more aboriginal relics than at any other spot in Salt Creek valley. It was no doubt the site of a workshop connected with the old Kaw village [the lower of two Kansas villages on the Missouri river, both of which had disappeared when Lewis and Clark visited the region in 1804]. . . . On the high hill, along what is known as 'Sheridan's Drive,' overlooking this camp site and the whole valley, is a group of ancient mounds, one of which was opened by Mr. McCoy, the government surveyor, in 1830, being the first Indian mound ever explored in Kansas. . . . A chain of prehistoric dwelling sites extends the whole length of the Valley, and mementoes of a vanished race are turned up by every plowshare."—"Salt Creek Valley," by George J. Remsburg, Leavenworth *Times*, February 15, 1905.

additional men for the surveying company. When he found I insisted on these, and he dare not refuse, he then insisted that I should go on a week, and then send for them. I let him know that I was in immediate want of them.

For five or six days previously I had informed him that I wished to leave the neighbourhood on monday morning. He still put the matter off. On tuesday early I wrote him I wished to leave that morning. He at length wrote me that they would be detailed that afternoon. On account of his delays we had not the requisite number of persons to assist us. He seemed to wish to subject us to inconvenience.

He had wheedled Maj. Beauchamp, the Sub. agt. to say he thought there was no danger. I saw Beauchamp and when I told him the story of the affair he appeared to feel embarrassed. I stated that no company, even down to one that came in a few days ago, ever thought of going almost half way to the mountains from State of Missouri without being prepared to defend themselves against the Pawnees. The Sec. War had thought an escort necessary— Maj. Riley, who lately commanded the garrison, had thot. two companies necessary— Genl. Clark, of St. Louis—Dougherty, Campbell, M. G. Clark, and others thot. one necessary, and every body would think an escort necessary and even Davenport never ventured to say one was not necessary until from my remark, he by saying so could withhold the escort.

Having discovered the disobliging disposition of Davenport on our first coming into this country, I had despaired of a competent escort, and therefore had confer[red] with Dougherty on the best method of accomplishing the work without one. It was hoped that when the Pawnees would be absent on their huntings, we might get thro. their country undiscovered. We, therefore, in council the other day gave them no idea of our going into their country.

Wednesday Oct. 6   My son overtook us with the six men, having found their horses, and brought on the men's provisions. On crossing a little creek near camp, mired a horse, and had to pull him out of the mud with ropes, &c. Our horses so heavily packed, & the men so awkward, and some of them drunk [so] that we had some difficulty to get on. Encamped on a branch of Stranger creek. Sent a man to aid the surveyors to find the camp. He awkwardly led them much astray. I heard him blowing, & shooting, and took a man and went out and fired my gun several times, before we discovered them coming in. Found honey today—

Thursday Oct. 7. Soon after we left camp, discovered a company which turned out to be Kanzas, who had been out hunting, & trapping. The company halted in a vale out of sight and more than a mile from us, and one rode across in great haste to meet us. I gave him a small piece of tobacco. He said there was a man or more with them, who wished to speak to me. I informed him that on such a hill I would stop to speak to them. On which he rode back in equal haste, and brought a half-breed who could speak English. In the evening three more came to our camp, on Stranger creek. This creek was so deep that the chain men had to swim it.

Friday Oct. 8 We found a good crossing for our horses, on Stranger Creek, a mile above our camp, and where was a good mill seat—water enough, now, to turn a grist mill most of the time.

Found a piece of gypsum here— Found a piece some days since on waters of Missouri. Encamped again on main Stranger creek.

Saturday Oct. 9 Discovered a large flock of elk. Sent three men, one of whom fired and wounded one of them. But we did not get him. Encamped on a small branch of Stranger, 26 miles from the garrison.

Thus far the country about the garrison and this way is very well supplied with springs of water, even at this time of great drought.

Sunday Oct. 10 Remained in camp on a small branch of Stranger. Jo Jim, whom I, the other day employed to go with us as interpreter, came to us. Brot. letter from M. G. Clark S. agt. for Kanzas. Clark advises that we take care to avoid depredation from both Kanzas, and Pawnees. A quarrel, a few days ago, took place between some white men hunting bees, and consequently trespassing on the Indians' lands, and in the affray a Kanza was killed.

Jo Jim can speak no other Indian language than Kanza. I have not been able to procure a man who speaks Pawnee. This is a serious misfortune, and much increases our liability to be injured by them.

Monday Oct. 11 We encamped on the main Sautrell.

Tuesday, Oct. 12 Encamped on a branch of Sautrell.

Wednesday, Oct. 13 Reached the mound we erected, some weeks ago, at the commencement of the Delaware outlet. In running from the garrison to this place a distance of nearly 46 miles, the surveyors struck within less than two chains of the mound, —distance, also, agreed with our calculations. I was much gratified with the accuracy of our work.

We encamped a little above the mound.

Thursday Oct. 14 — Grass for our horses, is every day becoming more scarce. The season is remarkably dry. The whole country around us, has burned over today. We had encamped in a creek bottom where there was least danger of the fire approaching us, and still, it sometimes seemed as though we should not escape. We were much annoyed by smoke and more than once, had to beat out the approaching fire. We did not leave camp. Some of the soldiers erected a couple of mounds.

Friday Oct. 15 — We steered our course due west and encamped on the sources of the Soldier. Difficult to find tolerable food for our horses. Had to beat out the fire to save a little spot for our horses. In a day the whole country put on its black and dismal dress. The dust arising from the burnt grass, and the blackened weeds and shrubbery, annoys our eyes, and blackens face, hands, and clothes.

Saturday Oct. 16 — Sent Jo Jim & a soldier, with two horses, to the garrison for our papers, and for some additional supplies for the soldiers. After much searching for food for our horses, stopped in, not a good place, on another branch of Soldier creek, some two or three miles from our work.

Sunday Oct. 17 — Remain in camp on the sources of Soldier creek. *Omitted in Note, Sep. 28.* Shane informs that since my talk to the Shawanoes respecting a school, Cummins the principal U. S. Indian Agt. for the Dels. and Shawanoes, had stated to the Shawanoes, that he had been directed by the Prest. of the U. States to say to them that if they would send some of their male youths to Johnson's school, in Kentucky, it would be well for them, that they would there be instructed at a cost to the Shawanoe nation of two hundred Dollars a head.[37]

Again. If they would accept of a school in their neighborhood, he had been requested by the Methodist congregation to inform them that they should be furnished with a mission in their place.

To the former, the Shawanoes replied that they wished to send their youths to school. But the tribe were poor, and could not spare the money it would cost them to send them to Ky. Moreover they would prefer sending to a school nearer at hand.

37. See footnote No. 29.

To the latter proposition they replied, that I had lately offered them a school. They had deferred their answer until I should be returning from the tour. But they had determined to accept of my offer.

Monday Oct. 18 — Had a little rain last night—the country is exceedingly parched with drought. When we got on to the praries, the ashes from the recently burned praries, and the dust and sand raised so by the wind that it annoyed us much, the wind rising, I found that the dust was so scattered that it became impossible to perceive the trail of the surveyors, who had gone a few hours ahead of the horses. While conversing with Calvin about the course we should go, we discovered the atmosphere ahead darkening, & as it had become cloudy, we fancied that a misting rain was coming upon us, and made some inquiry respecting the security of our packs. A few minutes taught us that what we had fancied to be rain, was an increase of the rising dust, sand, and ashes of the burnt grass, rising so much and so generally that the air was much darkened, and it appeared on the open praries as though the clouds had united with the earth. Our eyes were so distressed that we could scarcely see to proceed, It was annoying to our lungs. The black burnt grass, lodging on our hands and faces, and each one rubbing his watery eyes with pain, soon occasioned a most horrid appearance, our clothes also blackening fast. The wind blew incessantly and excessively severe.

We succeeded in finding a mile stone, and steering our course as well as we could—reached a wooded creek some four miles from our encampment. This afforded a partial relief from the wind and sand. Having left the horses and men in charge of Calvin, I with another man had just found the line along which the surveyors had passed, and was about to select a camping ground, when we met a man whom the Doctor [sent] to inform me that he could not proceed with his work, & that they waited for us in a wood a mile ahead.

It being very difficult for me to look at my pocket compass I told the soldier who had just returned, to lead us back. He set off with great confidence that he could find the way and in a few minutes was leading us north instead of west. He was unwilling to be called back, and insisted that he was right. On finding the surveyors, we encamped for the residue of the day. Even in this wood, and after the wind had somewhat abated, the black ashes fell on us considerably.

Tuesday Oct. 19 — The wind and dust were severe, but not so bad as yesterday. We worked all day— late before we encamped, which was on a large creek, supposed to be Vermillion.[38]

Wednesday Oct. 20 — Calvin surveyed today— Had to turn out of our way two miles or more to find food for our horses. Encamped on a branch of Blue river.

Thursday Oct. 21 — Again had to leave our course, with the packhorses, two or three miles to find grass. Late before the surveyors came into camp. We had got into a tract of a few miles square, which had not been burned. While in the act of pitching our tents, we discovered the fire coming towards us with alarming rapidity. We set fire in the grass in self defense.

The fires around us were sublime—the long lines and the flame ascending ten, fifteen, and sometimes 20 feet high. On seeing these praries on fire in such a dry time as this we cease to wonder that the wood does not increase faster—we only wonder that a vestige of wood is left. It was in the night before the surveyors got in to camp. We have seen sign of Beavers and Otters, for a few days.

Friday Oct. 22 — Crossed the trail of about ten waggons, and perhaps 7 horses which had gone out to the Rocky mountains, and returned since last spring, in the employ of trappers of fur—white men. Crossed an old beaten path. Reached & crossed Blue river,[39] and encamped not far west of it. Saw fresh sign of Indians—suppose they have discovered us, as we saw where one had been running. Men killed two Deer— Jo Jim & the soldier sent express to the garrison seven days ago, overtook us with flour, our papers, &c. Dougherty urges me to endeavour to establish a school on Missouri above the garrison as soon as possible, and believes that a mission there would be greatly encouraged by the Indians.

Saturday Oct. 23 — Encamped on a branch of Blue river. Grass poor— Nash killed a very fat buck. Fresh sign of Indians. Seen a trail of horses—some tracks show that the Indians had been running.

Sunday Oct. 24 — Blue river is a stream of beautiful clear water 99 yards wide, strong current, averaging one foot and a half in depth. Now very low. Heads near, and above the Grand island of

---

38. Vermillion creek rises in present Nemaha county, flows across present Pottawatomie county and empties into the Kansas river near present Belvue.

39. The Big Blue river is the largest tributary of the Kansas river. It rises in present Hamilton county, Nebraska, and enters Kansas through present Marshall county; forms the boundary between present Riley and Pottawatomie counties and joins the Kansas at present Manhattan. One hundred miles of its entire length of 250 miles are in Kansas.

the great Platt. It is a limestone country. Hilly near the river. Hills much washed, stony on sides, appearing white with the white limestone, sometimes of clay appearance—vallies & level up land good.

Oct. 24.
Waters of Blue river, north of Kanza—
108 miles west of Cantonment Leavenworth. At camp.

One of our horses, a hardy little fellow that I have long had in use, Broke his left hind leg in the night, by fastening it under the root of a tree, as he attempted to descend a bank ten feet high and almost perpendicular. The sentinel was driving him and another horse back to the company, when it occurred. I suppose the man had hurried them in the dark, and being hobbled before, the horse was forced down.

The grass is so poor for our horses, which are fast failing for want of food, that we deemed it indispensable to move on, in hope of reaching the Republican fork of Kanza, where we hope to find better food. Before we left camp we gave our poor little horse a bucket of water, and a lick of salt, & left him to hop about on his three legs until he dies—I have no hope of his recovering.

Carrol, who, on the first tour, was twice found asleep on post, was again detected in the same offence last night. On the former occasions he had escaped with a mere reprimand. It now appeared necessary to punish in some way. Immediately after breakfast, the company were convened, Carrol plead guilty and begged pardon for this time only. He plead with tears, and I soon became quite willing to let him off, provided I could do it in a way that would do us no injury in future. I asked if any of his associates would be security for his better behaviour. Several spoke, but so far from even requesting his pardon, they refused to vouch for his good conduct, expressed opinion that he ought to be punished. I told him then that I would compel him to carry a pack today— This I did not so much for a punishment really, as to show him that we *would* punish him, more severely for a repetition of the offence. I directed the corporal to prepare such a load as he deemed proper, reserving to myself the right to lighten it in case I thought it too heavy. The fellow padded on, and was very attentive to business in the run—

After searching much for green grass for our horses, we encamped on a branch as we suppose of Blue river. Grass poor indeed. Men killed two deer—some of the Deer are remarkably fat.

Monday Oct. 25 — Wind very high. Proceeding about three miles we came to a few acres of bottom land on a creek that had not been burnt, and where the grass was better than we had found it for a day or two, we encamped. Dried the venison we had lately killed.

Tuesday Oct. 26 — Wind very high, scarcely allowing us to pass. Encamped on a creek of the Republican, or Panee river.[40] Crossed a trail of Indians going to our left—lately—supposed to be Otoes or, Kanzas. Saw much iron ore today.

Found a hill of iron ore—indeed the most of the stone appears to be of that quality, though most of it is sandy.

Wednesday Oct. 27. — Passed some high rocky isolated hills, in which cliffs of sandy rocks appeared to contain much iron—much of the stone looked as if it had been melted in a furnace, and when broken exhibited the appearance of newly broken pot metal. The stone is shelly—the whole exhibiting volcanick appearance. We took some very curious specimens of hollow, and mineral stones.

We found Coperas on a creek further on. And immense rocks of soapstone above ground.

We had hoped to find food for our horses better on the river than on smaller streams. Today we reached the Republican, or Pawnee river, and to our great disappointment we found it more destitute of grass than any place we had seen where wood was to be found. The river runs over a bed of sand—the banks low, and all the bottom lands are a bed of sand white and fine, and now as dry as powder ought to be. I never before saw a river along which we might not find some rich alluvial moist bottoms, on which, at this season of the year could be found green grass. But here there is, in a manner *none*.

We examined along the river for grass until satisfied that none could be found and then turned back to a creek we had passed five miles back. We met the surveyors, and reached our creek a while in the night, having kept our poor horses in motion from 9 oclock in the morning. On reaching the creek we bogued along its banks by moonshine, a half a mile, and finding a little spot not burned over, we halted. Our poor horses had miserable fare. Some places along the river for half a mile or a mile in a place, there is no timber. A grove then occurs on one side, which, at a distance ap-

---

40. See "Ferries in Kansas, Part IV—Republican River," by George A. Root, *The Kansas Historical Quarterly*, v. 3, pp. 246-248.

pears, but on reaching it, no timber is found more valuable than cotton wood and Elm.

The scarcity of wood on the river and the sandiness & poverty of the bottoms, greatly discouraged me as to the country— While the great scarcity of food for our horses made us fear that we should not be able to proceed much further.

Yesterday killed a Raccoon— today killed a Deer and Turkey.

Thursday Oct. 28 Cannot proceed on our way westward today, for want of food for our horses— Surveyors went on to run a few miles, and to cross the river with their line. We sent down and up Coperas creek in search of grass. Moved camp a mile up the creek, and guarded the horses, unhobled, along the brink of the water, where was still a little green though coarse & hard, grass that had escaped the destruction occasioned by the great drought, and the ravages of the fire.

Friday Oct. 29 Our line was seven miles ahead of us. We started early. From appearances we were afraid to cross the river lest we should not be able to get food for our horses, and proceeded up a creek on the N. East side of the river, where after much searching we found a tolerable place, for these times.

Saturday Oct. 30 Started early, crossed the river—travelled and searched for grass till after sun set. Found a pretty good place. Surveyors urged on by our necessity for grass, made eleven miles. Encamped half a mile south west of the river, on a little creek. Our western line has now passed near the river 18 miles. The river averages in width 140 yards—though where measured it was only 126 yards. banks low—no rocks—all sand along it—its waters turbid—about half the bed covered with water—now very low average of water say 14 inches—tolerably brisk current. Prarie bottoms four or five miles wide—but little hill back—land tolerably good, except the sand near the river. Quick sand in the river. Epsom salts are deposited in the sand beaches so as to be perceiveable both to the eye, and by the taste. Pass two isolated ledges, or heaps of iron looking sand stone, one on each side of the river. Picked up pieces of an earthen pot, made by the aborigines in olden times. A few days ago I found the iron and brass parts of a short gun, in the Prarie—such as are much used by the Indians near the mountains. The wood part had been burned with the burning of the praries—one of our men found a knife. Night before last Jo Jim caught two Beavers in steele traps that he set. Saw tracks of horses & mules—

Indian sign—yesterday & today—not fresh. Many old tracks of Elks, tracks of one drove of Buffaloe. Crossed today three or four old paths leading to and from the river. Neither of our interpreters can tell whether we are below or above what is called the *old* Pani village,[41] though both are half-Indians, and have been in this country before. We know that we are *below*, but how far below we are at a loss to judge. Killed many fat turkies within two or three days. I shot one this evening.

Sunday Oct. 31 Remain in camp. Four men at a time, guarding the horses, and keeping them along the banks of a little creek now dry, where they find a little grass. At the commencement of the high land of the river, a mile from our camp, is a Cliff, two or three hundred yards long, of very coarse sandstone undergoing decomposition. The process has rendered the appearance of the pile romantic in the extreme, excavations ready to pull in immense rocks,—huge pillars standing alone, 15 or 20 feet high, castles resting on a kind of tripod, &c. are exhibited to the fancy. The stone is generally of a reddish yellow, parts, however, are white sandstone.

Monday November 1 We travelled about 4½ miles, and finding better grass than usual, encamped about 12 oclock— Surveyors went on further, & returned to camp. Passd. a very large encampment of Indians, made last spring—there must have been several hundreds of them. Killed six or seven rattle snakes on the open prarie. Killed two Deer & several turkies.

Tuesday Nov. 2 Dug out a root which bears a fruit like a small squash, the size of a pare on a vine resembling a squash vine. The root is three feet & a half long before branching and [blank in MS.] inches in diameter. I shot a deer, but had not time to follow it to recover it. Jo Jim caught a beaver, caught a badger yesterday and another today. Saw much Indian sign— Saw also Buffaloe & Elk sign. Left the river bottom. Country high, pretty fertile— Limestone land. Encamped on a creek of the river. Grass very poor—water extremely bad. Light of prarie fire discovered to N. West. Johnson, was lost and slept out last night. We discharged

41. McCoy's reference is doubtless to the Pawnee Indian village thought to have been established in present Republic county, S. 3, T. 2, R. 5W. The surveying party was below this location. John C. McCoy, a member of the party, states in his article "Survey of Kansas Indian Lands," *Kansas Historical Collections*, v. 4, p. 305: "On the 29th of October we reached the Republican, one hundred and thirty-four miles from Cantonment Leavenworth. This stream was called by the Kansas Indians Pa-ne-ne-tah, or Pawnee river. The river was twelve chains wide where we reached it, at a point near the present town of Clifton, in Washington county. Crossing to the south side, our course took us past near the present site of the town of Concordia. The terminus of our line, one hundred and fifty miles west of the initial points, was in what are now the limits of Smith county, on the top of a ridge west of Oak creek, not many miles from the present town of Cawker City."

several guns last night and this morning to notify him where we were.

Wednesday Nov. 3d. Jo Jim wounded a buffaloe, and others wounded another though neither could be found to day, and we have not time to stop to look after them tomorrow. Saw a flock of Antelopes. Old camping places of Indians seen. Encamped on a water of Solomon river.[42]

Thursday Nov. 4 Saw two Buffaloes early—did not stop to look after them. Saw a village of prarie dogs. Saw antelopes. In the evening saw five Buffaloes—wounded two, but had not time to follow them. Travelling in a small part of the country which had not been burnt, we were stopped by the fire. We set fire in self-defence, but had barely time to get our horses on to the small place we had burned in time to escape disaster from the approaching fires. For a while we were surrounded by flame, tho. not near enough to injure us, and enveloped in smoke. Encamped on a water of Solomon.

Friday Nov. 5 Completed the line of the outlet to 150 miles, and stopped. For some days we have discovered that our horses were failing so fast, that we must soon return, or lose them all. We have therefore risen before day & made extraordinary efforts to accomplish as much as possible while the horses could live. We are sure that we ought not to proceed further, and hope to get our horses back. We are beyond all Indian villages, and 50 miles, or more, into the country of Bufaloes—

Fired on a flock of Antelopes. Passed another Village of Prarie dogs. I fired on one, anxious to examine him, but he disappeared in his hole.

After we completed our survey, we turned on to a creek, and were looking for an encampment—the day calm & fair—when suddenly the atmosphere became darkened by a cloud of dust and ashes from the recently burnt Praries occasioned by a sudden wind from the north. It was not three minutes after I had first discovered its approach, before the sun was concealed, and the darkness so great, that I could not distinguish objects more than three or four times the length of my horse. The dust, sand, & ashes, were so dense that one appeared in danger of suffocation. The wind driving into ones eys seemed like destroying them.

---

42. See "Ferries in Kansas, Part V—Solomon River," *The Kansas Historical Quarterly,* v. 3, pp. 339-340.

I was more than a quarter of a mile from the pack-horses, with three men, only one of whom was immediately with me, when the storm commenced. Had I not feared that Calvin, with the horses and company, would continue to travel to reach me, and lose himself, I should have sought a low place and concealed my face until the storm had somewhat abated. I led on my horse, having the man who was with me to whip him on, sought the bank of the creek on which I had left the horses and proceeded on it until I reached them. Calvin had prudently halted in a low place, and was waiting for the abatement of the storm. We had great difficulty in making ourselves tolerably comfortable. One tent was prostrated after it was pitched. Mine could scarcely be made to withstand the wind, by tieing to trees.

The Doctor had taken three men and gone to examine some mineral hills. They sheltered for a while beneath a bank of the creek and about dusk reached our camp.

The storm commenced sun three quarters of an hour high in the evening, and blew tremendously all night. It had abated a little by morning. The dust was most annoying at the commencement. There was no clouds over us.

The termination of our line was about four miles north of Solomon river, in a district remarkable for minerals. Since we came into the vicinity of Republican, or Pawnee river, wood has been more scarce than previously. The creeks, however, are all wooded. Fuel would be sufficient for a considerable population—chiefly Elm, cottonwood, & willow near the rivers— farther from the rivers is more wood on the creeks, and of different kinds.

Some of the country between Pawnee & Solomon is of limestone character—though stone scarce generally—assuming more & more of a level character as we proceed westward— Soil generally good —some rich—other of 2d. quality. Water not so plenty nor so good as east of Pawnee.

We stopped 210 miles west of the State of Missouri. The country *is* habitable thus far.

Saturday Nov. 6. After a severe night, on us & our horses, which in addition to the wind and cold, were almost perishing with hunger, we set off as early as possible—the day freezing cold, and the wind excessive. Killed a poor Buffaloe on Solomon. Took a part of it. Searched much for grass. Travelled about 12 miles, and encamped on the north side of Solomon. Found a little spot not burnt—food miserable, yet better than we have had for a while. Passed some very large encamping places of Indians some made the last summer, and others longer ago. Many buffaloe sculs were placed together at one of them.

Sunday Nov. 7 — Remain in camp. Solomon is here about 70 yards wide, now lowwater at present, where the current is brisk, say 25 yards, shallow on ripples. Water transparent.—its shores, or rather sand beaches whitened with a deposit of salt, and in places, glauber salts. Glauber salts are deposited on the sand beaches of Pawnee river, & on the banks of [blank in MS.] creek where we terminated our survey.

About half a mile above our camp is a salt spring which is a great natural curiosity. (See description on other side).[43] Fresh horse track seen, either Indians, or a wild horse is near.

Monday Nov. 8 — We started early, & travelled till a half past three oclock— Encamped on the south side of Solomon, poor grass. Killed a Deer. Passed where Indians had been encamped hunting & trapping,—about 3, or 4 miles from where we had spent the two last nights. They had left there yesterday or early this morning—went towards Panee river. They had probably discovered us. Passed many old and large camps. Much sign of Bufaloe.

We had proceeded about four miles a little east of S. east, when we again came into a limestone country.

Tuesday Nov. 9 — Made about 22 miles and encamped near Solomon, crossed a little of running water, which was salt. Killed a deer, & Badger.

43. McCoy probably intended to add a description of the salt spring but failed to do so and there is only a blank page in the Journal. However, he described it as follows in his *History of Baptist Indian Missions*, p. 411: "On the Solomon river, a middle branch of the Kauzau, is a salt spring, which is a great natural curiosity. About one hundred yards from the bank of the river, in an extensive level prairie, is a mound of stone, formed by a deep ravine which surrounds it; it is one hundred and seventy yards in circumference at its base, and it rises above the bottom of the ravine thirty feet, and is level on the top, with a diameter of one hundred and twenty feet. The ravine, on one side, is about forty yards wide, and on the other ten. The summit of the mound is about a foot and a half higher than the adjacent plain. No stone of any kind is seen in the vicinity of the place, except that which composes the mound, which appears to be a secondary, shelly, and porous limestone. The sides of the mound, being stone, form a striking contrast with the outer bank of the ravine, which is only earth. The salt water forms a stagnant pool in the centre of the mound, fifty-five feet in diameter, and rising to a perfect level with the summit, so that a wind from any quarter causes the water to run over the opposite side of the basin. About half-way up one side issues salt water, which runs off in a small rivulet into Solomon river. Along this rivulet, and generally on the sides of the mound, salt is chrystallized in such quantities that it might be collected for use. The pool on the top is deep. Solomon river is, by the Kauzaus, called Nepaholla—meaning, water on the hill—and derives its name from this fountain; but the fountain itself is by them called Ne Wôh'kôn'daga—that is, 'Spirit water.' The Kauzaus, Pawnees, and other tribes, in passing by this spring, usually throw into it, as a kind of conjuring charm, some small article of value." Waconda, or Great Spirit Spring, is about two and one half miles southwest of present Cawker City in Mitchell county.

Wednesday　Traveled east about nine miles, and then ten miles
Nov. 10　E. S. E. Encamped on a water of Solomon (as supposed) Killed two deer & a badger. No limestone for 12 miles back—occasionally mounds & hill sides of iron looking sand stone. Soil good, for a few miles back resting upon sand of white & red colour, so that banks resembled an old lime kiln.

Thursday　So foggy that we could not see from one end of the line
Nov. 11　of company to the other. Set pocket compass, my son before, and I in the rear would observe the variation from the true course by the bend of our line. Often stopped to notice the compass. Finding this troublesome, and that the wind blew pretty constantly the same direction, I tied a ribbond to the end of my riding stick, and guided by the direction of the flag proceeded east until after noon, then bore southeast down Nishcoba—or Deep water.[44] Fell in with a flock of about 70 Elks. Killed three, and encamped on Deepwater.

Friday　Travelled Southeastwardly down Nishcoba, and en-
Nov. 12　camped on its south bank. We had intended to have travelled east from Solomon, until we fell in with Panie river, & made two attempts, but found that we should be thrown on to the smaller branches of streams, where we could find less food for our horses. Saw many elks. Killed a deer. Four Kanzas came to our camp & remained thro the night.

Saturday　Last night we had rain. The country here is moist, and
Nov. 13　consequently more pleasant to us, & better for the horses. Left Deepwater—travelled east—reached Panee river about one—proceeded down it east, and encamped on the point near the Junction of Panee & Smokey hill rivers. A horse tired and was left behind. Five Kanzas came to us and spent the night. Almost every place burnt over. Little food for our horses.

Sunday　Remain in camp. Found & brot. in the tired horse. Put
Nov. 14　our horses on to the south side of Smokyhill river, where we found a spot of bottom land not burnt. An old Kanza came to camp, & staid most of the day.

Monday　Crossed Republican river, & proceeded down Kanza on
Nov. 15　the north side. Two Indians, one an old man, overtook us running, in high state of perspiration, said a great company, returning from their Buffaloe hunt, had come to our camp since we

---

44. Chapman creek, flowing into the Smoky Hill river near present Chapman, Dickinson county.

started, and these two had run after us (some three or four miles) to speak to us, & to get a little tobacco. We gave them some, & left them. A horse tired. Left two men to bring him on, who reached camp before dark. Encamped near Kanza river.

Tuesday Nov. 16 — Branded our tired horse with a stirrip iron, and left him at camp. Encamped on Black paint creek, near an encampment of Indians, one of whom I hired to go and bring on, if he could, the tired horse to the Kanza agency.

Wednesday Nov. 17 — Met several Kanza hunters—give all we meet a little tobacco. Encamped on Kageshingah, on crossing crk.

Thursday Nov. 18 — Encamped on a small creek near Kanza river.

Friday Nov. 19 — Reached the Kanza agency. Obtained corn for our hungry and poor horses— spoke to Clark, the Agent respecting a school, &c. for the Kanzas— Made no definite arrangement. Clark promised to receive the tired horse.

Saturday Nov. 20 — Messrs. McCallister & Johnson, Methodist preachers, arrived last night. They purpose establishing a school &c. among the Kanzas. They, or, some others of that society had been here previously. I knew nothing of their intentions until since I spoke to Clark yesterday. They have, also, a few days since, made proposals to the Shawanoes to furnish them with a school, &c. I told them that our Society had made formal proposals to the Sec. War, a year and a half ago, to establish a mission among the Kanzas. Also, that I had spoken to the Shawanoes on my way up, & expected to receive their answer on my way down. But, I wished not to throw any obstacle in their way. They united in supposing there would be no disagreeing between them and us—manifested no solicitude about our propositions, and spake with a good deal of confidence relative to carrying forward their propositions. I think they will *not* likely do much for the Kanzas. Their circumstances are such as to require the exercise of faith & patient perseverance, in labourious, and often discouraging operations, rather beyond what we can expect from that denomination.[45]

45. Two Methodist missions were established in what is now Kansas in 1830. The Shawnee Methodist mission was located near present Turner, Wyandotte county. It was moved to present Johnson county in 1839. Thomas Johnson was the first missionary. His brother, William Johnson, was the first Methodist missionary to the Kansas Indians and evidence supports the theory that he began his work among them at the Kansas agency. Marston G. Clark, U. S. subagent at the Kansas agency wrote from that place to U. S. Indian Superintendent William Clark on November 21, 1830: ". . . Mr. McAllister & Mr. Johnson and myself have selected a site for a school house near the Agency. Those gentlemen say their school operations will commence at this place in a very short time. I am pleased with those gentlemen, and their views on the subject of teaching Indian children."—U. S. Indian Superintendency MSS., v. 6, pp. 78, 79.

I left the Doctor to bring on the horses and company generally by way of the garrison, where we have business, after he shall have rested and recruited the horses two or three days, and Calvin & I set out by way of Shawanoe Agency, taking two of the stronger of our horses. We had rain—no tent—fixed up a blanket, which partially sheltered us. No grass for our horses—had corn brot. with us from the agency.

Sunday Nov. 21   Passed the new settlement forming by the Delawares on their land. Spent a few minutes with Anderson, their aged principal Chief. He, and his people are much pleased with their new country, as he declared to me. Govt. has not assisted in removal. They, anxious to come set out upon their own resources. Most of the tribe have either arrived, or are on the road. All will be here in the Spring. There is much difficulty, and some scolding among the agents, & superintendent, &c. about furnishing the Delawares. Some hopes had been entertained of profitable business in removing them, that are disappointed, now the Indians have removed themselves. Govt. has not furnished provisions, except to a very small amount, and nothing will be done by the Sec. War, or the superintendent until I make my report, and an appropriation be made by Congress for expenses of that concern.

Monday Nov. 22   Agreeably to my promise gave notice to the Shawanoes that as they recollected what had passed as we went out, and as I had then promised to call on them on my return, I had done so—because I was the same man every day. If they had any thing to say to me, I was there ready to hear. Only Cornstalk & Perry were present—the others were absent from their villages.

They replied that, since I had passed Mr. Johnson—(the Methodist) had offered them a school, &c. They had answered him, that schools had been offered them repeatedly. They could not accept all—for there would not be room for them. They had been pleased with the talk I had given them relative to the manner of conducting schools, &c. and I had long been experienced in Indian matters, and they had therefore determined to accept of my offer. (This was *not* the time that the agent, Cummins, spoke to them for the Methodists, to whom they gave a similar answer.) They then said to me we are pleased with your views of the subject, and with your proposition, and cannot do otherwise than accept your offer— We do now accept it, & that matter is settled.[46]

46. There seems to have been a lack of agreement among the Indians themselves on the subject of the proposed mission; also a tendency to accept the proposal of the last one to solicit their consent. Richard Cummins, Indian agent, Delaware & Shawnee agency, wrote

Major Campbell, the subagent—in whose house we were, and who is my particular friend on this business, was transported with gladness that these two Chiefs had so cordially agreed to have a school, &c. Fish, and others were known to be friendly, and no unwillingness had been feared except from these two Chiefs. Campbell gave them his hand, and a present. I must now look out for missionaries & means, to build up affairs here, as soon as possible. May the Lord provide!

Sister Shane is sick—thinks she will not live long—has lately been very unwell,—wept freely when I conversed with her—said in her severe illness, she desired greatly to see me once more in the world, and now her requests had been granted. She did not fear to die, &c. Sick as she was she manifested a laudable solicitude for the establishing of a mission among the Shawanoes.

I made myself acquainted with the agency difficulties relative to the removal, and the provisioning of the Delawares, and promised to be the friend of Campbell on this, and some other Indian matters, when I should go to Washington. I also promised to attend to some of Shane's requests. Left Campbell's at 2 o'clock P. M. and lodged in Independence.

Tuesday, Nov. 23, at 8 o'clock P. M. slept at Young's— Wednesday, 24 slept at Davis', and on Thursday, Nov. 25, at 8 o'clock P. M. entered the dear circle of my family. For favours to them, and to us who have been absent, let me again erect an Ebenezer.— I was absent One hundred and two days.

to U. S. Indian Superintendent William Clark on January 13, 1831: "I have the satisfaction to state to you, that agreeable to your wishes expressive in a letter dated the 8th Nov. 1830, handed me by the Rev. Mr. McAllister & Thos. Johnson who were appointed to establish a school among the Shawnee Indians, that we have been able to get the consent of the Chiefs to establish a school among what is called Fish's or Jackson's band. The managers of the institution intend instructing the Indian children the arts of mechanism as well as that of literature. Mr. Johnson is at this time making arrangements, and I think shortly after the winter breaks will have the school in operation. I have great hope, that after this school is got into operation, the Indians within my Agency will not be so much opposed to complying with the wishes of the Government, in the arts of civilization."—U. S. Indian Superintendency MSS., v. 6, p. 96.

Ferries in Kansas

PART XI—GREAT NEMAHA RIVER

GEORGE A. ROOT

THE Great Nemaha river is formed by two branches—the northern and longer rising in Panama township, Lancaster county, Nebraska, in T. 7 N., and R. 8 E. The stream's course is to the southeast, through the northeast corner of Pawnee county, through Richardson county towards the southeast and east, where it is joined by the south branch. The Kansas branch (south fork) is formed by the junction of Hickory and Tennessee creeks in Nemaha county, which unite at a point about two miles south of Seneca, and flow northward slightly to the east of Seneca, past the village of Taylor Rapids and on into Nebraska, at a point near the eastern boundary of Range 13 E. The northern branch is joined in Richardson county, at the eastern edge of the city of Salem. From there the Great Nemaha flows in a slightly southeastern direction for about thirty miles to reach a point about fourteen miles east of the junction of its two branches, and then crosses the Kansas line three separate times within a space of about two miles, near the northeast corner of S. 5, T. 1, R. 18 E., on the old Diminished Iowa Indian reservation. From there the stream continues to the north and east for about five miles to join the Missouri river at a point about two miles north of the Kansas-Nebraska boundary.[1] The south branch of the river is approximately fifty miles in length, while the larger one is about 150 miles long. The Great Nemaha usually has a brisk current. It is broken at convenient intervals by rapids, which generally fall over rocks, and has sufficient fall to furnish power for milling purposes if dammed or otherwise controlled. The same can be said of nearly all its tributaries.[2]

The earliest mention of the river we have discovered is in the account of S. H. Long's expedition, in 1818-1820, in which it is spoken of as the Great Nemahaw.[3] Prince Maximilian, in the account of his travels, mentions the stream as the Great Nemawha.[4] Father Paul J. DeSmet, in his *Letters and Sketches*, mentions the stream in 1841-1842.[5] The word "nemaha" in the Otoe language signifies

---

1. Everts & Kirk, *Atlas of Nebraska*. Everts, *Atlas of Kansas*.
2. Parker, *Kansas and Nebraska Handbook*, p. 143.
3. Thwaites, *Early Western Travels*, v. 15, p. 132.
4. Ibid., v. 24, p. 110.
5. Ibid., v. 27, p. 227.

"water of cultivation," "ne," meaning water; "maha," denoting planting or cultivation.[6]

Very little is found in Kansas documentary history relating to ferries on the Great Nemaha, but from scattered data it is evident that an early-day trader named Roy or LeRoy operated the first ferry. George J. Remsburg, in a sketch of the Nemaha river, says that this early-day trader was John Baptiste LeRoy, of French-Canadian parentage, and originally from the French settlements in Illinois. The town of LeRoy, Ill., was named for the family. LeRoy was an interpreter for the Iowas, Sacs and Foxes, and also a trader with them, and it is thought that he may have come with the Indians in 1837. Their reservation embraced portions of what is now Brown and Doniphan counties, Kansas, and Richardson county, Nebraska. LeRoy married an Iowa woman and established himself on the Nemaha river near the mouth of the creek that bears his name. It is thought that he died among the Indians, living near St. Joseph, Mo., as a small stream coming out of the Blacksnake Hills south of that city is still known as Roy's Branch.

LeRoy had a trading establishment near the mouth of Roy's creek, in Brown county. It stood on the side of a hill overlooking both streams. His ferry was close to the north line of the state. This locality was probably the scene of a sanguinary battle between the Iowas and Otoes on one side and the Pawnees on the other. Mark E. Zimmerman, of White Cloud, learned of this battle from members of the Iowa tribe. To the Iowas the Nemaha Roy's creek site is known as the "Old Pawnee Village." It is thought to have been occupied as early as 1765.

Roy's ferry was located on a much-traveled route, and there must have been some sort of a crossing here at the time Kansas territory was created, for the first session of the territorial legislature established roads leading to that locality. It is said that most of the residents of this locality did their trading at Rulo, Neb.

In 1860, John W. Foreman and D. Vanderslice were granted authority by the territorial legislature to maintain a ferry across the Great Nemaha at a point near Elisha's creek. This act gave them a fifteen-year privilege for two miles above and two miles below.[7] No further history of this enterprise has been located.

Territorial roads had been established leading to the site of Roy's ferry as early as 1855, the first starting from the Wyandotte ferry

6. *Ibid.*, v. 15, p. 132.
7. *Private Laws*, Kansas, 1860, special session, p. 288. *House Journal,* 1860, special session, p. 461. *Council Journal*, 1860, special session, pp. 521, 538, 539.

on the Kansas river, and running by way of Delaware, Leavenworth, Kickapoo, Port William, Doniphan, Iola, and Iowa Point, to a point on the Kansas-Nebraska line, opposite Roy's ferry on the Great Nemaha.[8] Another ran from Doniphan to the Kansas-Nebraska line, via Roy's ferry to Iowa Point. James F. Foreman, Charles Blakesley and S. G. Fish were named as commissioners to view and mark out this thoroughfare.[9] Another road was projected by this same legislature, to start from a point opposite St. Joseph, Mo., via Whitehead, Great Nemaha agency, to Cramer's crossing of the Great Nemaha river, but apparently failed of passage.[10]

So far as is known this is the extent of ferrying on the Great Nemaha river in Kansas.

In the preparation of this story the writer has drawn heavily on newspaper articles written about the Great Nemaha river by George J. Remsburg.

8. *General Statutes*, Kansas, 1855, pp. 950, 951, 954.
9. *Laws*, 1857, p. 186.
10. *House Journal*, 1857, p. 46.   *Council Journal*, 1857, pp. 80, 89, 111, 112, 119.

Letters of a Kansas Pioneer
1855-1860
(Concluded)

THOMAS C. WELLS

Manhattan, K. T. Jany 3d, 1858.

My Dear Mother,

I RECEIVED you letter of 6th, ult. with pleasure, about ten days ago. I am glad to hear that you have a new minister settled in Peacedale & Kingston and that you like him so well. I hope he will be a man that will *wear well,* it is too frequently the case that a minister is liked, admired and applauded for a few Sabbaths, until the *novelty* is worn off, and then he is regarded as commonplace, disliked and perhaps scandalized, until he comes to the conclusion that he is doing little or no good in his present situation, asks for a dismission, and leaves the church to hunt another pastor. I would like to have father write as often as he can, but I do not know by what process of reasoning, you came to the conclusion that your "letters are not very interesting." I am sure I have never written anything that ought to lead you to think so, and, indeed, I do not think so. I can certainly give you the credit of being a good correspondent; you answer more punctually and generally write *fuller* letters than any other correspondent that I have. I hope you will continue to do the same.

It costs no more to send a letter to Kansas than to Kingston, and if you cannot write a long letter and make it interesting, we are glad to get a short one.

We had no public thanksgiving in Kansas. You would have liked it no better than we should have done, to have had "all your children" there on Thanksgiving day.

You ask my opinion about fathers building in Wakefield; I will give it and you may take it for what it is worth. *No, not at present;* and I will give my reasons. In the first place you are *now* very comfortably situated as you are. it will be time enough to build when you leave the bank, and *then* you may be better able to do so; you might hire a tenement while building. Secondly, I would advise no man to build a house if obliged to run largely in debt in order to finish it; better hire than do that; make your money before you spend it, is a good motto. Thirdly if you put all the money that you have, and more too, into a house, and then leave the bank I do not see how you are a going to *live;* you will have *nothing* laid by for a rainy day, and *nothing* to do any kind of business upon at present. If my reasoning is not good please give me better reasons to the contrary, and oblige.

No one, certainly, would rejoice more to have father settled in a home of his own, free from debt and embarrassment, and in a fair way to get a comfortable living, than myself; but, really, if he leaves the bank I do not see *how* he *can do so* in *Wakefield.*

He certainly would not attempt to live by farming or gardening in *W.,* he would have ten chances of success here to one there, at that kind of business. *What would he do?* I would have written in the same strain if *I* had been in any other part of the country than Kansas, even if I were living in W. I think I should have *said* substantially the same. Nevertheless, I did hope that if father ever left the bank you would all come and live near us. I would not *advise* you to *move* here *just now.* Wait and see what congress does for us this winter, and if our troubles are amicably settled I would like to have father come and make us a visit in the spring, and *see the country for himself,* he can then decide whether it would be wise to come here with his family. And now I will just state what appear to me, to be some of the advantages you would have in coming here instead of staying in W. You would be near at least *one* of your sons and his wife, whom I doubt not you would like as a daughter. You will have forty acres of good land, near a market (which I have already offered you) to commence upon. If you intend to get your living by farming you will have the benefit of my experience of two or three years which is certainly worth *something* and you would have to expend less, for a team and farming implements than you would in any other place as we could to *some extent* use the *same.* You could live with us until you could build a house for yourself. Being freed in a great measure from the demands of fashion, and the customs of a too aristocratic and extravagant east, your wants would be less, and you could live more *simply* and *cheaply,* yet no less *comfortably,* and not *lose caste* in the best of society around you. For the same reason I have written briefly &, I think, to the point, and with the feelings, if not the show of kindness and respect.

Manhattan, K. T. Feby 27th, 1858.

My Dear Mother

I have just finished writing a letter to Lizzie and will now commence one to you. We were very glad to get your last, began to think you were putting off writing a long time, and think it about time we heard from you again. Should have written this, in answer to your last, before, had I not just written to Herbert. Why do you most always put "Susy" in quotation marks when you write of Lizzie's little girl? Do you wish to hint of another "Susy" to me? Perhaps *you* think I would have done well to have tried to get *her* for my wife; *perhaps* I should, but I don't think so. I am well satisfied with the one that I have, and I think you would like her well if you were acquainted with her. I hope you may be sometime. I have never had reason to regret being married to her, and surely I have had time to get acquainted, *now*. I cannot help laughing when I think of my being uncle and you grandmother &c., it seems odd enough. I hope Henry will not confine himself so closely to his business as to injure his health, *that* is worth more than money. We hear from him every few months. We too have had a very mild and pleasant winter, but not so warm as the papers state that it has been in the east, so that flowers will bloom out of doors, we do not want it so warm as that in the winter, it cannot be healthy. Am glad to hear that the people continue to like Mr. Brown. What kind of a minister is Albert Palmer? Why does not Theodore write us? Does he improve any at school?

I am sorry that you and Herbert have been so much troubled with colds and coughs, you ought to be careful; that is the frequent cause and commencement of consumption. You had better come out here and live. I will warrant that you would not be much troubled with colds in this country. Glad to hear that father is so well. I thought from what you wrote that he was going to write soon and have been expecting a letter from him every week but none has come yet. I thought "Susy" and Atmore were pretty good friends before I left R. I. "Things looked like it" then. I *did* think from what you wrote that father thought of leaving the bank soon if he built a house in W. If he is really determined to spend the remainder of his days in W. and can build a house on his land without running in debt for it, perhaps it is the best thing that he can do. It would certainly be much pleasanter for him to have a home of his own, and as you say he could cultivate his land much more proffitably.

I have got any quantity of work to do this spring. Twenty five acres to plow and plant, a mile and three quarters of fence to build, &c. &c. The first two or three years are always pretty hard in a new country, but it is getting old very fast. It is nothing like what it was two years ago. (Feby 28th.) We are anxiously waiting to know what Congress will do in refference to Kansas at this session. The Lecompton Constitution, if confirmed by congress, will *never* be submitted to by the people of Kansas, *civil war first*. If Calhoun gives certifficates of election to the free state officers elected on 4th of Jany under that Constitution all may be right even if that swindle passes congress, for they will *all* of them immediately *resign* and leave the thing *dead,* without an executive department, and a *new* constitution *formed by the people* will be put in operation. We do not despair of a free state yet. The people of Kansas *will not* be the slaves of the administration or the South. There are wise heads here as well as in Washington and the plans of the slave power for our subjugation will be thwarted, *peaceably* if they can be, *forceably* if they must—*at all events Kansas must be free.*

Ella joins with me in sending love and hopes father will come and see us.

Do write often as you can and tell us how you all are &c. &c.

Yours very truly

Thomas C. Wells

Dear parents,   Manhattan, K. T. Mar. 13th 1858.

I received a letter from Mother yesterday morning and hasten to reply.

We were indeed surprised to hear that Theodore was in Beloit, it was entirely news to us. I hope it will prove to be a good move for him. It does seem most too bad that he should be obliged to leave school.

I am glad that Mr. Brown is the means of doing so much good, and that there is so much religious interest manifested in the societies over which he is pastor. I think it was unkind in you to write what you did about "five children" and as soon as they were old enough to be useful and to be company for you, if one should go to Europe, another to Africa &c., "you would then know how good it is." Would it please you better to have me come to R. I. and suffer with some disease of the lungs and die, than to remain in Kansas and enjoy excellent helth? I know that you would *not* have me do so. Were I sure that I should enjoy good health, in the east, I would sell out tonight if I had opportunity and come and settle near you; indeed, I would not have remained here so long as I have, would not have come back at all the last time did I not feel that justice to myself demanded it.

Wife and I, both of us frequently mourn that we are so far away from all our relations and would be glad to live nearer to them, but dare not on account of my health.

We have very good society here and we are pleasantly situated and like the country *very much*, and were you and some of Ella's friends out here would have no wish to leave.

Had I remained in R. I. I do not believe that I should be living now, and I dare not go back there to live, but as I could not do that I have done the next best thing that I could. I have tried my best to have you come and live near us. I have offered to pay father's expenses back, if he should come to see the country and not like it, have offered him land if he would come here and live, and to share my house with him until he could build one for himself; and he has not taken any notice of my propositions, made no reply to my letter. I do not think it is kind in him to do thus. I hope to get a letter from him soon.

You did not say that you were glad or sorry to get Ella's likeness, I would not have had it sent you did I not think you would like to have it. We would be *very glad* to have your likenesses. Will you not send them to us?

It was rainy this morning and I drew a plat of some of the sections near me and marked the names of the claim-holders on it, for father. I know *about* where a good many others live, but cannot tell *exactly* what quarter section they are on. I have written the names of a few that I am not certain about with pencil In the township east of me the *red* dotted lines indicate fractions and I do not know just what lots the claimants hold, where I have written their names with a pencil; they have a right to take four forty acre lots, in any shape they choose, if they are contiguous to each other. Manhattan city *proper* comprises those lots that I have marked thus (1) but the corporation extends one mile and three quarters north of the Kansas on the township line, and from thence directly east to the Blue river including all between those lines and the river. All the claim holders within the corporation have to pay a corporation tax of course. March 14th. The lines are so faint on this paper that I cannot see to follow them by candle light, but I think you can read what I have written, and I will not attempt to write it over again.

I will send you several copies of the minutes of the General Association of Congregational Ministers and Churches in Kansas.

It is quite warm here now and some of our farmers have commenced plowing—I shall commence, soon. Ella is not very well, she frequently expresses the wish that father would come and see us, and that some of my folks or her folks or both would come and settle near us.

Do write often. You do not know how much we enjoy a letter from home.   Yours truly and affectionately

Thomas C. Wells

Manhattan, K. T. May 22/58

My dear father & mother,

I received your long letter, mailed Apr. 3d, two or three weeks ago, and shall endeavor to answer it, as nearly as may be, in the order in which it was written. You must not think that I am provoked, or angry, or even "spunky" because I have not answered it before, the truth is that I have been so *very busy,* plowing, planting &c that I have not been able to find time to write. Neither do I *expect* father to leave his business often to write me a long letter, but I have thought that he might frequently add a few words to mother's letters, without spending a great deal of time to the neglect of other duties.

What mother wrote about "the children all going away" &c. was written as "your father says" &c as though *he* would have me feel that it was unkind in me to leave you and go so far away, however I am satisfied from his letter that he does not blame me for so doing.

I was not aware that I was usually very "*sensative* at any remark in mother's letters." I know that mother has "many cares," and that she does not generally enjoy very good health, though I was not aware that it had been unusually poor "for six months past" and am sorry to hear it, and I do not wonder that, sometimes, when sick or tired, or low spirited she should write things which she would not at another time, things which would convey false impressions, and that she should omit to speak of things that she had intended to notice; I would *not* blame her in the least for this, I doubtless do the same things myself, and for like reasons; you do not seem to have considered that I have a great deal to do, work hard, and frequently get *very tired*, am sometimes *most sick*, and once in a while though seldom feel a little "*blue*." You must remember too that I cannot always tell just what feelings may prompt a certain expression in your letters. I frequently mention things that I notice in your letters, which I do not understand or do not like, in order that you may explain if you feel disposed, and when you see anything objectionable in my letters I expect you to do the same.

As for writing a "blow up" or being "spunky" or anything of that sort it was farthest from my thoughts and I hope you will so consider it. The hardest expression that I have used in writing home was "unkind" and I know not how I could have used a milder term and expressed my feelings. Perhaps if either of you had at my age been obliged to leave home and be separated so far from your parents, you would have mourned over the necessity as much as I, and after thinking over every plan that might suggest itself for getting them to settle near you should at last make a proposition to them which you thought it *posible* might be excepted, perhaps I say, you would have thought it a little "unkind" if when they answered your letter they did not even notice your proposition. I am willing to think, however, that the neglect to notice was unintentional and pass it by.

I give mother the credit of being generally a very good correspondent and have wondered, sometimes, that she should write so long and so interesting letters as she has done and I hope will continue to do. If she sees anything that she does not like in my letters I hope she will mention it and I assure you I shall take it most kindly. I do wish I could see you both and talk with you. I hope I shall be able to make a visit east with Ella before many years but hope first that some way will be provided so that father can come and make us a visit in Kansas. Perhaps if Henry goes home as he talks of doing, he will, if nothing more, take charge of the bank long enough for father to make such a visit next fall. I am very glad father wrote me what he did about his purchases of house, land &c. I like to know how he gets along, and if he cannot make up his mind to come to Kansas and live am glad he has the prospect of a pleasant home in Wakefield, and that too without running in debt for it.

If you (father) wish to sell that lot in Kingston, we will sign the deed, of course, and you may apply one tenth, or less if you think that too much, to my notes at Bank. I would be glad to pay those notes but times are hard, it takes a good deal of money to get the necessaries of life, make improvements on my farm &c., and I would rather sell the stock, if the notes *must be paid soon*, than send the money from Kansas. As to what I wrote about Ella's dagueratype (by the way we had a copy of it sent us and I think it looks no more like her than I do—it was taken several years ago.) I did it more than any thing else for the purpose of finding out how you felt toward Ella. I had reason to fear, not from anything in your letters alone, however, that you and other eastern friends, had obtained an unfavorable opinion of her, although it had not, of course, been told me so in so many words. I am glad to learn that I was mistaken. I hope you will have an opportunity to become acquainted with her some time and have no doubt but that you will like her well. If ever I see you I will tell you the reason of my fears. Whatever idea you may have got from my letters I do not think that mother does not *love Theodore*, but I have feared that she did not show that love in such a way as to lead Theodore to *feel* it. I judged thus from T's letters to me before he went to Kingston to school. He wrote me that he could not stay at home, he wanted to go away some where, and would do so if he had to run away, and he wanted me to send him money that he might come to K, and he would pay me in work; That of course I would not do without your approval. I discouraged the feelings of discontent that he manifested, urged him to be a better boy, and try to obey and please you both as much as possible, and I did not doubt but that he would be far happier and find that you were interested in him and loved him. I wrote so strongly and scolded him so for thinking of running away, that he has not written us since, until very recently, since he has been in B. Theodore wrote me confidentially, and I hope you will not say anything about this to him, I think he feels differently now. As for the reason that T. left K., I acknowledge that I did get "tried" with him, and that he needed a "father's care" and I could not *"afford"* to keep him unless he showed more *interest* in my affairs, but still I should have tried to get along with him, and would not have sent him home for any of these things, he went of his own accord, and said that he did not like to have father alone and wanted to go and help him. Yet I thought then and so did others, that *one*, if not *the* great reason of his going was because he was homesick. (May 23d———

As to what I wrote about "Susy," I can scarcely help laughing, and yet I feel sorry that mother should take it so much to heart. I did not *think* of giving offence. I had noticed, that whenever

Mother wrote of Susy Cross, she always put "Susy" in quotation marks, and very naturally wondered what was the reason. I know that Susy Watson and I were always good friends in the east, and are now for aught I know, and I supposed that mother had done so as a kind of joke on me; I did not suppose that she wished to offend me, and I am sure she did not. Mother has not, however, given me any light on the subject and I am more curious than ever to know why she thus wrote "Susy."

Though as mother says, I "do not need letters to cheer me up" so much as when I first came to K. yet I feel as much interested to know how you all get along at home as I did then, and look for a letter from you now as anxiously and read it as eagerly, I think as I did then. As for criticising *your* letters I was not aware that I did so, any more than those of my *other* correspondents, I am sorry if I have written anything that has unnecessarily occasioned any bad feelings. I am glad to hear that you have a cow. I know you will enjoy it. I do not know how we could get along without one. Much obliged for the pepper seeds. Thank you, mother, for offering to write Ella how to make mangoes, &c. it will not be necessary however. You may write if you please how you make what you call "fritters."

I hear through Henry that Lizzie has another daughter, think she is doing up business pretty fast—two children in two years and a quarter. How is Saml getting along in his business now? I have not heard from them directly in some time. I hear nothing from the Lyme people yet. I wrote a letter to grandmother Johnson about two months ago. Am sorry to hear that she hurt her back a while ago.

Professor Smyth of Bowdoin College Maine preached at Manhattan this morning. He gave us a very good sermon from the text, Is there no balm in Gilead? Is there no Physician there.

Ella has got a letter from the M. E. Church and is going to unite with the Church of which I am a member. She does this entirely of her own accord, without *any* urging or persuading on my part. It will be pleasanter and better for us both I think to be members of the same Church. Had a letter from Amos not very long ago—also one from Dr Clarke.

And now my dear parents I must close. Hope there will be no occasion for the shedding of any more tears over my letters. If I do write any thing that displeases you, do write plainly about it immediately, and not wait until you get a large stock of grievances on hand.

With best wishes for your happiness in this world and the next I remain as ever
    Yours truly & affectionately
           Thomas C. Wells

Ella sends love and hopes you may come and see us. We are both pretty well now. Hope to hear that mother is better when you write again. Do write often.

Our ink is so miserable that I cannot write a decent letter.

         Manhattan, July 8th, 1858.
My dear Mother,

 I received a letter from you yesterday and hasten to answer it. I had begun to think my old friends had all forsaken me, as I had not heard a word from home for two and one half months and it is two months at least, I should think, since Lizzie, Henry or Theodore have written me. I received a letter from Grandmother Johnson and aunt Mariann about three weeks ago which I will endeavor to answer soon. I am always glad to hear from them, and from home and indeed from all my friends.

 Have you received my last two letters one written Apr 21st and the other about three weeks before? Ella thinks it was in my last that I asked you how to make fritters if that is so you must have received it. Much obliged for the receipts. I am glad Mr. Brown is liked so well and that his labors are so highly blessed in the conversion of souls. Wish we might have a revival here. I believe only one person has united with our church since it was organized, I mean by *profession*.

 I thought by Henry's last letter that he would be home before this time and was in hopes that he would get *initiated*, so that he could take charge of the bank and let father come and make us a visit this fall. By the way, you wrote nothing about father; Is he well, and how does he get along improving his land? How is your health now? better I hope. The "man" that called to see you "from Kansas" was Mr Peleg Westcott, I wonder whether he will come here again. he has a pretty good claim and would have brought his family here long ago if he could have sold property that he had in R. I. without too much sacrifice. What has Mr. Stedman been out west for? his health? or on business? Wish he had come far enough to see us. How did you like Whitinsville and the people there? Have you had any garden vegetables yet? We have had new potatoes, beets, and beans and had peas, turnips and radishes in June. Our garden looks finely now, and we shall have summer squashes and cucumbers in a week or two. Ella has quite a flower garden this summer. My sweet potatoes are doing very well. I do not remember whether I wrote you that I had some or not. How is Lizzie now? have you heard from her lately? and how does Samuel get along in his business? Does Bertie go to school now? I suppose he has got to be quite a large boy; he has not written us in a long time. Does Theodore like [it] in Beloit as well as ever?

We heard a speech from Ex. Gov. Stanton yesterday; he gave us a very good speech, very strong anti Lecompton. He is a fine looking man. The Steamboat Minie Belle[8] has made two trips to Manhattan this Summer—expect her up again soon. We have a daily mail now.

Corn and grain look finely; some farmers think they will get forty bushels of wheat to the acre. I never saw corn grow as it has this year.

We have a little pet prairie squirrel, you know I sent you one or two skins, he is real pretty. We have over a hundred this years chickens. Have a first rate cow, she gave milk over a year, gave nearly seven quarts a day within five weeks of the time she calved. We have picked about three quarts of wild raspberries this summer; they were real nice.

Have commenced building the Congregational Church, hope to have it ready for use before winter.

What kind of weather have you had this summer. The thermometer was up to 106° in the shade one or two days in *June* but we did not mind that more than you would 95° in the east. What did you do on the 4th? We went and picked raspberries.

We are both pretty well. Ella sends love. Hope you will write often
                                    Yours very truly
                                            Thomas C. Wells

My dear Mother,   Manhattan Feb. 24th 1859

It is a long time since I have written home. I have two of your letter[s] before me now, as yet unanswered, one mailed Dec. 30th and the other Feb. 2d. and my reasons for not writing before are the same as you sometimes give—*very* busy and *want* of *time*.

Farming in the west especially in a *new* country like this is very different from what it is in New England; there a farmer needs several hands to cultivate twenty or twenty five acres of corn and

---

8. See "The Kansas River—Its Navigation," by Albert R. Greene, in *Kansas Historical Collections*, v. 9, p. 342.

when they come to harvest they make short work of it, but here one man, with team, can plow, plant, and cultivate as many acres, but harvesting is a pretty long job.

A neighbor (Mr. Pattee) and myself have *shucked* or husked about thirty five acres of corn this *winter* and got it in, sixteen acres for him and the rest for me. We drive into the field with a two horse team, husk the corn as it stands, and throw into the wagon. I had several acres shucked on shares. You wonder why we did not get our corn in in the fall. You must *always remember* that this is a *new* country and only three years ago we *"settled"* or *"squated"* on the *naked* prairie, *everything* was to be done, and we cannot do that in three years. We had lived two winters in an *unplastered* house and we determined if possible to have at least one comfortable room this winter, and I did nearly all the work myself, then I had to attend court a week as juror, &c. &c., so that we did not commence on our corn until toward the middle of December.

I shall try to plan things differently this year so as to commence gathering my corn as soon as it is fit. You know I was a perfectly *green* hand at farming when I came here and have had to learn everything by experience; sometimes such knowledge has *cost* me *considerable* but take it all together I have got along very well. I shall have about six hundred bushels of corn to sell. It was the first crop on the land or I should have had much more. You know I lost all my old ground. Corn is worth but thirty cents here now, but we think the Pike's Peak emigration, &c., will raise the value to perhaps one dollar or more per. bush. in a month or two, even if it gets as high a[s] fifty cents per bush. it will [be] worth waiting for.

I am glad you write so often as you do, even if you are obliged to write short letters sometimes, we are always glad to hear from home. *Sometimes* we get most tired waiting for a letter but probably you *as* often have to wait a long time to hear from us. You are a very good correspondent, and I hope will continue so. We are *very* much obliged for the "pictures" you sent. Mother's looks very natural, better than father's which is most too light, but both are so good that it gives me much pleasure to look at them. We will try to get our miniatures, as soon as we can get them taken here, and send them to you. You can tell nothing by that likeness you now have of Ella, it looks no more as she does now than I do. Wish we had Herbert's and Theodores likenesses and also Lizzies and Samuels. I had a letter from aunt Mariann not long ago, and will try to answer it soon. Does Mr. Gillies have his printing office where he used to over Mr. Robinson's store? I should be very happy to receive a letter from aunt Elisabeth, and also from grandmother Wells. I have not heard from Dr. Clarke in a long time, I wish he would write.

I wish father to give J. A. Ward a receipt for me, for any money that he may receive from him on my account and when he pays the am't that I specified in my letter to him give a receipt in full. (I think the am't. was $35.) I supposed the dividends at the Banks were of sufficient am't to pay the discount on my notes and also a trifle on the principal at every renewal and so gave myself no uneasiness about it, but if necessary, I, of course, want father to use the money that he may receive of James A Ward for that purpose.

Perhaps if father can sell the stock for enough to pay the notes he had better do so, and square them up; I do not like to be in debt anywhere. If I get more money here than I need to pay current expenses, and make necessary improvements on my farm, I want to save it to defray the expenses of a visit east sometime, and if I did not want it for that, I could use money here to better advantage than to invest it in Bank stock. It *is "shamefull"* indeed, the way that Mr. Wright behaves toward his wife. I should not think she would live with him another day.

Several buildings will be put up on the College land this summer—two are already commenced—and it is expected the main building for school or College purposes will be built between now and next winter. It is probable that they will have something like a Seminary or high school for a few years, although they intend eventually to have a regular College. The trustees intend to put up public buildings for *educational* purposes only; and they have laid out their lands as a town or village where people can build and board the students &c. They call the *town* "Blue Mont," from a large hill or mountain near by and the College "Blue Mont Central." [9] A good chance for you and father to come and keep boarders!

We shall have a very neat and pretty church edifice when finished, which will be in a month or two I hope. We expect one or two more churches will be built during the coming season at Manhattan and a good many other houses, stores &c. There seems to be more than usual interest here now in religion. Besides the regular preaching, Sabbath schools, and so forth on the Sabbath, we have a *union* prayer meeting in the evening conducted in turn by the ministers of the four denominations. These meetings are well attended and

---

9. See "The Kansas State Agricultural College," by Prof. J. D. Walters, *Kansas Historical Collections*, v. 7, p. 169.

generally the time is well occupied. Besides this there are at least three prayer meetings held during the week at private houses. We are hoping and praying for a revival of religion here—that professing Christians may be quickened and many turned unto the Lord. Will not you pray for us that our faith may be strengthened and our prayers answered? We are too apt, especially, in a border country, to let the things of time occupy all our thoughts instead of laboring in earnest to save souls and build up the Redeemer's Kingdom. Is there much religious interest in South Kingstown now? Is Mr. Brown liked as well as ever? Ella says she is much obliged for the paper that father sent her, and she sends love to you both.

Ella's middle initial is S. not B. I send a *Herald of Freedom* once in a while. Our Manhattan paper does not get printed yet. I have got most tired waiting for it The man that they expected to conduct it failed to come, and they are now trying to get some one else.

We have had a very fine winter, most of the time quite warm and pleasant. There is a great deal of interest here on the subject of temperance now; a great many have joined the "Sons," and many of those that had been in the habit of using intoxicating drink. Our taxes are very high this year, owing, in part, at least, to a miserable set of county officers.

It is getting quite late and I must close, so good night to all.
      Yours truly
          Thomas C. Wells

The lines are so faint on this paper that I can scarcely see them at night, so you will excuse for not writing on them all the time. (Friday morning)

The frost is all out of the ground now.

        Manhattan, K. T. Apr 19/59.
My dear parents,

It is a long time since I wrote you, and still longer since you wrote a letter to me. Your last letter was dated Feb. 5th I believe. I have been watching the P. O. pretty closely lately in the hope of finding a letter from home, but not a letter comes. I hope none of you are sick.

We are as busy as ever, spring you know is an unusually busy time for farmers. I have sown my wheat and oats, my wheat is up and looks finely, and my oats if not up now, will be in a day or two. I have set out a good many forest trees and shrubs about the house, some of them will probably die, but I hope the greater part of them will live. I have a *small* forest of black locusts & cottonwoods growing. Have set out 25 or 30 peach trees and 16 apple trees, also a dozen or more Kansas plums. Ten of the apple trees were three or four years old and grafted the rest were last years seedlings. I think two or three of the plums that I set out last year will bear this year, they are now in full bloom. Have planted only some potatoes in my garden yet, though it is time some other seeds were in.

I have been making a good sized yard for my hens for a few days past, so that I can shut them up while the things ar[e] coming up in the garden; hope to get it done tomorrow and then will go at the garden. I have shot quite a lot of prairie chickens and ducks this spring, and have not spent much time about it either, they have been very plenty in my cornfield. There have been hundreds of *cranes* in the cornfield, and flying around, for a few days past. I should like to get one to examine, but they are very wild. They are very large birds almost or quite as large as turkeys. Hundreds and I don't know but I might say thousands of people are passing through here continually for Pikes peak. They come from all parts of the country, from various classes in society and they travel in all sort of ways. Some come with horses, mules, or oxen, and others come drawing handcarts, rolling wheelbarrows, or lugging packs on their backs.

They make a brisk trade for the merchants in town, and they almost double the price of corn for the farmers. I am afraid, however, that very many of them have much more *gold* in their possession now than they will have six months hence. Manhattan continues to grow and improve, some buildings are going up all the time—they have two steam saw mills there now.

They have let the contracts for the college building, both for the stone and wood work. They are going to work on it very soon— I do not know but they have already commenced. It is to be three stories high and I believe 40 ft x 60 ft on the ground. Two other buildings are now in process of erection in *Blue Mont* one a stone dwelling house about 25 ft x 30 ft the other a frame building 16 x 24 with ell, to be used in part for a store.

It was quite cold last week, so that it froze considerably nights, but it has been growing warmer for two or three days, and today it is uncomfortable with a coat on. The prairies begin to look quite green, and some of the earlier trees are putting out their leaves.

You were talking some of moving, when I last heard from you, I believe. Have you moved? Is business any better in the Bank than it was last year?

I hear quite often from Henry and occasionally from Theodore and Saml & Lizzie Had letter from aunt E. Hagadorn and *Uncle Frank* a few weeks ago.

Mr. Blood has been away two Sabbaths, and Mr. Paulson, a Methodist Minister from New Hampshire preached twice for us, and he gave us two *very* good sermons. It is expected that he will preach for the Methodists here next year, commencing soon. The Sunday evening meetings continue to be well attended, I believe, though I have not been able to attend for three Sabbaths.

Ella sends love. I hope to hear from you soon.

Yours truly
Thomas C. Wells

I enclose a few ducks feathers. We think they are very pretty. It lightens quite sharply in the North and I think we shall have a shower during the night.

[Ella S. Wells to Mrs. T. P. Wells]

Manhattan K. T. May 14th/59

Mrs. Ths. P. Wells
    Dear Mother

It has been a cold rainy day, so cold that I have [to] sit by a fire, something I have not had to do for a number of weeks before. I hope it will not be so cold long for I have worked very busily this week to get my flower seeds in and I fear they will rot. I have had more seeds to plant this Spring than ever I have had before and should feel very sorry [to] lose them. I had but few winter roots. nearly all of them lived. How I wish I could have some of your spare roots I love flowers so much. I took up a petunia last fall and put it in a segar box. (A flowerpot is out of the question here my friends sent me one but I had the misfortune to break it.) It commenced blooming in Mar. and has been in blossom ever since. I think very much of it house plants are so scarce here.

I have one sensitive plant up but they are so sensitive I fear this cold weather will kill it. I can plant them over again if it does. I brought the seed out with me. T. says he thinks you do not have them so I will send you a few seeds They have to be planted every year. they will not live long after frost comes but the seeds will ripen after the stalk is apparently dead. They do not require more than a quart of dirt, little less will do. I usually let two or three grow in a pot have one to touch and let the other grow they will be more sensitive if you do not let the wind blow them. I think them quite a curiosity. they will drop if a fly lights on them if kept out of the wind. keep the dirt pretty wet and warm when you plant the seeds. I don't know as all the seeds are good. Excuse me for writing so particularly about them I thought if you never had any you would like to know.

I was glad to get a line from you it seems a little different when it is directed to me although it is hard to write interesting letters to strangers as we are and strangers in each others locality. I sometimes tell T. when I read his letters that if folks were like mine they would like to know more of our every day life, he says he presumes you would but he can't write it "These women are so *curious* they want to know everything" I am glad you have a sewing machine and that you like it. Thank you for your kind wish that you could do my sewing I would like it very much although I am not driven with sewing just now. I got my sewing pretty well done up last winter for the first time since I was married I braided all the woolen rags I had and sewed them in a mat my first attempt at such work. I never saw any one do it except grandmother when I was a little girl. The forepart of winter I braided & sewed three husk mats that is work I never did until since I was married. I also cut & pieced all the new calico I had not enough for a spread but may be I shall have enough sometime. I will not buy new & cut it up but when one has small pieces I think it pays if one has the time. I expect you would say as many do were you to visit us that I was cut out for an *old maid*. I tell them I can't help it if having a place for everything & everything in its place is going to make me one I am willing to be one all my life. I am going to tell you something that T. has said repeatedly that I should not just to hecter him perhaps I am naughty but I do like to hecter him once in a while just for variety. That is that your son Thomas is Dea. & has been for more than a year. they have three Dea. here they choose one every year each to serve three years but at first they chose one for one year one for two & one for three years. he was chosen at first for one year now he is chosen for three. I felt to[o] bad at first to hecter him about it much but I have to a little now. the worst of it is I have to take care of the service & prepare bread & wine & I have nothing but grape jelly to make wine out of & I don't like to do it. Mrs. Blood says that is my cross but I don't think so. Our good neighbor Mr. Browning hectered us without mercy last year but has got chosen himself this so he keeps pretty still

You ask if I ride horseback. I have ridden a great deal but not much since we have had a buggy. I rode more or less for three years before I came out here. I have no saddle but T's. that does very well for a short distance I can gallop on that. I have ridden twenty three or four miles in a day since I came out here. I have ridden with another on the same horse many a time. I have heard my mother and grandmother tell of such things but never expected to do it. I have no chickens yet expect to have some next week. I have ten hens setting. We have between 70 & 80 fowls now. I have two little young doves & an old one we think much of them. It is getting late & I must close. I have written more than I intended when I commenced. I have written about ourselves as I would to my own relations thinking perhaps it would not be wholy uninteresting to you. We have not had a letter from Sister Lizzie in a very long time. hope she got our last letter. We are in usual health although I cannot endure much   T. says sometimes he has more sympathy for mother since he has had a wife your health is not good, but he did not realize that it made such a difference. My love to father & Herbert it is after ten o'clock & I must close. Hope we shall hear from you again soon.

Your aff daughter   Ella S. Wells

My dear father,   Manhattan, K. T. May 14, 1859.

We received your letter, and, also, one enclosed from mother to Ella, just three weeks ago today, and should have answered before had we not both been unusually busy,—Ella attending to her usual in door work, planting her flower seeds and planting some seeds for me in the garden, and I planting my garden, plowing my field &c. I am rather behind with my corn planting—have not done plowing yet— but hope to get all my corn in, as soon, at least, if not sooner, than I did last year. I did not finish planting until **May** 25th last year, and then had a very good crop. Corn ought to be planted here from the middle of April to the middle of May according to the season, though *some times* a very good crop is harvested from corn planted after the 1st of June.

The season is a week or two later than it was last **year.** I have been troubled about getting help this spring—have had two men, one left for Pike's Peak just when I needed him most and the other I sent away because he was a miserable poor hand to work. Though we have no relatives here we have very good neighbors and from what you write I should think that we visit and receive visits as often as you.

We attend meeting at the Methodist Church now as our church is being plastered &c., and will not be ready to occupy again in two or three weeks. The Methodists have a new minister this year, Mr. Paulson, from N. Hampshire a very interesting preacher, he preach[ed] twice for us when Mr. Blood was away. The Sunday evening union prayer meetings are still pretty well attended, but there does not seem to be so much interest manifested as a month or two ago. We hope and pray for better times. The "Association of Cong. Ministers and Churches" meets at Lawrance week after next, and I have been appointed or rather chosen one of the delegates from our church to that body, but think it *very* doubtful about my going. We have about thirty members connected with our church now.

They had speeches &c at the laying of the corner stone of the "Blue Mont Central College" last Tuesday afternoon, the first ceremony of the kind that has occured in Kansas. About three hundred people were present and some very good speeches were made. Quite a number of documents were placed in the cavity of the stone. The college building will be 40 ft. x 60 ft. on the ground and three stories high, all stone—underpinning corners, and window and door caps to be hewn, the rest rough work. It will be in full view from our house, half a mile distant. We are expecting to receive the first copy of the "Manhattan Express" [10] every day now. I cannot think of the name of the editor—he used to be connected with the "N. Y. Express" N. Y. City. I will send you a copy. Nearly all of the trees, both forest and fruit trees, that I set out this spring appear to be alive and growing. There are about two hundred in all.

Under the circumstances I am glad that you applied the money that you received of J. A. Ward, to my notes. I wish they were both paid up, and if Bank Stock should rise so that you think it advisable I hope you will sell my stock and pay my notes. If you will send us a deed made out in due form, or give me the boundaries so that I can write out a deed we will deed to you our right in the lot at K. and let you apply the $75. to my notes.

You wrote as though you *might* sell your place in W. before you occupied it. Did you mean only that such a thing was *possible* or that you really had some *intention* of doing so. I wish we lived nearer each other. The prairies look splendidly now, covered with a most beautiful green, and there are quite a variety of flowers in

---

10. First called *The Western Kansas Express.* Charles F. DeVivaldi was the editor and publisher.

bloom also. Most of our garden vegetables are up—of some the second planting.

Love to Mother and Herbert. Hoping to hear from home soon again I am yours affectionately   T. C. Wells

Has M. B. Sweet any property in S. Kingstown? he is owing considerable here.

[Ella S. Wells to Mrs. T. P. Wells]

Mrs. T. P. Wells.   Manhattan, K. T. July, 8th 1859.

    Dear Mother

I have had your letter almost three weeks, & I am ashamed to think it has not been answered, but it seems as if I had been unusually busy for the past month or two.

Perhaps you will wonder what I find to do, no one but my husband to do for. I should not have any more than I could do with ease if I confined my labors to the house, although a farmers wife who has to be Bridget mistress & all can always keep busy. But come to add to that 150 chickens 50 old hens shut up to feed & water, flower garden to take the whole care of & a good deal of labor in the vegetable garden & you may be sure I keep busy. I get so tired most every day that I have to lay down & that takes time. It is a good deal of work to pick & shell beans & peas & prepare vegetables, but as we are very fond of a boiled dinner I get one two or three times a week. T. comes as near scolding at me as he can because he says I try to do to[o] much, but when I see him driven with work that must be done that I cannot do I feel as if I must do all I can to help him.

If I were only strong I should not mind the work but as it is I often get so tired that writing or anything else seems a burden to me. I have been waiting to see if I could not find a little more of a leisure day to write but fear I shall not at present so please excuse a hasty scroll. I hope you are not out of patience looking for this. You say you would like me to write all about our house, Have I never sent you a rude plan of it & what is in it? I do not remember if not I will sometime when I am little more at leisure. That is if you would like it.

Have the seeds I sent you come up? mine are up and doing nicely. My flowers as a whole do first rate, some kinds the soil does not seem to agree with, but most of them do look nicely.

I enjoy it very much. I have the cypress vine I never saw it before it is real pretty full of buds. Have you got it? if not &

have seeds I will send you some in the fall, if you would like. I have that & morning glories planted in a circle with a stick in the middle & strings run from the circle to the top.

Our vegetable garden [grows?] nicely. I think much of a good garden. I shall have some summer squash tomorrow. We have had beets two or three weeks. they are as large as coffe cups now. We have had string beans & peas some time. we have carrots parsnips cabages asparigus salsify rubarb sage &c growing well. I think most of our sweet potatoes if they do well we shall have bushells of them this fall. If you are fond of them send your erand boy arround in the fall & we will give you a few bushells.

You say you should like me all the better for having things in their place. T. often says "mother will like you for that she likes to have things in order & will if it is a possiable thing" I am very glad, if anything makes me feel disagreeable it is to see a house look as if a gust of wind had been in at one door & gone out at another. You ask where we find market for our chickens we never have sold many we eat them as freely as we want & keep the hens to lay. Their eggs more than pay for keeping. Last year the wolves took as many as 75 I think.

I remember once last year I cooked two a week for eight weeks in succession. I get tired of them some times. I boil bake fry & make them in pies anything for a change. Did I ever tell you how many eggs I got last year? I will tell you now. please excuse me if I have done it before. 2905 of the number we sold 1818 none less than 20 cts. per. doz. thus far this year they have laid 2775 this year we have sold a few dollars worth for 10 cts a doz. but most of the time for 15 cts.

When T. read what you wrote about Dea wife "there" said he "I do feel all most provoked with you for writing that," but you know it will not do for a Dea. to get angry so I have the advantage of him You say you have those feathers in a wine glass perhaps you could put in some more. I saved a lot of them & as I can send them as well as not I will put in a few.

We had a Sabbath [s]chool before our church was impared by the tornado since then it has been broken up we expect to use the church again week from next Sabbath. M. B. Sweet owes T. a little but would not had he known he drank & acted so.

I must tell you we have 6 little pigs a few weeks old they can get out of the pen & run arround, they look real cunning.

T. bought me a couple of turkeys this week, they will be proffitable if they live & do well. You must excuse me for writing so much about our little affairs, life is made up of little things.

The college is getting up some the stone work is as high as the top of some of the lower windows, the longest side is toward us.

A dwelling house & store near the college has been occupied some time also Bro. Denison has the walls to a stone house up, so you see we are close to town.

I do wish you & father could come & see us. You would be pleased to see how quietly & happily we live. I am not as fond of society as most people; my home is everything to me. if I am happy there I am content & most certainly I am. I do sometimes long to see old friends at home but my husband is more to me than all the world besides so I get along very well.

T. sometimes says he has heard people say marriage divided the sorrows and doubled the joys of life but he never believed it until he tried it.

I will not finish this until he comes for I dare say he will have a word to write or send. Hope we shall hear from you again soon. T. thinks it a long time from one letter to another & I presume you do.

          Saturday afternoon.

Ths. sends his love & says he hopes to hear from one or both of you again soon & then we will try to write.

We are as well as usual. It is very warm & I am weary so I will close. Love to all.   Yours in love,
            Ella S. Wells.

      Manhattan K. T. Aug. 27th. 1859.

Mrs Thos P. Wells,
  Dear Mother,

Ella received your letter mailed Aug. 2d in due time and will answer it when she gets a little leisure. She is not very well and is very busy now. We have had a man with us for two or three weeks, and she has had considerable extra work to do, so that she is pretty well tired out. We are alone again now and I hope she will soon get well and strong again.

I am about sick today—have been threatened with a fever—but feel better than I did last night and hope to be able to go to work again Monday. I have been fencing in a pasture and getting up hay and have worked most too hard for this hot weather but hope a little rest will cure me up; I have been taking some medicine, however, to help along. I have now, besides cow-yard, stack-yard, dooryard &c around the house, a pasture of about 45 or 50 acres fenced in, and a field of about 37 acres. 20 acres of which is in corn. I hope to put in 12 acres of winter wheat this fall. My spring wheat and oats, especially the latter, did very well. We have a very good garden, and about half an acre of potatoes. Wish we could send you some of our vegetables and fine melons. We have about fifty fruit trees set out which are doing well.

Do you receive the *"Kansas Express"* regularly? and how do you like it? The foreman in the printing office ran away a few days ago and they have been able to print only half a sheet this week. I have been helping them for a day or two and they want me to stay until they can get another regular printer, which they hope to do in a week or so. I should have been helping them to day had I been well.

All kinds of stock are very cheap and money very scarce now, as many of our settlers are *obliged* to sell property at any price in order to obtain money to pay for their lands previous to the public sales which take place on and after the 29th day of Aug.

We went graping a few days ago, and got over two bushels of Kansas grapes, and Ella is making jelly today. The wild grapes here and all through the west and in California are very small, not much, if any, larger than good sized blueberries. We have no plums of any consequence this year, a late frost killed most of them and the curculio have made sad work among the rest. Our sweet potatoes are looking very finely, the vines if streched out would extend eight or ten feet all around the hills. I have not dug into any of the hills yet, and therefore do not know how well the tubers are growing. By the way, I would be glad if you would send us some grape seed in a letter.

I will send you some seeds of the wild sensative plants that grow on the prairie; they are perennial, very fragrant and very pretty. It would be a good plan to plant some of them this fall and those that are planted in the spring should be soaked twenty four hours before they are put into the ground. I will send, also, a few seeds of a yellow flower that grows on the bluffs. I would treat them in the same way. They both require a deep rich soil, but the seed should not be covered more than half an inch. It would be well to protect them by a little straw or coarse manure during the winter.

As I am rather tired I will write no more today. Hope to hear from you soon.

Ella sends love.   Yours truly   Thomas C Wells.

Manhattan, K. T. Oct 28th 1859.

Thos P. Wells, Esq.

My dear Father,

Your letter of Sept 18th was received about a month ago and I have been waiting only for time to answer it.

You write that mother and Herbert were in Lyme, had been gone some twelve days when you wrote—that would seem to us a long time to be separated, we have never been apart from each other twentyfour hours at one time since we were married. Had we either of us relatives to visit, within visiting distance, the case would doubtless be quite different.

You had been having *"very cold* weather," we had a light white frost on the night of the 5th of this month, but did not have a killing frost until the 17th and last night it froze a little again.

I wish you and mother too might come and see us and the country, guess you had better come and keep boarders (students) for the college now building. Keeping boarders is first rate business here if any one likes it. They are just putting on the roof to the college building. No, we do not cut stalks as you do in the east, it would be rather tiresome work should we attempt it for very many of the ears are higher than our heads and some of them as high as I can possibly reach; but we generally cut up a portion of our corn from the ground, before the leaves are dry and cure it for feed in the winter, though a great many do not, but turn their cattle into the field after their corn is gathered and let them pick for themselves. Most of my corn is very good, better than it was last year. Corn is not worth more than 25 cts a bushel here now. It does not pay very well to raise corn *to sell*, but we can make something by feeding it out to cattle, hogs, chickens, &c. My potatoes are very good but very few in a hill and that is the case generally here this year, as far as I can learn. I have about a dozen bushels of very fine beets, four or five of carrots, plenty of parsnips & cabbages, some salsify, about five bushels of sweet potatoes, and we have eaten all we wanted for a month past.

I would like to see your field and garden (as it was) I think you are getting to be quite a farmer Whether the "Express" *pays* or not I do not know. I believe they print about eight hundred copies a week, but the "Express" is not so interesting to me as the "Times" and I do not think it near so good a paper as Henry's "Citizen"

I am sorry that my note at the Bank has to lay over-due at all. I thought the dividends would always a little more than pay the discount. I would be glad to pay them both if I could, but that is out of the question at present. Whenever you *can sell* the stock for a *fair* price I wish you would, and apply the proceeds to the notes. I had no such form as I wanted to write a deed by, but I have written one which I think will answer, and will try to get it acknowledged, and send it in this letter. I shall be very glad to have you apply the money to one of my notes, and am very much obliged to you for attending to those notes for me.

I think it would pay well to keep sheep here if one had such a fence as would keep them at home, but a fence that will stop most cattle would not answer for sheep, and they would have to be got into a close yard every night to keep them from the wolves. I should have tried to get some sheep before now if I had a suitable fence around my pasture, and as soon as I am able to make it sheep proof I mean to buy a few.

It *does* cost a good deal to get corn to market now, but if we had a rail road up here, which we hope to have in two, three or four years, we *can afford* to raise it and send to St. Louis, the river boats will carry freight *down* very cheap. Wheat, when it does well, pays better than any other crop now it is worth $1.50 a bushel. I have $5\frac{1}{2}$ acres of winter wheat in this fall. I got only $15\frac{1}{2}$ bushels of *spring* wheat from two bush. sown, but it was my first trial it was sown too late and cut too late. I will hope to do better next time.

Flour of the best quality is worth $5. a hundred now, sugar $12\frac{1}{2}$ cts per lb. for light brown, molasses, very good 90 cts a gallon. Considerable molasses is being made here from the shorgum and it is very good. It is sold for 75 cts to 85 cts a gall. I have raised nearly wheat enough to keep me in flour this year but we have no flouring mills yet, (expect to have them next year), and I have it ground like Indian corn and make Graham bread of it. Our *tea* and *coffee* do not cost us one dollar a year.

Manhattan is building up as fast as could be expected when money is so scarce three or four building are going up nearly all the time. Pike's Peak travel does not affect our market very much, though it helps us a little. I do not think of any kind of seed but grape that I care to have you send me now.

I am sorry that Amos has done so poorly. I would like to see him very much. M. B. Sweet left the country some time ago and considerably in debt. He did not do much while here, he borrowed ten dollars of me a few days before he left and has not paid it.

Do they have any preaching at Kingston now? Ella sends love and says she will write when she is not so busy.

Are you all well? Do write often.

Yours very truly
T. C. Wells

Excuse the appearance of this as it is written by candle light.

Manhattan Kansas Territory
Monday, Dec. 26th, 1859.

Mrs. Thomas P. Wells
    Dear Mother,

I received two letters from you last Wednesday, one dated Dec 4th, and the other Dec 5, the latter though was pretty short, but it contained some grape seeds for which I am obliged.

It was all news to me that Lizzie had another little baby, I should think she would have her hands *full* now.

I received a couple of cards from Henry a week or two ago, and learned from them that he was married, before I heard from you. From what he had written I did not suppose he would be married quite so soon.

I am glad that you think Theodore has a good situation. We had a letter from him not long ago, and he appeared to be very well contented.

We would have liked very much to have been with you Thanksgiving day. I *hope* we may be able to come and make you a visit in two or three years; we talk of it a great deal, but it will be very expensive and we cannot afford it now, and even if we had plenty of money we would hate to leave our house and farm, except in pretty good hands. I do want to see you and father very much and so does Ella.

Is grandmother Wells well now? I would like to have her write to me—I wrote her a letter a long time ago.

Dr. Clarke has not written to me in more than a year I think. I wonder what has "come over the spirit of his dreams" that he cannot write. We will keep you duly informed in regard to the number of your grandchildren "in Kansas." None have made their appearance yet, and perhaps will not for some time to come, we do not believe in having too many irons in the fire at a time. We have had enough to do, thus far, to get an honest living, and keep out of debt, without having three or four babies to take care of &c.

You say that Eliza Hagard is engaged. Will she probably be married soon? Where is "Susy" now? is she engaged? or married?

What is Herbert doing? You have written nothing about him in a long time.

Our sweet potatoes are most gone, so you will not get any unless you come after them soon.

I wrote the deed and acknowledgement and omitted the date in both because I did not know when it would be *legally* finished. (and neglected to insert the date afterwards at the proper time) The date that father inserted was right.

We do not measure our corn when we get it in, and I cannot tell *exactly* how much corn I had this year, but probably between eight and nine hundred bushels.

Ella's sister Nancie is here now, has been here about a month. She is a *real* good sister and we hope she will make us a long visit. We wish she would settle near us when she gets married, and *perhaps* she will—but when—you must ask her. (Dec 27th.)

I have been out on a buffalo hunt, with two others, since I wrote you. We were away from home four days and a half, the first time that I have been from home all night since I was married. We took a good tent with us, and camped out every night. We went about eighty miles west of here, up the Smokey Hill and Solomon's fork. We did not kill any buffalo or even shoot at any, though we saw a plenty of them, and they are the most *ugly looking creatures* that ever I saw. The main herd had gone south, and those that we saw were all old fellows, and hardly worth killing; we would have killed one or two, however, or tried to, at least, had it not come up suddenly cold, and compelled us to go home.

The last night we were out it snowed quite hard nearly all night, the wind north and very cold; we managed to keep very comfortable during the night, but we almost froze riding home the next day. Although we got no buffalo meat, we were glad that we went; we passed through a very fine country and it was well worth such a trip to see the huge monsters. We got within a few rods of several of them, but it was nearly night and the caps on our rifles would not go so we did not shoot; we had other caps which we were going to try in the morning but, as I have written, we were driven home by the cold. Our nearest neighbors, Mr. Pattee and wife, have rented their place and gone back to New Hampshire for two or three years at least. We miss them very much.

I have not gathered all my corn yet, you know that is a winter job in the west. I have two men helping me now and hope to finish in ten days or two weeks of fair weather. I would prefer to have my corn gathered in the fall, but it is a long job to husk and crib 20 acres of corn, and I could hire no one to help me on *paying* terms until these men came along a few weeks ago. I give them every seventh load for husking and cribing, and their board *when at work.* Corn is worth 20 cts a bushel delivered.

Has any one heard any thing from Amos yet? You say that you have written me two letters now since I have written, but I have written more in this than you did in both of yours, so I shall consider that you owe me a letter now, and hope you will write quite soon.

Father owes me a letter too. Love to all. With best wishes I remain yours aff'ctly

T. C. Wells.

[Ella S. Wells to Mrs. T. P. Wells]

Mrs. T. P. Wells.   Manhattan, K. T. Dec. 27th/59

Dear Mother.

Your letter has remained a long time unanswered & I have but a few moments to spare this eve. but as Ths is finishing one to send to you tomorrow; I thought I would write a few lines, & send with it.

I find the longer I put off answering a letter the harder it is to answer. I was very busy while my garden lasted & then I was quite sick for me in the fall. So I have let one thing after another hinder me until now. I was anxiously looking for & worrying about sister for five or six weeks before she came, & now you may be sure we have a great deal to talk about as it is almost five years since I have seen a relative. We hope she will make us a long visit. She came all alone got along without trouble except being a good while on the way She has two trunks that have not yet arrived. My friends have sent me a good many presants but she does not tell me much about them. thinks it will be pleasanter if I don't know until I see them. I will try & think to put in some Cypress vine seeds. I expect to have a large garden if I live until another year. Sister has brought me quite a number of different kinds of seeds.

I am greatly obliged for the receipts you sent in your last.

I must close for it is quite late & I have to get up & get breakfast before light as Ths has two men getting in corn for a few days. My love to Father Herbert & a share yourself.

Affectionately your

daughter Ella S. Wells.

Manhattan, January 27, 1860.
Kansas Territory.

My dear Mother,

We received a letter from you last Friday, and as we always are, we were very glad to hear from home.

You write of getting letters from Henry and Dora on the same day that you received one from us, and say that it was "quite a treat" to get so many letters at once. I do not doubt that it was a "treat," but I do not think that you can *appreciate* a letter as we do until you, like us, have been, for a long time, far away from all your old friends and relatives.

Nearly all of *your* relations are near you, so that you can frequently visit them, while the best that we can do is to hear from *ours*, and I assure you that we are *very glad* to do that.

You say that I talked of coming to visit you in two or three years, two or three years ago, and you seem to think that there is not much more probability of our coming two or three years hence than now. Well, I do not know that there is; but this I do know, that *as soon* as we *can* come and feel that we are *doing right* we *intend* to come and *visit* you, at least, and if we once get east we *may not* come back here again, that will depend upon circumstances of which we know nothing now. *If* I knew that I could get into some good business east, that would be both healthful and profitable, I would sell out here as soon as I could get a good opportunity. Not that we are dissatisfied with the *country* or the *people*, here, or that we do not like our prairie home, but simply that we might be nearer to those we love. And yet, I assure you, it would be hard for us to give up our Kansas home, here we have lived and labored for several years, and they have been *happy* years—this has been our *first* home together—my own hands have helped to build our little house and the other buildings, and also the fences, here I have set out trees, here I have plowed and planted and harvested. We might move to some other place and be happy but no other place will ever seem to us like our first home in K. Sometimes I think that we had better make up our minds to spend our days here, but we do want to see you all, we want, *at least*, to come and make you a long visit, and we hoped to have done so before now, but that is easier to talk about than to do. It would take a good deal of money and of time.

We have not yet felt able to bear the expense of such a journey, and if we had a plenty of money, it would be very dificult to find any one with whom we would be willing to leave our house and farm.

So you must not think that because we do not come and see you, we do not want to, and very much too. We hope and expect to have a railroad up as far as here in *two or three* years from now and then it will not take quite so long to go from here to Rhode Island. And *if we wished to sell* our farm we could doubtless get considerable more for it then than now, for a railroad here would tend to increase the value of property considerably.

It *does* seem *too bad* for Amos to be alone in Texas, and especially when they are having such awful times there; but after all, I felt *relieved* to hear from him, for I feared that he was dead, it was so long since I heard a word from him. I wish we had good reason to think that he was a christian, and then if he should be taken away, we would feel that he had gone to a *"better country"* where there would be no more sorrow and no more sin.

If you should hear from him again do write me all that you learn about him. Do you think that Theodore is a christian? I do not get a letter from him *very frequently*. Let us pray for him and Amos, unto "Him that heareth the prayer of faith," that they may be converted and numbered among the "children of God." Nothing but the influence of the Holy Spirit can save them and that is promised in answer to prayer. I suppose that Herbert has got to be quite a large boy. I would like to have him write to me. I can hardly think of him only as a little boy that he was when I left Wakefield

Are they all well in Lyme? I have not heard from any of them in a long time.

On Tuesday night, Wednesday, and Wednesday night we had a real snow storm, but it is fast going off now. We had had neither snow or rain worth mentioning before this winter.

I had about a thousand bushels of corn this year. How much corn did father have off his two acres? We can only get 20 cts a bushel for ours, and mostly *store goods* at that, it is almost impossible to get *money* for anything at any price.

Ella says she is very busy today, and cannot write very well. She sends love.

Do you get the "Express" regularly? I do not think much of the editorials or selections generally, he lets his printer do most of the selections.

Do write as soon as convenient.

With much love I remain as ever,

          Yours truly
            T. C. Wells.

Manhattan, K. T. Apr 10/60

Mrs. T. P. Wells,
　Dear Mother;

I expected your last letter would have been answered *long* before now, but as was the case with you "various things" have prevented.

I have no one to help me this spring and with all the chores to do, and farm work to attend to you may imagine that I have my hands full.

I was glad to get a letter from grandmother with yours and will endeavor to answer soon.

I wish that Henry's desire of having you and father & Lizzie and her husband remove to Wisconsin might be realized; and if it should I assure you it would be a strong inducement for me to sell out here and settle somewhere near you. We, neither of us feel like going back to New England to live, for various reasons which I need not enumerate now, but we would be *very glad* to live within visiting distance of you and others of the family The longer we live here, however, the more attached do we become to our home, and although there are many things that we do *not* like, yet we are not sure that we should better ourselves by a removal.

I was very glad to learn that Amos is alive and well, even in Texas. I do not much blame him for wanting to remain in Texas until he gets able to pay "all he owes" I think that I would feel and do the same under similar circumstances.

You say that Mr. Belden is a very good minister &c. Our minister (Mr. Blood,) is a very good *man*, but *not* a good *preacher* if I am any judge of preaching. Some of the church like to hear him, however, and some do not. We are placed in rather an unpleasant situation, and do not know how or when we shall get out of it.

Does father get enough for taking charge of the "Times" to pay him for his trouble? Unless he gets very good pay I should think he would let it go rather than be so confined. You say that *some* of the selections in the "Express" are quite good. When you have said that you have said about all that you can for the paper. We think it rather a slim affair. If you do not care much about it I will not send a copy *regularly* next year.

It would not pay us to raise corn to sell at 20 cents a bush. if we made that our whole business, but corn does not need half the work to cultivate it here as in the east, and we can do a good deal at times when nothing else is pressing. I went through about three fourths of my corn last year with a cultivator once and back in each row and that is all that I did to it from the time I planted it until it was ready to harvest, and I got between forty and fifty bush. to the acre at that. I have no doubt but that I should have got more corn if I had worked it more, but I did not get time to do so.

Apr 11th. I did not have time to finish this last evening, and will try and write a little more now, as we are going down to Manhattan to meeting in a few minutes and can take it to the P. O. I have sown five acres of spring wheat which is up and looks very well considering it is so dry. I have got six acres nearly plowed on which I intend to sow oats. My winter wheat looks very well. I shall not plant more than 10 or 12 acres of corn this year. I shall want considerable myself to feed out. I am afraid you will never be able to enjoy a home of your own until you leave the Bank and when father gives that up I wish he would move fa[r]ther west if only in western N. Y. or Ohio, and perhaps I could sell out and move there too. Most anything from home is interesting to us, so please not wait until you have something which you think very interesting before you answer this. I do not see that your "powers of letter writing fail" at all, judging from your letters to us. We would be glad to hear from home oftener. That *old* Bible that you referred to is one that I picked up somewhere and saved as a curiosity. I do not care anything about it now. Where are my old lattin and greek books? I often wish I had them here to refer to.

The season is very forward, at least compared with last year. The plum trees are going out of blossom. Strawberries are in bloom. Apple and peach trees are leaving out and the prairies are beginning to look quite green. It is getting very dry, but things do not seem to suffer much from want of rain although we have not had any of consequence since Feb. But it is time for us to go and I must close. Love to Father and Herbert as well as yourself. In great haste,   Yours truly

                              Thomas C Wells

[Ella S. Wells to Mrs. T. P. Wells]

Manhattan, K. T. Apr 10th/60

Mrs. T. P. Wells,
Dear Mother,
Ths is writing so I will write a few words although I think he can write so much better & more interesting letters it is not of much use for me to add my mite.

We are having a very pleasant and open spring. Sister & I went Maying in March we got four different kinds flowers & some buds nearly ready to open. You spoke in a former letter of my enjoying it having her here it is very pleasant on many accounts but I do not expect she will stop any longer than autumn she does not like [it] well enough. I think she would have liked better had she got her trunks in season. She did not get them until the middle of Mar. & it was very unpleasant getting along as she had to. When she did get them some of her things were ruined. She had a bottle of black varnish that she used about painting the cork got out & it made black work where ever it went. We were so glad to get them that we get along with all bad marks. I expect to be very busy this summer with my flower garden & trying to have sister enjoy herself. I do not expect to accomplish a great deal except my work.

We both enjoy very good health now, but I can endure but little. I wish we could come & see you but I almost give up the idea when I think how much it costs & how difficult it will be for us to leave our place & stock. It is after nine o'clock, & I am weary so I will say good night. Love to father & Herbert & a share yourself.

Affec. your
Ella S. Wells.

Manhattan, Kansas T.
June 23d, 1860.

Dear Parents,
I had almost forgotten that I was owing you a letter. When Mother's letter came, which was more than a month ago, I was so *very* busy that I could not stop to answer it, and I have been busy enough ever since, but I did not intend that your letter should go so long unanswered. I have had no help this season have not hired a man for a day, so you will not wonder that I have had enough to do.

I have put in 5 acres of spring wheat, 6 acres of oats, 12 acres of corn & ½ acre of potatoes besides planting and taking care of a good sized garden, and doing all the *chores,* which last item is no inconsiderable matter, taking from 3 to 5 hours each day. I have planted about ⅛ acre of sugar cane (*shorgum*) this year. I can get the molasses made for half of it, if I strip the leaves off and haul it to mill, and what I have planted if it does well will make some 25 or thirty galls. at least. I intend to sow about an acre of buckwheat in a few days. It has been very dry this spring and summer thus far. We have not had a rainy day, only a *few showers,* since last Feby. In consequence of the drought small grains have not done well. My winter wheat did not *spread* any and is very *thin,* so that I can neither cradle nor mow it. What there is is well filled out and if I can get it gathered no other way I shall try to reap enough for seed with a sickle. I am in hopes that I can get a man to cut it for half of it, with a two horse *reaper.* There is probably not more than thirty bushels on the 11 acres. My spring wheat did not all come up good, what there is looks better than any that I have seen. But *very few* of my oats came up until a long time after they were sown, they are looking well now, however, and if the rest of the season is favorable I shall expect to get a fair crop. My garden is very backward on account of the dry weather. My corn looks well and is growing finely. I have commenced cultivating it. Sweet potatoes look well. We had a late *frost* which killed all the wild plums.

I commenced to answer your letter but have been writing about something else all the time. I should have enjoyed fishing in the Sankatucket with Dr. Clarke very much. Am glad to hear that he is happy with his new wife and I wish him *well* most truly. I wish father was able to give up the Bank (perhaps he is if he would but think so). I suppose he gets a little more leisure now that he has given up the *"Times."* I do not wonder that you both feel lonely sometimes, and I assure you that you do not wish that *we* were near you any more than we do, *or* that you were near us. I did not know but we would sell out this last spring, and if I had felt as discouraged then as I did a few weeks afterwards I think it likely that I should have sold even at a sacrifice; but I am glad that I did not. A man wanted to buy my farm and would probably have given $2,500. half cash and the rest in one year, but I wanted $3,500. and so he purchased else where. Besides my farm I have other property that I could probably sell for from $500. to $800. according to the *times.* I do not owe more than two or three dollars except my notes at Bank in R. I. If I get a good opportunity to sell out within a year or two I shall probably do so and settle nearer you. I like the country here well enough, but would like to be within visiting distance of my parents and old friends. We have a poor market now for anything. It is next to impossible to get any money at all. Times must improve, however, before long, they cannot grow much worse.

You ask about Morton B. Sweet. I have heard nothing of him for about a year. He was then going to fort Laramie or some other Government post with a government train. He left here very suddenly and considerably in debt. He had the name of drinking too much whiskey. He appeared well enough whenever I saw him, which was not very often. I well remember John A Brown & his sister Mary. Please remember me to them when you see them.

Remember me to all the Lyme friends when you write. I believe they have been owing me a letter for a long while. I would write them again, had I time to spare I have not been able to answer grandmother Wells' letter yet. Is she still in Rochester?

Congress has done us a great injustice by keeping us out of the Union so long. Had we been admitted when we were ready for it and desired it, we should doubtless have had a railroad from the Missouri river to Fort Reilly and other rail roads in other parts of the *state*. But capitalists will not take hold of such things much so long as we remain a Territory. If you can get time do write again *soon,* and I will *try* and answer *soon*. Hope I shall not have quite so much to do when I hear from you again.

Yours affectionately,
Thomas C. Wells

Ella says she would write some if she was not so tired. She joins me in love to you all. We are comfortably well and as *happy* as ever; hope you are the same, both *well* and *happy*.

Manhattan, K. T.
Oct. 19th, 1860.
Dear Father & Mother,

How do you do? Well, I hope—we are pretty well; Don't we look so?—only we are rather tired after a long journey, and probably show it in our faces. We received mothers letter of Aug. 24th in due time, but were very busy, cutting up corn &c. at the time and afterwards; on the 2d of Oct. we started for Leavenworth and when we came back found a letter from father. We were very glad to get both the letters and should have answered before but for want of time. Will now attempt to answer both. A short time after mother wrote her letter I had an opportunity to sell twelve and a half acres of land that I did not really need, for ($200.) two hundred dollars, half down and the rest on the first of next March. I sold the land, received the hundred dollars, and the note of a responsible individual (Rev. Mr. Denison,) for the balance. I tried for a long time to sell my farm, or sixty two and a half acres on the east, which contained most of my improvements, but could find no one that could raise any money. I might have sold easily *on time* and taken security by mortgage on the piece, but determined that I would stay here a year or two longer before I would sell thus.

The land will not decrease in value—it must rise—and next spring or next fall I may be able to sell for more than I now ask for my farm, or if I can get no more I may get the money down. Although the severe drouth has been very discouraging, and many will leave the country in consequence, yet it is not probable that we shall have another such season for many years if ever, and I think that a great many people will come to Kansas in the spring in the expectation of buying lands cheap from discouraged settlers. And if Kansas is admitted into the Union during the winter it will be the means of bringing a good many men with capital here, so that I think there is a fair prospect of my being able to sell in the spring, or at least within a year. The merchants here charge enormous proffits on almost all their goods, and seeing no prospect of my leaving here this winter, I concluded to go to Leavenworth and purchase what provisions &c. I needed. So I engaged a man to do my chores while I was gone, borrowed some wagon *bows* and *sheet* and fitted them to my lumber wagon, harnessed up my horses and started for Leavenworth, taking Ella with me, and leaving *sister* to take care of the house, &c., while we were absent. We went down on the south side of the Kansas fording that river at Manhattan, passed through Wabonsee, the Pottawatomie reserve, Topeka, Tecumseh, Big Springs, Lecompton, Lawrance and the Delaware reserve. We forded the Kansas again at Lawrance as it was very low. On our return we came through Grasshopper Falls, Rochester, Indianola, Louisville and St. George. We were gone nine days, slept in our wagon every night but one, and traveled at least two hundred and fifty miles. At Lawrance we found some friends with whom we spent a night. We found Leavenworth a very busy place of about two thousand inhabitants. We got our pictures taken there and think them pretty good only we were very tired and, Ella's especially looks too sober. We made our purchases without any difficulty. We found flour worth $3.40 per sack (98 lbs.) sugar 10¼ cts per lb. molasses—60 cts a gall. salt $1.90 per sack of 200 lbs. &c. &c. Here the same articles are selling for—, flour $5.00 and above, sugar 7 & 8 lbs for a dollar, Molasses 90 cts. and salt 3½ cts a lb. and other things in proportion.

We met with no accident on our journey and were glad to get home again. I have cut up most of my corn and shall have plenty of fodder for my stock. I shall probably get from 100 to 200 bush corn, probably not more than 100 bush that would be fit to sell, but a good many nubbins that I can feed to pigs and chickens. I shall fat and kill most of my hogs, and kill off a good many of my chickens. I think I shall not have to buy any corn for my own use. We got about two bush of very good sweet potatoes from 100 hills, and about half as many Irish potatoes as we planted! We bought a *few* potatoes in L. at 90 cts a bush and a few apples at $1.25 a bush. We raised about *2 bush* of squashes, no beets, turnips, carrots, cabbages, or any thing of the sort.

We had a letter from Lizzie and Samuel, telling of the loss of their baby &c. Samuel gave me a very kind invitation to spend the winter with them—said he could find enough for me to do. Thank you for the invitations you give us to spend the winter with you.

If you have a good opportunity to let your house and place do not save it for us, for it is very uncertain whether we shall be able to go east in the spring, and if we do go we can not tell now what we shall do. Depend upon this, that when we do leave Kansas, we shall want to make you a good visit and also Saml & Lizzie and others of our friends before we settle down in any kind of business. I am by no means certain that I could endure the sea air for any length of time   There has been much interest in religion here for several weeks. It commenced in the Methodist church and extended to the Baptist and Congregational Churches. We have had preaching every evening for about a week by Rev. Mr. Bodwell[11] agent of A. H. M. S. He is a very good man and an *earnest, practical* preacher. Our meetings have been well attended and much interest manifested. A dozen or more have asked the prayers of christians

---

11. The Rev. Lewis Bodwell (1827-1894), a native of Connecticut, came to Kansas in 1856 to serve as pastor of the Congregational church in Topeka. In 1860 he accepted the agency of the American Home Missionary Society. Six years later he was recalled to the Topeka church where he served until 1869, resigning on account of the ill health of his family. He then moved to Clifton Springs, N. Y. He took an active part in the struggle for freedom in Kansas.

in their behalf, and several of them hope that their sins are forgiven and their names written in the Lamb's book of life. I think Mr. B. will remain with us over the Sabbath. Mr. Blood has declined preaching here another year, and we know not whether we shall be able to get any one else immediately or not. Mr. Bloods time is out on the last Sunday of this month.

We had a glass and frame around our pictures, but have taken them off to send in a letter. They look better *in a frame*. Ella's likeness is not so good as mine.

We both send love and shall expect to hear from home soon.

Yours affectionately

T. C. Wells

Mr. Barker, a brother in law of Ella's, of Sherborn, Mass. made us a visit of several days a few weeks ago. You may imagine we were all much surprised to see any friend from N. E.

I got a letter from Mr. I. T. Goodnow yesterday. He says he called on you—thinks I had better remain here. What did he say of Kansas? T. C. W.

Kansas History as Published in the Press

An analysis of the composition of the population of Kansas was presented in an article published in *The Southwestern Social Science Quarterly,* of Austin, Tex., for September, 1935. The paper, "Some Demographic Characteristics of the Population of Kansas," by Carroll D. Clark and Roy L. Roberts, was read before the sociology section of the Southwestern Social Science Association meeting at Oklahoma City, Okla., April 20, 1935.

Cowley county history is featured in Walter D. Hutchison's column, "Folks Hereabouts," appearing frequently in the Arkansas City *Daily Traveler.* More of the county's history is also published in occasional feature articles under the heading "Cowley County Reminiscences."

Pre-movie days in Hutchinson as recalled by L. A. Meece to Elliott Penner, reporter, were described in an article printed in the Hutchinson *Herald,* January 26, 1936. A story quoting from James H. Birch's account of the Indian battle fought on site of Kinsley, on Coon creek, was recounted in the *Herald,* January 29. The battle is said to have occurred in May, 1848.

First white settlement in Allen county was discussed in articles appearing in the Iola *Daily Register,* February 20 and 21, 1936. The *Register* also conducted a questions and answers column on Allen county history under the title "Know Your County." The series, which ran for several weeks, started with the issue of March 9.

The history of the *Gove County Republican-Gazette,* which was founded at Gove City, April 9, 1886, was briefly reviewed in its issue of March 26, 1936.

Foreign settlements in Republic county were mentioned by Ida L. Smith in an article entitled "National Group Settlements" printed in the spring, 1936, issue of *The Aerend,* quarterly publication of Fort Hays Kansas State College. Included among the stories featured in the summer number were the following of historical interest: "Mirage [in western Kansas]," by Thomas Freeman; "The Fall of Rome [Ellis county]," by Jane Flood, and "Victoria Hunt Club Ball," by Paul King.

"Members of First Colored Family in Emporia Still Living," an article in the Emporia *Gazette* of April 9, 1936, reported. Joe Odair and his sister, Mrs. Ellen Burton, are the members who arrived in 1863.

Gove county's fiftieth birthday was observed with special ceremonies held at Gove City, September 2, 3, and 4, 1936. The *Gove County Republican-Gazette,* of Gove City, published several historical stories during the golden jubilee year. Included among these were: Excerpts from the first journal of the county commissioners, in the April 23 number, John F. Lindquist's reminiscences of the county, in the August 6 issue, and Lewis A. Lincoln's recollections, August 27. Mrs. A. M. Weir also contributed a series of articles on early Grinnell which appeared in the issues of August 13, September 3, 17, 24, and October 22. The valuation of Gove county's crops, livestock and taxable property for the past ten years was discussed by W. P. Harrington in the November 5 number.

Frankfort school history was briefly reviewed in the Frankfort *Daily Index,* May 15, 1936. The first school was organized in March, 1869.

Arkansas City's golfing history was recorded by Joe Bly in an article entitled "Tomato Cans Were Basis for First Golf Course in the City," appearing in the Arkansas City *Daily Traveler,* May 16, 1936.

Old-timers of Crawford county participated in the festivities held at Pittsburg, May 20, 1936, celebrating the sixtieth anniversary of the city's founding. A special historical supplement issued by the Pittsburg *Headlight* and *Sun,* May 19, included the following stories: "Franklin Playter a Major Figure Here During Early Days," "Pittsburg Has Been the Coal Capital of Kansas Many Years," "Churches Here Develop With City's Growth," "Tiny Settlement of 60 Years Ago Now Is Kansas Coal Capital," "G. W. Kidder Recalls Early Days in City," "Zinc Smelters Were Major Industry in Early Days Here," "First White Child Born in Crawford County [Elisha Black] Still Lives," "Schmidt 27th Man to Serve City as Mayor," "Water Supply Here Problem in Early Days," "City Was Live Camp in 1883," and "Recalls First City Platting."

Dighton's Christian Church, organized on May 26, 1886, celebrated the fiftieth anniversary of its founding, May 31, 1936. A brief history of the church was published in the Dighton *Herald,* June 4.

The history of Newton's Zion Evangelical Lutheran Church, which observed its golden jubilee, June 7, 1936, was reviewed in the Newton *Harvey County News*, June 4, *Evening Kansan-Republican*, June 6, and *Journal*, June 11.

Concord, Helena, and Mashenah, three ghost towns of Atchison county, were mentioned in the Atchison *Daily Globe*, June 10, 1936.

Biographical sketches of several of Smith county's pioneers were printed in the *Smith County Review*, of Smith Center, June 11 and 25, 1936.

The history of the Kansas Southwestern Railroad Co., organized August 27, 1885, as the Geuda Springs, Caldwell and Western Railroad Co., was reviewed in an article entitled "Kansas-Southwestern Bids Adieu to A. C.," in the Arkansas City *Daily Traveler*, June 25, 1936.

Fifty years of electric lighting in Great Bend was discussed in the Great Bend *Tribune*, June 30, 1936.

The life of Father Paul Mary Ponziglione, early Kansas missionary, was reviewed by Sister Mary Paul Fitzgerald in an article entitled "A Jesuit Circuit Rider," in the July, 1936, number of *Mid-America*, a Catholic historical magazine published at Chicago.

Dr. James C. Malin, associate editor of *The Kansas Historical Quarterly* and contributor of articles on Kinsley's boom and the farm population turnover in Kansas to the *Quarterly* during 1935, has written another paper in the series which was published in the July, 1936, issue of *Agricultural History*, sponsored by the Agricultural History Society of Washington, D. C. The article was entitled "The Adaptation of the Agricultural System to Sub-Humid Environment," and illustrated the activities of the Wayne Township Farmers' Club of Edwards county in 1886 to 1893.

The experience of Mrs. Frank Todd in a "Trip in Concord Coach From Newton to Wichita in the Spring of 1870," was related in Victor Murdock's column in the Wichita (Evening) *Eagle*, July 3, 1936.

A history of Corona lodge No. 137, I. O. O. F., instituted in Dodge City, July 6, 1876, was briefly sketched in the Dodge City *Daily Globe*, July 4, 1936.

The Wichita *Sunday Beacon* issued a 116-page anniversary edition, July 5, 1936. The occasion was the eighth anniversary of the taking over of the newspaper by Max, Louis and John Levand.

A history of the cattle industry in early-day Kansas was briefly outlined in the Dodge City *Daily Globe*, July 9, 1936.

Pioneering in the Walnut river valley of Butler county was recalled by George Tong, of Leon, in the Wichita *Sunday Eagle*, July 12, 1936.

Chanute *Tribune* reporters interviewed early-day railroaders of the vicinity to gather material for their "Railroad Week" feature stories published during the week starting July 13, 1936.

Liberal post-office history was reviewed in *The Southwest Tribune*, of Liberal, July 16, 1936. A new post-office building was dedicated July 18.

Names of business houses operating in Wichita in 1881 were printed in Victor Murdock's front-page column in the (Evening) *Eagle*, July 18, 1936.

Atchison's railroad history was sketched by John Burke in the Atchison *Daily Globe*, July 23, 1936.

Historic Dodge City places were discussed by a visitor writing in the Clyde *Republican*, July 23, 1936.

Alfred M. Landon, governor of Kansas, was formally notified of his nomination as the Republican candidate for president of the United States at special ceremonies held on the south steps of the state house in Topeka, July 23, 1936. The Topeka *Daily Capital*, *State Journal*, and the Wichita *Beacon* issued special notification-day editions honoring the governor and the state's distinguished guests.

Wichita history was reviewed in the sixty-fourth anniversary edition of the Wichita *Eagle*, issued July 26, 1936.

Utica's history was briefly outlined in the Utica *Star-Courier*, July 30, 1936. The city was incorporated on July 26, 1911.

A brief biography of Dr. Barnum Brown, curator of the American Museum of Natural History, New York, appeared in an article entitled "An Eminent Bone Hunter Got His Start Gathering Sea Shells in Kansas" in the Kansas City (Mo.) *Times*, July 30, 1936. Doctor Brown was born near Carbondale.

Chisholm trail history was briefly sketched in the Coats *Courant*, July 30, 1936.

"Eighty Years Ago Franklin, Kansas, Now Vanished, Was in the Limelight," was the title of a feature article in the Kansas City (Mo.) *Star*, August 1, 1936.

A review of the life of the late John Montgomery, publisher of the Junction City *Union* from 1888 to 1936, was printed in the *Union,* August 5, 1936.

The history of the First Methodist Church of Morganville, as written by Mrs. H. J. Merten and Mrs. W. H. Lennard, was published in *The Tribune,* of Morganville, August 6, 1936. The fiftieth anniversary of the building of the church was observed with ceremonies held August 2.

Barton county rural teachers for the 1936-1937 term were named in the Hoisington *Dispatch,* August 6, 1936.

The story of the Rev. Pardee Butler's enforced cruise on the Missouri river after expounding the cause of freedom in pro-slavery Atchison was retold in the Kansas City (Mo.) *Times,* August 7, 1936.

Several Kansas newspapers published articles in their summer issues recalling the grasshopper visitation of 1874. Included among these were: Wichita (Evening) *Eagle,* August 8 and 27, 1936; Clay Center *Dispatch,* August 11, and the Downs *News,* September 3.

Biographical sketches of Walter A. Huxman, governor-elect of Kansas, were printed in the Wichita *Sunday Eagle,* August 9, 1936, Kansas City (Mo.) *Star* and Wichita *Beacon,* November 8. A biographical sketch of Mrs. Huxman was also printed in the November 8 *Beacon.*

Great Bend's history was reviewed in detail in the Great Bend *Tribune's* forty-eight page sixtieth anniversary edition issued August 12, 1936. Extensive histories of the city's newspapers, schools, business houses, churches, telephone system, post office, clubs, electric lighting system, library, fire department, hotels, and railroads were printed. Pioneer biographies were sketched and names of the city's mayors and first county officials were featured. Included among the illustrations were a map of Barton county's oil pools, which accompanied a six-page history of the industry, and a plate showing points of interest in the Great Bend vicinity from 1806 to 1886. Sixty years' rainfall in Great Bend was recorded in table form. Other articles were headlined: "Egyptian Corn Introduced in County in Early '80's . . . ," "Mennonite Colony Moved Into Barton County in '70's, Securing Land in Pawnee Rock Vicinity," "Only Sign of Life Here When Don Dodge Came in '71 Was Dugout Where Post Office Stands," "Cyclone First Big Storm to Strike Here," "Pioneers Soon Learned Wheat the Best Crop," "County Lines Big Question in Early Days," "First Real Building Boom in Great Bend Took Place in 1878 . . . ," and "Mennonites Credited with Introducing Turkey Wheat. . . ."

St. Paul's Lutheran Church, also known as the Clark's Creek Church, which celebrated the seventy-fifth anniversary of its founding, August 16, 1936, is the oldest Lutheran church of the Missouri Synod in Kansas. A history of the church was sketched in the Junction City *Union,* August 12, and the Republic, August 13.

The Hoisington *Dispatch* issued an illustrated "Anniversary Edition" August 13, 1936, celebrating the "Fiftieth Anniversary of the Founding of Hoisington and Building of the Missouri Pacific Railroad to This Point." Included among the special articles were: "Barton County Officers From 1872 to 1936," "Charter That Started the City of Hoisington," "Early Real Estate Deals," "Townships Organized," "Old Army Trail," "First Hoisington Child," "The First Physician," "Early Newspaper History of Hoisington—Other Interesting Early Day Stories," "Hoisington High-school Graduates," "The Last Buffalo," "Down Through the Years," "The First Livery Barn in Hoisington," "First Commercial Club," "Official Happenings of Hoisington From the First Official Meeting," and "Hoisington, 1886-1936." Other stories reviewed Barton county post office and club histories. Names of city officials and biographies of prominent citizens were printed. Fifty-year residents of the community were named in a special column appearing from August 13 to September 10, inclusive.

Napoleon Boone was the "first white child born in Kansas 108 years ago in Jefferson county," George Remsburg recalled in an article published in the Atchison *Daily Globe,* August 15, 1936.

The story of the writing of "What's the Matter With Kansas," William Allen White's famous editorial of forty years ago, was told in the Kansas City (Mo.) *Times,* August 15, 1936.

Businesses operating in the vicinity of William and Market streets in Wichita before the erection of the post-office building on the northwest corner fifty years ago were described by Victor Murdock in the Wichita (Evening) *Eagle,* August 18, 1936.

Gen. James G. Harbord, Pershing's chief of staff during the World War, spent the early years of his life in the hills northwest of Bushong, Kan., the Kansas City (Mo.) *Times* recalled in an article published August 19, 1936.

Hoxie observed the fiftieth anniversary of its founding with a three-day celebration held August 20 to 22, 1936. Included among the writers contributing articles to the special edition of the Hoxie *Sentinel*, issued August 20, were: R. M. Martin, L. J. Wright, Fred C. J. Witt, F. A. McIvor, Mrs. Katherine Bieker, Mrs. F. M. Burr, Laura Lynam Rawson, Alice J. Turtle, and James Foster. A history of Sheridan county, as depicted in a pageant given at Hoxie, August 22, was published in the *Sentinel*, starting August 28.

Sod houses in Kansas were discussed in an article entitled "Kansas Woman [Mrs. George Crofton] Proud of Her Sod House, Where She Has Resided 50 Years," printed in the Wichita *Sunday Eagle*, August 23, 1936.

Introduction of electric lights in Dodge City in 1886 was recalled in the Dodge City *Daily Globe*, August 25, 1936.

Residents of Liebenthal, oldest of the Kansas settlements founded by emigrants from the lower Volga district of Russia, celebrated the sixtieth anniversary of the founding of their town, September 1, 1936. The history of the settlement was briefly reviewed in the Hays *Daily News*, August 31, and the La Crosse *Chieftain*, September 3.

Judge R. M. Pickler, Herbert L. Fryback, Walt W. Mills, W. C. Wolfe, Henry A. Clark, Frank W. Simmonds, W. H. Ransom, A. W. Relihan, L. C. Uhl, and A. C. Coolidge were among the contributors writing in the sixty-fifth anniversary edition of the *Smith County Pioneer*, of Smith Center, issued September 3, 1936.

Names of northeast Kansas old settlers registering at the Hiawatha fair, September 3, 1936, were printed in the Hiawatha *Daily World*, September 4.

"A Few of the Historic Early Churches of Kansas Stand Today as Landmarks," the Kansas City (Mo.) *Star* reported in a feature article published September 4, 1936.

The sixty-fifth anniversary of the Swedesburg Lutheran Church of Clay Center, which was organized September 4, 1871, was celebrated September 4, 5, and 6, 1936. Histories of the church appeared in Clay Center newspapers contemporaneous with the event.

An attractive pamphlet featuring the history of the Farmers State Bank of Lindsborg, which was chartered on September 4, 1886, was recently printed by the Bethany Printing Co., of Lindsborg. The historical sketch, prepared by J. O. Stromquist, was supplemented with biographies of men who were prominently identified with the organization and development of the bank.

The history of the Kansas department of the American Legion was briefly reviewed in the Wichita *Sunday Eagle*, September 6, 1936.

Gaylord celebrated the fiftieth anniversary of its incorporation on September 7, 1936. Historical sketches of the community were published in several issues of Smith Center newspapers.

The history of Olmütz, Barton county, was outlined by Rudy Mauler in the Hoisington *Dispatch*, September 10, 1936.

Argonia *Argosy* history was briefly reviewed in its issue of September 10, 1936. The newspaper was founded in October, 1913.

Recollections of J. L. Hodges, pioneer Kansas railroad man, were printed in the Pratt *Daily Tribune*, September 10, 1936. Mr. Hodges operated a short-line railroad from Liberal to Woods a few years ago.

The history of Rose school, District No. 27 of Butler county, was sketched in the Augusta *Daily Gazette*, September 11, 1936. The district was organized March 14, 1871.

A brief history of the Topeka chapter, Daughters of the American Revolution, was reviewed in the Topeka *Daily Capital*, September 13, 1936. The chapter, which is reputed to be the oldest in Kansas, was organized January 31, 1896.

The experiences of F. S. Kirk, of Wichita, during the opening of the Cherokee outlet in 1893 were recorded by Victor Murdock in the Wichita (Evening) *Eagle*, September 16, 1936. The article was headlined "At Opening of the Strip Forty-three Years Ago Today Horse Better Than Engine." Other articles recalling the historic event were published in the Arkansas City *Daily Traveler* and the Winfield *Daily Courier* of the same date.

"Battle of the Arickaree, Sept. 17, 1868, Ended an Indian Menace in Kansas," Paul I. Wellman reported in a Kansas City (Mo.) *Star* historical feature article appearing September 17, 1936.

A letter written by Donald Campbell, August 28, 1860, describing the journey of his party through Iowa and Nebraska on its way to make homes near Emporia was published in the Emporia *Gazette*, September 18, 1936. The letter is the property of Mrs. S. H. Bennett of Peabody, great-granddaughter of the writer.

The Syracuse Methodist Episcopal Church observed its fiftieth anniversary with special services held September 20, 1936. The church's history was reviewed in the Syracuse *Journal*, September 18.

Garden City's *Daily Telegram* celebrated the installation of Associated Press leased wire service in its plant with the issuance of a special section, September 22, 1936, featuring the city's newspaper history.

Thayer Methodist Church history was briefly sketched in the Thayer *News*, September 24, 1936. A new church building was dedicated by the congregation with services held September 27.

Pratt county's old settlers registering at their annual picnic held in Pratt, September 24, 1936, were named in the Pratt *Tribune*, September 25, and the *Union*, October 1.

The history of Ebenezer Methodist Church, Highland township, Clay county, was outlined in articles published in the Clay Center *Economist*, September 30, 1936, and *The Times*, October 1. The church observed its sixtieth anniversary February 12 and the event was celebrated on September 27.

Excerpts from the correspondence of the Rt. Rev. John Baptist Miège, S. J., first Vicar-Apostolic of the Indian Territory east of the Rocky Mountains, to his brother in France, were printed in *Mid-America*, Chicago, in its issue of October, 1936. The article, bearing the title "An Early Episcopal Visitation of Colorado: 1860," was edited by Thomas F. O'Connor and was translated from J. C. Garin's *Notices Biographiques sur Mgr. J. B. Miège Premier, Apostolique du Kansas* (Moutiers, 1886).

Articles relating to Kansas history appearing in current issues of the *Pony Express Courier*, of Placerville, Cal., include: "When Dodge City Was Wild and Woolly," by E. A. Brininstool, and "The Wind Wagon," by George J. Remsburg, in the October, 1936, issue; "Graves Along the Oregon Trail," by John G. Ellenbecker, in the November number.

"Early Days in Western Kansas" was the title of an article by J. G. Felts which was published in the *Logan County News*, of Winona, in its issues of October 1, 8, and 15, 1936. The history of the *News* was also reviewed by Mr. Felts in the October 1 issue.

"Getting the Railroads Into City of Wichita Stirred Up Emotions," Victor Murdock reported in the Wichita (Evening) *Eagle*, October 2, 1936. They were "carefully shuffled to the edge of the town and all ended up in the center of things."

Kansas history and industry were on parade at the Kansas Diamond Jubilee celebration, held in Wichita, October 7 to 17, 1936. Special "Diamond Jubilee" editions heralding the approaching exposition were issued by the Wichita *Sunday Eagle* and *Sunday Beacon*, October 4.

"Independence, Kan., Boasts Long List of Famous Persons," the Kansas City (Mo.) *Star* reported in a two-column article published October 8, 1936.

The history of the Strassburg community and its German Baptist Church was reviewed by Mrs. Jane Rupp in the Marion *Record*, October 8, 1936.

Horton celebrated the fiftieth anniversary of the founding of the city and the Rock Island Railroad Shops with a "Golden Jubilee Pageant," held October 12 to 15, 1936. Newspapers of the city issued anniversary numbers during the month, *The Tri-County News* on October 12 and the *Headlight* on October 29, the latter publication also observing its own golden anniversary. Stressed in both editions were histories of the city, railroad, churches, lodges, schools, and business houses. Photographs, biographies and reminiscences of pioneers, reprints from early Horton newspapers, congratulatory letters, and names of old settlers were also featured. The *News*, which contained 48 full-sized pages, published brief histories of the city's newspapers, political parties, clubs, patriotic organizations, hospital, early-day bands, electric light and water plants. Titles of several feature articles included: "Rock Island Building Through Northeast Kansas in 1886 Fathers the City of Horton," by F. J. Nevins; "Fire Fighting Equipment Has Improved Much in 30 Years . . . ," by Dr. Clyde Gray; "Famous Old Kickapoo Indian School Once Occupied Ground That Is Included in 'Horton Heights' District"; "H. C. Miller Horton's First Postmaster . . . ," by Bertha Coffland; "Captain J. R. Thompson Tells About the Soldiers of Horton"; "Chief Kennekuk, One of the Most

Famous of the Kickapoo Chieftains, a Unique Character in Northeast Kansas History," by George A. Root; "Horton High-school Graduates Down Through the Years." The historical supplement to the *Headlight* was issued in magazine form and contained 116 pages. Among other stories featured by the *Headlight* were a brief review of the Pony Express by W. R. Honnell; "A History of Muscotah," by Mrs. Ralph Ellson; "Fort Leavenworth Military Road," by George A. Root; "A Sketch of Our Kickapoo Neighbors," by George J. Remsburg, and "Some New Malden Memories," by G. W. Carpenter.

Solomon City's lodge, No. 105, A. F. & A. M., celebrated the sixty-fifth anniversary of its organization, October 19, 1936. A history of the lodge was briefly outlined in the Solomon *Tribune*, October 15.

Macksville observed the fiftieth anniversary of its founding with a celebration held on October 23, 1936. The Macksville *Enterprise* issued a special edition, October 15, featuring histories of the city and its schools, post office, newspapers, churches and business houses. Included among the historical stories were: "And Macksville Is Fifty Years Old," by J. C. Hinshaw, and "Early Experiences in Stafford County," by Mrs. C. A. Satterlee. Brief biographical sketches of pioneers were printed in this and the succeeding issue. On November 5, Mrs. John Lill's reminiscences of Cassoday were published.

Wichita's boom was recalled in a series of fifteen short articles featured on the front page of the Wichita (Evening) *Eagle*, starting October 16, 1936. The articles, contributed by Ralph Richards of Fort Scott, were labeled "Wichita As I Knew It."

Histories of the Washington Methodist Episcopal Church were printed in *The Washington County Register*, October 16, 1936, and the *Washington County News*, October 22. The church celebrated the seventy-fifth anniversary of its origin during the week beginning October 18. "Short Sketches of Kansas History" is the title of a new *Register* feature beginning with the October 16 issue.

Oakley's school history was sketched in the Oakley *Graphic*, October 23, 1936.

A two-column biography of Cyrus K. Holliday, one of Topeka's founders and promoter of the Santa Fé railroad, was published in the Kansas City (Mo.) *Star*, November 5, 1936.

Parkerville's history, as recounted by Mrs. Frank F. Prescott, was printed in the White City *Register,* November 5, 1936. The paper was read at the annual Pioneer Kansan picnic held in Wilsey, October 22.

A history of Wichita's school system was briefly sketched in the Wichita *Sunday Eagle,* November 8, 1936.

Osage City's Methodist Episcopal Church held its sixty-sixth anniversary homecoming, November 8, 1936. A history of the church was outlined in *The Journal-Free Press,* November 11.

Histories of Quinter and the Quinter Church of the Brethren were reviewed in *The Gove County Advocate,* of Quinter, November 12, 1936. The church commemorated its founding on August 14, 1886, with special services held November 14 and 15, 1936.

The history of *The Kiowa County Signal,* of Greensburg, formerly *The Progressive-Signal,* was sketched by A. W. Gibson in the *Signal* of November 12, 1936.

A two-column "Community History of Arrington," by J. M. Miller, appeared in *The Tri-County News,* of Horton, November 12, 1936.

Oatville's history was briefly recounted in the Wichita (Evening) *Eagle,* November 13, 1936.

Short introductory sketches of members of Topeka's artist group were printed in the Topeka *State Journal,* November 13 and 14, 1936.

Kansas Historical Notes

The Kansas Editorial Association held its annual meeting in Topeka, June 19 and 20, 1936. Tom A. McNeal, veteran Kansas editor, was honored with a testimonial banquet at the evening session on June 19. John Redmond, publisher of *The Daily Republican,* of Burlington, one of the speakers on the afternoon program, urged editors of Kansas "to pay more attention to the recording of current history as well as that of pioneer days." Newspapers should "contain the complete history week by week of the community and its institutions," he said. "Kansas newspapers always have coöperated with the State Historical Society to the extent of sending copies of each paper issued, but should send in all printed matter of historical nature which might be of value now or in future years."

Chase County Historical Society officers were reëlected at the annual meeting held in Cottonwood Falls, September 5, 1936. C. W. Hawkins, of Clements, continues as president; C. A. Sayre, of Cottonwood Falls, as vice-president; Henry Rogler, of Matfield Green, as secretary, and S. H. Baker, of Cottonwood Falls, as treasurer. Historians of the Society are preparing copy for the first volume of Chase county history which is to be published soon.

Forty-eight Kansas chapters of the Daughters of the American Revolution were represented in the organization's fourth annual pilgrimage to the Rev. Thomas Johnson hall at Shawnee mission, September 16, 1936. Mr. S. B. Haskin, of Olathe, was the principal speaker.

Bronze markers to be placed at the entrance of the old Indian mission burial ground east of Ottawa were dedicated at Ottawa, September 29, 1936, by the Gen. Edward Hand chapter of the Daughters of the American Revolution. Mrs. C. A. Gibson presided at the dedicatory program. Dr. S. P. Fogdall and Grace Meeker were the speakers. The inscriptions on the tablets read: "1845-1936. The Ottawa Indian Mission Burying Ground, graves of J. Meeker, founder, Chief Comechau and Notino, the Medicine Man. J. T. Jones, founder of O. U." "1845-1936. Jotham Meeker, first printer and publisher in Indian Territory (Kansas) at Shawnee 1833. Moved his press here 1849. Edward Hand Chapter D. A. R. 1936."

Several historic points in Douglas county were visited by members of the Douglas County Historical Society in two tours conducted by the Society on October 3 and 4, 1936.

Officers of the Riley County Historical Society were reëlected at the annual meeting held October 5, 1936. They are: C. M. Correll, president; Grace Givin, vice-president; Mrs. G. H. Failyer, secretary, and Mrs. John Flick, treasurer. On the new board of directors are: Mr. Correll, Mrs. E. M. Irish, Miss Givin, Charles Emmons, Mrs. Flick, Mrs. Failyer, Mrs. F. L. Murdock, Mrs. C. B. Daughters, Mrs. J. B. Mudge and Ada Billings.

The annual meeting for the election of officers of the Hodgeman County Historical Society was held at Jetmore, October 9, 1936. The officers are: L. W. Hubbell, president; E. W. Harlan, secretary; Mrs. Ora L. Teed, treasurer; Mrs. Leigh Newport, Lee Jackson, L. W. Hubbell, directors; Mrs. Margaret Raser, historian.

At a meeting of the Twentieth Kansas regiment association in Topeka, October 12, 1936, George Helwig was elected president and Frank Dodds, vice-president. Harry W. Brent was reappointed secretary-treasurer.

Four Centuries in Kansas, a new Kansas history by Bliss Isely, Wichita newspaperman, and W. M. Richards, Emporia educator, was published this summer by the McCormick-Mathers Company of Wichita. Designed for use in the public school system, the book is written in a straightforward and interesting style. It not only reviews Kansas' eventful past but describes the present-day resources and industries of the state. The 344-page book, attractively arranged, illustrated and printed, is a credit to its authors and publisher, and a worthwhile contribution to Kansas literature.

The Alumni Association of the University of Kansas has announced the issuance of a second and revised edition of Kate Stephens' book, *Life at Laurel Town*. The book, which presents a colorful picture of the people of Lawrence in the period following the Civil War, was first published in 1920. The second edition has some slight additions and carries real names of certain persons instead of the fictitious names used in the first edition. Miss Stephens has presented the edition to the Alumni Association. All income from sales goes to further the work of the association on behalf of the university. The book is priced at $2.50 a copy, postage paid. Address Alumni Association of the University of Kansas, Lawrence.

Western Kansas history has been recorded in Floyd B. Streeter's *Prairie Trails and Cow Towns,* recently published by the Mount Vernon Press, of Boston, Mass. Mr. Streeter, who is librarian of the Fort Hays Kansas State College, has made an extensive study of contemporaneous documents. His 236-page illustrated book represents a collection of several score subjects dealing with incidents occurring along the old wagon and cattle trails, life in the famous cattle-shipping centers of the early days and tales from the buffalo range.

Pioneer meetings or old-settler reunions are sponsored annually by citizens of many Kansas cities and towns. Most newspapers publish historical data contemporaneous with the gatherings in their individual localities. Following is a partial list of communities and dates of the meetings: Leavenworth "Pioneer Days," May 22-24, 1936; Hazelton, June 5; Wichita, June 6, October 10; Beloit, Ulysses, June 17; Gridley, June 20; Kingery township (Thomas county), June 21; Protection, July 4; Garden Plain (held at Wichita), July 19; Green, July 23-25; Nickerson, July 30, 31; Axtell, August 3-5; Jewell, Leoti, August 4, 5; St. Paul, August 6-8; Halstead, August 12, 13; Clyde, Cottonwood Falls, August 14; Baldwin, August 14, October 13; Larned, August 18, 19; Hanover "Days of '49," August 18-20; Finney and Haskell counties (held north of Sublette), August 19, 20; Deerfield, Ford, August 20; Belvidere, August 21; Oskaloosa, August 21, 22; Vermillion, August 25; Concordia, Lovewell, Mulvane, August 27; Sparks, August 27-30; Holton, August 28; Wabaunsee, August 30; Kensington, Gove City, September 2; Olathe, September 4, 5; Caldwell, September 7; Brookwood Park, September 12; Lawrence, September 14; Humboldt, September 14-19; Topeka, September 14, October 10; Fontana, Marion, Stafford, September 17; Weir, September 18, 19; Potwin, Pratt, September 24; Dodge City, September 26; Smith Center, September 30; Kirwin, October 6; Cherryvale, October 7; Mt. Hope, October 8; Fredonia, October 10; Herington, October 14; Horton, Rush Center, October 15; Clay Center, Howard, October 16, and Wilsey, October 22.

Index to Volume V

A

Abel, Anna H. 116
Abilene, cattle business of 10
— end of cattle trail at 12
— first Texas cattle to arrive at 8
— Jos. G. McCoy came to, in 1867 4
— Kansas Pacific Railway extended to, 4, 12
— note on cattle trail to 330
— Populist convention at 77
— Texas cattle, shipped east in 1868
  from 10
— — shipped from in 1867 9
— years of cattle trade 13
Abilene *Daily Reflector* 221
Abolitionists of the North 66
Academies, Kansas 57
Acansa river, name given Arkansas river
  by William Delisle 22
Adams, Charles Kendall 115
Adams, F. G. 352
— agent for Kickapoo Indians 15
Adams, H. B. 115
Addis, Miss M. L., president Shawnee
  County Old Settlers' Association 112
Aerend, The, publication of Fort Hays
  Kansas State College 107, 325, 419
Agricultural department, state 57
Agricultural History, Washington, D. C. .. 421
Agricultural History Society, Washington,
  D. C. 421
Ague and fever 158, 159, 164
  251, 298, 316, 426
Air planes, stream lined 66
Aitchison, R. T., Wichita 79, 81
Akansa river, early name of Arkansas river, 22
Alcove Springs, location of 210, 211
— named by members of Donner
  party 210, 212
Alcove Springs creek 211
Alex, Okla. 10
Alexander, T. P., pioneer hardware merchant, Florence, diary kept by 106
Alexander, stockade near 105
Alford, Susan D. 279
Ali-co-the, prominent Kickapoo 19
Allamead community, Lincoln county ... 105
Allen, Henry J., elected governor 77
Allen county 189
— note on first white settlement in 419
Alma, note on history of 325
Alma *Signal* 325, 332
Altamont, July 4, 1905, celebration, described in Altamont *Journal,* 1935 214
— note on history of 216
Altamont *Journal* 214, 216
Altenborg, John, director Lindsborg Historical Society 112
Alton *Empire,* consolidated with Osborne
  Journal 217
American Baptist Board of Foreign Missions 261, 263
American Geographical Society 118
American Guide Manual, a writers' project of the WPA 224
American Historical Association 116
American Historical Review 118, 121
American Home Missionary Society 417
American hotel, Chicago 162
American Legion, Kansas department, note
  on history of 426

American Museum of Natural History,
  New York 422
American Revolution 117-119
Amish farmers, residing near Yoder, remove to Iowa 223
Anadarko, Okla. 8
— Wichita agency at 7
Ancient, Free & Accepted Masons, Solomon City, note on history of 429
Ancient Order United Workmen, histories
  of local lodges published from time to
  time in the *Kansas Workman,* of Erie, 325
Anderson, ———, principal chief of Delawares 376
Anderson, John A. 57
Anderson, John F., interpreter for Kickapoo Indians 18
Anderson, W. P., agent of Kansas Pacific
  railroad at Abilene 12
Anderson, W. S., state master workman
  of Knights of Labor 205
Anderson county, note regarding early
  day recollections of B. F. Reiber 223
Andersons, the Missouri bushwhackers ... 66
Annals of Iowa, Des Moines 217
Anshutz, Carrie F. 108
Antelope 65, 252, 253, 257, 371
Anthony, Col. Daniel R., editor of
  Leavenworth *Times* 75, 218
— opposition to Knights of Labor 204
Anthony, George T., Tom McNeal's recollections of 75
Anti-Horse Thief Association, Hutchinson, note on activities of 328
Anti-Monopolist convention, met at Topeka 204
Anti-Monopoly party 202
Arapahoe county, Kansas 190
Arbitration, law passed by legislature in
  1886 for 193
— of industrial controversies, first legislation in Kansas for 51
— voluntary, legislation providing for
  tribunals of 49
Argentine, strike at plant of the Kansas
  City Smelting and Refining Co 191
Arickaree, battle of, September 17,
  1868 .... 214, 426
Arkansas 23
— party from, led to mouth of Little
  Arkansas in search of buried treasure, 6
Arkansas and Ninnescah Ferry, organization of 183
Arkansas City 23, 26, 31, 180
— bridge facilities at, impaired by flood, 31
— ferry at, rates on 29
— — preparations for free 28
— — woman's unusual experience while
  crossing on 28
— first bridge at, carried away by flood .. 27
— formerly Delphi 25
— freighting from 30
— note on golfing history of 420
— roads to and from 32
Arkansas City *Traveler* 27, 30- 32
  180, 182, 419-421, 426
Arkansas river 183, 184, 190, 260, 264, 345
— bed occasionally dry 22
— bridge at Wichita described 187
— Cimarron crossing, ferry at 190

(435)

436 GENERAL INDEX

Arkansas river, course of.............. 22
— cows drink river in two............ 23
— disappearance of water in channel in plains country 23
— disastrous floods in.................. 23
— discovery of underflow of............ 24
— drainage area of..................... 23
— ferries on, discussed by George A. Root 22-32, 180- 190
— — at mouth of Little Arkansas...... 185
— — first across in Sumner county..... 184
— first bridge in Wichita to span...... 188
— first crossing of, on Santa Fé trail.... 260
— flood, 1877.......................... 180
— — carried away toll bridge.......... 26
— high waters in 27, 31
— length of............................ 23
— little water in channel in 1871...... 184
— navigability of...................... 25
— shipments stranded on sand bars owing to shifting channels................... 25
— source of 22
— termed the Nile of America......... 22
— various names given to.............. 22
— westernmost ferry on, in Kansas..... 190
Arkansas River Bridge and Ferry Co., organization of.................. 183, 186
Arkansas River Ferry Company, date of charter 25
Arkansas territory, Indians to be restricted to regions west of......... 231
Arkansas Traveler, ferryboat at Arkansas City 30
Armourdale, strikers meetings held at... 42
Army trail, old, Barton county, mentioned 424
Arnott, F. M., cited.................... 30
Arrington, community history of, noted.. 430
— history reviewed in *Tri-County News*, Horton 108
Art, Indian............................. 57
Ash timber............................. 248
Astle, Etta Williams.................... 331
Atchison, David R............. 66, 158, 170
Atchison 15, 38, 40, 42, 48, 52
— history of, mentioned................ 217
— Missouri Pacific strikes of 1885 and 1886 .... 36, 37, 196, 197
— note on railroad history of........... 422
— overland trail from.................. 67
— stages out of....................... 15
Atchison Board of Trade, early circular of, reprinted in Atchison *Globe*...... 218
Atchison county........................ 108
Atchison *Daily* and *Weekly Champion and Press* 15
Atchison *Daily* and *Weekly Free Press*... 15
Atchison *Daily Champion*, cited..... 36- 39 41-43, 49, 204, 205
Atchison *Globe*... 217, 218, 320, 421, 422, 424
Atchison, Topeka & Santa Fe Railroad 26, 27, 193
— C. K. Holliday one of promoters of.. 429
Atkinson, — —,...................... 333
Atkinson, Gen. Henry, commanding western army..................... 348-350
Atmore, — —, mentioned.............. 383
Audobon, J. J. L., mentioned........... 119
Auglaize, Grand, branch of Osage river, 242
Augusta 32
— note on newspaper history of........ 223
Augusta *Daily Gazette*................. 426
Augusta *Journal*, founded March 17, 1887 223
Aunt Sally, steamboat, ascended Arkansas river to Arkansas City........... 25
Auplain river, twelve miles from Chicago, 230
Austin, Mr. and Mrs. — —, at Harmony mission 245
Austin, E. A............ 54, 62-64, 79, 81

Austin, E. A., elected second vice president Historical Society............. 80
— nominated for second vice-president Historical Society 64
Automobiles, first in Dodge City, and owners, described in Dodge City *Globe*, 109
— stream lined 66
Axtell, date of old settlers' meeting at... 433

B

Badger, William P., Kickapoo Indian agent 320
Badger, ... 373, 374
Bailey, John C., ferry location on Grasshopper 321
Bailey, Willis J., elected governor....... 77
Baker, S. H., Cottonwood Falls, treasurer Chase County Historical Society.. 431
Baldwin, date of old settlers' meeting at, 433
Bancroft, E. P., ferry operator......... 186
Band, first Kansas, article by Edward Bumgardner 278- 281
Bands, municipal.................. 106, 214
Banks, Robert, note regarding reminiscences of 213
Banson, — —, St. Louis............... 242
Baptist Board of Foreign Missions.. 122- 124
— letter of Isaac McCoy regarding outcome of treaty negotiations..... 137- 140
— William Staughton, corresponding secretary 125
Baptist Church................ 57, 284, 290
— First, Clay Center, note on silver anniversary of dedication of............. 328
— Manhattan 417
Baptist meeting house, near St. Louis... 325
Baptist missionary station, Carey, Mich., 339
Barber, Thomas, free state martyr...... 280
Barber County Index, Medicine Lodge... 326
Barber County Old Settlers' Association, note regarding annual meeting of 326
Barker, Mr. — —, Sherborn, Mass..... 418
Barnes, Lela, curator of manuscripts, Kansas State Historical Society, 114, 226, 338
— "Isaac McCoy and the Treaty of 1821," article by.................. 122- 142
— Journal of Isaac McCoy for exploring expeditions of 1828 and 1830, edited by 227-277, 339- 377
Barrows, Elder R. C., Oneida Christian Church organized by................ 214
Bartholomew, Elam, death of.......... 57
Bartholomew, Rev. J. E................ 58
— manuscript collection given Historical Society 57
Barton Brothers, ferry at Pierceville operated by 190
Barton, James, Cuba, settled in Republic county in 1871................... 220
Barton, T. J., ferry operator....... 181, 184
Barton, William, ferry operator.... 182, 184
Barton county.................. 23, 260, 426
— oil pools mentioned................. 423
— postal history mentioned............ 424
— rural school teachers........... 216, 423
Basketball, game devised by Dr. James A. Naismith 218
Battle, Arickaree................. 214, 426
— Black Jack.......................... 66
— Hickory Point....................... 66
— New Orleans........................ 11
— Osawatomie 66
— Tippecanoe 20, 343
Baum, J., St. Louis, Mo............... 269
Bay, Mr. — —, mentioned........ 229, 263
Beach, Rev. E. C., Garden Plain Methodist Church organized by.......... 109
Beadle's Dime Library, mentioned...... 57
Beans, mentioned 284

General Index 437

Bear, feet and unused portions buried by Indians 242, 243
— killed by McCoy's party 242
Beardslee, Grace, secretary Ness County Historical Society 112
Beaubien. See Bobia.
Beauchamp, Maj. ——, sub agent 361
Beavers 366
— trapped by Jo Jim during McCoy expedition 369
Beck, T. E. 222
Becknal, Mrs. —— 300
Bee hunting, on Indian lands 363
Bee trees 209, 250, 353, 355, 356
Beecher Bible and Rifle colony, eighty year memorial for 332
— note on 330
"Beecher's Bibles" 221
Beeks, Chas. E., Baldwin 80
Beezley, Geo. F., Girard 58, 80
Belden, Mr. —— 411
Bell, J. C. 119
Belleville municipal band 214
Belleville *Telescope* 220, 222
Beloit, date of old settlers' meeting at .. 433
— municipal band mentioned 106, 214
— rival of Glen Elder for county seat of Mitchell county 105
Beloit *Gazette*, note on history of 223
Belsha, George, St. Clair, Mo. 267, 277
Bemis, Eleanor S. 176, 284
— became Mrs. Thomas C. Wells 143
— *See, also*, Wells, Ella S.
Bennett, Abram, Indian agent at Kennekuk 324
Bennett, Mrs. S. H. 427
Bennington, municipal band 214
Bennington Presbyterian Church, note on history of 106
Bent county, Colo. 22
Benton, Col. Thomas H. 237
Bent's fort 70
Berkey, William 181
Berry, Mildred, Topeka 59
Berryman, J. W. 79, 81
Bertrand, Mr. —— 133
Bethany Printing Co., Lindsborg 426
Bethel School District, near Lincolnvale, fiftieth anniversary of erection of present school building 107
Betton, Frank H., commissioner of labor, 34 45, 191-193, 195
— engaged in lumber and milling business, 34
Bickerton, Capt. Thomas 325
Bicycle, first brought to Larned 218
Biddle, Maj. —— 136
Bieker, Mrs. Katherine 425
Big Blue river 149, 164, 167 319, 366, 367, 385
— bridge at Juniata carried away by ice, 165
— ferryboat built by Donner party at Independence crossing 208
— flood halts Donner party 208
— Independence crossing described by Bryant 210
— Juniata ferry operated by S. D. Dyer, 150
— largest tributary of Kansas river 366
— political complexion of settlers on east and west sides of 165
Big Cottonwood Crossing, Oxford known locally as 181
Big Nemaha river 345
Big Springs, mentioned 416
Biggs, John S. 214
Bigsby, Mrs. Guy (Nellie Colman), notes regarding her early history of Kanwaka 219, 327
Billings, Ada, director 432
Bingham, Mr. ——, appointed minister to Sault Ste. Marie 237

Binkley Brothers, operated store at Oxford 181
Binkley, John 181
Binkley, Lafe 181
Birch, James H. 419
Bird City, St. John's Lutheran Church, note on history of 328
Bird City *Times* 329
Bishop, G. S., diary of, mentioned 331
Biskie, H. A. 334
Bismarck Grove, Lawrence 281
Bison, Okla., formerly Buffalo Springs .. 8
Black, Elisha, first white child born in Crawford county 420
Black Dog trail of Osages 26, 189
Black Hawk war 150
Black Jack, battle of 66
Black locust trees 395
Black Paint creek 375
Black walnut timber 249
Blacksnake Hills, south of St. Joseph, Mo., 378
Blaine, James G. 202
Blaine county, Oklahoma 6
Blake, Mr. —— 237-239
Blakesley, Charles, road commissioner ... 380
Blanchard, Leola Howard, *Conquest of the Southwest*, quoted 190
Blizzard 65
— January, 1886, note on 331
—— featured in several Kansas papers in January, 1936 111
— middle 1880's mentioned 215
Blood, Rev. Chas. E., of Manhattan ... 169 295, 396, 397, 399, 411, 418
Blue Rapids 211
Blue river. *See* Big Blue river.
Blue sky legislation 57
Blue Springs, Scott county, Ky., Indian school at 354
Bluemont College, Manhattan 146, 393
— contract let for building 395
— corner stone ceremonies 399
— Joseph Denison one of founders 288
Bly, Joe 420
Boasa, Mr. —— 300
Boat, sunk in Kansas river 345
Bobia, Mr. —— 134
Bodwell, Rev. Lewis 417
Bogus laws 282
Bolles, Lucius 345
— corresponding secretary American Baptist Board of Foreign Missions 263
Bolton township, Cowley county ... 30- 32
Bonebrake, Fred B., Topeka 80
Bonner Springs *Chieftain*, Mrs. Frances Zumwalt Vaughn, editor 216
Bonsall, I. H. 29
Boomer wagons, ferrying of 26
Boone, Daniel 351
Boone, Daniel Morgan, farmer for Kaw Indians 351, 352
Boone, Napoleon, first white child born in Kansas 424
Booth, Henry 293, 308
Border Ruffians 169, 291
— encamped near Manhattan in 1856 ... 170
— under Atchison and Stringfellow 158
Border war 66
Borthwick, Martha, treasurer Ness County Historical Society 112
Boughton, Bessie, manuscripts given Historical Society by 58
Bourbon county 77
Bourgmont, French explorer, camped on Grasshopper 320
Bourne, E. G. 119
Bowen, Emanuel, name given by to Arkansas river 22
Bowlus, Thomas H., Iola 80
Bowman, Mrs. Thomas R. 58

438 GENERAL INDEX

Bows and arrows.................... 20
Boycott, of Topeka *Commonwealth*.. 47- 49
Boycotter, Topeka, issued during strike on Topeka *Commonwealth*.......... 48
Boycotts, in Kansas................... 46
Boyer, A. 105
Boyer, W. M., ferry incorporator...... 181
Boynton, C. B........................ 155
Braidwood, John R., Pittsburg, appointed inspector of mines.......... 35
Breechclout, Indian 20
Brent, Harry W., secretary-treasurer Twentieth Kansas Association....... 432
Brethren, Church of, Quinter.......... 217
Bridge, Grasshopper Falls, construction of 323
— Juniata, carried away by ice 165
— Oxford 183
— Sedgwick county, first move to from... 188
Bridges, C. R., employed to operate Arkansas City free ferry 28
Briggs, George M. 180
Briggs, James, note on early life in Kiowa county 214
Brigham, Mrs. Lalla M., Council Grove, 81
Bright, J. D. 335
Brininstool, E. A. 427
Brinsmaid, James B................... 58
Brokaw, C. L., Kansas City 81
Brooks, Mrs. Sarah, captured by Cheyennes 336
Brown, Mr. ——, mentioned by McCoy 236, 240, 264, 383, 390, 394
Brown, Mrs. ——, mentioned by McCoy 235, 383, 384
Brown, A. O., mayor of Parsons, 198, 200, 201
Brown, Dr. Barnum, native Kansan, curator American Museum of Natural History 422
Brown, E. S. 120
Brown, George W..................... 66
Brown, Ex-Gov. J. C., one of receivers of Texas & Pacific Railroad 194, 195
Brown, John 57, 66, 117
— Wadsworth Mound near Greeley, a lookout of 333
Brown, John, St. Louis, Mo. 272
Brown, John A. 415
Brown, Lewellyn 271
Brown, Mary 415
Brown, W. G. 120
Brown, W. R., ferry incorporator...... 25
Brown county, Kickapoo reserve in southwest corner of 15
— ferries operating within 379, 380
Browne, Chas. H., Horton 70
Browning, Mr. ——, of Fitchburg, Mass., mentioned 168, 288 291, 294, 300, 312, 397
Browning, Mrs. ——, of Fitchburg, Mass., mentioned 294, 300
Brummitt, D. R. 325
Bryant, Edwin 208, 209
— account of death of Mrs. Sarah Keyes written by 209, 210
Bryant, Dr. T. S., surgeon at Cantonment Leavenworth 360
Buchan, Wm. J., bill creating labor bureau sponsored by 33
— state senator, sketch of 33, 34
Buchanan, President James 73, 302
Buckskin leggins 18
Buckskin moccasins 17
Buffalo 13, 65, 70, 109, 185, 257, 370
— horns, as ornaments 18
— — spoons made from 255
— last killed in Stafford county in 1879. 216
— meat 284
— migrations, many trails through Indian country follow paths of 5

Buffalo overcoat 17
Buffalo Bill. See Cody, Wm. F.
Buffalo Springs, now Enid, Okla...... 7
Bull boats 185
Bull Moose movement................. 77
Bull wagon bosses..................... 332
Bumgardner, Edward 58, 81
— member State Historical Society...... 226
— "The First Kansas Band," article by 278- 281
Bunker Hill, Russell county, in 1875, note on 108
Burdick, Fannie 154, 284
Burlingame, coal mine strike at......... 193
Burlingame *Independent* 193
Burlington, Iowa, Oak street junior high school 114
Burlington *Republican* 431
Burnett, Abraham, Pottawatomie chief 131, 134
Burnett, John 133, 134, 136
Burns, C. C., mayor of Atchison........ 38
Burns, consolidated schools, note on..... 332
— First Methodist Church 333
Burns *Citizen* 332
Burns *News* 333
Burr, Mrs. F. M. 425
Burr Oak, note on early history of...... 328
Burr Oak *Herald* 327, 328, 334
Burt, F. I. 332
Burton, Mrs. Ellen..................... 420
Burton, Joseph R...................... 35
Busch, Rev. Geo., pastor Salem Lutheran Church, Lenexa 216
Bushong, Gen. James G. Harbord spent early years in hills near............. 425
Bushwhackers 66
Butler, Pardee, enforced cruise on "Missouri river by Pro-slavery men, mentioned 423
Butler county 189
— Rose School District No. 27, note on history of 427
Butterfield, Mr. ——, of Riley county.. 307
Butterfield's Overland Despatch 336
— stages on 68
Buzzard feathers as ornaments.......... 17
Byers, Otto P., of Chicago, had a part in railroad building in Kansas.......... 327

C

Cabot, John, mentioned........... 117, 118
Cabot, Sebastian, Muscovy company voyage of 118
Caldwell 5, 7, 8, 26
— cornerstone of new city building laid on February 27, 1936............. 221
— end of cattle trail at................ 12
— laid out by Wichita group........... 221
— years as a cattle town.............. 13
Caldwell *Daily Messenger*, "Cornerstone Edition" of 221
Calemink river 229
Calhoun, John 384
Calhoun, John C., Secretary of War.... 122
California, saved to Union by Pony Express 70
— Spanish land grants in.............. 72
Callaway county, Mo.................. 276
Cameron, Gen. Hugh.................. 202
Camp Beecher, Wichita on site of..... 189
Camp Gardner, Johnson county, transient camp 214
Camp Leavenworth 240, 340
— *See*, *also*, Cantonment Leavenworth and Fort Leavenworth.
Campbell, Alexander B., adjutant general 40, 42, 197, 199- 201
Campbell, Donald 427

General Index 439

Campbell, Maj. John, sub agent for
 Shawnee and Delaware agency... 342- 345
  348, 351, 358, 359, 362, 377, 378
Canadian river 326
Candler, —— —, cattle dealer of Indian
 territory 8
Canoes 229-231, 256
Cantonment Leavenworth 340, 341
  346, 347, 351-353, 355, 359, 367, 370
— Dr. T. S. Bryant surgeon of........ 360
Cape Horn 72
Capper, Arthur, Topeka............. 79, 81
— elected governor and U. S. senator... 77
— Shawnee County Old Settler's Association addressed by................ 112
Carbondale 422
— disastrous fire in coal mine in 1883,. 34
Carey, Mich......... 234, 237, 258, 262, 266
— Isaac McCoy a missionary at....... 227
— Mr. Reed sub-agent at............ 230
Carey mission, established on St. Joseph's
 river, Mich................... 122, 237
— McCoy moves family to............ 141
— named for celebrated Baptist missionary 141
— started erection of buildings at...... 141
Carlisle, Alex, said to be first rider on
 Pony Express out of St. Joseph, Mo.. 69
Carlson, A. W., director Lindsborg Historical Society 112
Carnegie Institute, Washington......... 118
Carney, Thomas, Leavenworth.......... 57
— governor of Kansas................. 73
Carpenter, A. B. & Co................ 291
Carpenter, Bertha 219
Carpenter, G. W................. 108, 429
Carpenters, wages per day in Manhattan
 in 1856 167
Carpet, Indian, made of rushes and iris.. 20
Carr, B. O., ferry operator............. 186
Carr, Frank O. 109
Carrie, Mr. and Mrs. W. C., Topeka.... 59
Carrol, —— ——, member of McCoy party,
 reprimanded for sleeping while doing
 guard duty 367
Carroll, Angus, bridge and ferry incorporator 183
Carroll, Gen. T. K., Paola............. 50
Carson, F. L., Wichita............. 79, 81
Carter, Edmund J., Gravois, Cooper
 county, Mo. 273
Cary, Harvey Myers.................. 58
Cary, Rev. Wm. B................... 106
Cass, Gov. Lewis, of Michigan..... 134- 136
  141, 230
— Isaac McCoy's visit to.............. 130
Cassoday, note on reminiscences of...... 429
Castanien, Pliny, newsman of Wichita
 Eagle 223
Catfish, three feet long................ 209
Catholic Advance, Wichita............ 213
Catholic church, in Kansas, note regarding history of.................... 213
— — note on first erected............ 330
— — Paola, note on history of........ 215
Catholic mission, St. Marys, mail held at, 151
Cattle, dealers of, Indian territory 8
— driven to Wichita by Chisholm...... 7
— first Texas to arrive at Abilene...... 8
— industry, Chisholm trail made famous
 by 8
— — in early-day Kansas, note on history of 422
— trails, Chisholm 189
— — — article on, by John Rossel.. 3- 14
— — multitude of, in Texas........... 10
— — through Indian territory, note on
 history of 325
Cawker City, Great Spirit Spring near.. 373

Cawker City, library of, Mrs. Adele
 Jennings, librarian 105
— municipal band of 106
— note regarding early days in 106
Cawker City *Ledger*................... 106
Cawker City *News* 105
Cedar creek, Jefferson county 319
— near Manhattan 149- 151
Cedar posts 305
Cedar Vale 32
Census, Kansas, law providing for, repealed by 1935 legislature 58
— Osborne county, 1870, mentioned 329
Central Branch of Missouri Pacific, Atchison round house wrecked by mob of
 strikers 197
— Union Pacific 15
Chachhaa Hogeree, Prairie village 353
Challiss, J. M., Atchison 64, 79, 81
Chandenois, an Indian accompanying
 McCoy 229, 239, 240, 243
  248-250, 261, 266
— game killed by 247
— injured while intoxicated 234
— kills turkey 256
— McCoy's praise of 250
— searches for stray horse........ 241, 242
Chanton, Mo. 261
Chanute *Tribune* 422
Chapman, E. B., of Topeka *State
 Journal* 223
Chapman creek 374
Chariton, Mo., early mention of........ 342
Chariton county, Mo. 275
Charity Masonic Lodge No. 263, Hazelton, note on history of............. 222
Charless, Joseph, Sr. 271
Chase county, history of, soon to be
 published 431
Chase County Historical Society.... 61, 79
— officers elected 431
Chautauqua, Ottawa noted for......... 333
Chebass, chief of Pottawatomies....... 142
Cheney, note on history of 111
Cheney *Sentinel*, cited........... 109, 111
Cherokee Indians, George Vashon agent
 for 350
— Jesse Chisholm a half breed 6
— western, of Arkansas 6
Cherokee outlet...................... 57
— opening of, mentioned 426
Chesbro, Jack 214
Cheyenne agency, Darlington, Okla..... 7
Cheyenne Indians, kill Benj. White and
 take daughter prisoner 336
Chicago, Ill., Isaac McCoy touched at,
 while setting out for exploring expedition 229
— once known as "Garden City of the
 West" 162
— prairie country in vicinity of........ 232
Chicago Fort (Fort Dearborn)......... 230
Chicago river, McCoy's party swim horses
 across 230
Chicago, Rock Island & Pacific Railway,
 closely follows line of Chisholm trail, 8
— Horton shops, fiftieth anniversary of
 establishment of 428
Chickasaw Indians 228, 239, 240
— decide not to accompany McCoy on
 exploring tour on account of lateness
 of season 238
— inspect lands west of Missouri....... 122
Chickasha, Okla. 8
Childs, Mr. —— ——,............... 293, 300
Childs, Lydia, mentioned.............. 119
Chills 164, 167
Chinese sugar cane................... 315
Chippewa Indians 123, 135

440 GENERAL INDEX

Chisholm, Jesse, a half-breed Cherokee,
  loyalist refugee 6
— biographical sketch 6
— — note on 326
— established trail which bears his name, 6
— guided by Indian trails through Indian territory 6
— herd of cattle collected by.......... 7
— J. R. Mead an associate of.......... 3
— note on shrewdness of.............. 328
— searches for buried treasure......... 6
— trading post of, at mouth of Little Arkansas 6, 10, 11
Chisholm, John, no trail to the north laid out by........................ 11
Chisholm creek 188, 328
Chisholm trail 189, 325, 330
— beginnings of 4
— branch trail laid out................ 12
— Chas. M. Harger's description of.... 13
— discussed in article by John Rossel, 3- 14
— disputes concerning origin of, and its location 10
— ended at Wichita................... 9
— extended from Indian territory to Texas 12
—footnote concerning 14
— made famous by cattle trade........ 8
— many trips over made by Joseph Stroud 5
— note on history of................. 422
— route of 8
— — note on 222
— was not for cattle.................. 7
Chisholm Trail Association............ 13
Chisum, Claiburne.................... 11
Chisum, John Simpson, cattleman, sketch of 11
Chittenden, H. M.................... 119
Choctaw Indians 228
— delegation accompanies McCoy to inspect lands west of Missouri........ 122
— desire not to accompany McCoy on exploring tour on account of lateness of season 238
— treaty of 1825 provided for schools for, 354
Cholera 150
— at Fort Riley...................... 154
— — deaths from 157
Christian Church, Dighton, note on history of 420
— Leon, note on history of............ 329
— Oneida, fifty-fifth anniversary celebrated 214
Christmas, in early Salina, note on..... 110
Chronicles of Oklahoma, Oklahoma City, 325
Chuck-kan-no river, present Delaware... 320
Church of the Brethren, Quinter, note on history of 217
Churches, historic early, note regarding, 425
Cimarron crossing, of Arkansas river, 70, 190
Cimarron Methodist Episcopal Church, note on fiftieth anniversary of...... 330
Cincinnati company, vote town shares towards building churches in Manhattan 303
Citizen-Patriot, Atwood 333
Civil War 65, 66, 68, 73
Civil Works Administration............ 55
Civilian Conservation Corps, camp newspapers published by, given Historical Society 59
Clark, Carroll D..................... 419
Clark, George A..................... 219
Clark, Henry A...................... 425
Clark, L. R......................... 110
Clark, Marston G., sub-agent for Kansas Indians 342, 348, 350 358, 362, 363, 375

Clark, Gen. William, Indian affairs superintendent 227-229 235, 238-240, 245, 267, 271, 342 345, 348, 349, 354, 355, 361, 377
— letter to Isaac McCoy, advises him to start on exploring tour............ 240
— McCoy calls on..................... 233
— — dines with 234
— — reports to, on return from exploring tour 264, 265
Clark county, note on early history of, 108
Clark County Clipper, Ashland, cited.... 108
Clarke, Dr. ——, of New England.... 286 291, 294, 301-304, 317, 389, 393, 406, 414
Clarke, Mrs. —— 309
Clarke, Ellis M...................... 333
Clarke, George W..................... 66
Clarke, Sarah Elizabeth, wife of Thomas P. Wells 143
Clark's Creek church (Lutheran), anniversary of 424
Clay, Henry 120
Clay Center, First Baptist Church, note on silver anniversary of dedication of. 328
— operated street cars in late 1880's.... 221
— St. Paul's Episcopal Church, fifty-fifth anniversary observed.......... 217
— Swedesburg Lutheran Church, sixty-fifth anniversary 425
Clay Center *Dispatch*.....217, 221, 328, 423
Clay Center *Economist*................ 427
Clay Center *Times*............... 328, 427
Clear creek, ford on, south of Kennekuk, 324
Clearwater 7
— First Presbyterian Church, note on... 214
Clemens, Edwin T.................... 222
Cleopatra 71
Cleve, Richard, Pony Express rider..... 331
Clifton, note on telephone history of.... 218
Clifton *News* 218
Clinger, F. S........................ 58
Cloud county, note regarding Arthur Selleck's reminiscences of 109
Clyde, date of old settlers' meeting at... 433
Clyde *Republican*.................... 422
Coal 251
— discovered by McCoy on Salt creek.. 361
— hauled long distances............... 193
— railroads grant low rate when hauled long distances 193
— southern Kansas, competing with Osage county 193
Coal mine, Carbondale, disastrous fire in 1883 at 34
Coats, Methodist Church, fiftieth anniversary of 326
Coats *Courant* 326, 422
Cody, William F................. 326, 332
— long ride made by while Pony Express rider 69
— outlaws hold up with disastrous results 69
— proposed bronze statue to mark spot where he spent boyhood days........ 218
Coffey county 77
— Hard Pan school, note on........... 330
Coffeyville, Woman's Relief Corps, note on early history of................ 328
Coffeyville *Leader* 328
Coffland, Bertha 428
Cohon (or Cohern), J., Shawnee express 342, 343
Colbert, principal chief of Chickasaw Indians 238
Colby, First Methodist Episcopal Church, note on anniversary of............ 333
Colby *Free Press-Tribune*....... 331, 333
Cold Springs, third station on Pony Express route west of St. Joseph...... 69

General Index

Coldwater, Methodist Episcopal Church, note on history of 216
Coldwell, John F., bridge and ferry incorporator 183
Collett, Mrs. Edith Phillips 107
Colonial Dames 61
Colonization attempts, Jewell county, note on 327
Colony, Beecher Bible and Rifle, note on, 332
Colorado, Arkansas river rises in mountains of 22
— — water of, monopolized by farmers of, 24
— ores of, refined at Argentine 191
— sandy soil east of Rocky Mountains.. 23
Colorado State Historical Society 336
Columbus, Christopher, mentioned.. 117, 118
Columbus, Cherokee county 35
Columbus (Miss.) *Press* 59
Colver, Mrs. Bessie 214
Comanche Indians 6
— boys rescued from, by William Mathewson 8
Comechau, Indian chief 431
Compromise of 1850 117
Concord, Atchison county ghost town... 421
Concord stage 15
— trip from Newton to Wichita in 1870 in, note regarding 421
Cone, Rev. Spencer H..... 261, 344, 347, 354
Confan, I. T., Belle Plaine 182
Confederates, Chisholm prevailed upon to aid 6
Congdon, W. M., state senator 33
Congregational Church, General Association of Kansas 386
— — met at Lawrence in 1859 399
— Manhattan 143, 166, 169, 290
                   303, 307-309, 318, 391, 417
— — organized in 1856 168
Congress, note regarding Kansans in, during first thirty years of statehood.... 109
— passed resolution authorizing appointment of committee to investigate labor troubles in various Mid-Western states, 196
Congressional Library, Washington, maps in 3
Conklin, P. J., early Kingman newspaperman 216
Conley, John, ferry operator 180
Connelley, William E. 116, 320
Connor, John, Delaware interpreter..... 343
                         344, 352-355, 357-359
Constitution, Kansas, some provisions of. 52
Constitutional prohibition, Gov. St. John's fight in favor of 75
Consular service, note on Kansans prominent in 329
Cook, Lieut. — — 351
Coolidge, A. C. 425
Coolidge 22
Coon creek, note on Indian battle on... 419
Copperas, found by McCoy's exploring party 368
Copperas creek 369
Corbett, Boston, as preacher 105
Corinth township, Osborne county, note on first electors 213
Corley, — —, murder of, mentioned.... 214
Cormack, John, Edwardsville, Ill. 269
Corn 282, 284
— boiled 255
— high price of 316
— Manhattan price, 1856 168
— — 1859 .... 392, 408, 411
— parched, McCoy's exploring party obligated to subsist on 244
Cornell University 115
Cornstalk, Shawnee Indian 376
Cornwall, Rev. Mr. — — 210

Coronado 218
— expedition of 22, 220
— horses brought to America by 68
Correll, Charles M., Manhattan 81
— president Riley County Historical Society 432
Cortez, horses brought to America by... 68
Cottonwood Falls, date of old settlers' meeting at 433
Cottonwood trees 395
— on Republican river 369, 372
Cougher, T. J. 197
Council City 147
Council Grove 70
— note on telephone history of 218
Council Grove, I. T., Chisholm's trading post at, abandoned at outbreak of Civil War 7
Council Grove *Republican* 218
County clerks, Kansas, first annual convention of, at Topeka 106
County seat wars, Kansas, mention of... 111
Court, first session in Missouri valley held at mouth of Kansas river in 1804... 334
Covenant Church, Marquette Mission.. 222
Covert, community, note on pioneers of.. 330
Cowboy band, Dodge City 110
Cowley county 23, 25
— all bridges destroyed by flood in 1877. 182
— ferries operating within .. 26-32, 180, 181
— first ferry license for Arkansas river issued in 26
— note on history of 419
Cowskin creek 183
Cox, Ida Ellen 110
Cox, J. J. 51
Coyotes, the ghouls of the prairie..... 70
Cramer's crossing, on Great Nemaha river 380
Crane, Frank S. 219
Crane, R. M., state senator 33
Crawford, S. J., colonel of colored regiment in Civil War 74
— governor of Kansas 73
— Tom McNeal's recollections of.... 74, 75
Crawford county, note regarding first white child born in 420
Crawford's opera house, Topeka 204
Creek Indians 237-239, 264, 266
— delegation accompanies McCoy to inspect lands west of Missouri 122
Creswell township, Cowley county ... 27, 30
Crofton, Mrs. George, note regarding sod house of 425
Crookneck squashes 284
Cross, Susy 388, 389
Crossle, Henry, St. Louis, Mo...... 270, 273
Crowder peas 308
Cuba municipal band, mentioned....... 214
Cultus Club, woman's organization, Phillipsburg, note on history of..... 110
Cummins, Richard W., Indian agent... 376
Curtin, A. G., ex-Governor of Pennsylvania 196
Cyclone, first big storm to strike Barton county, mention of 424
— Ottawa, note on 333

D

Daily Citizen, Topeka 35
— attitude of, during boycott of *Commonwealth* 47
Daily Eclipse, Parsons 194, 197
                              198, 201, 202
Daily Republican, Burlington 339
Darlington, Okla., Cheyenne agency at... 7
Darrow, Mrs. Mary E. 105
Daughters, Mrs. C. B., director 432
Daughters of American Colonists 61

General Index

Daughters of the American Revolution,. 61
— Gen. Edward Hand chapter, Ottawa, dedicate bronze markers at old mission burial ground................ 431
— — organized in 1889................. 333
— Kansas chapters represented at fourth annual pilgrimage at Shawnee mission, 431
— Topeka chapter, note on history of... 426
Daughters of 1812....................... 61
Davenport, Maj. William, of Sixth infantry 359, 360
— commandant at Fort Leavenworth.... 346, 349, 350, 357
— unfriendly towards McCoy........... 361
David, John G., ferry incorporator...... 182
Davies, Gomer T....................... 105
Davis, — —, mentioned by Isaac McCoy, 342, 377
Davis, A. A. 27
— known as "Peg Leg" Davis, ferry operator 26
Davis, Adley, assisted father operating ferry boat 26
Davis, Jefferson, appointed Secretary of War, became interested in railroad extension to the west.................. 4
— map made at instigation of.......... 5
Davis, John W., Dodge City............ 81
Davis, Jonathan M., elected governor... 77
Davis, S. K., road viewer.............. 190
Davis, Sophia 26
Dawson, John S., Hill City...... 54, 79, 81
Dean, John S., Topeka........... 62, 63, 80
Dedman, Samuel, of Pike county, Indiana, McCoy's exchange of letters with, 128
Deep Water creek, present Chapman creek 374
Deer 65, 150, 244, 247, 248, 250, 253, 258, 284, 355, 366, 367, 369, 370, 373, 374
— abundance of, along Neosho river.... 252
Deer creek, tributary of Arkansas river 27, 28
Deere, E. O., director Lindsborg Historical Society 112
Deerfield, old settlers' meeting held in.. 433
Deerskin moccasins 245
Delaware and Shawnee agency.. 341, 342, 376
Delaware Indians 339, 340, 350, 352, 354, 357-359
— Anderson chief of.................... 376
— invited to Lawrence Fourth of July celebration 279
— J. Connor interpreter 344
— Johnny Quick, second chief of........ 343
— name given Grasshopper river....... 320
— new settlement formed by........... 376
— start for Kansas without aid from government 376
— treaty, at St. Marys, Ohio........... 340
Delaware lands, iron ore found on...... 355
— McCoy's survey for establishing boundaries of 341
— mound ten feet square and six feet high to mark northern boundary..... 355
— sale of 322
Delaware outlet 340
— McCoy completes survey of........... 371
— mound erected by McCoy at commencement of 363
Delaware reservation 323, 416
— site of Fort Leavenworth reserved by McCoy in surveying of.............. 359
Delaware river 352
— also known as Sautrelle............. 354
— early effort to build bridge near mouth of 322
— ferries on, discussed by George A. Root 319-324
— floods in 319
— formerly called Grasshopper, history of, 319

Delaware river, largest tributary of the Kansas east of the Blue............ 319
— origin of name 319
Delisle, William, map of............... 22
— mentions Arkansas river as the Acansa, 21
DeLong, Mrs. Maud, daughter of Jefferson Riddle 322
Delphi, now Arkansas City............ 25
Democratic party 202
— Kansas, George W. Glick, first governor elected by 76
— — note on 222
Democratic Platform, Liberty, Mo., file of, acquired by Historical Society.... 59
Democratic state convention, labor resolutions passed by 203
Democrats 66
DeMott, Fred C., letter regarding Arkansas river ferry quoted................ 26
Denious, Jess C., Dodge City.......... 81
Denison, John 298, 303
Denison, Rev. Joseph, mentioned...... 287, 402, 416
— one of founders of Bluemont college.. 288
Denison, Mrs. Joseph.................. 287
Denison, Mariann 303
Denison, W. W., death mentioned...... 54
Denison, Texas, Missouri Pacific strike of 1885 36
Denton's ford on Arkansas river, ferry at, 29
Denver, James W., veto of bill for establishment of ferry over Grasshopper river 323
DeSmet, Father Paul J................ 378
Dewey, Admiral George, victory in Manila Bay subject of poem by E. F. Ware 109
Diamond School District 14, west of Green, Clay county, note on......... 329
Dickinson county 189, 221
Dighton, Christian Church, note on history of 420
Dighton Herald 420
Dixon, Mrs. Archibald, mentioned...... 120
Doctors, early-day 333
— walking six miles to summon......... 66
Dodd, W. E., mentioned 121
Dodds, Frank, vice-president Twentieth Kansas Association 432
Dodge, A. S., road viewer 190
Dodge City 24
— end of cattle trail at................ 11
— fight near, mentioned................ 110
— I. O. O. F. lodge in................. 421
— most famous of pioneer cattle towns.. 13
— note, early automobiles and owners... 109
— — historic places of 422
— — introduction of electric lights in... 425
— — wild and woolly days of........... 427
Dodge City Daily Globe...... 106, 109, 110, 421, 422, 425
Dodge City Journal.................... 106
Doerr, Mrs. Laura P. V., Larned.. 79- 81
Dog story, told by Tom McNeal....... 78
Doles, Mrs. Ellen T.................... 331
Doniphan 320
Doniphan county 217
— history of schools made............. 57
— Wathena first county seat of........ 21
Donner party, composition of.......... 208
— crossing of Big Blue river........... 208
— passed over Oregon trail in Kansas in 1846 208
Donoghue, David, Fort Worth, Tex..... 326
Doran, T. F., Topeka............. 78- 81
— address as president of Historical Society 65, 66
— short address introducing T. A. McNeal 71

General Index

Dougherty, Col. ——, of Texas........ 8
Dougherty, Maj. John, agent for Pawnees ..346-349, 351-355, 357-359, 362, 366
Douglas, A. A., mentioned.... 117, 120, 121
Douglas county, historic points in, visited 432
Douglas County Historical Society.. 219, 327
— historic spots in Douglas county visited by 432
— members visit Lecompton............ 336
— newly elected officers of............. 112
Douglass, Geo. L., Wichita, elected speaker 76
Douglass 32
Dover, Okla. 10
Downs *News* 213, 423
Doyle, Mr. —— 230
Dragoons, at Fort Riley................ 289
"Dramatic Kansas," paper by Olin Templin, of Kansas University, reviewed in Iola *Daily Register*.............. 108
Dred Scott decision, mentioned..... 117, 121
Droughts 65, 66
— country exceedingly parched with.... 365
— early day 214
— 1830 a year of.................... 363
— 1857 .... 310, 323
— 1860 .... 24, 414, 416
— mentioned by McCoy 369
Drum, Indian, monotonous music of 16
Drumheller, Daniel Montgomery, a Pony Express rider 222
Dudley, S. N. 58
Dugouts 181
— of large cottonwood trees, Donner party crossed Big Blue river in...... 208
Duncan, S. L., Wichita 187
Dunlap, John, ferry incorporator....... 182
Dunsmore, J. M., known as the "Bald Hornet of the Neosho" 76
— speaker of Populist house 76
DuPratz, Le Page 22
Dust bowl, southwest Kansas, note on history of 332
Dust storms 65
— mentioned by McCoy... 365, 366, 371, 372
— plow not to blame for 222
Dutch Henry's crossing, massacre at... 66
Dyer, ——, marriage to Miss Hanna.. 155
Dyer, G. M., Osawkee................. 322
Dyer, S. D., resident of Juniata 151, 152, 155, 158
— biographical sketch 150
— Sunday school held at house of...... 150
Dyer, Mrs. S. D. 150
Dyer, W. F., Osawkee 322

E

Early days in western Kansas.......... 428
Earthenware pot, made by aborigines, found by McCoy.................... 369
East Bolton, Cowley county........... 29
Eastern Star, Order of................ 223
Eaton, Mrs. E. A., recollections of Arkansas river ferry................. 26
Ebenezer Methodist Church, Highland township, Clay county.............. 427
Eberhardt, G. E., director Lindsborg Historical Society.................. 112
Economist, Clay Center 217, 218, 328
Edson, A. B.......................... 219
Education, Edwards county, note on history of 110
Edwards' *Atlas of Cowley County*.... 181
Edwards county............ 23, 25, 110, 421
Edwardsville, Ill. 233, 269
Effingham 324
Egyptian corn, introduced in Barton county 423, 424
El Dorado 32

El Dorado Junior College.............. 335
Election, 1857, Kansas, a Free State triumph 315
Elections, primary 57
Electric lighting, in Great Bend, mentioned 421
— introduced in Dodge city in 1886.... 425
— plant, Ottawa 333
Elisha's creek, ferry at................ 379
Elk 249, 251-253 258, 355, 356, 363, 370, 374
Elk Falls 32
Elkhart river, Indiana, McCoy selects site for mission on................. 131
Ellenbecker, John G., Marysville.... 79, 81 109, 331, 332, 427
— *Pony Express Courier*, contributor... 222
Elliott, Chas. S....................... 219
Elliott Addressing Machine Co......... 63
Ellson, Mrs. Ralph.................... 429
Ellsworth, Fred 219
Ellsworth, years as a cattle town....... 13
Ellsworth *Messenger* 214, 331
Ellsworth municipal band, mentioned... 214
Ellsworth *Reporter* 331
— published sixty-four years.......... 109
Elm, oak and walnut timber on Kickapoo reserve 16
Elm Creek township, Marshall county... 211
Elm Spring, Indian territory, branch of Chisholm trail started from........ 12
Elm trees 369, 372
El Paso, bridge at, washed out during flood in 1877...................... 185
— ferry, charges on................... 184
— now Derby, started in 1870........ 184
— Sumner county 30
El Paso Bridge Co., toll rates of... 184, 185
El Reno, Okla. 8
Embree, Mrs. Mary................... 80
— treasurer Kansas State Historical Society 63
Emerald, founded by Irish............. 334
Emigrant Aid Company................ 278
Emmons, Charles, director............ 432
Emory, Col. Wm. H., troops consolidated under command of................ 6
Empire-Journal, Osborne, note on history of 217
Emporia 42
— first colored family in, mentioned.... 420
Emporia *Gazette* 111, 427
Emporia *Republican*, published by C. V. Eskridge 25
Emporia State Normal School.......... 25
English, N. A., chairman Sedgwick county board of commissioners............ 188
"English Bill," mentioned............. 116
Enid, Okla........................... 7, 8
Episcopal Church, St. Paul's of Clay Center, note on history of.......... 217
Epley, Charles 328
Epp, J. R. 110
Epsom salts, along Republican river.... 369
Erwin, Joseph 274
Eskridge, C. V., ferry incorporator..... 25
Estes, Littleberry, mentioned by Isaac McCoy 261, 275, 342
Eudora, note on early history of....... 328
Eudora *Weekly News*, fiftieth anniversary of 328
Eureka high school 2
Evans, Abner A., LaFayette county, Mo., 274
Evans, Mrs. Mary 214
Evening Kansan-Republican, Newton... 421
Everett, Wm., Clay county, Mo........ 274
Ewing, C., mentioned by Isaac McCoy.. 342
Explorers, early, encountered dust storms in West 222

444   GENERAL INDEX

Exploring expeditions of 1828 and 1830, by Isaac McCoy, journal edited by Lela Barnes 227-277, 339-377

F

Fagan ——, superintendent of Missouri Pacific Railway................. 38, 43
Failyer, Mrs. G. H., officer Riley County Historical Society 79, 432
Fairchild, Frances 222
Fairview *Enterprise* 215
Fall River, note on schools in vicinity of, 328
Fall River *Star* 328
Famine 66
Farm creek, near Fort Clark........... 269
Farmers State Bank of Lindsborg, chartered in 1886..................... 426
Farms 331
Faulkner, C. E. 200
Fay, Edward T. 58
Fay, Mrs. Mamie Axline, Pratt........ 81
Fayette, Mo. 261, 275
Federal Archives Survey, work in Kansas progressing on 224
Felts, J. G............................. 427
Ferguson, James, sheriff of Wyandotte county 191, 198
"Ferries in Kansas," articles by George A. Root, "Arkansas River"... 22- 32
                                                       180- 190
—— "Grasshopper River"........ 319- 324
—— "Great Nemaha River"...... 378- 380
Ferry, Leonard S. 219
Ferry, Grasshopper Falls............... 323
Ferry boat, *Big Blue Rover*, constructed by Donner Party at Independence crossing 208
— operated by S. D. Dyer........ 165, 166
Fever and ague...... 158, 159, 251, 298, 316
Fidelity, St. Augustine's Church, note on history of 215
Finney county 23
— ferry operating within 190
— old settlers' meeting held in.......... 433
Fire department, Gypsum, mentioned.... 332
— Osborne, organized 1888 329
Fires, in Gypsum, note on............. 332
— in Ottawa 333
— *See, also,* Prairie fires.
Fish, E. A., ferry incorporator........ 180
Fish, Pascal 377
Fish, S. G., road commissioner........ 380
Fish, shot by Wesauogana.............. 251
Fisher, Mrs. Mattie.................... 331
Fishwaters, Mr. —— 240
Fitch, E. P., killed in Quantrill raid.... 280
Fitzgerald, Mary Paul.................. 421
Flags, U. S., over Major Langham's shanty 352
— requested by McCoy for use on exploring tour 342, 352
Flatboat, on Grasshopper near old Huron, 324
Flatboats, on Arkansas river........... 25
Flick, Mrs. John, officer Riley County Historical Society 432
Flies, bad 238
Flint Hills, note regarding springs in.... 110
Flint-lock musket 20
Flood, Jane 419
Floods 66
— Cowley county bridges destroyed during 1877 182
— Delaware river 319
— El Paso bridge carried away during... 185
— Gypsum valley, note on 332
— in Arkansas 180
Florence, T. P. Alexander pioneer hardware merchant of 106
Florence *Bulletin* 106

Flour, price in 1859 405
— scarcity of, at Harmony mission...... 244
Flournoy, ——, Independence, Mo..... 342
Fogdall, Dr. S. P...................... 431
Fool Chief, village of 352
Ford county 23, 260
Foreign settlements, in Republic county, 419
Foreman, James F., road commissioner.. 380
Foreman, John W., ferry operator 379
Forsythe, Mr. ——, mentioned........ 234
Fort Arbuckle 8
— troops of, set out for Fort Leavenworth 6
Fort Belknap, Texas................... 5
Fort Clark 231, 269
Fort Cobb 11
— troops at, set out for Fort Leavenworth 6
Fort Dearborn 230
Fort Dodge 70
Fort Dodge-Fort Hays trail........... 105
Fort Gibson, road from Fort Harker to, 189
Fort Hall 209
Fort Harker, trail to Wichita from..... 189
Fort Hays-Fort Dodge trail 105
Fort Hays Kansas State College. 57, 107, 419
— Floyd B. Streeter librarian at...... 433
— index of western Kansas newspapers preserved by, a WPA project 224
Fort Hays military reservation 111
Fort Laramie 415
Fort Leavenworth 279, 341
— Federal troops in Indian territory at beginning of Civil war ordered to, for mobilization 6
— first Kansas capital 325
— Isaac McCoy's foresight regarding site for 359
— military road from 67
— note on early history of 223
— old buildings at, still preserved..... 326
Fort Leavenworth-Fort Riley road. 150, 164
— relocation of 323
— crossed Grasshopper river near present Valley Falls 320
Fort Leavenworth military reserve, surveying of 360
Fort Leavenworth military road, note on history of 429
Fort Mann, Arkansas river said to be navigable to vicinity of 25
Fort Osage 352
Fort Riley 147, 282, 289, 300, 320, 415
— cholera raging at 154
— deaths from cholera at 157
— military road from Fort Leavenworth to 150, 164, 320
—— relocation of 323
— named for Maj. Bennet Riley 347
Fort Scott, S. D. Dyer a mechanic at.. 150
Fort Scott *Tribune* 330
Fort Scott *Tribune-Monitor* 336
Fort Sill, Okla. 7, 8
Fort Smith, Ark. 29
— Arkansas river navigable to 25
— federal garrison at 6
Fort Smith (Ark.) *Herald*, cited........ 23
Fort Washita, federal garrison at Fort Smith combined with............... 6
Fort Wayne 130, 131
                            135, 140, 252, 262
Fort Worth, Tex....................... 8
— Missouri Pacific strike of 1885....... 36
Fort Zarah 70
Forts, early Kansas, note on.......... 106
— in Ford county, investigation of..... 57
Foster, James 425
Fountain qui Bouille river, ferry planned for 190

GENERAL INDEX 445

Fouquet, L. C., Chandler, Okla., recollections of M. Greenway, operator of Wichita ferry 186
4-H Clubs, Kingman county, mentioned, 215
Four Mile community................. 217
Fourth of July, first Lawrence celebration of 279
— 1804, note on celebration of........ 334
Fox Indians 353
Fox river 268
— distressed looking whites living at mouth of 231
Frame, John, ferry operator........... 185
"Frank Heywood Hodder, 1860-1935," article by James C. Malin...... 115- 121
Frankfort *Daily Index* 420
— founded February 20, 1886.......... 220
Frankfort school history, note on...... 420
Franklin, Benjamin, quoted............ 140
Franklin, Douglas county, note on history of 423
Franklin county, note on early days of, 333
Franklin High School, Baltimore, Md....   2
Frazer, James, road commissioner...... 324
Fredonia 32
— note regarding court house at........ 111
Fredonia *Daily Herald* 111
Free Silver and Anti-Prohibition Party, Charles Robinson leader of.......... 76
Free State people, wrongs of........... 165
Freeman, Thomas 419
Freighting, from Arkansas City......... 30
Fremont, John C...................... 119
Fremont county, Colo.................. 22
French, Mrs. E. M., Jamestown, daughter of Benj. White, killed by Indians in 1868 336
French-Pottawatomie, Mo-she-No, a prominent member of............... 20
Frizell, E. E., Larned.................. 81
Fryback, Herbert L.................... 425
Frye, Johnnie, Pony Express rider, supplanted Alexander Carlisle........... 69
Fuhr, Frank 108
Fuhr, Lulu R......................... 58
Funston, "Fighting Fred".............. 111
Furs and robes, Chisholm returns with..   7

G

Gadsden Purchase 120
Garden City, boom of the 1880's described in Garden City *Daily Telegram*, 107
— note on newspaper history of........ 427
Garden City *Daily Telegram* 107, 427
— "Southwest Kansas Resource Edition" of 333
Garden Plain, date of meeting of old settlers of 433
Methodist Church, note on history of.. 109
Gardner, note regarding guerrilla visits to 215
Gardner *Gazette* 215
Garin, J. C.......................... 427
Garnett *Review* 109
Gas, artificial, in Ottawa, mentioned.... 334
Gasconade, Mo. 243, 273
Gasconade river, mills on.............. 242
Gaylord, fiftieth anniversary of incorporation 426
Geology, curious formations of, along Republican river 370
Georgia, emigrants bound for Kansas from 163
German Baptist Church, of Strassburg community, Marion county 428
German-Russians, migrate from Mexico to Russell 105
Geuda Springs, bridge completed at, in 1874 180
— Caldwell & Western Railroad Co..... 421
Geuda Springs, ferry on Arkansas near, operated by John Conley........... 180
Geuda Springs *News* 180
Ghost towns, in Kansas, mentioned.... 222
Gibson, Mrs. C. A. 431
Gibson, Thomas, Gasconade, Mo....... 273
Gilbert, Charles 188
Gill, Helen G. 116
Gillette, Almerin 45
Gillies, —— 284, 304, 392
Gillmore, Mrs. Isabel Mace, note on history of Henry Rohr Chapter of Order of the Eastern Star 223
Givin, Grace, officer Riley County Historical Society 432
Glauber salts, deposited on sand beaches of the Republican 373
Glen Elder, rival of Beloit for county seat of Mitchell county 105
Glen Elder *Sentinel* 105
Glick, George W., first Democratic governor of Kansas.................... 76
Goddard 223
Godsey, Mrs. Flora I., Emporia 64, 81
Golden, T. V., division superintendent of Missouri Pacific 198, 200
Goodnight, Charles, a partner of John Chisum 11
Goodnow, Isaac T........ 147, 149, 158, 165
                                    300, 309, 418
— one of founders of Bluemont College, Manhattan 146
Goodwin, G. H. 332
Goose, wild 247
Gordon, R. C., member ferry company.. 184
Gorham, Sylvia DeWitt 330
Gosa, Ottawa Indian...... 235, 242, 246, 248
                                249, 265, 266, 269
— accompanied McCoy on exploring tour, 229
— drunkenness of 234
Gould, Alfred, monument to............ 331
Gould, Fred, monument to 331
Gould, Jay 45, 46, 196
Gould Southwestern strike, short history of 194- 201
— states affected by................... 191
Gove City 420
Gove county, note on fiftieth anniversary ceremonies 420
Gove County *Advocate*, Quinter.... 217, 430
Gove County *Republican-Gazette*, Gove City 215, 420
— note on history of................... 419
Gove county teachers, 1935-1936, listed in Gove County *Republican-Gazette*, Gove City 215
Government road, from Fort Leavenworth to Fort Riley................. 150, 164
"Governors of Kansas," address on, by T. A. McNeal, before the Historical Society 71- 78
— surviving in 1935 77
Graduate Magazine, of University of Kansas 219
Graham, I. D......................... 58
Grand Army of the Republic, Ottawa... 334
Grand Auglaize, Mo................... 273
Grand Auglaize river, branch of the Osage, 242
Grand Island on Platte river.......... 366
Grand Pawnees, on Platte river........ 352
Grand river, Michigan, Baptist mission for Ottawas on 262
Grand river, Missouri 137, 244
Grant County Journal, Medford, Okla... 222
Grant-Johnson controversy, mentioned... 117
Grant township, Marion county, School District No. 9 107
Grape hunt 155
Grasshopper Bridge Company, failure of bill to establish 323

446 GENERAL INDEX

Grasshopper Falls 324, 416
— bridge constructed at 323
— ferry established at.............. 323
— laid out in 1859................... 320
Grasshopper river 352
— Bailey's ferry, close to Perry......... 321
— bill authorizing establishment of ferry at mouth of river, vetoed by governor, 323
— ferries on, discussed by George A. Root 319, 324
— ford west of Effingham 324
— length of 319, 354, 355
— name changed to Delaware....... 321
Grasshoppers 65, 310, 317
— in Harvey county, 1874, described by John S. Biggs in Sedgwick *Pantagraph*, 214
— may have given name to Grasshopper river 319
— near Manhattan, 1856 169
— visitations, in Kansas, years occurring, 320
— — 1857 313
— — 1874, note regarding 321, 423
Graves, W. W., *The Broken Treaty*, a story of the Osage country, issued in book form 217
Graves along the Oregon trail, note regarding 427
Gravois creek......................... 243
Gray, Dr. Clyde 428
Gray, John M., Kirwin 80
Gray county 23
— ferry operating within 190
Gray wolf 292
Grayson, Mr. ——, member of Donner party 209
Great American desert 65
Great Bend, building boom of 1878, mentioned 424
— history of, noted 423
— note on fifty years electric lighting in, 421
— sixty years' rainfall mentioned...... 423
Great Bend *Tribune* 421, 423
Great Nemaha agency 380
— John C. Anderson, interpreter at.... 18
Great Nemaha river, early mention of.. 354, 378
— ferries on, discussed by George A. Root 378-380
— length of 378
— source of 378
Great Plains region, Arkansas river traverses 22
Great Spirit spring, described by McCoy, 373
Greeley, Wadsworth mound near, a John Brown lookout 333
Green, Katherine, early days in Cawker City recounted in Cawker City *Ledger*, 106
Green, Nehemiah, preacher, became governor on resignation of Crawford.... 75
Green, Mrs. Willard 330
Green, Clay county 329
— date of old settlers' meeting at..... 433
Green Bay, Mich. 136, 234
Greenback party 202, 204
Greene, Albert R. 391
Greene, G. S. 269, 270
Greene, Max 190
Greenfield 32
Greensburg *News* 214
Greenway, M., ferry operator.......... 186
— recollections of L. C. Fouquet concerning ferry operated by.......... 186, 187
Greenwood county 189
Gridley, date of old settlers' meeting at. 433
Griffenstein, William, Wichita.......... 188
— crossed Arkansas river with wagon train 8
Grimsley, Thornton, St. Louis, Mo..... 272
Grinnell, note regarding early days..... 420
Grist mill, at Manhattan in 1856...... 166

Ground, Benjamin, St. Louis, Mo....... 269
Guerrillas, note on three visits to Gardner by 215
Guns 240
Gypsum, city auditorium 332
— fire department 332
— forty eight years ago............... 332
— mail service in, mentioned.......... 332
— municipal water system, note on..... 332
— note on early history of............ 332
— public schools, note on............. 332
Gypsum, deposits of, found by McCoy on Stranger creek 363
Gypsum *Advocate*, fiftieth anniversary edition of 332
Gypsum valley, note on floods in 332

H

Hackberry 248
Hackley, Capt. —— 135, 136
Hackney, Wm. P...................... 204
Hagadorn, E., mentioned 396
Hagard, Eliza 406
Hall, ——, Boston, dealer in band instruments 280
Hall, Mrs. ——, member of Donner party, twins born to 208
Hall, Mrs. Almira Belden 58
Hall, C. A., discharge of......... 194, 195
— foreman of woodworkers of Texas and Pacific car shops at Marshall, Tex... 194
Hall, Mrs. Carrie A., Leavenworth...... 81
Hall, Mrs. J. N....................... 336
Halstead, date of old settlers' meeting at, 433
Hamelton, Chas. A., leader in the Marais des Cygnes massacre 66
Hamilton, Clad, Topeka 81
Hamilton, George, director ferry company, 184
Hamilton, James, director ferry company, 184
Hamilton, John D. M., note on biography of 334
Hamilton county 22
— note on early history of............ 107
Hampden *Expositor* 59
Hanna, Miss ——, married to —— Dyer 155
Hanna, Mr. ——, mentioned.......... 154
Hanover, "Days of '49" celebration held in 433
Hanover bank, N. Y. 167, 170
Harbord, Gen. James G., Pershing's chief of staff during World War...... 425
Hard Pan school, District No. 3, Coffey county, note on 330
Hardeman county, Tenn. 11
Hardin, Mark 324
Hardy, Dr. Chas. W., Ottawa.......... 59
Harger, Chas. M., Abilene 14, 80, 219
— Chisholm cattle trail described by.. 13
Hargrove, L. B., sheriff 38, 39
Harlan, E. W., secretary Hodgeman County Historical Society............ 432
Harlow, Mr. ——, of Vermont 279
Harmony mission, Bates county, Mo.... 240, 243, 273
— McCoy's exploring party reach 244
— missionary force at................. 245
Harrington, Grant W. 220
Harrington, Wynne P. 420
Harris, John P........................ 333
Harrison, ——, McCoy bought horses of, 242
Harshberger, E. L. 335
Hartford, Vt., band 278
Hartley, John 111
Hartman, A. P....................... 220
Hartman, F. M....................... 220
Hartman, H. H....................... 220
Hartsock, Boone 82
— ferry at Arkansas City operated by.. 26

GENERAL INDEX 447

Harvey, Mrs. Isabelle C., Topeka... 79, 80
— member nominating committee 64
Harvey, James M., became governor and United States senator 75
— Mrs. Sara Keyes a great aunt of.... 212
— T. A. McNeal's recollections of..... 75
— three daughters of, reside on farm preempted by him in Riley county in 1859 212
Harvey county, grasshoppers in year 1874, mentioned 214
— relief furnished during winter of 1874-1875, note on 107
Harvey County News, Newton......... 421
Harwi, A. J., state senator 52
Haskell county 329
— note on early Sunday School history, 108
— old settlers' meeting held in 433
Haskin, Mrs. S. B., Olathe 81, 431
Hatfield, Rodolph, Wichita attorney.. 51, 52
Haucke, Frank, Council Grove 80
Haufbauer, John, ferry operator 184
Haven, notes on history of 331
Haven *Journal* 331
Hawk feathers, as ornaments 17
Hawkins, C. W., Clements, president Chase County Historical Society .. 79, 431
Hawley, James R. 202
Hay, cost of, along Pony Express route, 68
Hayes, R. S., first vice president of Missouri Pacific Railway at St. Louis, discusses strike matters 43, 44
Hays, Mrs. R. R. 217
Hays, high school history, notes on. 108, 331
Hays *Daily News* 108, 331, 425
Hazelton, date of old settlers' meeting at, 433
Hazelton *Herald* 222
Hazens, ——, leave Vermont for Kansas, 278
Hebrew, Mr. and Mrs. J. A........... 216
Hegler, Ben F., Wichita............... 81
Helena, Atchison county ghost town.... 421
Helwig, George, president Twentieth Kansas Association.................. 432
Henry, John A., ferry incorporator..... 183
Henry Rohr chapter, Order of the Eastern Star, note on history of......... 223
Herald of Freedom, Lawrence........59, 394
— P. B. Plumb foreman of............ 25
Herbert, Ewing 219
Herndon, A. G., Springfield, Ill......... 269
Hersey, T. F., surveyed cattle trail to Abilene 9
Hewitt, Dr. Charles.................... 218
Hiawatha 76, 196
— fair at, note regarding old settlers registered during 425
Hiawatha *Daily World*................ 425
Hickok, James B. (Wild Bill), in charge of Rock Creek, Neb., station on Pony Express route 69
Hickory 248, 249
Hickory Point, battle of................ 66
Hicks, ——, California cattleman...... 9
Hide Out and Rule schools, Fall River vicinity, note on history of.......... 328
Highland 15
Highway 73, Leavenworth county, proposed bronze statue of Buffalo Bill to be erected on...................... 218
Hill, Lloyd, Topeka.................... 59
Hillsboro *Star,* founded May 2, 1924... 327
Hindman, Gen. Thomas C., rescinds order that no quarter be given officers and men of colored regiments............. 74
Hing-gwi-men-o-ken, Delaware name for Grasshopper river 320
Hinshaw, J. C......................... 429
Historic spots, Kansas, mention of..... 334
— marker, erected on White's creek... 336
— Osborne county, note regarding..... 217

Historical Records Survey, instituted by the Kansas W. P. A................ 224
Historical Society. *See,* Kansas State Historical Society.
History and Literature Club, Horton's oldest woman's society, note on history of 327
Hobble, Frank A., Dodge City......... 81
Hoch, Edward Wallis, elected governor, 77
Hodder, Frank H........ 63, 64, 79, 81, 335
— articles published by............... 121
— author of *Government of the People of Kansas* 115
— biographical sketch, by James C. Malin 115-121
— book reviews written for various publications by 117-120
— date of death...................... 115
— elected president Historical Society... 64, 80, 115
— Kansas items published by.......... 116
— Lincoln materials for lectures prepared by, given Kansas Historical Society.. 118
Hodgeman County Historical Society, newly elected officers of............. 432
Hodges, George H., second Democrat to be elected governor of Kansas........ 77
Hodges, J. L., operated short-line railroad 426
Hogin, John C., Belleville.......... 79, 81
Hoisington, fiftieth anniversary, note on 424
— first child born at.................. 424
— newspaper history mentioned........ 424
Hoisington *Dispatch* 423, 426
— anniversary edition of.............. 424
Hole, Mrs. Agnes C., letter regarding ferry matters quoted 324
Hole, Franklin J. 324
Holladay Overland Stage Co., Frank A. Root, express messenger on.......... 15
Holladay stage coach lines............. 57
Holland, William, Farm creek, near Fort Clark 269
Hollembeak, Dr. G. W., early Dodge City doctor 110
Holliday, Cyrus K. 57
— one of Topeka's founders............ 429
Holmberg, J. A., director Lindsborg Historical Society 112
Holmes, Mrs. E. L., Lawrence......... 59
Holy Trinity Catholic Church, Paola, note on history of.................. 215
Holyrood *Gazette,* note on history of... 220
Homestead law, repeatedly defeated by Democrats 204
Honey 250, 353, 355, 356, 362
— found by members of Donner party.. 209
Honey locust 248, 249
Honnell, W. R.................... 66, 429
— address "The Pony Express".... 67- 71
— map of Pony Express route prepared by 67
Horn spoons 255
Hornet, The, mimeographed organ of Sun City schools, historical edition of... 109
Horse pistols 240
Horses, Isaac McCoy's efforts to prevent stealing of 355
Horton, date of incorporation......... 107
— fiftieth anniversary of, noted.... 428, 429
— "Golden Jubilee Pageant" held October 12 to 15, 1936..................... 428
— H. C. Miller, first postmaster of.... 428
— high school graduates, note on...... 429
— History and Literature Club, history of, noted 327
— note on history of.................. 107
Horton *Headlight* 107, 108, 327
— golden anniversary edition of.... 428, 429
Hose, Myrtle Curran 330

General Index

Hospital tax 192
Howard county, Mo. 276
Howes, Cecil 108, 109, 111, 221, 327, 335
Hoxie, H. M................... 41, 43, 196
— vice-president of Missouri Pacific railroad 38, 195
— willing to meet strikers............ 41
Hoxie, note regarding fiftieth anniversary of founding 425
Hoxie *Sentinel* 425
Hubbell, L. W., officer Hodgeman County Historical Society 432
Huerfano, Colo., ferry planned for.... 190
Huggins, W. L., Emporia.......... 79, 81
Hughes, W. F. 216, 220
Hulbert, Archer Butler, mentioned...... 120
Humboldt 32
— Methodist Church, seventy-fifth anniversary celebrated 110
— state road to Wichita from.......... 189
Humboldt *Union* 110, 186
Humphrey, James 45
Humphrey, Lyman U................. 52
— governor, Tom McNeal's recollections of 76
Hunnewell 26
Hunt, Elvid, *History of Fort Leavenworth*, quoted 359
Hunters 251
— accompanying McCoy 242
Huntersville, early days described in Hutchinson *Herald* 327
Huron, old, vestiges of old military road still visible near 324
Hutchinson, note on pre-movie days in.. 419
Hutchinson *Herald* 327, 419
Hutchinson *Record* 328
Hutchinson Typographical Union, note on founding of 330
Hutchison, Walter D................. 419
Huxman, Walter A., governor-elect of Kansas 423
Huxman, Mrs. Walter A.............. 423
Hypnotism, as first introduced in Wichita, note on 328

I

Illinois river 247
— McCoy party crossed by canoe 231
Independence 32
— note regarding famous persons of.... 428
Independence, Mo., Donner party's personnel as it left 208
Independence crossing, Big Blue river, Donner party halted by flood at...... 208
— location of 211
— why so named 211
Independence Methodist Episcopal Church, near Goddard, twenty-fifth anniversary 223
Independent Order of Odd Fellows, Dodge City 421
Indian 329
— agency, at Kennekuk 67
— — beef contracts at................ 11
— art 57
— battle, on Coon creek, 1848, note on, 419
— camping places on Solomon river ... 373
— carpet, made of rushes and iris..... 20
— cemetery, discovered by McCoy on Fort Leavenworth reservation 360
— corn 405
— customs, described 17, 18
— jubilee, Kickapoo-Pottawatomie, article by Frank A. Root 15- 21
— massacre, Lone Tree, in southwest Kansas 221
— mission burial ground, near Ottawa, bronze markers placed at entrance to.. 431

Indian missions, Methodist, in Kansas.. 57
— mounds, Kansas, Isaac McCoy first to explore....................... 361
— — on Ed Phillips place 324
— raid 215
— raids on Smoky Hill trail 336
— road, leading to Shawnee village..... 258
— scare, in Kirwin, in fall of 1878, note on 109
— sign 370
— trail, noted by Capt. Marcy 5
Indian territory...................... 26
— cattle dealers of 8
— Chisholm cattle trail started from.. 189
— federal troops located in, at beginning of Civil War.................... 6
— map prepared by Isaac McCoy for... 236
— Major Merril's map through 5
— surveys for railroads through territory of 5
Indianola 324, 416
Indians . 68, 284, 327, 336, 347, 357, 366, 369
— accompanying McCoy, become intoxicated while at St. Louis 233
— — growing impatient 244
— attending Kickapoo-Pottawatomie jubilee 15
— certain tribes permitted to examine lands west of Mississippi river and select locations 227
— eastern, removal of, to west planned. 227
— encampment of 370
— exceedingly careless and improvident.. 250
— ferried families across Arkansas river at Wichita in tubs 185
— log stockade in Osborne county, built for protection against, in early 1870's, 217
— McCoy's plans for removal to lands west of Missouri approved 122
— marked out easiest paths through the Indian territory 6
— massacre Kansas citizens on frontier.. 74
— removal of, to lands in west 230
— sanctioning public ownership of public utilities, note regarding 220
— southern 265
— — expected at St. Louis 262
— with McCoy party, obtained whisky and returned drunk 236
— *See, also,* names of tribes.
Industrial Court, Kansas 57
Infare, at S. D. Dyer's, described...... 156
Ingalls, John J. 66, 202
Interest rate, ten percent usual in early Kansas 289
Iola, First Methodist Church, seventy-fifth anniversary celebrated 110
Iola *Daily Register* 108, 110, 419
Iowa Indians 353
— diminished reservation of 378
— John B. LeRoy interpreter for...... 379
Ireland, Harry 333
Irish, Mrs. Eusebia Mudge 58
— director of Riley County Historical Society 432
Irish, founded Emerald 334
Iron, sand stone on Solomon river resembling 374
Iron ore, found on Delaware lands...... 355
—hill of, discovered by Isaac McCoy.... 368
Irons, Martin, district master workman of Knights of Labor.............. 194, 195
Irrigation, in western Kansas......... 24
"Isaac McCoy and the Treaty of 1821," article edited by Lela Barnes.. 122- 142
Isely, Bliss 330
— joint author of new Kansas history .. 432
Isham, Charles 214
Island Park, Gypsum 332
Ives, C. W., diary of................. 107

GENERAL INDEX   449

J

	PAGE
Jack's Ferry, Ray county, Missouri	274
Jackson, ― ―, member of McCoy exploring party	356
Jackson, Andrew, president	227
Jackson, Lee, director	432
Jackson, Mrs. Neva, telephone operator	324
Jackson county	341
Jacksonian, Cimarron	330
Jacquart, Bee	325
James' fork of White river	340
Jamestown	336
Jamison, J. C., attorney general of Missouri, at St. Louis to discuss strike matters	43
Jayhawkers	66
Jefferson, I. T.	7
Jefferson City, Mo.	244
Jefferson county	320
― ferries operating within	321-323
― first ferry license issued by county commissioners	322
― first white child born in Kansas within limits of	424
Jefferson Methodist Church, note on history of	213
Jenkins, Gaius	66
Jennings, ― ―, mentioned by Isaac McCoy	342
Jennings, Mrs. Adele, librarian Cawker City library	105
Jennings, Frank S., state senator	34
Jewell, date of old settlers' meeting at	433
Jewell county	217, 334
― note on early-day colonization attempts	327
J. H. Lucas, fastest steamboat on Missouri river	162, 163
Jingle Bob outfit	11
Jo Jim, a Kansas Indian interpreter	353, 356, 363, 364, 371
― beavers trapped by	369, 370
― deer killed by	355
Johnny Quick, Delaware. *See* Quick, John.	
Johns Hopkins University, *Studies in History and Political Science*	115
Johnson, ― ―, with McCoy's exploring expedition	370
Johnson, Grandfather ― ―	287
Johnson, Grandmother ― ―	287, 390
Johnson, Allen	121
Johnson, Andrew	327
Johnson, Harry	109
Johnson, Julia Esther	143
Johnson, Richard M., school planned by	354
Johnson, Samuel A.	335
Johnson, Rev. Thomas, Methodist preacher	375-377, 437
Johnson, William, first Methodist missionary to Kansas Indians	375
Johnson County Democrat, Olathe	216
Johnson-Grant controversy	117
Johnson's (or Johnston's) hotel, Detroit, Mich.	145, 161
Johnson's school, in Kentucky	364
Johnston, Gen. Albert Sidney, moved army from Fort Leavenworth to quell Mormon uprising	67
Johnston, John	133
Johnston, Mrs. William A., Topeka	79, 81
Jones, Mrs. ― ―, at Harmony mission	245
Jones, Horace, Lyons	81
Jones, Paul, Lyons	220
Jones, Samuel J., sheriff	170
Jones, Sue Carmody	330
Jordan, H. C.	335
Journal of Isaac McCoy for exploring expeditions of 1828 and 1830, edited by Lela Barnes	227-277, 339-377

	PAGE
Journal-Free Press, Osage City	430
Joy, Mrs. Sophia Kramer	213
Julesburg, Colo., station on old Pony Express route	69
Junction City	8
― Methodist Church, note on history of	326
Junction City *Republic,* cited	326
Junction City *Union,* cited	23, 423, 424
Juniata, ferry at, over Big Blue river	150
― government bridge across Blue carried away by the ice	165

K

Kageshingah creek	375
Kagey, Chas. L., Wichita	80
Kahrens, Joseph	217
Kalloch, Rev. Isaac S.	314
― pioneer editor and minister of Ottawa	333
Kambach, Mrs. Frank, secretary-treasurer Shawnee County Old Settlers' Association	112
Kandt, Henry W., note regarding early day reminiscences of	221
Kanopolis Methodist Episcopal Church, fiftieth anniversary	331
Kansas, birth of	65
― bonds, scandal growing out of sale of	73
― boycotts in	46
― Chisholm trail being marked by	14
― churches, note on early	425
― economic changes in during eighties	33
― far from treeless prairie	327
― hard times, mentioned	415
― history, reviewed in Topeka dailies	218
― Kaw Indian pronunciation of	260
― landmarks	57
― men in consular service	329
― monument erected at grave of ex-Gov. John W. Leedy	225
― newspapers of, coöperate with Historical Society	431
― regiments, First militia, sent to Parsons	201
― ― Second infantry	74
― ― Eighth infantry, colonel of John A. Martin	76
― ― Eleventh cavalry	25
― ― Nineteenth cavalry, Crawford resigns as governor to become colonel of	74
― ― Twentieth infantry, officers of	432
― seat of government temporarily located at Fort Leavenworth	325, 326
― seventy-fifth birthday anniversary	219, 220
― strike on Gould systems in	196
― territorial governor's lot not an enviable one	110
― trails through Indian territory headed towards	5
Kansas Academy of Science	278
Kansas Bureau of Labor and Industrial Statistics, creation of	34
Kansas Chamber of Commerce	62
― *Progress in Kansas* issued by	108, 111, 222, 334
Kansas Chief, Troy	321, 325
― founded by Solomon Miller, note on history of	332
Kansas City (Kansas), beginning of Missouri Pacific strike at	196, 197
― fiftieth anniversary of, 1936	220
Kansas City *Kansan,* "1936 Yearly Progress Edition" of	220
Kansas City, Mo.	42, 164
Kansas City (Mo.) *Journal*	36-38, 42, 43, 191, 192, 196, 197, 205
― Knights of Labor boycott against	46
Kansas City Smelting and Refining Co., strike at plant of, in Argentine	191, 193

29―5211

450 GENERAL INDEX

Kansas City (Mo.) *Star*, cited and quoted, 109, 110, 212, 218, 220, 222, 326, 327, 423, 425, 426, 429
Kansas City (Mo.) *Times*.............. 108, 111, 221, 327, 330, 335, 422-424
Kansas-Colorado water suit, for more equal distribution of Arkansas river waters 24, 25
Kansas conflict 111
Kansas Daily State Journal, Topeka 107
Kansas Daughters of the American Revolution 62
Kansas Day Club 219
Kansas Democrat, Topeka..... 193, 202, 206
Kansas Editorial Association, annual meeting of 431
Kansas Emergency Relief Committee, new project for Historical Society 55
— relief work under, discontinued...... 55
— supervision of workers in Historical Society under 54
— tasks assigned workers under 56
"Kansas Emigrants' Song," by Whittier, taboo on Missouri river 279
Kansas Frontier Historical Park, note on history of 111
"Kansas Historical Notes" 112, 224, 335, 336, 431-433
"Kansas History as Published in the Press" 105-111, 213-223, 325-334, 419-430
Kansas History Teachers' Association, new officers 335
Kansas Indians 253, 254, 265, 275, 320, 346, 350-352, 358, 363, 368, 370, 374, 375
— agency, at Kaw Indian farm 351
— Indian territory 27
— country west of Missouri purchased from 240
— deny ceding lands 345
— dress noted for scantiness...... 255, 256
— Half Breed lands 323
—— tract No. 20, south of Perry .. 319
— hunters, McCoy gives tobacco to .. 375
— hunting and trapping party of 363
— identified in language and friendship to Osages 255
— Jo Jim interpreter for 353
— McCoy has smoke with tribe...... 255
— M. G. Clark subagent for 342
— more wretched than Osages 255
— Ne-Woh-kon-daga, name given to Great Spirit Spring by 373
— reservation 240, 264
—— east line of 341
—— extent of 345
—— mound at corner of 355
—— survey of 340
— ride out from village to obtain tobacco from McCoy 256
— steal horses from Pawnees 351
— treaty of 1825, quoted 345
— villages of 254, 352
—— on Missouri river 264, 361
—— one hundred and twenty-five miles west of the Missouri line 256
— William Johnson first missionary to . 375
Kansas Industrial Court................ 57
Kansas legislature, 1855, bogus......... 293
—— known as Missouri legislature.... 155
—— road established by............... 324
— 1857, mentioned 322
— 1859, mentioned 25
— 1860, bills for establishment of ferries in western Kansas passed by 190
—— met in special session............ 185
— 1861, mentioned 321
— 1863, mentioned 321
— 1864, mentioned 321

Kansas legislature, 1871, mentioned 32
— 1872, mentioned 324
— 1875, mentioned 321
— 1885, labor legislation passed by..... 35
— 1886, arbitration laws passed by..... 193
—— met in special session........ 51, 52
— 1887, outstanding acts passed by.... 206
—— repealed some sections of militia law of 1885..................... 206
—— some measures that failed of passage 207
— 1891, overwhelmingly Populist....... 76
— 1935, law providing for decennial state census repealed by.................. 58
Kansas-Missouri border war, tragedies of, 66
Kansas-Nebraska bill 21, 117, 120, 121
Kansas-Nebraska boundary 378
"Kansas Newspaper Hall of Fame," sponsors of 336
Kansas official, Topeka................ 106
Kansas Pacific Railway................ 33
— line extended to Abilene 4, 12
— map issued by in 1874, a network of trails 10
— Texas cattle shipped east over...... 189
Kansas river 70, 148, 254, 257, 264, 341, 346, 351, 353, 359, 367, 375, 380, 391, 416
— crossed by Donner party............ 208
— Delaware river largest tributary east of Big Blue...................... 319
— description of lands along.......... 258
— Lewis and Clark expedition held first court session at mouth of.......... 334
— McCoy's description of............. 255
— timber along 256
Kansas Southwestern Railroad Co., note on history of...................... 421
Kansas State Board of Agriculture, census compiled under supervision of, discontinued by legislature............ 58
Kansas State College, Manhattan, 58, 335, 393
Kansas State Historical Society...... 2, 112
— accessions 60
— annual meeting, addresses........ 65-78
—— minutes 54-81
— appropriations 54
— archives department 58
— bonds sold 55
— contingent fund reduced by legislature, 54
— correspondence increased during last five years 54
— directors 80, 81
—— elected 79
—— meetings 54-64, 80
— Edwin C. Manning, president...... 25
— executive committee, members of..... 54
—— report 64
— Federal Emergency Relief Administration, work done in manuscript division by 58
— first capitol of Kansas 61
— Frank H. Hodder, president, death of, 115
— historical collections being indexed by federal help 56
— John Booth bequest fund........... 63
— John P. St. John scrap books given.. 58
— Jonathan Pecker bequest fund....... 63
— *Kansas Historical Quarterly*...60, 114, 336
— Kansas newspapers coöperate with.... 431
— library, information requested from.. 56
—— Kansas books and pamphlets added to 82-89
—— recent additions to........... 82-104
—— work accomplished by KERC workers in 56
— Lincoln materials given by Mrs. F. H. Hodder 118
— *List of Kansas Newspapers and Periodicals* published by................. 59

GENERAL INDEX 451

Kansas State Historical Society, local and county societies affiliated with....... 61
— McCoy journals in possession of..... 341
— McCoy papers given by Spencer McCoy 58
— map in possession of Historical Society 10
— marking historical sites............. 61
— membership, decreased by depression, 55
— — fee fund of 62
— Metcalf estate gives diaries......... 58
— museum, attendance and accessions... 59
— — work accomplished by FERA help in 59
— newspaper section 58, 59
— — shelves provided for............. 54
— nominating committee 79
— — report 64, 78, 79
— officers, elected 80
— — nominated 64
— Pike's Pawnee park................. 61
— private manuscripts accessioned..... 57
— secretary's report 54- 62
— Shawnee Methodist mission...... 60, 61
— some important documents and collections preserved by.................. 221
— subjects of research made in........ 57
— Thomas H. Bowlus fund............ 63
— treasurer's report 62, 63
Kansas State Journal, Lawrence.....280, 323
Kansas State Planning Board......... 57
Kansas State Teachers' College, Emporia, 335
Kansas Supreme Court, briefs of...... 56
Kansas State Teachers' College, Pittsburg 35
Kansas Weekly Herald, Leavenworth.... 323
Kansas Women's Republican Club, note on 218
Kansas Workman, Erie............... 325
Kanwaka community, Douglas county, notes on history of............ 219, 327
Kanzas News, Emporia, founded by P. B. Plumb 35
Kapioma, Kickapoo chief, killed by Texans 220
Karnowski, J. R..................... 334
Karstensen, Rev. K. J................ 213
Kearny county 23
Keeley, A. J., ferryman for Oxford ferry, 182
Keetley, Jack, Pony Express rider..... 69
Kelley, E. E., Garden City... 64, 79, 81, 331
— elected first vice president Historical Society 80
Kelley, Howard F., Seattle, Wash., newspaper volumes acquired from........ 59
Kellogg, C. M., member ferry company, 184
Kellogg, Lyman B., ferry incorporator.. 25
— positions held by.................. 25
Kelly, Mrs. Samuel J................. 58
Kelso, David 200
— attorney for Missouri Pacific Railroad, 198, 199
Kennedy valley, Douglas county...... 279
Kennekuk, chief of Kickapoos...... 428, 429
Kennekuk, town of, named for Kickapoo chief 7
— Kickapoo Indian agency at.......... 67
— old stage barn at.................. 324
— on Fort Leavenworth military road... 324
Kennekuk Anti-Horse Thief Association.. 67
Kennerly, Capt. Geo. H......235, 237- 240 267, 270, 272
— leader for McCoy exploring party.... 233
— resigned an Indian agency up the Missouri 233
Kensington, St. John Lutheran Church of 106
Kensington *Mirror* 106
Kent, James 117
Kent, William 117

Kentucky, Kansas lands compared to.... 259
Ke-o-Quack, Kickapoo chief..... 16, 19, 21
Keyes, Mrs. Sarah, date of death...... 209
— grave of, on Oregon trail, article by W. E. Smith 208- 212
— great aunt of James M. Harvey, of Kansas 212
— member of Donner party........... 209
Kickapoo Indian 320
Kickapoo Indian School, Horton....... 428
Kickapoo Indians, Chief Kennekuk a unique character of 67, 429
— Franklin G. Adams agent for........ 15
— John C. Anderson interpreter for.... 18
— Kapioma, chief, killed by Texans.... 220
— mode of bestowing presents on visitors 18, 19
— note concerning 429
— Pottawatomies intermarry with...... 15
— religious worship among............ 21
— reserve, in Brown county........... 15
— Wm. P. Badger agent for........... 320
Kickapoo parish 330
"Kickapoo-Pottawatomie Grand Indian Jubilee," article by Frank A. Root, 15- 21
Kidder, G. W....................... 420
Kildare, Okla. 26
Kimball, C. H., state senator...... 33, 200
Kimball, Edward, member Lawrence band 280
Kimball, Fred, killed in Quantrill raid.. 280
— member Lawrence band............ 280
Kimball, O. E., ferry incorporator..... 182
Kimball, Samuel, member Lawrence band, 280
Kincaid *Dispatch* 223
King, Paul 325, 419
King, Dr. Philip C., president Washburn College 56
King, William, St. Louis, Mo.......... 273
Kingery township, Thomas county, date of old settlers' meeting held in...... 433
Kingfisher, Okla. 7, 8, 10
Kingman county, notes on early days in 214, 216
Kingman County Farm Bureau and 4-H Clubs, mentioned 215
Kinkel, John M., Topeka............. 80
Kinsley 25
Kinsley *Graphic* 110
Kinzie, John, pioneer settler at Fort Dearborn 129, 134
— letter to Isaac McCoy giving his views on Indian education............... 120
Kiowa County Signal, Greensburg, note on history of..................... 430
Kiowa Indians 5
Kirk, F. S., Wichita, note regarding experiences of, during opening of Cherokee Outlet 426
Kirwin, Indian scare in vicinity of, in 1878 109
— note on early days in............. 108
Klews & McHenry, ferry and ferry rates, 321
Knapp, Dallas W., Coffeyville....... 79, 81
Knights of Labor..... 35, 45-47, 50, 51, 191 196, 201, 204
— Atchison 205
— boycott against Kansas City *Journal*.. 46
— — Topeka *Commonwealth* 46
— convention of, at Marshall, Tex...... 194
— general assembly of, urged formation of state bureaus of labor........... 33
— had charge of Missouri Pacific strike of 1885 37
— scheme for wreck of Missouri Pacific freight train traced to lodge of..... 198
Kochtitzky, Oscar, commissioner of labor statistics of Missouri, at St. Louis to discuss strike matters.............. 43

GENERAL INDEX

L

Labette City, state road to Meridian, Summer county 182
Labette county, C. B. Woodford sheriff of 198
Labor, element in gubernatorial campaign of 1886..................... 201
— legislation in 1885.................. 33
— problems, Governor Martin's administration, first year of, discussed by Edith Walker 33- 53
— — second year of, discussed by Dorothy Leibengood 191- 207
Labor Record, Hutchinson........... **330**
Labor's Tribune, Weir City, cited...... 35
LaCrosse *Chieftain*................... 425
LaCrosse *Republican* 105
LaFayette county, Mo.................. 274
Lake county, Colorado, Arkansas river rises in 22
Lake Michigan 136, 262
— Burnetts resided on 131
Lamar county, Texas 11
Land surveys, near Manhattan 301, 305
Landes, Kenneth K..................... 219
Landholders bank, Providence, R. I. 167, 173, 286
Landmarks, Kansas 57
— note on 327
Landon, Gov. Alf. M................... 66
— elected governor 77
— note on colonial ancestors of....... 327
— Republican candidate for office of U. S. president 422
Landon, John M., father of Gov. Alf. M. Landon 222
Lane, Gen. James H............ 57, 66, 280
Lane faction 73
Lane's fort, Brown county 107
Langham, Maj. Angus L., first surveys in Kansas made by............. 340, 352
Larned 80
— date of old settlers' meeting at...... 433
— first bicycle brought to, owned by L. H. Thorp 218
— note on telephone history of 218
Larned *Chronoscope* 106, 218
Latham station, Colo., Frank A. Root overland mail agent at............. 15
Lathrop, Asa S., Ottawa's first mayor.. 333
Law and Order League, formed at Parsons to preserve order during Missouri Pacific strike 201
Lawrence, Amos A..................... 66
Lawrence 15, 148, 416
— Border Ruffians threaten to destroy.. 170
— burning of, by Quantrill.......... 66, 280
— early band of, discussed by Edward Bumgardner 278- 281
— — furnished music at first commencement exercises at the University of Kansas 281
— — members and leaders of............. 280
— first Fourth of July celebration at... 279
— Kate Stephens' book portrays life in, following Civil War................. 432
— mills at 158
— people of, suffer at hands of Missourians 165
Lawrence *Democrat* 327
Lawrence *Journal-World* 219, 281
Lead and silver ores, refined at Argentine, 191
Leader-Courier, Kingman........... 215, 216
Leadville, Colo., Arkansas river arises near 22
Leahy, David D., mentioned....... 199, 328
Lease, Mary Ellen 66
Leavenworth, Col. Henry, ordered to select site for cantonment on Missouri river 341

Leavenworth 164, 166, 220, 415
— note regarding the news of admission of Kansas to Union 218
— "Pioneer Days" celebration held at.. 433
— population, 1860 416
— road from Grasshopper Falls to...... 324
Leavenworth county, boiler explosion in sawmill injured eight men........... 220
— "Buffalo Bill" Cody's early life spent in 218
Leavenworth *Standard* 202, 204
Leavenworth *Times* 75, 201, 204, 205 218, 220, 223, 325, 326, 361
Lecompton 416
— Chas. Robinson in jail at, charged with treason 73
— Douglas County Historical Society members pay visit to.............. 336
Lecompton Bridge Co................. 322
Lecompton Constitution 384
— frauds in connection with adoption of 221
Lee, Thomas Amory, Topeka.... 54, 64, 80
Leedy, John W., elected governor...... 77
— monument erected in memory of...... 335
Leftwich, T. E., publisher Larned *Optic*, 106
Leggins, buckskin 18
Legislature. *See* Kansas legislature.
Leibengood, Dorothy, social science instructor in Oak Street Junior High School, at Burlington, Iowa......... 114
— "Labor Problems in the Second Year of Governor Martin's Administration," article by 191- 207
Lenexa, Salem Lutheran Church, golden jubilee celebrated 216
Lennard, Mrs. W. H. and Mrs. H. J. Merten, note on their history of Morganville Methodist Church.......... 423
Leon Christian Church, note on history of 329
Leon Methodist Episcopal Church...... 219
Leon *News* 329
— "Fifth Annual M. E. Booster Edition," 219
Leoti, date of old settlers' meeting at... 433
LeRoy, John Baptiste, interpreter for Iowas, Sacs and Foxes.............. 379
— operated ferry on Great Nemaha river, 379
— trading house of 379
LeRoy Methodist Church, note on history of 219
LeRoy mission, established in 1858..... 219
LeRoy *Reporter* 219
Letter mail, going fifty miles for........ 151
"Letters of a Kansas Pioneer, 1855-1860" 143-179, 282-318, 381- 418
Levand, John 421
Levand, Louis 421
Levand, Max 421
Lewelling, L. D., elected governor...... 76
Lewis and Clark expedition, ancient Kaw villages visited by 361
— first court session in Missouri valley held by 334
Lewis, Mrs. Hiram, Wichita 59
Lewis, Edwards county, note on biographies of pioneers 110
Lewis *Press* 110
Lewistown, Ohio, Shawnee Indians from, 260
Lexington, Mo. 164
Leyman, Harriet 293, 300
Liberal post office, note on history of... 422
Liberty, Mo. 260, 261, 274
Library, Gypsum public, note on....... 332
— Haven, note on 331
— Congressional 56
Liebenthal, note on sixtieth anniversary of founding of town................ 425
— oldest of Kansas settlements founded by Russian emigrants............... 425

GENERAL INDEX 453

Lill, Mrs. John, note on her reminiscences of Cassoday 429
Lillard, T. M., Topeka 54, 81
Lilleston, W. F., Wichita 79, 81
Limestone 246, 248, 252, 254, 256, 265
Lincoln, Abraham 118, 222
Lincoln, Lewis A 420
Lincoln County News, Lincoln 105
Lincolnville 107
Lindquist, John F 420
Lindsborg, Farmers State Bank of, chartered in 1886 426
Lindsborg Historical Society, newly elected officers of 112
Lindsley, H. K., Wichita 81
Linn, note on history of 221
— originally named Summit 221
Linn-Palmer *Record* 221
Linn Study Club 221
Lipher, Mrs. —— 300
Liquor, used by Indians 21
Little, Ed C 77
Little Arkansas river 8, 185, 188, 328
— an ever-flowing stream 22
— Jesse Chisholm, leads party from Arkansas to, in search of buried treasure 6
—— settled with Wichita Indians at mouth of 6
—— trading post of 6, 10, 11
— Wichita Indians begin trek for 6
Little Grasshopper river, Atchison county, 319, 324
Little Platte river, Mo 341
Little Rock, Ark 27
Logan, John A 202
Logan County News, Winona, note on history of 428
Logan Republican 105
Lone Tree Indian massacre in southwest Kansas 221
Lone Tree school, Pottawatomie county, note on history of 213
Long, M. H 223
Long, Stephen H., expedition of, mentioned 319, 378
Long horn steers 13
Longrun (Kentucky) Association 124
Longton 32
Lonora, Missouri river steamboat 145
Loomis, Mrs. N. H., Omaha, Neb 110
Lost towns of western Kansas, note on .. 157
Louisiana, purchased by U. S 227
Louisville, mentioned 416
Lovejoy, Rev. Chas. H 172
Lucas, municipal band of 106
Lucas Independent, band convention issue of 106
Ludell, Trinity Lutheran Church near, celebrated fiftieth anniversary 333
Lumber, native 301, 306
— price per 1,000 feet at Manhattan in 1856 167
Luray, municipal band of 106
— record of fatal accidents in community, printed in *Luray Herald* 107
Lutheran Church 334
— Lenexa, golden jubilee celebrated 216
— Newton 421
— St. John's Evangelical, of Lincolnville, 213
— St. John's, of Bird City, note on history of 329
— St. Paul's, Geary county, seventy-fifth anniversary celebrated 424
— Trinity, near Ludell 333
Lykins, Johnston 237, 261, 263, 266
— footnote concerning 347
— teacher in McCoy's school 127
Lykins, Mrs. Johnston 263
Lyman, Hattie 312
Lyon, Gen. Nathaniel, at Wilson's creek, 74
Lyons, Mrs. Ida, first vice-president Douglas County Historical Society ... 112

M

McAllister, ——, Methodist preacher 375, 377
McCafferty, Mrs. ——, mentioned by Isaac McCoy 342
McCallister, ——, Methodist preacher. *See* McAllister.
McCarter, Mrs. Margaret Hill, Topeka 81, 218
McCleave, David Harold 58
McClees, Nelson, Wichita 188
McCord, ——, cattle dealer of Indian territory 8
McCormick-Mathers Company, Wichita, 432
McCoy & Martin, Kansas City, Mo., account book of for 1847-1848, given Historical Society 58
McCoy, Mr. ——, of Ohio 280
McCoy, Calvin. *See* John C. McCoy.
McCoy, Mrs. Christiana 126, 229, 232
— makes trip in canoe on Wabash .. 131, 132
McCoy, Delilah 135
McCoy, Isaac 358
— addressed council of Shawnee and Kaw Indians 345
— and the Treaty of 1821, article by Lela Barnes 122- 142
— anxieties of, regarding future of his missionary work 263
— appointed commissioner for removal of Indians to lands west of Missouri . 122
—— missionary to Wabash country 124
—— surveyor and agent to assist migration of Indians westward 122
— attacked with dysentery 246
— Baptist missionary 122, 227
— calls on Gen. Wm. Clark 233
— commissioned to survey Indian lands, 339
— dates and places of birth and death .. 122
— Delaware outlet survey completed ... 371
— dines with Gen. Clark 234
— employed drawing a map of the country west of Arkansas territory and west of Missouri 235, 236
— engages boarding and horsekeeping at a Mr. Brown's, near St. Louis 234
— established family at Fayette, Mo ... 339
— exploring expedition 1828, advised by Gen. Wm. Clark to proceed 240
—— chafes at delay of 237
—— decides to start on 239
—— detained near St. Louis by non arrival of Indians who were to accompany him 238
—— extent of land explored on tour ... 260
—— letter to Thomas L. McKenney regarding 228
—— party meets an escaping female in wilderness disguised as a boy .. 243
—— — reaches point 122 miles due west of Missouri boundary 253
—— procures rations at Harmony mission for tour 245
—— rate of pay given Indians accompanying 267
—— report of exploring tour to Gen. Wm. Clark 264, 265
—— retrospect of exploring tour .. 258- 260
— exploring expedition 1830, date of start 377
—— dust storm described by 371, 372
—— fire hazards encountered by 364
—— map, 1830, mentioned 320

General Index

McCoy, Isaac, exploring expedition 1830,
  number in party 361
— — party endangered by prairie fires.. 371
— — precautions taken to prevent Indians
  stealing horses of 355
— — return from exploring trip ... 377
— extracts from Journal of 229-268,
  341-377
— financial troubles of 123, 124
  126, 127, 128, 131
— gives drafts on Secretary of War for
  $5,000 234
— has smoke with Kansas tribe 255
— History of Baptist Indian Missions,
  quoted 359
— horseback journey to Philadelphia ... 140
— illness of 234, 247
— — while on way to St. Louis 232
— invited to attend council between
  Shawnees and Kansas Indians 344
— journal of, for exploring expeditions,
  articles by Lela Barnes, 227-277, 339-377
— journals and manuscripts of, in Historical Society 123
— learned art of making spinning wheels, 123
— letter to Gov. Lewis Cass regarding
  missionary matters 137
— manuscript collection in Kansas State
  Historical Society 228, 263
— married Christiana Polke 123
— pastor of Maria church 123
— planned for a seat of government for
  the Indians within Indian territory .. 260
— plans for removal of Indians to lands
  west of Missouri approved 122
— preached in Baptist meeting house near
  St. Louis 235
— preaches funeral sermon 236
— reaches St. Louis on return from exploring tour 264
— receives New Year's congratulations of
  Indians 142
— reception given by Indians to, described 254
— religious services held morning and
  evening on Sundays 252, 257
— — in Ottawa tongue held by 230
— removal to Carey, Mich............. 141
— — Fort Wayne, Indiana............. 127
— — Vincennes, Indiana territory..... 123
— requested to establish a school among
  the Shawnees 342, 343
— search for a stray horse 241, 242
— settled on Silver creek, Clark county,
  Indiana 123
— silver watch worn by, given Historical
  Society 59
— smoked pipe of peace with Indians on
  New Year's day 142
— some published works of 122
— spoke to Kaw agent respecting school
  for Kaw Indians 375
— statements of expenses of exploring
  tour 268- 277
— talks with Shawnees regarding school
  promised them 376
— tours made while in missionary work
  124- 127
— views regarding establishment of school
  for the Pottawatomies 132, 133
— visits Gov. Lewis Cass, of Michigan,
  for assistance for his mission 130
McCoy, Mrs. Isaac 229, 263, 341
McCoy, John Calvin, a son of Isaac, 235, 345
  346, 351, 352, 353, 357, 361
  365, 366, 372, 376
— baggage master during survey of Delaware lands 341
— letter quoted 352
— mention of Grasshopper river 319
— surveys of, mentioned 320

McCoy, Joseph G., Abilene cattle yards
  of 4, 8, 12
— advertising schemes of 9
— cattle buyer of Illinois 4
— extended cattle trail from Wichita to
  Abilene 189
— hired surveyor and extended cattle trail
  to Abilene 9
— induced Texas cattlemen to drive cattle to Abilene for shipment east 189
— methods of, in directing Texas cattle
  trade to Abilene 8, 9
— Sketches of the Early Cattle Trade,
  cited 3
McCoy, Marion, ferry incorporator 183
McCoy, Rachel....................... 135
McCoy, Dr. Rice 133, 345-347, 349, 351
— assistant surveyor 341
— engaged in practice of medicine 341
— resident of Kentucky 236
McCoy, Sarah, attending school in Cincinnati 236
McCoy, Spencer 58
— papers of John C. McCoy and Woodson McCoy, given Historical Society, 58
MacDonald, A. B.... 220, 222, 326, 331, 332
McFarland, Helen M., librarian, Topeka, 80
— "Recent Additions to the Library,"
  compiled by 82- 104
McFarland, Horace E., Junction City.. 80
McFeedy, J. 44
McGill, T. H., Russell in 1874-1876, described by, in Russell County News.. 111
McGlashen, C. F. 208
McIlwain, Charles, mentioned 119
McIntire, Mrs. Frank 58
— manuscripts given Historical Society
  by 57
McIvor, F. A. 425
McKenney, Thomas L., Indian Affairs,
  superintendent 227, 339
— letter to Isaac McCoy, regarding exploring tour in Indian country, 227, 228
— — regarding surveys of Indian lands.. 340
— letter to Gen. Wm. Clark, regarding
  survey of Delaware lands 348
McKinleys, father and son, lynching of,
  mentioned 214
McKinney, Wm. M., ferry across Grasshopper at Perry 322
Macksville, fiftieth anniversary of 429
Macksville Enterprise 429
McLain, Kathryn 108
McLean, Milton R., Topeka 79, 81
MacLennan, Frank P., editor Topeka
  State Journal 336
McMurtry, Levy, Callaway
  county, Mo.................... 262, 276
McNeal, Thomas A., ... 67, 79, 81
— address "The Governors of Kansas,"
  made before Historical Society .. 71- 78
— dog story told by 78
— personally acquainted with every Kansas state governor 71
— testimonial banquet in honor of 431
McNeil, L. E. and F. H. Poore, note regarding Methodism in Conway Springs, 214
McNulty, Joseph, old log hotel in Stockton erected by, in 1871 220
McPherson College 335
McPherson county 189
— genealogy of, note regarding 105
McPherson County Advertiser, McPherson 105
McShane, John, ferry operator 184
Madison county, Ill................... 277
Madisonian, Washington, D. C. 58
Magaukuk, a Pottawatomie Indian accompanying Isaac McCoy .. 229, 266, 270
— discovers bee tree 250

GENERAL INDEX 455

Mahan, Ernest 335
Mail routes, early 57
Mail service, in Gypsum, mentioned 332
Majors, Alexander 67
— old home of 67
Majors, Ben, son of Alexander Majors.. 67
Malin, Dr. James C................. 79, 81
— associate editor *Kansas Historical Quarterly* 114, 116, 421
— "Frank Heywood Hodder, 1860-1935," article by 115-121
— member nominating committee 64
— note regarding various articles written by 421
Malone, James, Topeka 80
Manhattan 25, 79, 212, 218, 338, 383
385, 386, 389-391, 393, 394, 396
398, 400, 402, 404-406, 408, 409
411-413, 416
— building activities in 1855 158
— building boom 311
— citizens of, start to relief of Lawrence, 170
— Congregational Church..... 143, 169, 318
— — organized at 168
— extent of, in spring of 1856......... 166
— literary society with library just starting 292
— map of, mentioned 293
— Methodist Church 399
— — being erected 307
— school house described 307
— steamboat makes two trips to 391
— Thomas Clarke Wells early settler in vicinity of 114
— threat to destroy 172
Manila Bay, Admiral Dewey's victory in, 109
Mann, S., road viewer 190
Manning, A. R........................ 332
Manning, Charles Burham 332
Manning, Edwin C., ferry incorporator.. 25
— president State Historical Society 25
Marais des Cygnes massacre, note on ... 330
Marais des Cygnes river 246
— bottoms along subject to inundation.. 248
— rampages mentioned 333
— timber a mile in width along 247
Maranville, Lea, president Ness County Historical Society 112
Marble, George Watson, editor *Fort Scott Tribune-Monitor* 336
Marcy, Capt. R. B..................... 6
— survey of the Mississippi Valley for railroad purposes made by 4, 5
— — topography carefully noted in 5
Marion 33
Marion county 32, 189
— Grant township 107
Marion Hill Lutheran Church, sixtieth anniversary celebration of organization, 334
Marion Methodist Episcopal Church, sixty-sixth anniversary celebrated.... 213
Marion *Record* 107, 213, 428
Marion *Review* 107, 213
Marmaduke, Gov. John S. 196
— at St. Louis to discuss strike matters, 43
— ordered out Missouri militia during Missouri Pacific strike 38
Marquette, explorer, Arkansas river mentioned by 22
Marquette Mission Covenant Church, thirty-fifth anniversary observed 222
Marquette *Tribune* 222
Marshall, Geo. H...................... 333
Marshall, T. L., state senator 35
Marshall, W. L....................... 119
Marshall, Tex., Gould Southwestern strike begun at 194
Marshall county 208
— school district No. 66, note on history of 220

Marshall County News, Marysville 109
Martin, McCoy &, Kansas City, Mo., account book of, given Historical Society, 58
Martin, A. H......................... 197
Martin, Gov. John A....... 39, 40, 42- 45
50, 71, 196
— appealed to, for military protection during Missouri Pacific strike 38
— called upon for military assistance in preserving order at Parsons 198
— colonel of Eighth Kansas 76
— dispatch to Superintendent Hoxie of Missouri Pacific Railway regarding strike situation in Kansas 41
— elected governor, Tom McNeal's recollections concerning 76
— Frank A. Root a partner of, in Atchison *Champion and Press* 15
— labor problems of, 1885 .... 33- 55
— — 1886 .... 191- 207
— nominated by acclamation 202
— opening speech of gubernatorial campaign delivered in Topeka 204
— with Kansas railroad commissioners, at St. Louis to confer with Missouri Pacific officials for adjustment of strike, 42
Martin, M. J., ferry incorporator 180
Martin, R. M......................... 425
Martin, Wm. B., Richmond, Ray county, Mo. 261, 274
Martin's river, present Delaware 320
Mary S. Wells chapter, No. 41, Order of Eastern Star of Osborne, fiftieth anniversary of 325
Marysville 25, 50, 211, 212
Mashenah, Atchison county ghost town, 421
Mason, Mrs. Henry F., Topeka, chairman nominating committee Historical Society 64, 78, 79, 81
Masonic Lodge, Hazelton 222
— Larned, organized in January, 1886.. 218
Masonic News, Kansas City 220
Massachusetts, emigrant aid society of.. 72
Massachusetts Baptist Missionary Society 124
Masters, Joseph G..................... 208
Mat, braiding woolen rags for 397
Mathewson, William, original "Buffalo Bill" 8
Mats, husk, mode of making 397
Mauler, Rudy 426
Maximilian, Prince, Nemaha river mentioned by 378
Mead, James R................... 23, 188
— associate of Jesse Chisholm 3, 7
— ferry operator 186
— "Reminiscences of Frontier Life," manuscript in Kansas State Historical Society 8
— takes goods for Jesse Chisholm over trail 8
— Trading post in North Canadian river.. 7
Meade Center, fiftieth anniversary of incorporation as third class city 108
Meade county, date of organization 108
— notes regarding early settlement and boundaries of 108
Meade *Globe-News*, special historical edition of 108
Mechem, Kirke, secretary of Kansas State Historical Society 62, 66, 80, 108, 111
— Memorial Craftsmen of Kansas, in Salina, addressed by 112
— note on early observance of Thanksgiving in Kansas 108
— report of 54- 62
— Shawnee Mission Indian Historical Society addressed by 336
Medical Bulletin, published by Sedgwick County Medical Society 329

GENERAL INDEX

Medicine Lodge, some incidents connected with 74, 75
Meece, L. A. 419
Meeker, Grace 431
Meeker, Jotham 57
— first printer and publisher in Indian territory 431
— founder Ottawa mission 431
Meluish, Anna, Ottawa 59
Memorial Craftsmen of Kansas, addressed by Kirke Mechem 112
Menard, Col. Pierre 234, 266
Mennonite colony, moved into Barton county, note regarding 424
Mennonites, credited with introducing Turkey Red wheat in Barton county, 424
Mercer, Joseph, Topeka 81
Meridian, Sumner county, state road from Labette City to 182
Merimack, Ohio, Shawnee Indians from, 260
Merril, Maj. ——, map made by ... 5, 6
Merrimack river, Mo. 273
Mershon, Clarence 107
Merten, Mrs. H. J. and Mrs. W. H. Lennard, note on their history of Morganville Methodist Church 423
Mescalero Apache reservation 11
Metcalf, Wilder S., estate of, diaries given Historical Society 58
Meteoric display, witnessed by Donner party 209
Methodist Episcopal Church 176, 213 290, 389
— Burns 333
— Cimarron 330
— Colby, note on fiftieth anniversary of founding 333
— Coldwater, note on history of 216
— Conway Springs, history of, noted... 214
— Garden Plain, note on history of ... 109
— Goddard 223
— Highland township, Clay county, note on history of 427
— Humboldt, seventy-fifth anniversary celebrated 110
— Iola, seventy-fifth anniversary celebrated 110
— Junction City, note on history of ... 326
— Juniata (South) 165
— Kanopolis, note on fiftieth anniversary celebration 331
— Kansas conference, 1856 280
— Lawrence, Sunday School 280
— Leon 219
— LeRoy 219
— Manhattan 399, 417
— Marion, sixty-sixth anniversary celebrated 213
— missions in Kansas established by in 1830 375
— Morganville, note on history of 423
— Norcatur, fiftieth anniversary celebrated 215
— Osage City, sixty-fifth anniversary home-coming, note on 430
— Potwin, founded fifty years ago..... 215
— Riley county, held quarterly meeting in grove 172
— Sedgwick, date incorporated 215
— Shawnee Indian school planned 343
— Solomon 216
— Syracuse, fiftieth anniversary 427
— Thayer, note on history of 427
— Washington, note on histories of ... 429
— Wichita (Grace) 333
Mexican War, mentioned 120
Mexicans, name for Arkansas river ... 22
Mexico, German-Russians migrate to Russell from 105

Meyer, H. A., president of Kansas City Smelting and Refining Co. 192
Miami Indians 130, 139, 140
— Mississinewa villages of 127
— William Turner agent for 127
Miami Republican, Paola 219
Mid-America, Chicago, Catholic historical magazine 326, 421, 427
Midway station, Nebraska, station on Pony Express route 69
Miege, Rt. Rev. John Baptist, S. J., note regarding correspondence of 427
Military road 324
— Fort Leavenworth 429
—— to Fort Riley 150, 320, 324
Militia, Kansas, Border Ruffians enrolled in 169, 202
—— law concerning amended 206
— Missouri state, ordered out during Missouri Pacific railroad strike 38
Mill creek 148
Miller, H. C., Horton's first postmaster, 428
Miller, J. M. 108
Miller, Nyle H. 60
Miller, Orman L., note on history of Lone Tree school 213
Miller, Sol, editor and founder, *Kansas Chief* 321, 332
Millikan, Martie 58
Mills, Walt W. 425
Mills, at Topeka and Lawrence 158
Mine inspection, enactment of law providing for 34
Mine inspector, annual visits required to make 35
Mineral hills, mentioned by McCoy 372
Miners, Osage county strikers, time inopportune for 193
— wages of, law requiring monthly payments 35
Minneapolis, municipal bank of, mentioned 214
— Presbyterian Church, note on early history of 106
Minneapolis *Better Way* 111
Minneola, most famous ghost town of Kansas 222
Minnich, J. Hont, ferry operator 184
Minnie Belle, steamboat, makes two trips to Manhattan in 1859 391
Mirage, in western Kansas, mentioned .. 419
Miry DeSein river. *See* Marais des Cygnes river.
Miry Swan river. *See* Marais des Cygnes.
Mississippi river......... 23, 229, 233, 267
— removal of Indians to west of....... 227
— valley of, railroad surveys in........ 4
Mississippi Valley Historical Association, 120
Missouri 258
— compromises, mentioned..... 117, 119, 120
— Indians to be restricted to regions west of 231
— John S. Marmaduke governor of.... 38
— southwestern, Texas cattle driven to after close of Civil War............ 4
— state militia, ordered out during Missouri Pacific Railroad strike......... 38
Missouri Historical Review 120
Missouri hotel, St. Louis............. 162
Missouri, Kansas & Texas Railway.. 40, 41
Missouri Pacific Railroad Co. 40, 44, 45, 202
— built to Hoisington................ 424
— H. M. Hoxie vice-president......38, 195
— officials of, notify city of Parsons that strikers were in possession of company property 198
— strikes 194, 206
—— ended satisfactory to strikers..... 43

General Index

Missouri Pacific Railroad Co., strikes, freight train wrecked by strikers traced to Knights of Labor...... 198
—— governors of Kansas and Missouri invoked as mediators 195
—— March, 1885, history of.......36- 46
—— Parsons situation.................. 199
—— public sentiment with strikers..... 64
—— strikers refuse paychecks, ignore notice of discharge and maintain perfect police system during period of 37
—— troops asked for, to preserve order, 201
— Wichita depot of.................... 185
Missouri river 21, 23, 57, 67, 68 70, 223, 233, 235, 243, 261, 264, 274, 321 336, 342, 354-356, 366, 378, 415
— discomforts of steamboat travel on, during low water................... 146
— *J. H. Lucas,* a steamboat on.... 162, 163
— "Kansas Emigrants Song" taboo on.. 279
— method of getting over sandbars..... 147
Missourians, circulating reports to discourage Northern immigration to Kansas 153
— going to Lawrence to vote.......... 149
— search trunks and boxes of freight of Kansans for Sharp's rifles.......... 165
Mitchell county, note on Arthur Sellick's reminiscences 109
Moberly, Mo., reduction of force in Wabash shops at.................... 45
Moccasins, deerskin 245
Mochilas, Pony Express riders carried valuables in 69
Mograin, Noel. See Mongrain, Noel.
Molasses, price in 1859 405
Mollie Dozier, steamboat on Missouri river 57
Money, scarcity of 315
Money creek 324
Mongrain, Noel, accompanies McCoy's exploring party............... 244, 245 247, 248, 252, 254, 257, 260, 261, 275
— described by McCoy 253
— half Osage, age of 244
— interpreter 240
Monitor-Press, Wellington 182, 326
Montezuma Press, founded as *Chief* 325
Montgomery, James 66
Montgomery, John, publisher of Junction City *Union* 423
Montgomery, Robert, letters to Isaac McCoy, containing particulars regarding treaty with Pottawatomies..... 133- 136
— teacher at McCoy's mission school... 133
Montgomery county, Mo............... 276
Monument, to Alfred and Fred Gould, who perished during blizzard of 1886, 331
— Trading Post 330
Moonlight, Thomas 204, 205
— nominated for governor by Democratic party 203, 204
Moore, Bert, of Winfield 30, 180
— statements regarding Shoo Fly and Ponca trails..................... 26
Moore, Ed. G. 330
Moore, Jim, Pony Express rider 69
Moore, Russell, Wichita 79, 81
Morehouse, Geo. P., Topeka 79, 81
Morgan, William Y., lieutenant governor, 77
Morganville, First Methodist Church, fiftieth anniversary of 423
Mormon war, Gen. Albert Sidney Johnston leads army to Utah to quell 67
Morrill, A. 181
Morrill, Edmund N. governor, Tom McNeal's recollections of 76, 77
Morrison, S. E., mentioned 119
Morrison, T. F., Chanute 80

Morse, Mrs. Emma Wattles 58
Morton, H. B., ferry incorporator 25
Morton County Farmer, Rolla 219
Mosely, Mrs. R. C. 213
Mo-shc-no, French Pottawatomie, footnote concerning 20
Mosier, Burr, member ferry company .. 184
Moss, Thomas S., ferry incorporator ... 182
Mott, F. O. 331
Mound, artificial, discovered by McCoy on summit of high hill 254
— at commencement of survey of Delaware outlet 363
Mounds, erected on Delaware lands, to mark reservation boundaries 355, 364
Mudge, Mrs. J. B. 432
Municipal bands, note regarding 214
Murdock, Mrs. F. L., director 432
Murdock, Marshall M. 24
— poem "The Nile of America," mentioned 22
Murdock, Victor...................... 109 326-328, 331, 340, 421, 424, 426, 428
— recollections of S. L. Dunkin, regarding Wichita ferry, recorded by 187
Murphy, John, bridge and ferry incorporator 183
Murray, John, Salt Springs Ferry operated by 180
Muscotah 320, 324
— note on history of 429
Muscovy company voyage, of 1553 118
Myers, Mr. —— 27
Myers, W. O. 334

N

Nach-uch-u-te-be river, present Delaware river 320
Naismith, Dr. James A., game of basketball invented by 218
Naomi Rebekah Lodge No. 61, Minneapolis, note on history of 111
Naoquah Kozhuk, Ottawa Indian, accompanied McCoy on exploring tour.. 229
Napawalla, Oxford first known as...... 181
Napoleon, Ark. 23
Narragansett *Times* 150, 151
Nation, Carrie 66
— note on saloon-smashing crusade of.. 327
National Bank of Topeka 63
National Tribune, Washington, D. C.... 59
National Youth Administration, local project operating under sponsorship of Kansas State Historical Society 224
Natoma, note on early history of....... 213
Navajo reservation 11
Nealley, Mr. —— 283, 285
Negroes, first colored family in Emporia, note on 420
Nelson, C. A., director Lindsborg Historical Society 112
Nelson, Carol Jean 219
Nemaha, meaning of word in Otoe language 378, 379
Neosho river 254, 257, 264
— McCoy searches for 251
— Osages living on 252
Neosho Valley Register, Burlington...... 59
Neptawa 181
Nesh-cosh-cosh-che-ba, or Swallow river, present Delaware 320
Ness County Historical Society, officers of, 112
Nevins, Allen 119
Nevins, F. J. 428
New England, second party to Kansas from 278
New England Farmer 307, 308
New Hampshire Historical Society 63
New Malden community, Atchison county, notes on early-day history of... 108, 429

GENERAL INDEX

New Mexico, Jesse Chisholm drives cattle to 7
— John S. Chisum large cattle owner of, 11
New York *Evangelist* 293
New York *Express* 399
New York *Observer*, cited 106
New York *Times*, Chisholm cattle trail described by 13
New York *Tribune* 176
New York *World* 13
Newhall, Samuel, member Lawrence band 280, 281
Ne-woh-kon-daga, Kaw name for Great Spirit spring 373
Newport, Mrs. Leigh, director Hodgeman County Historical Society 432
Newspaper, first established in Protection 215
News-Republic, Goodland 214
Newton, end of cattle trail at........ 12
— period as a cattle town 13
— Zion Evangelical Lutheran Church, golden jubilee of 421
Newton *Journal* 421
Niagara Falls, N. Y., suspension bridge. 144
Nickell, Joe, of Topeka *Capital* 327
Nickerson, date of old settlers' meeting at 433
Nile of America, Arkansas river so termed 22
Niles, Berrien county, Mich., Carey mission established near 141
Niles' Register, quoted 342
Ninnescah, ferry at 183
Ninnescah Ferry Company, chartered... 184
Ninnescah river 183
Nishcoba, or Deep Water creek, present Chapman creek 374
Nodewa river 345
Noonday, Indian accompanying McCoy on exploring tour 267, 270
Norcatur *Dispatch* 215
Norcatur Methodist Episcopal Church, fiftieth anniversary celebrated 215
Norman, Harry, of New York *World*... 13
Norris, Mrs. George, Arkansas City.... 80
North Canadian river 8, 10
— Beaver county, Okla. 320
— Chisholm and Mead join in trading venture to .... ` 7
Norton, G. H., ferry incorporator...... 25
Notino, Ottawa Indian 431
Nova School, Carmi township, Pratt county 223
Nyton, J. H., ferry incorporator 181

O

Oak 248, 251
— and elm and walnut on Kickapoo reserve 16
Oak creek, Smith county.............. 370
Oakley, fiftieth anniversary of founding of 107
— note on school history of........... 429
Oakley *Graphic* 107, 429
Oatville, note on history of........... 430
O'Connor, Thomas F.................. 427
Odair, Joe 420
Ogden, Maj. E. A., building Fort Riley, 320
Ogden, Riley county................... 316
Oil and Gas Journal, Tulsa........... 106
Oil producing center, Yoder now an.... 223
Oil wells, Kansas, first acid treatment of, 106
O-keet-sha, Kaw name, meaning stranger, 351
Oklahoma 6, 23, 26
— Chisholm trail being marked by..... 14
— surveys for railroads through territory included in 5
Oklahoma City, Okla., Council Grove just west of 7

Oklahoma State Highway Commission.. 325
Olathe *Mirror* 216
Old Pawnee Village, on Roy's creek..... 379
Old-Time Trail Drivers' Association, annual meeting at San Antonio...... 3
Oliver, Hannah P., Lawrence........... 81
Olmutz, Barton county, note on history of 426
Olson, Henry, director Lindsborg Historical Society 112
Olson, Nels 105
Omaha Indians 353
Onaga *Herald* 213
Oneida Christian Church, fifty-fifth anniversary celebrated 214
O'Neil, Ralph T., Topeka............. 80
Opothleyahola, sought refuge in Kansas.. 6
Order of Eastern Star, Osborne, note on history of 325
Oregon, Marcus Whitman missionary to.. 330
Oregon question 117, 119
Oregon trail 14, 70, 212
— article regarding grave of Sarah Keyes on, by Wm. E. Smith.......... 208- 212
— graves along the, note regarding..... 427
Oregon Trail Memorial Association, centenary celebration 208
Osage, Kaw Indian pronunciation of.... 261
Osage City 35
— coal mine strike 193
— Methodist Episcopal Church, sixty-sixth anniversary home coming 430
— miners delegate convention met at Burlingame 193
Osage City *Free Press* 193, 194
Osage County Democrat, Burlingame.... 193, 194, 205
Osage Indian, accompanying McCoy's exploring party, description of...... 245
— — desertion of 246
Osage Indians ... 247, 253, 255, 265, 275, 351
— country west of Missouri purchased from 240
— mother and child described.......... 246
— residing on Neosho river............ 252
— woman of, visits McCoy's camp to beg food 245
Osage mission, note regarding history of.. 215
Osage reservation 240
Osage river 243, 246- 248, 251, 254, 257, 258, 260, 264, 265
— Missouri, Grand Auglaize a branch of, 242
Osage trail 189
Osawatomie, battle of 66
Osawkee 320
— ferry license issued to Jefferson Riddle for 322
— steps for establishing bridge at...... 322
— toll bridge constructed at.......... 323
Osborn, Thomas A., elected governor.. 75
Osborne, band of 106
— fire department of, organized in 1888, 329
— new bridge, dam and lake completed at 329
— note on arrival of Pennsylvania colony at 329
Osborne county, first election in Corinth township 213
— log stockade, for protection against Indians, built in early 1870's.......... 217
— note regarding historic spots in...... 217
— organized in 1871 329
Osborne County Farmer, Osborne....... 217, 325, 328
Osborne County Farmers' Union, note on organization of 328
Osborne *Journal*, consolidation of Alton *Empire* with 217
Otero county, Colo. 22
Otis, Mr. — — 162

GENERAL INDEX 459

Otoe Indians 353, 368, 378
Ottawa 59
— a post office in 1864................ 333
— Asa S. Lathrop first mayor 333
— library, Reading Club nucleus of..... 334
— note on early history of 333
— noted for Chautauqua 333
— school district formed November, 1864 333
Ottawa *Herald*, seventieth anniversary edition of 333
Ottawa Indians 123, 135
140, 240, 265, 266, 268
— accompany Isaac McCoy on exploring expedition 122, 228, 229
— blacksmith and teachers for 137
— demands of, at treaty of 1821...... 138
— on Grand river 262
— speak same language as Pottawatomies with trifling variations 139
Ottawa Reading Club, nucleus of library, 334
Ottawa University 333
Otters 366
Overland Stage to California, Frank A. Root, author 2
Overland staging, out of Atchison 15
Overland trails, old, note on 332
— three met at Kennekuk 67
Overmyer, David, of Shawnee county.. 52
Owen, Mrs. E. M., president Douglas County Historical Society 112
Owens, — —, member legislature 1857-1858 323
Ox wagon 66
Oxford, known locally as Big Cottonwood crossing 181
— named for Osage Chief 181
— new concrete bridge near, dedicated.. 183
— pontoon bridge at 182
— settled in 1870 181
— Sumner county 30
Oxford Bridge and Ferry Co., organization of 182
Oxford Ferry Co., organization of 181
Oxford *Independent* 180
Oxford *Weekly* 181, 183
Oxford *Weekly Press* 182

P

Pacific railroad 117, 120
Pack horses 346
Packers, hired for exploring tour, described by McCoy as "poor sticks".. 259
Packmen, with McCoy's exploring tour.. 251
Paddock, Gaius, Madison county, Ill.... 277
Padouca Indian nation 320
Page river 231
Page's hotel, Lawrence, menu at 149
Paleontology, Joseph Savage a pioneer explorer of, in Kansas 278
Palmer, Rev. Albert 317, 383
Palmer, Ernest, member ferry company.. 184
Panee, Panie, Pawnee river. See Republican river.
Panees (Pawnees), war parties of....... 240
Pa-ne-ne-tah or Pawnee river 370
Paola 50
— Pleasant Hour Club, sixtieth anniversary of, observed................. 219
Parham, W. M., note regarding Phillips county history, discussed by..... 105
Parke, Benjamin, Indiana territorial judge 125
— temporary Indian agent following death of Thomas Posey............. 126
Parker, Effie 58
Parkerville, note on history of......... 430
Parr, Jacob, ferry at Denton's ford operated by 29
Parrish, Paul R. 58

Parrish, T. L., vice-president Kansas History Teachers' Association........ 335
Parsons, Mr. — —, formerly of Cape Cod 314
Parsons 33, 36, 38, 40, 42, 44, 45
— Law and Order League formed at.... 201
— Missouri Pacific strikes at... 196, 198, 199
— troops asked for 200, 201
Parsons *Daily Eclipse* 44, 45
Parsons *Daily Sun*, cited......... 35, 36, 44
45, 194, 198
Patrick, Col. — — 201
Patrick, Mrs. Mae C., Satanta 81
Pattee, Mr. — — 392, 407
Patterson, J. M., ferry incorporator..... 181
Paul, Prince of Wurttemburg........... 111
Paulen, Ben S., elected governor........ 77
Paulson, Mr. — — 399
Pawnee agency 31
Pawnee county 23
— first wheel made in county in 1881... 218
Pawnee County Historical Society...... 80
Pawnee Indians 255, 265, 352
355, 357-359, 361, 363, 373
— depredations of 348
— described 358
— John Dougherty agent for.......... 345
— Kansas Indians steal horses from.... 351
— lands of 354
— McCoy's efforts to conciliate........ 349
— republic, old village of.......... 345, 370
— towns of, mentioned 349
Pawnee river 370, 372- 374
— Republican also known as........... 368
Pawnee Rock 70
— vicinity of, mentioned 424
Paxico, note on early history of old town 223
Payne, Robert, St. Louis, Mo........... 271
Peach trees 395
Pearce, W. C., Garden City............ 110
Pearson, Benjamin F., author.......... 217
Pechowkee, Delaware chief............. 279
Peckham, C. W....................... 331
Pecos river 11
Peffer, Wm. A. 66
Penfield, F. C. 58
Penner, Elliott, reporter Hutchinson *Herald* 419
Pennsylvania colony, note on...... 329, 330
Perdue, Rosa M....................... 116
Perrin, Geo. H., road commissioner..... 324
Perry, — —, Shawnee Indian 376
Perry, Jefferson county 319
— John C. Bailey's ferry located near.. 321
— license for pontoon bridge issued..... 322
— McKinney's ferry at 322
Pershing, Gen. John J., Gen. James G. Harbord, chief of staff during World War 425
Peterton, coal mine strike at.......... 192
Philip, Mrs. W. D. Hays............. 80
Phillips, Maj. — —, paymaster, U. S. army 135
Phillips, Ed., resident near Effingham... 324
Phillips, Paul C. 119
Phillips, Wm. A...................... 66
Phillips county 57, 105
Phillips County Review, Phillipsburg.... 110
Phillipsburg, Cultus Club, a woman's organization 110
Phillipsburg *News* 108
Physicians, prominent in Wichita during first twenty-five years, note on...... 329
Pickler, Judge R. M. 425
Pierceville, ferry at 190
Pigeons, wild 231
Pike Pawnee Park 61
Pike, Zebulon M., monument to, blown down 61

GENERAL INDEX

Pike's Peak 398
— emigration 392
Pike's Peak travel 405
— passing through Manhattan 395
Pikes, John Brown 116
Pioneer Kansan picnic, held in Wilsey.. 430
Pistols, horse 240
Pittman, ——, mentioned............ 119
Pittsburg, churches 420
— coal capital of Kansas 420
— note on sixtieth anniversary of city's foundation 420
— water supply problem of early days, note on 420
Pittsburg *Headlight* 420
Pittsburg *Sun* 420
Place, Harold C. 222, 334
Platte river 352, 367
Playter, Franklin 420
Pleasant Hour Club, Paola, sixtieth anniversary of, observed 219
Plum trees 395
Plumb, Preston B. 202
— elected U. S. senator 75
— ferry incorporator 25
— positions held by 25
Plums, wild 155, 157
Plymouth, Brown county 107
Poetry, Kansas 57
Political revolution, in Kansas in 1890.. 76
Polke, Christiana, became Mrs. Isaac McCoy 123
Polke, William 262
— brother-in-law of Isaac McCoy..... 123
Polk's, point on road from Florence to Arkansas City 32
Pomeroy, Samuel C. 144
Ponca Indians 26
— agency of, on Salt Fork river...... 26
Ponca trail, Cowley county, route of, discussed 26
Pond Creek, I. T. 7, 8
Pontoon bridge, license issued to Thos. G. Smith for 322
— Oxford 182
— — carried away by flood 183
Pony Express 57, 66, 67
— Cold Springs third station west of St. Joseph........................ 69
— date of first riders east and west.... 70
— discussed by W. R. Honnell before Historical Society 67-71
— note on history of 429
— riders for.................... 69, 381
— saved California to Union 70
— stock and other equipment of 68
Pony Express Courier, Placerville, Calif. 222, 427
Ponziglione, Father Paul M., early Kansas missionary 215, 421
Poore, F. H. 214
Population studies 57
Populists, how title attached 111
— "Pops" a nickname for 66
— uprising of 57
Posey, Thomas, death mentioned 126
— Indian agent at Vincennes......... 125
Post offices, dead 108
Potatoes 284
— price at Manhattan, 1856 168
— shipped by ferryboat to Pawnee agency 31
Potowatomie Indians. *See* Pottawatomie Indians.
Pottawatomie creek, massacre of Pro-slavery settlers at crossing of 66
Pottawatomie Indians 135, 140
                           230, 240, 265-268
— adopted into Kickapoo tribe 15
— blacksmith and teachers for 137

Pottawatomie Indians, delegations accompany Isaac McCoy to inspect lands west of Missouri 122, 228
— intermarriage with Kickapoos 15
— Isaac McCoy's plans for establishment of school for, in Michigan territory 123
— Ottawas speak same language with trifling variations 139
— religious worship among 21
— reservation of 416
— Shawaunukwuk, accompanied Isaac McCoy on exploring tour 229
— visited by Isaac McCoy........... 131
"Pottawatomie-Kickapoo Grand Indian Jubilee," article by Frank A. Root. 15-21
Potter, Col. Jack 110
Potwin *Ledger* 215
Potwin M. E. Church, founded fifty years ago 215
Powderly, Terence V. 196
— Grand Master Workman of Knights of Labor 195
— head of Knights of Labor 48
Prairie 233, 252, 258
Prairie chickens 284, 296
Prairie dogs 70
— village of 371
Prairie fires 250, 316, 364, 366, 369-371
— seen by McCoy's exploring party in southwest Missouri 245
— started by McCoy's exploring party as signals to lost members of party, 356, 357
Prairie Pottawatomies 20
Prairie-du-Chien, treaty held at 353
Prairies, described 16
— Kansas, soil of, compared with Illinois 247
— mentioned by McCoy 232
— rolling, west of state of Missouri.... 246
Pratt county, note regarding old settlers registering at annual picnic 427
Pratt *Daily Tribune* 426, 427
— "Yearly Progress Edition" of, issued February 26, 1936 221
Pratt *Union* 427
Pratz, LePage du 22
Prentice, E. H., ferry incorporator 183
Prentis, Noble L. 40, 197
Presbyterian Church, Clearwater, organized February, 1874 214
— Minneapolis, note on history of..... 106
— Syracuse, fiftieth anniversary of..... 107
Prescott, Mrs. Frank F. 430
Preston, Ben 330
Preston *News* 223
Price, Ralph R., Manhattan 79, 81
Price raid 281
Priddle, Rev. C. V. 331
Primary elections 57
Prince, William, appointed Indian agent to succeed Thomas Posey 126
Pringle, Robena 335
Progress in Kansas, Topeka, issued by Kansas Chamber of Commerce.. 108, 111
                                   222, 334
Progressive-Signal, Greensburg......... 430
Prohibition amendment, passage of..... 76
Prophet Town, Wyandotte county 343
Pro-slavery settlers, massacred at Dutch Henry's crossing 66
Protection, date of old settlers' meeting at 433
— first newspaper of, mentioned...... 215
— townsite of 215
Protection *Post* 214
Providence (R. I.) *Journal* 293, 307
Provisions, prices at Leavenworth, 1860, 417
Prowers county, Colo. 22
Pruden, Capt. H. B., ferryboat operator, 31
Public library, Gypsum, note on 332

GENERAL INDEX 461

Public schools, Gypsum, note on 332
Pueblo, Colo., flood of June, 1921...... 23
Pueblo county, Colo. 22
Puritan Recorder 167

Q

Quantrill, William C., destruction of
 Lawrence by 66, 280
Quarles, W. 44, 45
Queens Daughters, Wichita, note on
 history of 213
Quick, John, second chief of Delawares. 343
 344, 346, 353, 356, 358, 359
Quick sands, in Republican river 369
Quindaro 15
Quinter, Church of the Brethren, founding of, notes on 217, 430
— history of, noted 430
Quivira, note on location of 326

R

Rabbit drives in Kansas, note on...... 107
Raccoon creek, Parke county,
 Indiana 126, 127
Raccoons 251, 369
Race, Mrs. Marion Kent, Chicago, Ill... 59
Rackensack, name applied to Arkansas
 river 22
Radio profession, note regarding some
 Kansans prominent in 223
Radios 66
Railroad building in Kansas, Otto P.
 Byers had part in 327
Railroad trains, stream lined........... 66
Railroaders, early day, note regarding.. 422
Railroads, Atchison, note on history of . 422
— getting into Wichita, note on........ 428
Rails 306
Rain, Silas, ferry incorporator 183
Rain storm, on banks of Big Blue river, 209
Rainey, George, pioneer of Oklahoma.. 6
Randolf, Mr. —— 287
Randolph, John, coined phrase "Dough
 Faces" 120
Rankin, Robert C., Lawrence........... 80
Ransom, W. H. 425
Raser, Mrs. Margaret, historian Hodgeman County Historical Society....... 432
Rattlesnakes, killed by Isaac
 McCoy 355, 370
Ravens, croaking of, a warning that enemies were near 257
Rawson, Laura Lynam 425
Ray county, Mo. 274
Raynesford, H. C., Ellis......... 58, 79, 81
"Recent Additions to the Library," list
 compiled by Helen M. McFarland,
 Kansas Historical Society
 librarian 82- 104
Red Bluff townsite, mentioned......... 211
Red Butte, Wyo. 69
Red Legs 66
Red river 6
Red river station, Chisholm trail to Kansas from 10, 325
Redmond, John, publisher Burlington
 Republican 431
Reed and Donner, caravan of.......... 208
Reed, ——, Baptist preacher, Wakefield,
 R. I. 284, 290, 302, 317
Reed, ——, sub agent at Carey, Mich... 230
Reed, Clyde M. 81
— dedicated new concrete bridge near
 Oxford 183
— elected governor 77
Reed, J. H., of Illinois, member of Donner party 209
Reed, Jim 230

Reed, N. A., Jr. 167, 176, 287
Reeder, Gov. Andrew H............. 325, 326
— Free State candidate for Congress.... 160
Reese, W. P. 58
Reiber, B. F., note regarding early recollections of 223
Reinhardt, Eileen 219
Relief, Harvey county, 1874-1875, note
 regarding 107
Religious worship among Kickapoo and
 Pottawatomie Indians 21
Relihan, A. W. 425
Remsburg, George J. 20, 107, 220
 320, 332, 361, 379, 424, 427, 429
— acknowledgments to 380
Rennick, ——, mentioned by Isaac
 McCoy 432
Reno county 23
Republic county, foreign settlements in,
 mentioned 419
— James Barton, of Cuba, settled in
 county in 1871..................... 220
— note regarding twenty-two ghost towns
 of 222
— Pawnee Indian village in............ 370
Republican party in Kansas.......... 66, 202
— note on history of.................. 222
— state convention of, resolutions regarding labor passed by................ 203
Republican river 351, 354, 367, 372, 374
— also known as Pawnee river.......... 368
— curious geological formations along... 370
— short description of................. 369
Reynolds, Mr. ——, of Manhattan.... 167
Reynolds, Dorothy 332
Rice, Dr. ——, St. Louis minister...... 163
Rice county 23
Richard, Rev. J. J. 334
Richards, David, operated first ferry across
 Arkansas river in Sumner county..... 184
Richards, Ralph 429
Richards, W. M., joint author of new
 Kansas history 432
Richardson, Mr. ——, ferry boat of... 183
Richmond, Mo. 261
Riddle, Jefferson, biographical sketch of, 322
— ferry operator 322
Riley, Maj. Bennet 347, 362
Riley County Historical Society 79
— old officers re-elected 432
Rinehart, George F., resident of Syracuse in middle 1880's 107
Rio des Acansas 22
Rio Napete, Mexican name for Arkansas river 21, 22
Ritter, John N., state senator 35
River, Auplain, twelve miles from
 Chicago 230, 231
River Page 231
Road, Florence to Arkansas City 32
— Fort Leavenworth to Fort Riley, relocation of 323
— Indian, leading to Shawnee village.. 258
— overland wagon..................... 15
— Santa Fé to St. Louis 249, 250
— state, Labette City to Meridian,
 Sumner county 182
— wagon, to Harmony mission station.. 243
Roads, to and from Arkansas City 32
— to and from Grasshopper Falls.. 323, 324
— to Roy's ferry 379, 380
Robbery, train, at Atchison, 1882, note
 regarding 217
Roberts, J. N., brigadier general 199
Roberts, Roy L. 419
Robey, Fernando, pioneer Wichitan, note
 on recollections of 331
Robinson, Mr. ——, mentioned....... 393
Robinson, Gov. Charles. 66, 76, 170, 280, 315
— California trip of 72

General Index

Robinson, Gov. Charles, faction of...... 73
— first state governor, Tom McNeal's recollections of 71-73
Robinson, G. I. 289
Robinson, John W., secretary of state.. 73
Robinson, Mrs. Sara T. D. 295
Rochester, mentioned 416
Rock, porous, snakes basking on....... 231
Rock City 32
Rock creek, Jefferson county 319
Rock creek, Neb., "Wild Bill" Hickok in charge of Pony Express station at, 69
Rock creek township, Nemaha county .. 319
Rock Island Magazine, cited 6
Rock Island shops, Horton, fiftieth anniversary of establishment of 428
Rock Ridge, on Pony Express route.... 69
Rocky Hill district, Lincoln county, note regarding early school days at....... 105
Rocky Mountains 65, 67, 366
— sandy country to the east of....... 22
Roff, Harry 222
Rogler, Henry, Matfield Green, secretary Chase County Historical Society 431
Rohrbaugh theatre, Ottawa 333
Rome, Ellis county, note on 419
Romine, J., Oxford 182
Rooks county, first election held in 1872, 216
— note on early life in 216
Rooks County Record, Stockton.... 216, 220
Roosevelt, Theodore 77
Root, Frank Albert, author and pioneer newspaperman 2
— biographical sketch 15
— Kickapoo-Pottawatomie grand Indian jubilee described by............ 15- 21
Root, George A., curator of archives, 2, 107 114, 219, 226, 338, 368, 429
— "Ferries in Kansas," articles by, on Arkansas river 22-32, 180-190
— — Grasshopper river 319-324
— — Great Nemaha river 378-380
Rooth, C. R., director Lindsborg Historical Society 112
Rose School District No. 27, Butler county, note on history of 426
Ross, Edmund G., voted to acquit Andrew Johnson 327
Ross, Harry E., former editor Burr Oak *Herald* 334
Ross, J. B., road commissioner 324
Ross, John, bass drummer, Lawrence band 290
Rossel, John, history instructor, Franklin High School, Baltimore, Md..... 2
— "The Chisholm Trail," article by.. 3- 14
Rothenberger, Frank, Osborne, old-timer of Osborne county 217
Roy, John Baptiste, operated ferry on Great Nemaha river 379
Royal Gorge, Arkansas river flows through 22
Roy's branch, named for John B. LeRoy 379
Roy's creek, Brown county, scene of sanguinary Indian battle 379
Roy's creek site, known to Iowa Indians as Old Pawnee Village 379
Roy's ferry, location of................ 379
— territorial roads established to....... 379
Rule and Hide Out schools, Fall River vicinity, note on history of......... 328
Runnymede 326
Rupert, Rev. Lynn H................. 326
Rupp, Mrs. W. E., Hillsboro.......... 81
— note regarding history of Marion M. E. Church, compiled by......... 213
Ruppenthal, Judge Jacob C., Russell, 58, 80
— index of all Russell county newspapers started under supervision of......... 224

Rural school teachers, Barton county, note on 216
Russel, — —, mentioned by Isaac McCoy 342
Russell, Majors & Waddell, Pony Express, operated by 68
Russell, W. G., Smoky Hill trail surveyed by 336
Russell, W. J., Topeka............ 79, 81
Russell, German-Russians migrate from Mexico to 105
— in 1874-1876, note on 111
— municipal band of 106
Russell county, dead post offices in, note on 108
— first acid treatment of oil wells in Kansas in 106
— indexing of all newspaper of, started, 224
— note regarding county court reporters, 110
Russell County News, Russell.......... 105 108, 110, 111
Russell Record 106
Russman, John, editor Holyrood *Gazette*, 220
Ryan, Ernest A., Topeka............ 79, 80
— member nominating committee....... 64
Rydjord, John 335

S

Sabbath school, held under a tree...... 172
Sac Indians 235, 353
— deserted settlement of.............. 247
— and Fox Indians, agency of......... 7
— — John B. LeRoy interpreter for.... 379
Sacramento, Calif................. 68, 70
St. Augustine's Church, at Fidelity, note on history of..................... 215
St. Charles, Mo. 243
St. Clair county, Ill.................. 277
St. George 416
St. John, John P., governor, Tom McNeal's recollections of 75, 76
— scrap books of, given Historical Society 58
St. John Lutheran Church, Kensington.. 106
St. John *News* 223
St. John's Evangelical Lutheran Church, Lincolnville, note on 213
St. John's Lutheran Church, Bird City, note on history of.................. 329
St. Joseph, Mich., missionary establishment at 266
— treaty of 229
St. Joseph, Mo..................... 68, 69
— trail from 67
St. Joseph's river, Michigan........ 122, 137
St. Louis, Mo. 233, 244, 269- 273
— City hotel 233, 269
— Isaac McCoy set out on exploring expedition of Indian country from...... 228
— levee described 163
St. Marie, Mich...................... 237
St. Mary's river, at Fort Wayne...... 252
St. Mary's treaty, Indians dissatisfied over outcome of..................... 137
St. Paul, date of old settlers' meeting at, 433
St. Paul *Journal*, cited................ 215
— W. W. Graves, editor.............. 217
St. Paul's Episcopal Church, Clay Center, fifty-fifth anniversary observed....... 217
St. Paul's Lutheran Church, Geary county, seventy-fifth anniversary of founding 424
St. Peter and St. Paul's river, name given Arkansas river by Spaniards of Coronado's expedition 22
Salem Church, old, Lyon county, destroyed by fire 111
Salem Lutheran Church, Lenexa, golden jubilee celebrated 216

GENERAL INDEX 463

Salina, Christmas in early day, note
  on 110
— municipal band mentioned 214
— note on history of city government.. 110
Salina Chamber of Commerce 110
Salina *Journal* 109, 110
Saline county 189, 332
— fifty years ago, note on 332
— note regarding minute books of 109
Saline river valley, note regarding first
  settlers in 332
Saloons, smashed in Kansas before
  Carrie Nation's crusade 327
Salt, Kansas, note on story of 334
Salt City 30, 31, 180
— ferryboat loaded with wheat and
  floated to Little Rock, Ark., from... 181
Salt City ferry, advertisement 181
Salt creek, Leavenworth county 357, 360
— prehistoric Indian encampments
  on 360, 361
Salt Fork river 26
Salt spring, mentioned by McCoy 373
Salt Springs Ferry Co., incorporators... 180
— ferriage charges of 180
Salvation Army, Wichita, note on 329
Samuel, ——, of Franklin, Mo. 261
Sand hills in southwest Kansas 190
Sandbars in Missouri river, method of
  getting over 147
Sandstone, formations of fantastic shape
  along Republican river 370
Sandzen, Birger, director Lindsborg
  Historical Society 112
Sangamon river, Illinois 232
Santa Fé Railroad. *See* Atchison,
  Topeka & Santa Fé Railroad.
Santa Fé road. *See* Santa Fé trail.
Santa Fé traders, on Arkansas 358
Santa Fé trail 14, 70
  190, 249, 250, 253, 257, 260, 267
— mounds raised by surveyors of 253
— protection for trade over 341
Satterlee, Mrs. C. A. 429
Sauk Indians. *See* Sac Indians.
Sault de St. Marie, Mr. Bingham appointed missionary to 237
Saunders, John I., note regarding his
  history of Cheney 111
Sautrelle (Delaware) river 320, 363
— dubbed "Sowtail" by Sol Miller 321
Savage, Forrest 278
— last survivor of Lawrence band 281
Savage, Joseph, pioneer explorer in
  Kansas paleontology 278
Saw logs, chopping for lumber 301
Saw mill, Leavenworth county, boiler explosion in 1861 injured eight men ... 220
— Manhattan 166
Sawtell, James A., Topeka 80
Say, Prof. Thomas, of Long's expedition, Grasshopper river mentioned by. 319
Sayles, W. A., ferry license issued to.... 188
Sayre, C. A., vice president Chase
  County Historical Society 431
Scalping knives 17, 20
Schafer, Joseph 119
Schattner, Fred 188
Schmidt, ——, mayor of Pittsburg 420
Schmitter, John 332
School, Districts 66 and 76, near Summerfield, notes on 213, 220
— for Indians, planned by Richard M.
  Johnson 354
— for Shawnees, considered 343, 364
— Haven Rural High 331
— history, Marion county 107
— teachers, rural, Barton county, note on, 423
—— Trego county, for 1935-1936, note
  on 216

Schoolcraft, Henry R. 136, 231
Schools, Doniphan county 57
— public, note on 332
Schultz, Floyd B., Clay Center 81
Scott, Chas. F., Iola 81, 219
Scott, Clark, bridge and ferry incorporator 183
Scranton, coal mine strike at 193
Searcy, Leonard, Liberty, Mo. 274
Sedalia, Mo., Missouri Pacific strike of
  1885 .... 36, 37
— strike on Missouri Pacific ordered from
  Knights of Labor headquarters at.. 198
— strikers meet at 42
Sedan 32
Sedgwick county 23, 33, 189
— ferries operating within 184-188
— first move for bridges in 188
Sedgwick Methodist Church, incorporated
  in 1875 215
Sedgwick *Pantagraph* 214, 215
Selleck, Arthur, note on reminiscences of, 109
Semple, Robert H. 50
— secretary Franklin Assembly Knights
  of Labor 44
Sen, Henry, falls of Grasshopper river
  discovered by 320
Sender, H. M., Kansas City, Mo 59
Seneca 69
Seneca County Press, Seneca Falls, N. Y., 105
Seneca *Courier-Tribune* 214
Seneca *Times* 214
Sensitive plants 396, 397
Shackleford, —— 261
Shadenoy, half Pottawatomie Indian.
  See Chandenois.
Shane, A., interpreter for Shawnees.... 258
  261, 262, 343, 345, 346, 351, 359, 364
Shane, Mrs. A. or Wiskehelaehqua..... 260
  342, 377
Shannon, Gov. Wilson 169, 170, 335
Sharkey, John, ferry operator 185
Sharp's rifles, Missourians search baggage of Kansans for 165
Shaw, F. E. 197
Shawaunukwuk, Pottawatomie, accompanied McCoy on exploring tour... 229
  252, 266, 270
Shawnee Baptist mission, founded by
  Johnston Lykins 347
Shawnee county, note on history of... 331
Shawnee County Old Settlers' Association,
  addressed by Sen. Arthur Capper... 112
— newly elected officers of 112
Shawnee Indians 265, 346, 375
— agency 342, 376
— and Delaware agency, location of... 342
— arrival in Kansas 260
— council house 345
— country of, well supplied with timber, 260
— Fish or Jackson's band 377
— invited to Lawrence Fourth of July
  celebration 279
— members accompanying McCoy attend
  dance given by 261
— prophet, Tenskwatawa 343
— reservation 148, 240
— school planned for 342, 343, 364
— settlement of, on Kansas river...... 260
— village 275, 344, 345
— — road leading to 258
Shawnee Methodist Indian mission..... 279
— Gov. A. H. Reeder and staff remove
  to 326
— Kansas D. A. R., annual pilgrimage to, 431
— located near Turner 375
— moved to Johnson county in 1839.. 375
Shawnee Mission Indian Historical Society 61
— addressed by Kirke Mechem 336

464   GENERAL INDEX

Sheldon, Rev. Chas. M., author 327
Sheldon, Elizabeth........... 283, 291, 302
                                306, 311, 317
Shepherd, John H., Howard county,
  Mo. 276
Sherburne, William, bridge and ferry
  incorporator 183
Sheridan, Gen. P. H. 74
Sheridan county, note on history of.... 425
Sheridan's drive, on Fort Leavenworth
  reservation 361
Sherman, Clarissa 143
Sherman, John 202
Sherman, Gen. Wm. T. 74
Sherman County Herald, Goodland 214
Shirer, H. L. 81
Shoemaker, F. C. 120
Shombre, Capt. Henry, Free State
  martyr 280
Shoo Fly creek, named for popular
  song 26
Shoo Fly trail, Cowley county, route of.. 26
Shroyer 211
Shumway, H. A., president Kansas History Teachers' Association........... 335
Sibley, Geo. C. 136
Sierra Nevada mountains, Donner party
  met disaster by starvation in 208
Sigma Delta Chi, fraternity 336
Siliman, Mr. ——, nephew of Gov.
  Cass 230
Silver and lead ores, refined at
  Argentine 191
Silver creek, Clark county, Indiana ... 123
Simerwell, Robert, Baptist missionary... 237
Simerwell, Mrs. Robert 263
Simmonds, Frank W. 425
Simmons, Mrs. India H., author 106
Simons, W. C., Lawrence 80
Simpson, Jerry 66
Simpson Baptist Church, note on history
  of 105
Simpson News 105, 109
Sioux Indians 353
Sipes, R. C., ferry incorporator..... 180
Sizemore, Mrs. Vera 221
Skeleton ranch, near Enid, Okla...... 7
Slade, Jack 222
Slater, Mr. —— 263
Slough creek, Jefferson county....... 319
Smies, Ed. A., Manhattan............. 217
Smith, ——, cattle dealer of Indian territory 8
Smith, ——, mentioned by Isaac McCoy, 342
Smith, Mrs. Caroline A., Manhattan.... 79
Smith, Frank B....................... 293
Smith, G. W., Davenport, Iowa........ 293
Smith, Herbert E..................... 111
Smith, Ida L......................... 419
Smith, Jedediah...................... 57
Smith, Jessica 335
Smith, Mrs. Luther, vice president Shawnee County Old Settlers' Association.. 112
Smith, W. S., Marysville............. 50
Smith, Walter, director ferry company.. 184
Smith, William E. 79, 81, 114
— "The Grave of Sarah Keyes on the
  Oregon Trail," article by 208-212
Smith County Pioneer, Smith Center.... 425
Smith county pioneers, note regarding
  sketches of 421
Smith County Review, Smith Center... 421
Smoky Hill river..................... 374
Smoky Hill trail, immigrant and stage
  road, bronze marker at Denver commemorating 336
Smyth, Prof. Egbert Coffin, of Bowdoin
  College 389
Snakes, seen by McCoy on exploring
  tour 231, 355, 370

Snyder, A. F., superintendent of Kansas
  City Smelting and Refining Co....... 192
Snyder, James, old resident of Effingham, 324
Snyder, Robert M., Jr................ 111
Soapstone, immense rocks of, mentioned
  by McCoy 368
Sod houses, note on.................. 425
Soil, on Kansas prairies, compared with
  that of Illinois................... 247
Solander, Mrs. T. T., Osawatomie.. 79, 81
Soldier creek............... 352-354, 364
Soldiers, Franklin county 334
Soller, August, Washington 80
Solomon City, Lodge No. 105, A. F. &
  A. M., sixty-fifth anniversary of
  founding 429
— Methodist Episcopal Church, dedication of building, 1935 216
— road to Wichita from 189
Solomon river 371- 374
— banks resemble an old lime kiln 374
Solomon Tribune 216, 429
Sotrael (Sautrelle), present Delaware
  creek 354
South Canadian river 10
South Carolina, emigrants from, bound
  for Kansas 163
South Kansas Tribune, Independence 213
South Pass 70
Southern Indians 237, 265
Southwest, note on stories about men and
  women who helped build 106
— trails through, indicated on surveys of
  Capt. R. B. Marcy 5
Southwest Social Science Association,
  note regarding meeting of 419
— *Southwestern Social Science Quarterly,*
  Austin, issued by 419
Southwest Tribune, Liberal 422
Spangler, Mrs. Caroline B., secretary
  Douglas County Historical Society .. 112
Spanish-American War 58
Spearville, note on history of 219
Spearville News 219
Speer, John, president Kansas State Historical Society 116
Speers & Walton, Arkansas City ferry
  projected by 30
Speers, W. H., biographical notes concerning 27
— ferry license issued to 26
— mill operator 27
Spencer, C. U., Emporia, organized printers on Topeka *Commonwealth* into a
  printers' assembly................. 48
Spiritualism 302
Spoons, made of buffalo horn 255
Spratt, O. M., Baxter Springs 79, 81
Spring creek, Sedgwick county 188
Springfield, Ill. 269
— Isaac McCoy's criticism of inhabitants
  of 232
Springs, in the Flint Hills, note on..... 110
Squashes, crook neck 284
Squatter Sovereign, Atchison, file of, acquired by Historical Society 59
Squirrels 244, 247, 355
Staats, Elmer B...................... 335
Stafford county, last wild buffalo killed in
  1879 216
— note on early experiences in 429
Standard, Leavenworth 195, 196
Stanley, W. E., Wichita 80
Stannard, Mr. —— 237
Stanton, Ex-Gov. Fred P.............. 391
State archives 58
State road, from Humboldt to Wichita.. 189
— Labette City to Meridian, Sumner
  county 182
State Savings Bank, Topeka 63

GENERAL INDEX 465

	PAGE
State Teachers' Association	25
Staudt, John G.	106
Staughton, Rev. William, corresponding secretary Baptist Board of Foreign Missions	125, 137, 140
Steamboat	234, 239
— J. H. Lucas, Missouri river boat,	162, 163
— Lonora, Missouri river boat	145
— Minnie Belle	391
Stecher, Chris	331
Stedman, Mr. ——	390
Steele, J. M., county clerk Sedgwick county	188
Stephens, Kate, author	432
Stevens, Caroline F., Lawrence	79, 81
Stevens, R. S. scandal connected with sale of bonds by	73
Stevens, Thomas C., papers of, given Historical Society	57
Stewart, A. H., a contributor of historical articles to Goodland papers	214
Stockade, near Alexander, on Fort Hays-Fort Dodge trial	105
— Osborne county, built in early 1870's for protection against Indians	217
Stockton, old log hotel built in 1871, by Joseph McNulty	220
Stogy shoes, described	17
Stone, Robert, Topeka	80
Stranger creek	351, 356, 357, 362, 363
Strassburg community, Marion county, note on history of	428
Street cars, operated in Clay Center in late 1880's	221
Streeter, Floyd B.	58, 325
— author	433
Strike, at Osage county coal mines	193
— on Gould system, states affected by	191
— strikers illegally hold Missouri Pacific property during period of trouble	42
Stringfellow, Benjamin F.	66, 158, 170
Stromquist, J. O.	426
Stroud, Joseph, many trips over Chisholm trail made by	5
Stubbs, Walter Roscoe, defeated for U. S. senate	77
— elected governor	77
Sublette, old settlers' meeting held near,	433
Sublette Monitor	108
— fiftieth anniversary of	328, 329
Sugar, price in 1859	405
Sugar cane, Chinese	315
Sugar tree, absence of, in Kansas	265
Suggs, W. W., directed cattle herds from Little Arkansas to Abilene	9
Summerfield, note on history of	219
Summerfield Sun	213, 219, 220
Summit, established in 1877, changed to Linn	221
Sumner, Col. E. V., at head of U. S. troops	170
Sumner county	23, 26
— ferries operating within	181- 184
— — first across Arkansas river in	184
Sumner County News, Wellington	326
Sumner County Press, Wellington	181
Sun City, Barber county	109
Sunday School	152
— early day	150
— Riley county	307
Surveying	374
Surveyors	301
— early Thomas county	331
— in Riley county	305
— of Santa Fé road, mounds raised by	253
— with McCoy exploring expedition	253, 353-355, 361-363, 365, 366, 368, 369
Sutter, John A., gold discovered in mill of, near Sacramento, Cal.	72
Sutton, Fred E.	217

	PAGE
Swallow river, present Delaware	320
Swedesburg Lutheran Church Clay Center, sixty-fifth anniversary	425
Sweet, Morton B.,	173, 307, 400, 401, 405, 415
Sylvan Grove, municipal band of	106
Syracuse Methodist Episcopal Church, fiftieth anniversary of	427
Syracuse Presbyterian Church, fiftieth anniversary of	107
Syracuse *Journal*	107, 427

T

Tabbo creek, Mo.	274
Tabor, Milton, note on his "Highlights of Kansas History from Coronado to Now"	218
— springs in the Flint Hills and the part they played in early history of Kansas, note on	110
Taylor, Rebecca Wells	107
Taylor, Roger, Montgomery county, Mo.	276
Taylor, William G.	327
Tecumseh, Indian chief	20, 416
Teed, Mrs. Ora L., treasurer Hodgeman County Historical Society	432
Telegraph line, completed to Pacific coast,	70
Telephones	57, 66
— Clifton, note on history of	218
— Council Grove	218
— Larned	218
— Ottawa, note on	333
Templin, Olin	108
— speaker at meeting of Douglas County Historical Society	112
Tennant, H. S., member Oklahoma State Highway Commission	325
Tenskwatawa, medicine man of Shawnees,	343
Terral, Tex.	10
Texas	8
— cattle, attempts to drive to market before Civil War	4
— — bedding grounds	13
— — first to arrive at Abilene	8
— — offered at $2 a head on the range without finding buyers	3
— — over Chisholm trail	8
— — selling price in the North	4
— — shipped east in 1868	10
— — — from Abilene in 1867	9
— cattlemen of, induced by J. G. McCoy to drive cattle to Abilene for shipment east	9, 189
— multitude of cattle trails in	10
— plains of, swarming with cattle at close of Civil War	3
Texas and Pacific Railroad	195
— Ex.-Gov. J. C. Brown one of receivers of	194
Thanksgiving in Kansas, note on early observance of	108
— 1858, no public celebration of	381
— often came in midst of hard times, but was celebrated anyway	109
Thayer, Eli	66
Thayer Methodist Church, note on history of	427
Thayer *News*	427
"The Grave of Sarah Keyes on the Oregon Trail," article by William E. Smith	208-212
Theatrical profession, some Kansans prominent in, named by Phil Zimmerman, of Lindsborg, in Topeka *State Journal*	223
Thoburn, Joseph B.	6
Thomas county, early surveyors	331
— note on early history of	330

30—5211

General Index

Thompson, ——, first cattle at Abilene driven from Texas by 8
Thompson, Capt. J. R................ 428
Thompson, W. F., Topeka 79, 81
Thornton & Thrash, Chariton county, Mo. 275
Thorp, L. H., first bicycle brought to Larned owned by 218
Thorstenberg, H. J., director Lindsborg Historical Society 112
Three Crossings, Wyo................ 69
Thunder and lightning, during a storm.. 162
Thurman, Harriet 58
Thurston, Mr. —— 288
Tichenor, Dr. William 325
Tiffany, Frank K. 329
Tiller and Toiler, Larned 218
Tilton, Charles, ferry incorporator 182
Timber 249, 254, 265
— a mile in width along Marais des Cygnes 247
— on Kansas river 256-258
— scarcity of, on uplands 259
Times, Clay Center 217, 329
Tinkler, Ella 332
Tippecanoe, Battle of 343
Tisdale 32
Tobacco 255, 258
— given to Indians by McCoy 261, 363, 375
— twists of 345
— worm, potatoes destroyed by 310
Todd, Ambrose 174, 178
283, 289, 291, 295, 308, 312
Todd, Mrs. Ambrose 294, 312
Todd, Mrs. Frank, note on her trip in Concord coach from Newton to Wichita, in 1870 421
Todson, Dr. George P................ 239
Toll bridge, across Arkansas river at Oxford 182, 183
— Arkansas City, carried away by flood, 26
— established at Osawkee 323
Tomahawks 17, 250
Tomson, Frank D., note on his impressions and reminiscences of Burlingame, 215
Tonance, E. S., ferry incorporator 181
Tong, George, of Leon 422
Topash, Pottawatomie chief 133
Topeka 416
— artist group of 430
— Congregational Church, Lewis Bodwell pastor 417
— eastern boundary of Kaw reservation short distance west of 341
— high school 335
— history 57
— mills at 158
Topeka *Commonwealth,* cited and quoted 26, 51, 52, 194, 195, 197, 204
— Knights of Labor boycott against ... 46, 47, 49
— printers assembly organized for 48
Topeka *Daily Capital* cited 35, 44
49, 110, 111, 194-196, 198, 205, 206
216-219, 319, 327, 330, 331
335, 422, 426
Topeka scrip, issued in 1856 111
Topeka *State Journal* 49
219, 220, 223, 329, 332, 422, 430
— Frank P. MacLennan editor of 336
Topenebee, chief of Pottawatomie Indians 131, 142
Torry, Charlie, witnessed hiding of fraudulent election returns on Lecompton constitution 221
Totten, Herbert C..................... 327

Trades-Union, Atchison ... 49, 51, 198, 204
— active in boycott against Topeka *Commonwealth* 48
Trading Post, monument erected at 330
Trafton, Rev. Mr., Methodist minister, 285
288, 291, 294, 300
Tragedies, in Luray community, note on, 107
Trail, from Fort Harker to Wichita ... 189
Trail Drivers of Texas, The, written by Texas trail drivers 3
Trails, Black Dog or Osage 189
— footnotes concerning 26
— mentioned by McCoy 366, 368, 370
— originating south of Wichita mountains, 5
— overland, three met at Kennekuk 67
— Texas a network of 10
Train robbers, battle with, mentioned .. 214
Train robbery, Atchison, in 1882, note on 217
Transient camp, Camp Gardner, Johnson county 214
Trappers 366
Treasure, buried, Jesse Chisholm leads party to mouth of Little Arkansas in search of 6
Treaties, to be held at Green Bay and Carey, Mich 234
Treaty, 1821 122-142
—— number Indians attending 136
—— ratified 141
— St. Joseph, mentioned 229
— St. Marys, Ohio, 1818, mentioned .. 350
Trego county school teachers, 1935-1936, listed in *Western Kansas World,* Wakeeney 216
Trembly, Wm. B., Kansas City 80
Tressin, Ida 332
Tri-County News, Horton ... 107, 108, 430
— anniversary edition of 428
Trichen, Dr. ——, of Wichita, moved stock of drugs from railroad terminus in Sedgwick county to Fort Smith .. 29
Trimble, Col. Wm. A., United States senator from Ohio 135, 136
Trinity Lutheran Church, near Ludell, fiftieth anniversary of 333
Turkey, wild 242, 256
258, 284, 355, 356, 369, 370
Turkey creek, Okla.................... 7
Turkey Red wheat, Mennonites credited with introduction of 424
Turner, William, agent for Miami Indians 127
Turtle, Alice J........................ 425
Turtles 152
— twenty-one pounder shot by T. C. Wells 150
Tuttle, Okla. 10
Typographical Union 202, 205
— Hutchinson, note on founding of.... 330
— No. 121, Topeka, fight of, against Topeka *Commonwealth* 48

U

Uhl, L. C............................ 425
Ulysses 325
— date of old settlers' meeting at 433
Underflow, of Arkansas river, discovered, 24
Union, Mo., a little village 241
Union Pacific Railroad 57, 71, 321
— Denver employees awaiting strike orders 45
— first capitol of Kansas restored by... 61
— golden spike driven to connect eastern and western divisions of 67
— Central Branch of 15

GENERAL INDEX

467

Union printers, on Topeka *Commonwealth*, start boycott 47
Union State Bank, Arkansas City 26
Union veterans, Gypsum, note on 332
United Foreign Missionary Society 240
United States, bureau of animal husbandry, cattle statistics of 10
— geological survey, Arkansas river flow ascertained by 24
— Highway No. 130 183
— Indian department 274
— Indian superintendency, St. Louis ... 57
— regiments, Second cavalry 336
— — — organized as Second dragoons in Florida in 1836 336
— — Sixth infantry 346, 359
— — 83rd. Colored infantry 74
— — 137th infantry 59
— Secretary of War 140, 229, 239
— Weather bureau 24
— — drainage area of Arkansas river given by 23
University of Kansas 108, 114, 121
218, 219, 336
— alumni association of 432
— *Humanistic Studies* 116
— Lawrence band furnished music at first commencement exercises of 281
University of Michigan 115
Updegraff, H. Harrison, ferry operator.. 185
Updegraff, W. W., state senator 185
Utica, note on history 422
Utica *Star-Courier* 422

V

Valley Falls *New Era* 320
Van de Mark, M. V. B., Concordia 81
Vanderslice, D., ferry operator 379
Vanderwilt, Ethel 216
Van Tuyl, Mrs. Effie H., Leavenworth 79, 81
Van Tyne, Claude H.................. 119
Vardeman, Rev. ——, of Kentucky ... 236
Varnum, Walter, treasurer Douglas County Historical Society 112
Vashon, George, Indian agent for Cherokees 350
Vassar, F. S......................... 329
Vaughn, Mrs. Frances Zumwalt, twenty-five years a reporter for Bonner Springs *Chieftain* 216
Venison 250
— McCoy party halt to dry 368
Vermillion river 366
Victoria Hunt Club ball 419
Vincent, —— 357

W

Wabash railroad line, rumors of strike on 45
Wabash river 127, 131
Wabaunsee 332, 416
— founded by Beecher Bible and Rifle colony 330
Wabaunsee County Truth, Wabaunsee .. 332
Waconda, or Great Spirit Spring, described by McCoy 373
Waddell, Russell, Majors &, Pony Express owned and operated by 68
Waddell, Samuel, St. Louis, Mo........ 270
Wadsworth Mound, near Greeley, a John Brown lookout 333
Waggener, Balie P.................... 40
Wagon, road, from settlements of Missouri to Harmony mission station ... 243
Wagon train, William Griffenstein crossed Arkansas river with 8
Wahusa creek, present Wakarusa 260

Waite, C. G., formerly of Tecumseh, bridge architect 323
Wakarusa creek 149, 260
Wakarusa war 325
Wakefield, Clay county 218
Wakefield, R. I., bank 167, 317
Walden, John R., note regarding his early history of Clark county 108
Walker, Bert P., Topeka 80
Walker, David 268
Walker, Edith, instructor history, Eureka High school 2
— "Labor Problems During the First Year of Gov. Martin's Administration," article by 33-53
Walker, Mrs. Ida M., Norton 79, 81
Walker, R., Oxford 182
Walker, Robert J..................... 57
Walker, W. H........................ 335
Walnut City 32
Walnut creek, flows across old Kickapoo reserve 16
Walnut river 25, 27
— valley of, Butler county, note on pioneering in 422
Walnut timber 248, 249
— elm and oak on Kickapoo reserve... 16
Walpole, W. J., ferry incorporator 180
Walters, J. D........................ 393
Walton, Amos, Arkansas City ferry operator 30
Walton, H., Isaac McCoy lodges with... 234
Wamego *Reporter* 213, 332
Wansley (on Wamsley), L. B., member ferry company 184
Wapaugkonetta, Ohio, Shawnee Indians from 260
Ward, James A............. 307, 393, 399
Ware, Eugene F., note on poem commemorating Dewey's victory 109
Wark, George H., Caney 81
Washburn College, Topeka, Dr. Philip C. King, president 56
— student employment project sponsored by 56
Washington County News, Washington, 429
Washington County Register, Washington, 429
Washington Methodist Episcopal Church, note on histories of 429
Washita river 6, 10
Water system, Gypsum, note on 332
Waterville *Telegraph*, founded by Frank A. Root 15
Wathena, Kickapoo chief, Ke-o-Quack married a daughter of 16
Wathena, Doniphan county, named for Kickapoo chief 21
Watson, Benjamin 162
Watson, Susy 389
Waurika, Okla....................... 8
Way, Lillian 58
Wayne Township Farmers' Club, Edwards county 421
Wea Indians 126
Wear, William W. 58
Webb, Claude 333
Weir, Mrs. A. M..................... 420
Wellington, note on sixty-fifth anniversary of founding 326
Wellington *Daily News* 326
Wellman, Paul I..................... 426
Wellman-Brown, Edith 332
Wells, Elizabeth (Frances Elizabeth)... 143
151-153, 167, 172, 383, 389-392, 396
398, 406, 411, 417
Wells, Ella S............ 291, 295, 299, 301
303, 304, 310, 312, 313, 317, 385, 386
388-391, 394, 398, 400, 402, 403
406-408, 410, 413, 415, 417

GENERAL INDEX

Wells, Emily P. 143
Wells, Grandma — — 393
Wells, Helen May 143
Wells, Henry (George Henry)..... 143, 152
    158, 160, 161, 167, 168, 173, 176, 284
    292, 294, 302, 304, 305, 307, 383
    387, 389, 396, 406, 409, 411
— letter to 169-171
Wells, Herbert Johnson 143, 172, 173
    284, 291, 295, 297, 300, 306-308, 312
    317, 318, 383, 392, 398, 400
    404, 407, 408, 412
Wells, Nathaniel, emigrant from Essex
    county, England 143
Wells, Theodore Backus 143, 158
    160-162, 164, 168-177, 283-287, 289, 290
    294, 295, 297, 304, 306-309, 314, 317
    318, 383, 384, 387, 390-392
    396, 406, 409
— letters to 299, 300, 312, 313
Wells, Thomas Clarke 114, 226, 338
— biographical sketch 143
— household experiences of 152
— "Letters of a Kansas Pioneer, 1855-
    1860" 143-179, 282-318, 381-418
— marriage of 285
Wells, Thomas Potter, letters of Thomas
    C. Wells to 143-147, 149-152
    158, 159, 173-179, 282, 283, 289, 290
    296-299, 304-311, 316-318, 384-390
    394-396, 398-400, 404-406, 413-418
Wells, Mrs. Thomas Potter, letters to, 147-149
    151-157, 159-169, 171-173, 175-179
    283-296, 300-304, 307-311, 313-315
    317, 318, 381-398, 400-403, 406-418
Wells-Fargo Express 336
Wesauogana, Indian of Ottawa tribe, ac-
    companied McCoy on exploring tour, 229
    233, 248, 270
— meets a cousin in St. Louis 235
West Kansas City (Kansas), Missouri
    Pacific strike of 1885 37
West Wichita 7
Westcott, Peleg 390
Western Home Journal, Ottawa, first is-
    sued on December 7, 1865 333
Western Kansas Express, Manhattan.... 403
    404, 411
— C. F. DeVivaldi, editor............. 399
Western Star, Coldwater 216
Wheat, price 1859 405
— shipped from Salt City to Little Rock,
    Ark. 181
Wheatley, E. E. 332
Wheatley, Ulilla 332
Wheeler, — —, of California, cattle
    owned by 9
Wheeler, Mrs. B. R., Topeka 81
Whelden, Mr. — — 300, 307, 312
Whelden, Mr. and Mrs. — — 293
Whisky 154, 229, 261
White, Benjamin, killed by Indians in
    1868, granite marker erected in mem-
    ory of 336
White, William A., Emporia, 57, 58, 79, 81
— note regarding his editorial "What's
    the Matter With Kansas" 424
White City Register 334, 430
White Cloud, Kansas Chief founded at, 332
— note on history of 331
White Plume, Kaw chief 345, 346, 352
White river, Missouri 340
White Rock 334
Whitehorn, Dr. — —, dentist of Man-
    hattan 294
White's creek, southeast of Jamestown,
    granite marker erected on 336
Whitfield, John W. 160

Whitman, Marcus, missionary to Oregon, 119
— note on 330
Whittemore, Margaret, notes on sketches
    of Kansas landmarks prepared by 327, 334
Whittier, John G. 281
— "Kansas Emigrants' Song," quoted .. 278
Whortleberris 155
Wichita 6-8, 11, 30, 222
— April, 1886, note on 328
— Arkansas river ascended to, by small
    craft 25
— banking history, note on 109
— boom, notes on 328, 429
— bridge, toll rates on 189
— business houses, 1881, note regard-
    ing 422
— date of old settlers' meetings at 433
— early-day business houses, note re-
    garding 424
— end of cattle trail at 12
— ferry 185, 190
— — first probably operated by M.
    Greenway 186
— — rates of ferriage on 188
— — some description of 187
— first bridge location 188
— church, note on building of 327
— — funeral, note on 327
— — Sunday School, note on 327
— getting railroads into city of, note on, 428
— Grace Methodist Episcopal Church,
    note on fiftieth anniversary celebration, 333
— note on history of 422
— period as cattle town 13
— prominent physicians during first
    twenty-five years, note on 329
— roads to and from 189
— Salvation Army, memorial plaque
    marks place where army first met fifty
    years ago 329
— school system, note on history of 430
— shooting up town of, note 331
— state road from Humboldt to 189
— Wichita Indians trek to site of 6
Wichita agency, Anadarko, Okla....... 7
Wichita Beacon 189, 223, 329, 333, 423
— anniversary edition of 421
Wichita Bridge Co., sells bridge to county, 189
Wichita Business College, note on history
    of 111
Wichita City, Library 58
Wichita Eagle 6, 8, 22, 108, 111, 223
    326-329, 331, 421-426, 428-430
— sixty-fourth anniversary edition of... 422
Wichita Indians, affiliated bands of, trek
    northward 6
— peace council at village of 6
Wichita mountains, trails originating
    south of 5
Wiggins, Eliza Johnston 325
Wiggins, Samuel, St. Louis, Mo....... 269
Wigwam, Delaware 346
Wilburn, — — 262
Wild Cat creek, Riley county 168
Wild grapes 156
Wild honey 362
Wild plums 155, 157
Wild turkeys 244, 247, 256, 258, 284
    356, 369, 375
— feathers as ornaments 17
Wilder, Abram, tenor drummer of Law-
    rence band 280
Willets, John F., gubernatorial candidate, 76
Williams, W. F..................... 331
Willow trees, on Republican river 372
Wilmarth, O., ... 279
Wilsey, Pioneer Kansas picnic held in... 430
Wilson, — — 304
Wilson, — —, California cattleman 9

General Index   469

Wilson, James, Grand Auglaize, Mo.... 273
Wilson, John H., Salina 79, 81
Wilson, Stephen J., note regarding
  guerilla visits to Gardner 215
Wilson, Thomas F., note on reminiscences
  of 329
Wilson, Woodrow, mentioned 118
Wilson State Bank, note on history of.. 222
Wilson *World* 222
Wilson's creek, Gen. Nathaniel Lyon at, 74
Winchester 324
Wind wagon, mentioned 427
Winds, high 365, 366, 368, 374
Winfield 25, 30, 32, 34
Winfield *Daily Courier* 426
Winnebago Indians 230
Wisconsin State Historical Society 121
Wiskehelaehqua, alias Mrs. Shane 342
Witt, Fred C. J...................... 425
Wolcott, Alexander, Indian agent at
  Chicago 135, 230
— letter to Isaac McCoy, with views on
  Indian reform 129, 130
Wolcott, Harry H., printer on Larned
  Optic 106
Wolf 252
— grey 292
Wolf claws, as ornaments 18
Wolfe, W. C........................ 425
Wolves, steal elk meat of McCoy's ex-
  ploring party 252
Woodford, C. B., sheriff of Labette
  county 198, 200, 201
Woodring, Harry H., assistant secretary
  of war 77
— elected governor 77
Woodson county 189
Woodsworth, Judge —— 309
Woodward, Chester, Topeka 80
Woolard, Sam F., Wichita 81
Wooster, L. D....................... 107
Wooster, Lorraine E., Salina.......... 81

Woman's Kansas Day Club............ 62
Woman's Relief Corps, Coffeyville, note
  on early history of................ 328
Worcester, Leonard, Greensburg, Ind.... 281
— leader Lawrence band.............. 280
Works Progress Administration, Kansas,
  Historical Records survey instituted
  by 224
— project, under sponsorship of Kansas
  State Historical Society 224
— — proposed 56
World War, mentioned 425
Worthington, Samuel L............... 271
Wright, Mr. ——, mentioned......... 393
Wright, L. J., mentioned............. 425
Wright, Neil 58
Wright, Samuel F., ferry operator..... 185
Wright, William 261, 275
Wright, William, ferry incorporator.... 180
Wurttemburg, Prince Paul of, note re-
  garding narrative of............... 111
Wyandotte city................ 33, 45, 321
Wyandotte Constitutional Convention, 73, 111
— John A. Martin, secretary.......... 76
Wyandotte ferry 379
Wyman, Walker D................... 58

Y

Yoder, an oil producing center......... 223
Yost, B. F., note on recollection of con-
  sular service 330
Young —— 377
Young, Dr. —— 140
Young, F. E., Stockton.............. 108
Y. M. C. A. college, Springfield, Mass., 218

Z

Zimmerman, Mark E., of White Cloud.. 379
Zimmerman, Phil, Lindsborg 223
Zion Evangelical Lutheran Church,
  Newton 421